PENGUIN CLASSICS DELUXE EDITION

SHAHNAMEH

ABOLQASEM FERDOWSI was born in Khorasan in a village near Tus, in 940 CE. His great epic the *Shahnameh*, to which he devoted most of his adult life, was originally composed for the Samanid princes of Khorasan, who were the chief instigators of the revival of Persian cultural traditions after the Arab conquest. During Ferdowsi's lifetime, the Samanid dynasty was conquered by the Ghaznavid Turks. Legend has it that Ferdowsi's lifework was not appreciated by King Mahmud of Ghazneh. He is said to have died around 1020 in poverty and embittered by royal neglect, though confident of his poem's ultimate fame.

A Fellow of the Royal Society of Literature, DICK DAVIS is currently professor of Persian at Ohio State University. His other translations from Persian include *Borrowed Ware: Medieval Persian Epigrams, The Legend of Seyavash*, and, with Afkham Darbandi, *The Conference of the Birds*.

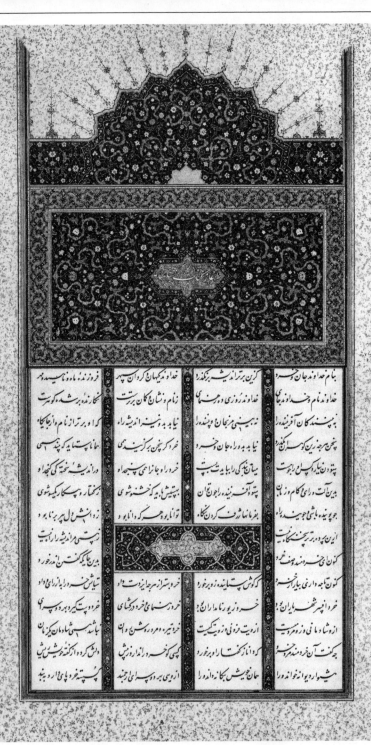

Shahnameh

The Persian Book of Kings

ABOLQASEM FERDOWSI

FiRDAWS
II

Translated by
DICK DAVIS

With a Foreword by
AZAR NAFISI

PENGUIN BOOKS

PENGUIN BOOKS
Published by the Penguin Group
Penguin Group (USA) Inc., 375 Hudson Street, New York, New York 10014, U.S.A.
Penguin Group (Canada), 90 Eglinton Avenue East, Suite 700, Toronto,
Ontario, Canada M4P 2Y3 (a division of Pearson Penguin Canada Inc.)
Penguin Books Ltd, 80 Strand, London WC2R 0RL, England
Penguin Ireland, 25 St Stephen's Green, Dublin 2, Ireland (a division of Penguin Books Ltd)
Penguin Group (Australia), 250 Camberwell Road, Camberwell,
Victoria 3124, Australia (a division of Pearson Australia Group Pty Ltd)
Penguin Books India Pvt Ltd, 11 Community Centre, Panchsheel Park,
New Delhi – 110 017, India
Penguin Group (NZ), 67 Apollo Drive, Mairangi Bay,
Auckland 1311, New Zealand (a division of Pearson New Zealand Ltd)
Penguin Books (South Africa) (Pty) Ltd, 24 Sturdee Avenue,
Rosebank, Johannesburg 2196, South Africa

Penguin Books Ltd, Registered Offices:
80 Strand, London WC2R 0RL, England

First published in the United States of America by Viking Penguin,
a member of Penguin Group (USA) Inc. 2006
Published in Penguin Books 2007

9   10   8

Copyright © Mage Publishers, 1997, 2000, 2004
Introduction copyright © Azar Nafisi, 2006
All rights reserved

Originally published in three volumes entitled *The Lion and the Throne*, *Fathers and Sons*,
and *Sunset of Empire* by Mage Publishers, Washington, D.C.

Illustrations provided by Dr. Ulrich Marzolph from his archive of Persian
lithographed book illustrations in Goettingen, Germany.

ISBN 978-0-14-310493-3
CIP data available

Printed in the United States of America

This translation is dedicated to Mohammad and Najmieh Batmanglij, with my gratitude and affection.

CONTENTS

FOREWORD

BY

AZAR NAFISI

I have two books in front of me. One is the galley for Dick Davis's *Shahnameh, The Persian Book of Kings;* the other is a much thinner book, designed for young readers and on its cover, above a Persian miniature painting of men on horses, is written in Persian: *Selections from Shahnameh,* by Ahmad Nafisi. In his introduction to this selection, my father mentions that the idea for this book goes back to the time he started telling stories from Persia's classical literature, beginning with Ferdowsi's *Shahnameh,* to my brother and me when we were no more than three or four years old and later to our children. My father always insisted that Persians basically did not have a home, except in their literature, especially their poetry. This country, our country, he would say, has been attacked and invaded numerous times, and each time, when Persians had lost their sense of their own history, culture and language, they found their poets as the true guardians of their true home. Citing the poet Ferdowsi and how, after the Arab invasion of Persia, he rescued and redefined his nation's identity and culture through writing the epic of Persian mythology and history in his *Book of Kings,* my father would say, We have no other home but this, pointing to the invisible book, this, he would repeat is our home, always, for you and your brother, and your children and your children's children.

Thus it was that like so many other Persian children my brother and I and later our children grew up with the *Shahnameh* and in the kingdom of imagination our father had created for us. Rostam, Tahmineh, Seyavash, Bizhan and the other fictional characters in Ferdowsi's stories became our brothers and sisters, cousins and neighbors. Ferdowsi's devoted readers throughout the centuries rewarded him by creating their own legends around him. When I was a married woman with children of my own, my father, in the same manner he used when I was a small child, would tell my children of the conflict between the noble poet Ferdowsi and the fickle king, Sultan Mahmud Ghaznavi. Dick Davis gives us the factual historical account, but we heard the popular one, the one that like the stories in the *Shahnameh,* while more akin to myth, revealed an important truth.

According to this version, Sultan Mahmud assigns *Shahnameh* to Ferdowsi, for which he promises to pay the poet a gold coin for every line. The king, as it seems to be the way with many rulers, does not fulfill his promise. Instead, he sends the poet silver coins, which Ferdowsi, despite his dire poverty, refuses. The king, finally realizing the worth of the poet, repents of his behavior and travels to the city of Tus to console the poet. He is too late: as his procession enters the main gate to the city it encounters another procession leaving the same gate with Ferdowsi's coffin. Implied in this legend, as in *Shahnameh* itself, is the truth that in the struggle between the poet and the king, the latter might win this world but to the former belongs the glory that comes with the conquest of that most absolute of all tyrants, time. Nearly a thousand years have passed, my father would say, the tone of marvel never missing from his voice, and we remember the king mainly because we remember the poet. It is the poet, he would declare, who is the final victor.

After the victory of the Islamic revolution, and especially during the years of the Iran–Iraq war, I took refuge in Persian poetry and literature when we would gather each week with a group of friends to read the classics of Persian literature with the well-known writer Houshang Golshiri. That was when I paid more attention not just to the stories but also to the miraculous language and poetry of *Shahnameh,* realizing that the poetry seemed so unobtrusive and supportive of the stories not because Ferdowsi was a lesser poet and a better storyteller but because he was so skilled a poet that the poetry became the story.

I realized then how right my father had been. For Persians, *Shahnameh* is like their identity papers, their conclusive evidence that they have lived. Against the brutality of time and politics, against the threat of constant invasions and destructions imposed on them by enemies alien and domestic, against a reality they had little or no control over, they created magnificent monuments in words, they reasserted both their own worth and the best achievements of mankind through a work like *Shahnameh,* the golden thread that links one Persian to the other, connecting the past to the present.

Now we have to be grateful to Dick Davis for weaving this golden thread into the fabric of another language. In his translation of these selections from *Shahnameh* he conveys the unique poetic texture of Ferdowsi's great epic. Yet we do not appreciate *Shahnameh* only for its Persianness, but also because it shapes and articulates those aspects of Persian culture that transcend time and space, defying limitations of history, ethnicity, nationality and even culture. This book, like literary classics, captures and articulates passions, urges, aspirations, betrayals, joys and anguish that are shared by all individuals no matter where they live and what language they speak. Ultimately, the English-speaking reader will be drawn to this book not only because it represents the best of Persian culture, but also because of its essential humanness. Reading *Shahnameh* will lead them to the amazing and yet inevitable discovery that celebrating our differences would have no meaning or substance if we did not simultaneously recognize our common humanity, our enduring connections and relations.

And because of this universal appeal the readers of this marvelous new English rendition of the *Shahnameh* can now experience with the readers before them from different cultures and nationalities the truth of the poet's prophecy when he wrote:

> *I've reached the end of this great history*
> *And all the land will fill with talk of me*
> *I shall not die, these seeds I've sown will save*
> *My name and reputation from the grave,*
> *And men of sense and wisdom will proclaim,*
> *When I have gone, my praises and my fame.*

INTRODUCTION

The *Shahnameh* is the national epic of Iran, or Persia as the country used to be called, composed by the poet Ferdowsi in the late tenth and early eleventh centuries C.E. Its subject matter is vast, being nothing less than the history of the country and its people from the creation of the world up to the Arab conquest, which brought the then new religion of Islam to Iran, in the seventh century C.E.

A difference from Western epics such as the *Iliad,* the *Odyssey* and the *Aeneid* immediately suggests itself: the Western poems deal primarily with one generation, while referring to others, and focus on a few leading characters who are contemporary with one another and so able to interact. The *Shahnameh's* great temporal span means that many generations are directly presented to us, and the cast of significant characters is thus far larger than is the case in Western epics. The current standard edition of the poem, which runs to nine volumes, includes over 50,000 lines (and by the criteria of English verse they are very long lines; each line has twenty two syllables, making it slightly longer than a heroic couplet, so that a more accurate computation for an English reader would be to say that it is over 100,000 lines long). In its great length, and in its multiplicity of characters and generations, as well as in other significant ways (e.g., in the existence of an ancient and still living folk tradition that continues both to feed the poem and feed off it, and produce new versions of familiar stories; as well as the relative uncertainty of the textual tradition), the *Shahnameh* often seems closer to Indian epics such as the *Mahabharata* and the *Ramayana* than to say the *Iliad*. The differences from Western epics should not however obscure the similarities, which are seen to be many when one examines particular episodes of the poem. For example, a staple theme of Western epic, both ancient and medieval, is a conflict between the king and the chief martial hero of the ethnicity at the center of the poem. The *Iliad*, which starts with such a conflict (between Achilles and Agamemnon), provides a prime example. This is also a major theme of the *Shahnameh*, one repeated over a number of generations and involving a number of feuding kings and heroes.

The Poem's Structure

How does Ferdowsi structure this huge panorama of conflict and epic adventure, which teems with so many characters and generations, and with so much narrative detail, that a hasty first impression of the poem must almost inevitably be that Ferdowsi has done what the British eighth century writer Nennius claimed to have done at the opening of his history when he wrote, "I have made a heap of all I could find"?

As is traditional for long medieval Persian poems, Ferdowsi precedes his narrative with an introduction that praises God and then passes to various other concerns before embarking on the stories themselves. The *Shahnameh* begins by exalting God, as the Lord of wisdom and the soul, and as being above all human comprehension. These three concerns, the nature of wisdom, the fate of the human soul, and the incomprehensibility of God's purposes, are to play major roles in the poem's unfolding:

> *Now in the name of God whose power controls*
> *Wisdom, and has created human souls,*
> *Exalted beyond all that thought or speech*
> *Is able to encompass or to reach,*
> *The lord of Saturn and the stars at night,*
> *Who gives the sun and moon and Venus light,*
> *Above all name and thought, exceeding all*
> *Of his creation, and unknowable . . .*

The exordium continues with a brief account of the creation of the four elements (earth, fire, air, and water) from which the world was fashioned, the creation of man (again wisdom is emphasized as being man's chief concern) and of the sun and moon. This is followed by a passage in praise of Mohammad, the prophet of Islam, and a passage on the poem's sources, which appears to be fairly circumstantial but is largely conventional in nature. The fact that Ferdowsi has utilized a passage (on the advent of Zoroastrianism) from the work of a previous poet (Daqiqi) is mentioned, and the introductory material concludes with praise of the Ghaznavid Sultan Mahmoud, from whom Ferdowsi clearly hoped for patronage (although legend has it that, as it happens, Mahmoud treated him very shabbily).

Once we get beyond this introductory material (which is omitted from the present translation), the fundamental structure of the poem is that of a royal chronicle, as its title, which means "The Book of Kings," suggests. Fifty kings (or, more accurately, fifty monarchs; three of them are queens) are named; their accessions to the throne, and their deaths (or abdications, or forcible removal from power) are meticulously recorded. The poem proceeds reign by reign, with increasingly frequent evocations of past kings and heroes, as well as occasional predictions of future reigns and events. However, the kings are by no means treated equally; some kings merit no more than a few lines, others many thousands. The reign of one king, Kavus, within whose reign many of the most famous legendary tales of the poem occur, occupies over three volumes of the standard nine-volume edition. Ferdowsi then shows more interest in some kings than in others; this must be partly because of the stories that were available to him (which gave him more to say about some kings than others), but it also suggests that certain themes, clearly exemplified in some reigns, were of particular interest to him. It is significant for example that the king we have just mentioned, Kavus, who bulks so large in the narrative as a whole, is one of the poem's worst kings, and in presenting the stories of his reign Ferdowsi constantly explores the dilemmas of a good man living under an evil or incompetent government.

The nature of the good man, the good hero, is a central focus of Ferdowsi's concern, and this suggests another recurrent characteristic of the poem, which is its strong ethical bias. The characters we seem most strongly invited to admire, especially in the poem's legendary tales, constantly ask themselves not, "How do I win?" but "How do I act well?" The ethical preoccupations of much of the poem dovetail with another of its concerns, in that, as with much medieval history and quasi-history, as well as being a chronicle it is a kind of "Mirror for Princes"; that is, a book that provides both positive and negative moral exempla for rulers (and others).

To describe the poem as primarily "a chronicle with ethical biases" suggests a certain aesthetic detachment from the material, which might be assumed to be presented largely as a moralized "historical" record. This however is far from true to the experience of reading the poem, which is almost everywhere imbued with a sense of emotional urgency, and even crisis, nowhere more so than in the closing pages when the work turns fairly unequivocally into a tragedy, the record of the passing of a deeply mourned civilization whose loss is seen as a disaster (here then is another difference from ancient Western epics, which do not end tragically).

The Historical Background

As is the case with major epics from other traditions the appearance of the *Shahnameh* marks a transitional moment. It is on the one hand a compilation and summing up of what is believed to have gone before, and in that sense it self-consciously marks the ending of an era, so that the poet writes with a sense of belatedness, of living irretrievably after the golden age he records. But it is also a beginning, in that a new tradition derives from it; the self-image of the people whose putative ancestors are celebrated in the work is cast, by the work itself, into a new mold. The author of the *Shahnameh,* Ferdowsi, lived at a time when such a recasting of the Persian tradition was almost uniquely possible—a little earlier or later and one cannot imagine his poem coming into existence in just such an emphatic and culturally redefining form. To understand the *Shahnameh* therefore it is necessary to know something of the time in which it was produced.

The great watershed of Persian history is the seventh-century Arab/Islamic conquest of the Sasanians, the last pre-Islamic dynasty that ruled Iran. From the perspective of the twenty-first century this occurred almost exactly half way through the historical record: there are approximately thirteen hundred years of recorded Persian civilization before this moment (from the sixth century B.C.E. and the foundation of the Achaemenid empire) and there are approximately thirteen hundred years from this moment to the present. The longevity and distinctiveness of Persian civilization during the pre-Islamic era were major factors in the ancient world, and though in the West political power shifted from the Greeks to the Romans, Persia remained more or less constant as the center of a continuous and specific tradition of civilization.

The Arab conquest of the seventh century C.E. came therefore as an overwhelming shock, especially since it must have seemed for a while as though Persian civilization would disappear as an entity distinguishable from the culture of other countries subsumed into the Caliphate. An Iranian scholar has dubbed the numbed aftermath of the conquest in Iran as "the two centuries of silence." One can gather something of the atmosphere of the early post-conquest years in the writing of a Zoroastrian (i.e. an adherent of the religion of pre-Islamic Iran) of the period: ". . . the faith was ruined and the King of Kings slain like a dog. . . . They have taken away sovereignty from the Khosrows. Not by skill and valor but by mockery and scorn have they taken it. By force they take from men wives and sweet possessions and gardens. . . . Consider how much evil those wicked ones have cast upon this world, than which ill there is none worse. The world passes from us."[1] After the conquest there were constant revolts against the new rulers, particularly in the central province of Fars, which had been the heartland of imperial Iran, and many towns had to be reconquered more than once. The Umayyad dynasty (661–750) had scant regard for Persian civilization and sensibilities, and treated even converts to Islam as second-class citizens if they were not of Arab stock (the majority of the indigenous population at this time was still not Moslem and at the beginning of the Islamic period their second-class status went without saying). The Abbasids who succeeded the Umayyads in 750 C.E. came to power partly as a result of a revolt that began in Khorasan (northeastern Iran) and were generally more sympathetic to Persian civilization and mores than their predecessors had been. The capital was moved to Baghdad, close to the ruins of the Sasanian capital of Ctesiphon—an ambiguous gesture that both reasserted the triumph of the Arabs over the Sasanians, but also signaled the more Persian-oriented direction that came to be taken by the caliphate. The caliph al Ma'mun in particular was known for his Persian sympathies; his mother was Persian and his chief minister, Fazl b. Sahl, who was also Persian, ensured that the Abbasid court, extraordinarily enough, adopted much of the ceremonial protocol of the Arabs' defeated enemy, the Sasanians. Iranians became prominent in the Abbasid civil service (the Barmaki [Barmecides] and Naubakhti families rose to par-

---

1. H.W. Bailey's translation of a passage from *The Great Bundahishn*, in his *Zoroastrian Problems in the 9th. Century Books*, 1943, p.195, cited by V. Minorsky, *Iranica*, 1964, p.257.

ticular prominence) and the Abbasid period saw a general Persianization of the court culture if not that of the caliphate in general. But the Arab yoke still clearly rankled and the early Abbasid period was marked by a series of spectacular revolts throughout Persia against rule from Baghdad.

A gradual weakening of the caliphal power meant that by the tenth century local dynasties controlled much of Iran, though they still nominally held power under the caliph's authority. In the west, including Baghdad itself for a while, the Buyids ruled; this was a dynasty that claimed descent from the Sasanians, revived for itself the Sasanian title of "King of Kings," and in its cultural allegiances seemed ready to embrace whatever would distinguish it from the Abbasids. It had strong Shi'a sympathies (the Abbasids of course were Sunnis) and the Buyid court also celebrated the ancient Zoroastrian festivals; this syncretic and quasi-nationalist amalgam is a curious foreshadowing of a much later period of Iranian culture, from the sixteenth century onwards. In the north east the Samanids ruled throughout the 10th century; this highly talented, energetic and culturally sophisticated dynasty claimed descent from Bahram Chubineh, a Sasanian general whom Ferdowsi treats at great length. It actively promoted an interest in ancient Iranian culture (as its claims to legitimacy of rule came largely from this source), commissioning translations and encouraging an antiquarian interest in the country's past. Most crucially for the later development of Persian literature, the dynasty used new Persian (the language that had developed since the conquest) rather than Arabic as its court language, and a court poetry of great brilliance, in Persian, soon began to flourish in Khorasan and Transoxiana, the area controlled by the Samanids.

Ferdowsi and His Sources

It was into this world that Ferdowsi was born, in 940 C.E., in a village near Tus, a town later to be supplanted in importance by its neighbor, Mashhad, but which was at the time one of the major cities of Khorasan. He was a "dehqan," that is a member of the indigenous landed aristocracy, a class which had survived the conquest in a severely attenuated form, and which had of course had to make its accommodations with the new civilization. It nevertheless saw itself as the repository of Persian/Iranian tradition and was regarded as "echt-Persian" in its sympathies (so much so that when the two peoples, Arab and Persian, are

contrasted in the literature of the period the word "dehqan" is some-
times used as the equivalent of "Persian"). Tus was generally controlled
by the Samanids, though its local ruler during part of Ferdowsi's lifetime,
Mansur b. Abd al-Razzaq, sometimes tried to play off the Samanids and
Buyids against each other, to his own advantage. The revival of interest
in indigenous Persian culture, fostered by the Samanids, was clearly of
fundamental importance in providing the milieu in which a project such
as the writing of the *Shahnameh,* which sought to celebrate the cultural
and ethnic inheritance of ancient Iran, could be undertaken. There is
also the fact that it was under the Samanids that poetry in Persian came
to be extensively written and so developed into a cultural force to be
reckoned with; this too indicates Ferdowsi's debt to the general ethos of
ethnic and quasi-national self-promotion created by the Samanid court.

Apart from those for a few relatively minor passages in the later parts
of the poem, Ferdowsi's sources have disappeared. The scholarly con-
sensus is that he used both oral and written sources, though the exact
proportion of the one to the other remains in doubt. For the later sec-
tions of the poem (from the advent of Sekandar—Alexander the
Great—onwards), he certainly utilized mainly and perhaps exclusively
written sources, some of which still exist, but for the earlier, legend-
ary and mythological sections, he may well have used primarily oral
sources.[2] One section of the poem, which was concerned with the
introduction of Zoroastrianism under king Goshtasp, was written by
Ferdowsi's predecessor, the poet Daqiqi, and Ferdowsi took over the
composition of the work when Daqiqi was murdered by a slave.

Ferdowsi's allegiances are apparent from the opening of the poem,
as much from his omissions as from what he includes. He begins with
the creation of the world, and the appearance of the first man/king,
Kayumars, and then passes on to kings who fight against supernatural
evil forces and establish the arts of civilization. Although there can be
no doubt whatsoever that Ferdowsi was a sincere Moslem (and there is
some evidence that like the Buyids he combined "nationalist" senti-
ment with Shi'a sympathies) he makes no attempt to include any ele-

---

2. This is the present writer's opinion, and was also that of the major Iranian scholar
Mehrdad Bahar as well as being shared by a few younger scholars. I emphasize though
that this is still very much a minority view, and that most scholars of the poem con-
tinue to believe that Ferdowsi used written sources for the whole work, supple-
mented by some oral material.

ments of the Qur'anic/Moslem cosmology in his poem, nor does he attempt to integrate the legendary Persian chronology of the material at the opening of his poem with a Qur'anic chronology. Unlike other writers who dealt with similar material, and who did attempt to intertwine the two chronologies (e.g. the historians Tabari and Mas'udi), he simply ignores Islamic cosmology and chronology altogether and places the Persian creation myths center stage. Further, the first evil person (as against supernatural being) in his poem is the usurping king, Zahhak, who brings disaster on Iran and who is identified as an Arab. The poem ends with the triumph of the Arab armies and the defeat of the Sasanians, and perhaps the most famous passage of this closing section is the prophecy by the Sasanian commander Rostam, the son of Hormozd, of the disasters that the conquest will bring on the country. The poem is thus framed by a fairly forthright hostility toward the Arabs and the political culture, if not the religion, they brought with them.

A Western reader who is unfamiliar with the poem, but who has been told that it deals with Iran's history before the coming of Islam, would naturally expect to find the early legendary material followed by stories relating to the Achaemenid monarchs—Cyrus, Darius, Xerxes and their successors. But the Achaemenids are virtually absent from the poem until just before the advent of Alexander the Great, that is until their decline. Further, the area of Iran which was their homeland, Fars, (or Pars, from which the word Persia is derived) is only rarely mentioned in the first two-thirds of the poem, and most of the place names that figure prominently in the pre-Alexander portion of the poem (e.g., Balkh, the river Oxus, the river Hirmand (Helmand), Kabul, Marv) are not within the confines of modern Iran. In fact the homeland of Iran in the *Shahnameh,* at least until the advent of the Sasanians, is Khorasan, which under the Samanids extended to the Oxus, and the material utilized in the earlier sections of the poem derives from the legends of this area and of Sistan—i.e. eastern Iran and what is now western Afghanistan. It has been surmised that during the dynastic upheavals between the conquest by Alexander and the emergence of the Sasanians in the third century C.E. (and particularly under the Parthians who derived from areas celebrated in these legends) this material gradually replaced the historical record of the Achaemenids who thus to all intents and purposes disappeared from the national record.

Themes, Preoccupations, and How the Poem Changes

The surface of the first half of the poem is concerned largely with tribal warfare, with the river Oxus defining the approximate territorial boundary between the factions; the obvious values celebrated are therefore those of tribal loyalty and military valor. The basic conflict is that between Iran and Turan, i.e. Khorasan and Transoxiana; the conflict is given a mythical origin in the story of the fratricidal conflict of Tur and Iraj. The inhabitants of Turan are referred to as "Turks"; this ethnic definition derives from the late Sasanian period when the area was in fact inhabited by Turkish tribes who did constantly threaten Iran. But the legends themselves must be older than this conflict, and, as the story of the common familial origin of the two peoples indicates, the stories, if they have any historical basis at all, must refer to ancient rivalries between different Iranian clans occurring perhaps around the time the Iranian people descended onto the Iranian plateau (a migration that is assumed to have happened some time before the beginning of the first millennium B.C.E.). The very earliest must refer to an even earlier period as they have parallels in Indian myth and legend (Jamshid of the *Shahnameh,* for example, has been identified with Yama, the Hindu Lord of the Underworld), and presumably derive from the time before the split between the Indian and Iranian divisions of the Indo-European peoples. Parallels with Western mythologies are also discernible: for example the story of Jamshid and Zahhak is not unlike that of Prometheus, in that a hubristic king introduces the arts of civilization to mankind, and is then kept in perpetual underground torment, except that the two halves of the tale are assigned to two actors within one story rather than to one.

Though most of them seem to have come from eastern Iran not all of the stories in the legendary section of the *Shahnameh* derive from the same tradition. Two different dynastic traditions are interwoven, and much of the interest of this part of the poem comes from the relationship between two dynastic families—the Kayanids, who rule Iran as a whole, and the house of Nariman (Sam, his son Zal, Zal's son Rostam, Rostam's son Faramarz) who rule in Sistan but who also function as the Kayanids' chief champions and advisors. This relationship is presented as a gradually deteriorating one: Sam is unquestioning in his loyalty to his Kayanid overlords, acting with the same loyalty toward bad kings as toward good; Zal is often critical of his kings' actions but always finally supports them; Rostam, who is the preeminent hero of the legendary section of the poem, is openly contemptuous of two of his kings (Kavus and Goshtasp) though he too, until goaded beyond endurance, acts with general loyalty; Rostam's son Faramarz rises in rebellion against his king and is slain.

What is perhaps especially interesting is that in these conflicts between the Iranian kings and their champions/advisors the latter are virtually always shown to be ethically superior to the kings they serve. Given the legendary and tribal nature of the stories, loyalty is obviously a prime virtue of the society described in the poem, but much of the poem's aesthetic interest derives from the fact that those who demand such loyalty are often morally inferior to those whom they govern, and that our sympathies are certainly with the governed rather than the governors. A similar situation can be found on the familial level. The three best known stories of the legendary section of the poem—those of Sohrab, Seyavash and Esfandyar—involve the deaths of sons; in each case the death comes about as a result of the father's actions, directly so with Sohrab, indirectly but equally culpably with Seyavash and Esfandyar. Again, the inferior in the relationship is shown as the innocent (this is particularly clear in the case of Seyavash). It is worth remarking also that all three of these slain sons have foreign, non-Iranian, mothers; Sohrab's mother is from Samangan, a frontier town with ambiguous loyalties, Seyavash's is from Turan, the traditional enemy of Iran throughout the poem, Esfandyar's is from "Rum" (Byzantium). Here too it seems as if the apparently monolithically authoritarian message of the poem is being somewhat called into question; just as loyalty to kings and fathers is a demand that produces a terrible human cost, so too the very centrality of Iran to the poem's values seems questioned by the sympathy we are invited to give to these sacrificed half-foreign princes. Indeed, Seyavash and his son Khosrow, who is presented as the perfect monarch of the legendary portion of the poem, both turn away from Iran for personal, ethical reasons.

Khosrow's abdication directs us to another complexity in the poem, its treatment of the notion of kingship. A surprisingly large number of kings in the poem abdicate, and prominent among these are two of the most ethically admirable of the poem, Feraydun and Khosrow. There is a story in the *Golestan,* by the thirteenth-century

Persian writer Sa'di, about a king who has a wonderful advisor whom he dismisses. The advisor takes up with a group of religious mendicants and there finds a spiritual peace he had never known at court. The country begins to go to rack and ruin and the king sends for his former advisor to return, saying he is the one man with enough intelligence to fill the post. The former advisor's answer is that it is precisely his intelligence that prevents him from resuming his position. The same problem, transferred to the ethical plain, haunts much of the *Shahnameh;* those ethically most fitted to rule are precisely those most reluctant to rule. The problem is graphically set out during Khosrow's self-communing before he finally resigns the throne.

The relatively frequent abdications, as well as other evidence such as the role Zal and Rostam play as kingmakers after the murder of the king Nozar, are further evidence of the eastern origin of the stories that make up the legendary part of the poem. Two traditions of kingship exist simultaneously in the work. One is that espoused by the Sasanians, through whom Ferdowsi must have received his sources; this is in essence the ancient Middle-Eastern notion of kingship, one that ties kingship to religion and to the sanction of God, that elevates the king to a quasi-divine position as God's representative on earth, and which derived from the pre-Iranian Babylonian dynasties. The other derives from "the practice of the steppe" and involves the acclamation of the king by his peers, the notion that the king can always be replaced if he becomes incompetent (or too old to rule effectively), and that he rules by virtue of his abilities and the consent of the nobility in general. The poem's "abdications" would seem largely to derive from this latter tradition, though in keeping with his practice elsewhere Ferdowsi frequently rewrites the topos as a problem of personal ethical choice. (There is a certain irony in the fact that of the two traditions of kingship it is the Eastern, less absolutist, one that seems to be authentically Iranian and the Western absolutist one that is ultimately Babylonian and non-Iranian; though due to the Achaemenids' espousal of the Babylonian tradition, and its adoption by subsequent Iranian dynasties, especially the Sasanians, it is this tradition that has come to be seen as essentially Iranian).

The figure of Rostam is of particular interest. He is the preeminent hero of the poem, and is presented as Iran's savior, but his origins (as the child of an Indian princess descended from an Arab demon king and of a man brought up beyond civilization by the fabulous Simorgh) proclaim him as having a peculiarly tangential relationship with Iran and its court and culture. He is in every sense a liminal figure, ruling in a border area, with connections to both the supernatural world (the Simorgh) and with the animal kingdom (his talismanic tiger skin). He displays many of the characteristics of the trickster hero, as this figure is found in many cultures, and indeed his patronymic ("Dastan") means "trickery." Further his ethic and way of being in the world often seem more primitive, and even gross, than those of the suave courtiers against whom he is often pitted, and it is notable that the weapons particularly associated with him (the mace, or club, and the lariat), are of the most ancient, and incidentally pre-metallic, kind. His legend would seem to incorporate extremely ancient layers of storytelling, some of them perhaps going back in origin to prehistory.

It should be apparent from even such a brief and necessarily incomplete summary of the themes of the poem's opening section that although it is undoubtedly an epic, and its superficial concerns are those of a dynastic chronicle, the relatively straightforward content we associate with such terms does not begin to do justice to the work's density and artistic complexity.

The poem passes from legendary to quasi-historical material with the appearance of Alexander, though in the earlier sections of this "historical" part the stories are given a more or less legendary treatment (Alexander for example is half-Iranian, his father being the Iranian king Darab, and in common with other Islamic versions of his legend he is presented as much as a seeker after knowledge and enlightenment as a world-conqueror). As with the Achaemenids, the historical record of the Parthians, who ruled Iran from the third century B.C.E. until the third C.E., is largely absent from the poem; this is almost certainly due to the success of the Sasanians in deliberately obliterating the memory of the dynasty they replaced.

The closing portion of the poem deals with the Sasanians; here the record is relatively complete and parts of the poem do approach the simplicity, even randomness, of a chronicle. There is also much more circumstantial detail to many of the stories recounted, and they clearly have not undergone the mythological weathering and constant refashioning of the legendary earlier narratives. Much of this section of the poem can be seen as a record of more or less direct propaganda for the glories of Sasanian civilization; the reforms of Ardeshir for example and a great deal of the narrative concerned with Khosrow (Kesra) Nushirvan, who is presented as the archetypal king of the poem's "historical" section much as Kay Khosrow is of the legendary section. Some themes of the earlier part of the poem continue to be treated; there is as much father-son conflict here as in the legendary section (albeit it is not presented in such starkly mythical terms), and the king-champion conflict receives one of its most extended treatments in the relationship between Bahram Chubineh and his two monarchs Hormozd and Khosrow Parviz. Bahram Chubineh is virtually the only would-be usurper of kingly power whom Ferdowsi treats relatively sympathetically, and this may well be because the Samanids, under whose nominal aegis Ferdowsi began his poem, claimed descent from this hero.

Often the stories in the poem's closing sections seem to be providing a kind of mirror image of the world of myth and legend of the poem's opening half. In the first half of the poem, prominent fathers (Rostam, Kavus, Goshtasp) are directly or indirectly responsible for their sons' deaths (Sohrab, Seyavash, Esfandyar), but in the second half prominent sons (Khosrow Parviz, Shirui) are held to be directly or indirectly responsible for their fathers' deaths (Hormozd, Khosrow Parviz). In the first half, the major champion is Rostam who, despite increasing provocation, attempts to maintain loyalty to the royal families of Iran and emphatically rejects the notion that he might ever be the king of the country. In the second half the major champion is Bahram Chubineh, who rebels against both of his monarchs and attempts to seize the throne for himself.

Most striking perhaps is the way that the role of women, and particularly non-Persian women, is redefined in the poem's second half. Virtually all of the significant women in the poem's mythological and legendary sections are non-Persian in origin (Sindokht, Rudabeh, Sudabeh, Farigis, Manizheh, Katayun) and, with the signal exception of Sudabeh, almost all of them are positively presented. Even Sudabeh, the first time we meet her, is a positive figure like Rudabeh and Manizheh, who defies her non-Persian father to be faithful to the Persian she loves. The most prominent female figure in the poem's second half is certainly Gordyeh, who is not foreign but Iranian, and represents the traditional and deeply Iranian virtue of loyalty to ancient mores. When foreign women do appear in the second half they are much less welcome than they had been in the legendary narratives. In the poem's earlier sections most of the narratives' major heroes have foreign mothers, but this doesn't prevent them from being seen as great exemplars of Persian virtues, and miscegenation is an accepted and generally welcomed fact. Indeed, perhaps the most positively presented king of the whole poem, Kay Khosrow, has only one Iranian grandparent; the other three are all Central-Asian Turks. But miscegenation is regarded with deep suspicion in the poem's second half, and that Hormozd has a Chinese mother and Shirui a Byzantine mother is seen in each case as a distinct negative. The preference here is for emphatic endogamy, although Ferdowsi is clearly embarrassed by the pre-Islamic laws that encouraged marriages within the immediate family, as is evident from his treatment of the daughter-father/Homay-Bahman relationship, and the way that he glosses over something earlier historians unequivocally recorded, that Gordyeh was married to her brother Bahram Chubineh.

One notable woman who has gone down in Persian legend as foreign in origin, and whose story is recounted by Ferdowsi, is Shirin. Unlike Nezami (the twelfth-century author of the better known romance version of her tale), Ferdowsi doesn't explicitly tell us that she is not a Persian, but given the suspicion of foreign consorts in the poem's second half, the unexplained scandal that surrounds her in his version of her tale, and the fact that her presence at court needs strenuous justification from her husband and king, Khosrow Parviz, perhaps point to this. This unexplained scandal is also an example of how not only the content of the tales changes in the poem's second half, but also Ferdowsi's method of telling them. In general, when reading the poem's earlier narratives, we have a clear idea of the ethical issues involved, and of where our sympathies are supposed to lie. We know that Seyavash is ethically superior to both Kavus and Sudabeh; that Piran Viseh acts from more morally admirable motives than does his king, Afrasyab; and that Goshtasp is at fault when he sends Esfandyar to bring Rostam to his court in chains. This moral clarity is often much harder to find in Ferdowsi's portraits of the central characters of his poem's later sections, many of whom are presented in a highly ambiguous and ethically unresolved fashion. Are we to approve or disapprove of Shirin? When we first meet her she is an abandoned woman and a figure of pathos; she elicits our sympathy. She is accused of some unspecified moral impurity and the charge is never really denied, merely evaded; we suspend judgment. She secretly murders her husband's favorite wife and assumes her position in the harem; we disapprove. She rejects her odious stepson, Shirui, and has a splendid speech of self-defense and a moving death scene; we approve, and this seems to be the final impression we are meant to bring away from her tale. But the figure she is most similar to from the poem's first half is the generally evil Sudabeh. Like Sudabeh she is a fairly ruthless and (probably) foreign royal consort who combines a dubious ethical reputation with an absolute hold on the king's affections, and at one point she seems to be about to become erotically involved with her stepson. With this comparison in mind we are again tempted to disapprove.

This moral ambiguity is not confined to Ferdowsi's portraits of female characters. Another prime example is that of the reformer Mazdak. We read that he is knowledgeable and that his words are wise, and when there is a famine the analogies he makes to the king concerning the populace's sufferings seem cogent and laudable. But the man who defeats him in argument is sponsored by Nushin-Ravan (Anushirvan), who is presented as one of the most admirable monarchs in the poem, and Ferdowsi explicitly tells us at the end of Mazdak's tale that a wise man would not act as he did. At the opening of his tale we seem meant to admire him; at the end we are virtually told to despise him. Perhaps the poem's most extreme instance of apparent authorial moral ambiguity, in the portrayal of a character, occurs in the account of Sekandar (Alexander), who is presented as both a barbarous conqueror and an ethically motivated searcher for enlightenment.

The reasons for this complexity, and ways in which it affects our experience of reading the tales, can be considered as separate, if related, issues. A major cause of some of the tales' ambiguities seems clear: Ferdowsi had much fuller sources for many of the quasi-historical narratives than he had for the legendary material, and some of these sources seem to have been quite radically contradictory of one another. The fact that he did not, apparently, attempt to resolve these contradictions seems significant. His method sometimes seems analogous to that adopted by a number of medieval Islamic historians (e.g., Tabari) who, when their sources offered differing versions of the same events, put down both versions, and then added, "But God knows best." Ferdowsi doesn't say this, and he doesn't explicitly tell us that he is recording different versions, but he (apparently) simply splices them together and leaves the contradictions intact in the one narrative. What is perhaps especially interesting is that in the pre-Sekandar portion of the poem we can sometimes see him choosing one version over another in the few instances when we know that he had more than one account available for a tale. For example, there were two versions as to why Rostam and Goshtasp quarreled. One was that Rostam despised Goshtasp's family as upstart, and Goshtasp resented this; the other was that Rostam vehemently denounced Goshtasp's adoption of the new religion of Zoroastrianism. The first version, which Ferdowsi follows, is found in Tabari's *History;* the second is in Dinawari's *History,* as well as in a number of works written after Ferdowsi's *Shahnameh,* e.g., the anonymous *History of Sistan.* This second version is wholly ignored by Ferdowsi. Here, for one of the legendary tales, we see him choosing one account over another, but in the historical sections of his poem his method seems to be more one of splicing than of choice and exclusion.

The contradictions are not only moral, but often factual. Sometimes these seem significant (Sasan has two differing lineages), often they seem simply incidental. Who, for example, is responsible for the blinding of King Hormozd? A prophecy says his wife will do it; we are told that members of a mob stirred up by Gostahm do it, unbeknownst to Hormozd's son, Khosrow Parviz. Khosrow Parviz is later accused of either having done it personally or of having instigated it. Ferdowsi apparently favors the second version (the mob), but he still includes the other two in his text.

When we compare the quasi-historical stories to those in the poem's legendary portion we see the truth of A. J. P. Taylor's aphorism, "History gets thicker as it approaches recent times—more people, more events, and more books written about them." One senses Ferdowsi dealing with these accumulating people, events, and books in his presentation of the historical narratives, which are thick with detail in a way that is quite absent from most of the earlier tales. If this multiplicity of detail can occasionally lead to contradictions, and sometimes to outright anachronisms (as in Sekandar's Christianity), it can also, paradoxically, give the tales a quotidian realism that is largely absent from the legendary material, as well as providing for sudden and arresting shifts of tone. Furthermore, the intensity of a number of the psychological portraits in this section (e.g., that of Bahram Chubineh) depends largely on the telling accumulation of such details. This concern with the quotidian brings another advantage: it is in the Sasanian section of the poem that we most often glimpse daily life outside of the court and the realm of the heroic. The occasional vivid vignettes of rural life that we encounter in the reigns of the later Sasanian monarchs contribute a kind of stylized realism that can be charming or sobering, depending on the circumstances recounted. In the same way, much of the humor of the poem also occurs in the Sasanian section, again frequently in moments located outside of the court. A new problem is that when Ferdowsi's sources lack detailed accounts, he must nevertheless give some version of what he believes to have happened. His apologetic and relatively perfunctory account of the Ashkanians (Parthians) was clearly caused by the fact that the Sasanians had fairly efficiently obliterated them from the historical record. Interestingly enough, this is something that Bahram Chubineh threatens to do to the Sasanians themselves. When the government of the Islamic Republic expunged from public life all positive references to the Pahlavis, even changing all the street names in the major cities, they were following ancient precedent.

From the opening of the poem the Persian courts are characterized as centers of both justice and pleasure. The ideal king will administer justice, which includes protecting the frontiers of the country against invasion, and his court will also represent a kind of earthly paradise whose pleasures include feasting, wine-drinking, the giving and receiving of gifts, hunting, and the celebration of the major festivals of the Zoroastrian year. The worst sins, for both the king and his subjects, are greed and excessive ambition. Erotic pleasure is hardly dwelt on in the poem's legendary section, although it is understood that this too is a constituent of the court's function as an earthly paradise.

In the stories from the "historical" section of the poem, erotic pleasure is sometimes brought into the foreground in a way that it had not been in the earlier tales, and the simultaneous association of both justice and pleasure in the person of the ideal king becomes more problematic. The three most positively presented kings of the post-Sekandar section of the poem are Ardeshir (the founder of the Sasanian dynasty), Bahram Gur, and Nushin-Ravan (Anushirvan the Just). Ardeshir is presented as a vigorous reformer who rewrites his country's legal code, energetically puts down internal dissension, and secures the country's borders against invasion. Nushin-Ravan is a man who inherits an empire and strives to administer it justly and according to ancient precepts, while remaining open to wisdom from other sources, especially India. The main difference between them and the more admirable legendary monarchs whom they succeed is the centralization of their administrative and cultural control. The sense of various centers of power (e.g., Sistan) only tangentially under the central government's authority, which is everywhere present in the legendary material, has largely disappeared from the narratives. Nevertheless, both these kings are re-embodiments, in Sasanian terms, of ideals that have been explicit throughout the poem's legendary section.

Bahram Gur, of whom Ferdowsi seems, in general, emphatically to approve, introduces a relatively new element into the poem, which is the emphasis on pleasure, especially the pleasure of erotic adventure, as the primary, and apparently often sole, activity of a monarch. Bahram Gur is presented as an ideal monarch who is largely preoccupied with sensual, private pleasure, but who is nevertheless just, and widely loved by his subjects, even if his vizier is worried about what he sees as the king's excessive attachment to women. Two stories—one beginning in comedy and ending in tragedy, the other wholly comic, which are placed back to back in his reign—also elaborate on another pleasure that had been taken for granted in the earlier sections of the poem, and this is drinking wine. The first story ends with wine being forbidden, and the second with this prohibition being abrogated as long as one does not drink to excess. It seems more than a coincidence that the outcome of the stories concerning wine in Bahram's reign reverses orthodox interpretation of the Qur'anic texts on wine, according to which the prohibition abrogates the implied permission to drink in moderation. At the end of the poem, when Rostam the son of Hormozd prophesies the disasters that will come to Iran as a result of the Arab invasion, Bahram Gur's reign is singled out as emblematic of all that the Arabs will destroy, and we realize that the emphasis on sensual pleasure and its attendant luxuries in his reign was deliberately presented as an alternative to the civilization brought by the Moslem Arab conquerors, which is characterized, by Rostam at least, in wholly negative and dour terms.

But despite Rostam's unequivocally bleak prophecy, the final episodes of the poem are profoundly ambiguous. Hormozd and Khosrow Parviz are complex, weak kings who seem to have inherited Bahram Gur's attachment to pleasure but have none of his panache or instinct for largess, and are unable to command the affection and loyalty of their subjects. They are followed by a virtual rabble. The sense of an empire destroyed as much by the weakness, extravagance, and squalid infighting of its rulers as by outside invasion pervades the poem's closing pages. Although the poet is emphatic in his lament for the civilization that was destroyed by the invasion, his depiction of the negotiations between the Arabs and the Persians seems at times weighted in the Arabs' moral favor. It is difficult to read the scene in which the laconic and almost naked Arab envoy Sho'beh confronts the arrogant Persian commanders, resplendent in their golden armor, as anything but an indictment of the Persians. Despite the undeniable epic grandeur of its best-known passages, the *Shahnameh* is never a simple poem, and the moral complexities it explores throughout its immense length come to a magnificent and unresolved climax in its last pages. If Ferdowsi's final claim is one of pride in his work, an emotion that seems almost as strongly present is that of bewilderment. As he frequently remarks whenever he has to record the untimely death of a character he admires, he cannot understand what the heavens arc about, and this sense of a repeatedly frustrated interrogation of God's purposes reaches its apogee in the poem's closing scenes.

But although in the narrative of the Sasanian reigns we may regret the absence of that epic force present in the earlier sections of the poem, there are other compensating virtues to this latter part, which often, incidentally, receives much less attention than the opening half. The circumstantial quality of much of the detail can give the scenes great vividness (e.g. the scene of the minstrel Barbad playing to Khosrow Parviz,) as well as pathos (e.g. the events leading up to the murder of Khosrow Parviz,) and tragic intensity (e.g. the suicide of Shirin, a scene that seems in its details to owe something to the story of Cleopatra's suicide over Antony's body in order to escape falling into the hands of Octavian, and whose ultimate source may be the story of Panthea in Xenophon's *Cyropaedia*). Few passages of any literature can equal the profound sense of the passing of a civilization that informs the closing pages of the *Shahnameh,* in which the cry that "Our long travails will be as nought" seems to call up the whole vast history of a country in its despairing summation. As the Zoroastrian chronicler quoted above wrote, "The world passes from us." These last scenes have a wonderful vividness and pathos; very telling for example is the way Ferdowsi emphasizes the pomp and wealth of the Iranian army and its commanders glittering in their jewels and gold, and then contrasts this with the hardiness and poverty of their Arab opponents. Two almost contradictory messages are being given to us at once; the wealth underlines the splendor that is about to pass, it brings home to us the sheer magnitude of what was about to happen, the gorgeousness that had been the indigenous Iranian civilization; but in the ascetic unconcern of the Arab warrior Sho'beh it also brings home the virtues of spartan simplicity, the laconic uncluttered force that an attitude of *contemptu mundi* can bring with it. In a brief scene of great richness and with consummate skill Ferdowsi sees and conveys both the glamor of the civilization that is dying and the valor of the new civilization that is emerging.

The Poem's Reception

If Ferdowsi began his poem under the Samanids, and in hopes of contributing to the revival of a politically independent Islamo-Persian civilization such as that promoted by the Samanids and their western neighbors the Buyids, he lived to see such hopes dashed within his own lifetime. In the closing years of the tenth century and the opening years of the eleventh the Samanid dynasty collapsed and eastern Iran was taken over by the Ghaznavid Turks under their energetic king Mahmud of Ghazneh. Whether Ferdowsi completely rewrote his poem or simply revised it to suit the new political climate is not known, but as it stands now the work contains frequent episodes of panegyric on Mahmud, though the irony of the author of a poem celebrating countless Iranian victories over the Turks writing such passages cannot have been lost on either the poet or the king. Legend has it that Ferdowsi's poem was not appreciated by Mahmud and that he died a poor and embittered man. The closing lines of the poem certainly attest to resentment at being poorly rewarded for what must have been virtually his life's work.

Just as the politics of Ferdowsi's own time seem to have affected the reception of his work so too modern politics have played a part in defining the poet's and his poem's reputation. The Pahlavi kings who ruled Iran from 1925 until 1979 were particularly interested in emphasizing Iran's pre-Islamic past as the ultimate source of Persian civilization, and to this end they assiduously promoted the study of Ferdowsi's poem, as it takes exactly this past as its subject matter. Since the Islamic revolution of 1979 in Iran the Islamic component of Persian culture has received emphatic state support, and the pre-Islamic period has been downplayed as a factor within the culture. In each case scholarship, both Western and Iranian, has tended to follow the current political fashion. Scholars writing on Iran before the revolution tended to emphasize a continuity of culture across the Islamic watershed; some recent writing tends to suggest that little of significance survived the conquest, that Iran became a wholly new cultural entity after its incorporation into the Islamic world. (Similar arguments as to the sources of national tradition can of course be found in other countries' histories; in Greece for example there are both partisans of continuity between ancient and modern Greek civilization, and those who assert that the coming of Christianity and the fashioning of a distinctive Byzantine civilization virtually negated all that had gone before in the culture.) But Ferdowsi's poem has survived other political vicissitudes and its immense value both as a literary work and as an unrivaled source of Iranian legendary material will certainly ensure its continued vitality as a component of the culture. Whatever else it is, the *Shahnameh* is the one indisputably great surviving cultural artifact that attempts to assert a continuity of collective memory across the moment of the conquest; at the least it salvaged the pre-conquest legendary history of Iran and made it available to the Iranian people as a memorial of a great and distinctive civilization.

The Translation

A word or two about the form of the present translation is perhaps appropriate. In Persian, the poem is written in one form throughout, couplets, which correspond quite closely in length to the English heroic couplet. But the stories of the *Shahnameh* have always enjoyed a vigorous popular life, told by itinerant story tellers called *naqqals,* and in this incarnation they have been recounted largely in prose with some episodes in verse. As Kumiko Yamamoto has put it in her fine book *The Oral Background of Persian Epics* (Leiden, 2003) "Prose is used to tell a story, and verse to mark the internal divisions of a performance . . . In terms of narrative structure too, verses which appear intermittently . . . are used, for example, to enhance dramatic effects, to express the internal feelings of characters, or to sum up the story.

Hence, verse functions as an attention-getter in the narrative, introducing different rhythms into the prose narration" (p.28). If therefore one wrote down a naqqal's performance, sticking to his formal choices, one would finish up with a prosimetrum, a text that is largely prose but contains passages of verse at significant moments of the narrative. The prosimetrum is a common medieval Persian form—Sa'di's *Golestan* is perhaps the most famous example—but it was also a not uncommon medieval European form; perhaps the best known European examples are the *De Consolatione Philosophiae* by Boethius and *La Vita Nuova* by Dante. To translate a medieval Persian poem into what had been a medieval Persian and European form seemed to be an undertaking that would not wholly traduce the formal qualities of the original.

There was a further reason for my choosing the form favored by the naqqals. The naqqali diffusion of the narratives of the *Shahnameh* has ensured, and been the most obvious manifestation of, these narratives' popular life within the culture. My aim in translating the *Shahnameh* was not to produce a text for scholars, but to make it available to a wide non-specialist audience. I hesitate to say a popular audience: perhaps no medieval literary artifact, from any culture, can have a truly popular existence now. We prefer our medievalism to be derivative and ersatz; *The Lord of the Rings* rather than *Beowulf, Camelot* rather than Malory or Chrétien de Troyes. Nevertheless there is still a world of readers, especially relatively young readers, who are not scholars, who might try Beowulf or Malory, and it was them I aimed to reach with my translation. I translated not for scholars, who after all have access to the original text, now in relatively good editions, but for that radically endangered species, the general reader. The naqqals' choice of form, the form of the popular diffusion of the stories of the *Shahnameh* in Persian, thus seemed all the more appropriate.

Given the poem's immense length, some passages have inevitably been omitted, and others are presented in summary form (the italicized prose passages are summarized translations of sections of Ferdowsi's text). In general, I did not omit passages within a given episode, and when I did it was usually because the poem had become highly repetitive. For example, in the later reigns there is an enormous amount of ethical advice handed out by kings either at their coronations or on their deathbeds. Much of this advice is extremely repetitive, and much of it I omitted. This of course changes the structure of Ferdowsi's poem, and ideally a reader should be aware of this. But our appetite for moral *sententiae* is considerably smaller than that of a medieval audience, and I did not feel I could try the patience of the general reader—who I again emphasize is my intended audience—too high. Conversely, in what I take to be the greatest stories of the poem, for example those of Seyavash and Esfandyar, virtually nothing is omitted. In particular I was scrupulous in translating everything that related to the interiority of the characters and the ethical dilemmas they face, simply because these seem to me to be among the most distinctive and aesthetically admirable sections of the poem.

The most substantial omission is the episode of the Twelve Champions, the Davazdah Rokh, which occurs during Kay Khosrow's war against Turan. The contemporary Iranian author Golshiri claimed that this episode is the heart of the poem, which only goes to show how far two devoted readers of the *Shahnameh* can, in all good faith, hold utterly differing views of it. The episode is highly repetitious (this is of course deliberate, but that does not make the repetitions any more palatable for a modern reader), and it also strikes me as otiose in its descriptions, and embarrassingly ethnocentric in its triumphalism. It is an extreme example of the kind of episode that can be found in ethnocentric epics the world over: but no other epic that I am aware of has an equivalent to the story of Seyavash, or to the story of Esfandyar, and since, for reasons of space, I had to make choices as to what could stay and what could go I felt I had much rather lose the Davazdah Rokh than either Seyavash or Esfandyar.

In working on this translation I have used various editions of Ferdowsi's text (which differs widely from manuscript to manuscript). For the stories prior to the tale of Esfandyar, my chief source has been the edition edited by Djalal Khaleghi-Motlagh (5 volumes, New York, 1988-1997). At the time of writing, only the earlier sections of the poem have been published in this edition. Sometimes, in the interests of producing a coherent narrative, it has proved to be impossible to follow this edition (for example, during the narrative of Zal's being tested by the sages of Manuchehr's court, where this edition, following what most scholars believe to be the oldest manuscript of the poem, gives too garbled an account to make narrative sense), and at these moments I have turned mainly to the so-called Moscow edition, edited by Bertels et al., (9 volumes, Moscow, 1966-1971). For the story of

Esfandyar, I have used Azizollah Jovayni's *Hemaseh-ye rostam o esfandyar* (Tehran, 1995). For the remainder of the stories, i.e. those after Esfandyar, I have used the Moscow edition. For a few moments, chiefly in order to add clarity to narrative details, I have used the nineteenth-century edition edited by Jules Mohl (reprinted Paris, 1976).

A Note on Four Words

The word *farr* refers to a God-given glory, and inviolability, bestowed on a king, and sometimes on a great hero. Its physical manifestation was a light that shone from the king's or hero's face. It has been suggested that the practice of saluting derives from an inferior's complimentary covering of his eyes with his hand, in order not to be blinded by the *farr* supposedly emanating from his superior.

The geographical term *Rum,* and its adjective *Rumi,* are particularly hard to translate consistently in the stories in the *Shahnameh*. The words refer to the civilizations that lie to the west of Iran, in Asia Minor and in Europe. Thus Sekandar the Macedonian is a Rumi, as are the Roman emperors who fought the early Sasanians, as also are the Byzantine emperors who fought the later Sasanians. For the sake of relative historical veracity I have translated the words in different ways in stories that occur in different epochs. Thus in the time of Sekandar I have translated Rum and Rumi as Greece and Greek, in the reign of Shapur I have used the terms Rome and Roman, and for the reigns of the later kings I have used Byzantium and Byzantine. This has the advantage of reflecting the actual enemies of Iran at the relevant periods, but it does also disguise the way in which for Ferdowsi these Western civilizations were one and continuous. Ferdowsi also uses *Rumi* (usually to describe cloth or armor) during the legendary stories, which take place in a nebulous prehistoric time, and here I have simply kept the word unchanged, as all translations would be anachronistic.

The Parthian and Sasanian capital was at Ctesiphon, on the River Tigris. In the reigns of the later Sasanian kings, Ferdowsi frequently refers to the city as "Baghdad" (he occasionally does this earlier in the poem too), and I have kept this usage in most instances, though it sounds and is anachronistic. The Abbasid (751 C.E.–1258 C.E.) capital of Baghdad was deliberately located close to the ruins of Ctesiphon, and materials taken from the ruins were used in its construction. In referring to Ctesiphon by the name of the Arab city that would almost literally take its place as the administrative center of a great empire, Ferdowsi seems to be simultaneously asserting a continuity of civilization across the divide of the conquest, and predicting the conquest itself.

The word *nard* is usually translated as "backgammon," and it is often said that the story of the importation of chess from India to Iran, and the Persian invention of backgammon in response, comes from the *Shahnameh*'s account of the reign of Nushin-Ravan. However, it is fairly clear from Ferdowsi's description of *nard* that the game referred to is almost certainly not backgammon, which does not, for example, involve kings. There were medieval variants of chess, at least one of which involved the use of dice to determine permissible moves, and it seems likely that it is one of these variants that Ferdowsi is describing, rather than backgammon. As we have no names for such variants I have left the word in Persian.

Dick Davis

A NOTE ON THE ILLUSTRATIONS

The immense popularity of the *Shahnameh*'s narratives and characters within Persian culture is indicated by the fact that they have been illustrated in a multitude of ways, from frescoes in palaces to sumptuous miniatures in court-commissioned manuscripts, to large screens painted in a direct and naïve style (somewhat similar to that used by cinema poster artists in the Indian subcontinent), which could be unrolled as a backdrop for a naqqal when he was telling a particular story. The illustrations used for this translation are taken from lithographs for popular nineteenth-century editions of the poem. They bring together traditional Iranian styles and the Western styles of illustration that were beginning to be known in Iran at this time, and in their combination of the homely and the heroic, the familiar and the fabulous, they give us a glimpse of the imaginative ways in which the poem's narratives have flourished within Persian popular culture.

Shahnameh

The Persian Book of Kings

THE FIRST KINGS

The Reign of Kayumars

What does the Persian poet say about the first man to seek the crown of world sovereignty? No one has any knowledge of those first days, unless he has heard tales passed down from father to son. This is what those tales tell: The first man to be king, and to establish the ceremonies associated with the crown and throne, was Kayumars. When he became lord of the world, he lived first in the mountains, where he established his throne, and he and his people dressed in leopard skins. It was he who first taught men about the preparation of food and clothing, which were new in the world at that time. Seated on his throne, as splendid as the sun, he reigned for thirty years. He was like a tall cypress tree topped by the full moon, and the royal *farr* shone from him. All the animals of the world, wild and tame alike, reverently paid homage to him, bowing down before his throne, and their obedience increased his glory and good fortune.

He had a handsome son, who was wise and eager for fame, like his father. His name was Siamak, and Kayumars loved him with all his heart. The sight of his son was the one thing in the world that made him happy, and his love for the boy made him weep when he thought of their being separated.

Siamak grew into a fine young man, and he had no enemies, except for Ahriman, who was secretly jealous of his splendor and looked for ways to humble him. Ahriman had a son who was like a savage wolf; this fearless youth gathered an army together, spread sedition throughout the world, and prepared to attack the king.

Siamak Is Killed by the Black Demon

Kayumars was unaware of these machinations, but the angel Sorush appeared before Siamak in the guise of a magical being swathed in a leopard skin, and told him of the plots against his father. The prince's heart seethed with fury and he gathered an army together. There was no armor at that time, and the prince dressed for war in a leopard skin. The two armies met face to face, and Siamak strode forward to attack, but the black demon sunk his claws into the prince's unprotected body and stretched the noble Siamak in the dust.

> Now in the dirt he laid the king's son low,
> Clawed at his gut, and struck the fatal bow.
> So perished Siamak—a demon's hand
> Left leaderless his people and his land.

When the king heard of his son's death, his world darkened with sorrow. He descended from the throne, weeping and beating his head, and scoring his royal flesh in an agony of distress. His face was smeared with blood, his heart was in mourning, and his days were filled with sorrow. The army was arrayed before the king, and a cry of grief went up from its ranks. Everyone wore blue as a sign of mourning, and all the animals, wild and tame alike, and the birds of the air, gathered and made their way weeping and crying to the mountains, and the dust sent up by the throng of mourners hovered in the air above the king's court.

They mourned for a year, until the glorious Sorush brought a message from God, saying, "Kayumars, weep no more, but be of sound mind again. Gather an army together and fight against this malevolent demon." The king turned his weeping face toward the heavens and prayed to the great god that evil strike those who think evil. Then he prepared to avenge the death of Siamak, neither sleeping at night nor pausing to eat in the day.

Hushang and Kayumars Fight Against the Black Demon

The great Siamak had a son, Hushang, who acted as his grandfather's advisor. This splendid youth seemed compounded of intelligence and courtliness. Kayumars lovingly brought him up as his own son, because Hushang reminded him of Siamak, and he had eyes for no one else. When his heart was set on war and vengeance he summoned Hushang and laid before him his plans and secrets. He said, "I shall gather an army together and raise a cry of lamentation in the demons' ranks. You must command these warriors, since my days are numbered and you must be the new leader." He gathered together fairies, leopards and lions, savage wolves and fearless tigers, birds and domestic animals, and this army was led by the intrepid young prince. Kayumars was in the rear, his grandson Hushang in the van. The black demon came fearlessly forward, and the dust of his forces rose into the heavens, but the king's fury and the wild animals' magnificence rendered the demons' claws harmless. When the two groups met, the demons were defeated by the animals; like a lion, Hushang caught the black demon in his grip, cleaving his body in two and severing his monstrous head. He laid him low in the dust and flayed his wretched body of its skin.

When Kayumars had achieved the vengeance he desired, his days came to an end, and the world was deprived of his glory.

> *You will not find another who has known*
> *The might of Kayumars and his great throne.*
> *The world was his while he remained alive,*
> *He showed men how to prosper and to thrive:*
> *But all this world is like a tale we hear—*
> *Men's evil, and their glory, disappear.*

The Reign of Hushang

The just and prudent Hushang was now master of the world, and he set the crown on his head and ruled in his grandfather's place. He reigned for forty years, and his mind was filled with wisdom, his heart with justice. Sitting on the royal throne, he said, "From this throne I rule over the seven climes, and everywhere my commands are obeyed." Mindful of God's will, he set about establishing justice. He helped the world flourish, and filled the face of the earth with his just rule.

The Discovery of Fire and the Establishment of the Feast of Sadeh

One day the king was riding toward the mountains with a group of companions when something long, and black suddenly appeared. Its two eyes were like bowls of blood affixed to its head, and smoke billowed from its mouth, darkening the world. Hushang considered care-

fully, then grasped a rock and flung it with all his royal strength at the
beast, which flickered aside, so that the rock struck against stony
ground and shattered. From the collision of the two stones a spark
leaped out, and the rock's heart glowed with fire. The snake was not
killed, but the fiery nature of flint was discovered, so that whenever
anyone struck it with iron, sparks flashed forth. Hushang gave thanks
to God that he had given this gift of fire, and from that time forth men
prayed toward fire. When night came Hushang and his companions
made a mountain of fire and circumambulated it. They had a feast that
night, and drank wine. The feast was named "Sadeh" and is Hushang's
legacy to us.

Then he took ore in his fist, and with fire he separated iron from its
rocky home. In this way he created the blacksmith's craft, fashioning
maces, axes, saws, and hatchets. Then he turned his attention to irriga-
tion, bringing water from lakes to the plains by means of channels and
canals, and so using his royal *farr* to lessen men's labor. In this way he
increased the land available for agriculture and the harvest, so that each
man could grow grain for his own bread and know the fruits of his own
toil.

Hushang used his God-given royal authority to separate animals
into those that are wild and can be hunted, like onager and deer, and
those suitable for domestic use, like cows, sheep, and donkeys. He
killed animals with fine pelts, like foxes and ermine, the soft squirrel,
and the sable, whose fur is so warm, and had fine clothes made from
them. Hushang toiled and spread justice, and consumed his due of the
world's goods, and then departed, leaving behind nothing but his good
name. In his time he struggled mightily, planning and inventing innu-
merable schemes, but when his days were at an end, for all his sagacity
and dignity, he departed. The world will not keep faith with you, nor
will she show you her true face.

The Reign of Tahmures

Hushang had an intelligent son, Tahmures, who was called "the Binder
of Demons." He sat on his father's throne and swore to preserve the
customs his father had instituted. He called his wise counselors to him
and spoke eloquently with them, saying, "Today the throne and crown,
the treasury and army, are mine; with my wisdom I shall cleanse the
world of evil. I shall restrict the power of demons everywhere and

make myself lord of the world. Whatever is useful in the world I will reveal and make available to mankind."

Then he sheared sheep and goats and spun their wool into fibers, from which he fashioned clothes; he also taught men how to weave carpets. He had flocks fed on grass, straw, and barley, and from among wild animals he selected the lynx and cheetah, bringing them in from the mountains and plains and confining them, to train them as hunters. He also chose hawks and falcons, and hens and roosters, who crow at dawn, and showed men how to tame these birds by treating them well and speaking gently to them. He brought out the hidden virtues of things, and the world was astonished at his innovations. He said that men should praise God, who had given mankind sovereignty over the earth's animals.

Tahmures had a noble vizier named Shahrasb, a man whose thoughts avoided all evil and who was universally praised. Fasting by day and praying by night, he was the king's star of good fortune, and the souls of the malevolent were under his control. Shahrasb wished the king's reign to be just, and he guided him in righteous paths, so that Tahmures lived purified of all evil and the divine *farr* emanated from him. The king bound Ahriman by spells and sat on him, using him as a mount on which to tour the world. When the demons saw this, many of them gathered in groups and murmured against him, saying the crown and *farr* were no longer his. But Tahmures learned of their sedition and attacked them, breaking their rebellion. He girded himself with God's glory and lifted his heavy mace to his shoulders, ready for battle.

All the demons and sorcerers came together in a great army, with the black demon as their leader, and their roars ascended to the heavens. But Tahmures suddenly confronted them, and the war did not last long; two-thirds of the demons he subdued by spells, and the other third by his heavy mace. He dragged them wounded and in chains in the dust, and they pleaded for their lives, saying, "Don't kill us, we can teach you something new and highly profitable." The king granted them their lives on condition that they reveal their secrets to him, and when he had freed them from their chains they had no choice but to obey him. They taught the king how to write, and his heart glowed like the sun with this knowledge. They did not teach him just one script, but almost thirty, including the Western, Arab, and Persian ways of writing, as well as the Soghdian, Chinese, and Pahlavi, showing him how the letters are formed and pronounced. For thirty years the king performed these and other noble actions; then his days were at an end and he departed, and the memory of his struggles was his memorial.

The Reign of Jamshid

All mourned when the Binder of Demons died. But his splendid son, Jamshid, his heart filled with his father's precepts, then prepared to reign. He sat on his father's throne, wearing a golden crown according to royal custom. The imperial *farr* was his. The world submitted to him; quarrels were laid to rest, and all demons, birds, and fairies obeyed Jamshid's commands. The royal throne shone with his luster, and the wealth of the world increased. He said, "God's glory is with me; I am both prince and priest. I hold evildoers back from their evil, and I guide souls toward the light."

First he turned his attention to weapons of war, and he opened the way to glory for his warriors. His royal *farr* softened iron, and his able mind taught men how to fashion helmets, chain mail, cuirasses, swords, and barding for horses. Occupied in this way for fifty years, he laid up stores of weapons. For another fifty years he gave his mind to the making of clothes for both feasting and fighting, using linen, silk, and wool, and fashioning fine stuffs and brocades from them. He taught the arts of spinning and weaving, dyeing and sewing. The world rejoiced in his reign, and he too rejoiced.

Then he spent fifty years gathering the men of different professions about him. He separated those whose business is prayer and worship, assigning the mountains to them as their dwelling place. Next he drew up ranks of men who carry lances, the lion-warriors who give splendor to their army and country, who are the throne's support and from whom a man's good reputation comes. The third group were those who work in the fields, sowing and reaping, and receiving no man's thanks, although no one reproaches them when it is time to eat. They are free men and quarrel with no one, and the world flourishes through their labor. As a sage once said, "It's only laziness that will make a slave of a free man." The fourth group were the men who work with their hands at various crafts and trades; they are contumacious people, and their hearts are always filled with anxiety. Jamshid spent fifty years arranging these matters, so that each man was aware of his appropriate duties and knew his own worth and rank.

Then he ordered the demons to mix clay and water and pack the mixture into molds for bricks. They made foundations of stone and plaster; then, using the science of geometry, they made the superstructure with bricks. In this way they built public baths and castles, and palaces that are a refuge against misfortune. He spent time extracting brilliant jewels and precious metals from rock, and so came into the possession of rubies, amber, gold, and silver. He used magic to solve the mysteries of how this could be done. He introduced the use of perfumes like benzoin, camphor, musk, sandalwood, ambergris, and rosewater, and he discovered cures for illnesses, showing men the way to good health. He revealed all these secrets, and the world had never known such an inquirer into her mysteries as he was. Next he turned his attention to water and ships, and so was able to travel quickly from country to country. Another fifty years passed in these labors, and nothing remained hidden from his wisdom.

The Festival of No-Ruz

Although Jamshid had accomplished all these things, he strove to climb even higher. With his royal *farr* he constructed a throne studded with gems, and had demons raise him aloft from the earth into the heavens; there he sat on his throne like the sun shining in the sky. The world's creatures gathered in wonder about him and scattered jewels on him, and called this day the New Day, or No-Ruz. This was the first day of the month of Farvardin, at the beginning of the year, when Jamshid rested from his labors and put aside all rancor. His nobles made a great feast, calling for wine and musicians, and this splendid festival has been passed down to us, as a memorial to Jamshid. Three hundred years went by, and death was unknown during that time; men knew nothing of sorrow or evil, and the demons were their slaves. The people obeyed their sovereign, and the land was filled with music. Years passed, the royal *farr* radiated from the king, and all the world was his to command.

> *Jamshid surveyed the world, and saw none there*
> *Whose greatness or whose splendor could compare*
> *With his: and he who had known God became*
> *Ungrateful, proud, forgetful of God's name.*

He summoned his army commanders and aged advisors and said, "I know of no one in the world who is my equal. It was I who introduced the skills and arts of living to mankind, and the royal throne has seen no one to compare with me. I arranged the world as I wished; your food and sleep and security come from me, as do your clothes and all of your comforts. Greatness, royalty, and the crown are mine; who would dare say that any man but I was king?" All the elders inclined their heads, since no one dared gainsay anything he said. But

> By saying this he lost God's farr, and through
> The world men's murmurings of sedition grew.

As a wise and reverent man once remarked, "If you are a king, be as a slave toward God; the heart of any man who is ungrateful to God will be filled with countless fears." Jamshid's days were darkened, and his world-illuminating splendor dimmed.

THE DEMON-KING ZAHHAK

The Tale of Merdas and His Son Zahhak

In those days, in the land of the Arabs, there was a good and fine king who sighed with fear before God. His name was Merdas, and he was a man of great generosity and justice. Each of the herds he had entrusted to his shepherds numbered a thousand, whether of cows, or Arab horses, or goats, or milk-giving sheep, and he freely gave milk to anyone who needed it.

This righteous man had a son, whose character had very little kindness in it. He was an ambitious youth named Zahhak, brave, turbulent in his moods, and of an evil disposition. Everyone called him Bivarasp, a Pahlavi word meaning "ten thousand horses," because he had ten thousand Arab horses, all with golden bridles. He spent most of his days and nights riding them, not into battle so much as to demonstrate his wealth and greatness.

One day at dawn Eblis appeared before Zahhak, presenting himself as a friendly well-wisher, and the youth was charmed by his conversation. Eblis said, "First I want your promise that our talk will be confidential, and then I will tell you what I have to say." The young man greeted him kindly, and answered, "I will tell no one about anything I hear from you."

Eblis said, "Listen to my advice. No one but you should be in charge here; with a son like you, why should an old, worn-out father go on ruling for so long? Take his place, you're the person best fitted for his position. If you listen to my advice, you will be the ruler of the world." Zahhak heard him out and considered his words, but the thought of shedding his father's blood troubled his heart. He said, "This is wrong; give me different advice, this is not something I can do." Eblis said, "If you don't follow my advice, you're breaking your promise; you'll stay as a wretched subject and your father will stay as ruler." And so he led the Arab into his trap, and Zahhak decided to obey him. He said, "Tell me how to do it, what's the best way to accomplish this? Don't make excuses now." Eblis replied,

> *"I will take care of how it's to be done;*
> *Your head will rise in heaven, like the sun."*

King Merdas owned a fine orchard, and he would go there in the dawn's darkness, to wash his head and body, and to pray. The servant who accompanied him did not bring a lamp. Eblis dug a deep pit there, and when the Arab king arrived in the orchard the next morning he fell into the pit and broke his back. The reverent man's good fortune was at an end, and his life departed. Then Eblis filled the pit in with soil and went on his way.

This noble king had taken pains to bring up his son in comfort; he had rejoiced in him and given him wealth. But his evil offspring broke faith with him and became complicit in his father's murder. I heard a wise man say that, no matter how much of a savage lion a man might be, he does not shed his father's blood, and if there is some untold secret here, it is the mother who can answer an inquirer's questions.

In this way the willful, unjust Zahhak seized his father's throne, placed the Arab crown on his head, and became the dispenser of largess and punishments to his people. When Eblis saw how effective his words had been, he gave some new evil advice. He said to Zahhak, "If you do my will, I will give you all you could wish from the world. Follow my orders and you will be king of the earth; its animals, men, birds, and fish will all be yours."

Eblis Makes Himself into a Cook

Next Eblis disguised himself as an intelligent, talkative young man, and appeared humbly before Zahhak. He said, "If the king will accept my service, I am an excellent cook." Zahhak welcomed him, had a place set aside for him, and gave him the key to the royal kitchens and pantries. At that time not many foods were known, and there were few dishes made from meat. The new cook made dishes from the flesh of birds and animals, feeding Zahhak on blood to build up his valor, as if he were a lion, all the while obeying all of his orders, and apparently submitting his heart to the king's commands. First he made a dish from egg yolks, to make him strong and healthy. Zahhak ate the dish and congratulated his cook, who received a reward for his labors. The cunning Eblis said, "May you live proudly and forever; tomorrow I shall prepare food which will nourish all your body." Then he left the king's presence and meditated all night on the wonderful dish he would make the following day.

In the morning the sun's topaz appeared in the blue dome of heaven, and the cook's heart was filled with hope as he brought in a dish made from partridge and white pheasant meat; when the king of the Arabs sat down to eat he gave his foolish head into Eblis's hands. On the third day the cook made dishes of chicken and lamb kebab, and on the fourth day, of veal cooked with saffron, rosewater, aged wine, and pure musk. When Zahhak stretched out his hand and ate, he was astonished at the man's skill. He said to him, "You are a well-meaning man; consider what it is that you desire, and ask me for it." The cook said, "May you live forever your majesty; my heart is filled with love for you, and my soul is nourished only by your glances. I have one request to ask of the victorious king, even though I am quite unworthy of it, and this is that he will command me to kiss his shoulders, and rub my eyes and face there." When Zahhak heard his words he had no notion of what the man was plotting and said, "I grant you your request, and may your name be honored for it." Then he said that the cook should kiss his shoulders, as if he were his bosom friend. The demon kissed the king's shoulders, and disappeared forthwith; no man had ever seen such a wonder in all the world.

Two black snakes grew from Zahhak's shoulders. In his distress the king looked everywhere for a solution, and finally he simply cut them off. But they grew again on his shoulders like the limbs of a tree. Learned doctors gathered about him and one by one gave their opinions; they tried every kind of remedy, but were unable to cure the king of his affliction. Then Eblis himself appeared in the guise of a wise doctor and said to Zahhak, "These growths were fated to appear; leave the snakes where they are, they should not be cut back. You must prepare food for them, and placate them by feeding them; this is the only thing you can do. Give them nothing but human brains to eat, and they should die from such food." And what was the evil demon's purpose in offering such advice, if not to empty the earth of mankind?

Jamshid's Reign Comes to an End

Meanwhile Persia was filled with dissension and revolt; the bright day darkened and men broke faith with Jamshid. His divine *farr* grew dim, and he gave himself to evil and foolishness. Petty kings and their armies sprang up on all sides, every province produced its own claimant to the throne, and they felt no love for Jamshid. A contingent made their way to the Arab lands, where they had heard there lived a terrifying lord with a face like a serpent's. Seeking a king, Persia's horsemen approached Zahhak: they greeted him as a sovereign, hailing him as the ruler of Iran. This serpentine creature came to Persia as quickly as the wind

blows, and there set the crown on his head. From every province he gathered together an army of Persians and Arabs, and attacked Jamshid on his throne, drawing the noose tight about him. When Jamshid saw that his good fortune had deserted him, he fled and went into hiding, grieving in darkness, abandoning his crown and throne, his sovereignty, armies and wealth, to Zahhak. For a hundred years no one saw him anywhere in the world, but then this infidel king reappeared on the shores of the Sea of China. He had hidden himself away from the serpent king, but could not escape him in the end. When Zahhak had him in his clutches, he gave him no time to plead his case but had him sawn in two, and filled the world with terror at his fate.

Jamshid's throne and glory were at an end, drawn away by time as amber draws away straw, and what profit to him were all the troubles he endured while he sat on his throne? He had lived for seven hundred years, bringing good and evil to light, but what good is a long life, since the world will never reveal her secrets to you?

> Her wine and honey will allay your fears,
> And her beguiling voices charm your ears—
> And when you're sure that she will never show
> Evil to you, she strikes the fatal blow.

The Reign of Zahhak

Zahhak reigned for a thousand years, and from end to end the world was his to command. The wise concealed themselves and their deeds, and devils achieved their heart's desire. Virtue was despised and magic applauded, justice hid itself away while evil flourished; demons rejoiced in their wickedness, while goodness was spoken of only in secret.

Two innocent young women were dragged from Jamshid's house, trembling like the leaves of a willow tree; they were Jamshid's sisters, the crown among his womenfolk. One of these veiled women was Shahrnavaz, and her chaste sister was Arnavaz. Zahhak trained them in magic and taught them evil ways, since he himself knew nothing but evil—murder, rapine, and the burning of cities.

Each night two young men, either peasants or of noble stock, were brought to Zahhak's palace. There, in the hope of finding a cure for the king's malady, they were killed and their brains made into a meal for the snakes. At the same time, there were two noble, upright men who lived in his realm; one was named Armayel the Pious, and the other, Garmayel the Perceptive. Together they talked of the king's injustice and the evil manner in which he was nourished. One said, "We should go and present ourselves as cooks to the king, to see if we can save at least one of each pair who are killed to feed the snakes."

They learned how to prepare numerous dishes and were accepted as cooks in the king's kitchens. When the victims were dragged before the cooks, and the time came for their blood to be spilled, the two men looked at one another with eyes filled with tears and with rage in their hearts. Unable to do more, they saved one of the two from slaughter, substituting the brains of a sheep, which they mixed with the brains of the man they killed. And so they were able to rescue one of each pair, to whom they said, "Hide yourself away in the plains and mountains, far from the towns." In this way they saved thirty victims a month, and when there were two hundred of them the cooks secretly gave them goats and sheep, and showed them a deserted area where they could live. The Kurds, who never settle in towns, are descended from these men.

Meanwhile Zahhak reigned ever more cruelly. If a warrior had a beautiful daughter hidden away in his house, Zahhak would accuse him of consorting with demons and kill him, and have the girl brought to him as his slave. He acted without regard for the customs of kings or the laws of religion.

Zahhak Sees Feraydun in a Dream

See what God did to Zahhak, when he still had forty years to live. Late one night he was sleeping with Arnavaz when he dreamed that three warriors suddenly appeared from an imperial palace. The youngest of the three was as tall as a cypress tree, the royal *farr* radiated from him, and he strode forward between the other two like a prince, ready for battle and bearing an ox-headed mace. He attacked Zahhak and smote him on the head with his ox-headed mace. The young man flayed him from head to foot, tied his hands behind his back, and set a yoke on his shoulders, then he dragged him to Mount Damavand with a group of onlookers following. Zahhak writhed in his sleep, and felt that his liver would split with terror; he cried out, and his pillared chamber shook with the noise. His beautiful serving girls sprang up at their master's scream, and Arnavaz said to him, "Tell me, my lord, what is troubling you; you are sleeping safely in your own house, it must be something in your soul that has terrified you. The seven climes are yours to rule, and animals, men, and demons watch over your safety."

The king said to his womenfolk, "You will not be able to conceal what I tell you, and when you hear this wonder you will despair of my life." Arnavaz replied, "You should tell us your secret; we might be able to suggest some remedy, since no calamity is without a remedy." The king described his dream, and Arnavaz said, "You should not neglect this. But your throne rules the world, which shines with your splendor, and all its animals, men, demons, birds, and fairies pay homage to your seal ring. Summon astrologers and magicians from every province; tell them what you have seen, seek out the truth of the matter, see in whose hands your life lies, and whether it is a man, a demon, or a fairy that threatens you. When you know this, that will be the time to make plans; don't tremble in fear at your enemies' malevolence." The king liked the advice of this woman, whose body was as elegant as a cypress tree, and whose face was as lovely as the stars.

The world was black like a raven's wing, when suddenly light appeared above the mountains; it was as if the sun were scattering topazes in a purple sky. The king summoned eloquent and learned sages from every quarter and told them of his heart-wrenching dream.

> He said, "Is it good or ill these signs portend?
> When will my earthly life come to an end?
> Who will come after me? Say who will own
> This royal diadem, and belt, and throne.
> Reveal this mystery, and do not lie—
> Tell me this secret or prepare to die."

The sages' lips were dry, and their cheeks wet with tears. They said to one another, "If we tell him what will happen, our souls will be worthless, and if he doesn't hear from us, we must wash our hands of life here and now." Three days went by, and no one dared speak to Zahhak; on the fourth he said, "Either be strung up on a gibbet alive or tell me my fate." All the sages bowed their heads, and their hearts were filled with terror, their eyes with tears. One of them, a wise and prudent man named Zirak, stepped forward. Anxiety seized his heart, but he spoke out fearlessly before Zahhak: "Rid your mind of vain thoughts, since no man is born from his mother but for death. Many worthy kings have sat on the throne before you and experienced great sorrow and great joy; each of them died and left the world in another's hands. Surround yourself with iron walls reaching to the sky, but you cannot remain here, another man will occupy your throne, and your good fortune will lie in the dust. This celestial ruler's name will be Feraydun; he is not born yet, his mother's time of anxiety and sighs is still to come. But when he is born he will be like a fruitful tree; when he grows to be a man he will lift his head up to the moon, and seek the crown and throne and royal belt. He will be cypress-tall, and on his shoulders he will carry an iron ox-headed mace, which he will bring down on your head; then he will bind you and drag you from your palace into the streets."

Zahhak asked, "Why should he bind me? What will make him hate me?" The sage replied, "If you are wise, you will know that a man does not do evil for no reason. His father will die at your hands, and this will fill him with the desire for vengeance. A cow called Barmayeh will be his wet nurse, and this too will be destroyed by you, and be an added cause of his hatred."

Zahhak heard him out, then fell from the throne in a faint, and the sage, fearing for his life, fled from the royal presence. When Zahhak regained consciousness he sat on his throne again and gave orders that the world be scoured for signs of Feraydun. He knew no rest, and could neither eat nor sleep; the brightness of his days had darkened.

The Birth of Feraydun

Many days passed, and Zahhak lived in fear. The noble Feraydun was born, and the world was renewed. He grew as tall as a straight cypress tree, and Jamshid's imperial *farr* radiated from him as if he were the sun. He was as necessary to the earth as rain, as fitting to the soul as wisdom. The turning heavens passed over Feraydun and cherished him with loving kindness. The cow called Barmayeh, the most splendid of all cows, was also born: she was like a peacock, and every hair of her body was a different color. Wise men, astrologers, and priests, gathered about her and said that no one in the world had ever seen such a cow, or heard of her like from the ancient sages.

In his search for Feraydun, Zahhak had filled the earth with rumors, and Feraydun's father, Abetin, fled in fear. But he fell into the lion's trap and was caught by some of Zahhak's malevolent guards. They trussed him up like a cheetah and took him before Zahhak, who killed him. When Feraydun's mother, Faranak, saw what had happened to her husband, she feared for Feraydun; sick at heart, she made her way to the meadows where the cow Barmayeh grazed. She went to the meadow's owner and wept bitter tears, saying, "Take this unweaned child into your safekeeping. Accept him as a father would from his mother, and nourish him with that splendid cow's milk. If you desire payment, my soul is yours, and my life will be hostage to your wishes." The keeper of the thickets and of the splendid cow answered, "I shall be as a slave to your son, and I will do as you have asked me." Faranak handed her son over to him and gave him lengthy advice on how to bring the boy up.

This protector was like a father to Feraydun, and for three years he fed him the cow's milk. But Zahhak did not rest in his search, and the world was filled with talk of the splendid cow. Faranak hurried to the meadows again and said to the man who had saved her son, "God has put a wise notion into my heart, and I must act on it, because my son is as sweet as life to me. I will leave this land of magicians and go with my boy toward India. I'll disappear from men's sight, and take this handsome child to the Alborz mountains."

She traveled with her son as quickly as a courier, and when she reached the uplands she was like a mountain sheep in her agility. There was a religious man living there, who had cut himself off from the cares of the world, and Faranak said to him, "Reverend sir, I have come here grieving from Iran. You should know that this noble child of mine will be the leader of his people; he will cut off Zahhak's head and cast his belt and crown in the dust. You must protect him, like a father who trembles for his son's soul." The good man accepted her son from her without a sigh.

One day news reached Zahhak of the meadow and of the cow Barmayeh, and like a maddened elephant he came there and killed her, together with all the other animals he could see nearby. Then he quickly made his way to the house where Feraydun had been living and searched it, but found no one. He set fire to the building and razed it.

Feraydun Questions His Mother About His Lineage

When Feraydun was sixteen years old he descended from the Alborz mountains to the plain, and came to his mother, asking her to reveal the secrets of his lineage to him. He said, "Who was my father? Who am I? What family am I from? Who can I tell people I am? Tell me what knowledge you have of all this." Faranak replied, "My ambitious son, I will tell you all you have asked. You are from the land of Iran, and your father was a man named Abetin. He was the scion of kings, a wise man and a warrior, who troubled no one. He was descended from Tahmures, from father to son. He was your father and a good husband to me; all the brightness of my days was from him. And then Zahhak, who delights in magic, tried to kill you and I hid you from him. What evil days I passed at that time! Your young, noble father sacrificed his life for yours, and I went to a wooded area no one knew of. There I saw a cow as lovely as a garden in springtime, of wondrous beauty from head to foot. Her keeper sat before her like a king, and I gave you to him. For many long days he brought you up, cradling you tenderly in his bosom, and feeding you the cow's milk, which made you grow into a fearsome warrior. Eventually the king heard of this cow and the meadow where she lived. He went there and killed your kind, mute wet nurse, and then he razed our home, sending its dust up to the sun, and made that tall building into a ruin."

Feraydun sprang up, enraged by his mother's words; his heart was filled with pain, his head with a longing for vengeance. Frowning in anger he answered his mother, "A lion becomes brave by being tested. The magician has acted, and now it is time for me to grasp my sword. With God's help I shall raise the dust of battle over Zahhak's palace." But his mother said, "This is unwise, you have no followers anywhere, whereas Zahhak is crowned and rules the world, and has an army ready for battle. If he wishes, he can summon to his side a hundred thousand warriors from each country. This is not how you should fight: don't see the world through a child's eyes.

> *Whoever drinks the wine of youth can see*
> *Only himself, and in that stupor he*
> *Will throw away his life. I seek for you*
> *Joy and prosperity in all you do."*

The Story of Kaveh the Blacksmith and Zahhak the Arab

Day and night Feraydun's name was on Zahhak's lips, in his greatness he feared his fall, and his heart was filled with terror at the thought of Feraydun. One day, seated on his ivory throne, with the turquoise crown on his head, Zahhak summoned the great men from every country to bear witness to his reign. He said to the sages gathered there, "You are wise, skilled men, and as all wise men know, I have a secret enemy. I do not underestimate even a contemptible enemy, and I fear that an evil fate awaits me. I must increase the size of my army, with men and demons, the two mixed together. I'm impatient to accomplish this and you must agree to it. Now a testament is to be written stating that your leader has sown nothing but seeds of righteousness, that he says only what is true, and that he is zealous in the pursuit of justice."

Out of fear of Zahhak, the great men gathered there witnessed the document; young and old, they signed their names to that evil monster's claims. At this moment the cries of someone demanding justice were heard at the door; the plaintiff was brought in and given a place in front of the nobles present. Zahhak frowned and said to him, "Tell us who has been unjust to you."

> *"I'm Kaveh, and a blacksmith, sire," he said,*
> *And as he spoke his clenched fists struck his head.*
> *"It's you whom I accuse, you are the one*
> *Whose fire's destroyed all that I've ever done.*
> *A king then, or a monster? Which are you?*
> *Tell us, your majesty, which of the two?*
> *If you reign over seven kingdoms, why*
> *Must our fate be to suffer and to die?*
> *Acquit yourself then, let me weigh your worth,*
> *And let your words astonish all the earth;*
> *And when we've heard you out we'll see*
> *The evils that the world has done to me,*
> *And why it is my son's brains have to feed*
> *Your snakes' insatiable and monstrous greed."*

Zahhak was astonished to hear such language; he returned Kaveh's son to him and tried to win him over by flattering words. Then he ordered Kaveh to sign the testament. But when Kaveh had read the document through, he turned to the assembled elders:

> *"You're in the demons' clutches now," he roared,*
> *"Your evil hearts no longer fear the Lord,*
> *And all your faces are set fair for hell;*
> *Your hearts believe Zahhak, you wish him well,*
> *But I will never sign, or give a thought*
> *To this corrupted tyrant and his court."*

He stood trembling with rage as he ripped the testament in two and flung it at his feet. Then, preceded by his stalwart son, he strode shouting from the palace into the public thoroughfare.

The elders said to the king, "On the day of battle the heavens do not dare to send cold winds against you, so why should this foul-mouthed Kaveh be allowed to grow red in the face before you as if he were a companion of yours? Why should he rip our testament to you in pieces and ignore your commands?" The king answered, "You will hear a wonder from me: when Kaveh appeared in the doorway and I heard his voice, it was as if a mountain of iron appeared in the palace between the two of us; and when he beat his head with his fists, I felt my heart break within me. I do not know what will come of this; no man knows the heavens' secrets."

When Kaveh left the court, a crowd gathered about him in the marketplace. He continued to shout his demands for justice, and he hoisted his leather blacksmith's apron on a spear as a rallying point. So many men crowded around that dust rose into the air, and Kaveh strode forward with the spear in his hand, shouting "You are God-fearing noble men, and if you're of Feraydun's party, free yourselves from Zahhak's chains; this king is Ahriman, and in his heart he is God's enemy." As he went forward an army of men gathered about him, and it was not a small one.

Kaveh knew where Feraydun was, and he made straight for the new commander's court. As the court caught sight of his approach, a thunderous cry went up, and when the prince saw the leathern apron, he took it as an omen of good fortune. He draped it in Rumi brocade, and adorned it with a device of jewels on a ground of gold, and made fringes for it of crimson, yellow, and purple; at the top of the spear he placed a splendid globe like the moon. He called the apron the Kaviani banner, and from this time forward any man who assumed power and placed the royal crown on his head would add new jewels to that blacksmith's leather apron. The Kaviani banner became so splendid with its brocades and silks that it shone in the night's darkness like the sun, and the world took hope from its brilliance.

The world continued in this way for a while, and the future was unclear. Feraydun saw that Zahhak's days were numbered; he crowned himself, and made his way to his mother. "I must leave now for battle," he said. "Your task is to pray to the world's creator, in good fortune and bad." His mother wept and prayed, "Great God, I place my trust in you; protect my son from evil, and clear the world of the unwise."

Feraydun quickly prepared for his departure, but kept his plans secret. He had two noble older brothers, Kiyanush and Barmayeh. He said to them, "Take heart and live in joy, my brave companions; the heavens can only turn for the better, and the royal crown will come back to us. Bring me skilled blacksmiths, and have a massive mace made." The two hurried to the blacksmiths' bazaar, and all its inhabitants who were eager for fame made their way to Feraydun. The prince took a pair of compasses and drew a picture of an ox-headed mace in the dust. The blacksmiths set to work, and when they'd forged the heavy mace, which glittered like the sun in the heavens, they took it to Feraydun. He was pleased with their work and gave them gold, silver, and clothes as a reward. He promised them a better future, and said, "If I can lay that monster beneath the earth, I shall wash the dust from your heads; I shall guide the world toward justice, remembering the name of God, from whom all justice comes."

Feraydun's War Against Zahhak

Feraydun lifted his head to the sun and prepared to avenge his father. He set off on the day of Khordad, when the omens were favorable, and under an auspicious star; an army gathered about him, and his glory rose up to the clouds. Strong elephants and oxen bearing the army's provisions preceded the column, and Kiyanush and Barmayeh were at the king's side as if they were his loyal younger brothers. And so Feraydun went forward like the wind, stage by stage, his head filled with thoughts of vengeance and his heart with justice.

Traveling quickly on their Arab horses, they reached a place where men who had devoted themselves to God lived. Feraydun dismounted and sent greetings to them. As the night darkened, a man came forward to welcome them: his musky hair reached to his feet, and his face was like that of a houri in paradise. This angelic figure came to the prince to teach him the secrets of magic, so that he would know the key to hidden things. Feraydun understood that this was a divine being and not an emissary of evil. His face flushed like the blossoms of the Judas-tree, and he rejoiced in his youth and good fortune. His cook made him a meal fit for a nobleman, and, when he had eaten, his head became heavy with sleep.

Feraydun's brothers saw the holy man's behavior, and how the prince's good fortune flourished, and they decided to destroy him. Feraydun was sleeping sweetly at the foot of a mountain, and late that night the two brothers slipped away from the army and climbed up to where a huge rock overhung the prince. They sent it tumbling down the mountainside to kill their sleeping brother, but by God's command the noise of the rock's fall woke Feraydun, and he stopped it in its descent by means of a magic spell; the rock halted and never moved again. Then Feraydun rose and prepared to continue on his journey, saying nothing to his brothers about what had happened.

He made for the River Arvand (if you do not know Pahlavi, this river is called "Dejleh" in Arabic, or the Tigris) and pitched camp on its banks, close to the city of Baghdad, and sent word to the ferryman there that he needed boats to transport his army across the river. But the man neither sent any craft nor came to talk with Feraydun. His answer was, "The world's king has told me in private that I am not to let so much as a mosquito cross this river without a permit sealed in the correct manner." Feraydun was enraged by this reply; his mind was focused on the coming battle and, undeterred by the river's depth, he mounted his brave horse Golrang and urged it into the water. His companions quickly followed suit, plunging their mounts in the river, so that the water rose above their saddles. The prince and his army reached the further bank and went on toward Jerusalem, which was called in Pahlavi "Gang Dezh Hukht" and was where Zahhak had built his palace.

When they were a mile from the city, the king saw a palace with walls that shone like the planet Jupiter in the heavens and were so high that they seemed to reach for the stars. He knew that this great palace, which seemed a place of joy and peace, was the home of the monster Zahhak, and he said to his companions, "I fear that anyone who can raise such a building on the dark earth is somehow secretly favored by fate. Rather than delay, we had better attack immediately." He shouldered his mace and urged his horse forward, bearing down on the palace guards like a fire, so that not one of them remained. This young, courageous warrior, who had no experience of the world, gave thanks to God and entered the palace on horseback.

There he came on an idol made by Zahhak, and its head reached into the sky. When Feraydun saw that it bore a name other than that of the Creator, he overturned it. With his mace he crushed the heads of the magicians and demons who were in the palace, then placed his foot on Zahhak's throne in victory. He had the black-haired women of the harem, whose faces were as splendid as the sun, brought before him. They had been brought up as idolaters and were trembling and terrified, as if they were drunk, but Feraydun commanded that their minds be purified, and their souls freed from darkness. He had them taught the ways of righteousness and cleansed them of their idolatry. Then Jamshid's two sisters stained their cheeks with tears and said, "May the old world be renewed by your good fortune! Tell us what star guides you, and what tree you are sprung from, that you have dared to attack the lion's sleeping quarters so bravely. How wretchedly we've passed our days, mistreated by that fool of a magician; what sufferings we have endured at that monster's hands! We have never seen anyone strong enough or valiant enough to seek his throne."

Feraydun answered, "Neither the throne nor good fortune will remain with one man forever. I am the son of the illustrious Abetin, whom Zahhak seized and murdered in Iran, and I seek Zahhak's throne in revenge. The marvelous Barmayeh cow was my wet nurse, and that innocent animal's blood too will be avenged by me. I have come from Persia bringing war, and I shall give the evil Zahhak no rest or peace until I have crushed his head beneath my ox-headed mace."

Arnavaz said, "Are you then King Feraydun, who will destroy magic and sorcery, and in killing Zahhak, free the world from tyranny? We are two princesses of the royal blood, and we cooperated with him only because we feared for our lives. My lord, think what it has meant to be married to such a serpent." Feraydun replied, "If the heavens are not in league with evil, I shall cleanse the world of this foul monster. Now you must tell me truly where he is lurking." These two beautiful women, who hoped to see Zahhak's head spitted on a lance, said, "He has fled toward India, to turn it into a land of sorcery, and there he slaughters innocents by the thousand. He is fearful of his fate, since it was predicted to him that the land would soon be rid of him, that his good fortune was at an end, and that a man would come who would seize his throne. This warning has filled his heart with fire, and nothing in life gives him pleasure now; he murders men and women, beasts of burden and wild animals, and mixes their blood in a vat, believing that if he washes his head and body there he might avert the astrologers' predictions. And still the snakes that grow from his shoulders continue to torment him; though he flees from country to country, this pain never ceases. But now he will return, since he is unable to stay anywhere for long." The hero listened while the lovely speaker unburdened her grief-stricken heart.

Feraydun and Zahhak's Viceroy
When Zahhak fled from the land, a man as lowly and wretched as a slave took his place on the throne and took command of his treasuries and palace. His name was Kondrow, and he was a fool who practiced injustice. This man burst into the audience chamber and saw that a new prince, as handsome as a cypress tree topped by the new moon, sat on the royal throne, while on one side of him sat Shahrnavaz, and on the other Arnavaz. Kondrow showed no emotion and asked no questions: he came forward humbly and made his obeisance. He said, "O king, may you live forever; you become the throne, and the *farr* that shines from you declares you worthy of sovereignty. May the seven climes be your slaves, and your head be raised above the clouds." Feraydun had him approach the throne and tell him the court's secrets, then he said, "Have the royal regalia cleansed, then have wine, musicians, and a banquet made ready; bring me whoever can please me with their music or knowledge, so that I can hold a feast worthy of my good fortune."

Kondrow did as he had been ordered; he had wine and musicians brought, and summoned nobles worthy of the honor to the prince's presence. When Feraydun saw the wine he called for music, and passed the night in festive celebration. But as dawn broke Kondrow left his presence, mounted his horse, and set off to join Zahhak. When he reached Zahhak he told him everything he had seen and heard. He said, "Proud king, the sign of your good fortune's eclipse has come. Three warriors attacked us with their armies; the central one is younger than the others, but in his stature he is like a cypress, and his face shines with royal splendor; he is younger than his brothers, but he leads them and is their superior. He carries a mace that is like a fragment of a mountain, and his glory outshines that of his companions. He rode into the palace, accompanied by his brothers, and took his place on your throne; then he destroyed all your idols and spells and flung your courtiers, both men and demons, from the castle walls, mixing their brains and their blood in death."

Zahhak said,

> *"There's nothing wrong in this; he is our guest,*
> *And everything may still be for the best."*

Kondrow replied, "When did a guest ever arrive flourishing an ox-headed mace? Or take your place on the throne and erase your name from the crown and royal belt, then convert your people to his own faith? If you think this man is your guest I wish you joy of him!" Zahhak said,

> *"Don't bother me with these complaints; don't whine!*
> *Demanding guests are an auspicious sign."*

Kondrow replied, "So I've heard, but listen to this: if this man is your guest, what business has he in your harem? He sits on the throne with Jamshid's sisters next to him and takes counsel with them; one hand fondles Sharnavaz's cheeks, while the other is kissed by Arnavaz's agate lips. And when night's darkness comes, he does more than this: he sleeps pillowed on musk—the musky hair of those two women who were your beloved companions." Hearing these words, Zahhak desired death and roared like a wild animal. He fell to cursing his wretched fate and said, "You will never be my castle's guardian again." His servant replied, "My lord, I think that you will never see your throne again. What was the point of making me the ruler of your country when you lacked all authority? Nothing like this has ever happened to you, so why don't you act in your own defense? You have been forced from power as a hair is forced out of dough."

Feraydun Captures Zahhak

Enraged, Zahhak ordered that his swift, keen-sighted horse be saddled, and with a massive army of warlike demons he set off for his palace. There, intent on vengeance, he clandestinely had his men take the outlying doors and roofs, but Feraydun's men saw this and swarmed to the attack. They were aided by all of the city's inhabitants who could fight, since they hated Zahhak. Like dew from dark clouds, bricks and stones rained down from the walls and roofs, and the narrow streets were cluttered with swords and arrows. All the young men of the city, and the old who had experience of warfare, deserted Zahhak and flocked to Feraydun. A cry went up from the fire-temple, "Even if the king is a beast of prey, young and old we shall all obey him, but we will not have this evil monster Zahhak occupy the throne." An army of men thronged the city, and such a cloud of dust went up that the sun was dimmed.

Jealousy of his rival's success made Zahhak seek another remedy. Separating himself from his men, he dressed himself in iron armor so that he was unrecognizable, seized a lariat of sixty lengths, and made his way onto the roof of the palace. From there he could see the black-haired sorceress Shahrnavaz, her cheeks as bright as day, her hair as dark as night, closeted with Feraydun and cursing Zahhak. He knew then that what had happened was fated by God, and that he would not escape from the evil fate that was in store for him. The fire of jealousy flared up in his mind, and forgetting his throne and the risk to his life, he let himself down into the palace with his lariat. He did not announce himself, but drew a glittering dagger, intent on shedding his handmaidens' blood. As Zahhak's foot touched the ground, Feraydun leapt forward like the wind and brought his ox-headed mace crashing down on Zahhak's head, so that his helmet was shattered. At that moment the angel Sorush appeared and said, "Do not strike him again; his time has not yet come. Now that you have broken his power, bind him and take him to where you see a pass between two mountains. He will live imprisoned within the mountain, and his people will never be able to reach him."

Feraydun lost no time in preparing strips of lion skin, with which he bound Zahhak's arms and body so tightly that a raging elephant could not have broken his bonds. Then he sat on Zahhak's golden throne and overturned the tyrant's evil customs. He had a herald cry at the palace gates, "You are wise and honored men; it is not right for you to be wielding weapons and riding out to war, in the same way that soldiers should not be artisans. Each group should follow its own calling, since if they follow one another's, the earth is filled with confusion. The evil tyrant has been captured, and the earth is cleansed of his power. Return in peace to your former occupations, and may you live long and happily!"

All the nobles and rich men of the city came to pay homage to Feraydun, who received them kindly, gave them advice and thanked them, and also gave thanks to God. He said, "This is my court, and my star will bring good fortune to your land, as my mace has freed the world from the monster's evil. I am lord of the entire earth, and I should not stay always in one place, otherwise I would have lived here with you for many long years." The nobles kissed the ground before him, and the din of drums rang out from the court. The bound Zahhak was led out, ignominiously flung on a pack animal's back, and taken to Shir-Khan. When they reached the mountains, Feraydun wished to kill Zahhak, but again Sorush appeared and spoke persuasively in his ear, telling him to take this solitary wretched captive to Mount Damavand. Feraydun did this, as quickly as a courier travels, and imprisoned Zahhak in Mount Damavand, loading chains on him, and confining him to a narrow cave that seemed to have no end. Heavy nails were driven into his body, avoiding his vital organs, and pinning him to the rock so that he would suffer there for a long time. And so he was left, hanging in chains, with his heart's blood staining the ground.

THE STORY OF FERAYDUN AND HIS THREE SONS

Feraydun Is Enthroned

When Feraydun became the world's sovereign and saw that there were no rivals to his rule, he prepared the royal throne and crown according to the custom of the Kayanid kings. He placed the crown on his head at the beginning of the month of Mehr, on an auspicious day. People turned toward wisdom, and the world was free from the fear of evil; quarrels were put aside, and a new festival was established. The nobles sat together rejoicing, each of them holding a cup of ruby wine, which glowed as brightly as the new king's face, and as the month began the world was renewed by his justice. He ordered that a fire be lit, and had ambergris and saffron sprinkled on the flames. In this way Feraydun instituted the festival of Mehregan, and the custom of taking one's ease and feasting at this time. This festival is still observed in his memory, and during the festivities you should try to let no sadness show in your face. Feraydun ruled for five hundred years, and not one of his days was given over to evil.

Faranak was unaware that her son had become king of the world and that Zahhak had been driven from the throne, his good fortune at an end. When news came to her that her son was crowned, she washed her head and body and prayed, bowing her head down to the ground, cursing Zahhak and praising God who had brought about such a happy turn of events. She secretly gave succor to the poor and unfortunate, telling no one else of her actions. For a week she distributed goods in this way, then she held a week of celebrations, opening wide the purse strings of her fortune, and making her home like an orchard filled with guests. All the wealth she had accumulated—the cloth and royal gems, the Arab horses with their golden gear, the armor, helmets, javelins, swords, and belts—she held nothing back, but had it all loaded on

camels, which she sent to her son's court with a message of congratu-
lation on his accession to the throne.

After Feraydun had received the homage of his people, he made a
tour of the world to become acquainted with its news and secrets.
Wherever he saw injustice, or an area that was not flourishing, he tied
the hands of evildoers as a king should, making the world an earthly par-
adise and planting cypresses and roses in the place of thorns and weeds.

Feraydun Sends Jandal to the Yemen

After fifty years had passed Feraydun was the father of three fine sons,
all worthy to wear the crown. They were

> *As tall as cypresses, fair as the spring,*
> *The image of their father and their king.*

Even before their father had named them they could hold their own
against elephants. The two older boys were sons of Shahrnaz, the
youngest the son of Arnavaz. When Feraydun saw their worth, he
asked his advisor Jandal to search the world for three princesses born
from the same mother and father, who would be worthy brides for his
sons.

Jandal was a wise and discerning man, and immediately he began to
make inquiries as to which kings in which countries had marriageable
daughters. He found no one in Iran who was worthy of this honor, but
then he came before Sarv, the king of the Yemen, as splendid as a
pheasant strutting among spring flowers; he kissed the ground and
showered flattery on this subject king. The king said to him, "May you
never cease to be praised; what orders do you have for me, what
instructions do you bring?" Jandal replied, "May you live in happiness
and the hand of evil never touch you. I am a lowly Persian subject and
bring you Feraydun's wishes for your wealth and prosperity as the
undimmed star of the Arabs. Feraydun says that there is nothing dearer
to a man than his sons, that his three sons are sweeter to him than his
sight, and that he seeks brides for them. I made inquiries, and have
heard that you have three unnamed daughters who are worthy of our
princes. These two noble families should be joined; this is Feraydun's
message, and may you answer as you see fit."

When the king of the Yemen heard this he withered like a waterlily that is plucked from the water. He said to himself, "If I don't see my three lovely daughters at my bedside, the brightness of the day will be like night's darkness to me. But I should keep my lips sealed about this; I must be in no hurry to give an answer. I'll consult with my advisors, and see what they say."

He had a suitable lodging prepared for Feraydun's messenger. Then he summoned his advisors and put the matter before them. He said, "I have three daughters, bright as lit tapers in their loveliness, and because of them Feraydun had laid a trap for me. He wants to separate me from these girls, who are as dear to me as my sight. His messenger proposes that Feraydun's three princes take my three girls as brides. If I say I am pleased at this development, I will not be telling the truth, and it is unfitting for a king to lie; besides, if I hand my daughters over to him, how will I endure the fire in my heart and the tears in my eyes? But if I reject his request, my life will be harried by his rage. It would be no light undertaking to provoke his wrath; he is the lord of the world, and you have heard how he dealt with Zahhak. Now, what do you propose that I do?"

The chieftains replied, "We do not see why you should twist and turn with every breeze that blows. Feraydun may be the lord of the world, but we are not slaves to do his bidding:

> To give good counsel's our appointed task,
> But spears and steeds are all the faith we ask;
> With daggers we will make the earth blood red
> And crowd the day with lances overhead.

If you approve of Feraydun's sons, make them welcome and keep silent. But if you want to find a way out of this and are still afraid of Feraydun, demand conditions that it will be difficult for him to fulfill." The king heard them out, but remained unsure what he should do.

The King of the Yemen's Answer to Jandal

He summoned Feraydun's messenger and spoke eloquently to him. "I am your king's subject, and will obey whatever he orders me to do. Tell him I said, 'You are a great man, and your sons are dear to you, especially as they are worthy to succeed you on the throne. My daughters too are dear to me, and if the king asked for my eyes, or for sovereignty over the Yemen, these sacrifices would hurt me less than never seeing my daughters again. But if this is the king's wish I cannot oppose it, and my three daughters will leave my kingdom when I have seen the king's princely sons. Their visit here will brighten the darkness of my days; and once I see the justice in their hearts, I shall grasp their hands in friendship, and give my daughters to them according to our customs, then quickly send them to back to you.'" When Jandal had heard his answer, he kissed the throne as was fitting and, calling down blessings on the king, he left the court and made his way back to the lord of the world. There he recounted all that he had seen and heard.

Feraydun called his sons to him and told them of Jandal's search. He said, "The king of the Yemen is a fine warrior; he has no sons, but his three virgin daughters are as his crown to him, and if the angel Sorush were to receive them in marriage, he would kiss the ground before them in homage. I have asked for these three as your brides and said all that is fitting; now you must go to him and speak eloquently on your own behalf. You must be wise and cautious, and listen carefully to all he tells you. Speak well when you answer him, and address his questions intelligently. You have been brought up as princes and must act appropriately. Be eloquent, perspicacious, and pure in your deeds; see that you are worthy of praise in any company. Tell the truth when you speak, and choose your words wisely. The king of the Yemen is a shrewd man, and he has few equals; he must not think of you as weak, because if he does, he will try to trick you. On the first day there will be a feast at which you will be honored. His three beautiful daughters will be there in their splendor, seated on thrones, each of them equal to the full moon in her beauty. The youngest will sit in front, the oldest will sit further back, and the middle one between them. The youngest will be placed next to the oldest of you, and the oldest next to the youngest, with the middle one between them. But you should be aware of this, and when he asks you which is the oldest, which is the middle one, and which is the youngest, you must be able to answer correctly. Say that the one who has been given the place of honor is the youngest, and the oldest is the one who has been placed lowest, with the middle one in her true place: in this way the business will turn out well for you." The three pure young princes heard their father's words, and when they left his presence they knew how they should act. They prepared for their journey, taking priests and an escort of warriors that glittered like the stars in heaven.

Feraydun's Sons at the Court of the King of the Yemen

When Sarv heard of the princes' approach, he had his army drawn up as splendidly as a pheasant's feathers and sent a welcoming party composed partly of members of his own family, partly of strangers. As the princes made their way forward, men and women came out to greet them, scattering jewels and musk mixed with saffron before them; their horses' manes were smeared with wine and musk, and their hooves trod on gold coins. The palace had been prepared for the princes and was like a paradise: filled with precious goods, its bricks were of gold and silver, and its walls were draped with brocade. As they dismounted before it their hearts swelled with confidence, and night seemed turned to day. The three daughters were presented by the king, and they were as Feraydun had predicted; each of them was as radiant as the full moon, and they sat as Feraydun had said they would. The king turned to the princes and said, "Which of these shining stars is the youngest, which is the middle one, and which is the oldest? You must indicate to me which is which." The princes answered as they had been instructed, and in this way seeled the eyes of deceit. The king immediately realized that his trick had failed and said, "The truth is as you say," and he gave the youngest to the youngest, the oldest to the oldest. And so they plighted their troth, with the three princesses blushing for shame at their father's behavior. Then the princesses returned to their own palace, their faces filled with beauty and charm, their lips with soft speech.

The King of the Yemen Casts a Spell on Feraydun's Sons

Now wine triumphed over wisdom, so that the princes were ready for sleep, and the three were conducted to a rose garden were they lay down on beds scented with rosewater. Then the Arab king practiced magic against them. He left the rose garden and raised a cold wind, intending that the young men would die of exposure; the plain and the garden froze and became so cold that even the crows did not dare fly there. The three princes sprang up in the cold, but with their knowledge of magic and their prayers they were able to overcome the king's spells, so that the cold did not harm them.

When the sun rose over the dark mountains, the deceitful king came quickly to the garden, expecting to find the faces of his sons-in-law blue with cold and their bodies frozen in death, so that his three daughters would stay with him. This was how he hoped to see them, but the sun and moon did not favor him; instead he discovered the three seated in princely glory and knew that his spells had failed. He gave an audience to the nobles of his country and opened the doors of his ancient treasuries, revealing long-hidden wealth. His three daughters, as lovely as the gardens of paradise, were brought before him, and he bestowed jewelry and crowns on them that were so heavy they were a torment to wear. Then he handed these three moons over to the princes' safekeeping and said before the assembled nobles and priests, "According to our customs, I give these three daughters of mine to these princes, who are worthy to marry them, and may they cherish them as their own sight, and hold them as dear as their own souls."

Then he had the brides' baggage strapped on spirited camels, and all the Yemen glittered with jewels. And so the train of embroidered litters wound through the countryside, and the young princes' caravan set off for Feraydun's court.

Feraydun Tests His Sons

> News came of their return: without delay
> King Feraydun set out to block their way.
> He longed to know their hearts, and by a test
> Lay all his mind's anxieties to rest.
> He took a dragon's form, one so immense
> You'd say a lion would have no defense
> Against its strength; and from its jaws there came
> A roaring river of incessant flame.
> He saw his sons; dust rose into the sky,
> The world re-echoed with his grisly cry.
> First he attacked the eldest prince, who said,
> "No wise man fights with dragon foes," and fled.
> Seeing his second son, he wheeled around.
> The youth bent back his bow and stood his ground,
> Shouting, "If combat's needed I can fight
> A roaring lion or an armored knight."

Lastly the youngest son approached and cried,
"Out of our path, fell monster, step aside.
If you have heard of Feraydun, then know
That we're his valiant, lion-like sons—now go,
Or I'll give you a crown that you'll regret!"
He saw how each son took the test he'd set
And disappeared. He left them there, but then
Came out to greet his princes once again—
Their king now, and the father whom they knew,
Surrounded by his royal retinue.

He came forward with the ox-headed mace in his fist, accompanied by the din of drums and his warlike elephants, with the chieftains of the army ranged behind him. When the princes saw their father they dismounted and kissed the ground before him. Their father took them by the hand and made much of them, and together they made their way to the palace, where Feraydun prayed, acknowledging that all good and evil come from the Creator. Then he summoned his sons to him, sat them on thrones, and said, "The dragon that wanted to consume the world with the fire of his breath was your father, out to test your manliness, and when he had seen your reactions he returned as himself, in his kingly state. Now I have decided on suitable names for you. You, the oldest, shall be called Salm, and may the world be as you would wish it: you sought safety (Salamat) when the monster threatened and did not hesitate to flee. You should call a warrior who does not fear elephants and lions a fool, not a brave man. Our middle son began impetuously, and the fire increased his bravery, and we will call him Tur; he is a brave lion who is able to bring down a raging elephant. Bravery in its place is a fine attribute, and the coward does not deserve a place of honor. As for our youngest son, a man who has both dignity and fierceness, who weighs matters carefully and is eager to fight, who chooses the middle way between earth and fire, as is right for an intelligent man, he is the most praiseworthy warrior in the world and will be called Iraj. May he remain magnanimous in all his doings, since from the outset he was like a lion and showed bravery in adversity. And now I am happy to name these beautiful young Arab women."

He called Salm's wife Arezu (Desire), Tur's wife he called Mah-e Azadeh Khui (A Free-Spirited Moon), and Iraj's wife, whose loveliness exceeded that of Canopus, he called Sahi (Tall and Slender). Next, astrological tables were brought, and Feraydun studied his sons' horoscopes. In Salm's he found the planet Saturn in Sagittarius; Tur's stars showed Mars soaked in blood, in Leo: when he looked at Iraj's stars he saw the Moon in Aries. These evil stars showed that trouble and warfare were in store for them.

THE STORY OF IRAJ

Feraydun Divides the World Between His Three Sons

Then Feraydun brought into the open a plan he had kept secret. He divided the world into three parts: one part consisted of the West, another of China and the land of the Turks, and the third of Persia, the land of warriors. The first area he gave to Salm, whom he ordered to select an army and set off to the West, where he was enthroned and acclaimed as the Lord of the Western Lands. He made Tur the master of Turan, and gave him sovereignty over the Turks and the land of China. Tur selected his army and marched to his new home, where he was enthroned and his nobles showered him with jewels and acknowledged him as the Lord of Turan. When the affairs of these two had been settled Feraydun turned to Iraj, on whom he bestowed Persia and the lands of the Arabs. He gave him the crown and sword, the seal and ivory throne, because he was worthy of them. Each of the three princely brothers sat in state in his own kingdom, and wise men proclaimed Iraj as the Lord of Persia.

Time passed, and Fate kept its secrets hidden. Feraydun grew old, and dust covered the garden of spring. Strength lessens as age creeps on, and as Feraydun's days darkened, so his sons grew stronger. Salm's heart leaped up in his breast, and his moods and manner changed: his spirit was overwhelmed by greed and desire, and he plotted with his counselors. He was dissatisfied with the portion his father had allotted him, and with the fact that the golden throne of Persia had been given to the youngest brother. His heart seething with fury and his face filled with frowns, he sent a messenger to his brother, the king of China. The message wished him long life and happiness and went on: "Look well at our story, the like of which no one has ever heard. We were three brothers, all worthy of the throne, and the youngest of us has

been blessed by good fortune. As I am the oldest and the most expe-
rienced, Fate should have favored me. And if I am left aside, shouldn't
the crown and throne belong to you, my lord? He gave Persia, the land
of heroes, and the Yemen, to Iraj; the Western Lands to me; and the
Turks and China to you. The youngest of us is the lord of Persia, and
there is no sense in this. There is no wisdom in our father's plans.
We two should grieve at his decision, which has done us a great
wrong."

The envoy quickly made his way to the court of Turan, where he
suavely repeated all he had heard and filled the king's head with vain
thoughts. When brave Tur heard these words he leaped up like a rag-
ing lion and said, "Tell your master this, 'Remember, my just lord, that
our father deceived us in our youth, that he planted a tree whose sap
is blood and whose fruits are poisonous. We must not hesitate to act;
it would be foolish to delay.'" The envoy brought back this message,
and once the secret was out between them, the two brothers, one from
China and the other from the West, met together and mingled poison
with their honey, discussing how they should act.

Salm's and Tur's Message to Feraydun

They chose a priest, an active, eloquent, perceptive man who would
remember whatever he was entrusted with. Salm spoke first, washing
his eyes of all shame before his father:

> "Let neither wind nor swirling dust delay
> Your journey as you hasten on your way.
> When you arrive at court, see that you tell
> King Feraydun his two sons wish him well:
> And then remind him of his age, that he
> Should fear God here and for eternity;
> A young man hopes for future joys, but men
> Whose hair is white will not see youth again.
> Tell him, 'God gave you all the earth to rule
> But you have acted like an evil fool;
> You had three sons, all valiant and brave,
> You favored one of them, to him you gave
> The crown of sovereignty—the other two
> Were disregarded and despised by you.

We are not less than him by birth; if he
Deserves the imperial dais, so do we,
And God will never look with favor on
Your preferential treatment of this son.
Snatch the crown off his worthless head, and give
Him some dark corner of the earth to live.
If you do not, we'll bring armed warrior bands
From China, Turkestan, and Western lands
To turn Iraj's day to dusty night
And humble Persia with our armies' might.'"

When the priest heard this harsh message, he kissed the ground and set off as quickly as wind-borne fire. He reached Feraydun's castle, which towered above him like a mountain, its battlements hidden among the clouds. Courtiers sat in the throne room, and beyond a curtain were the nobility; on one side lions and leopards were tethered, and on the other raging war elephants. The assembled warriors gave a roar like a lion's; it seemed to the messenger as though this were a celestial court, and that the warriors standing there were angelic beings.

Feraydun was told of the envoy's arrival and had the curtain drawn back so that his horse could enter. The envoy saw that Feraydun's face filled all eyes and hearts; that he was like a cypress in stature, that his visage was like the sun's, and that his hair was like white camphor about a red rose: his lips were all smiles, his gaze was modest and welcoming, kingly words adorned his lips. The envoy prostrated himself and covered the ground with kisses. Feraydun motioned him to rise and sat him on a worthy seat. First he asked about his two sons' health and welfare, then enquired solicitously as to the long, hard road the messenger had traveled. The envoy answered, "Great king, may the throne never be without you! Those you ask about live for your wellbeing; but I am merely a slave and not master of my own body. I have brought a harsh, angry message to the king, although I am guiltless of its contents. Tell me, my lord, if you would hear the young men's foolish words."

Feraydun's Answer to His Sons

Feraydun ordered him to speak, and he repeated the words he had heard. As Feraydun listened his mind seethed in anger, and he said, "You are a wise man, and there is no need for you to apologize for what you have said. My own eyes have foreseen this, and my heart suspected it. Tell those two corrupt and worthless fools, those two whose brains have been led astray by Ahriman: 'The king is pleased that you have shown your natures and says your greetings are worthy of you. You have forgotten the advice I gave you, and no trace of wisdom remains in your minds. Have you no fear or shame before God? Once my hair was as black as pitch, my stature was like the cypress's and my face shone like the full moon. But the skies turn, and have bent my back; they will bend yours too, and what is bent becomes unstable.

> I swear in God's name, by the earth, the sun,
> The moon, the crown, and throne; what I have done
> To you was just. I summoned men who are wise,
> Who know the stars and understand the skies,
> I spent long days in weighing up your worth,
> Apportioning the countries of the earth:
> The fear of God was in me, and I sought
> For justice on the earth and in my court.
> 'I'll give the world to my three sons', I said,
> But Ahriman has filled your heart and head.
> Ask yourselves now, Will God look kindly on
> The plans you've made, the evil things you've done?
> Listen: this story's one you ought to know,
> You'll reap the consequence of what you sow.
> This fleeting world is not the world where we
> Are destined to abide eternally:
> And for the sake of an unworthy throne
> You let the devil claim you for his own.
> I've few days left here, I've no heart for war,
> I cannot strive and struggle any more,
> But hear an old man's words: the heart that's freed
> From gnawing passion and ambitious greed
> Looks on kings' treasures and the dust as one;
> The man who sells his brother, as you've done,
> For this same worthless dust, will never be
> Regarded as a child of purity.
> The world has seen so many men like you,
> And laid them low: there's nothing you can do

> *But turn to God; take thought then for the way*
> *You travel, since it leads to Judgment Day.'* "

The envoy heard his words, kissed the ground, and turned away, leaving Feraydun's court as quickly as the wind.

When Salm's messenger had gone, Feraydun called Iraj to him and told him of what had happened. He said, "My two warlike sons are attacking from the west. Their stars have foretold their joy in evil, and the countries they were allotted are barren. Your brother will not be a brother to you while you wear the crown. From the ends of the earth, my two sons have declared open war: if you are ready to fight, open your treasuries and equip your men. Grasp this cup while it is still dawn, or at night supper will be at your expense. Look for no allies in this world; righteousness and innocence are your only friends."

The noble Iraj gazed at his reverend father and said,

> *"Our lives pass from us like the wind, and why*
> *Should wise men grieve to know that they must die?*
> *The Judas blossom fades, the lovely face*
> *Of light is dimmed, and darkness takes its place.*
> *The world is pleasure first, then grief, and then*
> *We leave this fleeting world of living men—*
> *Our beds are dust, for all eternity,*
> *Why should we plant the tree we'll never see?*
> *The starry heavens turn, and turn again,*
> *And all they bring mankind is blood and pain.*
> *The earth has seen so many men who wore*
> *Kings' robes and crowns, and will see many more:*
> *Vengeance has never been the royal way,*
> *And I shall not do evil, come what may.*
> *What are the crown and throne to me? Unarmed,*
> *I'll greet my brothers, whom I've never harmed,*
> *And tell them to forget their enmity.*
> *'Remember Jamshid,' I shall say, 'how he*
> *Was driven from this world he'd ruled, alone,*
> *Bereft of all his sovereignty and throne.*
> *My brothers, we'll endure this fate; we too*
> *Will taste the destiny that Jamshid knew.'*

I'll speak to them in kindness; this will be
Better than angry words and enmity."

Feraydun replied, "My wise son, your brothers look for war, while you look for reconciliation. I am reminded of the saying that one should not be surprised that the moon radiates moonlight: your answer is noble and your heart is filled with love. But what will happen to a man who knowingly places his head in the dragon's maw? Surely poison will destroy him, since this is the dragon's nature? My son, if this is your decision, prepare yourself, and choose a few companions from your troops to accompany you. In my heart's agony I will write a letter to these brothers of yours, in the hopes that I shall greet you once more with your body unharmed, since my soul's joy is in seeing you."

Iraj Visits His Brothers

The king wrote letters to the lord of the West and the king of China. He began with praise of eternal God and continued: "This letter is to advise two suns who shine in the heavens, two lords of war, two jewels among kings, and it is from one who has experienced the world, who has uncovered its secrets and turned night to day, who has wielded mace and sword and overcome all manner of difficulties. I no longer wish to wear the crown, to amass treasures, or to occupy the throne: I have suffered enough, and desire only the wellbeing of my three sons. Your brother with whom you are vexed, even though he has never breathed a word against anyone, has come to me disturbed by your anger. He prefers you to his sovereignty, and has acted nobly; he has left his throne and rides to you now, humbly, as your younger brother. Respect him and treat him well, and when he has been with you for a few days, return him to me safe and sound."

The king's seal was placed on the letter, and Iraj rode out from the palace. He went with a few companions, both young and old, the minimum necessary to accompany him on the journey, and as he drew near his brothers, he had no notion of their dark plans. They went out to welcome him as usual, and paraded their troops before him; when he saw their apparent kindness, Iraj's face relaxed. Two of them were filled with hatred, one with benevolence, and as they questioned one another, the conversation was to no one's satisfaction. Two men whose hearts were filled with a longing for vengeance, one whose heart was at peace, made their way to the commanders' camp. The army's eyes were fixed on Iraj, and the troops saw that he was worthy of the throne and crown. Their hearts were stirred by the sight of the young prince, and they turned to one another, praising him, saying Iraj deserved to be an emperor, and that no one but he should reign. Salm saw this from the sidelines and was troubled by the soldiers' behavior. He rode with his heart filled with rancor; blood suffused his liver, and his face was knotted with frowns. He cleared his pavilion of strangers and sat to consult with Tur. They talked about every aspect of the affair, about sovereignty and who reigned over which lands. In the midst of their conversation Salm said to Tur, "Why are our men huddled in pairs? As we returned here they were different from when we went out to welcome Iraj; the whole way back they all had their eyes fixed on him. My heart is darkened by this business of Persia, and the more I consider it the more my heart aches at it. I watched the men of our two armies, and they won't call anyone but him king from now on. If you don't uproot this upstart now, he'll drag you down from your throne."

Iraj Is Killed by His Brothers

They came to their decision, and throughout the night talked about how to accomplish it. When the veil was drawn back from the sun and dawn broke, dispelling sleep, their two worthless hearts were set on this, and they washed all shame from their eyes. They strode from their pavilion toward Iraj's tent; when he saw them approaching, kindness suffused his heart and he ran to greet them. The three brothers entered Iraj's tent, and the conversation ranged back and forth. Tur said, "If you are younger than us, why were you given the most important crown? You get Persia, its wealth, and the Kayanid throne and crown, while I have to make do with ruling Turks, and my younger brother has to suffer in the West. Our father favored you, the youngest son, when he made this division, but I will not allow this; neither the Kayanid crown, nor its throne, nor sovereignty, nor Persia should be yours."

When Iraj heard Tur's words, he answered him simply and straightforwardly: "You are my older brother and ambitious for glory; if you would be happy you must calm yourself. I don't want Persia, or the West, or China, or sovereignty, or authority over any country. Greatness that brings evil in its train is something for which we should weep. And if the heavens raise your saddle up to glory, finally your pillow will be the dust. I sat on the throne of Persia, it's true, but now I am tired of both the crown and the throne: I hand them both over to you, and may you harbor no hatred for me from now on. I've no desire to quarrel with you, and your heart should not be upset by anything I do. If it troubles you, and it means I cannot see you, I have no wish to rule in this world. I don't want anything except to be a subject, and may greed and the longing for grandeur never sway my heart!"

But Tur, who lacked all sense of righteousness, was annoyed by his brother's words, and frowned at them. He leapt up and grasped the golden throne on which he had been sitting and brought it crashing down on Iraj's head. Iraj begged him to spare his life and said, "Have you no fear of God, no shame before our father? Is this your decision? Don't kill me, because my blood will be upon your head.

> You have a soul yourself; how can you say
> That you will take another's soul away?
> Pity the ants that toil beneath your feet—
> They have their souls; to them their souls are sweet.

Don't make yourself a murderer. You'll never see me again; I will be content with a corner of the world, there to earn my bread in sorrow. How can you long to spill your brother's blood and torment our father's heart with such a crime? You wanted the world and now you have it; don't spill my blood, turning against God in this way." Tur heard his words but made no answer. He drew a dagger from his boot and split Iraj from head to foot, so that his body was veiled in blood. He plunged the poisoned dagger into his brother's trunk. Iraj's body buckled, the noble cypress was felled, and the blossoms of his face ran with blood. This is how the young prince died.

> O world, you nurtured him, but offered no
> Protection when his brother laid him low:
> I don't know whom you favor secretly,
> But we should weep for all we hear and see.
> And you, who murder kings, who live in fear,
> Learn from these criminals whose tale you hear.

Tur severed the mammoth warrior's head and had it filled with camphor and musk, and sent it with this message to their aged father, who had divided the world between them: "Here is the head of your darling, to whom you gave our ancestors' crown. Give him the crown now, and the throne if you wish; but this branch of the royal tree is no more." Then the two unjust brothers returned to their kingdoms, one in China, and one in the West.

Feraydun Learns That Iraj Has Been Killed

Feraydun watched the road, and the army watched with him, anxious for the return of the young king. When it was time for him to appear, his father prepared a turquoise throne for him, and a jewel-studded crown; wine and musicians were made ready, war drums were strapped on elephants, and the whole town was decorated. As Feraydun and his army busied themselves with these preparations, a cloud of dust rose above the road; from it emerged a camel on which sat a grieving, wailing messenger, and strapped to the animal's side was a coffin. This man rode up to Feraydun, sighing, weeping, and ashen-faced. Appalled by his words and manner, the king's companions removed the coffin lid and drew back the coverlet of silk within it, to reveal the severed head of Iraj. Feraydun fell from his horse into the dust, and the soldiers with him rent their clothes in grief. Their faces were blackened, their eyes rolled back in despair, and only the whites were visible.

The prince's return in such a manner threw the welcoming party into disarray; the banners were torn, the drums turned upside down, the nobles' faces became the color of ebony. The elephants and drums were draped in black cloth, the Arab horses in deep blue. The king walked, as did his soldiers, heaping dust on their heads; the nobles cried out in an agony of sorrow, clawing at their flesh as they mourned for the prince.

Brokenhearted, their king wailing in grief, the army made its way to the garden of Iraj; here the young prince had held court and presided over festivities. Clasping his young son's head to his breast, Feraydun entered the garden weeping. He looked at the imperial throne, and at his son's head which would never wear the crown again, at the garden's royal pool, the blossoming trees, the willows, and the quince trees. He saw this place of celebrations and ceremony emptied

of its nobility, and a cloud of dust rising up to the heavens. He burned the garden and clawed at his cheeks, wept, and tore his hair. His waist was girdled with blood, and he spread fire through the pleasure grounds, uprooted the flowerbeds, gave the cypresses to the flames, and with this act seeled tight the eyes of happiness. He cradled Iraj's head in his arms, and turned his face toward God. He said, "Lord of justice, look at this slaughtered innocent, his head severed by a dagger, his body devoured by lions. Burn the hearts of his two unjust brothers, and may they see nothing but sorrow in their lives. Burn their vitals, and have them suffer such agony that the wild beasts will pity their pain. I ask only that I be given a little time, my lord, until I see a child from Iraj's seed, who will bind on his belt for vengeance. When I have seen this, it is right that I lie where earth will be the measure of me."

He wept so long in this manner that the grass grew up to his chest; the earth was his bed, the dirt his pillow, and the bright world was dimmed before him. The doors to the court were closed, and Feraydun loosed his tongue, saying, "My young prince, my noble warrior, no one who wore the crown has died as you have died: your head severed by Ahriman, your body's shroud the lion's maw; the beasts mourn for you and find no rest or sleep. All the country's men and women have gathered together and sit weeping, their eyes wet with tears, their hearts filled with sorrow; their clothes changed to black and blue, they sit grieving for their king's death. What a day is this for them, in which they see all life as death."

Time passed, and in Iraj's harem Feraydun saw that one of his women, named Mah-Afarid, whom Iraj had greatly loved, was pregnant. The king was happy to see her secret, hoping that her child would be a means to vengeance for his son's death. When the time for her delivery came she gave birth to a girl, who was brought up in comfort and with tenderness. Had you surveyed this lovely girl from head to foot, you would say she was Iraj himself. When she had grown and the time came for her to marry, her face was as lovely as Canopus and her hair as black as pitch. Her grandfather promised her to Pashang, and married her to him after an appropriate time had passed.

THE VENGEANCE OF
MANUCHEHR

The Birth of Manuchehr

Mah-Afarid's daughter gave birth to a splendid child, one worthy of the crown and throne. As soon as the boy had been born a servant took him to Feraydun and said, "Good news, your majesty; look, here is Iraj." The king laughed, since it was indeed as if Iraj were alive again; he took the child in his arms and prayed to God, "May this day be remembered as auspicious, and may our enemies' hearts be defeated." Then he looked down at the child's face again and said, "Sprung from a pure mother and father, a noble branch has born fruit. Wine has been poured from a splendid goblet; he has a clear, open face (Manachehreh), and may his name be Manuchehr." Feraydun had the child brought up so attentively that the winds of heaven never touched him. The nurse who cared for him did not walk on the earth; her feet trod on musk, and a silk parasol shaded her head.

Throughout his childhood, no harm came to Manuchehr from the stars. Feraydun had him taught the arts of kingship, and his heart revived as Manuchehr grew. The army too favored the young man, and the king gave him a golden throne, a heavy mace, and a turquoise-studded crown. Then he handed over to him the keys to all his treasuries, as well as a royal enclosure made of brocade in various colors, within which were tents of leopard skin. He freely gave him Arab horses with golden bridles, Indian swords in golden scabbards, armor and helmets, bows from Chach, arrows of poplar wood, javelins and Chinese shields. He loved him so much that he thought it appropriate to give all these treasures, accumulated with such toil, to Manuchehr. Then he ordered the champions of the army and the country's nobles to come before him to acclaim the young man as king and to sprinkle emeralds over his crown. Great festivities were held, and it became clear who were wolves and

who sheep. Qaren of the Kaviani clan was there, as well as Shirui the
army commander, and Andian; the armies assembled, and Manuchehr
dominated them as his flock.

Salm and Tur Learn of Manuchehr

News that the imperial crown shone once more came to Salm and Tur.
Their unjust hearts feared the stars were turning against them; the evil-
doers' days were darkened, and they took counsel together. They
agreed they had to seek a remedy for their situation, and the only thing
they could think of was to send someone to Feraydun apologizing for
their past behavior. They sought out an envoy who would be able to
speak well and sincerely, and spoke flatteringly to him. Then, in fear of
what fate would bring them, they opened the treasury of the West and
chose from this ancient store a golden crown. They had elephants
richly caparisoned and filled chariots with musk and ambergris, gold
and silver coins, silks, and furs, and when all this had been made ready
the envoy presented himself before them, prepared for the journey.
They gave him a message to give to Feraydun, beginning with praise
of God and invoking blessings on Feraydun, wishing him long life,
health, and glory. Then they told him to say, "The eyes of these two
sinners are filled with tears of shame before their father; their hearts
burn with regret, and they beg for forgiveness. Wise men say that a
man is punished for his sins, that he suffers and his heart is filled with
anguish, and they say to the king that their hearts are tormented in this
way. But these things were written in our fates, they say, and our
actions have done no more than bring what was written to pass; even
lions that terrify the world, and dragons, cannot escape the snare of
fate. And then an evil and audacious demon emptied our hearts of all
fear of God, and made our minds his dwelling place. But we hope that
the king will pardon us, even though our sin is great, that he will put
it down to our ignorance, to the workings of the heavens, which now
save us and now destroy us, and thirdly to the demon who scurries
about the world and is ready for every mischief. If the king will not
look for revenge against us, our ways will be purified; let him send
Manuchehr to us, his suppliants, with a mighty army, so that we may
present ourselves before him, on foot, as his slaves. May we wash away
with our eyes' tears the tree of vengeance that has grown from all this

hatred. As the crown is renewed, we hasten to offer our tears and suf-
ferings, and we send treasure as an earnest of our good faith."

The Message of Salm and Tur Arrives at Feraydun's Court

His heart filled with words that had neither rhyme nor reason to them,
accompanied by elephants and treasure, the envoy came in splendor to
the court. When Feraydun heard of his approach he had the imperial
throne draped in Chinese brocade and the Kayanid crown made ready.
He sat on the turquoise-studded throne, like a cypress topped by the
full moon, wearing the crown, the royal earrings and torque, as befits
a king. Prince Manuchehr sat beside him wearing the royal diadem,
and the country's nobles stood ranged on each side, dressed in gold
from head to foot, bearing golden maces and shields. Wild animals
were tethered there with golden chains and collars, on the one side
lions and leopards, and on the other war elephants.

The warrior Shapur left the castle to welcome Salm's messenger,
who dismounted and ran toward the doorway. When he approached
king Feraydun and saw him crowned high on his throne, he bowed his
head and placed his face against the ground. The king motioned him
to a place on a golden throne, and the messenger began his speech:
"Great king, ornament of the crown, the throne, and royal seal, whose
throne transforms the world into a rose garden, and whose good for-
tune illumines the air, we are all slaves of the dust beneath your feet,
and live only for you." The king smiled on him and made him wel-
come, and the envoy repeated Salm's and Tur's message, that disguised
truth with lies. The king listened to his fluent talk asking pardon for
the two brothers and suggesting that Manuchehr visit them, when, as
his slaves, they would welcome him and transfer to him their crowns
and thrones, paying the blood-price they owed their father with silks
and gold, crowns, and royal belts. The envoy spoke and the king lis-
tened, and his answer was as a key that opens a lock.

Feraydun's Answer to His Sons

When the world's king had heard his evil sons' message, he answered
the envoy point by point. He said, "How can you hide the sun? The
hidden workings of their evil hearts are clearer than the sun in the
heavens. I've heard all you said, and now pay attention to my answer.

Tell those two fearless, shameless, unjust, malevolent wretches, that idle talk counts for nothing, and I will not indulge in it. If they feel such love for Manuchehr now, where is Iraj's body? It has been devoured by wild beasts, and his head was sent to me in a coffin. And now you've finished with Iraj, you wish to start on Manuchehr? You will only see him accompanied by an army, with an iron helmet on his head, bearing a mace and the Kaviani banner, the ground blackened by his horses' hooves. He will have the commander Qaren with him, and Shapur, Nastuh's son, will command the rear of his army. Sarv, the king of the Yemen, will be there in the vanguard to advise him. We look to wash the leaves and fruit of the tree of vengeance for Iraj in blood. Previously, we did not seek vengeance for him because we did not think the times were propitious; it would not have been suitable for me to fight against my two sons. But now that a noble branch has sprung from the tree that his enemies uprooted, you will find that a savage lion longs for vengeance for his grandfather's death, and that he comes with our champions, Sam the son of Nariman, and Karshasp, who is descended from Jamshid, that their army stretches from one mountain to another and pounds the earth beneath its feet. As for their demand that the king should wash all thoughts of revenge from his heart and forgive them, because this was the doing of the heavens, because their wisdom was clouded and their love overshadowed, I have heard all these futile excuses, and respond with the saying of a wise man, 'The man who sows the seeds of evil never sees one happy day, or the joys of paradise.' If God has forgiven you, why are you so afraid of your brother's blood? Have you no shame before God, with your black hearts and your tongues filled with lying words? You will be punished for this evil in both worlds; this act will not remain hidden. And then this sending an ivory throne, war elephants, and a turquoise-studded crown is supposed to make me give up my longing for revenge? I'm to sell princes' lives for gold? I'd rather my throne, crown, and glory were destroyed than do such a thing. Perhaps some dragon's spawn would accept a price for a priceless life, but who says that an aged father would do such a thing for his son's life? I've no need of this wealth you've sent, and there is no point in my talking any more on the subject. This father will never cease to long for vengeance while he lives. I've heard your message; hear my answer." Then to the envoy he said, "Spell this out to them, sentence by sentence. Now go!"

The envoy heard these terrifying words and observed Manuchehr seated on the throne. He withered away in fear, and rose trembling from his seat; there and then he sat in the saddle to depart. This noble young man saw in his soul all that was destined to happen, and that it would not be long before the heavens frowned on Tur and Salm. He sped like the wind, his head filled with the king's answer, his heart with foreboding.

When he reached the West, he saw a silken tent pitched on the plain, where the two kings waited for him. They made a space for him to sit and asked about the new king. They questioned the envoy concerning the crown and the imperial throne, King Feraydun and his army, the assembled warriors, and the state of the country. And then they wanted to know how the turning heavens had favored Manuchehr, who among the nobility was there, who the vizier was, the state of the treasury and who the treasurer was, how many cavalry were assembled there, who their leader was, and who the army commanders were.

The envoy said, "Let the man who has never seen the glories of spring see Feraydun's court. It is a place of spring-like joy, a heaven; the dust there is ambergris, the earth is gold. The heavens smile down on his palace; no mountain is as tall, no garden as vast. As I approached, the palace summit seemed hidden among the stars; there are elephants tethered on one side, lions on the other, and all the world bows before his good fortune. His elephants bear golden howdahs, his lions' collars are studded with jewels; drummers stand before the elephants, and the blare of brazen trumpets sounds from every side—the world seems to seethe, and the earth roar to the heavens. I entered the court and saw a king as radiant as the moon, seated on a turquoise-studded throne, his crown surmounted by shining rubies. His head was as white as camphor, his cheeks like rose petals; his heart seeks peace and his words are kindly. The world's hope and fear are in his hands, and you would say that Jamshid lives again in him. On his right sat Manuchehr, as tall and elegant as a cypress tree, as kingly in his heart and language as Tahmures the binder of demons. The warrior Qaren stood before him, and to his left was Sarv the king of the Yemen. Sarv is his vizier, victorious Karshasp is his treasurer, and no one has ever seen such wealth as is in his treasury. Two ranks of warriors line the palace walls, bearing golden maces and with golden diadems. Qaren, Andian, Shirui the destroyer of lions, and Shapur who is like a war elephant in his rage, are his commanders. The air is darkened when the war drums sound from their elephants' backs, and if they attack us, our mountains will be flattened like a plain, our plains encumbered like mountains; their hearts are filled with hatred, their faces with frowns, and war is their one desire."

He told them all he had seen, and the words he had heard from Feraydun. The hearts of the two criminals writhed in anguish, and their faces darkened. They sat and looked for some remedy, but their words had neither head nor tail to them. Then Tur said to Salm, "We must forget about peace and tranquility: that lion cub must not sharpen his teeth and become brave. How can he be devoid of talents, when his teacher is Feraydun? When grandfather and grandson conspire, something extraordinary will come of it. We must prepare for war, and make up for lost time."

They gathered forces from China and the West and led their cavalry out. The world was filled with rumors, and men flocked to their banners, but though their armies were limitless, their stars were already declining. The two armies made for Iran; their soldiers were hidden in helmets and armor, and war elephants and wealth accompanied the murderous brothers, whose hearts were bent on destruction.

Salm and Tur March Against Feraydun
Feraydun received news that their forces were nearing Persia and ordered Manuchehr to lead his army out on to the plain. He said:

> *"A young man of good fortune wins the day*
> *By patience; wisdom will entrap his prey—*
> *He lets the leopard follow him to where*
> *He has already laid his cunning snare."*

Manuchehr replied, "Great king, fortune has frowned on whoever opposes you with hatred in his heart, and his body and soul will soon be severed from one another. I have bound on my armor for battle and shall not loosen its knots until the battlefield's dust has obscured the sun. I have contempt for all their warriors; how can they dare to fight against me?"

He ordered Qaren to lead their troops out. The king's pavilion was pitched on the plain, with the royal banner fluttering in front. The warriors advanced in companies, and the plains and mountains were like heaving waves of the sea. The dust obscured the sun and darkened the bright day. Deafening war cries went up from every side, the Arab horses neighed, and the war drums resounded. For two miles elephants were drawn up before the camp; sixty of them bore golden howdahs studded with jewels, three hundred were loaded with baggage, three hundred were covered in iron armor with only their eyes visible. The king's tent was struck, and the army marched out from Tammisheh. Three hundred thousand armored cavalry, led by the warlike Qaren, each of them like a raging lion, and eager to avenge the death of Iraj, followed the Kaviani banner, their swords glittering in their fists. Manuchehr and Qaren emerged from the forests of Narvan to lead the army onto the open plain; the prince placed Karshasp in command of the left flank, Sam and Qobad had charge of the right. Outshining all others, Manuchehr, accompanied by Sarv, was as splendid as the full moon in the center of his forces. Qaren and Sam drew their swords from their scabbards, Qobad led the advance troops, and men from the clan of Taliman lay hidden to ambush the enemy. The army with its lion warriors and resounding drums was as splendid as a bride in all her finery.

Salm and Tur learned that an army intent on revenge was preparing for war. The two brothers led their troops out from among the trees, and the blood from their livers appeared as foam on their lips. The murderers advanced their troops, their minds filled with hatred; behind them lay the sea and the territory of the Alans. Qobad came forward to spy out the land, and when Tur heard of this, he rushed forward like the wind and said to him,

> "Go back to Manuchehr and say, 'And who
> Bestowed this armor and this sword on you?
> You have no father; from Iraj's race
> A girl was born, so who gave you the mace
> That signifies the royal sovereignty,
> Young king? Who gave you this authority?'"

Qobad answered, "Don't worry, I'll take your message exactly as you've said it. But if you reflected on this long and wisely, you'd know this is a terrifying business you've embarked on, and you'd be afraid to say these foolish words of yours. Don't be surprised if the wild animals weep for you day and night, because from the forests of Narvan to

China the land is filled with our horsemen and warriors, flourishing their swords when they see the Kaviani banner. Your heart and brain will split with terror when you see them, and you will not know the peaks of this land from its valleys."

Qobad went to the king and told him what he had heard from Tur. Manuchehr laughed and said, "No one but a fool would say such things. Thanks be to the God of this world and the next, who knows what is plain and what is hidden, and who is aware that Iraj is my grandfather and that the great Feraydun is my witness in this. When I fight, my lineage will be plain enough. I swear by the might of the God of the sun and the moon, that I will not let Tur rule for long; in the blinking of an eye, I shall display his severed head before the army. I shall have my revenge for Iraj's death, and trample Tur's reign beneath my feet."

Manuchehr Attacks Tur's Army

Manuchehr gave orders that tables be made ready for a feast, and that a place be set aside for wine and music. As darkness fell, he sent out sentries onto the plain. Qaren stood before the troops with Sarv, the king of the Yemen, and addressed them: "Nobles and lions loyal to the king, know that this is a war against Ahriman; keep yourselves ready, and live in the knowledge of God's protection. Whoever is killed in this battle will be received into Paradise, and his sins will be washed away. Whoever spills the blood of these warriors from China and the West and seizes their territory, his name will live forever, and he will earn the glorious praise of our priests. He will be given a diadem and throne from our king, who is the lord of strength and the dispenser of justice. When day dawns and two watches of the morning have passed, prepare to fight; ready your maces and Kaboli daggers. Keep to your ranks, and see that none advances his feet before the others." The commanders ranged themselves before the king and said with one voice, "We are your slaves, and live in this world only for the king. Whatever he orders we shall do immediately; for him we shall turn this plain to an Oxus of blood." Then each man returned to his own tent, meditating on the battle to come.

As dawn broke and darkness was dispelled, Manuchehr rose up in the midst of his forces, dressed in his armor, wearing a Rumi helmet, and grasping his sword; as one man, the troops thrust their lances into the air. They covered the face of the earth, their heads filled with fury, their foreheads with frowns. The king skillfully deployed the flanks and center of the army, and the ground seemed to heave like a floundering ship on the sea, or seethe like the waters of the Nile. The war drums on the elephants' backs were beaten, more drums were beaten before them, and the noise of trumpets resounded as if the battle were to be a festive celebration. The army moved forward like a mountain, and the two sides met in close combat. The plain became a sea of blood, as if red tulips had sprung up everywhere, and the elephants' legs glowed like pillars of coral. Until night came, and the sun disappeared, all the advantage was with Manuchehr, because the world's soul loved him.

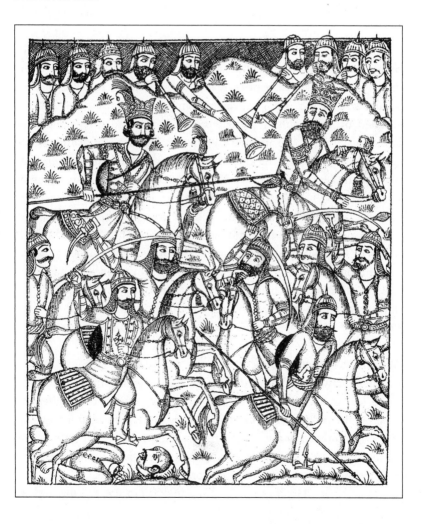

Manuchehr Kills Tur

Tur's and Salm's hearts seethed with fury, and they plotted an ambush, so that when night turned to day, the two warriors held back, and none of their men advanced to battle. When half the day had passed, their hearts were filled with hatred, and they hatched one useless plot after another. They said, "When night comes, we'll ambush them, and fill the mountains and plains with their blood."

Night came and day disappeared; darkness covered all the earth, and the two unjust brothers readied their soldiers for a night attack. But Manuchehr's spies had news of this and hurried to tell him what they had heard. Manuchehr handed his men over to Qaren, who took three thousand brave warriors and hid them where they would be able to waylay the enemy.

Tur set off with a hundred thousand troops in the darkness of the night; but as they neared the camp they came on the Persian forces drawn up behind their banner, ready for war. They had no choice but to attack, and the war cry went up from their midst. The sky was clouded by the cavalry's dust, and swords glittered in the dark like lightning; it was if the air itself caught fire, flashing like diamonds and burning the ground. The din of weapons deafened the fighters, and fire ascended into the heavens. The king lifted his head from where he had been lying in wait, and Tur had no means of escape. He tugged at his reins and turned to flee, as his soldiers' cries re-echoed around him. Manuchehr sped after him and, as he closed on him, flung a spear at his back. The sword dropped from Tur's hand, and Manuchehr grasped him, lifting him from the saddle and hurling him to the ground. There and then he severed his head and left his body for the animals to devour. Then he returned to his own camp, his mind filled with the turnings of fate, which bring now prosperity and now defeat.

Manuchehr's Letter to Feraydun

Manuchehr wrote a letter to King Feraydun, telling him of how the battle had gone. He began by invoking God, the lord of righteousness, purity, and justice, who is man's only protection against hardship, and called down his blessings on Feraydun, lord of the crown and mace, to whom belong justice, faith, and glory, from whose good fortune all righteousness comes, and from whose throne all splendor and beauty emanate. He continued, "I reached Turan successfully, and we prepared our army for war. We fought three battles in two days, both at night and under the shining sun. They tried a night attack but we were ready for them, because I had heard that they were going to attempt this trick as a last resort. We waylaid them, and I saw to it that their fists closed on nothing but air. As Tur retreated I pursued him and flung a spear after him, which pierced his armor, and then like the wind I lifted him from his saddle. I hurled him to the ground as if he were a monster and severed his head from his worthless body. I send you his head, as he once sent that of Prince Iraj in a golden casket. And now I shall deal with Salm."

He sent a swift messenger with the letter, and when the man arrived his face was filled with shame, his eyes with tears, since he wondered how he could show the severed head of the king of China to the Persian king, because no matter how evil a son might be, or how terrible his crimes, a father's heart would be wrung by such a sight. But he boldly came before the king and set Tur's head down before him. Feraydun called down blessings from the lord of justice on Manuchehr.

Qaren Captures the Castle of the Alans

News of the battle, and of the darkness that had obscured the moon, reached Salm. There was a castle to the rear of his forces, whose walls reached up into the blue heavens, and he decided to retreat there, to see how events would unfold. Qaren thought that if Salm were to avoid battle and reach this castle, it would be a refuge for him, as it was filled with all manner of wealth, and its granite walls rose out of the sea and reached up to the clouds, so that it could not be over flown even by the legendary homa. Qaren decided to make all haste and cut him off before he could do so.

He hurried to King Manuchehr and said, "If your majesty wishes, and will give authority and men to the humblest of his soldiers, I shall corner Salm, who can either fight us or attempt to flee. I shall need the royal banner and Tur's seal ring, and with them I shall be able to take Salm's castle. I and the warrior Karshasp, in the darkness of the night, will deal with this matter; but see that you say nothing to anyone."

When the air turned the color of ebony, they bound the war drums on their elephants, and the warriors set off toward the ocean. Qaren gave the command to Shirui and said, "I shall go in secret to the castle's commander, pretending to be a messenger. I'll show him Tur's seal, and as soon as I'm in the castle, I'll display the royal banner and draw my sword. You make for the castle, and my war cry will be the signal for your attack." The army waited near the castle, while Qaren went forward and showed the castle's commander Tur's seal. He said, "I've come from Tur, who told me to give up all thoughts of comfort and to travel night and day until I reached this place, where I am to make common cause with you, and take over the defense of the castle. If Manuchehr sends an army here with his banner, I'm to hold the castle, and if possible destroy his forces." When the castle's commander heard these words and saw Tur's seal ring, he opened wide the castle gates, believing what he heard and unaware of any subterfuge. He trusted the stranger, and his carelessness cost him his castle and his life.

As day began to dawn, Qaren unfurled the royal banner, as bright as the full moon, and uttered his war cry as signals for Shirui and his warriors. Shirui made for the castle gates, attacking the defenders, and bestowing crowns of blood on them. On the one side stood Qaren, on the other Shirui, above fire flashed from swords, beneath lay the waters of the sea, and by the time the sun attained the heaven's summit, the castle was in an uproar and its commander was not to be found. It was as if the castle itself had disappeared, and not a ship was to be seen on the sea; all that was visible was smoke rising up to the clouds. Fire flared, a wind rose, the cries of prisoners suing for quarter could be heard, and as the sun went down the sky, the castle was indistinguishable from the surrounding plain. Twelve thousand of the enemy were killed, and pitch black smoke billowed up from the fire. The whole surface of the sea turned as black as tar, and the plain was a river of blood.

The Attack by Kakui, Zahhak's Grandson

Qaren came to Manuchehr and told him of the battle he had fought. Manuchehr congratulated him, saying "May you live for ever as lord of your horse, saddle, and mace! As soon as you left me another army appeared; I've heard that it's led by the evil champion Kakui, a fearsome demon from Dezh Hukht Gang, and a grandson of Zahhak. He attacked with a hundred thousand men and cavalry and killed some of my lion warriors. And now Salm thinks of fighting, because this ally of his has arrived. I haven't faced him on the battlefield yet, but when he attacks I shall know what to make of him."

Qaren replied, "My prince, who can oppose you in battle? A leopard's skin will split with terror at the thought of it. Who is this Kakui, what is he? The wisdom of my heart, the purity of my mind, will fashion a scheme to deal with him, and no one like Kakui will set out against us from Dezh Hukht ever again."

Then the blare of trumpets and bugles, the cavalry's cries, and the din of war drums, were heard in the camp. The air turned the color of pitch, the ground that of ebony. It was as if diamonds were alive, like tongues of flame flickering in the darkness; cries from the give and take of combat sounded on all sides, and the air was filled with arrows' feathers, like a vulture's maw. Blood congealed on the warriors' hands as they gripped their swords, dripping down from the darkened blades; the earth seemed about to heave, like a cresting sea, when Kakui sprang forward, yelling his war cry and making straight for Manuchehr like a demon. The two faced one another like massive elephants, ready for combat. Kakui thrust a spear at Manuchehr's body; the king's helmet shuddered as the point passed through his armor and exposed his flesh. But Manuchehr struck at Kakui's neck with his sword and split his breastplate. For half the day these two blood-soaked men fought, until the sun sank in the sky. They attacked like leopards, and their blood was mixed with the dust, so that the plain and mountainside were drowned in blood, beyond all measure. Now Manuchehr was weary of battle, but he urged his horse forward with his thighs and grasped Kakui by the belt, lifting the mammoth warrior from his saddle, and hurled him down on the warm ground. He thrust his sword into Kakui's body, and so the life of this headstrong Arab, whose mother had borne him for this evil day, was dispersed on the wind.

Salm Flees and Is Killed by Manuchehr

Salm's head was emptied of all thoughts of vengeance, and he and his men fled toward the castle. Manuchehr's army came after them, but the way was so clogged with dead and wounded warriors that they had a hard time going forward. Mounted on his white charger, the young king was filled with rage; he cast off his horse's barding, to make better speed, and urged his mount into the retreating army's dust. He closed on the king of the West and cried out,

> "You unjust wretch, who killed your brother, who
> Desired his crown, that crown has come to you:

I've brought your crown for you, I've brought your throne—
The splendid tree you planted then has grown:
Wait for our sovereign Feraydun's reward,
Don't try to flee from me, my noble lord.
The tree you planted has borne fruit, you'll see
Its fruits served up to you immediately:
You nurtured them, you spun the silk that made
The thread by which your wretched life's betrayed."

As he shouted he rode forward, drawing level with Salm, and struck at his neck with his sword, so that Salm's body was split in two. He gave orders that the head be spitted on a spear and then he raised it into the clouds. Salm's army was astonished at the strength of his arm and dispersed like a flock without a shepherd, wandering aimlessly in groups in the plains, mountains, and caves. One of their number was a man of some eloquence, and they asked him to go to Manuchehr and say, "We are your subjects, and do not tread on the earth but at your command. Some of us owned flocks, and some farms and houses, and we were forced to join this army. Now we are all the king's slaves, and our hearts and souls are filled with love for him. If he wishes to fight against us and spill our blood, we lack the strength to oppose him: we lay our innocent heads before the king, at his mercy. He can do whatever he wishes with us, since he is the lord of our sinless souls."

The wise man repeated all this and Manuchehr listened in astonishment. His answer was, "I trample on all unjust desires, and renounce whatever is from Ahriman and not from God. Leave my sight, and may evil afflict all demons. Whether you are my enemies or my allies and well-wishers, the lord of victory has given me authority over you, and the innocent are distinguished from evildoers. Today is a day of justice, injustice is no more, and the heads of your commanders are safe. Follow the ways of love, and cast away your weapons." A herald cried from the royal pavilion, "Great champions, whose thoughts are noble, from now on do not spill blood thoughtlessly, since those who are tyrannical suffer an evil fate."

The enemy warriors touched their heads to the ground, and then took their weapons, armor, helmets, barding, maces, and Indian swords to Pashang's son, heaping them up before him like a mountain.

Manuchehr Writes a Letter to King Feraydun

Manuchehr dispatched a messenger bearing the head of the king of the West. He wrote a letter to his grandfather, describing his battles and the stratagems he had used. He began with praise of the Creator, from whom come victory and ability, beneath whose command all good and evil occur, who guarantees all oaths, calling down his blessing on the wise Feraydun, the king of the earth, destroyer of the plots of the wicked, possessed of knowledge and the divine *farr*. He continued, "By the king's strength I have destroyed the plots of those two sorcerers; I have cut off their heads and purified the land with my sword's steel. I shall come after this letter like the wind and recount all that has happened."

He ordered the warrior Shirui to gather the war booty into one place, load it onto elephants, and take all of it to the king. Then he had the brazen drums and trumpets sounded, and led his army from the seashore by the Chinese fortress to the court of Feraydun. As he approached Tammisheh, his grandfather longed to see him; the blare of brass trumpets rang out, and the army stirred in readiness. Elephants were loaded with turquoise thrones, and golden howdahs draped with Chinese brocade, banners, and fine stuffs, so that the world glittered with scarlet, gold, and purple. Like a moving black cloud the army marched from the sea of Gilan to Sari; their saddles, shields, and belts were of gold, their stirrups of silver. So they went forward, with elephants and treasure, to greet the young prince. Men from Gilan followed the army; they were like lions, with golden torques and hair as black as musk; in front of the king there were lions and elephants, followed by his warriors.

When Feraydun's banner appeared, Manuchehr's army formed its ranks. The prince dismounted, like a young sapling that has born new fruit, kissed the ground, and made his obeisance to the royal crown, throne, and seal ring. Feraydun ordered him to mount his horse, kissed him, and fondled his face with his hand. Then he turned his face to the skies and said, "Great lord of justice, you have said, 'I am the just lord, the succor of those who are oppressed.' You have dispensed justice and aided me, bestowing on me this crown and the imperial seal ring." Then he gave commands that Manuchehr sit on the royal throne and wear the crown. Shirui brought the captured wealth to the king's court, and Feraydun ordered that it be distributed to the soldiers.

Having done this he bowed to Fate's decree—
The leaf was withered on the royal tree.
He lived his life in mourning: ceaseless tears
And constant grief consumed his final years.
Weeping, the great king said, "My heart's delight,
My sons, have turned my day to endless night—
My sons slain wretchedly before my eyes,
Since all my plans were evil and unwise . . ."
And so, heartbroken, weeping for the past,
He lived tormented till Death came at last.
O world, from end to end unreal, untrue,
No wise man can live happily in you—
But bless'd is he whose good deeds bring him fame;
Monarch or slave, he leaves a lasting name.

THE TALE OF SAM AND THE SIMORGH

The Tale of Sam and the Simorgh

Now I shall tell an astonishing tale, taken from the stories our ancestors told. See what strange events Fate unfolded for Sam: listen well, my son.

Sam had no child, and his heart grieved at this. There was a beautiful woman living in his private quarters; her cheeks were like rose petals, her hair like musk. Her face was as splendid as the sun, and Sam had hopes that she would bear him a child. And this happened; after some time she gave birth to a beautiful boy, whose radiance lit the world, but although his face was as bright as the sun, his hair was completely white. Given how the child looked, Sam was not told of his birth for a week; all the women of his household wept over the boy, and no one dared tell Sam that this beautiful woman had given birth to a son who was an old man. Then a courageous wet nurse, who had a lion's spirit, came bravely before Sam and said, "May Sam's days be prosperous, and the hearts of those who wish him ill be torn out. In your women's quarters, a fine boy has been born from your beloved. His body is like pure silver, his face like paradise, and you will find no ugly spot on him. His one fault is that his hair is white; such is your fate, my lord."

Sam descended from his throne and went into the women's quarters. When he saw his son's white hair he despaired of the world, and lifting his face to the heavens, he complained bitterly. "O God, who is above all failings and faults, whatever you command is good. If I have committed a grave sin, if I have followed the ways of Ahriman, I repent and pray that God will grant me forgiveness. My grieving soul writhes with shame, and the hot blood boils in my heart. What shall I say about this ill-omened child when men ask about his black body, and his hair as white as jasmine? Shall I say he is a demon's child? He is like a leopard, whose skin is of two colors. No longer shall I call down blessings on Persia; I shall quit this land for shame."

He gave orders that the child be taken far away, to the place where the Simorgh has her home. They took the boy and laid him down in the mountains, then returned to the court. The day ended, and the champion's innocent son had no knowledge of white or black; his father had cast all kindness from his heart and acted evilly toward his unweaned child.

When the Simorgh's chicks grew hungry, she flew up from her nest; she saw an unweaned, crying baby lying on the ground; his cradle was of thorns, his wet nurse was the earth, he was naked, and no milk touched his lips. The black earth surrounded him, and above his head the sun shone in the summit of the heavens. Would that his mother and father had been leopards; they at least would have shaded him from the sun. The Simorgh flew down from the clouds, stretched out her claws and clutched him, lifting him up from the hot stones on which he lay. She flew with him back to her nest in the Alborz mountains, where she intended to take him to her chicks, thinking they could feed off him and pay no attention to his cries. But God had other plans, so that when the Simorgh and her chicks looked at the little child weeping bitter tears, something wonderful to relate happened: they took pity on him, staring in astonishment at his lovely face. She sought out the most delicate morsels of the chase for the boy, touching them to his lips, and in this way many days passed and the child grew into a fine young man. Men with caravans passing through the mountains would catch sight of this noble youth, whose body was like a cypress tree, whose chest was like a mountain of silver, and whose waist was as slim as a reed. Rumors of him spread through the world, since neither good nor evil ever remain hidden, and news of this glorious youth reached Sam, the son of Nariman.

The Dream of Sam, the Son of Nariman

One night Sam was asleep, his heart wearied with the cares of the world. He dreamed of a man from India, galloping toward him on an Arab horse, who brought him good news of that noble sapling his son. When he woke he summoned his priests and told them of the dream and of the rumors he had heard. "What do you say to this?" he asked. "What does your wisdom make of it?"

Young and old, all those present, said to Sam, "Lions and leopards in their stony lairs, the fish and the monsters of the sea, all love and nourish their children and give thanks to God for them; you have broken this bond of benevolence in casting out your innocent child. Turn to God and repent, since he is the guide to good and evil."

When dark night came and Sam slept again, his heart was filled with turmoil. In his dream he saw a banner fluttering on a mountain in India. Then a beautiful slave appeared, leading a mighty army; a priest was on his left, and a wise sage on his right. One of these two came forward and said coldly to Sam, "Presumptuous and immoral man, you have washed shame before God from your heart and eyes; what kind of a hero are you, if a bird has nourished your son? If it is a fault to have white hair, look at yourself, whose beard is white and whose hair is like the leaves of the willow. You despised your son, but God has been his protector, loving him more than a wet nurse would, while you were devoid of affection for him." Sam cried out in his sleep, like a lion caught in a trap.

When he woke, Sam called his counselors and the leaders of his army and set off for the mountains to reclaim what he had rejected. He saw a mountain whose peak reached the Pleiades, and on it a great nest woven from ebony and sandalwood. Sam stared at the granite slopes, at the terrifying Simorgh, and at its fearsome nest, which was like a palace towering in the clouds, but one not built by men's hands or from clay and water. He bowed his face down to the dirt, praising God who had created this bird, and this mountain whose slopes reached to the stars, acknowledging him as just and all powerful. He looked for a way to climb the mountain, seeking out wild animals' tracks, and said, "O you who are higher than all high places, than thought itself and the sun and moon, if this youth is indeed from my loins, and not the seed of some evil demon, help me to climb this mountain."

The Simorgh said to Sam's son, "You have endured the hardship of growing up in this nest, and now your father, great Sam, who is a champion among heroes, has come to this mountain searching for his son; he honors and values you now. I must give you back, and return you to him safe and sound." Listen to the youth's answer: "You have tired of my friendship, then? Your nest has been a noble home for me, and two of your feathers have been a glorious crown for me." The Simorgh replied, "When you see the throne and crown and the ceremonial of the Kayanid court, this nest will mean nothing to you. Go, see what fate has in store for you. Take these feathers of mine with you, so that you will always live under my protection, since I brought you up beneath my wings with my own children. If any trouble comes to you, if there is talk of good and ill, throw one of my feathers into the fire, and my glory will at once appear to you. I shall come to you in the guise of a black cloud and bring you safely back here."

Then she hardened her heart for their parting and lifted him up, soaring into the clouds, and set him down before his father. The youth's hair reached below his chest, his body was like a mammoth's, and his cheeks were as fresh as the spring. When his father saw him he wept, bowing his head before the Simorgh and paying homage to her. He stared at the youth, from head to foot, and saw that he was worthy of the Kayanid crown and throne. His chest and arms were like a lion's, his face like the sun, his heart was a champion's, and his arm was that of a swordsman. His eyebrows were pitch black, his lips like coral, and his cheeks the color of blood. Sam's heart felt the happiness of paradise, and he called down blessings on his son. He draped the boy's body in a champion's cloak, and they set off down the mountain. When they reached its base, Sam had a horse and royal clothes brought for his son; the army ranged itself before Sam, their hearts filled with happiness, and they set off on the return journey, preceded by elephants bearing drummers. The air filled with dust as they traveled, and the blare of trumpets, the din of drums, the clash of Indian cymbals, and the cavalry's cries accompanied them as they joyfully entered the city.

Manuchehr Hears of Sam's Expedition

The king heard that Sam had returned from the mountains in splendor: Manuchehr was pleased and thanked God for this good news. He sent Nozar hurrying to Sam to offer his congratulations and to tell Sam to come to the king so that he might see the face of this youth who had been brought up in a nest; then he could return to Zavolestan, to serve the king there.

Nozar reached Sam and saw the hero's son with him; Sam dismounted and the two embraced. He asked for news of the king and his warriors, and Nozar handed over his message. Sam kissed the ground and immediately set off for the court, as his king had commanded. Manuchehr came out with his entourage to greet him, and as soon as Sam saw Manuchehr's banner he dismounted and went forward on foot. Manuchehr ordered him to mount his horse, and the two set off together for the Persian court. Manuchehr sat in state on the throne and placed the royal crown on his head; on one side of him sat Qaren, on the other Sam. Then the chamberlain ushered in Sam's son, Zal, splendidly dressed, with a golden crown on his head, and bearing a golden mace. The king stared in wonder at his fine stature and handsome face, which seemed made to delight all hearts. He said to Sam, "Look after him well, for my sake; never cross him, rejoice in no one but him; he has the royal *farr*, the strength of a lion, a wise heart, and a sage's manner."

> And then Sam told the king of how and why
> He had decided that his child should die;
> He told him of the Simorgh and her nest,
> Of his regret, and his belated quest
> To find his son; throughout the world men heard
> Of Sam and Zal, and of this wondrous bird.

The king gave orders that sages, astrologers, and priests should inquire into Zal's horoscope, to see what the stars decreed for him. The astrologers studied the stars and said, "May you live forever in prosperity; he will be a famous champion, proud and intelligent, and a fine horseman." The king rejoiced to hear these words, and Sam's heart too was freed from sorrow. Manuchehr gave Sam a robe of honor which drew praise from everyone, as well as Arab horses with golden saddles, Indian swords in golden scabbards, brocades, silks, fine carpets, rubies, and gold; slaves from the west dressed in Western brocade with jeweled designs on a golden ground; trays of emeralds, golden and silver goblets set with turquoise and filled with musk, camphor, and saffron; cuirasses, helmets, barding, spears, arrows, bows, and maces; thrones worked in turquoise and ivory, ruby seal rings, and golden belts. And then he wrote and sealed a charter full of celestial praise for Sam, bestowing on him lordship over Kabol, Danbar, Mai, and India, the Sea of China as far as the Sea of Send, as well as Zavolestan as far as Bost.

When he had received the charter and these gifts, Sam called for his horse, rose and said to the king, "Kind king, lord of justice and righteousness, in this world, from the realm of the fish to the sphere of the moon, no one like you has ever reigned; no one has had your generosity, justice, nobility, and wisdom. The world is at peace because of you, you treat its treasures with contempt, and may the day never come when only your name remains to us." He bowed and kissed the throne, and then had the drums strapped on his elephants. All the town turned out to watch as he and Zal set off for Zavolestan. As he approached, news of his investiture preceded him, and the inhabitants decorated Sistan as though it were a paradise; the ground was of musk, the bricks of gold, and as Sam passed, people tossed musk, saffron, and gold and silver coins over him. The world was filled with rejoicing, with both the nobles and the common people joining in. All the nobility came before Sam saying, "May the young man's arrival here be auspicious," and then they called down blessings on Zal and showered him with gold coins.

Then Sam took his ease with wine and music, bestowing robes of honor on the wise and the noble, and all his courtiers competed to be honored the most.

Sam Bestows His Realm on Zal

Sam summoned the experienced men of the country to speak with them. "Noble and prudent advisors," he said, "the wise king's orders are that I lead an army to invade the Gorgsaran and Mazanderan. However, my heart and soul, my son, will remain here, while my eyes weep bitter tears at our separation. In my youth and arrogance I acted unjustly. God gave me a son and I abandoned him; in my ignorance I did not realize his worth. The great Simorgh took him, God assigned him to her care, and she brought him up until he was like a lofty cypress; I reviled him, she valued him. When the time had come for me to be pardoned, God returned him to me. Know that this youth is my refuge, and I leave him among you to remind you of me. Treat him well, advise him well, show him the path to a noble life."

Then Sam turned to Zal and said, "Act justly and generously; this is the way to seek happiness. Know then that Zavolestan is your home; all this realm is under your command. See that the land flourishes beneath your reign, and that you make your friends' hearts rejoice. The keys of the treasury are yours, and my heart will be glad or sorrowful according to how you prosper or fail." Young Zal said to Sam, "How can I live without you now? Now that we have been reconciled, how can you contemplate separation again? If ever a man was born in sin, I am that man, and it is right that justice is denied me. I ate dirt and tasted blood once, held in the great bird's claws; now I am far from my protector, and it is Fate that protects me. Of the world's flowers, my share is only thorns, but one cannot fight against God's decrees."

Sam said, "It is right to say what is in your heart like this; say it, say whatever you wish. But the astrologers have seen that a good star guides you, and they have said that here is your home, here is your army, and here is your crown. We cannot quarrel with the heavens, and it is here that your love must flourish. Now, gather a group of companions about you, horsemen and men eager for knowledge; learn from them, listen to them, gain all kinds of knowledge, and taste the pleasures they bring. Enjoy life and be generous, seek knowledge and be just." He spoke, and the din of drums rang out; the air turned pitch black, the ground was the color of ebony, and the ringing of bells and the clash of Indian cymbals was heard before the king's pavilion. Sam gathered his forces and set off for war. Zal accompanied him for two stages of the way, and then his father clasped him tightly in his arms and wept extravagantly. He commanded his son to return with happiness in his heart to the crown and throne. Zal took the journey home, pondering on how he could live so that he would leave a good name behind him.

He took his place on the ivory throne and placed the glittering crown on his head, resplendent with armbands and an ox-headed mace, a golden torque and golden belt. He was eager to learn and summoned knowledgeable men from every province, astrologers and priests as well as warriors and horsemen, and discussed all manner of subjects with them. Day and night he was closeted with them, discussing both weighty and trivial matters. Zal grew to be so learned that he was like a shining star; in all the world, no one had ever seen another man with his knowledge and understanding. And so the heavens turned, spreading a canopy of love over Sam and Zal.

THE TALE OF
ZAL AND RUDABEH

Zal Visits Mehrab in Kabol

One day Zal decided to travel about his kingdom, and he set out with an entourage of like-minded companions. They traveled toward India, Kabol, Danbar, Morgh, and Mai. They built palaces as they went, and called for wine and musicians to entertain them; they spent liberally, driving away all thoughts of sorrow, as is the way of those who live in this fleeting world. They reached Kabol, traveling in splendor, laughing, and with happiness in their hearts. The king there was Mehrab, a shrewd, wealthy man, who was fortunate in his dealings. He was as tall and elegant as a cypress tree, his face was as fresh as the springtime, and his gait was like a pheasant's. His heart was wise, his mind prudent; his shoulders were those of a warrior, and his mind that of a priest. When he heard of Zal's approach he left Kabol at dawn, taking treasure, richly caparisoned horses, slaves, and various other kinds of wealth such as gold coins, rubies, musk, ambergris, brocades woven with gold, silks, and samites, a crown encrusted with royal jewels, and a golden torque set with emeralds.

Hearing that a splendid welcoming party was coming to greet him, Zal went forward to receive them and entertained them with all due ceremony. He sat Mehrab on a turquoise-studded throne, a marvelous feast was spread before the two princes, and as the wine steward poured their wine, Zal took stock of Mehrab. He liked what he saw, and his heart was attracted by the king's behavior: when he stood up from the table, Zal saw how well built he was and said to his courtiers, "What finer man binds on a nobleman's belt than this?" One of the courtiers spoke:

> "In purdah, and unseen by anyone,
> He has a daughter lovelier than the sun.

Lashes like ravens' wings protect a pair
Of eyes like wild narcissi hidden there;
If you would seek the moon, it is her face;
If you seek musk, her hair's its hiding place.
She is a paradise, arrayed in splendor,
Glorious, graceful, elegantly slender."

Zal's heart began to seethe, and all peace and good sense departed from him. Night came and Zal sat plunged in thought, unable to sleep or eat for thinking of this girl whom he had never seen.

When the sun's sword touched the mountain tops, and the world's surface became the color of pale topaz, Zal held court and Mehrab came to visit him. As he approached, a cry of "Clear the way" went up, and Mehrab entered, like a tree that bears fresh fruit. Zal was pleased to see him and made much of him, honoring him more than anyone else present. He said, "Ask me for anything you wish, be it thrones, seal rings, swords, or crowns." Mehrab replied, "My king whom all obey, you are noble and victorious, and I have only one wish from you, one that will not be hard for you to fulfill, which is that you come as a happy guest to my palace, which you will illuminate like the sun itself."

Zal answered, "This is not advisable, your palace is not a place for me. Sam would not approve, and neither would King Manuchehr if he heard of it, if I became drunk with wine in the house of someone who worships idols. I'll listen favorably to anything else you ask." Mehrab made his obeisance before Zal, but in his heart he called him a faithless wretch. He strode from the court, calling down blessings on his host. Zal watched him go, and praised him according to custom, but because they were of different faiths, he kept his remarks to a minimum. None of the Persians looked kindly on Mehrab, since they considered him to be an idolatrous demon, but when they saw Zal speaking to him in such a friendly fashion, they one by one said favorable things about him, in particular that his women's quarters housed someone who was incomparable in her stature, beauty, dignity, and all that pertained to loveliness. Zal's heart was suddenly seized by the madness of longing, wisdom fled from his mind, and love flourished there. The chief of the Arabs, the lord of righteousness, has said of such matters,

> *"Whilst I'm alive my partner is my horse,*
> *Beneath the heavens my life will take its course,*
> *I'll never marry, to hear wise men speak*
> *Of me as one who's wanton, frail, and weak."*

Zal's heart became weary with the thoughts that beset him; his heart writhed at the thought of the gossip that was said of him, and the shame his passion might bring. And so the heavens turned, and Zal's heart became filled to the brim with love.

Rudabeh Talks with Her Slave Girls

At dawn one day Mehrab went to his women's quarters, where he saw two suns; one was his wife, Sindokht, and the other his lovely daughter, Rudabeh. Their apartments were decked out like a colorful garden in spring, filled with sweet perfumes and elegance. Mehrab was astonished at how lovely Rudabeh had grown, and he repeated the name of God over her as a blessing. She was like a cypress tree topped by the full moon, a moon that was crowned by her musky hair. She was dressed in brocade and jewels, and she seemed like a paradise filled with everything desirable. Sindokht said to her husband, "May evil never harm you; open your lovely lips and tell us where have you been today. Tell us what kind of person Sam's son is, this visitor who has an old man's hair. Does he belong on a throne, or in that nest where he was raised? Does he seem like a man at all? Does he follow in the footsteps of famous men who do noble deeds?" Mehrab replied, "My silver cypress, no hero in the world is worthy to follow in Zal's footsteps:

> *You'll see no other horseman to compare*
> *With Zal, he has no equal anywhere.*
> *As ruddy as the pomegranate flower—*
> *Youthful, and with a young man's luck and power;*
> *Fierce in revenge, and in the saddle he's*
> *A sharp-clawed dragon to his enemies;*
> *Possessed of mammoth strength, a lion's guile,*
> *His arms are mighty as the flooding Nile;*
> *He scatters gold when he's in court, and when*
> *He's on the battlefield, the heads of men.*

He has one fault—which after all's so slight
No one remarks on it—his hair is white."

Rudabeh had five kind Turkish slaves who were her confidantes. She said to these shrewd girls, "All five of you are my friends and know my heart and I wish all of you luck in your lives. I'm going to tell you a secret: I'm in love, and my love is like a wave of the sea that's cresting up toward heaven. My bright heart is filled with thoughts of Sam's son, and even when I sleep he never leaves me. The place in my heart where I should feel shame is filled instead with love, and day and night I think of his face. Now, help me, what do you think, what do you advise? You must think of some scheme, some way to free my heart and soul from this agony of adoration."

Her slave girls were astonished at this behavior from someone of Rudabeh's rank. They rose up like Ahriman and answered her forthrightly: "You are the crown of all the princesses in the world, praised from India to China, the jewel of your father's household; no cypress has your stature, the Pleiades are not as lovely as your face, your portrait has been sent from Qanuj to the king of the western lands. Have you no shame, have you considered what this would mean to your father? Do you want to embrace someone who has driven your father from his embrace, someone who was brought up by a bird in the mountains, who is a byword among men for his strangeness? No one has ever been born from his mother as an old man, and such a person will not have descendants. How can a young girl, whose lips are the color of coral, want to marry an old man? The world is filled with love for you, and your portrait is found in every palace; your face and hair and form are so lovely that the sun itself should descend from the fourth sphere to be your husband."

When Rudabeh heard their words, her heart beat fast, like a fire fanned by the wind. She shouted at them in fury, screwing up her eyes, her face trembling, her forehead filled with frowns, her eyebrows bent like a bow. "It's pointless to listen to such foolish talk; I don't want the Chinese emperor, nor the king of the West, nor the king of Persia. Sam's son, Zal, is the man I want; with his lion-like strength and stature, he is my equal. Call him old or young, he will be body and soul to me." The slave girls were taken aback by her response and said with one voice, "We are your slaves. Our hearts are filled with our love for you. We await your orders, from which nothing but good can come. May a hundred thousand like us sacrifice their lives for you, and may all the wisdom in the world come to your aid. May your black-eyed servants be filled with humility, and their faces blush with shame. If we must learn magic we will learn it, flying with birds and running with deer, seeling our eyes with spells and incantations, so that we can bring this prince to your side." Rudabeh's red lips smiled, and turning her saffron cheeks to them, she said, "If you bring us to one another's arms, and keep the promise you have made, you will be planting a noble tree whose daily fruit will be rubies."

Rudabeh's Slaves Go to See Zal

Then her slaves set about thinking of some way to help their helpless princess. They dressed themselves in Rumi brocade and wore chaplets of flowers in their hair. The five of them went down to the river bank, and in their tints and scents they were as lovely as the spring. It was the month of Farvardin, when the sun moves into Aries, and the year is renewed. Zal had come to the riverside to hunt; on the opposite bank the slave girls paused to pick flowers, and their own faces were like flowers as they gathered the blossoms into their arms. Zal watched from his throne and asked, "Who are those girls, who seem so fond of flow-ers?" A courtier answered, "They are from Mehrab's palace; his daugh-ter, whom people call the moon of Kabol, has sent them to gather flowers." Zal went closer to the girls and asked for his bow. On foot he approached the ducks swimming in the river and drew back the string from his bow; he watched for when one of the birds flew up from the river and then loosed an arrow at it. He brought it down in mid-flight, and its blood dripped into the river, reddening the water. One of the girls said to Zal's servant boy, who went to fetch the bird, "Who is that lion of a man? What kind of a man is he who shot that arrow, and whose king is he? Who would dare oppose such a warrior? We haven't seen a finer knight than he is, or a better shot with a bow." The hand-some boy bit his lip and said, "Don't talk about the king like that. He's the king of Zabolestan, Sam's son, and his name is Zal. The heavens don't turn above a finer knight, and the world will never see anyone more noble than he is." The girl smiled at the handsome boy and said, "Don't be so sure. There's a princess in Mehrab's palace who is finer by far than your king. Her stature is like a teak tree's, her color is that of ivory, and she wears on her head the crown of musk that God has given her. Her eyes are like two dark narcissi, her eyebrows are like a bow, her nose is like a silver reed, her mouth is small, like the contracted heart of a desperate man, and her hair falls in ringlets to her feet. Her mouth is so tiny that her breath can scarcely find passage there, and there is no one in all the world who is her equal for beauty. We have come here so that her ruby lips can become acquainted with the lips of Sam's son."

The boy left them and returned to Zal, who asked him what the girl had said that had made him smile so much and show his silver teeth in his blushing face. The boy told Zal what he had heard, and the hero's heart grew young at his words. He said to his handsome page, "Go and tell the girls to wait for a moment, so that they can take jewels with them as well as flowers." He asked for gold and silver coins, and jewels from his treasury, as well as five sets of clothes made of golden brocade. He told the boy to take these to the girls, but to do so secretly and tell no one, and to say to them that they shouldn't go back to the castle just yet because he had a message he wished to send. Slaves took the gifts to the girls and told them what Zal had said. One of the girls said to the page, "Words never remain secret for long unless they are between just two people. With three people they are no longer a secret, and four is like a crowd. Tell your prince that if he has a secret to impart, he should tell me face to face." Then the girls said to one another, "The lion has walked into the trap; now Rudabeh will have her heart's desire, and Zal shall have his, and everything has turned out for the best."

Zal's black-eyed treasurer, who was also his confidant in this matter, returned to the prince and told him all he had heard from the girls. Zal made his way to the beds of flowers on the riverbank, in hopes of arranging a meeting with Rudabeh. The princess's beautiful slave girls presented themselves and made their obeisance to him. Zal questioned them about their mistress, asking about her stature and beauty, her manner of speaking and wisdom, wanting to know if she was worthy of him. "Tell me everything," he said, "and see that you don't try to deceive me. If I find that you've spoken honestly, you'll be honored and rewarded, but if I find that you've lied in even the smallest detail, I'll have you trampled beneath the feet of elephants." The girls' faces turned the color of red juniper berries, and they kissed the ground before him. One of them said, "No noble mother has ever borne a man as fine as Sam, not in looks or stature, knowledge or purity of heart; and who is there to compare with you, brave lord, with your massive frame and lion strength? And thirdly, there is Rudabeh, whose face is like the moon, whose body is a silver cypress tree adorned in tints and scents; she is a rose, a jasmine flower, from head to foot, and her face is as radiant as Canopus shining above the Yemen. From the silver dome of her forehead her hair cascades in fragrant coils, looped with rubies and emeralds, down to her feet, her curls are links of musk entwined one with another, her ten fingers are silver reeds steeped in civet. You will see no idol as beautiful as she is in all of China; the moon and the Pleiades bow down before her."

The prince spoke urgently, but sweetly and gently, to a slave girl. "Tell me some way that I can reach her; my heart and soul are filled with love for her, and I long to glimpse her face." The slave girl answered, "With your permission, we shall return to the castle; we are all smitten with your glory, your handsomeness, and your words' sincerity. We shall report everything, changing nothing. We shall bring her musky head into your trap; we shall bring her lips to the lips of Sam's son. May the prince come to the castle walls with a lariat; he can loop it on the battlements, and so like a lion happily pursue his prey."

The Slave Girls Return to Rudabeh

The girls went on their way, and Zal returned to his camp; as he waited for the night it seemed to him that a year passed by. The girls reached the castle, each of them holding two posies of flowers. When the doorman saw them he grumbled; impatient words came from his troubled heart: "This is no time to be gadding about away from the castle. I'm astonished at your behavior." The girls responded in just as lively a fashion: "Today is different from any other day. There are no demons lying in wait among the blossoms. Spring has come and we have been to pick flowers; we have gathered these hyacinths." The doorman said, "This is no day to be doing such things. Zal's tents are no longer in Zabolestan; didn't you see the king of Kabol ride out from the castle to greet him? If he should come across you with these flowers in your hands, he'd knock you to the ground there and then."

The girls entered the castle and went to the princess, where they sat to tell her their secrets. They showed her the brocade and jewels Zal had given them, and Rudabeh asked about every detail of their encounter. "How did your meeting with Zal go?" she asked. "Has people's gossip exaggerated his qualities, or is he even better when you see him face to face?" The five girls all began to speak at once, vying for who should tell the princess what they had seen. "He's like a tall cypress tree; everything about him is elegant, and he radiates royal glory. The colors he wears, the perfumes, his height and build; he's a knight with a slim waist and a noble chest. His eyes are like two pitch-black narcissi, his lips are like coral, his cheeks ruddy as blood. His shoulders and trunk are like a lion's, his thighs are massive, his heart is learned, and he has a king's dignity. His hair is completely white; this is his only fault, and really it's nothing to be ashamed of; his curls are like silver links coiled together about his face, which is like the blossoms of the Judas tree. You think, 'He's just as he should be; and if he weren't like this he wouldn't inspire such love.' We told him he could see you, and he went back to his camp with his heart filled with hope. Now you must get ready to receive your guest, and tell us what answer we should take back to him."

The princess said to her slaves, "Then he's different from what people say. This Zal, who was brought up by a bird and was a youth who had withered away, with the head of an old man, has become as lovely as the blossoms of a Judas tree, tall and elegant, with a handsome face, from head to foot a hero. So, you boasted about my face to him, and reaped the reward for your words." As she spoke her lips broke into smiles, and her cheeks blushed the color of pomegranate blossoms. The slave girls said, "But now get ready, because God has granted your desires, and we pray that everything will turn out well."

Rudabeh's palace was as pleasant as springtime, and on its walls there were portraits of famous men. She had one of its rooms decorated with Chinese brocade, and she placed golden trays heaped with agates and emeralds there. Then she mixed wine, musk, and ambergris together and decorated the area with violets, narcissi, the blossoms of the Judas tree, branches of jasmine, and hyacinths. The drinking vessels were of gold set with turquoise, and held rose water. Rudabeh's face was as radiant as the sun, and the scents in her room rose up to the sun's sphere.

When the shining sun set, the doors to the private quarters of the castle were locked, and the keys hidden away. One of the slave girls went to Zal and said, "Everything is ready: come." The prince set off for the castle with all the haste and anxiety of a man going to meet his beloved. Rudabeh went onto the roof and stood there like a cypress tree topped by the full moon. When she saw Zal in the distance, she called out to him, "Welcome, bold young man. God's blessings be upon you, and may you tread on the heavens. I wish my slave girls happy hearts, because from head to foot you are as they described. But you have walked here from your pavilion, and I am afraid your royal feet have been irked by this." Zal heard her voice and, looking up, caught sight of her face; the roof shone with its light, and the earth glowed like a ruby. He answered her, "Heaven's blessings be upon you; your face is as lovely as the full moon. How many nights I have passed gazing at the stars, crying out to God, asking that he grant me a glimpse of your face. Now your voice and your sweet words have made my heart happy. But find some way for us to meet; how can I stay down here when you are on the battlements?"

Hearing his words, she loosened her hair, which cascaded down, tumbling like snakes, loop upon loop. She said, "Come, take these black locks which I let down for you, and use them to climb up to me." Zal gazed in astonishment at her face and hair, and said, "This would not be just. May the day never dawn when I strike at my soul like this, thrusting my spear into a wounded heart." He took a lariat from his page, looped it, and hurled it upwards without saying another word; the lariat caught on the battlements, and Zal quickly climbed up its sixty cubits. As he stepped onto the roof Rudabeh made her obeisance before him, then grasped his hands in hers. As if they were in a drunken stupor, they clasped hands and descended from the roof to Rudabeh's golden chamber, which glowed like a paradise. Rudabeh's slave girls stood before their houri, and Zal stared in wonder at her face, her hair, her stature, her splendor, her bracelets, her necklace and earrings, at her brocade dress woven with jewels like a garden in spring dotted with flowers. Her cheeks were like red tulips surrounded by jasmine, her face was surmounted by curl upon curl of musky hair. A sword-belt across his chest and wearing a diadem of rubies, Zal sat in princely splendor beside this glorious moon of beauty. For a while there was nothing but kisses, embraces, and wine; but then Zal said to Rudabeh, "If Manuchehr hears of this he will not agree to it, and Sam too will be loud in his opposition. But I despise their opinions and am ready to die if need be. I swear by almighty God that I shall never break faith with you. I shall pray before God as his slave, asking that he wash all anger and thoughts of vengeance from Sam's and Manuchehr's hearts. God will grant my request, and all the world will know you as my wife." Rudabeh replied, "And I too swear before God, and may he witness what I say, that no one shall be my master but Zal, the world's hero, the crowned prince on his throne, the lord of beauty and royal splendor."

> From moment then to moment their desire
> Gained strength, and wisdom fled before love's fire;
> Passion engulfed them, and these lovers lay
> Entwined together till the break of day.
> So tightly they embraced, before Zal left,
> Zal was the warp, and Rudabeh the weft
> Of one cloth, as with tears they said goodbye
> And cursed the sun for rising in the sky.
> Zal let himself down from the battlements,
> And made his way back to his army's tents.

Zal Consults with His Priests About Rudabeh

When the glittering sun rose above the mountain peaks, the warriors visited their prince and then each went his own way. Zal sent a messenger to summon knowledgeable men and priests to his court, and when they arrived he smiled, and with his heart filled with happiness he gave thanks to God who had woken his sleeping good fortune. Then he said, "Our hearts are filled with hope and fear of God; we hope for his grace and we fear sin, praising him to the best of our abilities, praying before him night and day. It is he who guides the sun and moon and leads our souls in the path of righteousness, who maintains the world which gives us such pleasure, who administers justice in this world and the world to come, who brings spring, summer, and autumn, who burdens trees with fruit and vines with grapes, who gives young men their power and beauty and old men the frowns on their faces, whose commands no man can gainsay since not an ant treads the earth without him. The world's peoples increase by coming together as couples, since a single person can produce no offspring. Only God is alone, having neither companion nor mate nor friend. All of creation lives in couples, and this is how being emerges from the hidden realm; this is so throughout the world, this is the heavens' will. If there were no couples in the world, authority would remain hidden; we see that no young man lives alone, and this is especially true if he is of good family, since then his might would pass from him. What is sweeter in the world than for a hero's soul to be gladdened by his children? And when the time comes for him to die, his life is renewed in his child; his name remains behind, so that men say, 'This is the son of Zal' and 'That is the son of Sam.' A son is an ornament to the crown and the throne; the man dies but his fortune lives on in his son.

"All this is my story; this is the rose, the narcissus, the flower at the heart of my tale. My heart has been snatched from me, my wisdom has fled; look at me now and tell me what medicine can cure me. I have not said this lightly, my mind is deeply troubled; my love is centered on Mehrab's palace, his land is like the heavens to me, and my heart is fixed on Sindokht's daughter. Now, what do you say to this? Will Sam agree to it? Will King Manuchehr? Will he consider it to be youthful impetuosity, or a sin? When a man seeks a wife, be he a commoner or a nobleman, he does what religion and custom demand; this is the way of faith, it is not a matter for shame, and no wise man quarrels with it. You are sages and learned priests, what do you say to me, what do you advise?"

But the priests and sages said nothing, their lips remained sealed, because Zahhak was Mehrab's grandfather, and the king had no love for him in his heart. No one said anything openly, but they thought, "How can wholesome food be joined with poison?" When Zal heard nothing from them, he was angered and tried another tactic. He said, "I know that when you consider this you blame me, but any man who makes a decision will hear himself blamed. If you will guide me in this, and free me from these chains, I shall do such things for you as no prince has ever done for his subjects."

Then the priests answered that they wished him well and desired his happiness. They said, "We are all your slaves, and it's our surprise that has silenced us. Mehrab is a nobleman, a warrior, and not to be taken lightly. He is descended from Zahhak, who was a demon, but even so he was the king of the Arabs. If Mehrab's ancestry doesn't trouble you, his family is not one to be ashamed of. You must write a letter to Sam— in this matter your wisdom is greater than ours and you will know what to say—so that he in turn will write to King Manuchehr, giving his opinion; Manuchehr will not ignore Sam's advice on such a matter."

Zal Writes a Letter to His Father Sam

Zal called for a scribe and poured out the contents of his heart. He began with praise of the world's just Creator, from whom come happiness and strength, who is the lord of the evening star, of Saturn and of the sun, of all that is and is not, who is one and whose slaves we are. He went on, "I invoke his blessing on Sam, the lord of the mace, the sword and helmet, who makes his grey horse curvet on the battlefield and leaves food there for the vultures, whose presence is a mighty wind in war, who rains down swords from the storm clouds, who distributes crowns and royal belts and places kings on their golden thrones; a man of all able qualities, and the greatest of these is his wisdom. I am as a slave to him, and my heart and soul are filled with love for him. I was born as he saw me to be, and the heavens dealt unjustly with me. While my father lived in comfort, in silks and samites, the Simorgh bore me to the mountains of India where she treated me as one of her squabs, and I depended on the food she hunted. My skin was burned by the wind, my eyes were blinded by dust, and though men said I was the son of Sam, he lived in glory while I lived in a nest, because God had ordained this. No one can escape God's justice, even though he fly beyond the clouds. A warrior's teeth can be like anvils, he might be able to crush a lance with them, his voice might make a lion's skin split with terror, but still he must obey God's will. Something heartbreaking has happened to me, something which men will not praise me for. But if my father, who is a brave man and a dragon in his wrath, will hear me out, all will be well.

"I weep for the daughter of Mehrab, I burn in the fire of my love for her. In the dark night the stars are my companions, my heart seethes in turmoil like the sea, I am beside myself with grief, and all men weep for me. My heart has seen injustice but I breathe only to obey you. You are the world's hero, what do you command? Free me from this pain, this agony of soul; let me marry Mehrab's daughter, according to our rites and customs. When you brought me from the Alborz mountains, you swore before your courtiers that you would never oppose me in my desires, and this is the one desire of my heart."

An envoy took three horses and set off as swiftly as fire from Kabol. Zal gave him his orders: "If one horse stumbles, you should not delay for an instant; mount another and press onward, until you're in Sam's presence." The messenger sped off like the wind, and when he reached the land of the Gorgsaran he saw Sam in the distance, hunting with his cheetahs on the mountain slopes. Sam caught sight of him and said to his companions, "A horseman is riding here from Kabol, and the mount he's riding is from Zavolestan. He must be an envoy from Zal; we should find out what he has to say, and ask him about Zal, Persia, and the king." At that moment the envoy, clutching a letter in his hand, reached Sam; he dismounted, kissed the ground, and called down God's blessings on the king. Sam questioned him and took the letter, and the envoy gave him Zal's greetings. Sam began to make his way down the mountain and opened the letter to read Zal's message; as soon as he had done so he stood rooted to the spot in astonishment. Zal's request did not please him; this was not how he had hoped his son would be. He said, "His words fit his nature, which has now become plain to me. These are the foolish whims a boy who was brought up by a savage bird would have," and he made his way back from the hunting grounds to his camp, his mind filled with foreboding. He said to himself, "If I say to him, 'This is not an advisable course of action; don't sir up trouble like this, be sensible,' I shall be known as one who gave his word idly and broke it. But if I say, 'Yes, you must follow your desires and do what your heart tells you,' then from that savage bird and this descendant of a demon, what kind of offspring will be born?" His heart was weighed down with worry, but he slept, and his sleep refreshed him.

Sam Consults with His Priests Concerning Zal

When he woke he summoned priests and wise men and consulted them. He began by questioning astrologers, and asked them what the outcome of a union between two who were as different as fire and water would be; surely it would produce a disaster like the war between Zahhak and Feraydun? He told them to consult the stars, and to see if any good could come of this. For many days the astrologers searched the skies, and when they came before him again they were smiling and said, "Fortune will join these two enemies as one." The chief astrologer said, "I bring you good news of the union between Zal and Mehrab's daughter: they will both prosper, and from these two will be born a great hero, a mammoth-bodied man who will conquer the world with his sword, who will lift the king's throne beyond the clouds. He will extirpate the race of evil from the earth and cleanse the world with his heavy mace. He will be a comfort to those who suffer, and he will close the gate of war and the pathways to evil.

> *"Persia will trust in him and in his fame,*
> *Her champions will rejoice to hear his name,*
> *Throughout his life the monarchy will thrive,*
> *In times to come his glory will survive;*
> *Before his name, inscribed on every seal,*
> *Persia and Rum and India will kneel."*

Relieved by the astrologers' words, Sam laughed and thanked them warmly, and gave them great quantities of gold and silver, because they had brought him comfort when he was afraid.

He called for Zal's envoy and said to him, "Speak kindly to Zal; tell him that this is a strange wish that he has, but that since I gave my word it would be unjust for me to look for some way to refuse him. At dawn I shall leave for Persia." Then he gave the messenger some silver coins and said, "Don't delay on your journey for an instant." When two watches of the night had passed, horsemen's cries, the din of drums, and blare of trumpets announced Sam's departure with his army for Persia. The envoy reached Zal with news of his good fortune, and Zal gave thanks to God for his happiness, distributing gold and silver coins to the poor, and being equally generous with his friends.

Sindokht Learns of Rudabeh's Behavior

A sweet-voiced serving woman acted as a go-between for Zal and Rudabeh, taking messages from one to the other. Zal summoned her and told her what he had learned. He said, "Go to Rudabeh and tell her, 'Purehearted moon of loveliness, when matters go from bad to worse, we soon see a key to open a way of escape. My envoy has returned from Sam with good news: Sam argued and blustered for a while, but finally he has agreed to our marriage.'" Then he gave the girl Sam's letter, and she hurried like the wind to Rudabeh to tell her the good news. Rudabeh showered her with gold coins and sat her down on a gold-worked throne; she gave her a muslin headscarf that was so finely woven the weft could not be told from the warp; it was embroidered in red and gold, and the gold was almost hidden by jewels. She also gave her two valuable rings, which glittered like the planet

Jupiter. Then she sent her back with many greetings and good wishes to Zal.

As the woman emerged from Rudabeh's apartments into the main hall of the palace, Sindokht caught sight of her. The woman blushed in fear, turning the color of red juniper berries, and kissed the ground before her queen. Sindokht became suspicious and said in a loud voice, "Where are you coming from? Tell me. You're always going back and forth from Rudabeh's apartments, and you avoid my eye when you do so. My heart suspects you of something. What are you up to? Are you the bowstring in this affair or the bow?" The woman replied, "I'm just a poor woman trying to earn my daily bread as best I can. Rudabeh wanted to buy some jewelry, and I brought her a golden diadem and a splendid ring set with precious stones." Sindokht said, "Show them to me and put my heart at rest." She replied, "I left both of them with Rudabeh; she wanted some other things, so I'm going to fetch them." Sindokht said, "Show me the money she paid you for them, and pour cold water on my anger." But the woman replied, "Rudabeh said she would pay me tomorrow; you can't ask to see something I haven't received yet."

Sindokht knew the woman was lying, and she hardened her heart against her. She began to search her roughly, looking in her bosom and sleeves, and when she found the fine headscarf embroidered by Rudabeh, she was enraged, and ordered her daughter to come before her. She clawed at her cheeks and wept, and said, "You are a noble woman and as beautiful as the moon, what whim has made you choose to act like someone from the lowest depths rather than someone who occupies a throne? What do you lack? Why are you behaving like a criminal? Now, tell your mother whatever secrets you are hiding, especially why this woman keeps coming to you. What is going on? Who is the man this scarf and rings were intended for? The Arab's wealth and crown have brought us both good and ill fortune, and you want to fling our standing and reputation to the winds like this? What mother ever gave birth to a daughter like you?"

Rudabeh was ashamed and stared at the ground. She began to weep, and tears coursed down her lovely cheeks. She said to her mother,

> "I wish I'd not been born, and then you would
> See nothing evil in me, nothing good.

You're wise, but love has made my heart its prey,
I think of Zal, Zabol's king, night and day;
I burn for him in love's tormenting fire,
My heart's consumed by passion and desire.
I weep my life away, without him I
Have no desire to live, I long to die.
He came to me, and hand in hand we swore
Our mutual love will last forevermore.
His envoy went to Sam, who angrily
Declared at first that he would not agree
To Zal's request, but bit by bit relented,
Argued, and stormed, and finally consented.
The letter that he sent to Zal was brought
To me here, by the woman whom you caught."

Sindokht was astonished at her words, and at first said nothing, but then thought that she liked the idea of Zal as a son-in-law. However, she said, "This isn't wise. There's no noble warrior who can compare with Zal; he's a great man, and the son of a hero, who has a fine reputation and is an intelligent, clear-sighted man. Zal has many virtues and only one fault, but that fault diminishes his splendor. The king of Persia will be angered by this, and he'll raise the dust of battle over Kabol. He has no desire for someone from our family to rule." Sindokht released the go-between and spoke kindly to her, saying she now knew what had been hidden from her. She saw that her daughter had lived cut off from the world and without anyone's advice. Then she lay down alone, filled with such anxiety that her skin felt bruised and broken.

Mehrab Learns of His Daughter's Love

Mehrab came from the court in good spirits, because Zal had been very attentive to him. He saw Sindokht lying down frowning and seeming troubled, and he said to her, "What's the matter? Why is your flower-like face filled with frowns?" She said, "I've been thinking for a long time about our palace and wealth, our Arab horses, our page-boys who have sworn loyalty to you, our gardens and royal enclosures, the beauty of our daughter, our reputation, knowledge, and prudence. Little by little the freshness and force of our lives leave us; misfortune will come, our enemies will inherit what is ours, our troubles will have been as vain as the wind. A narrow coffin will be our lot, and the fruit of the tree we have planted will be poison: we have watered it and labored over it, hung crowns and treasures in its branches, it has grown upwards to the sun and spread its shade, and now it is to be felled. This will be our end, and who knows where our peace is to found?"

Mehrab said to Sindokht, "You speak as if this were a new thing, but the fleeting world was ever thus, and wise men have always feared its ways. It raises one and casts another down, and heaven's will cannot be opposed. There is no point in agonizing over this, it won't change, we cannot fight against God's decrees." Sindokht said, "A priest will tell his child this parable of the tree to explain the ways of the world to him. I said it so that you would pay attention to what I have to say." She hung her head, and her rosy cheeks were wet with tears. "The heavens do not always turn as we would wish. Know then, that Zal, Sam's son, has set who knows what snares in secret to catch Rudabeh. He has captured her pure heart, and we must consider what to do about this. I have talked to her at length, but to no avail; her face is sallow with grief, and I can see that her heart is in turmoil."

When Mehrab heard this he sprang up and grasped his sword hilt; his body trembled, his face darkened, blood surged in his heart, his lips were cold with sighs, and he said, "I shall make a river of blood of Rudabeh this moment." Sindokht stood and, grasping him by the waist, said, "I am your slave, listen to me first, then do whatever you wish, and may wisdom guide your soul." But he twisted from her grasp and pushed her away, roaring like a maddened elephant. He shouted, "I should have cut that girl's head off when she was born. I didn't, I didn't do as my grandfather would have done, and now she comes up with this sorcery to destroy me. I could be killed for this and my reputation destroyed, why do you want to stop me from punishing her? If Sam and Manuchehr march against us, smoke from the sack of Kabol will cloud the sun, and neither the town nor our fields or crops will survive."

Sudabeh said, "Calm yourself, don't talk so wildly. Sam already knows, and there's no need to be so fearful and anxious. He's traveling from the land of the Gorgsaran to Manuchehr's court. The matter is not a secret any more, it's out in the open." Mehrab said, "Don't tell me such lies, woman; the wind does not obey the dust. If you could show me some way to manage this then I wouldn't be so worried. Who is there from Ahvaz to Qandahar who wouldn't like to be allied to Sam?" Sindokht answered, "My lord, may I never need lies to help me. What harms you obviously harms me, and I am devoted to your heart's well-being. I've told you the truth; this is the matter that's been troubling me. But if this marriage should happen, it wouldn't be so amazing after all, and the prospect should not worry us so much. Feraydun became king of Persia with the help of Sarv, king of the Yemen, and Zal is trying to do something similar. The world will not shine with splendor from earth, air, and water alone; fire must be there too, the elements have to mix. When a stranger joins your family, those who wish you ill are discomfited, because it makes you stronger."

As Mehrab listened to Sindokht his heart was filled with fury, his head with confusion. He said, "Bring Rudabeh to me." But Sindokht was afraid that he would harm her in his anger, and she answered, "First you must swear to deliver her back to me safe and sound; Kabol must not be deprived of her; she is a paradise, a rose garden, in her loveliness." She made him promise to renounce all thoughts of violence against their daughter, and Mehrab solemnly swore that he would not hurt her, but added, "The king will be furious with us for this; there won't be any country or mother or father or Rudabeh left when he has finished with us." Sindokht bowed before him and went smiling to her daughter, her face shining like the sun beneath the night of her black hair. She said, "Good news, the leopard has sheathed his claws and let the wild ass go free. Now, put on some fine clothes and go to your father, and see that you cry in front of him." Rudabeh replied, "What use are fine clothes? What are such worthless things when I lack the one precious thing I want? My soul longs for Sam's son; why should I hide what's obvious?"

But when she went before her father, as lovely as the sun rising in the east, she seemed drowned in rubies and gold; she was arrayed like a paradise, and as splendid as the sun in springtime. Her father stared at her in wonder and silently invoked God's blessings. Then he stormed at her, "You senseless child, when was such behavior ever right for a noblewoman? How can a fairy being like you marry that Ahriman?" She lowered her black eyelashes over her dark eyes, and did not dare draw breath. Her angry father raged at her like a roaring leopard, his heart filled with fury. She returned to her apartments heartbroken, and

her face was as sallow as saffron. Both the daughter and the king prayed
to God to aid them.

Manuchehr Learns of Zal's Engagement to Mehrab's Daughter

When Manuchehr learned that this diverse pair, Zal and Rudabeh,
intended to marry, he said to his priests and sages, "This will bring an
evil day to us. By war and policy I have delivered Persia from the
clutches of lions and leopards, and Zal's impetuous love must not be
allowed to raise up this defeated race so that they are our equals. By the
union of Mehrab's daughter and Sam's son a sharp sword will be
unsheathed, who on one side will not be of our people; this will be
like mingling poison and its antidote together. If their offspring follows
in his mother's footsteps, his head will be filled with malevolence
toward us; Persia will seethe with sedition and trouble, as he hopes to
gain her crown and wealth." All the priests approved his speech, and
said, "You are wiser than we are, and more able to do what is neces-
sary. Do what wisdom demands."

He summoned Nozar and his nobles to him and said, "Go to Sam
and ask him how the war has gone. Then tell him to come here before
he returns home." Nozar and his entourage set off with their ele-
phants and war drums. When they arrived at Sam's camp, he was
pleased to see them, and Nozar handed over his father's message. Sam
replied, "I shall do as he commands, and my soul will find peace
in seeing him." They set out tables for a feast, and the name of
Manuchehr was the first they remembered when they drank. They
passed the long night in pleasure until the bright sun reappeared; then,
to the din of drums, their mounts seemed to take wing as they sped
toward the court as Manuchehr had commanded.

When Manuchehr heard of their approach, a great cry went up
from Sari and Amol, and the army set off, filling the valleys with their
heavy lances, their shields woven in red and gold, their drums, trum-
pets, and cymbals, their Arab horses, elephants, and treasure. In this
manner, with its banners and drums, the army went to welcome Sam.

Sam Comes to Manuchehr

Sam dismounted as he drew near the court, and a way was cleared for
him to approach the king. Sam kissed the ground and went forward.

Manuchehr rose from his ivory throne, a crown set with shining rubies on his head, and motioned Sam to a throne near him. He treated him with appropriate kindness, asking him sympathetically about the war with the Gorgsaran and the demons of Mazanderan, and Sam answered all his questions one by one, recounting the story of his battles, the rout of their enemies, and the killing of Zahhak's descendant Kakui. As Manuchehr listened his crown seemed to reach to the moon with pleasure. He gave orders for wine and a banquet, to celebrate the extirpation of his enemies from the world. They passed the night feasting, and Sam's name was continually on the courtiers' lips.

When day broke Sam returned to Manuchehr's side. The king said to him, "Choose some chieftains and go from here to India; spread fire and sword there, burn Mehrab's castle and Kabol to the ground. Don't let him escape; he's dragon's spawn, always raising his war cry against someone, filling the peaceful world with war and trouble. Sever the heads of his allies, cleanse the earth of Zahhak's tribe." Sam replied, "I shall do this and satisfy the king's anger." He kissed the throne and touched his face to the king's seal ring. Then he and his army set off on their galloping horses for home.

Sam and Zal Meet

News of what Manuchehr and Sam were planning reached Mehrab and Zal. Zal was enraged; he flung back his shoulders and his lips quivered with anger. He left Kabol, saying, "If a dragon comes burning the world with his breath and wishes to conquer Kabol, he will have to cut my head off first." Angrily he made for his father's camp, his heart filled with anxieties, his head with the words he would say. As the lion cub approached the camp, all the army rose to greet him; the banner of Feraydun was set before them, and the elephants were draped in red, yellow, and purple cloths.

When Zal saw his father's face, he dismounted and walked forward. The chieftains on both sides dismounted, and Zal kissed the ground. His father spoke to him and Zal remounted his charger, whose saddle glittered with gold. The chieftains came forward anxiously, saying "Your father is angry with you; apologize, don't act stubbornly." Zal assured them, "There's no fear of that; I have blood in my veins, not dirt. If my father is wise, he won't bandy words with me, and if he

speaks angrily to me, I shall be ashamed and weep." They rode cheer-
fully into Sam's camp, where Sam dismounted and welcomed his son.
Zal kissed the ground and began.

He invoked God's blessings on Sam, and tears fell from his eyes. He
said, "May Sam be prudent and happy, and his soul incline toward jus-
tice. Diamonds are shattered by your sword, the earth weeps when you
ride out to battle, the world flourishes with your justice, and wisdom
and prudence are your soul's foundation. I alone have no part in this
justice of yours, even though I am your kin. I was raised by a bird,
when I ate dirt, but I have no quarrel with anyone in the world. I do
not know what crime I have committed—unless it is that the hero Sam
is my father—or whom I have harmed. When my mother bore me,
you rejected me and had me exposed in the mountains. You gave your
son over to grief, consigning me to the fire. Your quarrel is with God;
isn't it he who has created the colors black and white? I have nobility,
courage, and a hero's sword, and the lord of Kabol is my friend. He is
wealthy, prudent, and just, possessed of a throne, crown, and the mace
of sovereignty. I went to Kabol because you told me to; I did as you
commanded, taking your place when you went to the wars, and har-
vesting the fruit of the tree you had planted. Is this the present you
bring me from Mazanderan and your wars with the Gorgsaran, that
you will destroy the place I have chosen to live? Is this the justice you
bring me? I stand before you now as your slave and I deliver my body
to your anger. Cut my body in two with a saw if you wish, but do not
speak to me about Kabol."

> Sam listened to his son, and hung his head:
> "All that you're telling me is true," he said.
> "All that I did was wrong; your miseries
> Gladdened the hearts of all our enemies.
> And now, heart sore, you've come here as my guest
> To know if I will grant this last request.
> Be patient, while I find a way to bring
> Your cause persuasively before the king:
> I'll write a letter to him, you will be
> My trusted envoy to his majesty:
> I'll teach you what to say, and when you speak
> King Manuchehr will grant you what you seek.

If God's our friend, what we're about to do
Will hand your longed-for heart's desire to you."

Sam Writes a Letter to King Manuchehr

They summoned a scribe and dictated a detailed letter. Sam began with
praise of God, invoking his blessings on King Manuchehr, and contin-
ued: "As your slave I have reached the sixtieth year of my life: the sun
and moon have crowned my head with white camphor. I bound on my
sword belt as your slave and made war on sorcerers; the world has never
seen anyone ride his horse or wield his mace as I have done. I obliter-
ated the splendor of Mazanderan's warriors, and only I was able to
defeat the dragon that emerged from the River Kashaf, massive as a
mountain, broad as a valley, filling the earth with the foam from its lips,
terrifying the world's inhabitants. Its spittle burned vultures' wings, its
venom scorched the earth; it snatched monsters from the sea and eagles
from the air; the earth was emptied of people and flocks, every living
thing retreated before it. When I saw that no one dared oppose it, I
emptied my heart of fear and bound on my sword in God's name.
Seated on my massive mount, my ox-headed mace on my saddle, my
bow slung over my shoulder, my shield at the ready, I attacked like a
ravening monster: everyone who heard that I would try my mace against
this dragon bade me farewell as if I went to my death. I approached
and saw it was like a great mountain, with its hair trailing on the
ground, its tongue like a black tree, its gullet breathing fire, its eyes like
bowls of blood. It caught sight of me and roared and came forward in
fury. I felt there was a fire burning before me, the world swam like a
sea before my eyes, smoke rose up to the clouds. The ground trembled
at its roar, the earth swam with its poison. I too roared, like a lion, and
shot a diamond-tipped arrow, pinning one side of its mouth shut with
the tongue still hanging out. Another arrow pinned the other side of
its mouth, and a third went into its gullet. Blood bubbled up from its
entrails, and, invoking God's power, I struck my ox-headed mace
down on its head. I smashed it as I would an elephant's, and poison
flowed from the wound like the river Nile. The river Kashaf brimmed
with blood and turned yellow, and the earth was at peace again and
could rest. The world witnessed this combat; afterwards I was known
as 'Sam who kills with one blow,' and they showered me with gold

and jewels. When I came back from that battle my armor had been burned from my body and I was left naked, my horse's barding had been stripped away, and for years the countryside there was covered with nothing but burned thorns and scrub.

"I have placed my foot on the heads of chieftains and led my horse where lions had their lairs: for many years now the saddle has been my throne, and I have subdued Mazanderan and the Gorgsaran, never thinking of my home, but always mindful of your glory and happiness. But now my shoulders and the blows of my mace are not what they were, and I am bent with age. My son Zal, a hero who is worthy to fight on your behalf, has taken my place, and he has one secret request, which he will come to ask of you. In Kabol he has seen a beautiful young woman, as elegant as a cypress tree, as lovely as a rose garden, and he has become crazy with love for her. The king should not be angry with him, since anyone who sees him pities his despair: he comes before your throne with a heavy heart, and I ask that you treat him as befits a nobleman. It is not for me to teach you wisdom or how to behave."

When the letter had been written, Zal took it, and the trumpets blared as he mounted his horse.

Mehrab's Anger with Sindokht

Once all this became known in Kabol, Mehrab was filled with fury. He peremptorily summoned Sindokht and vented his anger with Rudabeh against her. He said, "I don't have the forces to stand up against Persia's king; I've no choice but to kill you and your vile daughter in public, in the hope that that will placate him." At his words, Sindokht sank down, and her resourceful heart was filled with foreboding. Then she ran to the radiant king, her arms folded submissively over her breasts, and said, "Hear me out, and if you want to do something other than I suggest, do it. If you have wealth that you're prepared to give up in order to save your life, then bring it, and something good may come of this night. No matter how long the night lasts, its darkness must finally come to an end: day will dawn, and when the sun rises the world will glitter like a ruby." Mehrab replied, "Don't talk old wives' tales to a warrior. Say what you know, fight for your life, or prepare for your body to be veiled in blood."

Sindokht said, "My lord, I hope you will have no need to shed my blood. I must go to Sam, it's I who must draw this sword from its sheath.

I shall risk my life and you, your wealth; give me treasure to take to him." Mehrab replied, "This is the key; we shouldn't worry about wealth. Take slaves, horses, thrones, and crowns, and be on your way. It may be that Kabol won't burn over our heads, and that his clouded heart will shine on us again." Sindokht said, "My lord, value your life rather than your wealth. But when I go looking for some solution to all this, you must not treat Rudabeh harshly. I care for her more than for anything in the world, and you must swear not to harm her." When her husband had sworn to this, she prepared to set out on horseback.

She dressed herself in gold-worked brocade, sewn with pearls and precious rubies. Then she poured out thirty thousand gold coins from the treasury, to which she added ten horses with golden trappings, fifty slaves with golden belts, fifty silver bridles and saddles for Arab and Persian horses, sixty slaves with golden torques, each bearing a goblet, one of which was filled with rubies, another with sugar, and the rest with musk, camphor, or gold. There were forty bolts of brocade with designs in gold and sewn with various jewels; two hundred Indian swords worked in silver and gold, the blades of thirty of which had been treated with poison; a hundred red-haired female camels, a hundred more to carry loads, a crown set with jewels, together with earrings, armbands and a torque, a golden throne studded with gems and as beautiful as the heavens, and four war elephants weighed down with carpets and clothes. When all this had been made ready she quickly mounted her horse and proceeded in state to Sam's court.

Sam Puts Sindokht's Mind at Rest

When she arrived she did not call out or give her name; instead she told the guards to say that someone had come as an envoy from Kabol, bringing a message from the warrior Mehrab to the world conqueror Sam. The chamberlain presented her news and was told to admit her. Sindokht dismounted and hurried before the king; she kissed the ground and made her obeisance before Sam and his noblemen. Then she had the slaves, horses, and other forms of wealth displayed one by one before Sam, and the column of gifts stretched for two miles. Sam was astonished at the sight and sat brooding on it, like a man in a drunken stupor; his arms were folded over his chest and he hung his head. He said to himself, "Where did all this come from, and why has it been brought here by a woman? If I accept these things from her,

Manuchehr will be angry with me, and if I return them, Zal will rise up in fury like the Simorgh." Finally he said, "Give these to our treasurer, as gifts sent in the name of a beautiful woman from Kabol." Sindokht was reassured. She had three lovely girls with her, pale skinned and as elegant as cypresses; each of them held a goblet filled with rubies, pearls, and other jewels, and they poured these out pell-mell before the king, then exited from the court.

Sindokht said, "Young men become as wise as old men listening to your advice: great men are instructed by you, and your glory illuminates the dark world. Evil's hands are bound by your goodness, and the path to God is opened by your mace. If Mehrab has sinned, his eyelashes are wet with tears. The inhabitants of Kabol are innocent; what has their leader done that they should be destroyed? They are slaves beneath the dust of your feet, the whole town lives for you. Fear the Creator of reason and might, of the evening star and the sun; he will not approve of such an act from you; do not bind on your belt for bloodshed."

Sam said, "Answer whatever I ask you, and don't try to evade my questions. Are you Mehrab's servant or his wife, whose daughter Zal has seen? Tell me about this girl's face and hair, her character and wisdom, so that I can see whether she's worthy of him. Describe her stature to me, how she looks, and her manner; tell me everything about how she seems to you, point by point." Sindokht replied, "My lord, greatest of lords, first you must swear with such solemnity that the ground will tremble at it, that no harm will come to me or to any of those I love. I own castles and palaces, treasure and slaves: when I know that I am safe here, ask me what you wish and I will answer, and so preserve my honor. Then I shall bring all the treasure hidden in Kabol to Zavolestan."

Then Sam took his hand in hers, gently caressed it, and swore as she had requested. Sindokht kissed the ground and told him what had been hidden. She said, "I am from Zahhak's family and married to Mehrab: I am the mother of the beautiful Rudabeh, for whom Zal is ready to sacrifice his soul. Throughout the night until day dawns, all of us call down God's blessings on you and on King Manuchehr. Now I have come to know what you wish, and to find out who your friends and enemies are in Kabol. If we have sinned and are unworthy to rule there, I stand before you here in my misery: kill those who are worthy to die, imprison those who should be imprisoned, but do not burn the hearts of the innocent inhabitants of Kabol, an act which will only brings dark days upon you."

Sam saw that he was dealing with a clear-sighted and intelligent woman, whose face was as lovely as the springtime, who had the stature of a cypress tree, whose waist was a slim as a reed, and who had the gait of a pheasant. He answered her, "I swear on my life that I shall keep faith with you. I approve of Zal's choice of Rudabeh as his wife, and may you, Kabol, and all who are dear to you live in safety and happiness. Although you are of another race than us, you are worthy of the crown and throne. This is the way of the world; there is no shame in it and there is no fighting with God's decrees: one is raised up and another cast down, one lives in wealth and another in want, one in happiness and another in misery. I have written a letter begging Manuchehr to look favorably on us, and Zal has taken it to him. He set off so quickly that it seemed he had grown wings, vaulting into the saddle without seeing it, and his horses' hooves seemed to take no account of the ground. The king will give him an answer; a smile will mean he agrees to our request. This prince who was brought up by a bird is in despair, the tears from his eyes moisten the earth at his feet, and if, in her love for him, his bride suffers as he does, it would be no surprise if the two of them died of grief. Show me the face of this child born of a dragon's race, and you will be rewarded."

Sindokht replied, "If you would make your slave's heart happy, ride to my palace. It will raise my head to the heavens in joy to bring a king like you to Kabol, where every one of us will be ready to sacrifice his life for you." Sindokht saw that Sam's face was all smiles, and that thoughts of revenge had been uprooted from his heart. She sent a messenger who rode as quickly as the wind to Mehrab, bearing the good news. "Forget all your suspicions and worries," she wrote. "Be happy in your heart and prepare to receive a guest. I shall come immediately after this letter and will not halt on the way."

The next day, as sunlight flowed into the world and men woke from sleep, Sindokht made her way to Sam's court, where she was greeted as the best of queens. She came before Sam and made her obeisance, and then spoke with him for a long time about her journey back to Kabol's king, and the preparations to receive Sam there as a guest. Sam said, "Go back, and tell Mehrab what you have seen here." Then he had a present prepared for her, consigning to her all that he owned in Kabol, including palaces, gardens, and farmland, and he also gave her flocks, carpets, and clothes. Then he took her hand in his and swore friendship with her, accepting her daughter, and giving her his warrior son, Zal. He concluded, "Stay in Kabol and be happy; have no fear of anyone who wishes you ill." Her face, which had been so downcast, blossomed again, and she set off home under a fortunate star.

Zal Delivers Sam's Letter to King Manuchehr

Manuchehr learned that Zal was approaching, and the nobles of his court went out to welcome him. A way was quickly cleared for him, and when he entered the court he kissed the ground and called down blessings on the king. For a long time he kept his eyes lowered, until the king bade him welcome and he approached the throne. The king asked him how he had endured the wind and dust of his journey, and he answered, "By your grace everything is made easy, and all troubles are a comfort." The king took the letter he carried, smiled, and acted affably toward him.

When he had read the letter Manuchehr said, "An ancient matter troubles my heart, and you have added to it. But your father Sam has written this letter with such anxiety and grief that I agree to your request and will think no more of the matter. I will see that you have your heart's desire, if this is what you wish, even though my heart is unsettled by it." Stewards brought in a golden table, and Manuchehr sat down before it with Zal and ordered the nobles to take their places beside them. When the king had finished eating, another area was prepared for them to drink together. Zal drank wine with the king, and then sat in his golden saddle and departed; throughout the night his heart was filled with thoughts, his lips with murmured words.

At daybreak he came to pay his respects to Manuchehr, who greeted him warmly, and, after he left, praised him in private. Then the king summoned priests, astrologers, and sages before the throne and commanded them to search the heavens. They spent three days with their astrolabes, laboriously studying the stars to know their secrets, and on the fourth they came before the king and said:

> "Our calculations show the water here
> Will be a mighty current, strong and clear:

The son of Zal and Rudabeh will be
A hero famed for all eternity.
Strength will be his, and swords, and praise,
Battles and banquets will fill all his days,
No eagle will outsoar him, and no lord
Will be his equal; with his glittering sword
He'll make the air weep, and his food will be
A roasted wild ass, spitted on a tree.
Prompt in his monarch's service, prompt to fight,
Persia's protector and stout-hearted knight."

The king said to them, "Keep what you have told me a secret." Then he summoned Zal so that they could question him.

Zal Is Tested

The sages sat with Zal and questioned him, to test his wisdom. One of them said, "There are twelve flourishing, splendid cypress trees, each of which has thirty branches."

Another said, "There are two fine, swiftly galloping horses, one black as a sea of pitch, the other white as clear crystal. They struggle and strive, but neither can overtake the other." A third said, "This is a wonder: there is a group of riders who pass by the prince, and sometimes there are thirty of them when you look, sometimes twenty-nine. One is not there, and then you count again and there are thirty." A fourth said, "You see a beautiful meadow filled with green plants and threaded with streams. A man comes there, holding a huge scythe, and he cuts down the plants, whether they are fresh or dry, never swerving aside as he does so." Another said, "There are two cypresses rising from the ocean, and a bird has built nests there. He sits on one at night and on the other during the day. When he flies up from the one its leaves wither and dry, and when he sits on the other it exhales the scent of musk. One is always withered, the other always fresh and fragrant." Another said, "In the mountains I discovered a flourishing city, but people left it, preferring a thorny waste, where they built houses towering up to the moon; they forgot the flourishing city and never mentioned it. Then an earthquake came, and their houses disappeared, and they longed for the city they had left. Now, explain these sayings to us: if you can do so, you will be turning dust to musk."

Zal sat deep in thought for a while; then he threw back his shoulders, breathed deeply, and answered the priests' questions, saying, "First, the twelve tall trees, each of which has thirty branches, are the twelve months of the year; twelve times the moon is renewed in her place, like a new king seated on his throne, and each month has thirty days; this is how time passes. As for the two horses who gallop swiftly as fire, the white and the black striving to overtake one another, they are night and day which pass over us across the heavens. Third, the thirty horsemen you spoke of who pass before the prince—of whom one is lacking, and then when one counts there are thirty again—these signify the fact that in some months one night is sometimes lacking. Now I shall unsheathe the sword of my speech and explain the two trees on which the bird builds its nests. From the sign of Aries to that of Libra the world lies in darkness until it passes into the sign of Pisces, and the two cypresses are the two halves of the heavens, of which one half is always withered and one fresh. The bird is the sun, which keeps the world in hope and fear. The city in the mountains is the eternal world, and the thorny waste is the fleeting world, which gives us now caresses and riches, and now pain and suffering. God counts your breaths and prolongs or breaks off your days; a wind arises and the earth shakes, and the world is filled with cries and lamentation. The man with the sharp scythe who cuts down both the fresh and withered plants, and who listens to no entreaties, is time the reaper and we are like the plants who are cut down, grandfather and grandchild alike, since he looks at neither young nor old but cuts down all in his path. This is the way of the world, and no man is born from his mother but to die."

When Zal finished his explanation, everyone there was astonished at his understanding. Manuchehr's heart was pleased; he enthusiastically applauded him and gave orders that a banquet as splendid as the full moon be held. They drank wine until the world grew dark and their wits were befuddled: the courtiers' cries resounded about the court, and when they left they did so happy and drunk, grasping one another's arms.

Zal Shows His Skill

When the sun's rays appeared above the mountains, and men woke from sleep, Zal came before the king like a ravening lion and asked permission to leave the court and rejoin his father. He said to the king, "I long to see Sam's face again, now that I have kissed the foot of your ivory throne and my heart has been gladdened by the sight of your crown and splendor." The king said to him, "Young hero, you must grant us one more day. It's love for Mehrab's daughter that makes you so eager to be off; what's this talk about missing Sam and Kabol?" Then he gave orders that cymbals, Indian bells, and trumpets be sounded in the great square.

Warriors gathered cheerfully there, bringing spears, maces, arrows, and bows. There was a huge tree that had flourished for many months and years in the square. Zal grasped his bow and urged his horse forward; he shot an arrow at the tree and the royal shaft pierced the great trunk. Then men bearing javelins set shields down; Zal asked his squire for a shield, squared his shoulders, and again urged his horse forward. He flung his bow aside, and grasped a javelin, which he hurled at three stacked shields with such force that it passed straight through them. The king turned to his noble warriors and said, "Which of you will fight him in single combat? One of you should challenge him." The warriors donned their armor, and their hearts were angry despite the cheerful remarks they made. They twitched their horses' reins and rode onto the square, grasping spears and shining lances. Zal charged forward, the dust rising from his horse's hooves, watching for which proud warrior would oppose him. Like a monster he galloped out of the dust, bearing down on a warrior and grasping him by the belt; he snatched him from the saddle with such ease that the king and his army stared in wonder. The assembly cried out that no one had ever seen his equal, and that the mother of any warrior who opposed him on the battlefield would be sure to wear the dark colors of mourning. No lion had ever given birth to such a hero; indeed he should not be considered a mere hero but a monster of war. And they said how fortunate Sam was, that he would leave such a brave horseman in the world as his heir when he died. The king congratulated him, as did the courtiers, and the company returned to the palace. There Manuchehr prepared such gifts for Zal that they astonished the noblemen present: there were valuable crowns and golden thrones, armbands, torques, and golden belts, as well as splendid sets of clothes, slaves, horses, and many other things.

Manuchehr Answers Sam's Letter

Manuchehr dictated an answer to Sam's letter: "Brave warrior, victorious as a lion in all your ventures: the heavens have not seen your like

in battles and banquets, in policy and beauty. Your fine son has come
to me, and I have learned of his wishes and the nature of his desire. I
have granted all he has asked for and spent many happy days in his
company. A lion like you, who has leopards as his prey, what else would
he sire but a warlike lion cub? I send him back to you with a happy
heart, and may evil keep its distance from him."

Zal left the court and dispatched an envoy to Sam with this mes-
sage: "I am returning from the king; my heart is happy and I come
with royal gifts, crowns, armbands, torques and ivory thrones." Sam
was so overjoyed to receive this message that despite his age, his youth
seemed to return to him. He dispatched an envoy to Kabol, telling
Mehrab of Manuchehr's kind treatment of Zal, of the happiness that
prevailed between them, and saying that both he and Zal would visit
him as soon as Zal returned.

The envoy galloped to Kabol, and shouts of joy rose into the skies
when he gave his news. The king of Kabol was beside himself with
pleasure that he was to be related to the ruler of Zabolestan; musicians
and entertainers were summoned, Mehrab's heart was cleared of all
anxieties, and there was a perpetual smile on his lips. He called Sindokht
to him and spoke kindly to her, saying, "You are a splendid wife, and
your advice has brought us from darkness to light. You have planted
such a sapling in the earth that princes pay homage to it. What you
planned for has happened, and all my wealth is at your disposal, be it
thrones or crowns or treasure." When Sindokht heard him she went to
her daughter to tell her the news, and said, "Good news, you will soon
see Zal; you have gained a husband who is worthy of you. A wife and
husband with your nobility of spirit will not endure the world's
reproaches. You rushed to fulfill your heart's desire, and now you have
found everything you sought." Rudabeh replied, "You are the king's
consort, and worthy of praise from everyone; the dust beneath your feet
is my pillow, and your commands are my soul's comfort. May the eye
of Ahriman be far from you, and your heart and soul always be filled
with joy."

Sindokht heard her, and then she set about preparing the palace for
their visitors. She had the audience hall decorated like a paradise, and
rose water, wine, musk, and ambergris were placed there. She laid
down a carpet worked in gold and sewn with emeralds, and another
whose design was made of pearls, each of which shone like a drop of

water. Then she placed a golden throne there, with Chinese patterns
on it, studded with jewels that framed carved reliefs, and its feet were
made of rubies. Next she turned her attention to Rudabeh, adorning
her like a paradise and writing magical incantations to the sun to pro-
tect her. She confined her in her golden apartments and gave no one
access to her. All of Kabol was made beautiful with colors, fine fra-
grances, and precious objects. Wine was brought, and the elephants'
backs were draped with Rumi brocade, on which musicians sat, wear-
ing golden diadems. The welcoming party was put together and slaves
went ahead scattering musk and ambergris, and spreading silk and
samite in the way. Musk and gold coins were scattered on the proces-
sion, and the ground was wet with rose water and wine.

Zal Returns to Sam

Meanwhile Zal made all speed homeward, like a flying eagle or a skiff
skimming the water. No one was aware of his approach, and so no one
went out to meet him, and suddenly a cry went up from the palace that
Zal had arrived. Sam went happily out to greet him and clasped him
in his arms, holding him close for a long time. When Zal had freed
himself from his father's embrace, he kissed the ground, and then
recounted all he had seen and heard. Sam and Zal sat on thrones beside
one another, and their lips were all smiles as they talked of Sindokht's
visit to Sam. Sam said, "A message came from Kabol, and the envoy
was a woman called Sindokht. She wanted a promise from me that I
would not act badly to her, and I gave her this, and then she asked for
everything so charmingly that I granted all of it. First she wanted
Zavolestan's prince to marry the princess of Kabol, then that you and
I visit her as guests, as recompense for the distress she had been
through. Now a messenger has come from her saying that this business
of her daughter has been settled; now, what should we tell this mes-
senger? What answer should we send Mehrab?" Zal was so happy that
he blushed like a tulip from head to foot, and he answered, "If you
think it's suitable, send a detachment of troops, and we'll come after
them; we can visit them, because we have a lot to discuss together."
Sam looked at Zal, and he understood very well what his son wanted;
he knew that Zal could not sleep at night and had no interest in any
conversation that did not concern Mehrab's daughter.

Sam gave orders that bells and Indian chimes signal their departure;

the royal pavilion was struck and a messenger was sent on ahead to announce to Mehrab that Sam, Zal, and a detachment of warriors and elephants would soon arrive. Mehrab had the drums sounded and trumpets blown, and drew up his army so that it glittered like a rooster's eye. The elephants and musicians, and the various banners of red, white, yellow, and purple silk, made the earth seem like a paradise: with the blare of trumpets and the sound of harps, the squeal of bugles and the ringing of bells, it seemed as if Judgment Day had come. This was the manner in which Mehrab went forward to welcome Sam, and when he saw him he dismounted from his horse and walked forward. Sam embraced him and asked him how fate had dealt with him: Mehrab for his part called down blessings on both Sam and Zal and then mounted his swift charger again, like the new moon rising above the mountains. He placed a golden crown studded with jewels on Zal's head, and the group arrived in Kabol happily laughing and chatting together. The town was so full of the sounds of Indian chimes, lutes, harps, and trumpets that it seemed to be transformed; the horse's manes were soaked in musk, wine, and saffron, and drummers and trumpeters were mounted on elephants. Three hundred slaves carrying golden goblets filled with musk and jewels called down blessings on Sam and then scattered their goblets' jewels before him, and whoever came to the festivities wanted for nothing.

Sam smiled and said to Sindokht, "How long are you going to keep Rudabeh hidden?" In the same manner Sindokht replied, "And where is the gift you will give, if you wish to see the sun?" Sam answered, "Ask me for whatever you wish." They went to the golden apartments, in which the happiness of spring awaited them. There Sam looked at Rudabeh and was overcome with wonder; he did not know how to praise her adequately, or how to keep his eyes from being dazzled by her splendor. Then he commanded Mehrab to come forward, and the marriage was solemnized according to ancient custom. Zal and Rudabeh were sat side by side on one throne, and agates and emeralds were scattered over them. Rudabeh wore a splendid diadem and Zal, a jewel-studded crown. A list of the treasures he was giving them was brought by Mehrab, and as it was read out, it seemed men's ears could not listen until its end. From there they went to a banqueting hall, where they sat with wine cups in their hands for a week, and then returned to the palace where the festivities went on for three more weeks.

At the beginning of the following month Sam began his journey home to Sistan, together with Zal, their elephants and drums, and the troops who had accompanied him. Zal had howdahs and litters made for Mehrab's women folk, and a palanquin for Rudabeh, and she, Sindokht, Mehrab and their family set out for Sistan. They traveled happily, praising God for his gifts, and arrived in high spirits, laughing and smiling. Then Sam bestowed sovereignty over Sistan on Zal and unfurled his auspicious banner to lead his troops once again toward the land of the Gorgsaran and Bactria.

ROSTAM, THE SON OF ZAL-DASTAN

The Birth of Rostam

It was not long before Rudabeh's cypress-slim form began to change; her belly filled out, her body grew heavy, and the Judas blossoms of her face turned as sallow as saffron. Her mother said to her, "My soul, what's happened that you look so yellow?" She replied, "My lips moan day and night; my time has come, and I cannot give birth to the burden within me. My skin feels as though it were stuffed with stones, or that it contained a mass of iron." Rudabeh endured this until the time for her to give birth came closer, and she could neither sleep nor rest. Then one day she fainted, and a cry went up from Zal's palace; Sindokht was informed, and she clawed at her face and tore out her musky hair. The news reached Zal that the leaves of his noble cypress tree had withered away, and he came to her pillow, sick at heart and with tears in his eyes. Then he remembered the Simorgh's feather and smiled, and he told Sindokht to take heart. He brought a brazier and lit a fire, in which he burned a little of the Simorgh's feather. Immediately the air darkened, and the bird appeared, ready to do his bidding, like pearls raining down from a dark cloud; I say pearls, but it was peace to the soul that she brought. Zal made his obeisance before the bird and praised her. The Simorgh said to him, "Why are you sad, why are the lion's eyes wet with tears? A cub eager for fame will be born to you from this silver cypress:

> He'll master all the beasts of earth and air,
> He'll terrify the dragon in its lair;
> When such a voice rings out, the leopard gnaws
> In anguished terror its unyielding claws;

Wild on the battlefield that voice will make
The hardened hearts of iron warriors quake;
Of cypress stature and of mammoth might,
Two miles will barely show his javelin's flight.

"For him to be born into the world, you must bring a glittering knife, and a man familiar with spells. First, make the beautiful Rudabeh drunk with wine, and so drive fear and worry from her heart. Don't watch as the sorcerer begins his incantations to bring out this lion from within her body: he will cut open the cypress's belly, and she will feel no pain. Then, driving all fear and anxiety from your heart, you must sew up the wound where the sorcerer cut her. Pound the herb I will describe to you in milk and musk, and dry the mixture in the shade. Massage this into her wound, and you will see it heal within the day. After this, stroke her body with my feather, since its shadow will be auspicious. You should rejoice at this and give thanks to God; it was he who gave you this royal tree, which every day brings you greater good fortune. Do not be sad at this turn of events; your noble sapling is about to bear fruit." She plucked a feather from her wing and let it fall, then flew upwards and was gone. Zal retrieved the feather, and did as the Simorgh had told him. This was a wonder, and the world watched, weeping and apprehensive. Sindokht cried desperate tears, wondering when the baby would be delivered from her daughter's body.

A skilled priest came, and made the lovely Rudabeh drunk with wine. She felt no pain as he cut open her side, and turned the baby's head toward the opening. He brought the child forth so painlessly that no one in the world had ever seen such a wonder.

The child was like a lion, a noble son,
Tall and handsome, lovely to look upon;
And all who saw this mammoth baby gazed
In wonder at him, murmuring and amazed.

For a day and a night the mother slept from the effects of the wine, and her heart knew nothing of what happened. They sewed up her wound and massaged the scar with the mixture the Simorgh had described. When she woke from her sleep and spoke to Sindokht the onlookers gave thanks to God and showered her with jewels and gold coins. She smiled when she saw her noble child, because she saw the signs of royal glory in him, and said, "I escaped (*rastam*) from my peril, my pain came to an end," and so they named the boy Rostam.

They sewed a doll of silk, that was the same height as this lion who had not yet tasted milk, and stuffed it with sable fur. Its face shone like the sun and the evening star. They traced a dragon on its bicep, placed a lion's paw in its hand, tucked a lance beneath its arm, and put a mace in one hand and reins in the other. Then they sat it on a charger surrounded by servants, scattered gold coins over the group, and sent this image of Rostam with his mace to Sam.

Festivities were held from Zavolestan to Kabol; all the plain was filled with the sound of trumpets and the drinking of wine, and there was a banquet for a hundred guests in every corner of the kingdom. Musicians were everywhere in Zavolestan, and commoners and noblemen sat together as intimately as the warp and weft of one cloth. They took the image of the unweaned Rostam to Sam, whose hair prickled with pleasure. "This silken doll resembles me, and if his body is half this size, his head will touch the clouds." Then he called for the messenger to come forward, and showered gold coins over him till they covered his head. The joyful din of drums rang out from the court, and the royal square glittered like a rooster's eye. Sam called for wine and musicians, distributed gold coins to the poor, and held such a banquet that the sun and moon gazed down in wonder. He answered Zal's letter, beginning with praise of Creator and the good fortune that had come to them; next he praised Zal, the lord of the sword and mace, and then turned to the silken doll, who displayed the shoulders of a warrior and the glory of a king. He told Zal that he should preserve it so carefully that no breath of wind could harm it, and added that he had prayed night and day that he would live long enough to see a hero grow from Zal's seed, and now that this child had been born to them, their chief duty was to pray for his life.

Sam Comes to See Rostam

So the world went forward, and things that had been hidden were revealed. Ten wet nurses were set to suckle Rostam, since it is milk that gives a man his strength. When he was weaned, his food was oak apples and meat; he ate enough for five grown men and people were astonished at his appetite. When he was eight spans high, he seemed like a noble cypress tree, and his face shone like a star, at which the world stared in wonder. He seemed to be Sam himself, in his stature, appearance, opinions, and behavior. When news reached brave Sam that Zal's son had grown to be like a lion and that no one in the world had ever seen such a young man with his warrior-like qualities, Sam's heart beat faster and he longed to see the boy. He entrusted his army to a commander and went with a detachment of experienced fighters toward Zavolestan, led there by the love he felt for Zal's son.

When Zal heard of his father's approach, he had drums strapped on elephants and the earth turned the color of ebony beneath the cavalry's hooves. He and Mehrab and the governor of Kabol set out as a welcoming party; a pebble was thrown into a goblet, which was the signal for the soldiers to mount, and a great cry went up on all sides. All the valley was filled with troops, the earth turned as black as pitch and the air was dark with dust. The neighing of Arab horses and the trumpeting of elephants could be heard for five miles. One elephant bore a golden throne, on which sat Zal's son, with his cypress-stature and huge shoulders and chest. On his head was a crown, he wore a belt about his waist, and carried a shield in front of his body and a heavy mace in his hand. When Sam appeared in the distance, the army divided into two columns, and Zal and Mehrab, the youth and the warrior of many years, dismounted and bowed their heads to the ground, calling down blessings on the hero Sam. As Sam caught sight of the lion cub on the elephant's back his face opened like a blossom; they led the boy forward on his elephant and Sam stared at him, taking in his crown and throne. Brave Sam called down blessings on him, saying "My lion cub, incomparable child, may you live long and happily!"

Rostam kissed the throne and, what was wonderful, praised his grandfather in a new way:

> "Live happily, my lord, the sturdy root
> From which I, Rostam, am the newest shoot.
> I'm Sam's devoted slave, and while I live
> The pleasures feasting, sleep, and comfort give
> Will not beguile me. Helmets, armor, bows
> That I can draw against our country's foes,

My saddle and my horse, my mace and sword,
These will be all my life, my noble lord.
My face resembles yours, and when I fight
May I resemble you in dauntless might."

Then he climbed down from the elephant's back, and Sam took him by the hand, kissing his eyes and head, and the elephants and drums stayed still and silent. They set off for Gourabeh, smiling and chatting as they rode, and when they arrived they sat in the palace on a golden dais, feasting in happiness. They spent a month in this manner, untroubled by hardship, and music accompanied their feasting, with each of them singing in turn. In one corner of the dais sat Zal, in the opposite corner Rostam, with his mace in his hand, and between them was Sam, with the feathers from the lammergeyer, signifying royal glory, depending from his crown. He stared in awe at Rostam, and from time to time he would call down blessings on the youth's arms and shoulders, his reed-like waist and noble chest. Then he turned to Zal and said, "You could question a hundred generations and never hear of one who was born in such a manner. There is no one in the world who is as handsome as he is, or who has his stature and shoulders. Come, let us drink wine in celebration of this happiness, and may it drive all sorrow from our hearts, since the world is fleeting; we arrive and depart, and as one grows old another is born."

They drank their wine, and in their cups they praised
Zal after Rostam. But Mehrab was dazed
With drink, and in his drunkenness he said
The arrogant ideas that filled his head.
"I don't consider Zal as anything,"
He said, "and Sam's as worthless as the king.
Rostam and me, we are the heroes here,
The clouds daren't pass above us, out of fear.
And I'll renew Zahhak's power, you'll soon see,
And all of you will have to bow to me."

But Zal and Sam laughed at Mehrab's boastful words.

At the beginning of the month of Mehr Sam set off once more. He said to Zal, "My son, see that you act justly, with your heart ready to serve your kings, choosing wisdom over wealth, always keeping your hands from evil deeds, and striving to do God's will. Know that the world tarries for no man; take care of what I say, follow my advice, and tread only in the path of righteousness. I feel in my heart that my time here is coming to an end." Then he said farewell to his son and grandson, admonishing them not to forget his words. Chimes sounded from the court, and the blare of trumpets was heard from the elephants' backs. Sam left for Bactria; his heart was filled with love and he spoke kindly to his son and grandson, whose faces were stained with tears, and whose hearts were filled with his precepts, as they accompanied him for three stages of the way. Then they turned back, and Sam continued on his long journey.

THE BEGINNING OF THE WAR
BETWEEN IRAN AND TURAN

The Last Days of Manuchehr

Manuchehr had lived for one hundred and twenty years, and the time had come for him to prepare for his last journey. His astrologers came to him and told him of the evidence of the skies; they could not see that his days would continue, and he should be ready to leave the world. They gave him the bitter news that the glory of his sovereignty was dimmed, and said to him, "You will go to another place, and may you meet with God there. There is no fighting against death; you must do now whatever is necessary before your departure."

When he heard the astrologers' advice, Manuchehr altered his court's customary procedures. He summoned priests and sages and opened his heart before them. He had Nozar brought before him, and spoke with him at length. He said, "This royal throne is an illusion, a wind, and you should not tie your heart to it for eternity. I have striven with dangers and difficulties for a hundred and twenty years, known great happiness and success, and faced my enemies in battle. The glory of Feraydun inspired me, and with his advice I turned all injuries to my advantage. I fought against Salm and savage Tur, and took revenge for the death of my grandfather, Iraj. I rid the earth of misery, founded cities and fortresses. But now it is as if I had never seen or known the world; the reckoning has passed and gone into darkness. Life has less potency than death; it is a tree whose leaves and fruits are poison. I have endured pain and sorrow, and now I bestow the imperial throne and treasure on you: I give you the royal crown, as Feraydun gave it to me. Know that when you have experienced the world and it has gone by, you must return to a better place, but the traces you leave behind you will last for long years. They must be such that they bring you praise, and men say of you that you were a man of pure race who enacted the pure faith. See that you do not swerve aside from God's faith; it is this which brings good counsel. Never leave God's way, since both good and bad come from him. After I have gone, an army of Turks will come and they will decide who sits on Persia's throne and who wears her crown. You have hard work ahead of you, and those you confront will sometimes be wolves, sometimes sheep."

When he had finished speaking tears stained his cheeks, and Nozar wept bitterly for him.

> He closed his royal eyes, coldly he sighed,
> And Manuchehr, Iran's great sovereign, died.
> All that remains now is his royal name,
> And words are all that constitute his fame.

The Reign of Nozar

After the period of mourning for his father had ended, Nozar lifted the Kayanid crown above Saturn. He sat on Manuchehr's throne and held court, summoning his people and distributing wealth among them. But not many days passed before his mind turned toward injustice. Murmurings were heard on every side, and the world grew weary of this new king whose heart lived only for wealth and money, who had abrogated his father's customs, acted cruelly toward his priests and advisors, and despised all men. Peasant revolts sprang up, and pretenders to the throne appeared; when the cries of protest spread and all the world was in turmoil, this unjust king was afraid and sent an envoy to Sam, who was fighting against the Gorgsaran, with a message filled with flattery and asking for his help.

When this letter reached Sam, he heaved a cold sigh. At cockcrow, the din of drums and bugles was heard, and from the land of the Gorgsaran advanced an army whose size would put the green oceans to shame. As he drew near Persia, her nobles went out to greet him; they gathered quickly when they heard of his approach and came before him on foot. They spoke at length about the injustices of Nozar, a king who had foolishly forsaken his father's ways. They said, "The world has been ruined by his depredations, and his good fortune sleeps. He does not follow the ways of wisdom, and the royal *farr* has departed from him. There would be nothing wrong if the hero Sam were to take his place on the royal throne. The world would flourish beneath his justice; Persia and her people support him, we are all his slaves, our souls live for him, and we will be obedient to his will."

But Sam answered them: "How could this please God? While Nozar, who is of royal lineage, sits on the throne, how could I wear the crown? Such a thing is impossible, and no one should listen to such talk. If even a daughter of Manuchehr occupied the throne and wore the royal crown, my pillow would still be the dust and my eyes would rejoice to see her. If Nozar's heart has departed from his father's ways, this has not been going on for long. The iron is not yet so rusted that its splendor cannot be restored. I shall restore his divine *farr* and make the world look for his love again. Give up these ideas, and reaffirm your loyalty to the king. If you do not obtain God's mercy and the king's love, Nozar's anger will engulf the world in flames."

The nobles regretted what they had said and reaffirmed their loyalty, and the world was restored to peace by Sam's presence of mind. The nobles went before Nozar and expressed their contrition, and reaffirmed their status as his subjects. The glory of Nozar's reign was restored, his royal *farr* returned, and once more he ruled in peace. Sam advised Nozar on how to act justly and then received the king's orders to return to battle. He left the court with fine gifts from Nozar: thrones, crowns, rings, slaves, horses with golden bridles, and two golden goblets filled with red rubies.

Pashang Learns of Manuchehr's Death

And so the heavens turned, dissatisfied with Nozar and feeling no love for him. News of Manuchehr's death reached the army of the Turks, and those who wished Persia ill talked of the troubles that beset Nozar's reign. When the Turkish commander Pashang heard of this, he decided to invade Iran. He talked constantly of his father, Zadsham, and sighed bitterly over what had happened to Tur, remembering all that Manuchehr and his army had done. He called the chieftains and nobles of the country together, men like Akhvast, Garsivaz, Barman, and Golbad, who was a ravening lion in battle, as well as Viseh, who had command of his armies. His favored champion was his son Afrasyab, who came quickly at the summons. He talked of Salm and Tur and said, "We should not hide our desire for revenge against the Persians beneath our robes. Whose mind is not incensed to think of their actions?

Everyone knows what they have done to us,
How evil they have been, how infamous.
But we must dry our eyes—it's time now for
Revenge, rebellion, and relentless war!"

When Afrasyab heard his father's words he forgot all thoughts of rest, food, or comfort. He stood before his father, his heart filled with the longing for revenge, and said:

"Against wild lions I can stand and fight,
I am the match for Persia's monarch's might.
If Zadsham had but drawn his warlike sword
The world would not be ruled by Persia's lord:
If he'd been eager for a warrior's fame
Turan would not be overwhelmed with shame,
But his descendants can wage war, and we
Will crush these Persians with our victory."

Pashang's ambition flared up when he saw Afrasyab, with his lion's shoulders and mammoth's might, his shadow that seemed to stretch for miles, his tongue like a cutting sword, and his heart like a foaming sea. He ordered him to unsheathe his sword and lead the army against Iran. He saw his son as a worthy commander, someone fit to raise his head up to the sun, who after his own death would inherit the kingdom. When Afrasyab left his father's presence, his head was filled with the longing for vengeance, his heart with impatience for battle.

While preparations for war were being completed, Afrasyab's brother, Aghriras, came to their father full of foreboding. He said, "My father, you are an experienced man, and you are the chief of the Turks, but consider: it is true that Manuchehr is gone, but Sam still commands their armies, and they have warriors like Karshasp and Qaren as well as many others. You know what that ancient wolf did to Tur and Salm. My grandfather Zadsham was the king of Turan and the leader of the Turkish armies, his helmet touched the moon's sphere, but he never talked as Afrasyab is now doing, and never read in the book of vengeance during a time of peace. It would be better if we gave up these thoughts of rebellion, which will bring disaster on us."

Pashang said to his son, "Afrasyab is like a male lion set on the hunt, a war elephant ready for battle, and a grandson who does not seek revenge for his grandfather's shame is not worthy of his lineage. You should go with him to give him good advice. When the clouds loose their burden on the plains, and the mountain slopes and deserts turn to good pasturage for our horses, and plants grow to the height of heroes, when the world turns green with spring's vegetation, that is the time to pitch your tents on the plains. When your heart rejoices in the spring's verdure and flowers, you should lead our army to Amol. Trample Dehestan and Gorgan beneath your cavalry's hooves, and make their rivers' waters ruby-red with blood. That was where Manuchehr set off from on his war of vengeance against Tur. See if you can confront Qaren or Karshasp there and overcome them; make our ancestors' souls happy by your victories, and burn in the fires of chagrin the hearts of those who wish us ill." And Aghriras said to his ambitious father, "I shall make their rivers flow with the blood of vengeance."

Afrasyab Invades Persia

When spring's new growth gave the plains the appearance of silk, the Turks prepared for battle. Armies gathered from Turan and China, and joined with warriors armed with maces from the west. So massive were their forces that they had neither center nor edge, and Nozar's fortunes began to fade. The news that a Turkish army was approaching the Oxus reached Feraydun's successor, and the Persian armies left the imperial palace to gather on the plain. Under Qaren's command, they set off for Dehestan, with Nozar following in the rear. The world was filled with rumors, and as the army came near Dehestan, the sun was obscured by their dust. Nozar's pavilion was pitched in front of the town; he had no desire to fight within the city walls and did not delay there for long.

Campaigning in Arman, Afrasyab chose two Turkish chieftains, one named Shamasas and the other Khazbaran, gave them a force of thirty thousand cavalry, and sent them to march on Zavolestan, where they were to attack Zal. News had come that Sam was dead and that Zal was building him a tomb; Afrasyab was overjoyed at this, since he saw that the Persians' fortunes were declining. He marched on Dehestan and pitched his pavilion opposite the town. Who could count his forces? But multiply four hundred by a thousand and you will have some notion of their army's size. The very mountains and sands

seemed to seethe with their presence, and all the desert was filled with warriors. On King Nozar's side there were a hundred and forty thousand men, all mounted and ready for war. Afrasyab surveyed his army, and at nightfall sent a messenger with a letter to Pashang, saying, "We have sought to conquer the world and it is within our grasp; if we reckon up the forces at Nozar's disposal, we see they are mere prey for us, and we shall hunt them down. And Sam is no longer there to fight for his king; Zal is busy building him a tomb and does not have the strength to fight against us. Shamasas has taken Zavolestan and wears their glittering crown. It is good to strike at the right moment and to consult with those who are friendly and wise. If a man hangs back when he should act, he will not have such an opportunity again." The messenger seemed to grow wings as he sped toward the king of Turan, whose splendor was like that of the sun.

The Combat Between Barman and Qobad; Qobad Is Killed

When dawn showed above the mountains, the advance troops of Afrasyab's army reached Dehestan. There was a Turk among them named Barman, and he said, "I will shock these sleepers awake." There were two parasangs between the armies, and all the weapons and machinery of war were ready. Barman surveyed Nozar's army and saw Nozar's pavilion. He went to the commander of the Turkish forces, told him of what he had observed, and said, "How long do we have to hide our prowess? If the king will permit, I will challenge one of their men to single combat; then they will see my valor and consider no one but me to be a warrior." The wise Aghriras said, "And if Barman is defeated our frontier forces will be disheartened, and we shall suffer a setback. We must choose some anonymous warrior, and then we shall not be biting our nails waiting for the outcome." Afrasyab's face flushed with shame as he listened to Aghriras, and with a frown on his face he said to Barman, "Put on your armor and string your bow; you are the best of our warriors, and there will be no need to bite our nails when you fight."

Barman returned to the battlefield and shouted toward Qaren, the son of Kaveh, "What warrior from Nozar's army will fight against me in single combat?" Qaren looked round at his men to see who would step forward to fight, but none of the famous fighters gave any answer, except for the ancient warrior Qobad. The wise commander frowned at this; Qobad was his brother and his words enraged him. He was so angry that tears stood in his eyes; how could it be that from all this great army and all these young warriors, an old man should be trying to fight? Qaren was upset by Qobad's behavior and in front of the army he said to him, "You've reached the age when you should forget about fighting, particularly against someone fresh, young, and confident like Barman; he's a horseman with the heart of a male lion, and he lifts his head above the sun in his pride. You are an important leader of this army and an adviser to the king. If your white beard is reddened with blood, all our warriors will lose heart; our army will be broken, and the hearts of our friends will despair."

Now listen to Qobad's answer to the warlike Qaren. He said, "The turning heavens have allotted me my life. My brother, you must know that our bodies are born to die, and that warriors live to wear their helmets in war. From the time of the great Manuchehr until today my heart has lived in sorrow. A man cannot reach the heavens while he is alive; he is the prey of death, which pursues us all. One dies from a sword blow in the midst of battle; vultures and ravening lions devour his body, spears and swords slash his head. Another dies in his bed, but it is certain that we must all die. If I am to leave this splendid world, my strong brother will take my place here; he will build me a royal tomb, and perform the rites that love dictates. He will wrap my head in camphor, musk, and rose water, and lay my body down for its eternal rest. Allow me this, my brother; farewell, and may you flourish in the world."

When he had finished speaking he grasped his spear and went out to the battlefield like a maddened elephant. Barman said to him, "Time has delivered you to me: it would be better for you to wait, since fate itself is ready to demand your life from you." Qobad replied, "The world has given me my time. A man will die when his time has come, and cannot die before then." At that he urged his black horse forward, giving no respite to his warlike soul. From dawn until the sun cast lengthened shadows, the two tried their strength against one another.

> But Barman was victorious at last;
> He sped onto the battlefield and cast
> A lance that struck Qobad, piercing his back;
> His spine was smashed. Slowly he toppled, slack
> And lifeless, from the saddle to the ground;
> Thus died the hero, aged, and renowned.

Barman returned to Afrasyab, his cheeks glittering with triumph, and he was given a robe of honor the like of which no nobleman or subject had ever seen.

When Qobad was killed, Qaren led his forces out and the two armies met like the mingling of two mighty oceans, so that the earth seemed to

shake with their encounter. Qaren rushed forward, and from the side of
Turan, Garsivaz was equally quick to attack. The neighing of horses and
the dust sent up by the armies obscured the sun and moon; the diamond
glitter of steel weapons was dulled by blood. Dust swirled like rain clouds
made vermilion by the sun, clouds reverberated with the din of drums,
and swords ran with blood. Qaren urged his horse this way and that,
wielding his sword like fire, as if diamonds rained down coral, except
that the coral was men's souls. When Afrasyab saw his prowess he led his
men toward him, and the two fought until night appeared over the
mountains, and still their desire for vengeance remained unsatisfied.

As night fell Qaren led his forces before Dehestan and came to
Nozar's pavilion, his heart wrung by his brother's death. Nozar saw
him and wept tears from eyes that had been unable to sleep. He said,
"My soul did not mourn like this even after Sam's death: may Qobad's
soul be as resplendent as the sun, and may it be your fate to remain in
this world eternally. There is no escape from the death we are born to,
and the world is nothing but a cradle for the grave." Qaren replied,
"Since I was born I have dedicated my body to death: it was Feraydun
who placed this helmet on my head, so that I could ride out to avenge
Iraj. Since that day I have not loosened my sword-belt nor laid down
my sword. Now my brother, a man filled with dignity and wisdom, has
died, and this will be my end, too. May you live forever; today when
battle overtook Pashang's son, and part of his army was destroyed, he
chose fresh troops, then saw me with my ox-headed mace and came
after me eager to fight. I came so close to him that we looked one
another in the eye, but then he wove a magical spell, and both light
and color disappeared before my sight. Night fell and the world turned
dark, and my arm was unable to strike. It seemed that time itself was
ending, and that the sky had retreated beneath the earth, and we had
to draw back from the battle in the dust and darkness."

Afrasyab's Second Attack

On both sides the army rested, and on the second day they renewed
the battle. The Persian forces formed ranks as was customary during
the Kayanid kings' wars, and when Afrasyab saw them he had his
army's brazen drums beaten and their ranks drawn up. The sun seemed
to go into hiding behind the dust sent up by the armies' cavalry, the
give and take of battle from both sides began, and the plains became

indistinguishable from the mountain slopes. The two armies clashed with such force that blood flowed like a river: wherever Qaren attacked, blood mingled with the dust, and where Afrasyab's dust rose up, the plain streamed with blood. From the center of his troops Nozar rode out against Afrasyab, and the two leaders

> *Then flung such spears at one another, each*
> *Writhed like a snake in twisting out of reach.*

The battle lasted until nightfall, when Pashang's son began to gain the upper hand. Most of the men in the Persian army had been wounded, and the forces of Turan carried the battle into their positions. The Persian troops turned back helplessly and fled across the plain. Nozar's heart was grief-stricken, since the stars had clouded his crown with dust. When the din of drums died away on the battlefield he summoned Tus, who came together with Gostahm, their lips filled with sighs, their souls with sorrow. He said, "What pain there is in my heart!" and he wept even as he spoke. Blood seemed to fill his heart, cold sighs escaped from his lips, and he remembered his great father's words: "From Turan and China a mighty army will invade Iran; your heart will be wrung by them, and your army broken." "Now," he said, "the king's words have been borne out, and the day he predicted has come. No one has ever read in a book chronicling the famous and their deeds of such a huge army as has been led here from Turan. You must go to Pars and collect my family and take them to Rabeh-kuh in the Alborz mountains. Hide your departure from your troops, because if they find out, their hearts will break; it will be like further wounding a wounded man. But in this way one or two people of Feraydun's seed might be saved from this innumerable host of enemies. I do not know if we shall see one another again; tonight we shall make a last effort at resistance. Keep a watch day and night, and stay aware of what is going on in the world. If you hear bad news about our army, and that our imperial glory has been darkened, do not fall into despair, because the heavens have ever been thus, killing one man in battle, and giving another happiness and a crown. A man who has been killed is like one who has died; he quivers for a moment, and then is at rest." Then he embraced his sons and wept. Tus and Gostahm left Nozar's presence, their cheeks wet with tears, and their souls filled with anxiety.

Nozar and Afrasyab Fight for a Third Time

The army rested for two days, and on the third, as dawn broke, Nozar was forced to fight. Afrasyab descended on his forces like a seething ocean, and shouts mingled with the blare of trumpets, and the sound of Indian chimes rose up from the royal pavilion. The din of drums was heard in the tents and the warriors donned their iron helmets. No one had slept in Afrasyab's camp; the night had been spent in preparing the army and sharpening swords and javelins. The valley was filled with troops advancing with their heavy maces; the mountain slopes and plains disappeared, and troops were deployed from sea to sea. Qaren placed himself in the center of his forces, so that they would protect the king; Taliman commanded the left flank, and Shapur, Nastureh's son, the right. From dawn till dusk neither the mountains, nor the sea, nor the plains could be seen. But when the spears' shadows lengthened, the Persian forces were broken, and as their luck declined, so the Turks gained the upper hand. Shapur's troops were routed, and Shapur himself lay dead. The Persians fled from the Turks toward Dehestan and occupied the citadel; there were only a few approaches to the fortress and they fought hard throughout the day and night to defend them. In this way they gained some respite. Nozar established himself there, and the way was blocked to the enemy's cavalry.

Afrasyab dispatched a Turk called Qarakhan to Pars, telling him to go by a desert road and cut off the Persian baggage train. When Qaren heard that Afrasyab had sent out a detachment of troops in the night, his fury knew no bounds and he came to Nozar like a leopard, saying: "Look what this deceitful king has done to you; he has sent innumerable troops against our army's womenfolk, and if he captures them, our nobles will be in despair; they will hide their heads in shame. I must pursue this Qarakhan; you have provisions here and flowing water, and the troops are loyal to you. Wait here, and keep up your spirits, as befits a brave king." But Nozar replied, "This is not advisable; none of my commanders can compare with you. Gostahm and Tus left to see to the baggage train when the drums sounded at dawn. They will catch up with the women and look after them appropriately."

They sat to their food and called for wine, and for a while they dispelled sorrow from their hearts. Then soldiers gathered in Qaren's quarters, and their eyes were as filled with tears as winter clouds are with rain. They spoke of this and that, and then said, "We must go to Pars; we cannot accept this decision. If the Persian womenfolk are captured by our enemies, if they take our wives and children prisoner without our putting up a fight, who will ever dare lift a lance again in these plains, who will be able to rest or sleep?"

Shirui, Keshvad, and Qaren discussed this at length and finally, when half the night had passed, decided to leave. Gazhdahom was holding a fortress to which Barman had laid siege with his elephants, blocking the way forward. It was he who had inflicted a wound on Qaren when he killed his brother, and Qaren longed for vengeance. He attacked like a lion and gave Barman no chance to retreat, hurling a spear into his waist and shattering his spine; Barman's forces lost heart and fled from one another in disorder, and Qaren and his troops pushed on toward Pars.

Nozar Is Captured by Afrasyab

When Nozar learned that Qaren had left, he came hurrying after him, hoping to escape the evil fate that threatened to trample him underfoot. As soon as Afrasyab heard about Qaren's flight across the desert, he gathered his troops and set off in pursuit. They made good speed and closed on the Persians, pursuing him through the night until dawn. The world was darkened with the dust sent up by the galloping riders, and finally it was Nozar who was captured, together with one thousand two hundred of his troops. The captives were led in chains before Afrasyab.

Then Afrasyab gave orders that his men were to search the caves, mountains, deserts, and rivers to prevent Qaren from escaping. But he was told that Qaren had already departed, because he was worried about what would happen to the Persian women, and had killed Barman. Afrasyab said to Barman's father, Viseh, who grieved for his son's death, "Leopards hesitate to attack Qaren, but you must take troops and go after him, to avenge your son's death."

Viseh Finds His Son Dead

Viseh set off with a detachment of soldiers, but before he caught up with Qaren, he saw his son sprawled dead on the battlefield and countless warriors of Turan lying there dead with him. Their banners were torn, their drums overturned, their shrouds were red as tulips, their faces vermilion with blood.

Qaren learned that Viseh was advancing against him; he sent a detachment of his men on Arab horses to Zavolestan, and with the rest he went out from Pars onto the plain, illuminating the world with his splendor. To his left he saw an army approaching, and a black banner emerged from the dust; at the head of the troops he saw Viseh, the Turkish commander. The two armies drew up their ranks and advanced on one another, and from the center of his men Viseh called out: "The wind has swept away your crown and your great throne. All the lands from Qanuj to the borders of Zavolestan, and from there to Bost and Kabol, are in our hands now; it is our portraits that are painted on the walls of their castles. Where will you find a resting place now that your king has been captured?" Qaren replied, "I am Qaren, and water will not wash away my prowess. I did not leave out of fear, or because of rumors; I fought with your son, and now that you are looking to avenge his death, I shall fight with you."

The left and right flanks of the armies went forward, and the sun and moon were dimmed by dust. The armies clashed, and a river of blood flowed across the ground. Qaren's forces prevailed over Viseh's, and Viseh turned back from the battle. Many of his men were killed when he fled, but Qaren did not pursue him. Viseh made his way back to Afrasyab, weeping for his son's death.

Shamasas Attacks Zavolestan

The Armani leader whom Afrasyab had sent against Zavolestan was Shamasas. He and Khazbaran led thirty thousand warlike troops across the Oxus and marched with their swords and maces as far as the River Hirmand.

At this time Zal was in mourning and building a tomb for his father, and Mehrab was diligently carrying out the functions of government for him. He sent a envoy to Shamasas with a message: "May the commander of Turan's army wear the crown of sovereignty forever. I am descended from the Arab king Zahhak, and I have no great love for Zal's rule. I allied myself with his family because I had no choice, in order to preserve my life. Now this castle is the center of my power, and all Zavolestan is in my hands. Zal is in mourning for his father, and my heart is cheered by his grief; I would be happy if I never saw his face again. Give me time, and let me send a messenger to Afrasyab, so that he can know the secrets of my heart, and in this way silence those who speak against me. I shall send him appropriate gifts, whatever is fitting for a king, and if he orders me to appear before him I shall stand before his throne ready to serve him. I shall hand over my sovereignty to him, and my heart will be content with his approval. I shall send him the wealth I have accumulated and cause no trouble for his warriors."

In this way he snared the Turanian warriors' hearts, while at the same time he sought for a way to escape from the threat they presented. He sent an envoy to Zal, saying, "Fly as quickly as a bird, open your wings; tell Zal what you have seen and tell him to lose no time in getting here. Say that two champions like leopards have come here from Turan to make war on us. Their army is encamped on the banks of the Hirmand, and so far the gold I have bribed them with has tangled their feet and impeded their progress. But if you delay in your response, our enemies will achieve what they desire."

Zal Comes to Mehrab

The envoy reached Zal, whose heart flared up like fire at the news. He set off with his army to join Mehrab, and when he saw Mehrab and considered how prudently he had acted, he said to himself, "Why should I fear Turan's army? What's this Khazbaran to me? No more than a fistful of dirt." He said to Mehrab, "You have acted wisely, and I applaud all you've done. Now, in the darkness of the night, I shall go and show them what I'm capable of. They will know soon enough that I have returned, and that my heart longs to fight against them."

Zal slung a bow over his shoulder, and each of the arrows he took was as massive as the bough of a tree. He spied out the enemy encampment and then shot the arrows into three different areas of the camp. Uproar ensued, and when night turned to day, the troops gathered round the arrows.

> They said, "These arrows must be Zal's, since no
> Brute force but his could match them to the bow."

Shamasas said, "Khazbaran, if you had not been so eager for wealth, there would be no Mehrab left by now, no army, no more treasure to plunder, and no Zal to terrify you like this." Khazbaran replied, "He is one man, he's not Ahriman, and he's not made of iron; don't worry about fighting with him, I'll deal with him when I find him."

When the shining sun began to climb in the sky, the din of drums rang out on the plain; within the city could be heard drums and trumpets, as well as the clashing of cymbals and Indian chimes. Zal led his men onto the plain, together with their tents and elephants; rank upon rank gathered there, and from a distance the dust sent up made the plain look like a black mountain. Khazbaran, armed with his mace and shield, attacked Zal, swinging his mace against Zal's chest. His breastplate shattered, Zal turned back, and the warriors from Kabol followed him. He donned new armor and returned to the fray like a lion; his father's mace was in his hand, his head was filled with fury, and blood welled in his heart. He brought his ox-headed mace down on Khazbaran's head, and the ground was spotted with his blood like a leopard's hide. Zal flung him down and left him sprawled lifeless, then went onto the plain between the two armies. He called for Shamasas: "Come out and fight; the man who daren't come out has no heart for a fight." But when Shamasas saw Zal's mace he hid himself away among his troops. In the dust of battle Zal came on Golbad encased in armor; he fitted an arrow to his bow and it struck Golbad's waist, piercing his body armor, and pinning Golbad to his saddle. The army watched in horror, and Shamasas in particular lost heart, and his face turned sallow. Shamasas and his troops fled in disorder, and Zal and Mehrab came after them in hot pursuit. So many men were killed that it seemed there was no earth left for the soldiers to tread upon, and the Turkish troops flung down their armor and fled toward their king.

When Shamasas reached the desert, Qaren, Kaveh's son, appeared in the distance; he was returning from his encounter with the troops of Viseh, whose son he had killed with such contempt. Qaren realized who he was facing and why they had come to Zavolestan. He had the trumpets sounded, and the two armies came face to face. Dust obscured the sun as many of Shamasas's men were wounded and others taken prisoner. Shamasas escaped with a few men, fleeing from the dust of battle.

Afrasyab learned of the death of his chieftains; his heart filled with the fire of grief and his cheeks were stained with tears. He sprang up in anger and said, "Where is Nozar? Viseh can take his revenge on him." When Nozar heard this, he knew that his days were numbered. A group of soldiers came gossiping and shouting to find him and dragged him with his arms bound in front of Afraysab. As soon as he saw Nozar approaching, Afraysab thought of his ancestors and of his desire to avenge their humiliation. He said to Nozar, "You deserve whatever evil comes to you," and called for a sword. He severed King Nozar's head with a blow to his neck and flung his lifeless body to the ground. So perished Manuchehr's heir, and the throne of Iran remained empty.

The captives were dragged in, and they pleaded for their lives. Aghriras came forward to intervene on their behalf and began to argue with Afrasyab. He said, "To kill so many unarmed captives is not a noble act but a base one. It would be better if they were not harmed; hand them over in chains to me, and I'll imprison them in a cave and have them well guarded. They will die wretchedly there, but you should not shed their blood." Afrasyab responded to his brother's request and handed the prisoners over to him; they were taken weeping and wailing to Sari.

Afrasyab's Rule in Persia

Afrasyab made all speed from Dehestan to Rey, his horses sweating with exhaustion. There he placed the Kayanid crown on his head and held open court, distributing gold coins.

Gostahm and Tus received news that the glory of the imperial crown had dimmed, and that the king's head had been severed with a sharp sword. They tore out their hair and clawed at their faces, and lamentation was heard throughout Iran. These chieftains' heads were smeared with dust, their eyes were filled with tears, and their clothes torn. They made for Zavolestan, speaking of the king, and longing for him in their souls. They went mourning to Zal, and said:

> *"Alas for Nozar and his bravery,*
> *His might, his crown, his magnanimity;*
> *Protector of Iran, prop of the state,*
> *King of the world, most glorious of the great,*
> *Scion of Feraydun, of unmatched worth,*
> *Whose horses' hooves subdued the willing earth;*
> *We'll dip our swords in poison and avenge*
> *His unjust death, relentless in revenge.*
> *The heavens weep to see our wretched fate,*
> *And you must put aside your robes of state*
> *To mourn beside us, to lament and keep*
> *This vigil with us while we grieve and weep."*

The whole company joined them in their weeping, groaning as if they were burning in fire. Then Zal said, "Until the Day of Judgment my sword shall not see its scabbard; my horse beneath me will be my throne, my feet will be nowhere but in the stirrups, and my crown will be my helmet. I shall not sleep or rest until I have taken my revenge; the rivers flow with less water than my eyes flow with tears. May the king's soul be resplendent among his glorious peers, and may you comfort yourselves with the knowledge of God's justice, so that your hearts find peace. We are all born for death; we belong to death, and we have given our heads into its keeping."

News reached the Persian captives in Sari that Zal and his companions were preparing an attack. They were disturbed by this, and in their anxiety they could not eat or sleep. They were afraid of what Afrasyab would do and they sent a message to Aghriras, saying: "You are a great lord, famed for your goodness, and we live only because of your words: we are all your slaves. You know that in Zavolestan Zal reigns and that the king of Kabol is with him there, together with other warriors like Barzin, Qaren, Kherdad, and Keshvad, the destroyer of armies. These are great heroes who will not hesitate to use their strength in Persia's defense, and when they ride out to war they can pierce a man's eye with a lance thrust. Afrasyab will be infuriated by their attacks, and he will turn his anger on his prisoners. For the sake of his crown he will have all our heads roll in the dust, even though we are innocent of any crime. If Aghriras will agree to set us free, we shall scatter throughout the world, and we shall praise him before chieftains and nobles, and pray that God protect him."

The wise Aghriras replied, "I cannot do this. My enmity toward the king will be plain, and that Ahriman will be enraged with me. But I shall try to help you in another way, one which will not provoke my brother. If Zal attacks, when he comes close to Sari I shall hand you over to him, and then evacuate Amol without fighting, and so bring shame on my head." The Persian nobles bowed their faces to the ground, and when they had expressed their gratitude to him, they sent an envoy from Sari with a message for Zal. The message said, "God has been merciful to us; the wise Aghriras has become our ally. He swears that if two men come here as Zal's representatives from Iran he will not fight, but evacuate the area around Amol and lead his army to Rey; if this isn't done, not one of us will escape from the claws of that dragon

Afrasyab." When the message was read to Zal, he said, "Now, my war-like leopards, which of you whose heart is blackened by war will under-take this mission and so raise his head to the sun?" Keshvad slapped his hand to his chest and said, "I am prepared to do this." Zal called down blessings on him and said, "May you live happily for as long as the sun and moon exist."

An army set off from Zavolestan to Amol, and news of this reached Aghriras, who had the brazen trumpets blown and led his men toward Rey, leaving all the prisoners in Sari. When Keshvad reached Sari he freed them, and gave each of them a horse, and the group set off on its journey from Amol to Zavolestan. At the news of Keshvad's return in triumph, Zal distributed money to the poor and gave the messenger one of his own robes. Zal went out to welcome Keshvad, as was appropriate, and wept over the captives who had escaped from the lion's clutches. He brought them into the city with great honor and had palaces allotted to them, so that they lived again as they had done under Nozar, with their own wealth, thrones, and crowns.

Aghriras Is Killed by His Brother

When Aghriras arrived in Rey from Amol, Afrasyab learned what he had done and said to him, "What do you think you are up to, mixing honey and bitter colocynth like this? I told you to kill them, and that this was no time for caution or high-mindedness. It's not for a warrior to worry about wisdom, that's not what brings him glory in battle; a fighting spirit and wisdom have nothing to do with each other." Aghriras replied, "A little shame and a sense of honor are not out of place; whenever you think of acting evilly, fear God and do no harm to anyone. The crown and royal belt have seen many like you, but they stay in no one's possession for long." The king sprang up like a mad-dened elephant, and for an answer drew his sword. And then this faith-less fool slashed his brother in two with a blow to the waist.

Zal heard about what had happened to Aghriras and said, "His good fortune grows dim, and his throne desolate." He had the brazen trumpets blown, and drums strapped onto his war elephants, and he drew up his army that glittered as splendidly as a rooster's eye. He led his men toward Pars, seething with anger as he marched. From sea to sea the plains were filled with men, and the faces of the sun and moon were obscured by dust. When Afrasyab learned that Zal had mobilized his forces, he prepared for the defense of Rey. The advance troops of the two armies fought day and night, and many warriors and chieftains were killed on both sides.

One night Zal talked at length about Afrasyab, and his own warriors' battles and those of his allies. Then he said, "If a king is to be fortunate and his soul to be luminous, he must be of royal lineage, and also he must be someone who is aware of tradition and the past. The army is like a ship, and the king on his throne is both the wind and the ship's pilot. Although both Gostahm and Tus are fine warriors, neither is worthy of the crown and throne; we need a king who is fortunate, who is endowed with the divine *farr,* and with wisdom." They searched among Feraydun's descendants for someone who would be worthy of the throne. They could find no one but Zav, the son of Tahmasp, to renew the glories of Feraydun's crown. Qaren, together with priests and the lords of the marches, took the good news to him that he would inherit the crown, since Zal and all the army wished him to be king. Zav accepted their choice and took his place on the throne.

The Reign of Zav, the Son of Tahmasp

Zav ascended the throne on an auspicious day, and Zal swore loyalty to him. An old man in his eightieth year, Zav reigned for only five years. In that time he made the world young again with his justice and goodness; he stopped the army from committing crimes and prevented them from arbitrarily arresting people and killing them, and he communicated in his heart with God.

At that time the world was suffering from a famine; the ground was desiccated and the plants withered, no winds blew, no rain fell from the heavens, and bread was worth its weight in gold. For eight months the two armies faced one another but did not fight, because their strength had been broken by the famine. People said to one another, "It is our fault that this evil has fallen on us from the heavens." From both armies cries of hunger could be heard, and a messenger from Afrasyab came to Zav saying, "Our fate in this fleeting world is nothing but pain and grief. Let us divide our lands and invoke God's blessings on one another. Our nobles are exhausted by war, and this famine means we must not delay in making peace." They swore that they would not harbor hatred for one another in their hearts, that they would divide their lands justly and according to precedent, and that they would bear no grudge against one another for the past. Beyond the Oxus, and into China and Khotan, was to belong to Afraysab, and Zav and Zal had no power beyond the border where the Turks' tents were pitched; for their part the Turks would not advance into Iran. Although Zav was an old man, the world was renewed under his rule; he led his army to Pars, and Zal returned to Zavolestan.

Then the mountain tops echoed with thunder; the world flourished again with the colors and scents of flowers, and the land filled with streams, gardens, and flowing water. The earth was as lovely as a young bride, because when men do not have tigerish natures she is not harsh and grudging to them. Zav called his nobility together to give thanks to God, saying, "Abundance has replaced famine, and God held the keys to this change." Everywhere festivities were held, and men emptied their hearts of all anger and enmity. So five years passed without suffering, but when Zav reached the age of eighty-six, his sun-like face faded; this kind, just man died, and the good fortunes of Iran faded.

Afrasyab Learns of Zav's Death

Afrasyab evacuated Rey and crossed the Oxus. But Pashang, whose heart was filled with hatred and his head with thoughts of war, sent him no greetings. Afrasyab dispatched a messenger to him, but for months, for a year, Pashang would not receive him. Pashang's heart was sated with the throne and crown, he felt like a rusted sword, and he grieved for the death of Aghriras. He sent an envoy to Afrasyab saying, "You should have been a friend to Aghriras, but you shed your brother's blood and fled from that savage brought up by a bird. I want no more to do with you, and you will never see me again."

Time passed, and the tree of calamities bore bitter fruit. Information reached the Turks that Zav had died and that the Persian throne was empty. All the world's ears were filled with the news, "The imperial throne lies idle." Pashang sent Afrasyab a letter saying, "Cross the Oxus and lead an army into Persia; do not wait until someone occupies their throne. I am sending you into war against our enemy; so far it is only your brother whom you've harmed." Afrasyab mustered troops and led them from the plain of Sepinjab to the Oxus, and the earth seemed like a heaven raining down Indian swords. When news reached Iran that Afrasyab claimed the throne, the Persians turned to

Zal and addressed him harshly: "Gaining control of the world was an easy matter for you, then? Since Sam died and you have been our champion, we have not known one day of happiness. An army has crossed the Oxus and is bearing down on us, obscuring the sun with the dust it sends up. If you have a solution to this crisis, put it into effect, because the Turkish leader will be here soon enough." Zal said to the nobles, "Since I have bound on my belt to fight, no horseman like me has ever sat in the saddle; no one can wield my sword or mace, and I have fought night and day. I have feared nothing but old age, and now that my back is bent and I cannot flourish my Kaboli dagger as I once did, Rostam has grown to be like a tall cypress and deserves the diadem of greatness. He needs a war horse, and none of our Arab horses are equal to the task. We must find him a mammoth mount, and I will inquire everywhere for one. I shall ask Rostam if he agrees to my plan and remind him that he was born to fight against the seed of Zadsham. I shall see if he is ready for the task." All the cities of Iran rejoiced to hear his words; Zal sent out messengers in every direction, and had armor manufactured for his horsemen.

ROSTAM AND HIS HORSE RAKHSH

Rostam Chooses a Horse

> Zal said to Rostam, "You have grown so tall,
> Your cypress body towers above us all.
> The work that lies ahead of us will keep
> Our restless spirits from their food and sleep;
> You're still a boy, not old enough to fight,
> Your heart still looks for pleasure and delight,
> Your mouth still smells of milk, how can I ask
> You to take on this seasoned warrior's task,
> To fight with lion warriors, and beat
> Them back until they scatter in defeat?
> What do you say to this? What will you do?
> May health and greatness always partner you!"
> And Rostam answered Zal: "Pleasure and wine,
> Feasting and rest, are no concern of mine—
> Hard-pressed in war, or on the battlefield,
> With God to aid me, I shall never yield.
> I need to capture with my noose a horse
> Of mountain size and weight, of mammoth force,
> I need a crag-like mace if I'm to stand
> Against Turan, defending Persia's land.
> I'll crush their heads with this tremendous mace
> And none shall dare oppose me face to face—
> Its weight will break an elephant, one blow
> From it will make a bloody river flow."

Zal was so moved by his son's words that his soul seemed about to leave his body.

Rostam Chooses Rakhsh

Zal had all the herds of horses that were in Zavolestan, as well as some from Kabol, driven before Rostam, and the herdsmen explained to him the royal brands that they bore. Whenever Rostam selected a horse, as soon as he pressed down on it, the horse's back would buckle beneath his strength, so that its belly touched the ground. But then a herd of horses of varying colors from Kabol was driven past him, and a gray mare galloped by; she had a chest like a lion's, and was short-legged; her ears were pricked like glittering daggers, her fore and hindquarters were plump, and she was narrow-waisted. Behind her came a foal, of the same height and breadth of chest and rump as his mother, black eyed and holding his tail high, with black testicles, and iron hooves.

> *His body was a wonder to behold,*
> *Like saffron petals, mottled red and gold.*

Rostam watched the mare go by, and when he saw the mammoth-bodied foal he looped his lariat, and said, "Keep that foal back from the herd." The old herdsman who had brought the horses said, "My lord, you can't take other people's horses." Rostam asked who owned the horse, since its rump bore no trace of any brand. The herdsman said, "Don't look for a brand, but there are many tales told about this horse. No one knows who owns him; we call him 'Rostam's Rakhsh', and that's all I know. He's been ready to be saddled for three years now, and a number of nobles have chosen him; but whenever his mother sees a horseman's lariat she attacks like a lioness." Rostam flung his royal lariat, and quickly caught the horse's head in its noose; the mother came forward like a raging lioness, as if she wanted to bite his head off. But Rostam roared like a lion, and the sound of his voice stopped the mare in her tracks. She stumbled, then scrambled up again and turned, and galloped off to join the rest of the herd. Rostam tightened the noose and pulled the foal toward himself; he pushed down with all his hero's strength on the foal's back, but the back did not give at all, and it was as if the foal was unaware of Rostam's hand. Rostam said to himself, "This will be my mount; now I can set to work. He will be able to bear the weight of my armor, helmet, and mace, and my mammoth body." He asked the herdsman, "Who knows the price of this dragon?" The herdsman replied, "If you are Rostam, then mount him and defend the land of Iran. The price of this horse is Iran itself, and mounted on his back you will be the world's savior." Rostam's coral lips smiled, and he said, "It is God who does such good works."

He set a saddle on Rakhsh, and his head whirled with thoughts of war and vengeance. He opened Rakhsh's mouth and saw that he was a swift, strong, courageous horse. Each night Rostam burned wild rue before him to ward off evil; from every side Rakhsh seemed to be a magical creature, swift in battle, with large haunches, alert and foaming at the mouth.

> *Rakhsh and his noble rider seemed to bring*
> *To Zal's reviving heart the joy of spring.*

Zal opened the doors to his treasury and distributed gold coins, careless of today and tomorrow.

ROSTAM AND KAY QOBAD

Zal Leads His Army Against Afrasyab

Then from the back of an elephant he threw a pebble in a goblet as a sign to mount and gave a shout that could be heard for miles. The din of drums and blare of bugles mingled with the sounds of Indian bells and the trumpeting of elephants: the Day of Judgment seemed to have come to Zavolestan, as if the earth were crying out to its dead, "Rise." Rostam led the army, followed by the land's experienced warriors; it was spring time as they set out, and the world was filled with blossoms and flowers.

Afrasyab learned of Zal's approach, and from then on he could neither rest nor eat in his anxiety. He led his army toward the river at Rey, where the marshy reed beds are. The Persian army left the desert and made for the battlefield, until only two parasangs separated the two sides. Zal called a council of his experienced advisors and said to them: "You have seen the world and are wise in its ways; we have drawn up our army here and hope for a favorable outcome. But we are not of one mind as we were, and this is because the throne lacks a king; everything is unsure now, and the army has no leader. We need someone of royal lineage to take his place on the throne and bind on the belt of authority. A priest has told me of such a king, one who possesses the royal *farr*, and whose good fortune is still young. This is Kay Qobad, who is descended from Feraydun; he is an imposing man, wise, and just." Then Zal turned to Rostam and said, "Take your mace now and throw back your shoulders; choose a group of companions and ride quickly to the Alborz mountains. Greet Kay Qobad respectfully but do not delay your return; you must be back here in two weeks, so do not rest for any reason along the way. Say to him, 'The army is asking for you, and it has prepared the royal throne in your honor.'" Quick as the wind, Rostam

bound on his belt and set off to fetch Kay Qobad. He brought him to
Zal during the night, saying not a word to anyone about his arrival, and
Zal sat with him and his advisors for a week, discussing what should be
done.

The Reign of Kay Qobad

On the eighth day the ivory throne was made ready, and the royal
crown suspended above it. Kay Qobad seated himself there and placed
the jeweled crown on his head. The chieftains were gathered—men
like Zal and warlike Qaren, Kherdad, Keshvad and Barzin—and they
scattered jewels over the newly crowned king. He listened to what they
had to say about Afrasyab and reviewed his troops. On the following
day the noise of preparations was heard from the royal pavilion, and
Qobad led his army out. Rostam put on his armor, and the dust he
raised made him seem like a maddened elephant. The ranks of the
Persian army marched to war, ready for bloodshed: one wing was led
by Mehrab, the king of Kabol, and the other by Gazhdahom. Qaren
was in the center, together with Keshvad, the breaker of armies. Zal
followed them, with Kay Qobad, and it was as if there were fire on the
one side of him, wind on the other. In front of the troops the Kaviani
banner fluttered, dyeing the world scarlet, yellow, and purple, like a
ship lifted on a wave above the Sea of China. The plains and moun-
tain slopes were a mass of shields, and swords glittered like torches;
from end to end the world was like a sea of pitch over which twinkled
a hundred thousand candles. You would think the sun would lose its
way, with the squeal of the trumpets and din of the army.

Rostam's Combat with Afrasyab

Once battle was joined, Qaren was involved in every charge, some-
times riding to the left, sometimes to the right, everywhere eager for
bloodshed. When Rostam saw how he fought, he went to his father
and said, "Tell me what position the evil Afrasyab keeps during battle.
What does he wear? Where does his banner flutter above the troops?
Is that shining purple banner his? I will grasp him by the belt today and
drag him down from his saddle." Zal answered, "Listen to me, my son,
look after yourself today; that Turk is a fire-breathing dragon in com-
bat, a cloud that rains down disaster. His banner is black, as is his
armor; his arms are encased in iron, and his helmet is of iron. All the

surface of his iron armor is chased with gold, and his black banner is
affixed to his helmet. Keep yourself safe from him, because he is a
brave man, and fortune favors him with victory." Rostam said, "Don't

trouble your soul about me; the world's creator is my ally, and my
heart, my sword, and my arm are my refuge."

Then as the trumpets sounded Rostam urged his brazen-hoofed
Rakhsh forward, and when Afrasyab caught sight of him he paused in
wonder at this immature youth. He said to his warriors, "Who is that
dragon who has escaped from his bonds? Who is he? I don't know his
name." One of his men replied, "That is Zal's son. Can't you see that

he has come here with Sam's mace? He's young, and eager to win a name for himself." Like a vessel lifted high on a wave, Afrasyab went ahead of his army, and when Rostam saw him he gripped his thighs against Rakhsh and lifted his heavy mace to his shoulders. As he drew level with Afrasyab he brought his mace crashing down on the king's saddle, then reached out and grasped at his belt, lifting him from his leopard-skin saddle. He wanted to take him back to Qobad, as a trophy from his first day of battle, but his strength and the weight of Afrasyab between them were too much for the belt, which split, so that Afrasyab's head lay in the dirt, and his cavalry quickly gathered about him and hid him in the dust they sent up. When the king slipped out of his grasp like this, Rostam bit the back of his hand in anger. "Why," he said, "didn't I tuck him under my arm, instead of hanging on to his belt?"

Bells rang out from the elephants' backs, and the din of drums could be heard for miles, when they brought the good news to Qobad, that Rostam had broken the center of the Turks' army. They said, "When Rostam reached the Turkish king, his black banner disappeared; Rostam grasped him by his belt and flung him down to the ground, so that a cry of consternation went up from the Turks." Qobad sprang to his feet, and his army surged forward like a sea whipped up by the wind. Everywhere was the sound of weapons clashing, the glitter of daggers, the shock of wood against armor. Protected by their golden helmets and golden shields, men's heads became dazed by the shock and din of blows. It was as if a cloud had rained vermillion down by magic, staining the earth with red dye. One thousand one hundred and sixty brave warriors were killed at a stroke, and the Turks fled before the Persians, retreating to Damghan; from there they made their way to the Oxus, sick at heart and weary, filled with rumors and reproaches, their armor shattered and their belts loosened, unheralded by trumpets or drums, bereft of their strength.

Afrasyab Sees His Father

From the river bank Afrasyab went to his father in despair, his tongue filled with words. He said, "Exalted king, you sinned when you looked for vengeance in this way. First, no one in the past ever saw great kings break their word. And Iraj's seed has not been eradicated from the land, and no antidote has been found for this poison. When one goes, another takes his place, and the world will not remain without a leader. Qobad has come forward and placed the crown on his head, and has opened up a new way to warfare. And a horseman has appeared of Sam's race; Zal named him Rostam. He came forward like a hideous monster, and the ground seemed scorched by his breath. He attacked everywhere, striking with his sword and mace; the air was filled with the sound of his mace's blows, and my soul was not worth a fistful of dirt before his might. He shattered our army, and no one in the world had ever seen such a wonder. He caught sight of my banner and brought his mace down on my leopard-skin saddle; then he grasped at my belt and lifted me up as if I weighed no more than a mosquito. My belt split, and I fell from his grasp on the ground, and my men dragged me away from him. I see no alternative to making peace, because your army cannot withstand his onslaught. The lands which Feraydun bestowed on Tur have been given to me, and you should renounce this ancient longing for revenge. You know that being told about something is not the same as seeing it; something is always lacking when you only hear about a subject. War with Iran seemed like a game to you, but this has proven to be a hard game for your army to play. Consider how many golden helmets and golden shields, how many Arab horses with golden bridles, how many Indian swords with golden scabbards, and how many famous warriors Qobad has ruined. And worse than this, your name and reputation, which can never be restored, have been destroyed. Don't think of past resentments, try to be reconciled with Kay Qobad. If you decide on any other course of action, armies will converge on you from four directions; from one side Rostam, a blazing sun against whom there is no defense, will attack; from another Qaren, who has never looked on defeat; from a third Keshvad, with his golden diadem, who has attacked Amol; and from a fourth Mehrab, the lord of Kabol, who leads Zal's armies."

Pashang Sues for Peace

The king of the Turks' eyes filled with tears as he listened in silence to Afrasyab's words. He told a scribe to bring paper and ink made from musk; the calligraphy of the letter this man wrote was so beautiful that it was worthy of a master, and it was decorated with colors and images. Pashang dictated: "In the name of the lord of the sun and moon, who has bestowed authority on us; may his blessings be on the soul of

Feraydun, who is the warp and weft of our ancestry. If, in his ambition for the crown and throne, Tur acted evilly toward the Iraj, and there is much to be said about this, their quarrel must now be put to rest. Manuchehr has taken revenge for what happened to Iraj, and Feraydun showed us the true way when he divided the lands into separate realms. We should commit our hearts to this division and not ignore the customs and wisdom of our ancestors. At that time Tur's imperial tents were pitched in Transoxiana, and the River Oxus marked the border. Iraj did not covet this area; he was given the land of Persia by Feraydun. If we break this agreement and go to war, we make life hard for ourselves, we wound ourselves with our own swords, and provoke God's wrath, so that we shall inherit nothing, neither in this world nor the world to come. We should respect the division that Feraydun made between Salm, Tur, and Iraj, and renounce all thoughts of vengeance, for these lands are not worth the disasters we have brought on ourselves. Our heads have grown as white as snow, and the ground has been dyed vermilion with Kayanid blood, but in the end a man owns only the earth in which he lies; five cubits of ground are all we inherit, linen covers us, and we lie in the grave. Ambition's door leads to sorrow and suffering, and our hearts remain heavy while we live in the fleeting world. If Kay Qobad will accept our terms, if his wise mind will incline to justice, none of our men will think even in their dreams of crossing the Oxus, and the Persians will not come here, except to bring greetings and a message of peace; in this way our two countries will live prosperously and happily."

The king sealed the letter and dispatched a detachment of men to take it to Kay Qobad. The messengers handed over the letter, and also spoke at length. Kay Qobad answered, "We did not attack first. It was Tur who committed the first crime by destroying Iraj, and in our own time Afrasyab crossed the Oxus and invaded Iran. You have heard what he did to King Nozar, so that even the beasts of the field grieved for him. And the way he acted with the wise Aghriras was not worthy of a chivalrous man. If you regret these evil acts, and will renew our treaties, I harbor no ambitions or desire for revenge, since I am prepared to leave this fleeting world. I grant you your side of the Oxus, in the hopes that Afrasyab will be content with this." And he wrote out a new treaty, planting a tree in the garden of greatness.

But Rostam said to him, "Your majesty, do not look for reconciliation in place of war; peace is not what they deserve; let them see what I can do with my mace in their land." The king replied, "I have never seen anything better than justice: Pashang is Feraydun's grandson, and he and his son have had enough of warfare. A wise man should not seek to be underhanded or unjust. I have written a charter on silk granting you suzerainty over Zavolestan, as far as the Sea of Sind. May you wear the crown and sit on the throne there, illuminating the world. Give Kabol to Mehrab, but keep your spear points dipped in poison, for wherever there is a kingdom, there is warfare, however great the realm may be." He placed a golden crown on Rostam's head and a golden belt about his waist, as a sign that he gave these territories into his keeping. Rostam kissed the ground before him. Then Qobad said, "May the throne never be without Zal; the world is not worth one of his hairs, and he serves to remind us of the great men of the past." He sent Zal clothes of royal cloth of gold, and a belt and crown set with rubies and turquoises. On five elephants they placed howdahs set with turquoises that glittered more splendidly than the waters of the Nile, and draped the howdahs in cloth of gold. Qobad sent Zal treasures the like of which no man had ever seen, with the message, "I wished to send you a more splendid present, and if I live a long life I will see that you want for nothing in this world." He distributed suitable gifts to Qaren, Keshvad, Barzin, Kherrad, and Pulad, and these included gold and silver coins, swords, shields, crowns, and belts.

Kay Qobad Travels to Estakhr in Pars

Then he set out for Pars, where the key to all his treasures lay. His palace was at Estakhr, where the Kayanid kings ruled in glory. The world paid him homage as he ascended the throne, ruling with wisdom and splendor and according to custom. He said to his nobles, "From end to end the world is mine, and if an elephant fights with a mosquito, this is a breach of justice and faith. I want nothing but righteousness in the world, because to provoke God's anger will bring want to our land. Ease comes from effort, and wherever there is water and earth, there is my treasure. The cities and armies are mine, and my kingdom depends on the army. Live safely, protected by the lord of the world; be wise and live at peace. May those who have wealth enjoy it and share it, and be grateful to me that I enable them to do this. And whoever is hungry and cannot feed himself by his labor, my court will be his pasture, and

I will welcome all who come to me." Then he remembered the example of past heroes and made the world flourish with his justice and generosity.

In this way he lived at peace for a hundred years; what kings have there been in the world who can compare with him? He had four wise sons: the first was Kay Kavus, the second Kay Arash, the third Kay Pashin, and the fourth Ashkas. When he had reigned for a hundred years, his strength began to wane; he knew that death was near and that the green leaves of his life had withered. He summoned Kavus and spoke to him of justice and generosity. He said, "I am ready for my last journey. Lower my coffin into the ground and take your place on the throne, this throne that passes from us before we know, and whose servants are without wisdom: I feel I am still that man who came so happily with his companions from the Alborz mountains. If you rule justly and righteously, you will be on a journey to the heavens; and if greed and ambition snare your mind, you will be unsheathing a dark sword that will be used against you."

He finished speaking, and then departed from the splendid world, exchanging his palace for a coffin. This is the world's way, which raises us from the dust and disperses us on the wind.

KAY KAVUS'S WAR AGAINST THE DEMONS OF MAZANDERAN

The Reign of Kay Kavus

If a noble tree grows tall and is then damaged in some way, its leaves wither, its roots weaken, and its summit begins to droop; and if it snaps, it must give way to a new shoot that, when spring comes, will bud and blossom like a shining lamp. If a sickly branch grows from a good root, you should not curse the root for this. In the same way, when a father cedes his place to his son and acquaints him with the secrets of life, if the son then brings shame on his father's name and glory, then call him a stranger, not a son. If he slights his father's example, he deserves to suffer at the hands of fate. This is the way of the ancient world, and you cannot tell what will grow from a given root.

When Kavus took his father's place, all the world was his slave. He saw that he owned treasures of all kinds, and that the earth was his to command: the throne was his, the royal torque and earrings, the golden crown set with emeralds, and Arab horses with streaming manes, and he considered no one in the world to be his equal.

One day he was in a pleasure garden, seated on a golden throne with crystal feet, drinking wine with the Persian chieftains and talking of this and that. A musician, who was in reality a demon, came asking for audience with the king. He said, "I'm renowned in Mazanderan for my sweet voice; if I'm worthy to appear before the king, let me approach his throne." The chamberlain went behind the curtain and said to the king, "There is a musician at the gate with a lute; he sings very sweetly." Kavus gave orders to admit him, and they sat him down with his instrument. He began to sing:

> "My country is Mazanderan—may she
> Abide forever in prosperity;

Her gardens bloom with roses all year long,
Wild hyacinths, a myriad tulips throng
Her mountain slopes; her climate's sweet and clear,
Not hot, not cold, but springtime all the year;
Her perfumed air revives the soul—it seems
Rose water rushes in her mountain streams;
In every month wild tulips can be seen
Dotting the hillsides' and the meadows' green;
Her serving girls are lovely to behold,
And there's good hunting there, and wealth, and gold."

While Kavus was listening to this song, he conceived the idea of conquering Mazanderan with his army. He said to his warriors, "We have spent our time feasting, and while a brave man idles his time away, weak enemies grow strong. My throne is greater than that of Jamshid or Zahhak or Kay Qobad, and my justice is greater than theirs. I should be greater than them in my accomplishments as well; a king should be ambitious to conquer the world." When the nobles heard what he had to say, none of them approved. They frowned, and their faces turned sallow; none of them had any desire to make war on demons. No one said anything openly, but they sighed in silence. Tus, Gudarz, Keshvad, Giv, Kherrad, Gorgin and Bahram said, "We are your slaves and tread the earth at your command." But later they sat together and discussed the king's words: "What kind of a calamity is this? If what the king said in his cups isn't forgotten, we and Iran are facing a disaster. There will be no country, water, or land left to us. Even Jamshid, with his crown and his seal ring by which he had birds and demons under his command, never thought of fighting against the demons of Mazanderan. And Feraydun, who had such knowledge and was skilled in magic, never considered this as a possibility." Then Tus said, "Brave lords, experienced in battle, there is one solution, and it should not be hard to achieve what we desire. We must send a messenger to Zal saying, 'Come immediately; if your head is smeared with mud, do not stop to wash it clean.' He should be able to give the king wise advice, to tell him that it's Ahriman who has put this idea in his mind, and that one should never open doors behind which demons wait. It may be that Zal can make him change his mind; if he cannot, then our fortunes, good and bad, are at an end."

After they had discussed the matter at length, they dispatched a courier. He made good speed, and when he reached Zal he passed on his message: "The nobles send greetings to Zal, the son of Sam. A strange event has happened, and our minds are unable to deal with it. If you are not prepared to help us, no one here will be left alive and our land will disappear. Ahriman has led our king astray; he has no intention of living as our ancestors did, he wastes the wealth he took no pains to accumulate, and he intends to attack Mazanderan. If you pause even long enough to scratch your head, the king will have left and thrown to the winds all the trouble you took in Kay Qobad's service. Evil thoughts have twisted the king's soul, so that everything that you and your lion cub Rostam have done seems so much wind to him."

Zal was deeply troubled to hear that the leaves of the royal tree had turned yellow in this way. He said, "Kavus is an arrogant man who has not experienced the heat and cold of this world. A king should be someone over whose head the sun and moon have passed for many years. He thinks nobles and commoners alike tremble before his sword, and it will be no surprise if he pays no attention to my advice. It will hurt me if he doesn't listen to me, but if I make light of this in my heart and forget my loyalty to the king, neither God, nor the king, nor Iran's heroes will approve of me. I will go to him and give him what advice I can. It will be best for him if he accepts it; but, if he insists on what he has decided, the roads are open, and Rostam will be there with the army."

Zal spent the long night deep in thought, and when the sun raised its crown above the horizon he set off with his chieftains to the king. News reached Tus, Gudarz, Giv, Bahram, Gorgin, and Roham that Zal was approaching Iran, and that his banner was now visible. The army's commanders went out to meet him, calling down blessings on him and conducting him to the court. Tus said to him, "We are grateful that you have decided to help Iran's nobles and are going to this trouble on our behalf. We all wish you well and are filled with respect for the glory of your crown." Zal replied, "When a man has lived for some years he remembers the advice of his elders, and this is why the heavens deal justly with him. We should not withhold our advice from Kavus, because he certainly needs it. If he ignores the wisdom of what we suggest, he will live to regret it." With one voice they replied, "We are yours to command, and consider no one else's advice to be of any value compared with yours."

The group entered the court, with Zal going ahead and the other nobles with their golden belts following him. When Zal saw Kavus sitting in state on the throne, he bent his arms submissively across his chest and lowered his head. He said, "Lord of the world, whose head is lifted higher than those of all other noblemen and chieftains, no one has seen a king like you occupying the throne, or a crown like yours, and the heavens have never heard of good fortune like yours. May all your years be filled with victory and prosperity, your heart always filled with knowledge, your head with wisdom." The king made much of him and sat Zal beside himself. He asked him about the difficulties of his journey, about news of the heroes of his land, and about Rostam. Zal said to the king, "May you live victoriously and happily; your good fortune makes all of them prosperous, and they rejoice proudly in your patronage." Then he began to speak respectfully of the matter at hand, and said, "The days pass over us, and the heavens revolve over the dark earth: Manuchehr has left this splendid world, leaving behind treasures and palaces, and we also remember Zav, Nozar, and Kay Qobad. These kings, with their great armies and commanders, never thought of attacking Mazanderan:

> It is a land of demons, wizardry,
> Smooth lies, and spells, and secret sorcery;
> If you attack them, you won't see again
> The gold you throw away there, or the men;
> No one has conquered them—no, not by stealth,
> Or by invasion, or corrupting wealth;
> Forget the conquest of Mazanderan,
> No king has ever thought of such a plan.
> These chieftains are your subjects, but like you
> They are the slaves of God in all they do.
> Don't shed their noble blood, or out of greed
> Plant in the ground ambition's evil seed,
> Because it grows into a tree whose roots
> And lofty branches nourish loathsome fruits."

Kavus replied, "I don't need your thoughts on this matter. I have more strength, glory, and wealth than Jamshid or Feraydun, and I have a greater army and more courage and treasure than Manuchehr or Kay Qobad, who never considered attacking Mazanderan. The world is ruled by my sharp sword; you drew your sword and conquered the earth, and why should I not show the world what I can do? They will submit to me or I shall force them to do so with the power of my sword; either I shall empty Mazanderan of inhabitants, or I shall impose heavy taxes on them. They are contemptible in my eyes, sorcerers and soldiers they are all alike, and you shall hear that the world has been cleared of them. Stay behind then with Rostam and be Persia's protector. The world's creator is my ally, and those demons' heads are my prey. If you will not help me in this war, at least do not tell me to reconsider my plans."

Zal could see no sense in the king's words and said, "You are the king and we are your slaves, and we spoke only out of our hearts' concern for you. Whether you speak justly or unjustly, we must breathe and walk according to your will. I have said the things I should say, the things that were in my heart. A man cannot draw death forth from his own body, or seel up the world's eyes with a needle, or escape from necessity by holding back from it; even the king cannot do these three things. May the shining world favor you, and may you never recall my advice; may you not regret your actions, and may your heart be wise and bright with faith."

Then Zal quickly bade the king farewell, his heart clouded with anxiety by this news of the king's departure. When he left the court, the sun and moon were dark before his eyes. Tus, Gudarz, Bahram, and Giv accompanied him. Giv said to Zal, "I hope God will guide Kavus, because if God does not, we may as well consider him lost. May greed and necessity and death be far from you, and your enemies be unable to harm you. Wherever we go we hear only praise of you, and after God Iran places her hopes in you. You made this hard, thankless journey for the sake of her heroes." One by one they embraced Zal as he set out on his return to Zavolestan. As soon as he had gone, Kavus gave orders that Tus and Gudarz should prepare the baggage train and lead the army toward Mazanderan.

Kavus Reaches Mazanderan

When night turned to day and the warriors set off for Mazanderan, Kavus entrusted Iran to Milad's keeping, giving him his seal ring and authority and the keys to his treasury. He said, "If enemies appear, then draw the sword of warfare; Rostam and Zal will be your refuge from any evil." On the next day the din of drums rang out, and Gudarz and Tus marched at the head of the army. Kavus accompanied them, lending luster to the army's march, and as the sun set he pitched his camp before Mount Aspruz. This place, where Kavus had decided to rest and sleep, was the home of monstrous demons; it was a place that even elephants feared. Kavus had cloth of gold draped over his throne, and the air was filled with a delicious scent of wine. All the chieftains sat before Kavus, and they spent the night with wine and companionable talk. At dawn they rose and came belted and helmeted before the king, who ordered Giv to take a thousand warriors with maces and to lead the way into Mazanderan. "Whoever you see," he said, "young or old, separate their souls from their bodies; burn any buildings you come across, turn the day into night, so that these demons will understand that the world is to be emptied of sorcery." Giv bound on his belt, left the king's presence, and selected a group of men from the army. He marched with them to the borders of Mazanderan, and there rained down swords and maces on the inhabitants. Neither men, nor women, nor children were spared by his sword; he burned and plundered the towns and brought poison instead of healing into the inhabitants' lives. He had come to a city that was like a paradise, filled with all manner of pleasure. In every street and building there were more than a thousand serving girls wearing torques and earrings, and even more whose faces were as radiant as the moon, wearing diadems; there was golden treasure scattered everywhere, with here gold coins and there jewels, and there were countless flocks of animals in the surrounding countryside. You would say that it was a veritable paradise. They took news to Kavus of the glory and splendor of this place, saying that Mazanderan was the partner of heaven, that all of this city was adorned like an idolater's temple with Chinese brocade and flowers, that the women there were like houris, and their faces were like the blossoms of the pomegranate tree.

The Iranians had been looting the area for a week before the news reached the king of Mazanderan, and his heart was filled with pain, his head with anxiety. One of the demons of his court was called Sanjeh, and his soul and body were lacerated by this news. The king said to him, "Go as the sun traverses the sky to the White Demon; tell him that a huge army led by the Iranian king Kavus has arrived here and is looting Mazanderan. Say that if he does not come to our aid, he will soon see no one left alive here." Sanjeh took the warlike king's message to the White Demon, who replied, "Do not despair of fate; I will come immediately with a mighty army and drive them out of Mazanderan."

When night came, a black cloud spread over the army, making the world as dark as an African's face. The earth seemed like a sea of pitch, from which all light had gone into hiding. There seemed to be a huge tent of smoke and pitch looming over them, and men's eyes were baffled by the darkness. When night had passed and day came, the eyes of half the men in the Persian army were darkened, and their leaders' heads were filled with fury against the king. Many men perished because of this; the army had never known such a disaster. The king was also blinded, and his actions brought evil on his army: their wealth was looted, and his soldiers led into captivity. In his misery Kavus said, "A sensible advisor is more valuable than treasure." The Persians suffered in this way for a week, and now none of their army was able to see. On the eighth day the White Demon roared:

> *"Kavus, you're like a willow, fruitless and afraid.*
> *And you once thought your army could invade*
> *Mazanderan, and that your strength is like*
> *A maddened mammoth's when you choose to strike!*
> *Since you have occupied the Persian throne,*
> *Wisdom's deserted you, good sense has flown.*
> *Here is the end of everything you sought,*
> *Here is the punishment for which you fought!"*

Then he chose twelve thousand demons armed with daggers and set them to guard the Persians, filling their chieftains' minds with grief. The demons fed them on a handful of bran, so that their days were filled with suffering, and took all the king's treasures, including his crown set with rubies and turquoises, and gave them to Mazanderan's army commander, Arzhang. The White Demon said to him, "Tell the king that he need talk no more about Ahriman; the Persian king and his army will never look on the bright sun and moon again. I have not killed them, but only so that they will know how pain differs from pleasure. They will die slowly, groaning in despair, and no one will pay any attention to their complaints." When Arzhang heard this message, he set off for the king of Mazanderan, taking the Persian warriors as prisoners and their treasures and horses with fine trappings as plunder.

King Kavus Sends Word to Zal of What Has Happened

Then, sick at heart, Kavus sent a warrior to go as quickly as a flying bird or wind-borne smoke to Zal and Rostam in Zavolestan, and to say to them, "Fortune has dealt me a heavy blow, and dust has dimmed my throne and crown. The turning heavens have given my wealth and my army of famous warriors, as splendid as roses in springtime, to the demons; the wind you said would come has borne everything away. Now my eyes are darkened and my fortunes are confused; my royal head is bowed with weariness: wounded, and in Ahriman's clutches, my wretched body gives up its soul. When I remember the advice you gave me, cold sighs rise up from within me. I did not act wisely, I did not follow your advice, and my lack of wisdom has brought disaster on me. If you do not come to my help now, all that we have gained will be lost."

The messenger told Zal all he knew and all he had seen and heard. Zal clawed at his skin in grief, but he said nothing, either to friends or to enemies. In his heart he saw clearly the evils that Kavus was suffering far away. He said to Rostam, "We must neither eat nor drink nor delight in our sovereignty, because the king of the world has been snared by Ahriman, and disaster has come to the Persian army. You must saddle Rakhsh and grasp your sword for vengeance. Fate has brought you up for this day. In this battle against Ahriman you must not rest or draw breath; cover your chest with your tiger skin, and drive all thoughts of sleep from your mind. What man who has seen your lance can feel easy in his soul? If you fight against the sea, it is turned to blood, and at the sound of your voice, mountains crumble to the plains; Arzhang and the White Demon must have no hope of escaping from you with their lives. Your heavy mace must smite the neck of the king of Mazanderan and shatter it to pieces."

Rostam replied, "The way is long, how shall I go without soldiers to accompany me?" Zal said, "There are two ways there from this kingdom, and both are filled with difficulties and dangers. One is the way that Kavus took; the other lies through the mountains and will take two weeks. You will meet with lions and demons and darkness, and your eyes will be bewildered by what they see. If you take the shorter way, you will come on monstrous things, and may God come to your aid then. It is a hard way, but set Rakhsh along it and you will survive its perils. In the dark night, until daybreak, I shall pray to God that I shall see your shoulders and chest again, and your sword and mace in your hand, and if God wills that a demon turn your days to darkness, can any man avert this from you? What comes to us must be endured. No one can stay in this world forever; and even if he remains here for a long time, he is finally summoned to another place. If a man leaves behind him a noble reputation, he should not despair when he has to depart."

Rostam replied to his father, "I have bound my belt on in readiness to obey you. The great warriors of the past did not choose to walk into hell, and those who were not tired of life did not choose to face ravening lions, but I am prepared for whatever I encounter and I ask for no ally but God. I shall sacrifice my body and soul for the king and smash these sorcerers and their talismans. I shall rescue the Persians who are still living, and I will leave neither Arzhang, nor the White Demon, nor Sanjeh, nor Kulad Ghandi, nor Bid, alive. I swear by the one God who has created the world, that Rostam will not dismount from Rakhsh until he has bound Arzhang's arms in a rock-like knot and placed a yoke on his shoulders, and Rakhsh has trampled Kulad's head and brains beneath his hooves." Zal embraced Rostam and invoked many blessings on his head, and Rostam, with his cheeks flushed and his heart firm in its resolve, mounted Rakhsh. Rudabeh came to her son, her face wet with tears, and Zal too wept bitterly over him. They bade him farewell, not knowing whether they would ever see him again. So passes the world, and a wise man knows of its passage, and with every day that goes by, your body becomes more free of the earth's evil.

THE SEVEN TRIALS OF ROSTAM

The First Trial: Rakhsh's Combat with a Lion

Rostam rode out from Sistan in high spirits, his face flushed with joy. By riding Rakhsh through the dark night as well as the bright day, he covered two days' journey in one. He became tired and hungry, and he saw a plain ahead of him filled with wild asses. He urged Rakhsh forward with his thighs, and the ass he fixed on was unable to outrun him; no animal could escape Rakhsh's speed and Rostam's lariat together. The lion Rostam threw his lariat, and its noose dropped over the brave ass's head. Then he lit a fire with the point of an arrow and piled thorns and scrub onto the blaze, and after he had killed and skinned the beast, he cooked it in the flames. He needed neither a table nor cooking pot, but simply ate the flesh and threw away the bones. He removed Rakhsh's reins, and let him wander in the meadow there; then he made himself a bed of reeds and trusted in the safety of a place where he should have been afraid. The reed bed hid a lion's lair, and no elephant dared disturb the reeds nearby.

When one watch of the night had gone by, this ravening lion returned to its lair. He saw a mammoth warrior sleeping among the reeds, and a horse awake and standing in front of him. He said to himself, "First I must bring down the horse, if I'm to get my claws on its rider." He charged toward Rakhsh, whose spirit flared up like fire. Rakhsh brought his front hooves down on the lion's head and sank his sharp teeth into his back. He threw it down on to the ground, tore it to pieces, and rendered this savage animal harmless. When Rostam woke he saw that this lion's world had indeed become dark and comfortless, and he said to Rakhsh, "You are an intelligent animal, who told you to fight with lions? If you had been killed, how could I have ridden to Mazanderan with this heavy mace and helmet and this bow and lariat of mine? If you had woken me, I would have made short work of your combat with this lion."

Rostam's Second Trial: Rostam Finds a Spring of Water

When the sun rose above the mountain's summit, Rostam woke uneasily from a sweet sleep. He rubbed Rakhsh down, put his saddle on him, and prayed to God. A hard road lay ahead of him, and he had to go forward unsure of what he might encounter. Rakhsh's legs became weary, and his rider's tongue was afflicted by the heat and his thirst. Rostam dismounted, and with his lance in his hand, staggered forward like a drunken man. He looked for some way to save himself and raised his face to the heavens, saying, "Just lord, you bring all pains and difficulties to an end, and if my pains are pleasing to you, my treasure is amassed in another world. I travel in the hopes that God will have mercy on King Kavus, and that I will be able to free the Persians from the clutches of demons, according to God's commands. They are sinners and abandoned by you, but they worship you and are your slaves. Many of their mammoth bodies have been bruised and broken, they are weakened and maddened by thirst." Then Rostam fell on the hot earth, and the flesh of his tongue was split open with thirst. At that moment he saw a ram with fat haunches running in front of him, and he thought, "Where does this ram find water for itself? Surely this is God's mercy, to show this animal to me at such a moment?" He gripped his sword in his right hand, and invoking God's name, rose to his feet. Holding his sword he followed the ram, leading Rakhsh by the reins with his other hand. The ram led him to a stream, and Rostam turned his face to the skies and said, "Whoever turns away from the one God has no wisdom in him; when difficulties hem us in, he is our only source of help." Then he called down blessings on the ram and said, "May your pastures always be green and cheetahs never consider you as prey; may the bow of any man who shoots an arrow at you be broken and his arrows lost, because Rostam has survived through you, and if it were not for you he would now be thinking of his shroud, and preparing to be the prey of dragons or wolves." Then he lifted off Rakhsh's saddle and washed all his body in the clear water, so that he glittered like the sun. When he had drunk his fill, he turned his mind to hunting; his quiver was full of arrows, and with his bow he brought down a wild ass with a body as massive as an elephant's. He stripped it of its hide, and when he had lit a fire he dragged it from the stream and cooked it in the flames. He fell to his meal, tearing out the bones with his hands, then went back to the stream and drank copiously again. He was now ready to sleep and said to Rakhsh, "No fighting with anyone tonight. If an enemy appears, wake me up; don't look for a confrontation with any demons or lions." Then he lay down and slept with his lips sealed, and Rakhsh wandered here and there cropping the grass till midnight.

Rostam's Third Trial: Combat with a Dragon

A dragon, from which no elephant had ever escaped, appeared on the plain. Its lair was nearby, and even demons were afraid to cross its path. As it approached it saw Rostam asleep and Rakhsh standing awake, alert as a lion. He wondered what had lain down here in his sleeping place, because nothing ever came this way, neither demons nor elephants nor lions; and if anything did come, it didn't escape this dragon's teeth and claws. It turned toward Rakhsh, who trotted over to Rostam and woke him. Rostam was immediately alert, ready to fight, but he gazed about him in the darkness, and the fearsome dragon disappeared. In his annoyance Rostam chided Rakhsh for waking him. He slept again, and again the dragon emerged from the darkness. Rakhsh stamped on Rostam's pillow and pawed at the ground, and once more Rostam woke. He sprang up, his face sallow with apprehension, and gazed about him, but he saw nothing except the darkness. He said to his kind, wise horse, "You should sleep in the night's darkness, but you keep waking me up; why are you in such a hurry for me to be awake? If you disturb me again like this, I'll cut your feet off with my sword. I'll go on foot, dragging my lance and heavy mace to Mazanderan." For a third time he lay his head down to sleep, using Rakhsh's barding as his mattress and bedcovers. The fearsome dragon roared, his breath seeming to flicker with flames, and Rakhsh galloped away, afraid to approach Rostam. His heart was split in two, fearing both Rostam and the dragon. But his agitation for Rostam urged him back to the hero's side; he neighed and reared up, and his hooves pawed violently at the ground. Rostam woke from a sweet sleep, furious with his horse, but this time God produced a light so that the dragon could not hide, and Rostam made him out in the darkness. He quickly drew his sword, and the ground flashed with the fire of combat. He called out to the dragon, "Tell me your name, because from now on you will not see the world to be as you wish. It's not right for me to kill you without my learning your name." The fearsome dragon said, "No one ever escapes from my claws; all of this plain is mine, like the sky and air above it. Eagles don't dare fly over this land, and even the stars don't look down on it." It paused, and then said, "What is your name, because your mother must weep for you?" The hero replied, "I am Rostam, the son of Zal, who was the son of Sam, of the family of Nariman." Then the dragon leaped at him, but in the end he could not escape from Rostam, because when Rakhsh saw the strength of its massive body bearing down on Rostam, he laid back his ears and sank his teeth into the dragon's shoulders. He tore at the dragon's flesh, and the lion-like Rostam was astonished at his ferocity. Rostam smote with his sword and lopped the dragon's head off, and poison flowed like a river from its trunk. The ground beneath its body disappeared beneath a stream of blood, and Rostam gave a great sigh when he looked at the dragon, and saw that all the dark desert flowed with blood and poison. He was afraid, and stared in horror, murmuring the name of God over and over again. He went into the stream and washed his body and head, acknowledging God's authority over the world. He said, "Great God, you have given me strength and intelligence and skill, so that before me demons, lions and elephants, waterless deserts and great rivers like the Nile, are as nothing in my eyes. But enemies are many and the years are few." When he had finished his prayer, he saddled Rakhsh, mounted, and went on his way through a land of sorcerers.

Rostam's Fourth Trial: He Kills a Witch

He rode for a long time, and when the sun went down in the sky he saw a landscape of plants and trees and running streams, as if it were a garden belonging to a young man. He saw a stream that glittered like a pheasant's eye, and next to it a golden goblet filled with wine. There was also a roasted chicken, and bread, with a saltcellar and candied fruits nearby; it was a feast for sorcerers, who had quickly disappeared when they heard him approaching. Rostam dismounted and lifted the saddle from Rakhsh's back. He was astonished to see the chicken and bread, and sat down beside the stream. He lifted the golden goblet filled with wine, and next to it was a lute, as if the desert were a hall that had been made ready for a feast. Rostam picked up the lute and began to play it, composing a song about himself as he did so:

> *"This is the song of Rostam, who's been given*
> *Few days of happiness by Fate or heaven.*
> *He fights in every war, in every land;*
> *His bed's a hillside, or the desert sand.*
> *Demons and dragons are his daily prey,*
> *Devils and deserts block his weary way.*
> *Fate sees to it that perfumed flowers, and wine,*
> *And pleasant vistas, are but rarely mine—*
> *I'm always grappling with an enemy,*
> *Some ghoul or leopard's always fighting me."*

His song reached the ears of one of the sorcerers, a witch, who disguised herself as a young girl, as beautiful as the spring and lovelier than any painting. She came to Rostam, full of tints and scents, and sat down next to him and questioned him. Rostam silently gave thanks to God that on the plains of Mazanderan he had found this feast and wine, and now he had found a beautiful young wine stewardess too. He didn't know that she was a villainous sorcerer, an Ahriman disguised in spring's colors. He placed a bowl of wine in her hand and praised God who is the author of all good things. But as soon as he mentioned God's kindness, the witch's face changed; her soul had no comprehension of such things, and her tongue could not utter such praise. She turned black at the sound of God's name, and when Rostam saw this, as quick as the wind he looped his lariat about her, and before she was aware, had trapped her head in its coils. He said to her, "What are you? Tell me. Show me yourself as you are." Suddenly there was a withered old woman in his lariat's coils, ugly, deceitful, and vicious. Rostam slashed her in two with his dagger, and the other sorcerers' hearts were terrified when they saw this.

Rostam's Fifth Trial: The Capture of Olad

From there he journeyed on, like a man anxious to reach his goal, galloping onward till he came to a place that had never seen the brightness of the sun. Dark night fell, as black as an African's face, and neither the stars nor the sun nor the moon were visible. It was as if the sun were chained somewhere, and the stars caught in the coils of a lariat. He let his reins go slack, since he could see neither slopes nor streams in the darkness, and then emerged into the light, and the ground was like green silk, bright with young wheat shoots. The ancient world seemed to have grown young again, covered in green growth, and with streams flowing here and there. Rostam's clothes were soaked with sweat, and he was sorely in need of rest and sleep. He stripped his tiger skin from his chest and took off his helmet, which also felt drowned in sweat. He lay both of them down in the sun and prepared to rest. He removed Rakhsh's bridle, and let him wander at will in the young wheat. When his tiger skin and helmet had dried he put them on again, then lay down on a pile of vegetation, like a lion.

But a man who had been sent there to keep animals out of the wheat saw Rakhsh and ran shouting toward him. Then he saw Rostam and slashed at his legs with a stick, and when Rostam woke the man yelled at him, "You Ahriman, why did you let your horse wander in the wheat, spoiling the property of someone who's never done you any harm?" Rostam was infuriated by his words; instead of answering, he sprang up and seized the man by the ears, twisting them, and tearing them off his head. The man quickly retrieved his ears from the ground, screaming in astonishment at what Rostam had done. The owner of this land was a man called Olad, a fine, brave young man, and the injured servant went wailing to him, carrying his bloody ears in his hand. He said, "I went to get a horse out of the wheat and the streams; it belonged to a man like a black devil, wearing a leopard skin corselet and an iron helmet, an Ahriman or a sleeping dragon, and when he saw me he jumped up and said not a word but ripped my ears off and flung them on the ground." Olad was with a group of noblemen, out hunting in the meadows, and they had come on a lion's spoor, but when he heard this astonishing tale from his servant he tugged at his reins and made for where the man indicated Rostam was. As Olad and his companions approached him, Rostam mounted Rakhsh and drew his glittering sword and rode toward them like a threatening cloud. Olad said to him, "What's your name? What kind of a man are you, and which king have you sworn loyalty to? Quarrelsome lions can't pass this way."

Rostam said, "My name is cloud, if a cloud can fight like a lion; it'll rain down spears and sword blows and lop noblemen's heads off. If my name penetrates your ears, it'll freeze your blood. Have you ever heard, in any company, of the bow and lariat of Rostam? You know what I call a mother who bears a son like you? A sewer of shrouds, or a mourner at a wake. Bringing your cronies here against me is as pointless as throwing walnuts at a dome in the hope that they'll stick there." Then he looped his lariat on his saddle and drew his death-dealing sword, and every blow he made with it lopped off two heads; he was like a lion that descends on a flock of lambs, and the ground was soon strewn with the dead. The plain filled with the dust of scattering horsemen, as they fled to the mountains and caves. Rostam went after them, the dust turned the day to night, and as he caught up with Olad he flung his lariat and noosed his head with it. He dragged him down from his horse and bound his arms and said to him, "If you tell me the truth, if I find no lies in you, you'll tell me where the White Demon is and how to find Kulad Ghandi and Bid, and where Kavus is imprisoned, and you'll show me who did this evil act. Do this, and you won't regret it; with this mace I'll depose the king of Mazanderan, and you'll rule here in his place, as long as you don't lie to me."

Olad said, "Drive anger from your heart, and for once look at what you are doing. Don't separate my soul and body for no reason; you'll get from me everything you wish. I'll show you where the White Demon lives and, what you're really hoping for, the place where Kavus is imprisoned; I'll show you the way there. From here to where Kavus is held is a hundred parasangs; from there to where the Demons are, it's another hundred, and the way is a difficult one. In those two hundred parasangs you'll see an immeasurable cavern; it's a horrific place between two mountains, and even that auspicious bird the homa couldn't fly over those summits. There are twelve thousand warlike demons living there and keeping watch at night; Kulad Ghandi is their leader, and Bid and Sanjeh are their guards. You will see one of them with a body like a mountain, with a chest and shoulders ten cubits wide. Despite your great strength and horsemanship, and the way you wield your mace and sword, it will go badly for you if fight against demons like this. After you pass this area you'll come to a plain so strewn with rocks that a deer could not pick its way across it; a demon is lord of the marches there, and all the other demon warriors there are under his command. Once you leave his territory you'll come to a river which is two parasangs across, and beyond it is the land of dog-

headed men and those who have soft feet, and it is like a huge build-
ing three hundred parasangs in width. The area is called Bargush, and
from there to where the king of Mazanderan has his seat is an ugly and
difficult journey. More than six hundred thousand horseman roam the
land there; they are all wealthy and have fine armor, and not one of
them is wretched or poor. They have one thousand two hundred war
elephants, and there is no room for them in the cities. Even if you're
made of iron, you can't survive in that land alone; Ahriman's file will
wear you down!"

Rostam laughed and said:

> *"Just show me how to get there, then you'll see*
> *How all these warriors fare when faced with me.*
> *You'll find out what one mammoth man can do*
> *Against their king's demonic retinue;*
> *Protected by the world Creator's will,*
> *Helped by my sword and arrows and my skill.*
> *When first they glimpse my body's strength and might,*
> *And see the massive mace with which I fight,*
> *Their skins will split with fear: headlong they'll ride,*
> *Routed, with tangled reins and terrified.*
> *All that I want is that you'll show me how*
> *To reach Kavus: come on, get moving now!"*

Rostam's Sixth Trial: Combat with Arzhang

Rostam rested neither in the bright day nor the dark night, but pushed
on toward Mount Aspruz, where Kavus had led his army and been
defeated by the demons' magic. When half of the night had passed, a
wild noise could be heard on the plain, and fires and candles could be
seen burning all over Mazanderan. Rostam said to Olad, "Where is this
place, with fires burning to the left and right?" Olad replied, "It's the
border with Mazanderan, where the inhabitants only sleep for two
watches of the night; their leader Kulad, Arzhang, and Bid, as well as
all the warriors who follow the White Demon, are making those wild
cries and shouts." Rostam slept again, and when the sun rose he used
his lariat to tie Olad tightly to a tree. Then he hung his grandfather's
mace from his saddle and rode into Mazanderan, his heart filled with

schemes of conquest. He wore a royal helmet on his head, and his cuirass of tiger skin was soon soaked with sweat. He set off to find Arzhang, and when he came on the demon's army he gave a great cry that seemed to split the sea and mountains. Arzhang heard this shout and came rushing out of his tent: Rostam saw him and urged his horse forward, bearing down on him like fire. He grabbed him by the head and ears, and holding on to his shoulders with his other hand tore the demon's head off, like a ravening lion, and flung it covered in blood into the crowd of warriors. When the demons saw his mace, their hearts and claws split with terror, and, careless of their homes and homeland, fathers stumbled over sons in their efforts to flee. Rostam drew his sword and slaughtered many of them, and as the sun went down in the sky he galloped back to Mount Aspruz.

He freed Olad from the lariat's coils, and they sat together at the foot of a tall tree. Rostam asked him the way to the city where King Kavus was, and then he immediately set off, following Olad as his guide. As they entered the city, Rakhsh neighed like a cloud growling thunder. Kavus said to the Persians, "Our troubles are over, I heard Rakhsh's neigh, and it has refreshed my heart and soul." At that moment Rostam appeared, and as he approached Kavus, the other Persians gathered round him. They made their obeisance before him, lamenting their lot and questioning him about the perils of his journey. King Kavus embraced him and asked after Zal. Then he added, "Rakhsh will have to gallop unseen by those sorcerers; if the White Demon hears the earth has been cleared of Arzhang, your troubles will be numberless, and the earth will be filled with the demons' armies. Go to the White Demon's home now, exert yourself, use your sword and arrows, and may God help you to bring these demons's heads down to the dust. You're going to have to cross seven mountains, and at every stage you'll see a band of demons. A horrifying cave will appear before you, I've heard it's like a pit, and filled with terrors. Its entrance is crowded with warrior demons who fight like leopards. The White Demon lives in that cave, and he is both the hope and fear of those warriors, but if you can destroy him, they too will be destroyed, because he is their leader. Our warriors' eyes are darkened with sorrow, and I live sightless and bewildered in the darkness; doctors have told us there is hope of a cure if we use a balm made from the blood and brains of the White Demon. This is what a learned doctor told us, that if we drop three droplets of this balm into our eyes, like tears, the darkness will clear completely."

Rostam prepared to leave, to do battle with the White Demon, and he said to the Persian captives, "Stay vigilant till I return. I am going to fight with the White Demon; if he bends my back in defeat, you will remain here a long time in misery, but if the lord of the sun grants me success under a lucky star, you will see your homes again, and your thrones, and the royal tree will bear fruit once more."

The Seventh Trial: Combat with the White Demon

Rostam set out prepared for battle, longing for revenge and his mind focused on the coming combat. When Rakhsh reached the seven mountains and the bands of warrior demons, they saw an army of demons crowded about the entrance to a bottomless cavern. Rostam said to Olad, "You have answered honestly all I have asked you; but now the battle begins in earnest, and you must reveal to me the secrets of how to proceed." Olad said, "When the sun becomes warm, the demons sleep; then you can overcome them, but you must wait until then. Now, you won't see any of them even sitting down, except for some of their guards who are sorcerers, but then you will be victorious over them, if God is your ally."

Rostam was in no hurry to go forward, and he waited until the sun was high in the sky. Then he tied Olad up in the coils of his lariat, mounted Rakhsh, drew his sword from its scabbard, and roared out his name like thunder. He descended on the demons and severed their heads with his sword blade; none of them stood against him in battle, none of them was eager to make a name for himself by fighting with him. Then he went forward looking for the White Demon, his heart filled with fear and hope. He saw a pit like hell, and in the darkness the demon's body was still invisible. Rostam stood there for a while, his sword gripped in his hand; he couldn't see anything, and this was not a time to run away. He rubbed his eyes and peered into the pit's darkness, and made out a mountain there, hiding the pit behind its bulk. It was the color of night, its hair was white like snow, and the world seemed to be filled with its stature and breadth. It moved on Rostam like a black mountain, wearing an iron helmet, its arms protected by iron armor. Rostam's heart was filled with fear, and he thought that this might be one situation from which he would not escape. But he sprang forward like a maddened ele-

phant and slashed with his sharp sword at the demon's trunk. The force
of his blow severed a leg at the thigh, but the wounded demon attacked
him, and the two locked together like an elephant and a lion. Each
repeatedly tore flesh from the other's body, and the ground beneath them
was turned to mud with their blood. Rostam said to himself, "If I sur-
vive today I shall live forever," and the White Demon said to himself, "I
despair of my sweet life, and even if I escape from the clutches of this
dragon, with a leg severed and my skin lacerated, I shall have no author-
ity left in Mazanderan with either the nobility or their subjects." Then
Rostam gave a great roar and clutched the demon by the neck, and
threw him to the ground. He plunged his dagger into him and hacked
out his heart and liver. All the cave was filled with the demon's great
bulk, and the world seemed like a sea of blood.

Rostam came out of the cave, freed Olad from his bonds, and tied
his lariat to his saddle. He gave Olad the Demon's congealed liver, and
the two of them set off to Kavus. Olad to him, "You are a lion in war
and have conquered the world with your sword. My body still bears
the marks of your lariat where I bowed my neck in your bonds, but
you gave my heart hopes of a reward, which I now ask for. To break
your word would not be worthy of a lion warrior blessed with good
fortune like yourself." Rostam replied, "I shall bestow Mazanderan on
you, from border to border, but there are still long, difficult days of
struggle ahead, in which we will see both good and bad fortune. We
have to drag the king of Mazanderan down from his throne and fling
him into a pit, and our daggers have to sever the heads of thousands
upon thousands of demons. When these things have been done I shall
make you the lord of this earth and not betray my promise."

Kavus's Sight Is Restored

Then the great champion reached King Kavus and said to him: "You
are a king who loves knowledge; now delight in the deaths of those
who wish you ill. I ripped open the belly of the White Demon, and
his king can repose no more hopes in him. I have torn the demon's
liver from his side; what are the victorious king's orders for me now?"
Kavus called down blessings on him, and said, "May the crown and
royal seal ring never be without your help. The mother who bore you
should be blessed; my good fortune has increased because of your two
parents, since now the elephant who defeats all lions is my subject."

When they brushed the king's eyes with the White Demon's blood, the darkness there cleared. An ivory throne was brought, with a crown suspended above it, and the king took his place there as the ruler of Mazanderan, surrounded by Rostam and his other chieftains, men like Tus, Fariborz, Gudarz, Giv, Roham, Gorgin and Bahram. So a week passed with wine and music, and Kavus gave himself over to pleasure and enjoyment. On the eighth day the king and his chieftains mounted their horses, shouldered their massive maces, and dispersed into Mazanderan. They rode according to the king's orders, as quickly as fire burns through dry reeds, bringing fire and the sword to the cities there. Then the king said to his men, "The just punishment for sin has been meted out, and now you must hold back from slaughter. We must send an intelligent, dignified man, someone who knows when to act quickly and when to delay, to the king of Mazanderan, to wake up his heart and trouble his mind." Rostam and the other chieftains were pleased at the notion of sending a message to this king, one that would bring light into his dark soul.

Kavus Writes a Letter to the King of Mazanderan

On white silk, a wise scribe wrote a letter filled with promises and threats, with sweetness and ugliness. It began, "Praise to God, from whom virtues are made manifest in the world, who has given us wisdom and created the turning heavens, who has created travail and difficulty and love, who has given us the power to do good and evil, the lord of the turning sun and moon. If you are just and follow the true faith, you will only hear blessings from men, but if you harbor evil and do evil, punishment will come to you from the turning heavens. Do you not see how God has dealt with you, raising the dust of battle over your demons and sorcerers? If you are aware of what fate brings, if wisdom is your teacher, then keep the crown of Mazanderan, and come to my court as my subject. You will not be able to withstand Rostam if he makes war on you, and you have no choice but to pay me taxes. If you do what I say, you can keep your sovereignty over Mazanderan, and, if you do not, what happened to Arzhang and to the White Demon will happen to you, and you should despair of life."

The king summoned Farhad, a warrior famous for the way he wielded his steel sword, and told him, "This letter is filled with good advice; take it to that demon who has escaped from the captivity he deserves." Farhad kissed the ground and took the letter to the land of the Gorgsaran, fierce warriors who fought with daggers, where men dwelt whose feet were made of leather; the king of Mazanderan held court there, surrounded by his warlike chieftains. When he heard that a messenger from Kavus was approaching on horseback, he chose a few men from his retinue and told them that this was the time to show their mettle. He said, "Today we can't separate what is demonic from what is human: be like leopards when you welcome him, see that you provoke him in such a way that even the wisest of men would fight back." They went out to greet him with their faces filled with frowns, but nothing went according to their plan. One of them took Farhad's hand and squeezed it, mangling the muscles and bones, but Farhad's face did not even turn sallow, and he showed no sign of feeling any pain. They took Farhad to their king, who questioned him about Kavus and the difficulties of his journey, and then handed the letter, written on silk with musk mingled with wine, to a scribe, who read it aloud. When the king heard of Rostam's battle against the White Demon, his eyes reddened with blood and his head filled with roars of lamentation. In his heart he said, "The sun will hide away, night comes, rest and sleep will leave me: the world will never be at rest because of this Rostam, whose name will not remain obscure." He grieved for Arzhang and the White Demon, and for the deaths of Kulad Ghandi and Bid. When he had heard the king's letter through, his eyes were wet with bitter tears, and he sent his answer to Kavus:

> "Can wine replace the waters of the sea?
> And you imagine you can threaten me?
> Your throne cannot match mine, and I command
> A thousand thousand warriors in this land.
> When they attack like savage lions they'll keep
> Your Persians' heads from their refreshing sleep,
> The dust of battle I send up will hide
> The plains and hills and every mountainside."

When Farhad heard his belligerent language, he did not wait for a letter to be written, but tugged at his reins and galloped back to the Persian king, where he recounted what he had seen and heard, tearing the veil aside from what had been hidden before. He said, "Their king is higher than the heavens, and his high hopes are no lower. He turned his head aside at my message, and the world is contemptible in his eyes." Rostam said to Kavus, "I will deliver our people from this shame. I must take him a message, and its words must be like a sword drawn from its scabbard. A letter as cutting as a sword blade must be written, a message like a roaring thunder cloud; I will go as the messenger and my words will make blood flow in the rivers there." King

Kavus answered, "The crown and royal seal ring are resplendent because of your deeds; when you bear someone a message, elephants' hearts and lions' claws split with terror."

King Kavus Writes a Second Letter to the King of Mazanderan

He summoned a scribe, who dipped his pen in black ink, and the king dictated this message:

> *"Your words are foolish, and a man who's wise*
> *Will not resort to such unworthy lies:*
> *Empty your mind of all such talk, and bow*
> *Down like a slave; you are my subject now.*
> *And if you don't, my men from sea to sea*
> *Will celebrate another victory;*
> *The dead White Demon's soul will haunt your plains*
> *And feed the hungry vultures with your brains."*

When the king had sealed the letter, Rostam hung his massive mace from his saddle and set off for the king of Mazanderan. As he was approaching, news reached the king that Kavus had sent another messenger, one who was like a lion or a war elephant, with a lariat of sixty loops fixed to his saddle, and a fast galloping horse under him. The king of Mazanderan chose a few of his chieftains and sent them out to welcome the new messenger. When Rostam caught sight of them, he saw a tree with huge branches at the roadside and tore it up by the roots, flourishing it in his fist like a lance. The welcoming party stopped where they were in astonishment, and Rostam flung down the tree and rode up to them. There was a lengthy exchange of greetings, and then one of the party gripped Rostam's hand and squeezed it, attempting to hurt the hero. Rostam smiled, and the group stared in wonder at him. Then Rostam squeezed the hand in his, and its owner turned pale, fainted from the pain, and fell from his horse to the ground. When he revived he quickly made his way to the king of Mazanderan and there recounted everything he had seen, from beginning to end.

There was a horseman whose name was Kolahvar; he tyrannized over Mazanderan, his nature was like a savage leopard's, and his dearest wish was to fight in wars. The king had him summoned and said to him, "Go to this messenger and show him what you're made of. Do such things that his face is filled with shame, and he weeps hot tears." Like a ravening lion Kolahvar went to the champion, his face filled with frowns and growling questions like a leopard. He gave Rostam his hand and squeezed Rostam's hand so hard that it was bruised from the pain. Rostam remained impassive, then squeezed Kolahvar's hand in return, and the nails fell from Kolahvar's fingers like leaves from a tree. With his hand hanging uselessly at his side, Kolahvar reported back to his king, showed him his hand, and said, "A man can't hide his pain from himself: it would be better if you made peace with this warrior than went to war with him. Don't overreach yourself; you won't be able to withstand men like him, and your best course is to agree to pay them taxes. If you accept their terms you'll be doing the best thing for Mazanderan, both for its chieftains and the common people; this way we'll get rid of the danger, and that's better than being terrified out of our wits."

At that moment Rostam entered the court like a savage lion. The king looked at him, then motioned him to a suitable seat and questioned him about king Kavus and his army. Then he said, "Are you Rostam? You have his heroic strength." Rostam replied, "I don't know if I'm worthy even to be Rostam's servant. I can't do the things he does; he is a champion, a hero, a great horseman." Then he handed over the willful king's letter, adding that his sword would bear fruit when it lopped off chieftains' heads. The king was astonished and angry when he heard the letter, and said to Rostam:

> "Tell your king this, 'Your arrogant attempt
> To cow me with your words provokes contempt.
> If you are Persia's sovereign lord, if you
> Are like a lion in all you think and do,
> I am Mazanderan's great king, my throne
> And golden crown and army are my own,
> And you're a fool to summon me, to say
> I should submit to you; kings don't display
> Such pride to other kings, or try to seize
> The thrones of others by such strategies.
> Pride comes before a fall. Now turn around,
> Go back to Persia, to familiar ground,

Because if I and my great army once attack,
You'll be defeated, routed, driven back,
And if I meet you face to face, you'll find
How vain the words are in your foolish mind.'"

Rostam looked directly at the king, his warriors, and his chieftains; he hardly heard what the king was saying, he simply felt more eager to fight him. He refused to accept the king's gift of clothes, horses, and gold; the crown and belt he was offered excited his contempt. His heart filled with rage and the longing for battle, he returned to Kavus and described for him all he had seen and heard in Mazanderan, then added, "Think nothing of them, take courage, and prepare for war against these demons. I feel only disdain for their horseman and heroes."

The King of Mazanderan Makes War on Kavus and the Persians

When Rostam left Mazanderan, the king of sorcerers began to prepare for war. He had the royal pavilion taken from the city and led his armies onto the plain. The dust they sent up obscured the sun, and neither the sea nor the mountains nor the plains were visible. The elephants' feet trampled the ground as the army set off, and no one hesitated. When King Kavus heard that the demons' forces were approaching, he first commanded Rostam to prepare for battle, and then turned to Tus, Gudarz, Giv, and Gorgin, with orders that that the army prepare and make ready its spears and shields. The chieftains' pavilions were pitched on the plain of Mazanderan, and Nozar's son Tus commanded the right flank, while Gudarz commanded the left. The mountains re-echoed with the blare of brazen trumpets, and the warriors gathered there made the whole hillside seem like a mass of iron. Kavus was in the center, with ranks of soldiers around him on every side, and Rostam, who had never known defeat in war, was at the army's head.

There was a famous warrior in Mazanderan who carried a heavy mace on his shoulders when he went into battle. His name was Juyan, and he was ambitious, a good fighter with his mace, and had an imposing voice. His cuirass glittered on his body, and the sparks from his sword blows burned the ground. He came in front of the Persian army, and the mountains and plains echoed as he roared, "Who will fight with me, who will draw forth dust from water?" King Kavus said to the Persians, "Aren't you ashamed, that no one responds to his challenge? Are your hearts and eyes so abashed and downcast by this demon's voice?" None of his brave warriors answered him, and it was as if the whole army had withered at the sight of Juyan. Then Rostam tugged at his reins and rode up to the king flourishing his lance. He said, "Give the order, your majesty, and let me confront this demon." Kavus replied, "No Persian wants to fight him; the task is yours."

Rostam grasped his death-dealing lance in his fist and urged Rakhsh forward. He went onto the battlefield like a maddened elephant, pulled on his reins, gave his war cry that made the whole plain tremble, and a cloud of dust rose into the sky. He called out to Juyan, "You are ugly and evil, and your name will be struck from the list of warriors. Your fate is decided now; the woman who bore you will weep for you." Juyan replied, "Don't be so sure of yourself when you confront Juyan and his cold dagger; your mother's heart will break, and she will weep over that cuirass and helmet of yours." When Rostam heard Juyan's reply he raged like a savage lion and rode straight at him, flinging his lance at Juyan's waist, where it cut through the coat of mail, severing the fastenings of his armor and piercing his trunk. Rostam dragged him from his saddle, spitted like a hen, and hurled him to the ground, his armor cut to pieces, his mouth filled with blood. The warriors of Mazanderan were appalled to see this, their hearts gave way within them, their faces turned sallow, and all the battlefield was filled with talk of Rostam's feat. The king of Mazanderan called out to his army, "Take courage and fight, attack like leopards."

The din of drums and blare of trumpets rang out on both sides, the sky was darkened and the ground turned the color of ebony. The sparks struck by swords and maces were like lightning flashing from dark clouds, and the air was filled with the scarlet, black, and purple of banners.

> The demons' cries, the darkened atmosphere,
> The din of drums, the horses' neighs of fear
> Shook the firm land—no man had seen before
> Such fury, or such violence, or such war;
> The clash of weapons filled the air, and blood
> Flowed from the heroes like a monstrous flood—

The earth became a lake, a battleground
Where waves of warriors broke and fell and drowned;
Blows rained on helmets, shields, and shattered mail
Like leaves whirled downward in an autumn gale.

The battle raged for a week, and on the eighth day King Kavus took his crown from his head and stood weeping before God. He bowed down, rubbed his face in the dust, and said, "Great lord of truth, creator of justice and purity, grant me victory over these fearless demon warriors, and renew my imperial throne." Then he put a helmet on his head and came before his troops. A cry went up, and the blare of brazen trumpets rang out, and Rostam rushed forward like a mountain. Kavus ordered Tus to bring forward the war elephants from the rear of the army, and Gudarz, Zangeh-Shavran, Gorgin, and Roham strode forward like wild boar, with their great banners seven cubits high streaming above them, while Farhad, Kherrad Borzin, and Giv accompanied them. First Rostam launched an attack on the center of the enemies' forces, soaking the ground with their warriors' blood, then like a wolf bearing down on sheep, Giv crossed over from the right flank to the left, and on the right Gudarz brought forward armor, shields, drums and other equipment. From dawn until the sun sank in darkness, blood flowed in the rivers like water, faces lost all trace of shame, courtesy and kindness, and the sky seemed to rain down maces. Piles of the dead lay on every side, and the plants were smeared with men's brains. Trumpets and drums resounded like thunder, and the sun disappeared behind an ebony cloud. Rostam and a large detachment of troops made for where the king of Mazanderan fought, but for a long time the king held out, refusing to give ground. The ambitious hero, the killer of kings, called on God's help and handed his squire his lance; then he flourished his mace, filling the air with his war cry, leaving elephants dead and demons senseless, so that elephants with their massive trunks lay lifeless for miles. Now Rostam called for lances again and rode straight toward the king of Mazanderan; he flung a lance at his belt where it dislodged his spine, but in sight of the Persian warriors, the king used magic to transform his body into a mountainous crag, and Rostam bit on his lance in astonishment.

At that moment King Kavus and his men, accompanied by their elephants and war drums, rode up. He said to Rostam, "Great hero, what's happened to make you stand staring for so long?" Rostam replied, "When the worst of the fighting was over, and my fortunes had begun to shine with success, I saw the king of Mazanderan with his massive mace on his shoulders. I gave brave Rakhsh the reins and flung a spear that struck the king's waist. I thought I'd see him fall from the saddle, blood streaming from his body, but he turned into that crag of granite, and so escaped from the perils of war and my prowess."

Every man in the Persian camp who had any strength in his grip tried to lift the granite rock that enclosed the king of Mazanderan, but it could not be shifted from its place. Then Rostam opened his arms, and without testing its weight, lifted the rock, while the army looked on in wonder. He walked with the craggy mass, while a crowd of men followed him, calling down blessings on him, and scattering gold coins and jewels over him. He carried it to the space in front of the king's pavilion, where he flung it down and placed it at the Persians' disposal. He addressed the rock, "Either come out from hiding behind cowardice and sorcery, or I shall batter this rock to pieces with steel crowbars and an ax." When he heard this, the king of Mazanderan transformed himself into a cloudy mass, wearing a steel helmet and encased in body armor. Rostam seized him by the arm, and laughed as he dragged him before king, to whom he said, "I've brought that mountainous crag, whose fear of axes has made him tired of fighting with me." Kavus looked at the king of Mazanderan's face and saw nothing there that was worthy of a throne or crown. He remembered the suffering he had been through and his heart ached at the thought of it; his mind filled with wind, and he told his executioner to hack the man to pieces with a sharp sword.

He sent someone to the enemy encampment with orders that whatever wealth was there, including coins, thrones, crowns, belts, horses, armor, and gold, should be piled into heaps. Then he had the soldiers come in groups, and he rewarded each man appropriately, giving the most to those who had undergone the most. He gave orders that the demons who were still recalcitrant, and of whom the people still went in terror, should have their heads cut off, and their bodies were to be scattered on the common highway. Then he went to a place of prayer and prayed privately to God; he remained there for a week, prostrating himself in supplication and praise. On the eighth day he opened the doors to his treasury and distributed goods to all who needed them; he spent a week in this way, giving men freely whatever they required. Now that justice had been served, he delayed for a third week in Mazanderan, calling for the music of the harp, his drinking companions, and wine served in goblets set with rubies. During this time, Rostam said to the king, "Every man has his uses, and I asked Olad to be an honest guide for me, which he was. I encouraged him to hope for Mazanderan as a reward for his honesty. It would be right for the king to bestow a robe of honor on him and have his chieftains swear allegiance to him for as long as he lives." When the king heard his loyal champion's words, he placed his hand on his heart as a sign of agreement and summoned Mazanderan's chieftains to come before him. After he had spoken with them about Olad for a while, he had Olad enthroned, and then set off on the return journey to Pars.

Kavus Returns to Iran and Dismisses Rostam

As Kavus entered Iran, the army's dust obscured the sky, and the noise of men and women celebrating his return rose up to the sun. All the land was decorated in his honor, and everywhere men called for wine and musicians. The world was renewed by the king's renewal, and a new moon rose above Iran. When Kavus took his place on the throne, victorious and happy, he opened the doors to his ancient treasuries and had paymasters come from every area to receive gold for their people. The army commanders arrived before the king, clamoring to see Rostam, and when the hero entered the court he wore a crown and was seated on a throne next to Kavus, who arranged for gifts that were worthy of him: a throne set with turquoise and ornamented with rams' horns, a royal crown set with gems, a set of imperial clothes made of cloth of gold, splendid bracelets and torques, a hundred maidservants as lovely as the moon and wearing golden belts, a hundred more with musky hair and fine clothes and jewelry, a hundred Arab horses with golden trappings, a hundred black-haired camels with golden bridles, royal brocade from Rum, China, and Persia, a hundred purses of gold coins, a goblet set with rubies and filled with pure musk, another set with turquoises and filled with rose water, and all manner of tints and scents and other goods.

A scribe wrote a charter on silk, using ink made from musk, wine, and aloes, in which Rostam was confirmed in his sole lordship over Sistan. Kavus praised him, and said, "May the crown and royal seal ring never lack your support, may kings value you in their hearts, and may your soul be filled with humility and obedience." Rostam bent forward and kissed the throne. Then the city was filled with the din of drums, and everyone took part in the festivities; decorations were hung on the houses, and the noise of cymbals and brazen trumpets filled the air. And so Rostam departed and the king sat on his throne, making the world bright with his righteousness and observance of ancient ways. With the sword of justice he smote the neck of sorrow, and in his heart there was no thought of death. The earth was filled with green growth and streams, and all the world was as lovely as the garden of Aram. The king grew powerful through his just ways and faith, and the hands of Ahriman were tied. The world learned that King Kavus had returned from Mazanderan and once again sat crowned on the throne. Everyone was astonished that he had attained such magnanimity of soul, and men lined up outside his court with offerings and gifts.

The world seemed heaven then, on every side,
Justice prevailed, and riches multiplied.

THE KING OF HAMAVERAN
AND HIS DAUGHTER SUDABEH

The Barbary Kingdom

Kavus decided to tour the borders of his kingdom. First he traversed the marches of Turan and China, and then, preceded by the blare of trumpets and the din of drums, he entered the land of Makran, where the country's nobility greeted him with tribute and presents. From there he went on to Barbary, whose king decided to give battle rather than pay tribute. So many troops were at his command that the sun was darkened by the dust sent up by their horses' hooves, and in the gloom a man could not distinguish his own hand from the reins he held. The king of Barbary's men came forward in countless bands, surging one after another like the waves of the sea.

Gudarz saw their forces, readied his mace for battle, and, with a thousand armored horsemen flourishing lances and bows, bore down on the enemy troops. The onslaught broke the center of the enemy's line; their troops were routed and their king fled from the battlefield.

When the old men of the city saw how the wind of battle blew, they came, contrite and wretched, before Kavus, saying:

> *"We are your humble servants, and we bring*
> *The tribute we've collected to our king;*
> *Grateful, obedient to your rule, behold*
> *In place of coins we offer jewels and gold."*

Kavus made much of them and forgave them and conferred new laws upon them. Then, to the noise of cymbals, chimes, and trumpets, he proceeded toward Bactria and the Caucasus. When news reached these areas that King Kavus was approaching, the nobles came out to greet him, bearing presents and tribute. From there he went on to Zabolestan, where Dastan's son Rostam was his host. The king stayed with him for a month, spending the time either feasting with music and wine, or hunting with hawks and cheetahs.

But in the rose garden a thorn appeared; when all the world seemed ordered and at peace, dissension arose among the Arabs. A rich nobleman raised the standard of revolt in Syria and Egypt and the people turned from Kavus. When the king learned that a rival for the throne was challenging him, the thunder of war drums rang out and preparations to leave Zabolestan began. Kavus led his army to the seashore and there innumerable boats were built and launched. A thousand leagues the army sailed and made landfall where three countries meet; on the left was Egypt, on the right Barbary, and ahead the waters of Zareh, beyond which lay Hamaveran. News reached these areas that King Kavus had entered the waters of Zareh, and the three countries joined their armies with one another on the Barbary Coast.

The combined forces of these allies covered the deserts and mountains; the lion had no place for his lair, the wild ass found no way through the plains; the leopard on his crag, the fish in the depths, the eagle in the clouds—all were displaced, there was no room for any animal in all that mighty mass of soldiers.

When Kavus disembarked his men, mountain and desert disappeared, the world seemed nothing but swords and armor; the very stars drew their light from glittering lances. The mountains shook with the blare of trumpets, the earth trembled beneath horses' hooves, and such a din of drums thundered out that the land of Barbary seemed to have become one enormous army encampment.

A tucket sounded from the Persian lines, and Gorgin, Farhad, and Tus rode forward. Further down the line, Gudarz, Giv, Shidush, and Milad also rode out; their lances dipped in poison, they let their reins fall slack on their horses' necks and, bent low over the pommels of their saddles, they charged the enemy. War cries and the clash of arms resounded; Kavus attacked from the army's center, and his troops followed close behind him. The world was darkened by their dust, and crimson blood rained down, spattering the ground as thick as dew, until it seemed red tulips had sprung up between the rocks. Sparks sprang from the clashing blades, the ground was awash with blood, and the three armies were so overwhelmed by the Persian forces that they fell back in utter confusion.

The first to capitulate was the king of Hamaveran; he flung away his sword and massive mace and sent a courier asking for quarter. He said he would deliver weighty tribute in the form of horses, weapons, thrones, and crowns if Kavus would not lead his army against Hamaveran itself. And having heard the message, Kavus answered that, as his former enemy now acknowledged Kavus's crown and authority, he would live safely, under the Persian monarch's protection.

The Tale of Sudabeh

> Then someone took Kavus aside and said: "This king
> Has sired a daughter lovely as the spring,
> More stately than a cypress tree, and crowned
> By hair like black musk, like a noose unbound,
> Her tongue is like a dagger lodged between
> Lips sweet as sugar cane; she is a queen
> Arrayed like paradise, a paragon
> As pure and splendid as the vernal sun,
> Fit for a monarch, if one should decide
> To choose this moonlike beauty as his bride."

Kavus's heart leapt up within his breast; he chose a wise and subtle man from his retinue and ordered him to go to the king of Hamaveran and say from him: "Those nobles who best understand the ways of the world seek to be allied to me, since the sun draws its light from my crown and the earth is but a support for my ivory throne, and all who are not protected by my shadow wither away. Now I seek an alliance with you, washing my face with the waters of reconciliation. I have heard that you have in purdah a daughter who is worthy to be my wife, for she is pure in her lineage and pure in her body and praised in all cities by all people; and if you find a son-in-law like myself, the son of Qobad, then the light of heaven has indeed treated you with favor."

The courier hurried to the king of Hamaveran's court; warmly and with eloquence he greeted the king on behalf of Kavus and delivered the message with which he had been entrusted. When he heard the courier's words the king of Hamaveran's heart grew heavy with sorrow and foreboding, and to himself he said, "He is a sovereign, world-conquering and victorious, but she is my only daughter in all the world, and to me she is dearer than life itself. But if I slight this

courier and treat him contemptuously, I have no means to fight the
war that will ensue. It is best that I should close my eyes to this effron-
tery and allay my heart's anger." Then he said to the courier, "These
desires of your king have no end. He asks of me the two things I have
held dearest, and there is no third to equal them. He has taken my
wealth that was the prop of my rule, and he takes my daughter, who
is the delight of my heart. My life is mine no more, and I resign to
him all that he demands."

In sorrow he called his daughter Sudabeh to him and spoke to her
about Kavus, saying, "An eloquent messenger has come here with a
letter from the king: He wishes to snatch from me my heart, my rest,
and my life, because he asks for you. What do you say to this? What
are your wishes in the matter? What is your opinion?" Sudabeh
answered, "Since we have no choice, it is better not to grieve at this.
The lord of all the world can take whole countries if he so wishes.
Why should you grieve at an alliance with him? This is a joyful devel-
opment, not a cause for sorrow." The king of Hamaveran saw that
Sudabeh was not opposed to the match; he summoned Kavus's mes-
senger and motioned him to a place higher than that of all his courtiers.
Then they drew up the alliance according to the rites and usages of
their religion and time.

The heavy-hearted king prepared the bridal procession: three hun-
dred slaves and forty litters, a thousand mules and horses and a thou-
sand camels loaded with brocade and gold coins, and, for the bride
herself, a litter splendid as the moon, preceded and followed by beasts
bearing her personal wealth. The troops accompanying her were
dressed like denizens of Paradise; so colorful they were, the earth
seemed covered by a carpet of wild flowers. When she came before
Kavus he looked at her face and saw her smiling ruby lips, her two nar-
cissus eyes, her nose fine as a silver reed. Lost in astonishment he stared
and invoked God's blessing on her. He called an assembly of wise men
and priests; before them he acknowledged that Sudabeh was worthy to
be his bride, and so the marriage was performed according to their
rites and customs.

The King of Hamaveran Plots Against Kavus
But the king of Hamaveran was sick at heart and sought for some way
to improve his situation. After a week had passed, on the eighth day he

sent a messenger to Kavus saying, "If the king will come as my guest to my palace, the country of Hamaveran will be honored to entertain his splendor and majesty." He secretly hoped to find a way both to regain his daughter and to escape from paying tribute. But Sudabeh realized that her father was planning some kind of violence during the festivities and said to Kavus, "This is not advisable, Hamaveran is no place for you. He is plotting to harm you during the festival, and you should not place yourself at his mercy. All this is on my account and will be a cause of sorrow to you."

But Kavus had no regard for the opinion of anyone from her country and did not believe her. He and his nobles set off for the promised festivities in Hamaveran. A whole city, called Shaheh, had been devoted to the celebration, and when Kavus entered it, all its inhabitants made their obeisance before him, scattering in his path jewels and saffron, gold coins and ambergris. The town was filled with the sounds of music and song, woven together like the warp and weft of fine cloth. Seeing Kavus, the king of Hamaveran dismounted, together with his courtiers, and, from the palace entrance to the audience hall, trays of pearls, rubies, and gold were emptied before Kavus, while musk and ambergris rained down upon his head. Within the palace Kavus was seated in triumph on a golden throne. He passed a week with the wine cup in his hand, happy and rejoicing, and day and night the king of Hamaveran stood before him like a servant ready to carry out his wishes, and in the same way the king's courtiers served the Iranian nobles. And so the visitors felt safe and welcome and had no suspicion of any harm or trouble. But all this had been planned and foreseen by the king of Hamaveran and he sent the news to Barbary, whose leaders were of one mind with him. When their army arrived, the king of Hamaveran was overjoyed, and one night, when the Iranians were defenseless and unprepared, trumpets sounded the attack. Kavus was suddenly seized, together with Gudarz, Giv, Tus, and the rest of his entourage.

There was in that country a mountain that rose from the depths of the sea; its peak pierced the clouds and on its slopes was a fortress so high that it seemed embraced by the heavens. Kavus and his nobles were sent in chains to this castle and flung within its walls, where they were guarded by a thousand warriors. Kavus's royal pavilion was sacked, and the gold there and his crown were plundered by the nobles of

Hamaveran. The pavilion itself was trampled underfoot. Two columns of veiled women were led out, and in their midst was a litter containing Sudabeh, who was to be taken back to her father's court. When Sudabeh saw her women in this state, she ripped her royal clothes from her body and tore at her musky hair and scored her face with her nails. She wept, and screamed at her father's envoys that they were dogs, and cried out to them:

> *"No man who is a man will praise this act,*
> *You could not chain him when his troops attacked;*
> *Hearing his drums, your hearts were overthrown,*
> *Then he was armed, his warhorse was his throne,*
> *You quailed before Gudarz and Giv and Tus—*
> *Then was the time for you to chain Kavus!*
> *But no, you lie and break your oaths and cheat*
> *And ambush him with welcoming deceit.*
> *I will not part from him or leave his side;*
> *Though he should die I will remain his bride."*

This outburst was reported to her father, who was enraged. He took her at her word and had her sent to the fortress where her husband was kept in chains, and there she comforted him, ministering to him in his sorrow and misfortune.

Afrasyab Renews the War

News spread throughout the world that the king of Iran was in captivity. Many claimants to the crown appeared, among them Afrasyab, who roused himself from his life of eating and sleeping and taking his ease, and once again attacked Iran. The war lasted for three months, at the end of which the Iranian army was routed; many men, women, and children were enslaved and the remaining Persians were gripped by despair. A number of fugitives made their way to Zabolestan, where they entreated Dastan's son Rostam to save the country, saying:

> *"You are our refuge, our last hope, our one*
> *Protection now that King Kavus has gone;*
> *Alas, Iran will be destroyed, a lair*
> *For leopards and wild lions will flourish there,*

> *Our land will be a wasted battleground*
> *Where evil kings will triumph and be crowned."*

Rostam wept at their words, and his heart was filled with pain and sorrow. He answered them, "I and my army shall prepare for war, and I shall rid the land of Iran of these Turkish invaders."

Rostam's Message

Rostam sent messengers to the king of Hamaveran and, secretly, to Kavus. To the former he said: "You tricked the king of Iran and went back on your oath. To stoop to such ruses is not the way of chivalry. Either you release King Kavus or prepare to do battle with me." But the king of Hamaveran answered, "King Kavus will never descend to the plains again, and if you come to Barbary your welcome will be swords and heavy maces; the chains and prison that hold him await you too. I and my army shall confront you; this is how we deal with invaders."

In response Rostam gathered an army together and took it over sea and dry land to the borders of Hamaveran. There he set about plundering the countryside, and all the land ran with rivers of blood. News reached the king of Hamaveran that Rostam had saddled Rakhsh and was laying his land waste and that this was no time for delay. He led his army out from the city to confront the Persians and the bright day was darkened by their dust.

But seeing Rostam's massive weight and height and the great mace he carried on his shoulder, the king's troops' hearts failed within them and they fled back toward the city. The king sat with his councillors and asked for two young men to go as couriers to Egypt and Barbary. The letters they bore said that the three countries were close and had always shared in joy and misfortune, and that if they came now to the aid of Hamaveran there was nothing to fear from Rostam, but that if they did not, Rostam would eventually bring disaster on their heads too.

When they learned that Rostam's army was nearby, their hearts quaked with fear. But they mustered troops and set out for Hamaveran; so great was their number that there was not space on the plain where they were drawn up for an ant to walk. Seeing these forces, Rostam secretly sent a message to Kavus: "The kings of three countries have risen against me, and if I fight their forces they will be routed in such utter confusion that they will not know their heads from their feet. But this war must not have bad consequences for you, and from such evil men we must expect an evil response. The throne of Barbary is nothing to me if its capture means harm to my king." The courier heard the message and took it by hidden ways to Kavus, who answered, "Do not concern yourself about me; it was not for me that this world was created, and thus the heavens have ever turned, mingling poison with sweet draughts and war with peace. The world's Creator is my support and his greatness and benevolence are my refuge. Give Rakhsh his head, and do not leave a single one of our enemies alive, in the open or in hiding." When Rostam heard this message, he prepared for battle.

Rostam Fights with the Three Kings

The next day the armies were drawn up in battle order; on the side of Hamaveran there were a hundred war elephants; behind them were countless jostling banners—red, yellow, and purple—and the army stretched for two miles. When Rostam saw their lines, he said to his men, "You see their mounts' necks and manes, but keep your eyes on the points of their lances; though they are a hundred thousand and we are but a hundred horsemen, it is not greater numbers that will win this battle." Spears and arrows glittered in the air, the earth swam with blood like a wine vat; so many lances thronged the sky it seemed a bed of close-packed reeds, and abandoned armor and severed heads, still helmeted, lay scattered on the ground. Rostam urged Rakhsh forward but avoided combat with lesser men; instead he rode after the Arab king and flung his lariat, catching the king by the waist; he jerked him down from the saddle with the violence of a polo mallet striking the ball, and Farhad bound his arms. Sixty of this king's noblemen were taken prisoner, and the king of Barbary was also captured along with forty of his warriors. The king of Hamaveran was defeated and promised to hand over Kavus and his noblemen to Rostam.

Kavus, along with Giv, Gudarz, and Tus, was released from his fortress prison, and Rostam delivered to the Persian treasury the arms of three countries, the treasure of three kings, their pavilions, hosts, crowns, and thrones and whatever other things of value he saw. Then Kavus had brought before him a gold-caparisoned palfrey on which was a golden litter; the frame was of aloe wood studded with jewels and its couch was of Rumi brocade, worked with turquoise and rubies on a jet-black ground. He had Sudabeh sit within the litter, and when she took her place there, he saluted her sunlike splendor. He led his army out of the city to their camp, and, augmented by the forces of Egypt, Barbary, and Hamaveran, the number of his forces now exceeded three hundred thousand.

Kavus Sends a Message to Afrasyab

When Rostam had informed the king of Afrasyab's new incursions into Iran, Kavus sent the Turanian leader a letter: "Leave the land of Iran, repent of your overreaching pride; I hear nothing but talk of you and your depredations. Turan is your homeland, and you rejoice in its wealth, but blindly you turn always to evil. You want for nothing, do not then strive for excess; such longings will bring you only pain and endless sorrow. Accept your subordinate status and so save your skin. You know well enough that Iran is my land and that the world trembles before my might. No matter how brave a leopard may be, it dare not confront the lion's claws."

When this message reached Afrasyab, his mind was filled with hatred, his heart with rage. He sent his answer: "Such idle talk can come only from one who is low-minded; if Iran is your country as you claim, why did you long to conquer Mazanderan? Hear then the truth: Iran is mine for two reasons—first, that I am descended from the son of Feraydun, and second that I have overcome its inhabitants by the force of my sword. My sword will lop the summits from the mountains and bring down eagles from the dark clouds. My banners are unfurled, and I have come prepared for war."

Hearing his answer, Kavus put his vast army on a war footing and led them from Barbary into Syria; for his part, Afrasyab marched forward and his army clouded the heavens with their dust. The world was deafened by the blare of trumpets and the din of drums, the land was overspread with iron armor, the air was blackened by thick dust. In the shock of battle Afrasyab's fortunes declined; two sections of the army of Turan were slain, and when he saw this, Afrasyab's mind churned like fermenting wine that bubbles without fire beneath it. He cried out, "O my brave warriors, best of my troops, lions of Turan, it is for such a day that I have trained and nourished you; throw your hearts into the battle and drive back Kavus; with lances and swords fall on the Iranian troops. Capture the lionhearted Rostam, noose his head and haul him from his mount. I shall give my own daughter to whoever subdues Rostam; I shall exalt his glory higher than the moon's sphere."

When they heard him, the Turanians attacked with renewed force, but all their efforts were in vain and Afrasyab fell back toward Turan, heartsick and with two parts of his army destroyed. Seeking sweetness and pleasure from the world, he had found only bitter poison.

For his part, Kavus returned in triumph to Pars; he reigned in splendor, giving himself up to the pleasures of court life. He sent out great warriors, wise and just men, to confirm his rule in his possessions, in Merv and Nayshapur and Balkh and Herat; the world was filled with justice and the wolf turned harmlessly from the lamb. On Rostam, Kavus bestowed the title of Champion of all the World.

Kavus Is Tempted by Eblis

Then one morning the devil Eblis addressed a convocation of demons, in secret and unbeknownst to the king: "Under this king our lives are miserable and wretched: I need a nimble demon, one who knows court etiquette, who can deceive the king and wrench his mind away from God and bring his royal glory down into the dust; in this way the burdens he has placed upon us will be lightened." The demons heard him, but none at first responded, out of fear of Kavus. Then an ugly demon spoke up, "I'm wily enough for this." And so saying, he transformed himself into a handsome, eloquent youth, one who would grace any court.

It happened that the king went out hunting, and the youth saw his opportunity. He came forward and kissed the ground; handing Kavus a bouquet of wild flowers, he said, "Your royal *farr* is of such splendor that the heavens themselves should be your throne. The surface of the earth is yours to command; you are the shepherd and the world's nobles are your flock. There is but one thing remaining to you, and when this is accomplished your glory will never fade. The sun still keeps its secrets from you; how it turns in the heavens, and who it is that controls the journeys of the moon and the succession of night and day, these are as yet unknown to you."

The king's mind was led astray by this demon's talk, and his mind forsook the ways of wisdom: He did not know that the heavens are immeasurable, that the stars are many but that God is one, and that all are powerless beneath his law. The king was troubled in his mind, wondering how he could fly into the heavens without wings. He asked learned men how far it was from the earth to the heavens; he consulted astronomers and set his mind on a foolish enterprise.

He gave orders that men were to go at night and rob eagles' nests of their young; these squabs were to be placed in houses in pairs and reared on fowl and occasional lamb's meat. When the eagles had grown

as strong as lions and were each able to subdue a mountain goat, Kavus
had a throne constructed of aloes wood and gold, and at each corner he
had a lance attached. From the lances he suspended lamb's meat; next
he bound four eagles tightly to the structure. Then King Kavus sat on
the throne, his mind deceived by the wiles of Ahriman. When the
eagles grew hungry they flew up toward the suspended meat and the
throne was lifted above the ground, rising up from the level plain into
the clouds. The eagles strained toward the meat to the utmost of their
capacity, and I have heard that Kavus was carried into the heavens as far
as the sphere of the angels. Others say that he fought with his arrows
against the sky itself, but God alone knows if these and other such sto-
ries are true. The eagles flew for a great while, but finally their strength
gave out and their wings began to tire; they tumbled down from the
dark clouds, and the king's throne plummeted toward the ground. It
finally came to rest in a thicket near Amol and, miraculously, the king
was not killed. Hungry and humiliated, Kavus was filled with regret at
his foolishness; he waited forlornly in the thicket, praying to God for
help.

Once Again King Kavus Is Rescued
While he was begging forgiveness for his sins, the army was searching
for some trace of him. Rostam, Giv, and Tus received news of his
whereabouts and set off with a band of soldiers to rescue him. Gudarz
said to Rostam:

> *"Since I was weaned of mother's milk I've known*
> *The ways of kings and served the royal throne;*
> *I've seen the world's great monarchs and their glory,*
> *But never have I heard so mad a story*
> *As this we hear now of Kavus, this fool*
> *Who's so unwise he's hardly fit to rule."*

The heroes reached Kavus and furiously reproached him. Gudarz said:

> *"A hospital is where you need to be,*
> *Forget your palaces and sovereignty;*
> *You throw away your power, you don't discuss*
> *Your plans and foolish fantasies with us.*

Three times disaster's struck you down, but still
You haven't learned to curb your headstrong will:
First you attacked Mazanderan, and there
Captivity reduced you to despair;
Then, trusting to your enemies, you gave
Your heart away and so became their slave;
And now your latest folly is to try
Your strength against the ever-turning sky."

Shamefaced and humble, Kavus replied, "All that you say is true and just." He was placed in a litter, and on his journey home humiliation and regret were his companions. When he reached his palace again, his heart remained wrung with sorrow, and for forty days he waited as a suppliant before God, his head bowed in the dust. His pride was humbled, and shame kept him locked within his palace. Weeping and praying, he neither granted audience nor feasted, but in sorrow and regret had wealth distributed to the poor.

But when Kavus had wept in this way for a while, God forgave him. King Kavus reestablished justice in the world, and it shone equally on nobles and commoners alike. Justice made the world as rich and splendid as a fine brocade, and over all the king presided, majestic and magnificent.

THE TALE OF SOHRAB

Rostam Loses Rakhsh

At dawn one day Rostam decided to go hunting, to drive away the sadness he felt in his heart. Filling his quiver with arrows, he set off for the border with Turan, and when he arrived in the marches he saw a plain filled with wild asses; laughing, his face flushed with pleasure, he urged Rakhsh forward. With his bow, his mace, and his noose he brought down his prey and then lit a fire of brushwood and dead branches; next he selected a tree and spitted one of the slaughtered asses on it. The spit was as light as a feather to him, and when the animal was roasted he tore the meat apart and ate it, sucking the marrow from its bones. He sank back contentedly and slept. Cropping the grass, his horse Rakhsh wandered off and was spotted by seven or eight Turkish horsemen. They galloped after Rakhsh and caught him and bore him off to the city, each of them claiming him as his own prize.

Rostam woke from his sweet sleep and looked round for his horse. He was very distressed not to see Rakhsh there and set off on foot toward the closest town, which was Samangan. To himself he said, "How can I escape from such mortifying shame? What will our great warriors say, 'His horse was taken from him while he slept?' Now I must wander wretched and sick at heart, and bear my armor as I do so; perhaps I shall find some trace of him as I go forward."

Samangan

The king of Samangan was told that the Crown Bestower, Rostam, had had his horse Rakhsh stolen from him and was approaching the town on foot. The king and his nobles welcomed him and enquired as to what had happened, adding, "In this town we all wish you well and stand ready to serve you in any way we can." Rostam's suspicions were laid to rest and he said, "In the pastures, Rakhsh wandered off from me; he had no bridle or reins. His tracks come as far as Samangan and then peter out into reeds and the river. If you can find him, I shall be grateful, but if he remains lost to me, some of your nobility will lose their heads."

The king responded, "No one would dare to have done this to you deliberately. Stay as my guest and calm yourself; tonight we can drink and rejoice, and drown our worries with wine. Rakhsh is such a world-renowned horse, he will not stay lost for long."

Mollified by his words, Rostam agreed to stay as the king's guest. He was given a chamber in the palace and the king himself waited on him. The chieftains of the army and the city's nobility were summoned to the feast; stewards brought wine, and dark-eyed, rosy-cheeked girls sought to calm Rostam's fretfulness with their music. After a while Rostam became drunk and felt that the time to sleep had come; his chamber had been sweetened with the scents of musk and rosewater, and he retired there for the night.

Tahmineh

When one watch of the night had passed, and Venus rose into the darkened sky, a sound of muffled whispering came to Rostam's ears; gently his chamber door was pushed open. A slave entered, a scented candle in her hand, and approached the hero's pillow; like a splendid sun, a paradise of tints and scents, her mistress followed her. This beauty's eyebrows curved like an archer's bow, and her ringlets hung like nooses to snare the unwary; in stature she was as elegant as a cypress tree. Her mind and body were pure, and she seemed not to partake of earthly existence at all. The lionhearted Rostam gazed at her in astonishment; he asked her what her name was and what it was that she sought on so dark a night. She said:

> "My name is Tahmineh; longing has torn
> My wretched life in two, though I was born
> The daughter of the king of Samangan,
> And am descended from a warrior clan.
> But like a legend I have heard the story
> Of your heroic battles and your glory,

Of how you have no fear, and face alone
Dragons and demons and the dark unknown,
Of how you sneak into Turan at night
And prowl the borders to provoke a fight,
Of how, when warriors see your mace, they quail
And feel their lion hearts within them fail.
I bit my lip to hear such talk, and knew
I longed to see you, to catch sight of you,
To glimpse your martial chest and mighty face—
And now God brings you to this lowly place.
If you desire me, I am yours, and none
Shall see or hear of me from this day on;
Desire destroys my mind, I long to bear
Within my woman's womb your son and heir;
I promise you your horse if you agree
Since all of Samangan must yield to me."

When Rostam saw how lovely she was, and moreover heard that she promised to find Rakhsh for him, he felt that nothing but good could come of the encounter; and so in secret the two passed the long hours of night together.

As the sun cast its noose in the eastern sky, Rostam gave Tahmineh a clasp which he wore on his upper arm and said to her, "Take this, and if you should bear a daughter, braid her hair about it as an omen of good fortune; but if the heavens give you a son, have him wear it on his upper arm, as a sign of who his father is. He'll be a boy like Sam, the son of Nariman, noble and chivalrous; one who'll bring down eagles from their cloudy heights, a man on whom the sun will not shine harshly."

Then the king came to Rostam and asked how he had slept, and brought news that Rakhsh had been found. Rostam rushed out and stroked and petted his horse, overjoyed to have found him; he saddled him and rode on his way, content with the king's hospitality and to have found his horse again.

Sohrab Is Born

Nine months passed, and the princess Tahmineh gave birth to a son as splendid as the shining moon. He seemed another Rostam, Sam, or

Nariman, and since his face shone bright with laughter, Tahmineh named him Sohrab (Bright-visaged). When a month had gone, he seemed a year old; at three, he played polo; and at five, he took up archery and practiced with a javelin. By the time he was ten, no one dared compete with him and he said to his mother, "Tell me truly now, why is it I'm so much taller than other boys of my age? Whose child am I, and what should I answer when people ask about my father? If you keep all this hidden from me, I won't let you live a moment longer." His mother answered, "Hear what I have to say, and be pleased at it, and control your temper. You are the son of the mammoth-bodied hero Rostam and are descended from Dastan, Sam, and Nariman. This is why your head reaches to the heavens; since the Creator made this world, there never has been such a knight as Rostam." Secretly she showed him a letter that Rostam had sent, together with three rubies set in gold; then she said, "Afrasyab must know nothing of this, and if Rostam hears of how you've grown, he'll summon you to his side and break your mother's heart." Sohrab answered, "This is not something to be kept secret; the world's chieftains tell tales of Rostam's prowess; how can it be right for me to hide such a splendid lineage? I'll gather a boundless force of fighting Turks and drive Kavus from his throne; then I'll eradicate all trace of Tus from Iran and give the royal mace and crown to Rostam, I'll place him on Kavus's throne. Next I'll march on Turan and fight with Afrasyab and seize his throne too. If Rostam is my father and I am his son, then no one else in all the world should wear the crown; when the sun and moon shine out in splendor, what should lesser stars do, boasting of their glory?" From every quarter swordsmen and chieftains flocked to the youth.

War Breaks Out Again

Afrasyab was told that Sohrab had launched his boat upon the waters and that, although his mouth still smelled of mother's milk, his thoughts were all of swords and arrows. The informants said that he was threatening war against Kavus, that a mighty force had flocked to him, and that in his self-confidence he took no account of anyone. Afrasyab laughed with delight; he chose twelve thousand warriors, placed them under the command of Barman and Human, and addressed his two chieftains thus: "This secret must remain hidden. When these two face each other on the battlefield, Rostam will surely be at a disadvantage. The father must not know his son, because he will try to win him over; but, knowing nothing, the ancient warrior filled with years will be slain by our young lion. Later you can deal with Sohrab and dispatch him to his endless sleep." Afrasyab sent the two to Sohrab, and he entrusted them with a letter encouraging the young warrior in his ambitions and promising support.

The White Fortress

There was an armed outpost of Iran called the White Fortress; its keeper was an experienced warrior named Hejir. Sohrab led his army toward the fortress, and, when Hejir saw this, he mounted his horse and rode out to confront him. Sohrab rode in front of the army, then drew his sword and taunted Hejir, "What are you dreaming of, coming to fight alone against me? Who are you, what is your name and lineage? Your mother will weep over your corpse today." Hejir replied, "There are not many Turks who can match themselves against me. I am Hejir, the army's brave commander, and I shall tear your head off and send it to Kavus, the king of all the world; your body I shall thrust beneath the dirt." Sohrab laughed to hear such talk; the two attacked each other furiously with lances. Hejir's lance struck at Sohrab's waist but did no harm, but when Sohrab returned the blow, he sent Hejir sprawling from his saddle to the ground. Sohrab leapt down from his horse, intending to sever his enemy's head, but Hejir twisted away to the right and begged for quarter. Sohrab spared him, and in triumph preached submission to his captive. Then he had him bound and sent to Human. When those in the fortress realized that their leader had been captured, both men and women wailed aloud with grief, crying out, "Hejir is taken from us."

Gordafarid

But one of those within the fortress was a woman, daughter of the warrior Gazhdaham, named Gordafarid. When she learned that their leader had allowed himself to be taken, she found his behavior so shameful that her rosy cheeks became as black as pitch with rage. With not a moment's delay she dressed herself in a knight's armor, gathered her hair beneath a Rumi helmet, and rode out from the fortress, a lion eager for battle. She roared at the enemy's ranks, "Where are your heroes, your warriors, your tried and tested chieftains?"

When Sohrab saw this new combatant, he laughed and bit his lip and said to himself, "Another victim has stepped into the hero's trap." Quickly he donned his armor and a Chinese helmet and galloped out to face Gordafarid. When she saw him, she took aim with her bow (no bird could escape her well-aimed arrows) and let loose a hail of arrows, weaving to left and right like an experienced horseman as she did so. Shame urged Sohrab forward, his shield held before his head to deflect her arrows. Seeing him approach, she laid aside her bow and snatched up a lance and, as her horse reared toward the clouds, she hurled it at her opponent. Sohrab wheeled round and his lance struck Gordafarid in the waist; her armor's fastenings were severed, but she unsheathed her sword and hacked at his lance, splitting it in two. Sohrab bore down on her again and snatched her helmet from her head; her hair streamed out, and her face shone like a splendid sun. He saw that his opponent was a woman, one whose hair was worthy of a diadem. He was amazed and said, "How is it that a woman should ride out from the Persian army and send the dust up from her horse's hooves into the heavens?" He unhitched his lariat from the saddle and flung it, catching her by the waist, then said: "Don't try to escape from me; now, my beauty, what do you mean by coming out to fight? I've never captured prey like you before, and I won't let you go in a hurry." Gordafarid saw that she could only get away by a ruse of some kind, and, showing her face to him, she said, "O lionhearted warrior, two armies are watching us and, if I let them see my face and hair, your troops will be very amused by the notion of your fighting with a mere girl; we'd better draw aside somewhere, that's what a wise man would do, so that you won't be a laughing stock before these two armies. Now our army, our wealth, our fortress, and the fortress's commander will all be in your hands to do with as you wish; I'll hand them over to you, so there's no need for you to pursue this war any further." As she spoke, her shining teeth and bright red lips and heavenly face were like a paradise to Sohrab; no gardener ever grew so straight and tall a cypress as she seemed to be; her eyes were liquid as a deer's, her brows were two bent bows, you'd say her body was a bud about to blossom.

Sohrab said, "Don't go back on your word; you've seen me on the battlefield; don't think you'll be safe from me once you're behind the fortress walls again. They don't reach higher than the clouds and my mace will bring them down if need be." Gordafarid tugged at her horse's reins and wheeled round toward the fortress; Sohrab rode beside her to the gates, which opened and let in the weary, wounded, woman warrior.

The defenders closed the gates, and young and old alike wept for Gordafarid and Hejir. They said, "O brave lioness, we all grieve for you, but you fought well and your ruse worked and you brought no shame on your people." Then Gordafarid laughed long and heartily and climbed up on the fortress walls and looked out over the army. When she saw Sohrab perched on his saddle, she shouted down to him:

> "O king of all the Asian hordes, turn back,
> Forget your fighting and your planned attack."
> She laughed; and then, more gently, almost sighed:
> "No Turk will bear away a Persian bride;
> But do not chafe at Fate's necessity—
> Fate did not mean that you should conquer me.
> Besides, you're not a Turk, I know you trace
> Your lineage from a far more splendid race;
> Put any of your heroes to the test—
> None has your massive arm and mighty chest.
> But news will spread that Turan's army's here,
> Led by a stripling chief who knows no fear;
> Kavus will send for noble Rostam then
> And neither you nor any of your men
> Will live for long: I should be sad to see
> This lion destroy you here—turn now and flee,
> Don't trust your strength, strength will not save your life;
> The fatted calf knows nothing of the knife."

Hearing her, Sohrab felt a fool, realizing how easily he could have taken the fortress. He plundered the surrounding settlements and sulkily said: "It's too late for battle now, but when dawn comes, I'll raze this fortress's walls, and its inhabitants will know the meaning of defeat."

But that night Gazhdaham, Gordafarid's aged father, sent a letter to Kavus telling him of Sohrab's prowess, and secretly, before dawn, most of the Persian troops evacuated the fortress, traveling toward Iran and safety.

When the sun rose above the mountains, the Turks prepared to fight; Sohrab mounted his horse, couched his lance, and advanced on the fortress. But as he and his men reached the walls, they saw very few defenders; they pushed open the gates and saw within no preparations for battle. A straggle of soldiers came forward, begging for quarter.

Kavus Summons Rostam

When King Kavus received Gazhdaham's message, he was deeply troubled; he summoned his chieftains and put the matter before them. After he had read the letter to his warrior lords—men like Tus, Gudarz (the son of Keshvad), Giv, Gorgin, Bahram, and Farhad—Kavus said, "According to Gazhdaham, this is going to be lengthy business. His letter has put all other thoughts from my mind; now, what should we do to remedy this situation, and who is there in Iran who can stand up to this new warrior?" All agreed that Giv should go to Zabol and tell Rostam of the danger threatening Iran and the Persian throne.

Kavus wrote to Rostam, praising his prowess and appealing to him to come to the aid of the throne. Then he said to Giv, "Gallop as quickly as wind-borne smoke and take this letter to Rostam. Don't delay in Zabol; if you arrive at night, set off on the return journey the next morning. Tell Rostam that matters are urgent." Giv took the letter and traveled quickly to Zabol, without resting along the way. Rostam came out with a contingent of his nobles to welcome him; Giv and Rostam's group dismounted together, and Rostam questioned him closely about the king and events in Iran. After they had returned to Rostam's palace and rested a while, Giv repeated what he had heard, handed over the letter, and gave what news he could of Sohrab.

When Rostam had listened to him and read the letter, he laughed aloud and said in astonishment, "So it seems that a second Sam is loose in the world; this would be no surprise if he were a Persian, but from the Turks it's unprecedented. I myself have a son over there, by the princess of Samangan, but he's still a boy and doesn't yet realize that war is the way to glory. I sent his mother gold and jewels, and she sent me back an answer saying that he'd soon be a tall young fellow; his mouth still smells of mother's milk, but he drinks his wine, and no doubt he'll be a fighter soon enough. Now, you and I should rest for a day and moisten our dry lips with wine, then we can make our way to the king and lead Persia's warriors out to war. It's possible that Fortune's turned against us, but if not, this campaign will not prove difficult; when the sea's waves inundate the land, the fiercest fire won't stay alight for long. And when this young warrior sees my banner, his heart will know his revels are all ended; he won't be in such a hurry to fight anymore. This is not something we should worry ourselves about."

They sat to their wine and, forgetting all about the king, passed the night in idle chatter. The next morning Rostam woke with a hangover and called again for wine; this day too was passed in drinking and no one thought about setting out on the journey to Kavus. And once again on the third day Rostam ignored the king's summons and had wine brought. On the fourth day Giv bestirred himself and said, "Kavus is a headstrong man and not at all intelligent; he's very upset about this business and he can neither eat nor sleep properly. If we stay much longer here in Zabolestan, he will be extremely angry." Rostam replied, "Don't worry about that; there's not a man alive who can meddle with me." He gave orders that Rakhsh be saddled and that the tucket for departure be sounded. Zabol's knights heard the trumpets and, armed and helmeted, they gathered about their leader.

Rostam and Kavus

They arrived at the king's court in high spirits and ready to serve him. But when they bowed before the king, he at first made them no answer, and then, addressing Giv, he burst out in fury, "Who is Rostam that he should ignore me, that he should flout my orders in this way? Take him and string him up alive on the gallows and never mention his name to me again." Giv was horrified at Kavus's words and remonstrated, "You would treat Rostam in this way?" The courtiers stared, struck dumb, as Kavus then roared to Tus, "Take both of them and hang them both." And, wildly as a fire that burns dry reeds, he sprang up from the throne. Tus took Rostam by the arm to lead him from Kavus's presence and the warriors there watched in wonder, but Rostam too burst out in fury and addressed the king:

> "Smother your rage; each act of yours is more
> Contemptible than every act before.
> You're not fit to be king; it's Sohrab you
> Should hang alive, but you're unable to."
> Tus he sent sprawling with a single blow
> Then strode toward the door as if to go

But turned back in his rage and said, "I am
The Crown Bestower, the renowned Rostam,
When I am angry, who is Kay Kavus?
Who dares to threaten me? And who is Tus?
My helmet is my crown, Rakhsh is my throne,
And I am slave to none but God alone.
If Sohrab should attack, who will survive?
No child or warrior will be left alive
In all Iran—too late, and desperately,
You'll seek for some escape or remedy;
This is your land where you reside and reign—
Henceforth you'll not see Rostam here again."

The courtiers were deeply alarmed, since they regarded Rostam as a shepherd and themselves as his flock. They turned to Gudarz and said, "You must heal this breach, the king will listen to no one but you; go to this crazy monarch and speak to him mildly and at length, and with luck we'll be able to restore our fortunes again." Gudarz went to Kavus and reminded him of Rostam's past service and of the threat that Sohrab was to Iran, and when he had heard him out, Kavus repented of his anger and said to Gudarz, "Your words are just, and nothing becomes an old man's lips like wisdom. A king should be wise and cautious; anger and impetuous behavior bring no good to anyone. Go to Rostam and remind him of our former friendship; make him forget my outburst." Gudarz and the army's chieftains went in search of Rostam; finally they saw the dust raised by Rakhsh and caught up with him. They praised the hero and then said, "You know that Kavus is a brainless fool, that he is subject to these outbursts of temper, that he erupts in rage and is immediately sorry and swears to mend his ways. If you are furious with the king, the people of Iran are not at fault; already he regrets his rage and bites the back of his hand in repentance."

Rostam replied, "I have no need of Kay Kavus: My saddle's my throne, my helmet's my crown, this stout armor's my robes of state, and my heart's prepared for Death. Why should I fear Kavus's rage; he's no more to me than a fistful of dirt. My mind is weary of all this, my heart is full, and I fear no one but God himself." Gudarz replied, "Iran and her chieftains and the army will see this in another way;

they'll say that the great hero was afraid of the Turk and that he sneaked away in fear; they'll say that if Rostam has fled, we should all flee. I saw the court in an uproar over Kavus's rage, but I also saw the stir that Sohrab has created. Don't turn your back on the king of Iran; your name's renowned throughout the world, don't dim its luster by this flight. And consider: The army is hard pressed, this is no time to abandon the throne and crown."

Rostam stared at him and said, "If there's any fear in my heart I tear it from me now." Shamefaced, he rode back to the king's court, and when he entered, the king stood and asked his forgiveness for what had passed between them, saying, "Impetuous rage is part of my nature; we have to live as God has fashioned us. This new and unexpected enemy had made my heart grow faint as the new moon; I looked to you for help and when you delayed your coming, I became angry. But seeing you affronted by my words, I regretted what I had said." Rostam replied, "The world is yours; we are all your subjects. I have come to hear your orders." Kavus said, "Tonight we feast, tomorrow we fight." Entertained by musicians and served by pale young slaves, the two then sat to their wine and drank till half the night had passed.

The Persian Army Sets Out Against Sohrab

At dawn the next day the king ordered Giv and Tus to prepare the army; drums were bound on elephants, the treasury doors were opened, and war supplies were handed out. A hundred thousand warriors gathered and the air was darkened by their dust. Stage by stage they marched till nightfall, and their glittering weapons shone like points of fire seen through a dark curtain. So day by day they went on until at last they reached the fortress's gates, and their number was so great that not a stone or speck of earth was visible before the walls.

A shout from the lookouts told Sohrab that the enemy's army had come. Sohrab went up onto the city walls and then summoned Human; when Human saw the mighty force opposing them, he gasped and his heart quailed. Sohrab told him to be of good cheer, saying, "In all this limitless army, you'll not see one warrior who'll be willing to face me in combat, no, not if the sun and moon themselves came down to aid him. There's a great deal of armor here and many men, but I know of none among them who's a warrior to reckon with. And now in Afrasyab's name I shall make this plain a sea of blood." Cheerful and fearless, Sohrab descended from the walls. For their part the Persians pitched camp, and so vast was the number of tents and pavilions that the plain and surrounding foothills disappeared from view.

Rostam Spies on Sohrab

The sun withdrew from the world, and dark night spread her troops across the plain. Eager to observe the enemy, Rostam came before Kavus. He said, "Let me go from here unarmed to see just who this new young hero is, and to see what chieftains are accompanying him." Kavus replied, "You are the man for such an undertaking; take care, and may you return safely."

Rostam disguised himself as a Turk and made his way quickly to the fortress. As he drew near he could hear the sound of drunken revelry from the Turks within. He slipped into the fortress as a lion stalks wild deer. There he saw Sohrab seated on a throne and presiding over the festivities; on one side of him sat Zhendeh-Razm and on the other were the warriors Human and Barman. Tall as a cypress, of mighty limb, and mammoth chested, Sohrab seemed to fill the throne. He was surrounded by a hundred Turkish youths, as haughty as young lions, and fifty servants stood before him. In turn, all praised their hero's strength and stature and sword and seal, while Rostam watched the scene from afar.

Zhendeh-Razm left the gathering on some errand and saw a warrior, cypress-tall, whom he did not recognize. He came over to Rostam and said, "Who are you? Come into the light so that I can see your face." With one swift blow from his fist, Rostam struck out at Zhendeh-Razm's neck, and the champion gave up the ghost there and then; he lay motionless on the ground, never returning to the feast. After a while Sohrab noticed his absence and asked after him. Retainers went out and saw him lying prone in the dirt; neither banquets nor battles would concern him again. They returned wailing and weeping, and told Sohrab that Zhendeh-Razm's days of feasting and fighting were over. When Sohrab heard this, he sprang up and hurried to where the warrior lay, and the musicians and servants with tapers followed after him. He stared in astonishment, then called his chieftains to him and said, "Tonight we must not rest but sharpen our spears for battle: A wolf has attacked our flock, eluding the shepherd and his dog. But with

God's aid, when I ride out and loose my lariat from the saddle, I'll be revenged on these Iranian warriors for the death of Zhendeh-Razm." And with this he returned to the feast.

For his part Rostam slipped back to the Persian lines, where Giv waited on watch. Rostam told Giv of how he had killed one of the enemy, and then he went to Kavus and gave him news of Sohrab, saying that the new hero had no equal in either Turan or Iran, and that he was the image of Rostam's own grandfather, Sam. He told Kavus of how he had killed Zhendeh-Razm, and then he and the king called for musicians and wine.

Sohrab Surveys the Persian Camp

When the sun had flung its noose into the sky, and rays of light shot through the empyrean, Sohrab armed himself and went up onto a tower on the city walls; from there he could see the Iranian forces spread out below. He summoned Hejir and, after promising wealth if he was truthful and prison if he was not, he said to him, "I want to ask you about the leaders and champions of the other side, men like Tus, Kavus, Gudarz, Bahram, and the famous Rostam; identify for me everyone I point out to you. Those multicolored pavilion walls enclosing tents of leopardskin; a hundred elephants are tethered in front of them, and beside the turquoise throne that stands there, a banner rises emblazoned with the sun and topped with a golden moon; there, right in the center of the encampment—whose place is that?" Hejir replied, "That is the Persian king's court, and there are lions there as well as elephants."

Sohrab went on, "Over to the right, where all the baggage and knights and elephants are, there's a black pavilion around which are countless ranks of soldiers; the banner there bears an elephant as its device, and there are gold-shod knights on guard before it; whose is that?" Hejir answered, "The banner embroidered with an elephant belongs to Tus, the son of Nozar." "And the red pavilion that so many knights are crowded round, where the banner shows a lion and bears in its center a huge jewel, whose is that?" "The lion banner belongs to the great Gudarz, of the clan of Keshvad."

"And the green pavilion, where all the infantry are standing? Where the banner of Kaveh is; look, a resplendent throne shines there, and on it is seated a hero who's head and shoulders taller than all those who stand in front of him. A magnificent horse, with a lariat slung across its saddle, waits next to him and neighs toward its lord every now and again. The device on the banner there is of a dragon, and its staff is topped with a golden lion." Hejir answered, "That's some lord from Tartary who's recently joined forces with the king." Sohrab asked the new lord's name, but Hejir said, "I don't know his name; I was here in this fortress when he came to our king." Sohrab was saddened in his heart, because no trace of Rostam was to be seen.

He questioned Hejir further, pointing out an encampment around a banner that bore the device of a wolf. "That belongs to the eldest and noblest of Gudarz's sons, Giv," Hejir replied. "And over toward where the sun is rising, there's a white pavilion thronged about with foot soldiers; their leader's seated on a throne of teak placed on an ivory pedestal and he's surrounded by slaves?" "That is Prince Fariborz, the son of King Kavus." "And the scarlet pavilion where the soldiers are standing round the entrance, where the red, yellow, and purple banners are; behind them towers a taller banner bearing the device of a wild boar and topped with a golden moon?" "That belongs to the lion-slaying Goraz, of Giv's clan."

And so Sohrab sought for some sign of his father, while the other hid from him what he longed to know. Once again he asked about the tall warrior beneath the green banner, beside whom waited a noble horse bearing a coiled lariat. But Hejir answered, "If I don't tell you his name it's because I don't know it myself." "But this cannot be right," Sohrab said. "You've made no mention of Rostam; the greatest warrior in the world could not stay hidden in this army camp; you said he was the foremost of their heroes, keeper of the country, and ward of the marches." "Perhaps this great warrior has gone to Zabolestan, for now is the time of the spring festival." Sohrab answered: "Don't talk so foolishly; his king has led their forces into the field; if this world champion were to sit drinking and taking his ease at such a time, everyone would laugh at him. If you point out Rostam to me, I'll make you a wealthy and honored man, you'll never want for anything again: But if you keep his whereabouts hidden from me, I'll sever your head from your shoulders; now choose which it's to be."

But in his heart the wily Hejir thought, "If I point out Rostam to this strong Turkish youth, who has such shoulders and who sits his horse so well, out of all our forces it'll be Rostam he'll choose to fight against. With his massive strength and mighty frame, he could well kill Rostam, and who from Iran would be able to avenge the hero's death? Then this Sohrab will seize Kavus's throne. Death with honor is better than aiding the enemy, and if Gudarz and his clan are to die, then I have no wish to live in Iran either." To Sohrab he replied, "Why are you so hasty and irritable? You talk of nothing but Rostam. It's not him you should try to fight with; he would prove a formidable opponent on the battlefield. You wouldn't be able to defeat him and it would be no easy matter to capture him either."

Sohrab Issues His Challenge

When Sohrab heard such slighting words, he turned his back on Hejir and hid his face. Then he turned and struck him with such violence that Hejir sprawled headlong in the dirt. Sohrab went back to his tent and there donned his armor and helmet. Seething with fury, he mounted his horse, couched his lance, and rode out to the battlefield like a maddened elephant. None of the champions of the Persian army dared confront him: Seeing his massive frame, his martial figure on horseback, his mighty arm and glittering lance, they said, "He is another Rostam; who would dare look at him or oppose him in combat?"

Then Sohrab roared out his challenge against Kavus, "What prowess have you on the battlefield? Why do you call yourself King Kavus when you have no skill or strength in battle? I'll spit your body on this lance of mine and make the stars weep for your downfall. The night when I was feasting and Zhendeh-Razm was killed, I swore a mighty oath that I'd not leave a single warrior living in all Persia, that I'd string Kavus up alive on a gallows. Is there one from among all Persia's fighting champions who'll oppose me on the battlefield?" So he stood, fuming with rage, while not a sound rose from the Persian ranks in answer to his challenge. Sohrab's response was to bend low in the saddle and bear down on the Persian camp. With his lance he severed the ropes of seventy tent pegs; half of the great pavilion tumbled down, the sound of trumpets rang in the air, and the army scattered like wild asses before a lion. Kavus cried out, "Have someone tell Rostam that our warriors are confounded by this Turk, that I've not one knight who dares confront him." Tus took the message to Rostam, who said,

> "When other kings have unexpectedly
> Asked for my services, or summoned me,
> I've been rewarded with a gift, with treasure,
> With banquets, celebrations, courtly pleasure—

> *But from Kavus I've witnessed nothing more*
> *Than constant hardships and unending war."*

He ordered that Rakhsh be saddled and, leaving Zavareh to guard his encampment, he rode out with his warriors beside him, bearing his banner aloft.

When he saw the mighty Sohrab, whose massive frame seemed so like that of Sam, he called to him, "Let's move aside to open ground and face each other man to man." Sohrab rubbed his hands together, took up his position before the ranks of waiting soldiers, and answered, "Don't call any of your Persians to your aid, you and I will fight alone. But the battlefield's no place for you, you won't survive one blow of my fist, you're tall enough and have a fine chest and shoulders, but age has clipped your wings, old man!" Rostam stared at the haughty young warrior, at his fist and shoulders, and the way he sat his horse, and gently said to him:

> *"So headstrong and so young! Warm words, and bold!*
> *The ground, young warrior, is both hard and cold.*
> *Yes, I am old, and I've seen many wars*
> *And laid low many mighty conquerors;*
> *Many a demon's perished by my hand*
> *And I've not known defeat, in any land.*
> *Look on me well; if you escape from me*
> *You need not fear the monsters of the sea;*
> *The sea and mountains know what I have wrought*
> *Against Turan, how nobly I have fought,*
> *The stars are witness to my chivalry,*
> *In all the world there's none can equal me."*
> *Then Sohrab said, "I'm going to question you.*
> *Your answer must be honest, straight, and true:*
> *I think that you're Rostam, and from the clan*
> *Of warlike Sam and noble Nariman."*
> *Rostam replied, "I'm not Rostam, I claim*
> *No kinship with that clan or noble name:*
> *Rostam's a champion, I'm a slave—I own*
> *No royal wealth or crown or kingly throne."*

And Sohrab's hopes were changed then to despair,
Darkening before his gaze the sunlit air.

The First Combat Between Rostam and Sohrab

Sohrab rode to the space allotted for combat, and his mother's words rang in his ears. At first they fought with short javelins, then attacked one another with Indian swords, and sparks sprang forth from the clash of iron against iron. The mighty blows left both swords shattered, and they grasped their ponderous maces, and a weariness began to weigh their arms down. Their horses too began to tire, and the blows the heroes dealt shattered both the horse armor and their own cuirasses. Finally, both the horses and their riders paused, exhausted by the battle, and neither hero could summon the strength to deliver another blow. The two stood facing one another at a distance, the father filled with pain, the son with sorrow, their bodies soaked with sweat, their mouths caked with dirt, their tongues cracked with thirst. How strange the world's ways are! All beasts will recognize their young—the fish in the sea, the wild asses on the plain—but suffering and pride will make a man unable to distinguish his son from his enemy.

Rostam said to himself, "I've never seen a monster fight like this; my combat with the White Demon was as nothing to this and I can feel my heart's courage begin to fail. A young, unknown warrior who's seen nothing of the world has brought me to this desperate pass, and in the sight of both our armies."

When their horses had rested from the combat, both warriors—he who was old in years and he who was still a stripling—strung their bows, but their remaining armor rendered the arrows harmless. In fury then the two closed, grasping at one another's belts, each struggling to throw the other. Rostam, who on the day of battle could tear rock from the mountain crags, seized Sohrab's belt and strove to drag him from his saddle, but it was as if the boy were untouched and all Rostam's efforts were useless. Again these mighty lions withdrew from one another, wounded and exhausted.

Then once more Sohrab lifted his massive mace from the saddle and bore down on Rostam; his mace struck Rostam's shoulder and the hero writhed in pain. Sohrab laughed and cried, "You can't stand up to blows, it seems; you might be cypress-tall, but an old man who acts like a youth is a fool."

Both now felt weakened by their battle, and sick at heart they turned aside from one another. Rostam rode toward the Turkish ranks like a leopard who sights his prey; like a wolf he fell on them, and their great army scattered before him. For his part Sohrab attacked the Persian host, striking down warriors with his mace. Rostam feared that some harm would come to Kavus from this young warrior, and he hurried back to his own lines. He saw Sohrab in the midst of the Persian ranks, the ground beneath his feet awash with wine-red blood; his spear, armor, and hands were smeared with blood and he seemed drunk with slaughter. Like a raging lion Rostam burst out in fury, "Bloodthirsty Turk, who challenged you from the Persian ranks? Why have you attacked them like a wolf run wild in a flock of sheep?" Sohrab replied, "And Turan's army had no part in this battle either, but you attacked them first even though none of them had challenged you." Rostam said, "Evening draws on, but, when the sun unsheathes its sword again, on this plain we shall see who will die and who will triumph. Let us return at dawn with swords ready for combat; go now, and await God's will!"

Sohrab and Rostam in Camp at Night

They parted and the air grew dark. Wounded and weary, Sohrab arrived at his own lines and questioned Human about Rostam's attack. Human answered, "The king's command was that we not stir from our camp; and so we were quite unprepared when a fearsome warrior bore down on us, as wild as if he were drunk or had come from single combat." Sohrab answered, "He didn't destroy one warrior from this host, while I, for my part, killed many Persians and soaked the ground with their blood. Now we must eat, and with wine drive sorrow from our hearts."

And on the other side, Rostam questioned Giv, "How did this Sohrab fight today?" Giv replied, "I have never seen a warrior like him. He rushed into the center of our lines intending to attack Tus, but Tus fled before him, and there was none among us who could withstand his onslaught." Rostam grew downcast at his words and went to King Kavus, who motioned him to his side. Rostam described Sohrab's massive body to him and said that no one had ever seen such valor from so young a warrior. Then he went on, "We fought with mace and sword and bow, and finally, remembering that I had often enough pulled heroes down from the saddle, I seized him by the belt and tried to drag him from his horse and fling him to the ground. But a wind could shake a mountainside before it would shift that hero. When he comes to the combat ground tomorrow, I must find some way to overcome him hand to hand; I shall do my best, but I don't know who will win; we must wait and see what God wills, for he it is, the Creator of the sun and moon, who gives victory and glory." Kavus replied, "And may he lacerate the hearts of those who wish you ill. I shall spend the night in prayer to him for your success."

Rostam returned to his own men, preoccupied with thoughts of the coming combat. Anxiously, his brother Zavareh came forward, questioning him as to how he had fared that day. Rostam asked him first for food, and then shared his heart's forebodings. He said, "Be vigilant, and do nothing rashly. When I face that Turk on the battlefield at dawn, gather together our army and accoutrements—our banner, throne, the golden boots our guards wear—and wait at sunrise before our pavilion. If I'm victorious I shan't linger on the battlefield, but if things turn out otherwise, don't mourn for me or act impetuously; don't go forward offering to fight. Instead, return to Zabolestan and go to our father, Dastan; comfort my mother's heart, and make her see that this fate was willed for me by God. Tell her not to give herself up to grief, for no good will come of it. No one lives forever in this world, and I have no complaint against the turns of Fate. So many lions and demons and leopards and monsters have been destroyed by my strength, and so many fortresses and castles have been razed by my might; no one has ever overcome me. Whoever mounts his horse and rides out for battle is knocking at the door of Death, and if we live a thousand years or more, Death is our destiny at last. When she is comforted, tell Dastan not to turn his back on the world's king, Kavus. If Kavus makes war, Dastan is not to tarry, but to obey his every command. Young and old, we are all bound for Death; on this earth no one lives forever." For half the night they talked of Sohrab, and the other half was spent in rest and sleep.

Sohrab Overcomes Rostam

When the shining sun spread its plumes and night's dark raven folded its wings, Rostam donned his tigerskin and mounted Rakhsh. His iron helmet on his head, he hitched the sixty loops of his lariat to his saddle, grasped his Indian sword in his hand, and rode out to the combat ground.

Sohrab had spent the night entertained by musicians and drinking wine with his companions. To Human he had confided his suspicions that his opponent was none other than Rostam, for he felt himself drawn to him, and besides, he resembled his mother's description of Rostam. When dawn came, he buckled on his armor and grasped his huge mace; with his head filled with battle and his heart in high spirits, he came onto the field shouting his war cry. He greeted Rostam with a smile on his lips, for all the world as if they had spent the night in revelry together:

> *"When did you wake? How did you pass the night?*
> *And are you still determined we should fight?*
> *But throw your mace and sword down, put aside*
> *These thoughts of war, this truculence and pride.*
> *Let's sit and drink together, and the wine*
> *Will smooth away our frowns—both yours and mine.*
> *Come, swear an oath before our God that we*
> *Renounce all thoughts of war and enmity.*
> *Let's make a truce, and feast as allies here*
> *At least until new enemies appear.*
> *The tears that stain my face are tokens of*
> *My heart's affection for you, and my love;*
> *I know that you're of noble ancestry—*
> *Recite your lordly lineage to me."*

Rostam replied, "This was not what we talked of last night; our talk was of hand-to-hand combat. I won't fall for these tricks, so don't try them. You might be still a child, but I am not, and I have bound my belt on ready for our combat. Now, let us fight, and the outcome will be as God wishes. I've seen much of good and evil in my life, and I'm not a man for talk or tricks or treachery." Sohrab replied, "Talk like this is not fitting from an old man. I would have wished that your days would come to an end peacefully, in your bed, and that your survivors would build a tomb to hold your body while your soul flew on its way. But if your life is to be in my hands, so be it; let us fight and the outcome will be as God wills."

They dismounted, tethered their horses, and warily came forward, each clad in mail and helmeted. They closed in combat, wrestling hand to hand, and mingled blood and sweat poured from their bodies. Then Sohrab, like a maddened elephant, struck Rostam a violent blow and felled him; like a lion leaping to bring down a wild ass, he flung himself on Rostam's chest, whose mouth and fist and face were grimed with dust. He drew a glittering dagger to sever the hero's head from his body, and Rostam spoke:

> "O hero, lion destroyer, mighty lord,
> Master of mace and lariat and sword,
> Our customs do not count this course as right;
> According to our laws, when warriors fight,
> A hero may not strike the fatal blow
> The first time his opponent is laid low;
> He does this, and he's called a lion, when
> He's thrown his rival twice—and only then."

By this trick he sought to escape death at Sohrab's hands. The brave youth bowed his head at the old man's words, believing what he was told. He released his opponent and withdrew to the plains where, unconcernedly, he spent some time hunting. After a while Human sought him out and asked him about the day's combat thus far. Sohrab told Human what had happened and what Rostam had said to him. Human responded, "Young man, you've had enough of life, it seems! Alas for this chest, for these arms and shoulders of yours; alas for your fist, for the mace that it holds; you'd trapped the tiger and you let him go, which was the act of a simpleton! Now, watch for the consequences of this foolishness of yours when you face him again."

Sohrab returned to camp, sick at heart and furious with himself. A prince once made a remark for just such a situation:

> "Do not make light of any enemy
> No matter how unworthy he may be."

For his part, when Rostam had escaped from Sohrab, he sprang up like a man who has come back from the dead and strode to a nearby stream where he drank and washed the grime from his face and body. Next he prayed, asking for God's help and for victory, unaware of the fate the sun and moon held in store for him. Then, anxious and pale, he made his way from the stream back to the battlefield.

And there he saw Sohrab mounted on his rearing horse, charging after wild asses like a maddened elephant, whirling his lariat, his bow on his arm. Rostam stared at him in astonishment, trying to calculate his chances against him in single combat. When Sohrab caught sight of him, all the arrogance of youth was in his voice as he taunted Rostam, "So you escaped the lion's claws, old man, and crept away from the wounds he dealt you!"

Sohrab Is Mortally Wounded by Rostam

Once again they tethered their horses, and once again they grappled in single combat, each grasping the other's belt and straining to overthrow him. But, for all his great strength, Sohrab seemed as though he were hindered by the heavens, and Rostam seized him by the shoulders and finally forced him to the ground; the brave youth's back was bent, his time had come, his strength deserted him. Like a lion Rostam laid him low, but, knowing that the youth would not lie there for long, he quickly drew his dagger and plunged it in the lionhearted hero's chest. Sohrab writhed, then gasped for breath, and knew he'd passed beyond concerns of worldly good and evil. He said:

> "I brought this on myself, this is from me,
> And Fate has merely handed you the key
> To my brief life: not you but heaven's vault—
> Which raised me and then killed me—is at fault.
> Love for my father led me here to die.
> My mother gave me signs to know him by,
> And you could be a fish within the sea,
> Or pitch black, lost in night's obscurity,
> Or be a star in heaven's endless space,
> Or vanish from the earth and leave no trace,
> But still my father, when he knows I'm dead,
> Will bring down condign vengeance on your head.
> One from this noble band will take this sign
> To Rostam's hands, and tell him it was mine,
> And say I sought him always, far and wide,
> And that, at last, in seeking him, I died."

When Rostam heard the warrior's words, his head whirled and the earth turned dark before his eyes, and when he came back to himself, he roared in an agony of anguish and asked what it was that the youth had which was a sign from Rostam, the most cursed of all heroes.

"If then you are Rostam," said the youth, "and you killed me, your wits were dimmed by an evil nature. I tried in every way to guide you, but no love of yours responded. Open the straps that bind my armor and look on my naked body. When the battle drums sounded before my door, my mother came to me, her eyes awash with tears, her soul in torment to see me leave. She bound a clasp on my arm and said, 'Take this in memory of your father, and watch for when it will be useful to you'; but now it shows its power too late, and the son is laid low before his father." And when Rostam opened the boy's armor and saw the clasp he tore at his own clothes in grief, saying, "All men praised your bravery, and I have killed you with my own hands." Violently he wept and tore his hair and heaped dust on his head. Sohrab said, "By this you make things worse. You must not weep; what point is there in wounding yourself like this? What happened is what had to happen."

The shining sun descended from the sky and still Rostam had not returned to his encampment. Twenty warriors came riding to see the battlefield and found two muddied horses but no sign of Rostam. Assuming he had been killed, they sent a message to Kavus saying, "Rostam's royal throne lies desolate." A wail of mourning went up from the army, and Kavus gave orders that the drums and trumpets be sounded. Tus hurried forward and Kavus told him to have someone survey the battlefield and find out what it was that Sohrab had done and whether they were indeed to weep for the fortunes of Iran, since if Rostam had been killed, no one would be able to oppose Sohrab and they would have to retreat without giving battle.

As the noise of mourning rose from the army, Sohrab said to Rostam, "Now that my days are ended, the Turks' fortunes too have changed. Be merciful to them, and do not let the king make war on them; it was at my instigation they attacked Iran. What promises I made, what hopes I held out to them! They should not be the ones to suffer; see you look kindly on them."

Cold sighs on his lips, his face besmeared with blood and tears,

Rostam mounted Rakhsh and rode to the Persian camp, lamenting aloud, tormented by the thought of what he had done. When they caught sight of him, the Persian warriors fell to the ground, praising God that he was alive, but when they saw his ripped clothes and dust-besmeared head and face, they asked him what had happened and what distressed him. He told them of the strange deed he had done, of how he had slaughtered the person who was dearer to him than all others, and all who heard lamented aloud with him.

Then he said to the chieftains, "I've no courage left now, no strength or sense; go no further with this war against the Turks, the evil that I have done today is sufficient." Rostam returned to where his son lay wounded, and the nobles—men like Tus, Gudarz, and Gostaham—accompanied him, crowding round and saying, "It's God who will heal this wound, it's he who will lighten your sorrows." But Rostam drew a dagger, intending to slash his own neck with it; weeping with grief, they flung themselves on him and Gudarz said, "What point is there in spreading fire and sword throughout the world by your death, and if you wound yourself a thousand times, how will that help this noble youth? If there is any time left to him on this earth, then stay with him and ease his hours here; and if he is to die, then look at all the world and say, 'Who is immortal?' We are all Death's prey, both he who wears a helmet and he who wears the crown."

Rostam replied, "Go quickly and take a message from me to Kavus and tell him what has befallen me; say that I have rent my own son's vitals with a dagger, and that I curse my life and long for death. Tell him, if he has any regard for all I have done in his service, to have pity on my suffering and to send me the elixir he keeps in his treasury, the medicine that will heal all wounds. If he will send it, together with a goblet of wine, it may be that, by his grace, Sohrab will survive and serve Kavus's throne as I have done."

Like wind the chieftain bore this message to Kavus, who said in reply, "Which warrior, of all this company, is of more repute than Rostam? And are we to make him even greater? Then, surely he will turn on me and kill me. How will the wide world contain his glory and might? How will he remain the servant to my throne? If, some day, evil's to come to me from him, I will respond with evil. You heard how he referred to me:

'When I am angry, who is Kay Kavus?
Who dares to threaten me? And who is Tus?'"

When Gudarz heard these words, he hurried back to Rostam and said:

"This king's malicious nature is a tree
That grows new, bitter fruit perpetually;

You must go to him and try to enlighten his benighted soul." Rostam gave orders that a rich cloth be spread beside the stream; gently he laid his wounded son there and set out to where Kavus held court. But he was overtaken on the way by one who told him that Sohrab had departed this world; he had looked round for his father, then heaved an icy sigh, and groaned, and closed his eyes forever. It was not a castle the boy needed his father to provide for him now, but a coffin.

Rostam dismounted and removed his helmet and smeared dust on his head.

Then he commanded that the boy's body be covered in royal brocade—the youth who had longed for fame and conquest, and whose destiny was a narrow bier borne from the battlefield. Rostam returned to his royal pavilion and had it set ablaze; his warriors smeared their heads with dust, and in the midst of their lamentations they fed the flames with his throne, his saddlecloth of leopardskin, his silken tent of many colors. Rostam wept and ripped his royal clothes, and all the heroes of the Persian army sat in the wayside dust with him and tried to comfort him, but to no avail.

Kavus said to Rostam, "The heavens bear all before them, from the mighty Alborz Mountains to the lightest reed; man must not love this earth too much. For one it comes early and for another late, but Death comes to all. Accept this loss, pay heed to wisdom's ways, and know that if you bow the heavens to the ground or set the seas aflame, you cannot bring back him who's gone; his soul grows old, but in another place. I saw him in the distance once, I saw his height and stature and the massive mace he held; Fate drove him here to perish by your hand. What is it you would do? What remedy exists for this? How long will you mourn in this way?"

Rostam replied, "Yes, he is gone. But Human still camps here on the plains, along with chieftains from Turan and China. Have no rancor in your heart against them. Give the command, and let my brother Zavareh lead off our armies." The king said, "This sadness clouds your soul, great hero. Well, they have done me evil enough, and they have wreaked havoc in Iran, but my heart feels the pain you feel, and for your sake I'll think no more of them."

Rostam Returns to Zabolestan

Rostam returned then to his home, Zabolestan, and when news of his coming reached his father, Zal-Dastan, the people of Sistan came out to meet him, mourning and grieving for his loss. When Dastan saw the bier, he dismounted from his horse, and Rostam came forward on foot, his clothes torn, with anguish in his heart. The chieftains took off their armor and stood before the coffin and smeared their heads with dust. When Rostam reached his palace, he cried aloud and had the coffin set before him; then he ripped out the nails and pulled back the shroud and showed the nobles gathered there the body of his son. A tumult of mourning swept the palace, which seemed a vast tomb where a lion lay; the youth resembled Sam, as if that hero slept, worn out by battle. Then Rostam covered him in cloth of gold and nailed the coffin shut and said, "If I construct a golden tomb for him and fill it with black musk, it will not last for long when I am gone; but I see nothing else that I can do."

> This tale is full of tears, and Rostam leaves
> The tender heart indignant as it grieves:
> I turn now from this story to relate
> The tale of Seyavash and his sad fate.

THE LEGEND OF SEYAVASH

A Turkish Princess Is Discovered

One day at cockcrow Tus, Giv, and a number of other knights rode out from their king's court; taking along cheetahs and hawks, they set off for the plain of Daghui to hunt for wild asses. After they'd brought down a great quantity of game, enough for forty days, they saw that the land before them was black with Turkish tents. In the distance, close to the border between the Persian and Turkish peoples, a thicket was visible, and Tus and Giv, followed by a few others, rode over to it. To their astonishment, they discovered a beautiful young woman hiding there, and Tus said to her, "How is it a girl as radiant as the moon is in this thicket?" She answered, "Last night my father beat me; he came back drunk from a feast and, as soon as he saw me, he drew a dagger and began shouting that he would cut my head off, and so I fled from our home."

The knights asked her about her family, and she explained that she was related to Garsivaz who traced his lineage back to Feraydun. Then they asked how it was that she was on foot. She said that her horse had collapsed in exhaustion, that the quantity of gold and jewels she'd brought with her, together with her crown, had been stolen from her by bandits on a nearby hill, and that one of them had beaten her with the scabbard of his sword. She added, "When my father realizes what's happened, he'll send horsemen out to find me, and my mother too is sure to hurry here to stop me going any further."

The knights could not help but be interested in her, and Tus said quite shamelessly, "I found this Turkish girl, I rode on ahead of the rest of the group, she's mine." Giv responded, "My lord, didn't you and I arrive here together, without the others? It's not fitting for a knight to get so argumentative about a slave girl." Their words became so heated that they were ready to cut the girl's head off, but to resolve the matter one of the company suggested they take her to the Persian king's court, and that both should agree to whatever the king decided.

And so they set out for the court, but when Kavus saw the girl he laughed and bit his lip and said to the pair of them, "I see the hardships of the journey were well worth it, and we can spend a day telling stories about how our heroes went hunting with cheetahs and snared the sun. She's a delicate young doe, and prey like that's reserved for the very best." He turned then to the girl and said, "What family are you from, because your face is like an angel's?" She answered, "My mother's nobly born, and my father's descended from Feraydun; my grandfather is Garsivaz, and his tent is always at the center of our encampment." Kavus said, "And you wanted to throw to the winds such a fine lineage, not to speak of your lovely face and hair? No, you must sit on a golden throne in my harem and I'll make you the first of all my women." She answered, "My lord, when I saw you, of all heroes I chose you for my own."

> *Enthroned within his harem now—arrayed*
> *With rubies, turquoise, lapis, gold brocade—*
> *She was herself an unpierced, precious gem,*
> *A princess worthy of a diadem.*

The Birth of Seyavash

When spring with all its glorious colors came, Kavus was told that his encounter with this radiant beauty had resulted in the birth of a splendid son. The loveliness of the boy's face and hair was rumored throughout the world; the king, his father, named him Seyavash and had his horoscope cast. But the horoscope was not auspicious; taking refuge in the will of God, Kavus was saddened to see that the stars did not augur well for the boy's future.

Shortly afterwards Rostam came to the court and addressed the sovereign: "It's I who should undertake the education of this lion cub; no courtier of yours is more suited to the task; in all the world you won't find a better nurse for him than I shall be." The king pondered the suggestion for a while and, seeing that his heart had no objection to it, he handed into Rostam's arms his pride and joy, the noble infant warrior. Rostam took the boy to Zavolestan and there constructed a dwelling for him in an orchard. He taught him how to ride and all the skills appropriate for a horseman; how to manage bridle and stirrups, the use of bow and lariat; how to preside at banquets where the wine goes round; how to hunt with hawks and cheetahs; what justice and injustice are; all that pertains to the crown and throne; what wise speech is; what warfare is and how to lead his troops. He passed on to him all the arts a prince must know, toiling to teach the boy, and his labors bore good fruit. Seyavash became a prince without a peer in all the world.

Time passed and now the youth was hunting lions with his lariat. He turned to Rostam and said, "I need to see my king; you've taken great pains in teaching me the ways of princes, and now my father must see the skills that Rostam's taught me." Rostam gathered presents for him— horses, slaves, gold, silver, seal-rings, crowns, thrones, cloth, carpets— and whatever his own treasury could not supply he sent for from elsewhere. He had Seyavash splendidly equipped, since the army would be observing him, and to keep the boy's spirits up, he accompanied him part of the way. His people decked the road in splendor, mixing gold and ambergris and sprinkling the mixture on him as he passed. Every house and street was decorated and the world was filled with joy, gold coins were scattered beneath the horses' hooves, their manes were smeared with saffron, wine, and musk; in all Iran there was not one sad soul.

Seyavash was welcomed at the court with great pomp and ceremony; festivities were held and Kavus lavished gifts on his son, reserving only the royal crown, saying that the boy was as yet too young for such an honor. But after eight years had passed he made him lord of Kavarestan, the land beyond the Oxus, and the royal mandate was inscribed on silk according to ancient royal custom.

Sudabeh's Love for Seyavash

Now when the king's wife, Sudabeh, saw Seyavash, she grew strangely pensive and her heart beat faster; she began to waste away like ice before fire, worn thin as a silken thread. She sent someone to him saying, "If you were to appear in the royal harem one day it would cause no alarm or surprise." Seyavash replied:

> "I don't like harems and I won't agree
> To plots and intrigues, so don't bother me."

At dawn the following day Sudabeh hurried to the king and said, "Great lord, whose like the sun and moon have never seen, whose son's a matchless paragon, dispatch this youth to your harem where his sisters and your women can set eyes on him; we'll do him homage and give him presents, and the tree of loyalty will bear sweet fruit." Kavus replied, "Your words are wise, your love is equal to a hundred mothers' love." He called Seyavash to him and said, "Blood ties and love will not stay hidden long; you've sisters in my harem, and Sudabeh loves you like a mother. God has created you in such a way that everyone who sees you loves you, and those who are your kin should not have to be content with glimpsing you from a distance. Pay a visit to my womenfolk, stay with them for a while and let them honor you." But when Seyavash heard the king's words, he stared at him in astonishment:

> He strove to keep his heart unstained and clean
> And pondered what it was the king might mean:
> Perhaps Kavus felt some uncertainty
> And meant to test his faith, or honesty.
> He knew the king was sly and eloquent,
> Watchful and warily intelligent.
> He thought, "And if I go there, Sudabeh
> Will corner me and pester me to stay."
> He said, "Send me to men of proven sense,
> To councilors of deep experience,
> To those who'll teach me how to fight, who know
> How I should wield a sword, or shoot a bow,
> Who know how kings hold court, how courtiers dine,
> The rules that govern music, feasts, and wine:
> What will I gather from your women's quarters?
> Since when has wisdom lived with wives and daughters?
> But if these are your orders, I will do
> Whatever seems appropriate to you."

The king replied, "Rejoice, my son, and may wisdom always guide you; I've heard few speeches so eloquent and it does a man good to hear you talk like this. But don't be so suspicious; be cheerful, drive away such gloomy thoughts. Now, your loving sisters and Sudabeh,

who loves you like a mother, are all waiting for you in the harem."
Seyavash said, "I shall come at dawn and do as you command."

There was a man, whose heart was cleansed of all evil, called Hirbad,
and he had charge of the king's harem. To this wise man Kavus said,
"When the sun unsheathes its sword, pay attention to what Seyavash tells
you." Then he told Sudabeh to prepare jewels and musk to scatter before
his son. When the sun rose above the mountains, Seyavash came to his
father and made his obeisance before him; Kavus talked to the boy for a
while then summoned Hirbad and gave him his orders. He said to
Seyavash, "Go with him, and prepare your heart for new delights."

The two went off together lightheartedly enough, but when
Hirbad drew back the curtain from the harem's entrance, Seyavash felt
a presentiment of evil. The womenfolk came forward with music to
welcome him; he saw bowls of musk, gold coins, and saffron on every
side, and as he entered gold, rubies, and emeralds were scattered before
his feet. He trod on Chinese brocade worked with pearls and saw fac-
ing him a golden throne studded with turquoise and draped in gor-
geous cloth; there sat the moon-faced Sudabeh, a paradise of tints and
scents, splendid as Canopus, a tall crown set on the thick black curls
that fell clustering to her feet. Beside her stood a slave, her head
humbly bowed, her mistress's gold-worked slippers in her hands.

As soon as she saw Seyavash enter, Sudabeh descended from the
throne. She walked coquettishly forward, bowed before him, and then
held him in a lengthy embrace. Slowly she kissed his eyes and face,
gazing as if she could never grow weary of him. She murmured,
"Throughout the day and for three watches of the night I thank God
a hundred times for your existence. No one has ever had a son like you,
no king has ever had a prince like you." Seyavash knew what all this
kindness meant, and that such friendship was improper; he hurried
over to his sisters, who greeted him respectfully and sat him on a
golden throne. After spending some time with them he returned to the
king's audience hall, and the harem buzzed with chatter: "That's what
I call a real prince, so noble and so cultivated . . .," "He seems an angel,
not a man at all . . .," "And his soul just radiates wisdom . . ."

Seyavash went to his father and said, "I have seen your harem; all
the splendor of the world is yours, and you can have no quarrel with
God. In treasure and power and glory you surpass Jamshid, Feraydun,

and Hushang." The king was overjoyed at his words and had the castle decorated like a spring garden; father and son passed the time with wine and music, giving no thought to the workings of Fate. At night-fall Kavus made his way to the harem and questioned Sudabeh: "No secrets from me now, tell me what you thought of Seyavash, of his behavior, of how he looks, of his conversation. Did you like him? D'you think he's wise? Is he better from report or when you see him face to face?" Sudabeh replied, "The sun and moon have never seen your equal, and who in all the world is like your son? This is not some-thing to be secretive about! Now, if you agree, I'll marry him to one of his own kin; I have daughters from you and one of them would surely bear him a noble son." Kavus replied, "This is my desire exactly; the greatness of our name depends on it."

When Seyavash came to his father the following morning Kavus cleared the court and said: "I have one, secret, unfulfilled request of God: that my name should live through a son of yours, and just as I was rejuvenated by your birth, so you will know delight in seeing him. Astrologers have said you will father a great son, to keep our name alive in the world. Now, choose some noble girl as your consort; look in King Pashin's harem, or there is King Arash's clan; look about for someone suitable." Seyavash said, "I am the king's slave, obedient to his wishes; but Sudabeh shouldn't hear of this, she won't like it. And I'm having no more to do with her harem." The king laughed at Seyavash's words; he thought all was firm ground and had no notion of swampy water lurking beneath the straw. "You worry about choosing a wife," he said, "and don't give Sudabeh a thought. She speaks well of you and only wants what's best for you." Seyavash showed pleasure at his father's words and bowed before the throne, but inwardly he still brooded over Sudabeh's intentions.

Sudabeh Tries Again
The next day Sudabeh sent Hirbad to Seyavash, saying, "Tell him to put himself to the trouble of honoring us with his noble presence." Seyavash came to the harem and saw her seated on her throne, her crown set on her bejeweled hair, her beautiful womenfolk standing by, as if the palace were a paradise. She descended from her throne and sat him there, then stood before him submissively, her arms folded across her chest, like a serving girl. She motioned to the young women, lovely as uncut jewels,

and said, "Look on this place, and on these gold-crowned virgin girls whose characters are compounded of coyness and modesty. If one of them pleases you, tell me: go forward and examine her face and stature." Seyavash glanced at the girls, but they were all too shy to return his gaze. One by one they passed before his throne, each silently reckoning her chances of being chosen. When the last had gone by, Sudabeh said, "How long will you stay silent? Won't you tell me which one you like? Your face is like an angel's, and anyone who glimpses you in the distance wishes you were hers. Look carefully at these girls, and choose whichever's suitable for you." But Seyavash sat there silent, thinking that it would be wrong to choose a wife from among his enemies; the story of what the king of Hamaveran had done to Kavus came to his mind, and the fact that Sudabeh was this man's daughter and, like him, was full of wiles and hatred for the Persian people. As he opened his mouth to answer, Sudabeh removed her veil and said:

> "The moon's of no account beside the sun,
> And now you see the sun. Come now, choose one
> Of these young virgins, and I'll have her stand
> Before you as your servant to command.
> But first, swear me an oath you'll never try
> To wriggle out of: King Kavus will die,
> And when that happens I will turn to you:
> Value me then as he was wont to do.
> I stand here now, your servant girl, I give
> My flesh to you, the soul by which I live;
> Take anything you want from me, I swear
> I won't attempt to slip free from your snare."
> She clutched his head and ripped her dress, as though
> All fear and shame had left her long ago.
> But Seyavash's cheeks blushed rosy red,
> Tears filled his eyes, and to himself he said,
> "May God who rules the planets succor me
> And save me from this witch's sorcery.
> If I speak coldly to her she'll devise
> Some spell to make the king believe her lies.
> My best course is to flatter her; to calm
> Her heart with glozing chat and gentle charm."

And so he said to Sudabeh: "Who in all the world is your equal, who is fit for you except the king? Your daughter is enough for me, no better bride for me exists. Suggest this to the king and see what he replies. I swear I'll look at no one else until she's grown as tall as I am. As for this liking you've conceived for my face, well, God has made me as you see me; but keep this as our secret, tell no one, and I too will keep the matter dark. You are the first of all our womenfolk, and I think of you as my mother." Then he left, with sorrow in his heart.

When Kavus arrived in the harem, Sudabeh told him of Seyavash's visit, saying that he had seen all the young women there but only her own daughter had pleased him. Overjoyed, the king had the treasury doors flung open and a great treasure prepared, while Sudabeh watched in wonder. She was determined to bend Seyavash to her will by any means possible, or, if she could not, to destroy his reputation.

Once more she sat upon her throne arrayed in all her splendor and summoned Seyavash. She said, "The king has prepared treasures for you, crowns and thrones such as no man has ever seen, immeasurable quantities of goods, enough to weigh down two hundred elephants. And he's going to give you my daughter as a bride. But look at me now; what excuse can you have to reject my love, why do you turn away from my body and beauty? I have been your slave ever since I set eyes on you, weeping and longing for you; pain darkens all my days, I feel the sun itself is dimmed. Come, in secret, just once, make me happy again, give me back my youth for a moment. I'll reward you with far more than the king has offered—bracelets, crowns, thrones. But if you refuse me and hold your heart back from my desires, I'll destroy you with the king and make him look on you with loathing."

Seyavash replied, "God forbid I should lose my head for the sake of my heart, or ever be so disloyal to my father as to forget all manliness and wisdom. You are the king's consort, the sun of his palace; such a sin is unworthy of you." Then Sudabeh sprang from her throne and stretched out her claws at him, crying, "I told you all the secrets of my heart and now you want to ruin me, to make me a laughingstock?" She tore her clothes, clawed at her cheeks, and screamed so loudly the sound was heard in the streets. A tumult of wailing went up from the palace and its gardens, and hearing it, Kavus sprang from his throne and hurried to the harem. When he saw Sudabeh's scratched face and the palace abuzz with rumors, he asked everyone what had happened, never suspecting that his hard-hearted wife was the cause of all this. Sudabeh stood wailing and weeping in front of him, tearing at her hair, and said, "Seyavash came to my throne room and clasped me tightly in his arms, saying he had never wanted anyone but me; he flung my crown aside and tore my clothes from my breasts."

Kavus questioned her closely, and in his heart he said, "If she is telling the truth, and is not simply trying to stir up trouble, the only possible solution is for Seyavash to be executed. The wise say that, in cases like this, honor demands blood." He cleared the harem of everyone but Sudabeh and Seyavash, and then, turning first to Seyavash, calmly said, "You must hide nothing from me. You didn't do this evil, I did, and now I must bear the consequences of my own foolish talk; why ever did I order you to go to the harem? Now I must suffer while you tell me what happened. Keep your eye on the truth now, and tell me exactly what occurred."

Seyavash told him the story and of how wild with passion Sudabeh had been, but Sudabeh broke in, "This is not true, he wanted no one in the harem except me. I reminded him of all the king had given him, of our daughter and all the treasure that was to be his, and I said I'd add more in gifts to the bride; but he said he wanted only me, and that without me girls and treasure were nothing to him. He flung his arms about me, his embrace was unyielding as a rock, and when I wouldn't do what he wanted, he yanked at my hair and scratched my face. I'm pregnant with a child of yours, my lord, and I suffered so much I thought I would lose our baby there and then; the world turned dark before my eyes."

Kavus said to himself, "I can't trust what either of them says; this is not something to be decided quickly, crises and worry cloud a man's judgment. I have to search out carefully which of the two of them is guilty and deserves to be punished." To this end he sniffed at Seyavash's hands and at his arms and body. Next he turned to Sudabeh, and on her he smelt the scents of wine, musk, and rosewater. There was no trace of such scents on Seyavash; there was no evidence that he had touched her. Kavus grew grim, despising Sudabeh in his heart, and to himself he said, "She should be hacked to pieces with a sword." But then he thought of Hamaveran and of the outcry that would arise if

Sudabeh were harmed, and also he remembered how when he had
been in captivity there, alone and friendless, she had ministered to him
day and night; the memory of this tormented him and he said noth-
ing. Thirdly, she was a loving woman and he felt she should be forgiven
for her faults. And fourthly, he had young children by her, and he
could not bear the thought of their grief if anything should happen to
their mother. But Seyavash was innocent, and the king recognized his
righteousness. He said to him, "Well, think no more of all this; follow
the ways of wisdom and knowledge. Mention this matter to no one;
we mustn't give gossip any kind of encouragement."

Sudabeh's Plot Against Seyavash

When Sudabeh realized that Kavus despised her, she began to plot
against Seyavash, nourishing the tree of vengeance with her wiles. One
of her intimates was a witch who was enduring a difficult pregnancy,
and Sudabeh gave her gold, persuading her to take a drug that would
abort the twins she carried. Sudabeh said she would tell Kavus the
babies were hers, and that she had miscarried because of Seyavash's evil
behavior. The woman agreed; when night fell she swallowed the drug,
and two ugly devil's spawn were still-born from her. Sudabeh hid her
and then lay groaning on her bed as if in labor. Her maidservants came
running and saw the two dead devil's spawn on a golden salver, while
Sudabeh screamed and tore at her clothes. Kavus woke trembling at the
noise and was told what had happened to his wife. He hardly drew
breath for the rest of the night and at dawn he hurried to the harem,
where he saw Sudabeh stretched out, her quarters in an uproar, and the
two dead babies lying pathetically on the golden salver. Her eyes awash
with tears, Sudabeh said, "See the work of this paragon of yours, and
like a fool you believed his lies!"

Kavus was sick at heart; he knew this was something he could not
ignore and he brooded on how to resolve the situation. He had
astrologers summoned; he told them of Sudabeh's history and of the
war with Hamaveran, then showed them the dead babies, and asked
their opinion. The men set to work with their astrolabes and charts and
after a week declared that poison did not turn to wine by being placed
in a goblet, and that these two babies were not Sudabeh's or the king's,
but the spawn of an evil race. For a week Kavus kept his own council,

but then Sudabeh appealed to him again saying, "I was the king's companion in adversity, and my heart's so wrung with grief for my murdered babies I hardly live from one moment to the next." But Kavus turned on her and said, "Be quiet, woman, enough of these sickening lies of yours." Then he ordered the palace guards to search high and low throughout the city for the babies' mother; they found her nearby and dragged her before the king. For days he questioned her kindly and made her promises, then he had her tied up and tortured, but she refused to confess. Finally he gave orders that she was to be threatened with execution and that, if she still stayed silent, she be sawn in two; but her only reply was that she was innocent and did not know what to say.

When Kavus was told of her response he went to Sudabeh and informed her of what the astrologers had said, but Sudabeh's reply was that they only said this because they were afraid of Seyavash. She added that, even if he felt no grief for their dead children, she had no other recourse than him and was content to leave the resolution of this quarrel to the world to come. She wept more water than the sun draws up from the Nile, and Kavus wept with her.

He dismissed her and summoned his priests and explained the situation. They advised that he try one of the two by fire, for the heavens would ensure that the innocent would not be harmed. He had Sudabeh and Seyavash called and said that in his heart he could trust neither of them unless fire demonstrated which of the two was guilty. Sudabeh's answer was that she had demonstrated Seyavash's guilt by producing the two miscarried babies, and that he should undergo the trial as he had acted evilly and sought to destroy her. Kavus turned to his young son and asked him his opinion. Seyavash replied that hell itself was less hateful than her words, and that if there were a mountain of fire, he would pass through it to prove his innocence. Torn between his love for Sudabeh and his regard for his son, Kavus decided to go ahead with the trial. He had a hundred caravans of camels and another hundred of red-haired dromedaries bring wood, and servants piled it into two huge hills, between which was a narrow pathway such as four horsemen might with difficulty pass through. While the populace watched from a distance,

> *Kavus had priests pour thick pitch on the pyre;*
> *Two hundred men dashed out to set the fire*

And such black clouds of smoke rose up you'd say
Dark night usurped the brilliance of the day.
But then quick tongues of flame shot out and soon
The plain glowed brighter than the sky at noon,
Heat scorched the burning ground, and everywhere
The noise of lamentation filled the air;
They wept to see the prince, who came alone
On a black horse before his father's throne;
His helmet was of gold, his clothes were white
And camphor-strewn, according to the rite
That's used in preparation of a shroud.
Dismounting from his horse, he stood, then bowed.
Gently his father spoke, and in his face
The prince saw conscious shame and deep disgrace.
But Seyavash said, "Do not grieve, my lord,
The heavens willed all this, and rest assured
The fire will have no strength to injure me;
My innocence ensures my victory."

When Sudabeh heard the tumult she came out on the roof of her palace and saw the fire; muttering to herself in rage, she longed for evil to befall the prince. The whole world's eyes were fixed on Kavus; men cursed him, their hearts filled with indignation. Then Seyavash wheeled, urging his horse impetuously into the fire; tongues of flame enveloped him and both his horse and helmet disappeared. Tears were in all eyes, the whole plain waited, wondering if he would re-emerge, and when they glimpsed him a shout went up, "The young prince has escaped the fire!" He was unscathed, as if he'd ridden through water and emerged bone dry, for when God wills it, he renders fire and water equally harmless. Seeing Seyavash, all the plain and city gave a great cry of gratitude, and the army's cavalry galloped forward scattering gold coins in his path; nobles and commoners alike rejoiced, passing on the news to one another that God had justified the innocent. But Sudabeh wept and tore at her hair and scored her cheeks with her nails.

Seyavash appeared before his father and there was no trace of fire or smoke or dust or dirt on him; Kavus dismounted, as did all the army, and the king clasped his son in his arms, asking his pardon for the evil that had been done. Seyavash gave thanks to God that he had escaped

the flames and that his enemy's designs had been destroyed. The king heaped praise on him and the two walked in state to the palace, where a royal crown was placed on the prince's head and for three days the court gave itself up to wine and music.

But on the fourth day Kavus sat enthroned in majesty, his ox-headed mace in his hand, and peremptorily summoned Sudabeh. He went over what she had claimed, then said, "Your shameless behavior has tormented my heart for long enough; you played foul tricks against my son, thrusting him into the fire; you used magic against him, and no apology will avail you now. Leave this place and prepare yourself for the gallows; you do not deserve to live and hanging is the only fit punishment for what you have done." She answered, "If my head's to be severed from my body, I am ready, give your orders. But I want you to harbor no resentment against me in your heart, so let Seyavash tell the truth—it was Zal's magic that saved him." But the king burst out, "Still at your tricks? It's a wonder you're not hunchbacked with the weight of your impertinence!" And then he turned to the court crying, "What punishment is suitable for the crimes she has committed in secret?" All answered, "The just punishment is that she suffer death for the evil she has done." Kavus said to the executioner, "Take her and hang her in the public way, and show no mercy." When all abandoned

Sudabeh in this fashion, the women of the court broke into loud lamentation, and Kavus turned pale, his heart wrung by their cries.

Seyavash said to the king, "Torment yourself no more about this matter; forgive her for my sake. Now, surely, she'll accept good guidance and reform her ways." And to himself he said, "If Sudabeh's destroyed, the king will regret it eventually, and when that happens he'll blame me for her death." Kavus, who had been looking for some excuse not to kill Sudabeh, replied, "For your sake I forgive her." Seyavash kissed his father's throne and then rose and left the court; the women of the harem flocked about Sudabeh, bowing before her one by one.

And after some time had passed the king's heart once again inclined to Sudabeh, and his love was such that he could not tear his eyes from her face. Once again her evil nature reasserted itself and she began to weave her secret spells, plotting against Seyavash. And, listening to her, Kavus once again began to turn against his son; but, for the moment, he concealed his suspicions.

Kavus Learns of a New Attack on Iran

News came to the lovesick Kavus that Afrasyab and a hundred thousand Turkish cavalry were menacing his borders. Reluctant to give up his life of ease and pleasure, he summoned a council and addressed them thus: "God did not make this Afrasyab of earth, air, fire, and water, as he did other men. How often has he sworn peace with us, but as soon as he can gather an army together, he forgets all his oaths and promises. There's no one but myself who can confront him and turn his day to darkest night; if I don't eclipse his glory he'll attack Iran and lay waste our territories as swiftly as an arrow flies from the bowstring." His advisors said, "Your army is sufficient without your presence; why waste wealth recklessly? Twice already your rashness has delivered the kingdom into your enemies' hands. Choose some warrior worthy of war to carry out this task for you." He answered, "But I see no one here who can confront Afrasyab; no, it's my boat that must be launched for this undertaking. Now leave me, and let me prepare my heart for what's to come."

Hearing this, Seyavash grew pensive, and thoughts crowded his mind like a dense thicket. To himself he said, "I should fight this war, and I must persuade Kavus to give command of our armies to me. In this way God will free me both from Sudabeh and my father's suspicions; and besides, if I can overcome such a force, I shall win fame for myself." He strode forward, his sword belt buckled on, and said, "I am capable of fighting with the king of Turan, and I shall humble his heroes' heads in the dust."

His father agreed to his request and made much of him, loading him with new honors and giving him treasure with which to equip the army. Then Kavus summoned Rostam and said to him, "No mammoth has your strength, and you showed your unparalleled wisdom and discretion when you raised Seyavash. Now he's come to me, his sword belt buckled on, talking as if he were a young lion. He wants to lead the expedition against Afrasyab; you're to accompany him, and see you never take your eyes off him. If you are watchful, I can sleep easily, but if you relax your vigilance, then I must bestir myself. The world rests safely because of your sword, and the moon in its sphere is yours to command." Rostam said:

> "I am your slave, obedient to you,
> Whatever you command me I shall do;
> My refuge is prince Seyavash, and where
> His crown is, heaven too, for me, is there."
> Heartened by Rostam's words Kavus replied,
> "May wisdom be your spirit's constant guide!"

Preceded by the din of fifes and kettledrums, the proud commander Tus appeared at court and the king flung open his treasury doors to equip the assembled warriors. Helmets, maces, sword belts, armor, lances, and shields were distributed, and the king sent the key to the treasury where uncut cloth and other wealth was stored to Seyavash, saying that he was to administer it as he saw fit. He chose twelve thousand cavalry, men from Pars, Kuch, Baluch, Gilan, and the plain of Saruch, and twelve thousand infantry; for leaders he chose men like Bahram and Zangeh, Shavran's son, and he also selected five priests to hold aloft the Kaviani banner.

Seyavash gave orders that they assemble on the plain outside the palace, and so crowded did the area become, it seemed there wasn't room for one more horseshoe; before the host the Kaviani banner

floated like a glittering moon. Kavus came out, quickly inspected the
troops, and addressed them:

> "May fortune favor you! May all who fight
> Against you be deprived of sense and sight;
> As you set out, may health and luck be yours,
> May you return as happy conquerors."

War drums were strapped on the elephants' backs; Seyavash gave the
order to mount and advance. His eyes awash with tears, Kavus accom-
panied them for the first day's journey. Finally father and son embraced,
each weeping like a cloud in springtime, and each felt within his heart
that he would not see the other again. Kavus turned back to his court,
and Seyavash led his warlike army on toward Zavolestan, where Zal,
Rostam's father, awaited them. There a month passed with wine and
music; Seyavash spent his time with Rostam, or with Rostam's brother
Zavareh, or seated cheerfully with Zal, or hunting wild game through
the reed beds.

But after a month Seyavash and Rostam led the army forward, leav-
ing Zal and his hospitality behind. Men flocked to their banner from
India and Kabol, and as they neared Herat, troops poured in from
every side. The heavens still smiled on them as they approached Talqun
and Marvrud, and so they went forward toward Balkh, injuring no
one, not so much as by an unkind word.

On the enemy's side, swift as the wind, Garsivaz and Barman
led their army forward; the leaders of the vanguard, Barman and
Sepahram, heard that a new prince, mighty as a mammoth, was lead-
ing an army forth from Iran. Quick as a skiff that cleaves the waves,
they dispatched a messenger to Afrasyab, telling him of Seyavash and
his great army and that warriors like Rostam, death's harbinger,
accompanied him. They pleaded with him to come at once, with fresh
troops, for the wind was in the sails of their venture and the ship
plunged forward.

But Seyavash confronted them before any answer could arrive, and
Garsivaz, hemmed in by Iran's troops, had no choice but to give bat-
tle; he decided to make a stand before the gates of Balkh. Two great
battles were fought on separate days, and then Seyavash staged a suc-
cessful infantry attack against the city's gates. As the Persians poured

into the city, Sepahram led the Turanian retreat back across the Oxus
to Afrasyab.

Seyavash Writes a Letter to His Father

As soon as Seyavash and his army had entered Balkh, he ordered that
a fitting letter, inscribed on silk, with ink compounded of musk,
spices, and rose water, be written to the king. He began by thanking
God from whom all victories proceed, who rules the sun and the
revolving moon, who exalts kings' crowns and thrones, who raises to
glory and strikes down in sorrow whomsoever he wishes, and whose
ways are beyond all human why or wherefore. Having invoked God's
blessings on his father, he continued: "By the grace and *farr* of the
world's king, I came to Balkh in high spirits and favored by fortune.
We fought for three days and on the fourth, victory was ours; Sepahram
has retreated to Termez, and Barman fled like an arrow shot from a
bow. My troops occupy the countryside as far as the Oxus and the
world submits to my glory. Now, if the king so orders me, I shall lead
our army further and continue the war."

When this letter reached the Persian king he felt that his crown and
throne had been elevated to the heavens, and he prayed to God that
this young sapling of his should grow and bear ripe fruit. In his happi-
ness he had an answer written as splendid as spring, as cheerful as par-
adise: "I pray to God who rules the sun and moon and maintains the
world that he keep your heart happy and free from sorrow and disas-
ter, and that victory, glory, and the crown accompany you forever.
Impatient for battles of your own, armed with fortune, skill, and righ-
teousness, you led off your army, although your lips still smelled of
mother's milk. May your body ever keep its skill and your heart always
attain to its desires. But now that you have the upper hand, you should
hold back somewhat. Make good use of the time you've gained; see
that the army doesn't scatter, fortify your camp:

> "This Turk you're dealing with is sly and base,
> Malevolent, and of an evil race;
> He's powerful, imagining that soon
> He'll lift his head above the shining moon.
> Be in no hurry now for war; hold back,
> Let Afrasyab advance, let him attack;

When once he's crossed the Oxus he will see
Carnage destroy his dreams of victory."

He set his seal to the letter and called for a messenger, ordering him to
make all haste to Seyavash. When Seyavash saw his father's missive, he
kissed the ground and banished all thoughts of sorrow from his heart;
he laughed and touched the letter to his head, took note of its con-
tents, and in his heart felt only loyalty to its commands.

But, for his part, the lion-warrior Garsivaz fled like wind-blown
dust to the king of Turan, where bitterly and plainly he told him how
Seyavash, aided by Rostam and an infinite army of famous fighters,
had attacked Balkh. He said, "To each one of us there were fifty of
them, armed with ox-headed maces, and their bowmen surged for-
ward like a fire. The eagle does not fly as they flew. For three days and
nights they fought, until our leaders and horses were exhausted, but
when one of their side grew tired, he retired from the battle and
rested, then returned with renewed vigor." But Afrasyab leapt up like
flame and screamed, "What's all this babble about sleep and rest?" He
glared at him as if he'd hack him in two, then yelled in fury and drove
him from his presence. He gave orders that a thousand of his hench-
men be summoned for festivities and that the plains of Soghdia shine
with Chinese splendor.

Afrasyab's Dream

Afrasyab passed the day with them in pleasure, but as the sun sank from
sight, he hurried to his bed and tossed and turned there in the bed-
clothes. When one watch of the night had passed he trembled and
cried out in his sleep, like a man delirious with fever. His servants ran
to him in an uproar, and when Garsivaz heard that the light of the
throne was dimmed, he hurried to the king's bedchamber and saw him
lying there sprawled in the dirt. He took him in his arms and said,
"Come, tell your brother what has happened." Afrasyab answered,
"Don't ask me, don't say anything to me now; hold me tightly in your
arms for a moment and let me gather my wits." After a while he came
back to himself and saw his chamber filled with lamenting retainers.
Torches were brought and, shaking like a wind-blown tree, he was
helped to his bed. Again Garsivaz questioned him: "Open your lips,
tell us this wonder."

The great Afrasyab answered him thus: "May no one ever see such a dream again; I've never heard that any man, young or old, has passed such a night. In my dream I saw a plain filled with snakes, the world was choked with dust, and eagles thronged the sky. The ground was dry and parched, as though the heavens had never blessed it with rain. My pavilion was pitched to one side, and our warriors stood around it. A dust storm sprang up and toppled my banner, and then on every side streams of blood began to flow; they swept away my tent, and my army that numbered over a thousand was mere lopped heads and sprawled bodies. Like a mighty wind, an army attacked from Iran; what lances they brandished, what bows! Every horseman had a head spitted on his lance and another head at his saddle; clothed in black, their lances couched, a hundred thousand of them charged my throne. They flung me from my seat and bound my arms behind me; I stared desperately around but saw none of my own people there. A haughty warrior dragged me before Kavus, and there on a shining throne sat a young man of no more than fourteen. When he saw me bound before him, he roared like a thunder cloud and hacked me in two with his sword. I screamed with the pain, and my screams awoke me."

Garsivaz said, "The king's dream can only mean what his friends would want for him: you will attain to your heart's desire and those who wish you ill will be destroyed. We need a wise, experienced dream interpreter; we should call our priests and astrologers to the court."

Wondering why they'd been summoned, a group appeared at court. Afrasyab had them enter, seated the most distinguished in the front, and chatted a little with each man. Then he said, "My wise, pure-hearted councilors, if I hear a word about this dream of mine from anyone in the world, I shall not leave a single head here on its body." Then, to allay their fears, he distributed a great deal of gold and silver among them and described his dream to them. When the chief priest had heard the dream he was afraid and asked pardon of the king, saying, "Who among us could interpret this dream, unless the king promises to deal justly with us when we give him our opinion?" The king promised they would come to no harm, and an eloquent spokesman for the group began: "I will reveal the inner meaning of the king's dream. A young prince accompanied by experienced councilors will lead a mighty and vigilant army here from Iran; the boy's father has had his horoscope cast and it predicts that our country will be destroyed. If the king fights with Seyavash, the face of the world will turn crimson as brocade with the blood that's shed; the Persians will not leave one Turk alive, and the king will regret giving battle. And if the young prince should be killed by the king, Turan will be left with no king to lead it, this land will be convulsed by a war of vengeance for Seyavash. Then you will recall these truths, when our land is ruined and depopulated; and, even if the king became a bird, he could not outsoar the turning heavens that look on us at times with fury, at times with favor."

When he heard this Afrasyab was alarmed and put all thoughts of war from his head; he told Garsivaz at length of the destruction that had been prophesied if he fought with Seyavash. He concluded, "Instead of looking for world dominion, I've no choice but to sue for peace. I'll send him gold, silver, crowns, thrones, and countless jewels, and I'll withdraw from the territories they ceded before. Then perhaps this disaster can be averted and my tears will damp this fire down. If I can seel Fate's eyes with gold, then the heavens may look favorably on me again. But we can only read what Fate has written; justice is whatever the heavens will for us."

At sunrise the country's nobles came to court, wearing their diadems of office and with loyalty in their hearts. Having gathered together his wisest and most experienced men, Afrasyab addressed them:

> "In all my life, Fate's given me no more
> Than battles, conflict, and unending war.
> How many from this noble company
> Have been destroyed in war because of me;
> How many gardens are now overgrown,
> How many cities sacked and overthrown,
> How many orchards fought through; far and wide
> My troops have scarred and scoured the countryside.
> And when the king's unjust, goodness must flee,
> Hiding itself in stealth and secrecy;
> The wild ass suffers an untimely birth,
> And rivers fail and dry throughout the earth,
> The hawk's squabs grow up blind, beasts' teats turn dry,
> The musk-deer makes no musk to know him by;
> Righteousness flees from crookedness in fear,
> On all sides dearth and misery appear.

But tired now of the evil ways I trod,
I long to trace the virtuous paths of God;
In place of sorrow, pain, and enmity,
I'll nourish knowledge, justice, amity;
Through me the world will be at rest; no more
Will death surprise us, and untimely war.
Iran and wide Turan are mine by right,
How many kings pay tribute to my might!
If you agree hostilities should cease,
I'll write to Rostam now, proposing peace;
To Seyavash I'll send rich tokens of
My hopes for harmony and mutual love."

One by one his councilors agreed to peace and reconciliation, saying that he was their king and they his slaves. When they had left, Afrasyab turned to Garsivaz and said, "Make ready for the road, don't waste words; choose two hundred warriors and prepare gifts for Seyavash: Arab horses with golden saddles, Indian swords with silver scabbards, a gem-encrusted crown, a hundred camel-loads of carpets, two hundred slave girls and as many boys. Tell him we've no quarrel with him, that we make no claim on Iran. Say, 'We accept that Soghdia, the land as far as the Oxus, is ours; thus it has been since the time of Salm and Tur, when all the world was turned upside down and the innocent Iraj was slain. I pray that God will grant us peace and happiness, that your good fortune will bring peace to the world, and that war and evil will disappear. You are a king yourself; speak to the king of Iran, see if you can soften his warlike ways.' Flatter Rostam, take him slaves and horses with golden bridles, load him with gifts so that our plan is successful, but, as he's not a king, don't present him with a golden throne."

When Garsivaz had gathered the gifts together, they made a splendid show. He hurried to the Oxus and sent a nobleman ahead to Balkh to announce his coming. As soon as Seyavash heard of Garsivaz's approach, he consulted with Rostam as to what should be done.

Garsivaz arrived and Seyavash commanded that he be admitted to the court; seeing him, he stood, smiled, and asked his pardon. Garsivaz paused at a distance and kissed the ground; shame was apparent in his face, and his heart was filled with fear. Seyavash motioned him to a place near the throne and asked after Afrasyab. Garsivaz sat and took stock of the prince's splendor and then addressed Rostam, "When Afrasyab heard of your coming, he sent me here with a trifling present for Seyavash." He signaled that the gifts be paraded before Seyavash; the road from the city gates to the court was thronged with the slaves and valuables he'd brought, and no one could reckon their value. Seyavash was well pleased with what he saw and he listened to Afrasyab's proposals. The wary Garsivaz kissed the ground, made his obeisance, and left the court.

Rostam said, "We should entertain him for a week before we give an answer. We must think carefully and consult with others." A house was fitted up for Garsivaz and stewards sent to look after him, while Seyavash and Rostam turned the proposal over at length. Rostam was suspicious of the speed with which Garsivaz had come and, as was prudent, had scouts posted to keep an eye on the approaches. Seyavash questioned him, then said, "We have to get to the bottom of why they are seeking peace; what's the best antidote for a poison like him? Who are his closest kin? If he were to send a hundred of his warrior relatives here as hostages, that would show us his real objectives. God forbid he's holding back simply out of fear, and that under this show of good intentions he's actually beating his war drums. Once we've arranged all this we should send someone to my father Kavus to persuade him to give up his dream of vengeance." Rostam agreed, "You're right; this is the only way to conclude the treaty."

At dawn the next day Garsivaz appeared at court, belted and crowned as was appropriate; he kissed the ground before Seyavash and greeted the prince. Seyavash said, "I have been weighing your words and deeds carefully; the two of us agree that we should wash all thoughts of vengeance from our hearts. Take this answer to Afrasyab: 'If you are plotting an attack on us, know that he who sees the ends of evil should refrain from evil and that a heart adorned with wisdom is a priceless treasure. If there is no poison hiding in this draught you offer, if malevolence has no place in your heart, then let Rostam choose a hundred of your kin, whose names will be given to you; you will send these men to me as guarantors of your good faith. Further, you will evacuate those Iranian towns you occupy, withdraw to Turan, and cease to plan for war. There should be only righteousness between us; I for my part will not prepare for war, and I shall send a letter to King Kavus advising him to recall our armies.'"

Garsivaz dispatched a horseman, saying, "Gallop to Afrasyab and don't pause for sleep on the way; tell him that I've accomplished all he wished for, but that Seyavash demands hostages before he'll renounce this war." When the message was delivered, Afrasyab writhed inwardly, uncertain what he should do. He communed with himself: "If I'm to be deprived of a hundred of my own kindred, my court's power will be broken, there'll be no one left here who has my well-being at heart; but if I refuse him these hostages, he'll think all I've said is a lie. I shall have to send them if he won't agree to any other terms." He counted off a hundred of his kinsmen, according to the list drawn up by Rostam, presented them with gifts and robes of state, and sent them to the Persian prince.

Then he gave orders that the drums and trumpets be sounded; the royal pavilion was dismantled and his army evacuated Bokhara, Soghd, Samarkand, Chaj, and Sepanjab, moving toward Gang without excuses or delay. When Rostam learned of their withdrawal he ceased to worry; he hurried to Seyavash, told him what he'd heard, and said, "Since things have turned out well, Garsivaz should be allowed to return." Orders were given that a robe of honor be prepared and that weapons, a crown, and a belt, together with an Arab horse with a golden bridle and an Indian sword in a silver scabbard, be brought. When Garsivaz saw the prince's gifts, he seemed as astonished as a man might be who saw the moon descend to the earth. He left full of praises for the prince, and his feet seemed to skim the ground in gratitude.

Seyavash sat on his ivory throne, the crown suspended above him. He searched his mind for someone eloquent, who could give words persuasive force; he needed some nobleman from the army who would get on well with Kavus. Rostam said to him, "Who is going to dare open his mouth about such a subject? Kavus is as he always was, his anger is always there, neither less nor more. All I can suggest is that I go to him; I'd split the earth open if you ordered me to, and I think only good can come of my mission." Seyavash was overjoyed at his words and gave up all thoughts of looking for another messenger.

Seyavash Writes a Letter to Kavus
The prince and Rostam sat down together and talked at length. Seyavash summoned a scribe, and a letter was written on silk. He began by prais-

ing God who had given him victory and glory, whose orders none can evade, the Lord of wealth and dearth, Creator of the sun and the moon, Bestower of the crown and throne, who knows all good and evil. The letter continued: "I reached Balkh rejoicing in my fate, and when Afrasyab heard of my coming the clear water in his goblet turned to pitch. He knew that difficulties hemmed him in, that his world was darkened and his luck at an end. His brother came offering me wealth and beautiful slaves, begging the king of the world for peace, and resigning authority to him. He promised to keep to his own territories, to leave Iran's soil, and to harbor in his heart no thoughts of war. He sent a hundred of his relatives to me as guarantors of his word. Rostam comes to you asking that you pardon him, since he is worthy of our kindness." Rostam set off for the king with a contingent of men, his banner fluttering overhead.

For his part Garsivaz returned to the king of Turan and told him of Seyavash, saying, "As a prince he has no equal for handsomeness or nobility of action, for intelligence or kindness or dignity or eloquence; he's brave, speaks well, is a good horseman, and he and wisdom are like old companions." The king laughed and said, "Policy beats warfare, then, my brother! I was disturbed by that nightmare I had, which is why I looked for some way out of this. Well, I've accomplished what I wanted with gold and treasure."

Meanwhile Rostam reached the king of Iran's court. As he entered, Kavus descended from the throne and embraced him, asking after his son and their battles and wanting to known why Rostam had returned. Rostam began by praising Seyavash, then handed over the letter. While the secretary was reading it to him Kavus's face grew black as pitch and he turned on Rostam: "He's young, I know, and has seen nothing of the world's evil, but you, who have no equal in the world, whom all great warriors long to match themselves against, haven't you seen Afrasyab's wickedness, and how he has deprived me of rest and sleep? I should have gone, I longed to fight with him, but they told me not to, saying I should let the young prince manage things. And where God's punishment was called for, you let yourselves be beguiled by wealth he's looted from the innocent and by a hundred misbegotten Turks, bastards whose fathers no one can name. What does he care about such hostages? They're water under the bridge to him. But if you've taken leave of your senses, I'm not tired of warfare yet: I'll send someone resourceful to Seyavash, tell him to burn Afrasyab's presents and to send the hostages in shackles here, where I'll hack their heads off. And as for you, you must lead your army into enemy territory where, like wolves, they're to plunder all they find until Afrasyab comes out to fight you."

Rostam replied, "My lord, don't upset yourself about this, but listen to me for a moment. The world is now subservient to you, and you yourself advised the prince not to advance across the Oxus, but to wait for Afrasyab to attack. And so we waited, but he sued for peace. It's not right to attack someone who's looking for peace and reconciliation. And the righteous will not look kindly on someone who breaks his oath. Seyavash fought like a fearless leopard, and what else was he fighting for but the crown and throne, wealth and security, and our homeland Iran? He has gained all these, and there is no point in wildly looking for war now; don't darken your bright heart with such muddied notions. If Afrasyab reneges on his promises, then we can fight; we're not tired of battle, and that will be the time for swords and warfare. Don't ask your son to break his oath; lies do not become the crown. I tell you plainly, Seyavash will not go back on his word and he would be horrified to know what you're planning."

Then Kavus started up, glaring at Rostam in fury, and said, "So everything comes out now, does it? So it was you who put these thoughts in his head, you who tore the desire for vengeance from his heart? You only looked for your own ease and comfort in all this, not for the glory of our crown and throne. You stay here; Tus is the one to strap war drums on his elephants and complete this business. I'll send a messenger to Balkh, and the message he takes will be a bitter one. If Seyavash can't agree to my commands, then he's to resign command of the army to Tus and return here with his companions, and I'll deal with him as he deserves."

Rostam was enraged and replied, "The heavens themselves don't lord it over me; if you think Tus a better warrior than Rostam, you'll learn soon enough how rare men like Rostam are." And he stormed from the king's presence with hatred in his heart, his face flushed with anger. Kavus immediately summoned Tus and ordered him to set out. Tus had drums and trumpets sounded to muster the army for the journey.

Kay Kavus's Answer to Seyavash

Kavus summoned a scribe and had him sit beside him. He dictated a letter full of belligerent, angry words. Having praised the God of war and peace, Lord of the planets Mars and Saturn and of the moon, Creator of good and evil and of kingly glory, he went on: "Young man, rejoicing in your strength and fortune, may the crown and throne be yours forever. If you have neglected my commands, it's because the sleep of youth has beguiled you. You've heard what this enemy did to Iran when he beat us in battle. Now is no time for you to fall for his wiles; if you don't want fortune to forsake you, don't push your young head into his trap. Send these hostages you've secured here, to my court; it's no surprise if he's deceived you, he's done it to me often enough, persuading me by his glozing words to call off my attacks. I said nothing about a truce, and you've disobeyed my orders, enjoying yourself with pretty girls instead of getting on with the war. And as for Rostam, he can't get enough of gifts and riches. But it's conquest by the sword that you should depend on, it's conquered land that gives a king glory. When Tus arrives he'll sort out your affairs. You're immediately to load the hostages with chains and mount them on donkeys. Fate won't look kindly on this truce of yours; when the news spreads in Iran, it'll cause an uproar. Get on with your task of vengeance; attack by night and make a second Oxus of their blood. Then Afrasyab won't stay sleeping long; he'll advance to give battle. But if you feel sorry for that devil incarnate, if you don't want to break your word to him and have no stomach for war, then hand the army over to Tus and get yourself back here."

When Seyavash received the message and saw its graceless language, he called over the courier, who told him how Rostam had been received, and about Tus and Kavus's rage. Seyavash was saddened to hear of the treatment meted out to Rostam, and he fell to brooding on his father's actions, on the day of battle, and on the Turkish hostages. He said:

> "A hundred noble knights, all innocent,
> Of royal lineage: and if they're sent
> To King Kavus he'll neither ask nor care
> About their lives, but hang them then and there.

And what excuse can I then bring before God? The world hems me in with evil: if I make war on the king of Turan, God and my own men will condemn me; and if I hand over the army to Tus and return to Kavus, evil will come to me from him, too. I see evil to the left and to the right, and evil ahead of me. Sudabeh has brought me nothing but evil, and I don't know what else God has in store for me."

He summoned two noblemen from the army, Bahram and Zangeh, cleared his tent of everyone else, and sat them down. He told them what had happened to Rostam and went on, "Countless evils surround me; the king's kind heart was like a leafy tree bestowing shade and fruit, but everything was turned to poison when Sudabeh deceived him. His harem became my prison, and my life's laughter turned to misery; the fruit of her lust was the fire I passed through. I chose war as a means of escape from her clutches. And when we came to Balkh and defeated the enemy, they retreated from our land and sent us presents and hostages. Our priests advised us to turn aside from war, as we had secured all we had fought for and there was no point in shedding more blood. I will not order further fighting, since I fear to break my oath. Disobedience to God is contemptible, and if I turn from righteousness, I shall forfeit both this world and the world to come; I shall be as Ahriman would wish. And, if I fight, who knows to which side Fate will give the victory? Would that my mother had never borne me, or that in being born I had died; my fate is like a massive tree whose fruit is poison and whose leaves are sorrow. I have sworn a binding oath before God and if I break it disaster will erupt on every side. The whole world knows I have made peace with the king of Turan; everyone will revile me, and I shall deserve it. And how can God look kindly on me if I turn again to vengeance, cut myself off from the ways of faith, and flout the laws of earth and heaven? I shall leave this place and seek out somewhere where my name will be hidden from Kavus; but may all be as God wills. Zangeh, I ask you to undertake a heavy responsibility; go quickly to Afrasyab's court and return to him the hostages and presents he has given us. Tell him what has happened." And to Bahram he said, "I leave our armies, elephants, and war drums, together with this frontier area, under your command. Wait till Tus comes and then hand everything over to him; count out to him all the treasure, every crown and throne, item by item."

Bahram's heart was wrung with sympathy for his commander's pain; violently he wept and cursed the country of Hamaveran. The two noblemen sat grief-stricken, then Bahram said, "This is not the way forward; without your father there is no place for you in all the world. Write the king another letter, ask for Rostam back. If he tells you to fight, fight. Best not to bandy words with him; there's no shame in apologizing to your father. We'll wage war as he commands us to; don't brood on this, flattery will bring him round. The crown and throne, the army and court, all will be useless without you. The king's brain is like a brazier filled with coals, and all his plans and wars are mere folly."

But Seyavash could not accept their advice, since the heavens secretly willed another fate for him. He answered them: "The king's command transcends the sun and moon for me, but neither commoner nor noble, neither lion nor mammoth, can oppose God; a man who disobeys God's commands abandons himself to bewilderment. I can neither plunge these two countries into warfare again nor go back to the king with his orders neglected and there face his wrath and disappointment. If you are alarmed at my orders, ignore them; I shall be my own messenger and leave this encampment."

Hearing this, the warrior's hearts failed within them; as if seared by fire they wept at the prospect of separation from their commander, fearing what fate held in store for him. Zangeh replied, "We are your slaves, sworn to serve you, faithful unto death." Seyavash said, "Go to Turan's commander and tell him what has happened to me; say that this truce has meant sweetness for him, but only pain and poison for me. Say that I will not break the oath I swore to him, and that if this means I am to be exiled from the throne, then God is my refuge, the earth will be my throne and the heavens my crown. Tell him I cannot go back to my father. Ask him to allow me free passage through his territories, to wherever God wills I should wander. I shall seek out some distant country where my name will remain hidden from Kavus, where I shall not have to hear his reproaches and can rest awhile from his fury."

Zangeh's Mission to Afrasyab

Taking a hundred warriors as escort, Zangeh reached the Turkish king's capital. As he approached, Afrasyab rose from the throne, embraced him, and made much of him. When the two were seated Zangeh handed over a letter and repeated all he had been told. Afrasyab's heart was wrung by what he read and heard, and his head whirled with confused notions. He had Zangeh billeted according to his rank and then summoned Piran. Clearing the court, he shared with him Kavus's childish talk, which showed his evil character and his plans for war. As Afrasyab spoke his face clouded with anxiety; worry and sympathy for Seyavash filled his heart. "What," he asked, "is the remedy for all this? What would it be best for us to do?"

Piran replied, "May you live forever, my lord. In all matters you are wiser than I am, and more able to carry out what must be done. But this is my opinion: whoever has the opportunity to help this prince, either secretly or openly, either by giving him wealth or taking pains on his behalf, should do so. I've heard that in stature, sense, dignity, chivalry, and all that's fitting for a prince, there's no nobleman in all the world who is his equal. But seeing is better than hearing, and we have seen how nobly he acted over the hundred hostages he held, opposing his father on their behalf. He's cast aside hopes of the crown and throne and is turning to you for help. It would not be wise or right, my lord, to let him simply pass through our territories; our noblemen would blame you for this and you would sadden the prince. And then consider, Kavus is old, he cannot reign for much longer; Seyavash is young, he possesses the royal *farr*, and he will soon inherit the throne. If my lord acts wisely in this matter he will write to Seyavash welcoming him as a father would. Give him a place in this country, offer him respect and kindness; marry one of your daughters to him, treat him with honor and dignity. If he stays here with you, it will bring peace to your land, and if he returns to his father Fate will look kindly on you. Iran's king will be grateful to you and the world's noblemen will praise you. If Fate brings Seyavash here, our two countries will rest from warfare, as the world's creator would wish."

When Turan's commander had heard Piran out and looked at the facts, he brooded for a while, weighing what should be done. Then he said, "Your advice pleases me; no one in the world has your experience and wisdom. But there's a proverb that seems apposite here:

> Bring up a little lion cub, and you
> Will be rewarded when his teeth show through;

Forgetting all the kindness he's been shown
He'll maul his master when his claws have grown."

But Piran said, "May the king look at this matter wisely: will a man display his father's bad qualities when he has opposed those very qualities? Don't you see that Kavus's days are numbered, and that this being so, he must die soon? Then with no trouble at all Seyavash will inherit his country and its treasures and glory; our country and his, and their crowns and thrones, will then be yours. And is this not the height of good fortune?"

Afrasyab's Answer to Seyavash

Hearing this, Afrasyab took a wise decision and called in an experienced scribe. He began his letter with praise of the world's creator and continued: "May this God bless the prince, lord of the mace and sword and helmet, who is righteous and who fears God, in whose soul there is no injustice or crookedness. I have received Zangeh's message, and my heart is grieved at your king's treatment of you. But what else does a fortunate man seek for in the world than a crown and throne? And these you have; all of Turan will do your bidding, and I feel the need of your kindness. You'll be my son and I will be like a father to you, a father who seeks to serve his son. Kavus has never shown you the kindness I will; I'll open my treasury to you, assign you a throne, and keep you as my own child so that you will be a remembrance of me in the world when I am gone. If I let you pass through my kingdom, commoners and nobles alike will condemn me, and you will find the going hard beyond my borders, unless you have supernatural powers. You'll see no land there and will have to cross the Sea of China. But God has made this unnecessary for you; stay here and live at ease; my army, territories, and wealth are at your disposal. And you won't have to search for excuses to leave: when you and your father are reconciled, I'll load you with presents and willingly send you on your way to Iran. You won't be at odds with your father for long; he is old and will soon grow tired of his differences with you. Once a man reaches sixty-five the fire of anger begins to fail in him. Iran and all its wealth will be yours. I have accepted God's command that I succor you, and no harm will come to you from me."

Afrasyab sealed the letter and, having given Zangeh gifts of gold and silver, a splendid cloak, and a horse with a gold-worked saddle, he sent him on his way to Seyavash. Zangeh reported to his prince what he had seen and heard, and Seyavash rejoiced at this, but at the same time his heart was filled with sorrow and anxiety that he had to make a friend of his enemy, since when did cooling breezes ever blow from a raging fire? He wrote to his father, saying, "Despite my youth I have always acted wisely, and the king's anger against me grieves my heart. His harem was the cause of my first sorrow, making me traverse a mountain of fire, and in my trial the wild deer wept for me. To escape such shame I set out for war, riding confidently against its monstrous claws. Two countries rejoiced at the peace I fashioned, but the king's heart hardened against me like steel. Nothing I did pleased him, and since he is sick of the sight of me, I shall not stay in his presence. May happiness always inhabit his heart, while sorrow drives me to the dragon's maw. I do not know what will become of this, or what secrets of good and ill the heavens hold in store for me."

Next he gave orders to Bahram: "Keep your fame bright in the world; I hand over to you my crown and royal pavilion, the wealth I've levied, and the throne, our banners, cavalry, elephants, and war drums. When the commander Tus arrives, hand them over to him just as you've received them." He selected three hundred horsemen for his own use, together with a quantity of coins, jewels, and armor. Then he summoned his officers and addressed them: "Piran, sent by Afrasyab, has already crossed to our side of the Oxus. He bears a secret message for me, and I shall go out to welcome him. You must remain here; you are to regard Bahram as your leader and to obey his orders." The warriors kissed the ground before Seyavash.

Seyavash Travels from Iran to Turkestan

As the sun set, and the air grew dark and the world forbidding, Seyavash led his men toward the Oxus, his face obscured by tears. At Termez the streets and roofs were decorated to welcome him, so that spring with all its tints and scents seemed to have come, and each of the towns they passed through seemed like a bride arrayed in splendor. At Qajqar he dismounted and rested for a while. When news of his approach arrived, Piran chose a thousand knights and rode out to welcome him, taking as a gift four richly caparisoned white elephants and a hundred horses with gold-worked saddles. As soon as Seyavash saw his banners and heard the elephants' trumpeting he hurried toward him. The two embraced and Seyavash said, "Why have you troubled yourself by travelling like this? My only hope has been to see you alive and well." Piran kissed his head and feet and his handsome face and gave thanks to God, saying, "O Lord of what is hidden and what is plain, if I had seen such a man in a dream it would have restored my youth to me." To Seyavash he said, "I praise God that I see you before me as clearly as the daylight. Afrasyab will be like a father to you, and all on our side of the Oxus are as your slaves. I have over a thousand henchmen who are yours to command, and if you can accept an old man's service, I stand ready to obey you."

> The two rode forward then, their cheerful chat
> Wandering at random over this and that;
> The towns they passed were filled with music's sound,
> And scattered musk and gold obscured the ground.
> But seeing this, the prince's eyes grew dim,
> Old, melancholy memories troubled him;
> His heart recalled great Rostam's land, Zabol,
> The grandeur and the beauty of Kabol—
> Then all Iran beset him, place by place,
> He blushed for shame and turned away his face;
> But wise Piran saw all his misery
> And bit his lip in pain and sympathy.

They rested a while and, gazing in wonder at him, Piran said, "You seem like one of the ancient kings. You've three qualities which together make you unique: first, that you're of the seed of Kay Qobad; another, that you speak so honestly and eloquently; and third, that your countenance radiates grace." Seyavash replied, "You are renowned throughout the world for your good faith and kindness, for your hatred of evil and Ahriman; swear to me now and I know you will not break your word. If my presence here is good, I should not weep; but if it is not good, then tell me, show me the way to another country." Piran said, "Don't dwell on the fact that you've left Iran; trust to Afrasyab's kindness and be in no hurry to leave us. His reputation is bad in the world, but this is undeserved; he's a God-fearing man. He's wise and cautious in his councils and is not given to making hasty, harmful decisions. I'm related to him, and I'm both his champion and adviser. In this land over a hundred thousand horsemen are mine to command; twelve thousand are from my own tribe and, if I wish, will wait on me day and night. I've weapons, territory, flocks of sheep, and much more in reserve; I can live independently of everyone. All that I have I place at your disposal if you will agree to live here. I've accepted you as a trust from God, and I shall let no harm come to you; though no one knows what Fate holds in store for him." Seyavash was comforted by these words; his spirits revived and they sat to their wine, Piran as a father, Seyavash as his son.

Cheerful and laughing, they pressed on to Gang, a beautiful site where the Turkish monarch held court. Afrasyab came rushing out on foot to greet them, and as soon as he saw the king approaching, Seyavash dismounted and ran forward. They embraced, kissing each other's eyes and head, and Afrasyab said, "The world's evil sleeps. From now on neither revolt nor war will break out; the leopard and the lamb will share one watering place. Brave Tur set the world in a turmoil, but now our countries are tired of war. They have fought for too long, blind to the ways of peace; through you we shall rest from battles and the longing for blood-revenge. The land of Turan is your slave, the hearts of all here are full of love for you. All I have, my body and my soul, are yours. May you live healthily and happily here; all our treasures are yours. I will treat you with a father's love and always smile upon you."

Seyavash replied, "May your lineage never forfeit its good fortune." Then Afrasyab took Seyavash's hand, led him to the throne, and sat down. He gazed at Seyavash's face and said, "I know of nothing like this in all the earth. In the world men are not like this, with such a face, such stature, such royal *farr*." And turning to Piran he said, "Kavus is old and sadly wanting in wisdom if he can give up such a noble and accomplished son."

Afrasyab had one of his palaces set aside for his guest; it was spread with gold-worked carpets, and a golden throne with legs fashioned like the heads of buffalo was placed there. The walls were hung with Chinese brocade, and a multitude of servants was assigned to it. Seyavash entered, and its arch seemed to touch the heavens; he sat on the throne lost in thought until a servant called him to dine with the king. The meal passed in pleasantries, and then the courtiers sat to their wine while musicians played in the background. Afrasyab pledged his heart to Seyavash and swore he'd know no rest without him. They drank till darkness fell; by the time everyone was tipsy Seyavash had forgotten about Iran, and in this drunken state he returned to his own quarters. Afrasyab said to his son Shideh, "Take some of our nobles at dawn to Seyavash, as he's waking up, and have them present him with gifts—slaves, fine horses, gold-worked boots—and have the army take him cash and jewels. Do this in a dignified, becoming way." The king himself sent many more gifts, and so a week passed by.

Seyavash Displays His Skills Before Afrasyab

One evening the king said to Seyavash, "Let's get up at dawn tomorrow and enjoy ourselves at polo; I've heard that when you play, your mallet's invincible." Seyavash agreed and the next morning they made their way laughing and joking to the field, where the king suggested they divide up their companions, with Seyavash heading one team and he the other. But Seyavash said, "I can't be your rival, choose some other opponent and let me ride on your side, if you think I'm good enough." Afrasyab was pleased by this and thought everyone else's remarks mere chaff in the wind by comparison. Nevertheless he insisted, "By the head and soul of Kavus, you're to play against me; and see you do well, so that no one says I've made a bad choice for an opponent." Seyavash replied, "I and all the warriors here, and the game itself, are yours to command." For himself the king selected Golbad, Garsivaz, Jahan, Pulad, Piran, Nastihan, and Human, who was known for being able to scoop the ball from water. To Seyavash's side he sent some of his own henchmen, including Ruin and the famous Shideh, Andariman, who was a great horseman, and Ukhast, who was like a lion in battle. But Seyavash said, "Which of these men is going to try for the ball? They all belong to the king, and I'll be the only one playing on my side. If you'll allow me, I'll choose some of my own men." The king agreed and Seyavash selected seven Iranians who were worthy of the honor.

At the field's edge drums thundered out, cymbals clashed, and trumpets blared. The ground seemed to shake with the din, and dust rose into the sky as the horsemen took the field. The king struck the ball up toward the clouds; Seyavash urged his horse forward and before it touched the ground he smote the ball so hard that it disappeared from sight. Afrasyab ordered another ball to be tapped toward Seyavash; the prince lifted it to his lips and the sound of trumpets and drums rang out. Then he mounted a fresh horse, tossed the ball into the air, and hit it such a blow with his mallet that it seemed to rise to the moon's sphere, as if the sky had swallowed it. The king laughed out loud, and his nobles were startled enough to exclaim, "We've never seen a horseman with such skills." Afrasyab said, "This is how a man who has God's *farr* is!"

A royal pavilion had been erected at the field's edge and there Seyavash sat with the king, who gazed happily at his princely guest. Then he called to the warriors, "The field, mallets, and balls are yours!" The two sides fell to, and dust rose up, obscuring the sun. The Turks strove hard to get possession, but without success; Seyavash was alarmed by the Persians' behavior and called out in Pahlavi, "This is a playing field, not a battlefield for you to be raging and struggling like this; give way, and let them have the ball for once." The Persians let their reins go slack and stopped encouraging their horses. The Turks struck the ball and rushed forward like fire. When Afrasyab heard the Turks' shout of triumph he realized what that sentence in Pahlavi had meant. He said to Seyavash, "I've been told that you have no equal as a bowman." Seyavash drew his Kayanid bow from its casing and Afrasyab asked to look at it and have one of his men test it. He praised it highly and handed it to Garsivaz, ordering him to string it. Garsivaz struggled to notch the string, but to his chagrin was unable to. Seyavash took the bow from him, knelt, bent back the shaft and strung it. The king laughed and said, "Now that's the kind of bow a man needs; when I was young I had one just like that, but times have changed. There's not another man in Iran or Turan who could manage this bow in battle, but Seyavash with his great chest and shoulders wouldn't have any other."

A target was set up at the end of the lists; without saying a word to anyone Seyavash mounted his horse, yelled his war cry, and galloped forward; one arrow struck the center of the target and, as the warriors watched, he notched another (made of poplar wood, with four feathers) to the string and in the same charge again transfixed the target.

Gripping the reins in his right hand he wheeled around and once again sent an arrow home. Then he slipped the bow over his arm, rode back to the king, and dismounted before him. The king stood and called down blessings on him, and the two made their way happily back to the palace.

They sat to food and wine, accompanied by courtiers worthy of the honor, and after a few draughts had been downed and the company was growing merry they toasted Seyavash. While they were still feasting Afrasyab conferred a splendid robe on Seyavash, a horse with all its trappings, a sword and diadem, clothes and a quantity of uncut cloth the like of which no one had ever seen, silks, purses stuffed with coins, turquoises, male and female slaves, and a goblet filled with rubies. He ordered that all this be counted out and then conveyed to Seyavash's palace. He commanded his kinsmen to think of themselves as a flock of which Seyavash was the shepherd. Then he turned to the prince and said, "We must go hunting together; we'll enjoy ourselves, and the hunt will put sad thoughts out of our minds." Seyavash said, "Whenever and wherever you wish."

And so one day, accompanied by a group of Turkish and Persian warriors, they started out with cheetahs and hawks for the hunt. Seyavash spied a wild ass on the plain and left the group behind as he set off like the wind in pursuit. His reins grew light, his stirrups heavy, as he galloped forward over the rough terrain. He caught up with the ass and slashed it in two with his sword; the two halves were absolutely equal in weight (as if his hands were a balance and the ass weighed silver) and when the king's companions saw this they exclaimed, "Here is a swordsman worthy of the name!" But to one another they murmured, "An evil has come to us from Iran. Our leader is put to shame by him; we should oppose the king in this." Seyavash rode on through gullies, over mountains and across the plain, bringing down prey with arrows, sword, and lance, piling up carcasses everywhere, until the group was sated with hunting and made its way cheerfully back to the king's palace.

Whether in good spirits or gloomy, the king wished to be with no one but Seyavash; he took pleasure in his company alone, no longer admitting Garsivaz and Jahan into his confidence. Day and night he spent with Seyavash, and it was Seyavash who was always able to bring a smile to his lips. In this way, with all its mingled joy and grief, a year went by.

Piran's Advice to Seyavash and to Afrasyab

Seyavash and Piran were sitting one day, chatting of this and that, when Piran said, "You're like a man who's only passing through this country; what will remain of Afrasyab's kindness to you when you die?

> You're now the close companion of our king,
> As loved by him as pleasure is in spring,
> And you're Kavus's son—your glory here
> Has raised you to the moon's auspicious sphere,
> And this is where you ought to lead your life.
> But you've no brothers here, no kin, no wife,
> You're like a solitary flower beside
> An empty field; you need to choose a bride.
> Forget Iran, its sorrows and its wars;
> When once Kavus has died, Iran is yours.
> Here in the royal castle's women's quarters
> The king has three incomparable daughters,
> And Garsivaz's household boasts of three
> Descended from a noble ancestry,
> And I myself have four girls, each of whom
> Will be your slave if you will be her groom.
> But best would be if you can marry one
> Of Afrasyab's girls; you will be his son.
> The finest of them's Farigis, whose grace
> Knows no competitor in any place;
> She's tall and slender as a cypress tree,
> Her hair's a musky crown; you'll never see
> A woman more accomplished or more wise.
> If you should wish to gain this noble prize
> I'll be your messenger and go-between
> To ask the king if she can be your queen."

Seyavash gazed at Piran and said, "What God wills cannot stay unfulfilled; if this is heaven's course, then I cannot oppose it. If I'm not to reach Iran again, or see Kavus's face again, or that of the great Rostam who brought me up, or Bahram's or Zangeh's, or the faces of any of our warriors, then I must choose a home here in Turan. Be as a father to me and arrange this marriage, but keep it secret for now." Having said this, he sighed repeatedly, and his eyelashes glistened with tears. Piran replied, "A wise man doesn't fight with Fate; if you once had friends in Iran, you've entrusted them to God and left them behind. Your home is here now."

Piran bustled off to the court and waited for a while near the throne until Afrasyab said, "Why are you standing here? What's on your mind? My army and wealth are at your disposal, and if I've some prisoner whose release will be dangerous for me, I'll set him free if you should ask. Now, what do you want from me?"

The wise councilor answered, "May you live for ever; I've all the wealth and power I need. I bring a secret message from Seyavash. He says to you, 'I am grateful for the fatherly welcome you have given me here; now I need you to arrange a marriage for me. You have a daughter called Farigis, and I should be honored if I were considered worthy of her.'" Afrasyab grew pensive and replied, "I've gone through this before and you didn't agree with me. A man who nourishes a lion cub will regret it once the lion's grown. And astrologers have predicted that the union of these two will produce a prince who will conquer the world and destroy Turan; the first crown he will seize will be mine:

> Why should I plant a tree whose bitter root
> Will only serve to nourish poisoned fruit?

A child that comes from Kavus and Afrasyab will mingle fire and flood; how can I know whether he will look kindly on Turan? And if he favors Iran, then it will be as if I've purposefully taken poison. A man doesn't deliberately pick a snake up by the tail. As long as he's here I'll treat him like a brother, but that's all."

Piran said, "Any child of Seyavash will be wise and good-natured. Pay no attention to what astrologers say; arrange matters for Seyavash. A prince of our two peoples will be lord of both Iran and Turan, and both countries will be at peace after long warfare. There can be no more splendid lineage than that of Feraydun and Kay Qobad. And, if heaven has another fate in store for us, thinking will not change it. This is a splendid chance, the answer to all you have desired."

The king replied, "I hope your advice turns out well. I accept your suggestion; see that the matter is carried out appropriately." Piran bowed, left the court, and hurried to Seyavash. He went over what the

king had said, and that night the two washed all sorrows from their
hearts with wine.

Seyavash Becomes Related to Afrasyab

When the sun raised its golden shield into the sky, Piran said to
Seyavash, "Bestir yourself, you're to be the princess's guest, and I'm
ready to do whatever you order me to in this affair." Seyavash was
uneasy in his heart and shamefacedly said to Piran, "Do whatever you
think's appropriate; you know I've nothing to hide from you." Piran
bustled off to his house and had his wife Golshahr choose a splendid
wedding gift: uncut cloth, gold woven Chinese brocade, trays of emer-
alds, beakers of turquoise filled with musk and sweet-smelling wood,
two princely crowns, two torques, a necklace, two earrings, sixty
camel-loads of carpets, three sets of clothes with designs worked in red
gold and jewels, thirty camel-loads of silver and gold, a golden throne
and four chairs of state, three pairs of slippers worked in emeralds,
three hundred slaves with gold caps, a hundred more bearing gold
beakers. All this, together with ten thousand dinars, was taken to
Farigis by Golshahr and her sisters. She kissed the ground before the
princess and said, "The sun is to be joined with the planet Venus;
tonight you must go to the prince and shine in his palace like the full
moon."

And so Farigis, resplendent as the full moon, came to the young
prince. The festivities lasted a week; no one, not even the birds of the
air or the fish in the sea, slept during that time; from end to end, the
earth was like a garden filled with happiness and music-making.
Afrasyab loaded his son-in-law with gifts and gave him a charter writ-
ten on silk, making him lord of the lands that stretched to the Sea of
China, and in confirmation of his sovereignty he sent a golden throne
and crown to Seyavash's palace.

A year went by, and then one day a messenger from Afrasyab
arrived at Seyavash's palace. The king said, "It would be right for you
to separate yourself from me somewhat. I've given you the land that
stretches toward China; make a tour of your territories and choose
some city that delights your heart. Make that your happy home, and
never swerve from righteousness."

Seyavash was pleased at this advice; he had fifes and kettledrums
sounded, the baggage train fitted out, and litters prepared for Farigis

and the women of her entourage. As he led out his army Piran accompanied him with his own troops, and the two made their way toward Piran's homeland, Khotan. There the prince stayed as Piran's guest for a month, feasting and hunting. When the month was over the din of drums rang out at cock-crow and, with the army led by Piran, Seyavash entered the appanage he had been granted by Afrasyab.

When it was known they had arrived, the local chieftains gave them a splendid welcome, filling the land with the sound of harps, lutes, and flutes.

> They reached a fertile and well-watered place,
> Possessed of every strength and natural grace:
> The setting's natural limit was the sea,
> A highway marked the inland boundary,
> To one side mountains reared above the plain,
> A place of hunting grounds, and wild terrain;
> The streams, the groves of trees, made weary men
> Feel that their ancient hearts were young again.

Seyavash said to Piran, "I shall build here, in this happy place: I'll raise a splendid city filled with palaces and porticoes. My capital will be worthy of the crown and throne and will soar as high as the moon's sphere." Piran replied, "My lord, do as you see fit. I will contribute everything necessary; knowing you, I have no more need for wealth or land." Seyavash said, "All my treasure and goods are from you; I see you striving everywhere on my behalf. I'll build a city here such that everyone who sees it will be amazed." But the astrologers reported that the site was inauspicious, and when Seyavash heard this the reins slackened in his hands and tears fell from his eyes. Piran asked, "My prince, why should this grieve you so much?"

> And Seyavash said, "As the heavens roll
> They cast my spirit down and sear my soul.
> The wealth with which my treasury is filled,
> The goods I've sought, the palaces I build,
> Will pass into my enemy's fell hand.
> Before long, death will take me from this land.

And why should I rejoice when I foresee
That others will sit here in place of me?
I'm not long for this world, and soon, God knows,
I'll need no palaces or porticoes;
My throne will then be Afrasyab's, and he
Though innocent connives to murder me.
And so the ever-turning skies bestow
Now joy, now sorrow, on the world below."

Piran said, "O my lord, why do you bewilder your soul in this way? Afrasyab has cleansed all evil from his heart and renounced all thoughts of vengeance; and while the soul stays in my body I will stay faithful to you. I won't let even the wind so much as disturb your hair." Seyavash said, "Your reputation is unsullied, and I see only goodness come from you. You know all my secrets; I bring you tidings from God himself, for I am privy to the secrets of the turning heavens. I will tell you what must be, so that later when you see how the world turns you will not wonder at my fate. Listen then: not many days will pass before I shall be slain, although I am innocent of sin; another will inherit my throne and palace. You are true to your word, but the heavens will otherwise. Slander and an evil fortune will bring evil on my innocent body. Iran and Turan will rise against one another and life will be overwhelmed by vengeance. From end to end our lands will suffer, swords will usurp the time; innumerable red, yellow, black, and purple banners will throng the skies of Iran and Turan; endless the pillage and slaughter, the theft of accumulated treasure; countless the countries whose streams will turn brackish, their soil trampled beneath war horses' hooves. Then the lord of Turan will regret what he has said and done; but when smoke rises from his pillaged cities, regret will be useless. My spilt blood will set Iran and Turan to wailing, and all the world will be in turmoil. Thus He who holds the world has written, and it is by his command that what has been sown is reaped. Come, let us rejoice and feast while we may; the world passes; why tie your heart to it, since neither our efforts nor the wealth we delight in will remain?"

Hearing him, Piran's heart was stricken with grief, and to himself he said, "If what he says is true, I am the cause of this evil. It was I who expended so much effort to bring him to Turan, I then who sowed the seeds of this war of vengeance. I took the king's words as so much wind when he said as much to me." But he consoled himself, "Who knows the secrets of the heavens? He remembers Iran, Kavus, and the days of his greatness, and it is this that's disturbed him." As they rode forward all their talk was of the mysteries of fate, but when they dismounted they put the subject aside and called for wine and musicians. For a week they feasted, telling tales of the ancient kings; on the eighth day a letter came from Afrasyab ordering Piran to lead his troops on a tour of inspection, collecting tribute as he went. First he was to travel to the Sea of China, then to the border with India and the Indian Ocean, and from there to Khazar in Turkestan.

The shout to assemble went up from the doorway of Piran's tent; to the din of drums troops amassed to receive their orders, and then the columns set out on the itinerary the king had commanded.

Afrasyab's Letter to Seyavash

One night, at about the time men sleep, a messenger from Afrasyab came hurrying to Seyavash. The letter he bore was filled with kindness: "Since you left I am never happy. I have identified a place here in Turan where you could live; however cheerfully and splendidly you pass the time where you are, return to my kingdom and confound those who are envious of your good fortune."

Seyavash gathered his troops and set off to the appointed place, as the king had commanded him. With him came a hundred camel-loads of dirhems, forty of dinars, and a thousand red-haired Bactrian camels made up the baggage train. Ten thousand swordsmen guarded the litters carrying the women of his court, and the thirty camel-loads of precious goods—rubies, turquoise, torques, crowns and earrings, sweet smelling woods, musk and ambergris, brocade and silk, as well as goods from Egypt, China, and Persia. He came to the chosen place, named Khorram-e Bahar (The Joy of Spring), and there constructed a city of palaces, porticoes, public squares, orchards and gardens; the place was like a paradise, and in the desert wastes he made roses, hyacinths, and tulips grow. On his palace walls he had frescoes painted showing royal battles and banquets. One was of King Kavus with his crown, torque, and royal mace; Rostam stood next to his throne, and with him were Zal, Gudarz, and the rest of Kavus's entourage. On the opposite wall Afrasyab was painted, together with his warriors and the chieftains

Piran and Garsivaz. At each corner of the city was a dome that reached to the clouds; and there, their heads among the stars, musicians would sit and sing. The city was called Seyavashgerd, and the world rejoiced in its existence.

On his return journey from India and China, Piran came to visit Seyavash. He was curious to see what the prince had done with the site and hurried forward, together with a crowd of well-wishers worthy of the honor. The prince and his troops came out to greet him; seeing him in the distance Piran dismounted, as did Seyavash, and the two embraced. They walked together through the city, where so recently there had been only a wilderness of thorns, and Piran praised Seyavash and the magnificent buildings and orchards he saw laid out on every side. He said, "If you were not endowed with knowledge and the royal *farr,* how could you ever have founded such a place? May it last as your memorial until the end of the world, and may you and your descendants live here as victorious kings until then."

When he had seen a portion of the city he reached Seyavash's palace and turned toward Farigis's quarters. The princess scattered coins before him in welcome, asked about the hardships of his journey, and seated him on a throne, while her servants stood in waiting for his orders. He praised all he saw, and then they turned to feasting, wine, and music. They spent a week in this way, at times lighthearted and cheerful, and at times quite drunk. On the eighth day Piran handed over gifts he had brought from his travels: rubies and other princely gems, coins and jewel-studded crowns, silks, horses with saddles of leopard skin and gold-worked bridles; to Farigis he gave a diadem and earrings, a necklace, and a gem-encrusted torque.

After leaving Seyavashgerd Piran returned to his own land of Khotan. Entering his women's quarters he said to his wife, Golshahr, "Whoever has not set eyes on paradise should travel where I have been, to see the angel Sorush enthroned in splendor. Go for a while, and refresh your soul with the sight of Seyavash's city." Then, quick as a skiff that cleaves the waves, he traveled on to Afrasyab. He listed the countries he had visited and the tribute he had levied, then mentioned Seyavash, saying all he had seen and answering the king's questions: "Heaven's glories do not equal that city, nor is the sun more splendid than Seyavash. I saw a city unparalleled in all of Persia and China: wisdom and that prince's soul have combined to make a paradise of gardens, public places, and flowing streams. From a distance Farigis's palace glitters like a vast jewel. Men revile the world, but you have no cause for complaint now. If Sorush himself were to descend from the blue heavens he would not be possessed of such magnificence, glory, and wisdom as is your son-in-law. And our two countries rest from war, returning to life like a man who has lain unconscious and revives again."

The king was happy to hear these words, believing that the tree of his good fortune had borne fruit. He told Garsivaz what he had heard, and said, "Visit Seyavashgerd and see what kind of a place it is. Seyavash has given his heart to Turan and forgotten Iran; he's renounced its crown and throne and said farewell to King Kavus, Gudarz, and Bahram. In the thorn-brakes here he has created a city; he has built Farigis tall palaces and treats her with honor and respect. When you see him, speak kindly to him and act with suitable deference, whether out hunting, seated at court with his Persian entourage, or drinking and feasting. Take him abundant presents—whatever you can lay your hands on in your treasury—and give Farigis presents, too, and congratulate her on her good fortune. If your host welcomes you with smiles, stay in his pleasant city for two weeks."

Garsivaz Visits Seyavash

Garsivaz chose a thousand Turanian knights and set off in high spirits for Seyavashgerd. Hearing of his approach Seyavash and a detachment of troops hurried out to meet him; the two embraced and Seyavash enquired after the king's health. He welcomed Garsivaz to the palace and had his escort billeted appropriately. On the next day Garsivaz brought Seyavash the king's letter together with a robe of state; when Seyavash saw the robe the king had bestowed on him, his spirits opened like a flower in springtime. He and his nobles took Garsivaz about the city, and when they had surveyed it, building by building, they returned to the palace. There they saw Farigis wearing a diadem studded with turquoise, seated on her ivory throne, and surrounded by maidservants. She descended and welcomed Garsivaz, asking after the king and her hometown. Garsivaz seethed with resentment, but his outward behavior was punctilious and respectful. In his heart he said, "Let another year pass and Seyavash will have no time for anyone: he has sovereignty here, a crown and power, wealth, land, and an army." But though inwardly he writhed in anguish and his face turned pale, he hid what was in his heart, saying to Seyavash, "Your efforts have been rewarded; may you live for many years enjoying your good fortune." Two golden thrones were placed in the palace, and there Garsivaz and Seyavash sat, while musicians played heart-bewitching music on harps and lutes.

At sunrise on the next day Seyavash and Garsivaz went out to an open space to play polo. Garsivaz threw down the ball and Seyavash struck it so hard that it disappeared as though the heavens had swallowed it, while his opponent's mallet struck only dust that spurted up from the plain. Thrones were set at the edge of the field for the two heroes, who watched as their men displayed their prowess with javelins. Garsivaz suggested that Seyavash himself show his martial valor before the Turks, and he assented.

Seyavash Displays His Skill to Garsivaz

The prince exchanged his throne for his saddle. Five suits of mail, each heavy enough to tire a man, were bound together and set up at the field's end, while all the army watched. Seyavash owned a spear that had belonged to his father, who had used it in the war against Mazanderan; this he grasped and then like a maddened elephant he charged, plunging the spear into the suits of mail, shattering their fastenings and scattering them at will. Garsivaz's men collected the broken remnants from the field. Then the prince had four Gilani shields—two made of wood and two of iron—bound together as a target. He called for his bow, and thrust six poplar wood arrows in his belt; three more he kept in his fist, and one he notched to the bowstring. Then he galloped toward the target and loosed the first arrow: it pierced all four shields, as did all ten of his arrows one after another, while young and old roared their approval.

Garsivaz said, "My prince, in all Iran and Turan you have no equal. But let's you and I engage in a wrestling match, grasping each other's belts and straining to throw one another, here, in front of our troops. I'm the foremost warrior of the Turks, and you won't see many horses to rival mine; there's no one else here who's fit to oppose you. If I can throw you from your saddle to the ground, you'll have to accept that I am the better warrior and have the better mount, and if you succeed in throwing me, I'll never show my face on a battlefield again." Seyavash replied, "Don't say such things: you are a great lord and a great warrior, your horse is superior to mine, and I reverence your helmet. Choose some other Turk to face me." Garsivaz said, "It will only be a friendly contest, for a moment, with no malice or hard feelings involved." But Seyavash replied, "It would not be right; where I fight is no place for you. When two men oppose one another, they may smile but their hearts are filled with fury. You're the king's brother and your horse's hooves tread down the moon. I'll do whatever you order me to, but I can't consent to this. Choose some lion warrior from among your companions, set him on a fine, fleet horse, and if you're still intent on having me fight, you'll see his head in the dust." Garsivaz laughed, and turning to his Turks called out, "Which of you wants to humble the greatest of warriors, and so be renowned throughout the world?" No one responded, till Gorui spoke up, "If no one else will oppose him, I'm his match." Seyavash frowned at this, but Garsivaz said, "My lord, he has no equal in our army." Seyavash said, "If I'm not going to fight with you, combat with anyone else is contemptible. But choose two, and I'll fight against both together." A Turk called Damur joined Gorui, and Seyavash faced them, while they circled him. Then he lunged forward and grabbed Gorui by the belt, dragging him from his saddle to the ground, all without having to use his lariat. Next he wheeled toward Damur and seized him by the neck, lifting him lightly from his horse, so that all the onlookers were astonished. As if he were carrying a mere ant rather than a warrior, he rode over to Garsivaz, dismounted, released Damur, and sat down laughing on his throne. Garsivaz was secretly enraged by what he had seen and his face flushed. The two returned to the palace and spent a week feasting according to Persian custom, drinking wine and listening to singers, flutes, and lutes.

On the eighth day Garsivaz and his entourage made preparations to leave. Seyavash wrote a friendly letter to Afrasyab and loaded Garsivaz with presents.

> At first the journey home was filled with praise
> Of Seyavash and all his princely ways,
> But Garsivaz said, "When this Persian came,
> The only gift he brought for us was shame.
> Our king has welcomed him—to our disgrace,
> Humiliation stares us in the face.

Great Gorui and brave Damur, two men
Whose like Turan won't quickly see again,
Were forced by this high-handed Persian knight
To look like fools who don't know how to fight.
And this won't be the end of it; I fear
The consequences of his presence here."

And so he talked until they reached Afrasyab's court, muddying the streams of goodwill toward Seyavash. When they arrived, Afrasyab questioned him eagerly, and after he had read Seyavash's letter he laughed aloud, in the best of spirits. Malignant Garsivaz saw the king's gladdened face, and as evening came he left the court, his heart a mass of pain and hatred.

All night he writhed in anguish, and when night's black cloak was torn aside he made his way to Afrasyab again. The court was cleared of strangers and the two sat together. Garsivaz began, "Your majesty, Seyavash is not the man he was; he receives messengers from King Kavus and also from Rum and China; he drinks Kavus's health and a mighty army has gathered around him. Soon he will be a threat to you. If evil had not darkened Tur's heart, he would not have slain Iraj, but since that time our two countries have been like fire and water, each heartsick at the other; and you are crazy enough to want them to unite? You might as well attempt to trap the wind. If I had hidden this evil from you, the world would have condemned me."

The king's heart was hurt by this report, and he began to brood on Fate and its sorrows. He said, "Affection sprung from our common blood guides you to speak like this. Let me weigh the matter for three days; if wisdom agrees with your assessment, I'll say what remedy to adopt."

On the fourth day Garsivaz appeared at court, his sword belt tight about his waist, his diadem of office on his head; Afrasyab summoned him and went over the matter of Seyavash. He said, "How you remind me of our father, Pashang! And who else have I in the world besides you? It's you I must tell my secrets to, and you must plumb them thoroughly and give me your advice. That dream I had, which upset me for a while and confused me, prevented me from fighting against Seyavash. But no harm's come to me from him; since he's bid farewell to the throne of Iran and wisely woven his fate with mine, he has never once disobeyed my orders. And I've treated him well; I gave him a country to rule over, and wealth, and I've made no mention of our grievances against him. I've made a blood alliance with him; I gave him my daughter, the light of my eyes, and I've renounced all thoughts of vengeance against Iran. If, after all this, I were to suspect him, the world would rebuke me; I haven't the least excuse to move against him. If I were to harm him our nobles would condemn me, I'd be a byword for bad faith everywhere. And if I harmed an innocent man could God who rules the sun and moon approve of this? I can see no other solution than to summon him to my court and then send him back to his father: if it's sovereignty he wants, he can take his quarrel elsewhere."

Garsivaz said, "My lord, you can't treat this matter so lightly. If he goes back to Iran now, our whole country will be destroyed. Whenever you welcome a stranger into your family he becomes privy to all its secrets; if you try and distance yourself from him now, who knows what insanity may come from this? He'll be your enemy, and you'll be rubbing salt into open wounds. As has been well said, the man who brings a leopard up sees only trouble as his reward."

His words seemed true to Afrasyab, who regretted what he had done and foresaw only disaster. He replied, "I see no good in this affair, neither in its beginning nor in its end. We must look for what the heavens reveal; in every situation delay is better than haste. Wait until the sun has shone on this for a while, until we get some sense of God's will, and who it is that heaven's light looks favorably upon. If I summon him to court, I'll be able to sound his secrets, and if I bring disloyalty to light, then I shall have to harden my heart against him; no one can blame me then, since evil deserves punishment and there's an end to the matter."

But Garsivaz, intent on vengeance, said, "You are wise and honest, my lord, but consider: if Seyavash, with all his power and royal *farr*, with his God-given might, with that mace and sword of his, should come here, to your court, then the sun and moon will be darkened for you. Seyavash is not the man you saw; his crown outsoars the heavens. And you would not recognize Farigis, who seems beyond all earthly needs. Your army would go over to him, and you'd be left like a shepherd with no flock. If the army sees a prince as handsome, generous, and wise as he is, it's not going to be content with you as its sovereign. And you can't simply keep him in his own city, grateful to you for what you've done for him and still willing to serve you. No one has ever seen a lion and an elephant mate, or fire above while water flows below.

> *If someone wraps a lion cub in silk,*
> *A little whelp, who's not yet tasted milk,*
> *It keeps its nature still, and, once it's grown,*
> *Fights off an elephant's attack alone."*

Then Afrasyab became despondent and beset by care; old memories of ancient wrongs and thoughts of vengeance filled his heart.

From then on Garsivaz visited him continually, filling the king's heart with calumny, until one day Afrasyab cleared the court and said to him, "Go and visit him; don't stay long, but give him this message from me: 'Don't you have any desire to quit your round of pleasures and see someone else? Come here with Farigis for a while; I need to set eyes on your face again and enjoy your wise company. There is good hunting in our mountains, and wine and milk in our emerald goblets. We can spend time pleasantly together, and when you wish to return to your own city, you'll be seen off with music and festivities. Why is it forbidden for you to drink with me?'"

Garsivaz Visits Seyavash for the Second Time

His heart filled with malevolence, his head with deceit, Garsivaz hurried off on his mission. When he was close to Seyavashgerd he selected a smooth-talking soldier and said to him, "Go to Seyavash and say to him from me, 'My noble and ambitious lord, I beg you by the soul of Turan's king, and by the soul and crown of King Kavus, not to trouble yourself to come out of your city to greet me. Your fame, *farr*, lineage, crown, and throne raise you above such concerns, and the winds themselves stand ready to serve you.'"

The envoy arrived and kissed the ground before Seyavash, who was saddened by Garsivaz's message; he withdrew and pondered for a while over what it might mean, saying to himself, "There is some secret hidden here." When Garsivaz reached the court Seyavash went out on foot to meet him, questioning him about his journey, the king, and affairs of state. Garsivaz handed over Afrasyab's letter, which delighted Seyavash, who exclaimed, "I'd outface swords and adamantine walls for his sake; I'm ready to travel to his court; you and I shall link our reins and ride together. But first we must feast and drink in these golden gardens, for the fleeting world is a place of sorrow and grief, and woe to him who does not seize pleasure where he can."

Garsivaz said in his heart, "If I return to the king with him, his chivalry and wisdom will trample my plans underfoot; my words will count for nothing, and my council will be seen as a lie. I must make some scheme to lead him astray." For a while he stood in silence, staring at Seyavash's face. Then tears flowed from his eyes, and seeing this, Seyavash asked in sympathy, "My brother, what is it? Is it a sorrow you can't talk about? If your tears are because you're upset with Turan's king, I'll ride with you now and fight against him until I know why he's humiliating you; and if some formidable enemy has appeared in your life, I'm ready to help you in any way I can. Or if Afrasyab is at odds with you because someone has been slandering you and so replaced you in his favor, tell me about it so that I can help look for a remedy."

Garsivaz replied, "No, there's nothing like this between me and the king, and I've no enemies my wealth and martial skill can't deal with. Thoughts of our lineage welled up in my heart, and I remembered true tales from the past. How evil first came from Tur, who lost God's *farr;* you've heard of how he schemed against the humble Iraj and so began the endless vendetta of our peoples, and how from then until the time of Afrasyab, Iran has been like fire and Turan like water, never mingling in one place, always rejecting wisdom and good council. And Turan's king is worse than Tur; his ox had not been skinned yet, who knows what he'll do? You don't know how evil his nature is, but if you watch and wait, you'll see. Think first of how with his own hand he stabbed Aghriras. The two were brothers, of the same mother and father, and yet he killed Aghriras, who had committed no crime. And there have been many other innocent nobles whom he has destroyed. My concern is that you remain vigilant and safe; since you came here, no one's been harmed by you, you've always striven for justice and decency, and the world has been made more splendid by your knowledge. But Ahriman has filled the king's heart with resentment against you. I don't know what God wills in all of this. But you know that I'm your friend whatever good or evil should appear; I don't want you to think later on that I knew of this and didn't warn you."

Seyavash replied, "Don't trouble yourself about this. God is with me, and the king has given no sign that he wishes to destroy me. If he were angry with me, he wouldn't have distinguished me by giving me a country to rule over, together with his own daughter, wealth, and troops. I'll return with you to his court and make his darkened moon splendid again. Wherever truth shines out, lies lose their luster. I shall show Afrasyab my heart, brighter than the sun in the heavens. Be cheerful, and give up these dark suspicions."

Garsivaz said, "My kind lord, don't imagine he is as you once saw him. For all your knowledge and stature, you can't distinguish pretence from goodness, and I fear bad luck will come of this. He has tricked you, blinded you with glory. You were foolish to rejoice when he made you his son-in-law; he lured you away from your own people and gave a great feast and made you his familiar, so that the world began to gossip about it. You're not a wiser man than Aghriras, and you're no closer to him than he was; before their horrified troops Afrasyab cleaved his brother's waist in two with a dagger. Take this as a lesson, and put no trust in the fact that you're related to him. There, I have told you what's in my heart. You abandoned your father in Iran and made a place for yourself here in Turan; you trusted our king's talk and became his friend in sorrow. But this tree you planted has bitter roots and its fruit is poison." His heart was filled with treachery, but he sighed as he spoke and his eyelashes were wet with tears.

Seyavash stared at him in bewilderment, and tears streamed from his eyes; he remembered the prophecies of his evil destiny, that the heavens would deprive him of love, that he would not live long but die while still a young man. His heart was wrung and his face turned pale, his soul was saddened and sighs escaped his lips. He said, "However I look at this, I cannot see that I deserve punishment. No one has heard that I have done or said anything wrong. If I have made free with his wealth, I've also striven on his behalf, and whatever evil comes to me I shall not swerve aside from his commands. I'll accompany you, without my troops, and we'll see what has turned the king against me."

Garsivaz replied, "Ambitious lord, it would be better for you not to come. A man should not step heedlessly into fire or trust himself to ocean waves. You'd be rushing into danger and lulling your good luck to sleep. I will act for you in this and throw cold water on the fire. Write an answer setting out the good and evil of the situation; if I see that he has no thoughts of vengeance and that the days of your glory are renewed, I'll send a messenger here on horseback, lightening the darkness of your days. I trust in God, who knows what is open and what is hidden, that the king will return to righteous ways, leaving aside crookedness and evil. And if I see that his mind is still dark, I'll send a messenger immediately, and you should wait no longer but leave at once: it's not far from here to the borders, a hundred and twenty parasangs to China, and three hundred and forty to Iran. In the former everyone looks favorably on you; in the latter your father longs to see you and the whole country is yours to command. Don't delay, but write to both countries and be prepared to fly to either."

> No longer vigilant, no longer wise,
> Prince Seyavash believed his specious lies.
> He said to him, "I put my trust in you,
> I acquiesce in all you say and do;
> Go, plead my cause before the king, and seek
> For righteousness and justice when you speak."

Seyavash Writes to Afrasyab

He summoned a scribe and dictated his letter. After invoking God and praising wisdom, he addressed Afrasyab: "O wise beneficent king, may you live forever. You summon me and I am grateful; but you have summoned Farigis, too, and she has been ill for some time. She hardly touches her food and has not the strength to walk. She keeps to her bed, and I sit beside her pillow. My heart is filled with anxiety, seeing her hovering between this world and the next. When her illness eases she will be ready to serve you: but my worry for her well-being is the reason I cannot visit you now." He had the letter sealed and handed it to Garsivaz, who asked for three of his fastest horses and rode day and night back to Afrasyab's palace.

On the fourth day he reached the court, and when the king saw him exhausted from the journey he asked him why he had hurried back so quickly. Garsivaz replied, "When evil threatens there's no time for delay. Seyavash treated everyone with contempt; he didn't come out to meet me, he wouldn't listen to what I said, he didn't read your letter, he kept me standing before his throne. Letters were constantly coming to him from Iran, but the gates of his city were closed against me, and troops flocked to him from Rum and China. If you don't deal with him soon, your fist will close on wind and nothing more; he'll make war on us and seize both Iran and Turan. And once he leads his men to Iran who will dare attack him? I've told you what I've seen, now suffer in the crisis you created."

When Afrasyab heard him, ancient wrongs revived in his mind. In his anger he said nothing to Garsivaz, but fire roared in his heart and his head seemed filled with wind. He ordered fifes, cymbals, trumpets, and Indian chimes to be sounded and led his army out from Gang: once more he planted the tree of vengeance.

While the deceitful Garsivaz was straining in the stirrups on his journey home, Seyavash made his way to the inner apartments of his palace. His face was pale and his body trembled. When Farigis saw him she said, "My lion lord, what's made you lose your color like this?" He answered, "My love, I have no honor left here in Turan; if Garsivaz speaks truly, my life has come full circle."

> Queen Farigis clutched wildly at her hair
> And clawed her rosy cheeks in her despair,
> Blood clogged her musky curls, tears stained her face,
> Distractedly she cried, "Leave, leave this place,
> But where in all the world will welcome you?
> Now, quickly, tell me what you plan to do;
> Your father's rage excludes Iran, you say,
> China would shame you, Rum's too far away—
> Your only refuge in the world is He
> Who rules the sun and moon eternally.
> May years of pain destroy the scoundrel who
> Corrupted the king's heart and slandered you."

And Seyavash said, "Garsivaz will be arriving at Afrasyab's court about now."

Seyavash's Dream

On the fourth night Seyavash slept in Farigis's arms; he began to tremble and started up from sleep, roaring like a maddened elephant. Beside him his wife said, "My prince, what is it?" Then she called for tapers, and for sandalwood and ambergris to be burned before him. Again she asked, "My king, what did you see in your dream?"

Seyavash said, "Tell no one what I've dreamed. My love, my silver cypress tree, I saw an endless river, and on the further shore a mountain of fire, and men with lances crowded the bank. The fire began to overwhelm my city, Seyavashgerd. On one side there was water, on the other fire, and between them was Afrasyab mounted on an elephant. He saw me and frowned, and blew on the fire to make it flare up." Farigis said, "This can only have a good meaning; sleep now for the rest of the night."

But Seyavash rose and called his troops to the palace courtyard. His dagger in his hand, he began to prepare for battle and sent out scouts to watch the road from Gang. When two watches of the night had passed, one of the scouts galloped back from the plain, saying, "Afrasyab and a great horde of soldiers have appeared in the distance; they are hurrying this way." And then a courier brought a message from Garsivaz: "Save yourself; nothing I said had any effect and the fire sends out clouds of threatening smoke. Decide what you must do and where you should lead your army." Still Seyavash did not suspect his behavior, believing all that he told him. Farigis said, "My wise king, don't think of me, put no trust in Turan but saddle a swift horse and flee. You must stay alive; save your own head and give no thought to anyone else."

Seyavash replied, "My dream was true, and the glory of my life darkens; my time on earth draws to its close and only bitterness remains. But this is the heavens' way, bestowing now pleasure and now sorrow; if my palace reached to the stars, still the world's poison would have to be tasted; and if I lived for one thousand two hundred years, still my resting place would be the dark earth. You are five months pregnant, and if the fruit maturing in your womb should grow to ripeness, you'll be delivered of a splendid prince. Name him Kay Khosrow, and may he be a consolation for your sorrows. Soon, by Afrasyab's command, my luck will sink to sleep; though I am innocent they will cut my head off, and my crown will be soaked in my vitals' blood. I'll have no coffin, shroud, or grave, no mourners to lament my death; I shall lie like a stranger in the dirt, my head severed from my body by a sword blow. The king's bodyguards will drag you naked through the streets, and Piran will come to beg you from your father.

He'll take you in your wretchedness to his castle; a warrior will come from Iran and lead you and your son secretly across the Oxus. Your son will be placed on the throne, and from the fish in the sea to the birds of the air all creation will serve him. A huge army will come from Iran intent on vengeance; the world will be filled with tumult. Armies will clash in the war of my revenge, the earth will groan from end to end in torment, and Kay Khosrow will throw the world into confusion." This was his farewell to Farigis: "Dearest wife, I must leave; harden your heart, and bid farewell to ease and luxury." She scored her cheeks and tore out her hair, her heart filled with grief for her husband, her eyes with tears. The two clung to one another in their grief, then, weeping and heartsick, Seyavash left her apartments.

He went to the stables where his Arab horses were kept and found black Behzad, who on the battlefield outran the wind. Lifting off his halter Seyavash wept, took Behzad's head in his arms, and whispered in his ear, "Let no one near you until Kay Khosrow returns; he will replace your bridle. Then you must bid farewell to this stable and bear him out to war and vengeance." He hamstrung all the other horses, wild as a fire that burns through reeds; then he and his warriors set out for Iran, their faces blinded by tears.

Afrasyab and Seyavash Meet

But after they had traveled half a parasang they were confronted by the army of Turan. Seeing them in their armor, with their swords at the ready, Seyavash buckled on his breastplate and said to himself, "Garsivaz spoke the undeniable truth." Each side eyed the other's ranks; before this neither had felt any enmity for the other. Turan's cavalry held back out of fear of Seyavash. The Iranians drew up in battle order and prepared for bloodshed: all of them were ready to fight alongside Seyavash; neither delay nor reproaches would be of any use now. They said, "If we're killed we won't go down to the dust alone; they'll see what battle with Persians means and not consider us contemptible." Seyavash said, "There is no sense to this; this battle has neither head nor tail to it. We'll shame ourselves, and my gift to my father-in-law is to make war on him. But if the heavens decree that I shall be destroyed by evil, I have no strength or desire to oppose God's will. As the wise have said, there is no point in striving against an evil fate." Then he called out to Afrasyab, "Great and glorious king, why have you come with your army ready for war; why do you wish to kill me, though I am innocent? You will stir up the armies of our two countries, and fill the land with curses."

Garsivaz replied, "You senseless fool, when has such talk ever been worth anything? If you're so innocent, why have you come before the king armed? A show of bows and shields is no way to welcome a monarch."

The sun rose as Garsivaz spoke, and Afrasyab ordered his men to draw their swords and roar their war cry as if Judgment Day had come. He said, "Grasp your weapons, and make this plain a sea of blood to float a ship on."

There were a thousand Persian warriors there, all good fighting men, but they were surrounded on all sides and slaughtered. Seyavash was wounded by arrows and lances and fell from his black horse; as he lay in the dust Gorui wrenched his hands behind his back and bound them tight as a stone. They set a yoke on his shoulders and dragged him on foot, hemmed in by soldiers, his face bleeding, toward Seyavashgerd; the prince had never seen such a day as this.

Afrasyab said, "Take him off the road, to a stony place where no plants grow, and cut off his head. Let his blood sink in the hot soil there; fear nothing, and be quick about it." But the army cried out as with one voice, "Great king, what is his sin? Why would you kill someone for whom the very crown and throne will weep? In the days of prosperity do not plant a tree whose fruit will be poison."

Piran's clear-sighted younger brother, Pilsom, was there. He said to Afrasyab, "The fruit of this tree will be pain and sorrow; the wise say that one who acts circumspectly has little to regret, that reason soothes anger, that haste is the work of Ahriman, bringing guilt to the soul and pain to the body. There's no sense in cutting off a subject's head pre-cipitately. Keep him in chains until time teaches you the best course; act when wisdom's wind has touched your heart. A wise king does not sever a head that's worn a crown. And, if you kill this innocent, his father Kavus and Rostam, who brought him up, will seek revenge. Men like Gudarz, Gorgin, Farhad, and Tus will bind war drums on their elephants; the mammoth-bodied Giv, who despises all enemies, and Kavus's son Fariborz, a lion who never tires of battle, will ready themselves for a war of vengeance. The plains will be thronged with warriors; neither I nor any like me in this company will be a match for them. But Piran will be here at dawn; wait and hear his advice."

Garsivaz said,

> *"Pay no attention to a young man's prattle:*
> *Vultures feed on their warriors killed in battle;*
> *If you're afraid of vengeance, this will be*
> *Sufficient cause for Persia's enmity.*
> *You've done enough harm—must you once again*
> *Listen to raw advice from foolish men?*
> *If this prince calls, from Rum's and China's borders*
> *Swordsmen and troops will flock to hear his orders.*
> *You've wounded the snake's head—now you're afraid,*
> *And want to wrap its body in brocade?*
> *Well, spare him if you wish, but I won't be*
> *A part of it, you've seen the last of me;*
> *In some dark cave I'll hide myself away*
> *And live in fear until my dying day."*

Then Damur and Gorui came forward, plausibly twisting their words: "Don't worry about spilling Seyavash's blood, delay is wrong when there's work to do. Take Garsivaz's good advice and destroy your enemy. You set the trap and caught him, don't hesitate now. You have the leader of the Persians in your grip, now break the hearts of those who oppose you. You've destroyed his army already, how do you think the Persian king is going to look on you? If you had done nothing against him from the beginning, this could have been overlooked; but now it's better if he disappear from the world entirely."

The king replied, "I've seen no sin in him, but the astrologers say that hardship will come because of him. But if I spill his blood, a whirlwind of vengeance will arise from Iran. I have brought evil on Turan, and sorrow and pain on myself. To free him is worse than killing him, and killing him is grief and agony to me. But neither wise nor evil men know what the heavens will bring."

Farigis heard this talk and came before the king, her cheeks bloodied, her hair smeared with dust, wailing and trembling with pain and fear. She said, "Great king, why will you make a widow of me? Why have you given your heart to lies? In your glory you cannot see the misery before you. Don't cut off an innocent prince's head; the ruler of the sun and moon will not approve of this. Seyavash abandoned Iran and, with all the world to choose from, made his obeisances to you; he renounced his crown and throne and father's goodwill for your sake. And he became your ally and support; what more do you want from him? Who has deceived you? And I am innocent, do not mistreat me, for the world is fleeting, casting one into a pit of misery and raising another to glory; but both descend to the dark earth finally. Do not listen to malignant Garsivaz's lies and so make yourself an emblem of evil throughout the world. You've heard what the Arab tyrant Zahhak suffered at Feraydun's hands, and what the great king Manuchehr did to the malevolent Salm and Tur. In Kavus's court live men like Rostam, who is contemptuous of Turan and at whose name the world trembles, Gudarz of whom lions are terrified, Bahram, and Zangeh, the son of Shavran. You are planting a tree whose leaves will bring blood and whose fruit is vengeance. The world's glory will darken and curse Afrasyab; you are ruining yourself, and you will have long years in which to remember my words. You're not out hunting now, bringing down some wild ass or deer; you're destroying a prince, and the throne and crown will curse you. Do not cast the land of Turan to the winds, or make this an evil day that you'll regret."

Having said this she gazed at Seyavash's face, wailing and clawing her cheeks. The king pitied her but seeled up the eyes of wisdom and said, "Leave, get back to the palace; what do you know of what I mean to do?" They took Farigis and locked her in a dark room deep in the palace.

Seyavash Is Killed

Garsivaz looked at Gorui, who turned his face aside, and stepped before Seyavash, abandoning all chivalry and shame. He grasped the prince by the hair and began to drag him away; Seyavash cried out, "Great God, who rules our earthly state and destiny, bring forth a bough from me that will be like a shining sun to my people, who will seek revenge for my death and renew my ways in my own land." Pilsom followed him, his eyes awash with tears, his heart filled with sorrow. Seyavash said to him, "Farewell; may Fortune weave her threads with yours forever; convey my greetings to Piran. Tell him the world has changed, that I had other hopes of Piran when I was like a willow tree bending before the wind of his advice. He told me that when my luck turned he would be at my side with a hundred thousand infantry and cavalry, that he would be like a pasture for my foraging. But now that I'm haled before Garsivaz, on foot, despised and wretched, I see no one here to befriend me or to weep for me."

Garsivaz and Gorui dragged him away from the army and the city to a waste place on the plain. Gorui took the dagger from Garsivaz, and when they had reached the appointed place they threw the prince's mammoth body to the ground. Knowing neither fear nor shame, they held a gold dish at his throat to catch the blood and severed the head of that silver cypress tree. The prince's head sank into endless sleep, never to awake. Gorui took the dish to the place that Afrasyab had ordered, and emptied it. A wind rose up, and darkness obscured the sun and moon; people could not see one another's faces, and all cursed Gorui.

> I turn to right and left, in all the earth
> I see no signs of justice, sense, or worth:
> A man does evil deeds, and all his days
> Are filled with luck and universal praise;
> Another's good in all he does—he dies
> A wretched, broken man whom all despise.

Seyavash's palace resounded with lamentation; his slaves cut off their hair, and Farigis too cut her musky tresses and bound them about her waist and clawed at her cheeks' roses. Loudly she cursed Afrasyab, and when he heard her cries he ordered Garsivaz to drag her into the streets, and there to strip her and have her beaten, so that she would miscarry the seed of Iran, saying, "I want nothing to grow from Seyavash's root, neither a tree nor a bough nor a leaf; I want no scion from him worthy of a crown or throne."

One by one the nobles of his entourage condemned him, saying that no one had ever heard of a king or minister who had given such an order. Pilsom came weeping and heartsick to Lahak and Farshidvard and said, "Hell is better than Afrasyab's realm, and this land will know no rest or peace now; we should go to Piran and seek help for these tormented women."

They saddled three fine horses and hurried to Piran's castle, where

they arrived covered in sweat and dust. They told him that Seyavash
had been dragged on foot, bound, and with a yoke placed about his
neck; that he had been forced to the ground by Gorui with his face
twisted up like a sheep's while a basin was held to catch his blood; that
his head had been severed and that his body lay like a silver cypress
felled in a meadow. They said that a heathen shepherd of the deserts
would not slit a man's throat in such a way, that all the land mourned
for Seyavash, and that tears stood in all eyes like dew.

Piran fell from his throne in a faint, and when he came to he tore
at his hair and clothes and heaped dust on his head. Pilsom said to him,
"Hurry, pain is heaped upon pain: Farigis will be killed, guards have
dragged her by her hair to the court; don't turn your back on her
distress."

Piran had ten good horses brought from his stables and in two days
and nights the group arrived at Afrasyab's court. They saw the gates
thronged with warders and executioners, and Farigis dragged forward,
as if insensible, by guards with drawn swords in their hands. The court
was in a tumult, weeping and lamenting and condemning Afrasyab,
saying that he would have Farigis hacked in two, that this horrific
crime would utterly destroy his sovereignty and that no one would ever
call him king again. Piran rode forward like the wind, and everyone
with any sense rejoiced. Farigis saw him through her bloody tears and
said, "See what evil you have brought upon me, you have thrown me
living into the fire." Piran dismounted and tore at his clothes in grief;
he told the guards crowded about the gates to delay carrying out their
orders.

Then, weeping and heartsore, he rushed before Afrasyab and said,
"Great king, live prosperously and wisely: what evil has darkened your
benevolence, what demon has gained power over you, destroying all
shame before God in your soul? By killing the sinless Seyavash, you've
thrown your own honor and glory in the dust. When this news reaches
Iran the court will go into mourning, and their nobles will lead a great
army here intent on vengeance. The world was at peace and God's
ways prevailed, and now some demon has burst from hell and deceived
the king's heart: curses on the devil who perverted your heart! For long
years you'll regret this, living in pain and sorrow. And now that you've
dealt with Seyavash, you turn against your own child? But Farigis has
no desire for glory or sovereignty; don't make yourself a byword for

cruelty by killing your pregnant daughter; you will be cursed through-
out the world for as long as you live, and when you die hell will be
your home. If the king would brighten my soul he will send her to my
castle; and if you fear her child, wait until it is born; I'll bring it to you,
and then do to it whatever evil you wish."

Afrasyab replied, "Do as you say; you have made me unwilling to
shed her blood." Heartened by this, Piran went to the gates, paid off
the guards, and took Farigis away from the court and its lamentations.
He brought her to Khotan and, when they arrived, entrusted her to
Golshahr, his wife, saying, "Hide this lovely woman away; look after
her well." Days passed, and Farigis, whose glory lit the world, grew
heavier.

The Birth of Kay Khosrow

On a dark, moonless night, when birds and beasts were sleeping, the lord
Piran saw in a dream a candle lit from the sun. Seyavash stood by the can-
dle, a sword in his hand, crying out in a loud voice, "This is no time
for rest; rise from sleep, learn how the world moves onward; a new
day dawns and new customs come; tonight is the birthnight of Kay
Khosrow."

Piran trembled in his sleep and woke; he roused Golshahr and said,
"Go to Farigis; I dreamed of Seyavash, more splendid than the sun,
who said to me, 'How long will you sleep? Rise, and run to the feast
of Kay Khosrow, who will rule the world.'"

When Golshahr reached Farigis she saw that the princess had
already borne her son. She ran back lightheartedly, shouting the news
to all the world, and said to Piran, "He's like the sun and moon
together; come and see the little marvel, see what God has created in
his goodness; you'll say he's ready for a crown, or for a helmet and bat-
tle." As soon as Piran saw the prince he laughed and scattered coins for
him; his great stature seemed more fitting for a one-year-old child than
a newborn baby. Gazing at the child, Piran wept for Seyavash and
cursed Afrasyab. To his nobles he said, "If I am killed for this, I'll say
it: I shall not let Afrasyab get his clutches on this child, even if he
throws me to wild beasts."

At the time the sun unsheathes its sword, as Afrasyab was waking
up, Piran came hurrying in; after the room was cleared, he approached
and said, "Sun king, world conqueror, wise and versed in magic arts,

another subject was added to your rule last night. He seems a capable, intelligent child and is as fair to look on as the moon. If Tur could live again he'd long to see him, for he resembles Feraydun in majesty and glory. No picture in a palace is as magnificent as this prince; in him the royal splendor is renewed. Now distance evil thoughts from your mind, mercy will become both your crown and your heart."

> *God cleansed all hatred from the monarch's mind;*
> *He knew that Seyavash had been maligned;*
> *He sighed for him, tortured with pain and guilt,*
> *Mourning his malice and the blood he'd spilt.*

He said, "I've heard enough about this newcomer; everyone talks about him. The land is full of disturbances because of him, and I remember what I was told; that from the mingled line of Tur and Kay Qobad a great king would be born, the world will turn to him, and all the cities of Turan will pay him homage. But let what must come, come; there's nothing to be gained by worry and grief. Don't keep him among your courtiers; send him off to the shepherds, and see that he doesn't know who he is or why he is there." He said whatever came into his head, thinking that this ancient world was young and malleable.

Piran left the court in high spirits, giving thanks to God and praising the king. He traveled home deep in thought. Once there he summoned shepherds from the mountains and said, "Keep this boy as dearly as your own souls, keep him safe from wind and dust, see that he wants for nothing and never suffers." He gave the shepherds many gifts, and sent a wet nurse with them.

By the time the boy was seven years old his lineage began to show. He fashioned a bow from a branch and strung it with gut; then he made a featherless arrow and went off to the plains to hunt. When he was ten he was a fierce fighter and confronted bears, wild boar, and wolves. Soon, still using the same rough bow he'd made, he progressed to leopards and lions. By now he would take no orders from the shepherd who looked after him, and so his guardian descended from the mountains and went whining to Piran. He said, "I've come to complain to your lordship about our young hero; at first he hunted deer and didn't look for lions or leopards. But now it makes no difference to him whether he's after a lion or a deer. God forbid any harm should come to him; I'm yours to command my lord." Piran laughed, and said, "Lineage and skill won't stay hidden long!"

He rode to where the young lion was living and ordered him to step forward. Seeing the boy's noble stature, he dismounted and kissed his hand. Then he gazed at him, taking in the signs of kingly glory in his face; his eyes brimmed with tears and love filled his heart. He folded the boy in his arms and held him there for a long time, brooding in his heart on the boy's fate. He said, "O Khosrow, follower of the pure faith, may the face of the earth be bright for you." Khosrow replied, "My lord, everyone speaks well of your kindness, and I see you're not ashamed to embrace a shepherd's son." Piran's heart was wrung at these words; he blushed and said, "My boy, you call to mind our ancient heroes; the world is yours by right and you're deprived of it. No shepherd is kin to you, and I could tell you much more about this." He called for a horse and royal clothes for the young man, and, as the two rode together back to Piran's castle, Piran grieved in his heart for Seyavash. He kept the boy by him and brought him up; but though he delighted in his company, he feared for him because of Afrasyab, and his anxiety gave him no rest. And so the heavens turned for a few years more, and Afrasyab's heart grew milder. One night a messenger arrived summoning Piran to the king's presence. When he arrived Afrasyab said to him, "Every night my heart is filled with thoughts of evil and sorrow. I think of that child of Seyavash and it's as if he has darkened all my days. How can it be right for a shepherd to bring up a descendant of Feraydun? If it's fated that evil will come to me from him, my precautions won't change God's will. If he can forget about the past, let him live happily, and I will, too; and if he shows any signs of evil, then he'll lose his head, as his father did."

Piran replied, "My lord, you need no councilor to advise you. What does a little child who's ignorant of the world know about the past? Don't trouble yourself about this matter any more. What's that saying, 'The teacher's stronger than the father, and a mother's love counts most of all'? Now, for my sake, swear me an oath, as solemn as those sworn by the ancient kings, that you won't harm the boy." Afrasyab's granite heart softened at Piran's words, and he swore a solemn royal oath:

> *"By day's bright splendor, by the dark blue night,*
> *By God who made the earth and heaven's light,*
> *Who made earth's beasts and human souls, I say*
> *I shall not harm this child in any way."*

Piran kissed the ground and said, "Just king, without peer or equal on the earth and in the heavens, may wisdom always guide you, may time and space be as the dust beneath your feet."

Piran Takes Kay Khosrow to Afrasyab

Piran hurried back to Kay Khosrow, and his cheeks glowed with happiness. He said to Khosrow, "Drive wisdom from your heart; if he talks about battles answer with banquets, appear before him like a fool, talk as an idiot talks. If you can keep clear of sense, you'll get through today safely." Then he placed the Kayanid crown on his head and buckled the Kayanid belt about his waist. He had him mounted on a high stepping horse, and the two came to Afrasyab's court while crowds gathered to gaze with tears in their eyes, and heralds called before them, "Clear the way, a new prince approaches."

When they reached the court the grandfather's face was wet with tears of shame; then he stared at his grandson, saying words of friendship but revolving evil in his mind. He gazed for a while at the youth's stature and splendor, and as he looked his face turned pale. Watching him, Piran began to tremble and despaired of Khosrow's life. The king's face seem closed and forbidding, but then kindness entered his heart.

He said, "Young man, you are new to the court; tell me what you know about the shepherd's life. What do you do with your sheep, how do you lead them to their pasture?"

Khosrow answered, "There's no hunting; I've no bow or bowstring or arrows."

Then Afrasyab asked him about his teachers, and the good and evil fortune he had seen.

Khosrow answered, "Where there's a leopard, the hearts of sharp-clawed men burst with fear."

Thirdly he asked him about his mother and father, about Iran, and about his food and where he slept.

Khosrow answered, "A fierce dog can't bring down a ravening lion."

The king laughed at his replies and turned to Piran saying, "His mind's awry; I ask him about the head and his answer's all about feet. No good or evil is going to come from him; men intent on revenge don't behave like this. Go, hand him over to his mother, and set someone trustworthy to look after them. Let them go to Seyavashgerd. Keep bad councilors away from him, but give him whatever he needs in the way of money, horses, slaves, and so forth."

Hurrying a little, Piran hustled Kay Khosrow from Afrasyab's presence; they reached home safely with Piran well pleased by what had happened and convinced that the evil eye was seeled. He said, "God's justice has bestowed a new tree on the world, and now it gives its fruit." He opened wide the doors of his ancient treasury and equipped the prince with all he needed—silks, swords, jewels, horses, armor, crowns, belts, thrones, purses of coins, carpets, and cloth and everything else he might require.

Then he sent Farigis and Kay Khosrow to Seyavashgerd, which had become a wilderness of thorns; even the beasts of the field came to pay homage to them, and men gathered from every quarter and bowed before them, saying, "From the noble tree's uprooted stock a new shoot has sprung. May the evil eye be far from our universal lord, may Seyavash's soul be filled with light." The ground of the ruined city revived and the weeds turned to tall cypresses. From the place where Seyavash's blood had been spilt a green tree sprang up; on its leaves the prince's face could be seen, and its scent was like the scent of musk. It flourished in the winter's cold as freshly as in spring, and it became the place where those who mourned for Seyavash gathered together.

> *This crone will see her infant suck and play,*
> *And while he sucks she'll snatch her breast away;*
> *Such is the world to which our hearts are bound*
> *Before we're hurried pell-mell underground.*
> *If Fortune raises one above the skies*
> *Fortune will cast him down before he dies;*
> *Turn from this world's inconstant vanity*
> *And put your trust in God's eternity.*

*W*hen Rostam learned of Seyavash's death he dragged Sudabeh from Kavus's harem and killed her for her part in the young prince's downfall. He then attacked Turan and laid much of it waste in a war of vengeance. Afrasyab however escaped and lived to fight another day.

The Persian hero Giv was sent to Turan to find and bring Kay Khosrow, and his mother Farigis, to Iran. After their hazardous journey, crossing the river Oxus to the Iranian side, Kay Khosrow was acclaimed by the Persian court as Kavus's heir. Only Tus demurred, as he believed that both he and Fariborz had a better right to the throne than Khosrow.

Khosrow became the ruler of Iran, and his grandfather Kavus retreated into the background. Khosrow immediately began preparations for a lengthy campaign to subjugate Turan and bring Afrasyab to justice for his murder of Seyavash. The malcontent Tus was made commander of the Persian army, and sent on a preliminary expedition against Turan.

FORUD, THE SON OF SEYAVASH

When a great warrior embarks on war he should not trust his army to an enemy; only tears which no doctor can cure will come of this. Someone who is from a noble family but who cannot achieve any kind of greatness is made savage by his failure. It is unwise for a king to trust any man who remains subject to others and unfulfilled in this way. If the heavens deny him his desires, his loyalty to the king is always suspect; there is no goodness in him, and ambition always gnaws at his heart. When you hear this tale through, you will know the nature of such a man.

Tus Leads His Army to Turan

The sun had reached its zenith, bringing Aries beneath its sway, and the world was filled with a golden light like white wine. From Tus's encampment the din of drums and the squeal of trumpets rang out; the land resounded with war cries and the neighing of horses, and the air was dark with the dust of armies gathering. The sun and moon were obscured, and everywhere the clatter of armor and the trumpeting of elephants could be heard.

Red, yellow, blue, and purple banners thronged the sky, and in the center was the banner of Kaveh, surrounded by horsemen from the clan of Gudarz. A tucket sounded, and Kay Khosrow appeared at the entrance to his tent, crowned and carrying his mace. Wearing golden boots as a sign of office, Tus went forward with the banner of Kaveh. He was followed by chieftains descended from Nozar, each wearing a torque and a diadem; one by one they paraded before Khosrow.

The king addressed them: "Tus leads this army; he bears the Kaviani banner, and you must be ready to obey his orders. Following royal custom, he should harm no one on the march; let no chill wind

touch farmers, craftsmen, or any other civilian. Fight only with oppos-
ing warriors; harm no one who offers you no harm, for the world is
fleeting and we are not here long. Under no circumstances should you
pass through Kalat; if you do so your enterprise will fail. May the soul
of Seyavash be as the sun; may his place in the other world be one of
hope. He had a son, by a daughter of Piran; the boy closely resembled
his father. He and I were born at the same time, and he was like me
when we were young, open and cheerful in his manner. He lives now
in Kalat with his mother, ruling the area in royal splendor. He knows
none of our Persian chieftains by name; you must not ride that way.
He has a fine army, besides which the road through his territory lies
over a difficult mountain pass. He himself is a brave warrior and horse-
man, of noble lineage and with a champion's strength. Take the
way through the desert; there is no point in passing through a lion's
territory."

Tus replied, "May Fortune always favor your desires; I shall travel as
you have commanded, since your commands bring only success."

Quickly Tus led off his troops and Kay Khosrow retired to take
council with Rostam and his nobles and priests. They spoke of
Afrasyab, of Kay Khosrow's anxieties, and of his father's suffering.

The army progressed, stage by stage, until they came to a place
where the road divided. In one direction lay a waterless desert, and in
the other Kalat and the road to Jaram. The elephants with their war
drums in the van of the march paused until Tus arrived; the men
waited to see whether he would obey orders or take the road the army
itself would have preferred. When he reached them Tus talked with his
officers about the hot, waterless way; he said to Gudarz, "Even if the
dust of this desert were of amber and its sands of musk we would still
have a weary journey ahead of us, and we will need water and rest.
Therefore it's better that we make for Kalat and Jaram, and we can rest
at Mayam for a while. On both sides of the road the area is cultivated
and there's flowing water; why should we put ourselves to the trouble
of slogging through the desert? I've been through Jaram once before,
when the army was led by Gazhdaham, and it's not a difficult journey,
except there's a bit of going up and down hillsides. It's best we go this
way then, and not count off the desert parasangs."

Forud Learns of the Approach of the Persian Army

Forud was told that the face of the sun was dimmed by an approaching army's dust, and that the earth seethed like a rushing river with horses and elephants. "Your brother," they said, "is bringing an army up from Iran, seeking revenge for the murder of his father." Forud was an inexperienced youth; when he heard this his heart was filled with anxiety, and his soul darkened. He went out to inspect the surrounding mountainside and had the gates to his castle fastened behind him. He gave orders that no herds or flocks of sheep were to be left on the plains or mountain pastures, that all of them were to be brought within the perimeter wall. When he had supervised the flocks being brought up the mountainside he returned to the castle and secured the gates. From Jaram the din of distant drums resounded, and toward Mayam dust obscured the sky.

Forud's mother was Jarireh, who still grieved in her heart for Seyavash. Forud came to her and said,

> *"Dear mother, from Iran an army comes*
> *Led by great Tus, with elephants and drums;*
> *What's your advice? What tactics should we try?*
> *If they attack us how should we reply?"*

His mother said, "My son, you're always so eager to fight, but God forbid such a day should dawn for you. Your brother Kay Khosrow is now the new king of Iran; he knows very well who you are, and that you and he had the same father. Piran gave me to your father from the first, and if he hadn't done so Seyavash would never have taken a Turkish wife. You are of noble, royal descent on both sides. If your brother is seeking revenge in order to vindicate the spirit of Seyavash, you should join him and prepare yourself for war. Put on your Rumi armor and ride out to battle, your heart filled with rage, your head ringing with war cries. Go in the van of your brother's army; as he is the new king, so you will be the new champion seeking revenge. It is fitting for even leopards and sea monsters to grieve at Seyavash's death, and for the birds of the air and the fish of the sea to curse Afrasyab; no heroic prince like Seyavash will ever appear again in the world, neither as regards glory or civility or dignity or justice. You are this great man's son, you're every inch a king and you should ready yourself to exact revenge, to show whose blood runs in your veins. Observe this approaching army and find out who is leading it. Call your warriors about you and prepare gifts—wine, fine robes, noble horses, tables of food, swords, helmets, barding, armor, Indian daggers. In all the world, your brother is a sufficient treasure to you; may you lead his army on this war of revenge, you as the new champion, he as the new king."

Forud said to his mother: "Which Persian should I speak to? On the day of battle, which of them can I depend on? I know none of them by name, and none of them have sent any messages to me."

Jarireh replied, "My prince, when you see their army's dust in the distance, search the ranks for Bahram and Zangeh, the son of Shavran. Have them show you proof of who they are, for you and I need have no secrets from them. Don't be separated from these two; they were your father's lieutenants when he was a prince. May you and your good name live forever; may Seyavash's soul abide in glory. Now, keep what I tell you in mind; go out with Tochvar and with no other soldiers. When you ask who is who in their army, Tochvar will be able to tell you."

Forud said, "Mother, you're like a lion, and it's your councils that give our tribe its splendor."

> A lookout ran in from the walls and cried,
> "The Persian army fills our mountainside,
> The plain and passes are all thronged with men,
> You'd say we'll never see the sun again;
> The way up to our castle's like a sea
> Of banners, elephants, and cavalry."

Tochvar and Forud galloped out of the castle gates, but the young man's luck was dimmed by dust, and when the heavens turn aside, neither rage nor kindness suffice.

Forud said to Tochvar, "Don't keep from me anything I ask you; when we see the Persian chieftains with their banners and maces of office, and golden boots, tell me the names of everyone you know." They made their way to a high point from which they could look down on the groups of Persians below. There were so many golden helmets and golden shields, golden maces and golden belts, that a man would say there was no gold left in any mine on earth and that a cloud had passed overhead and rained down jewels. There were cavalry and infantry, swordsmen and lance bearers, and their drums thundered with such a noise that the vultures of the air cowered away in fear; thirty thousand warriors, armed and ready for combat, crowded the mountainside. Forud and Tochvar stared in astonishment at the mass of men and their gear.

Forud said, "Now, tell me the chieftains' banners, and don't hide anything from me." Tochvar replied, "The banner with the device of an elephant belongs to Tus, and those horsemen with glittering swords who crowd around it are his bodyguard. The banner behind him, with the device of a shining sun, belongs to your father's brother, Fariborz. Behind him, the huge banner that's surrounded by such a mass of warriors, the one with a shining moon, belongs to young Gostaham, Gazhdaham's son, whose valor makes elephants tremble in terror. The one beyond that, with the device of a wild ass, stands before the brave warrior Zangeh, the son of Shavran. The banner studded with stars, with a red ground and a black silk fringe, belongs to Bizhan who in battle stains the sky with blood. The banner with the dark, lion-terrifying tiger belongs to Shidush, a huge mountain of a man. The one behind that, with a buffalo, with all the lance bearers crowded around it, belongs to Farhad, who seems blessed by heaven in all he does. The banner with the wild boar on it belongs to Gorazeh, and the one bearing the device of a wolf belongs to the chieftain Giv."

Tus Sees Forud and Tochvar on the Mountainside

When the Iranians caught sight of Forud and Tochvar high on the mountain, Tus was furious and ordered the elephants with their war drums to halt. He said, "This will alarm our soldiers; a nimble horseman must ride up to the summit and see who those two warriors are, and what they're doing up there. If they're our men they'll be whipped with two hundred lashes, and if they're Turks they're to be caught and brought here. If they're killed in the encounter then their bodies are to be dragged in the dust; we should do this without fear of any consequences. If they're spies sent in secret to count our number, let them be hacked in two where they are, and their bodies tossed from the mountainside."

Bahram, of the tribe of Gudarz, volunteered, saying, "I'll ride up to the summit and do as you command." He urged his horse out of the army's ranks; determinedly, he made his way up the mountain. Forud turned to Tochvar and said, "Who's this approaching us with such contempt? He's in such a hurry he seems quite unconcerned by us; he's riding a fine dun horse and has a lariat looped at his saddle." His councilor answered, "He's not someone to be handled roughly; I don't know who he is, but I think he's one of Gudarz's men. When Khosrow returned to Iran from Turan, one of the king of Turan's helmets went missing; I think he's wearing it, and his armor seems royal, too. He's surely one of Gudarz's clan, but let's ask him."

> Bahram approached the top, and roared aloud
> As if he were a threatening thundercloud,
> "Who are you on the mountain's summit there?
> Our trumpets blare, our drums' din fills the air,
> And can't you see our army's countless horde
> Led by great Tus, our leader and our lord?"

Forud replied, "You've been offered no scorn, don't speak scornfully to us. Talk civilly, as a knight should, and keep your cold, contemptuous words unsaid. You're not a lion and I'm not a wild ass; this is no way to behave with me. You're no greater than I am, neither as a warrior, nor as a man, nor in brute strength. You've a head, feet, a heart, a brain, sense, a loud voice, and eyes and ears; look, I have all those, too, so don't threaten me. I'm going to question you, and if you answer me as befits a knight, I shall be pleased."

Bahram replied, "Say on, then, you in the sky up there while I'm down here on the ground!"

Forud said, "Who is leading this army off to war?"

Bahram answered, "Tus leads us, with the Kaviani banner and his war drums; he's accompanied by chieftains like Gudarz, Giv, Shidush, Farhad, Gorgin, Gostaham, Zangeh, and Gorazeh."

Forud said, "Why haven't you mentioned Bahram? The list is incomplete without him. Of all the clan of Gudarz, he's the one that I want to hear about, but you say nothing about him."

Bahram replied, "Well, my lion-warrior, and what have you to do with Bahram?"

Forud said, "This is what I heard from my mother. She said, 'When the army approaches you, welcome them and ask for Bahram, and also for another warrior called Zangeh, the son of Shavran; these two were brought up with your father, they shared the same wet nurse, and you should try not to miss them.'"

Bahram replied, "May fortune favor you; are you the fruit of that royal tree? Young prince, are you Forud? If so, long may your shining soul flourish!"

He said, "Yes, I'm Forud, a sapling from that toppled cypress."

Bahram said, "Show me your body, uncover the mark of Seyavash." Forud showed him his upper arm, on which there was a dark mole, like a dash of amber on a rose petal, such that no painter could reproduce it, even with a pair of Chinese compasses. Bahram knew then that the person before him was descended from Qobad and of the seed of Seyavash. He dismounted and made his obeisance to Forud and then ran up the mountain toward him. Forud too dismounted and sat on a rock and said to Bahram, "Great leader, lion in battle, seeing you alive and well, I could not be happier if my eyes beheld my father here; I came to this summit to find out which chieftains were with the Persian army and who was leading it. I shall hold as splendid a feast as my means allow, in order to delight your commander. I shall distribute horses, swords, maces, and all manner of other goods, and then I shall set out with you to Turan, intent on vengeance. I am the right man to prosecute this war; in the saddle I am like a mounted fire, burning all before me. Tell your commander to come up the mountain so that he and I can spend a week together laying plans, and on the eighth day, when the war drums ring out and Tus is seated in the saddle, I shall in bitterness of heart, and with a fury that no man has ever equaled, prepare myself to avenge my father's death."

Bahram replied, "My young, noble, chivalrous prince, I shall tell Tus all that you have told me, and I shall kiss his hand asking him to respect your wishes; but our leader is not a wise man and he has little time for advice. He has skill and wealth and is of the blood royal, but he has scant respect for the king. He's always quarreling with Giv, Gudarz, and the king about Fariborz and the succession, and he constantly says, 'I am of the seed of Nozar, I am worthy to be king of the world.' He's likely to ignore my words, or to be infuriated by them and attack me. He's a willful, unpredictable man. Apart from myself, don't let anyone else who comes in search of you catch sight of your helmet; if someone else comes, don't greet him. And then Tus dislikes me in his heart, because he wishes that he and Fariborz were rulers. He said to me, 'See who's on that mountain, don't ask him why he's there but let your mace and dagger speak for you. Why should anyone be on that mountain today?' If he takes your message calmly, I will bring you the good news and lead you to the army; if anyone else comes, do not trust him. Not more than one warrior should ride up to you at a time, this is our leader's way; if anyone approaches consider him well, and if need be, retreat to your castle and bar the doors."

From his belt Forud drew a mace; its handle was of gold and encrusted with turquoise. He said to Bahram: "Take this as a remembrance from me and keep it whatever happens; if Tus welcomes me, all will be well and there will be many other presents—horses, saddles, crowns and royal jewels."

When Bahram returned to Tus he said, "May wisdom fill your faultless soul: the man we saw was Forud, the son of King Seyavash, who was slain despite his innocence. He showed me the birth sign of those descended from Kavus and Kay Qobad."

> But evil Tus replied, "These men you see,
> These drums and trumpets, all belong to me;
> My orders when I sent you there were clear:
> 'Don't say a word to him, but bring him here.'
> So he's a prince, is he? And who am I,
> According to this castle in the sky?
> What have I seen from your Gudarz's clan?
> Nothing but brazen traitors, to a man.
> A lion doesn't guard that mountainside;
> One useless horseman made you run and hide."

Rivniz Fights with Forud

Tus turned to his troops: "Great fighters, destroyers of our enemies, I want an ambitious warrior who'll face this Turk in combat, who'll sever his head with a dagger and bring it here to me." Rivniz, Tus's son-in-law, responded to the call; this battle would be his last.

Bahram said to him, "Champion, fear the Lord of the sun and moon and don't rush into something that will dishonor you. If a knight rides out against that prince, he won't escape with his life." Tus was angered by Bahram's words and he ordered a few warriors to ride up toward the summit of the mountain. But as they were leaving Bahram called out to them, "Don't think this will be an easy task. It's Kay Khosrow himself who's on that mountain, and a hair of his is worth more than any hero. If anyone here never saw Seyavash's face, then let him ride up the mountainside to see it now." When they heard this the warriors returned to camp.

But Tus's son-in-law, whom the heavens watched with scorn, took the way from Jaram toward Mount Seped, his heart filled with a furious longing for combat.

When Forud caught sight of him, he readied his bow, and said to Tochvar, "Tus has treated my overtures of peace with contempt. The knight riding up toward us is not Bahram, and anxiety fills my heart. Watch him, and tell me whether you recognize him; and why is he clothed from head to foot in iron armor?" Tochvar replied, "This is Rivniz, the one brother among forty sisters, all as lovely as the spring. He's deceitful, untrustworthy, a flatterer; but he's also young and brave and Tus's son-in-law."

Forud said, "This is no time to be praising him, when he's about to fight me. As soon as he gets closer I'll send him back to his sisters' skirts. If he feels the wind of my arrows and lives, no longer count me as a man. Now, should I shoot at his horse or at him; you're experienced at this, what do you advise?" Tochvar said, "Shoot at the rider, and let Tus grieve for him. Tus knows that in the goodness of your heart you offered him peace, but he's foolishly decided to make war on you, and in so doing he shames your brother."

When Rivniz was a bowshot away, Forud drew back his Indian bow and loosed an arrow of poplar wood, which pierced the knight's helmet, pinning it to his skull. He fell, and his horse turned, dragging Rivniz's head in the dust. Tus was watching from the heights in Mayam, and when he saw this the mountainside blurred and darkened before his eyes. But as the wise say, an evil nature is repaid in kind, not once but many times.

Tus's Son, Zarasp, Fights with Forud

Then Tus said to Zarasp, "Make your heart bright as fire, put on knight's armor, exert yourself and avenge our fallen champion; if you do not, I see no one who will." Zarasp prepared for combat and placed his helmet on his head; his heart was filled with a longing for revenge, and his head whirled with impatience.

The lion warrior said to Tochvar, "Another rider is coming. Look and see if you recognize him; is he a prince, or one of the common soldiers?" Tochvar replied, "The time has come to fight in earnest; this is Tus's son, Zarasp, who won't turn his horse aside from a raging elephant. He is married to one of Rivniz's sisters and has come to avenge his brother-in-law. As soon as he can make out your helmet, loose an arrow against him, so that this crazy commander Tus will realize we're not to be despised."

Forud urged his horse forward and as he did so loosed an arrow toward Zarasp: it pierced the armor at his waist and entered his body. Blood flowed from the wound, and his soul departed; he fell, and his horse turned and galloped back to camp. A great cry went up from the Persian army, and Tus wept with rage and grief; in haste he pulled on his armor, lamenting for the two dead warriors and shaking like a leaf. Like a mountain he sat in the saddle, as if he were astride some great elephant, then grasped the reins and set off toward Forud, his heart filled with a longing for revenge, his head whirling with grief and pain.

Tus Fights with Forud

Tochvar cried out to Forud, "A moving mountain approaches our mountain: it's Tus, their commander, who's come to fight against you in combat. You should not pit yourself against an experienced monster like this; get into the castle and bar the gates, and then we'll see what Fate decrees. Now you've killed his son and son-in-law you can't expect a friendly welcome from him."

Forud was young and flared up against Tochvar saying, "When battles are to be fought—whether it's against Tus or a raging elephant or a ravening lion or a sea monster or a tiger—a man gives himself to combat heart and soul; he doesn't start smothering the fire with mud."

Tochvar, in his experience, said, "Princes do not despise good advice. Even if you were made of iron and could rip a granite mountain up by its roots, you're still one solitary knight. If thirty thousand Persian warriors come up this mountain to fight against you, not only your castle but the very stones of this mountain will be razed and not a jot will survive. And the expedition to avenge your father's death will suffer a setback that will never be reversed." But he did not say what should have been said long before and, following the advice of this worthless councilor, Forud gained only war and death.

The prince tugged at the reins, turning his horse toward the castle, and notched another arrow to his bow. Within Forud's castle walls were eighty female attendants; they were watching from the battlements, and when they saw the young hero turn back, their spirits sank.

Tochvar addressed Forud: "If you're determined to oppose Tus it's better you don't destroy him; kill his horse beneath him, because a Persian prince won't fight on foot even if hard-pressed. And then one arrow might not finish him; his henchmen are certain to follow him up the mountain. You have never faced his fury, and you can't deal with both him and them." Forud heard him and drew back his bow; the arrow struck Tus's horse, which lowered its head and fell lifeless to the ground. Enraged, Tus made his way on foot back down the mountain, his shield slung around his neck, his body caked in grime. Forud yelled taunts after him, "What happened to the great champion then, who runs away on foot from a single horseman? What kind of a show does that make in front of his army?" The women on the battlements laughed, and Jaram re-echoed with their scornful cry,

> "The old man ran from the young hero's bow,
> Straight down the mountain, quick as he could go."

When Tus reached the base of the hillside, warriors clustered about him saying, "You've come back safe and sound and this is no time for tears." But Giv turned aside, ashamed to see his leader return on foot. He said, "This young man has gone too far; if he's a prince, and wears the earrings of his office, how can he treat our great army so contemptuously? We're not here to agree to whatever he wants to propose. Even if Tus was hasty and overbearing, this Forud is making a mockery of our mission. We came here to sacrifice our lives in a war of vengeance for Seyavash; we should not forget this. Forud has destroyed Zarasp, a great knight descended from Nozar, and he left Rivniz's body weltering in its own blood. What further humiliations are we waiting for? Even if he were Jamshid's son and had Qobad's brain, he's still embarked on the course of an ignorant fool."

Giv Fights with Forud

As he spoke he fastened on his armor; he mounted his horse, which was like a mighty dragon, and set off toward Jaram. When Forud saw him, a cold sigh escaped his lips and he said, "This army has no sense of its luck, good or bad; one after another they come, each braver than the last, shining like the sun in Gemini. But this is not a wise course, and a head without wisdom is like a body without a soul. If they aren't victorious, I fear for their war of vengeance, unless Khosrow comes to Turan, and then he and I shall stand shoulder to shoulder in this war for our father and crush our enemies like dirt in a fist. Now, tell me, who is this haughty warrior, over whose weapons they'll have to weep?"

Tochvar looked down the mountainside and, unaware of the effect of his words, was like one who sows thorns in a meadow. He said, "This man is a terrible dragon whose breath can bring birds down from the sky. He has destroyed three armies from Turan, orphaned innumerable children, crossed mountains, rivers, and deserts, deprived countless fathers of their sons, and placed his foot on the neck of slain lions. It was he who took your brother to Iran, getting him across the Oxus when no boat could be found. His name is Giv, and he's a mammoth of a man, a raging flood in battle. No arrow will pass through his breastplate: he wears Seyavash's armor when he fights and fears neither lances nor poplar wood arrows. Shoot your arrow at his horse and see if you can wound that. Then he'll have to dismount and go on foot back to camp as Tus did, his shield slung about his neck."

Forud drew back his bow and the arrow flew, piercing the horse's chest. Giv toppled from his collapsing mount and began to make his way back down the mountain. A laugh of derision went up from the battlements, and Giv seethed with chagrin beneath their taunts. The Persian warriors went to him saying, "Thanks be to God it was your horse that was wounded, and not you."

But his son Bizhan, who was a headstrong youth, railed against him: "My father's a conqueror of lions, he's outfaced raging elephants, so why did a single horseman make you turn tail like this? You always used to be in the thick of the fighting, and now because your horse is wounded you run off like a drunkard!" Giv said, "When my horse was wounded I'd no choice but to quit the field," and then angrily reproached Bizhan for his presumptuous remarks. Bizhan turned his back on him; Giv exploded in rage and struck at him with his horsewhip, shouting as he did so, "Haven't you been told you should think before picking a quarrel? You've neither sense nor brains nor wisdom, my curses on whoever brought you up!"

Bizhan's heart was filled with bitter fury, and he swore a solemn oath before God that he would not take saddle from horse until either he had avenged Zarasp or died in the attempt. He went to Gostaham, his heart filled with grief, his mind with rage, and said, "Lend me a horse that can ride up that mountain; I'm going to put my armor on and show just who is a man and who isn't. A Turk has installed himself on that summit in full view of the army. If we leave here there will be a lot of hard riding to do, and I've only two horses that can carry a

man in full armor; if one of them's killed here, I'll never find his equal either for speed, strength, or endurance."

Gostaham replied, "This is not sensible; you should not go rushing into disaster. Think of Zarasp, Rivniz, our matchless leader Tus, your father who brings down lions—all of them seen off by this Turk; no one can defeat that granite mountain and enter the castle unless he has a vulture's or a Homa's wings."

Bizhan said, "Don't break my heart; I'll tear myself limb from limb if

I don't do this. I've sworn by the moon, by God who holds the world, and by our sovereign's crown that I'll not come down from that mountain until I have avenged Zarasp or am slain like him."

Gostaham replied, "This is not the road you should be taking; wisdom knows nothing of such fury."

Bizhan burst out, "Then I shall go on foot to avenge Zarasp, keep your horses!"

And Gostaham said, "I would not have one hair of your beard harmed. I've a hundred thousand horses, their tails braided with royal jewels; choose one and have him saddled, and if he's killed, so be it."

He owned a splendid horse, swift as a wolf, lean-bellied, tall and eager for combat. Bizhan, filled with youth's ambition, had him armored with barding. But when he thought of Forud's prowess, Giv's heart was thrown into anxiety. He called Gostaham to him, and they talked about youth's impetuous fire; he sent back with him Seyavash's armor and royal helmet. Gostaham gave them to Bizhan who put them on as quickly as he could and set off in high spirits, accoutered as a mighty warrior, up Mount Seped.

Bizhan Fights with Forud

The young prince turned to Tochvar: "Another of their men is coming. Look there, and tell me the name of this young chieftain for whom they'll soon have to weep and wail."

Tochvar replied, "Iran has no warrior like him; he's Giv's only son, and his father loves him more than his wealth and his own soul. He's a brave champion, victorious as a lion. Again, shoot at the horse; you must not break the Persian king's heart by killing this lad. And anyway, he too is wearing the armor that Giv wore, and it's proof against arrows and lances. He's likely to fight on foot and you won't be his equal then; look at that sword he bears, glittering like diamonds."

Forud loosed an arrow at Bizhan's horse, which fell as if lifeless; Bizhan disentangled himself from his falling mount and began to climb up to the summit, his drawn sword in his hand.

> He shouted to Forud, "Courageous knight,
> Wait where you are and see how lions fight;
> Know that this unhorsed warrior won't turn back
> But sword in hand I'll climb your mountain track;

Wait for me, face me man to man, and then
See if you ever want to fight again!"

When he saw that Bizhan was not withdrawing, Forud shot an arrow at him, but Bizhan lifted his shield and harmlessly deflected it. He reached the summit and readied his sword; Forud retreated, and the battlements behind him rang with shouts. Bizhan ran after him, and with his sword hacked at the barding of Forud's horse; he pierced it, and the horse fell in the dust. Forud scuttled into the gatehouse of his castle and the sentinels immediately barred the gates behind him. Those on the battlements hurled rocks down at Bizhan, knowing that no time should be lost. Bizhan yelled back, "You were mounted and ran away from a man on foot. Aren't you ashamed of yourself? Where are your courage and fame now, Forud?"

When Bizhan got back to Tus he boasted, "My lord, that knight could humiliate a whole plain full of soldiers; you shouldn't be surprised if the hail of his arrows turned a granite mountain to water, there's no greater fighter anywhere." Tus's response was to swear an oath of vengeance, saying, "I'll raze his castle and see the dust of its ruins obscure the sun; I'll fight a battle of revenge for Zarasp and destroy that malignant Turk; I'll make the stones of his castle glisten like coral with his blood."

Jarireh's Dream

When the shining sun disappeared and dark night spread its army across the sky, a thousand horsemen entered the castle of Kalat as reinforcements. The gates were fastened behind them, and the night was filled with the sound of armaments and the bells of their horses' gear.

Jarireh, Forud's mother, slept at her son's feet, and the darkness was filled with pain and sorrow for her. She dreamed of a great fire that raged in their castle, and then spread until the whole mountain was a mass of flame which consumed the castle and all the women in it. She started up from sleep, her soul in anguish, and went on the battlements to gaze out on the world. She saw all the mountain filled with the glitter of spears and armor, and ran weeping to Forud, saying "Wake up, my son, the stars have turned against us; all the mountainside is thronged with our enemies, and their spears and armor threaten our gates!"

The young prince said, "Dear mother, do not cry.
If Fate has willed that I am soon to die
You weeping will not make my death delay;
Each man must leave on his allotted day.
My father too was young when he was killed,
Now I must bow to what the heavens have willed.
As he was put to death by Gorui
So this Bizhan intends to murder me.
But I will fight; if I'm to die, I'll slaughter
All who attack, and I'll not beg for quarter."

He distributed helmets and armor to his men; then he placed a helmet
on his own head, tightened the belt about his Rumi armor, and
grasped his royal bow.

Forud Fights with the Persians and Is Killed

When the shining sun rose into the sky's vault, the war cries of chief-
tains rang out on all sides, mingling with the clatter of heavy maces
and the din of drums, bugles, fifes, and Indian chimes. Forud led the
Turkish troops out from the castle, and the top of the mountain was so
clogged with dust, arrows, and maces that it seemed like a sea of pitch.
The ground had disappeared, there was hardly room to fight, and the
rocks and precipitous mountain slopes alarmed the horses.

Battle was joined and, as the sun journeyed across the sky, Forud's
army steadily lost ground. On the heights and in the gullies the Turks
were killed; Fortune was against the young man, although he himself
still fought like a lion and the Persians watched him in wonder. But
when he saw that all his companions had been killed, and that he could
not fight on alone, he tugged at the reins, turned, and fled up the
mountain to his castle. Roham and Bizhan lay in ambush for him, and
as he approached Bizhan appeared on horseback in front of him and
bore down on him. As soon as he saw Bizhan's helmet Forud readied
his mace, but as he did so Roham rode out of the ambush behind him,
yelling his war cry, an Indian sword in his grasp. He struck a mighty
blow that caught Forud on the shoulder, severing his arm, and render-
ing him unfit for battle. Forud groaned with the pain and urged his
horse forward; he reached the castle gates, which were slammed to and
bolted behind him.

Jarireh ran to him and took him in her arms, and she and their attendants bore him to an ivory couch. At the hour of his death he was still too young to have worn the crown. His mother and the women cut off their musky tresses, and Forud struggled for life while wailing surrounded his couch and anguish filled the castle. Barely opening his lips, Forud said, "It's right for you to mourn; the Persians will come now intent on plunder, they will enslave you and raze my castle and its ramparts to the ground. Those of you who pity me, whose faces burn for my sorrow, go to the battlements now and cast yourselves down from them, so that not one of you remains for Bizhan to boast of. He it is who has taken my life from me, who has destroyed me in the days of my youth." After he had said this, his cheeks turned sallow, and in pain and grief his soul departed.

The womenfolk fled to the battlements and all of them threw themselves down on the rocks beneath. Jarireh set fire to the castle and fed it with their treasures. Then she went to the stable and with a sword slashed the remaining horses' bellies and lacerated their legs, and the horses' blood spattered her face. Lastly she made her way back to where Forud lay. She drew a dagger from the folds of his clothes and ripped open her belly with it; she placed her face against her son's and died.

The Persians had torn up the gateposts and poured into the castle, intent on plunder. But when Bahram came on Forud and Jarireh his heart broke with grief. Weeping, he turned to the Persian troops and said, "This man has died even more wretchedly and terribly than his father did. Seyavash was not killed by a mere squire, and his mother did not die beside him; neither was his castle burned like a reedbed nor his chattels and treasures destroyed. Fear God, my friends, and the turning of the heavens, whose arm is long in apprehending evil-doers and who is merciless to sinners. Have you no shame before Kay Khosrow, who spoke so gently and at such length to Tus, who sent you here to avenge the death of Seyavash and who gave you such wise council? When he learns of his brother's spilled blood, you will lose all favor with him. And what good can be expected from men like Roham and that hot-head Bizhan?"

Meanwhile Tus and his entourage of Persian chieftains, including Gudarz and Giv, made their way up the mountainside to Kalat, their war drums sounding as they came. Entering the room where Forud and his mother lay dead, they saw Bahram seated beside the bodies, weeping and lamenting, and Zangeh to one side, a group of warriors clustered about him. Forud lay on the ivory couch like a toppled teak tree, his face fair as the full moon, and it was as though Seyavash himself lay there, asleep in his armor. Gudarz and Giv and the other warriors wept to see him, and Tus too wept bloody tears, both for his son and for Forud. Gudarz, Giv, and the others there turned on him and said, "A commander should not act hastily, and rage ruins all he does. Through rage and haste you have thrown this young prince, with all his splendor and nobility, to the winds; and the same passions destroyed both Rivniz and Zarasp, who counted Nozar among their ancestors. Without wisdom, ability and rage together are like a sword eaten away by rust."

Tus ordered that a royal tomb be built on the mountain top. Within it, on a golden couch, they placed the prince's body dressed in cloth of gold and with a golden belt. His head was embalmed with camphor and his body with rosewater and musk. The tomb was sealed, and the army moved on; so passed this lionhearted prince.

A fter Forud's death, Tus led the Persian army deep into Turan, and Afrasyab's counselor, Piran, was put in charge of Turan's defenses. Success had made the Persians careless, and Piran was able to inflict a severe defeat on them by ambushing them at night.

Kay Khosrow eventually heard of Tus's insubordination in attacking Forud, and of his army's defeat at the hands of Piran. He angrily recalled Tus and appointed Fariborz as commander in his place. But the Persians suffered defeat again, and the remnants of their broken army fled back toward Iran. Turan allied itself with other Asian peoples and nations, including China, in the hope of finally defeating Iran. Rostam began to intervene in the conflict and the tide of battle turned in Iran's favor: Afrasyab and his allies were routed, although Afrasyab managed to escape again, and the border areas between Iran and Turan were once more under Persian control. At this point Rostam, who could now move about Turan more or less at will, encountered a notorious demon, the Akvan Div.

THE AKVAN DIV

Listen to this tale, told by an old Persian. Here is what he said:

One day Kay Khosrow rose at dawn and went to a flower garden to hold court. He had spent the first hour of the day there, surrounded by his chieftains—Gudarz, Rostam, Gostaham, Barzin, Garshasp (who was descended from Jamshid), Giv, Roham, Gorgin, and Kharrad—when a herder of horses came in from the plains with a request for help.

"A wild ass has appeared in my herd," he said. "He's like a demon—a div—who has slipped his bonds, or you could say he's like a savage male lion. He's constantly breaking the necks of my horses. He's colored just like the sun, as if he'd been dipped in liquid gold, except for a musk-black stripe that runs from his mane to his tale. He's as tall as a fine bay stallion, with big round haunches and sturdy legs."

Khosrow knew very well that this was no wild ass, since a wild ass is never stronger than a horse. He turned to Rostam and said, "I want you to deal with this problem; go and fight with this animal, but be careful, for it may be Ahriman who is always looking for ways to harm us." Rostam replied:

> *"Your Fortune favors any warrior who*
> *Fearlessly serves your royal throne and you:*
> *No dragon, div, or lion can evade*
> *My fury and my sword's avenging blade."*

He mounted his great horse Rakhsh and, lariat in hand, left the king and his courtiers to their pastoral pleasures. When he arrived at the plain where the herdsman kept his horses, the wild ass was nowhere to be seen. For three days he searched among the horses, and then on

the fourth he caught sight of him galloping across the plain like the
north wind. He was an animal that shone like gold, but beneath his
hide all was ugliness and sin. Rostam urged his horse forward, but as
he closed on the wild ass he changed his mind. He said to himself, "I
shouldn't kill this beast with my dagger; I ought to noose it with my

lariat and take it still alive to the king." Rostam whirled his lariat,
intending to snare it by the neck, but as soon as the ass saw the lariat,
he suddenly disappeared from before the hero's eyes. Rostam realized
that he was not dealing with a wild ass, and that it would be cunning
he would have to call on, not strength. He said, "This can only be the
Akvan Div, and somehow he must be made to feel the wind of my
sword's descent. I've heard from a knowledgeable man that this is the
area he haunts, but it's strange that he should take on the shape of a
wild ass. I must find some trick by which my sword can stain that
golden hide with blood."

Then once again the beast appeared on the plain, and Rostam urged
his horse forward. He notched an arrow to his bow, and as he rode like
the wind, the arrow flew ahead like fire. But at the moment he drew
back his royal bow, the ass once again disappeared. For three days and
nights Rostam rode about the plain, until he began to feel the need for
water and bread, and he was so exhausted that his head sank down and
knocked against the pommel of his saddle. Looking around, he caught
sight of a stream as inviting as rosewater; he dismounted and watered
Rakhsh, and as he did so he felt his eyes closing in sleep. He loosened
the girth and removed the poplar wood saddle from Rakhsh's back and
set it down as a pillow beside the stream. He spread out his saddle cloth
and lay down to sleep on it, while Rakhsh cropped the grass nearby.

When the Akvan Div saw Rostam asleep in the distance, he trans-
formed himself into a wind rushing over the plain. As soon as he
reached the sleeping hero he dug out the soil all round him, and then
lifted him up toward the heavens on a great crag of excavated earth.
Rostam woke and was alarmed; his wise head whirled in confusion,
and as he wriggled this way and that the Akvan Div called out to him:

> "Hey, Rostam, mammoth hero, make a wish!
> Am I to throw you to the ocean fish,
> Or hurl you on some arid mountainside?
> Well, which is it to be, then? You decide."

Rostam realized that in this div's hands all wishes would be turned
upside down. He thought, "If he throws me down on a mountain, my
body and bones will be smashed. It'll be much better if he throws me
in the sea, intending the fishes' bellies to be my winding sheet."

> Rostam replied, "The Chinese sages teach,
> 'Whoever dies in water will not reach
> The heavens, or see Sorush; his fate will be
> To haunt this lower earth eternally.'
> Throw me upon some mountain top, and there
> I'll terrify a lion in its lair."

When the Akvan Div heard Rostam's request, he roared and bore him toward the sea.

> "I'm going to hurl you somewhere," he replied,
> "Beyond both worlds, where you can't run or hide."

Then he flung him deep into the ocean's depths; but as he descended through the air toward the water, Rostam drew his sword and with this he kept off the sharks and sea monsters that made for him. With his left arm and leg he swam, and with the right he warded off attacks. He struck out immediately, as befits a man used to fighting and hardships, and after a short time, by going steadily in one direction, he caught sight of dry land.

Once he had reached the shore and given thanks to God who had delivered him from evil, he rested and took off his wet tiger skin, spreading it beside a stream until it was dry. He threw away his soaked bow and armor and set off, leaving the sea behind him. He found the stream by which he had slept and where he had been confronted by the evil-natured div.

But his splendid horse Rakhsh was nowhere to be seen in the pastures there, and Rostam railed against fate. Angrily he picked up the saddle and bridle and set off through the night in search of him. As dawn broke he came on a wide meadow filled with clumps of trees and flowing streams. There were partridges everywhere, and he could hear the cooing of turtle-doves; then he found Afrasyab's herdsman, asleep among the trees. Rakhsh was there, charging and neighing among the herd's mares, and Rostam whirled his lariat and snared him by the head.

He rubbed Rakhsh down, saddled him, slipped the bridle over his head, and mounted. Then calling down God's blessing on his sword he set about rounding up the horses. Their thundering hooves woke the bewildered herdsman, who called to his companions for help; grasping lariats and bows, they came galloping to see who the thief was who had dared come to their meadow and challenge so many of them. When Rostam saw them he drew his sword, roared like a lion, "I am Rostam, the son of Zal," and fell upon them. When he had slaughtered two-thirds of them, the herdsman turned and fled; Rostam followed in hot pursuit, an arrow notched to his bow.

It happened that at this time Afrasyab was coming to this very meadow, in a hurry to inspect his horses. He arrived with his entourage and with wine and entertainers, intending to relax for a while in the place where the herdsman watered the herd every year.

But as he drew near the spot there was no sign of either the herdsman or his horses. Then he heard a confused noise coming from the plain, and in the distance he saw the horses galloping and jostling one another, and Rakhsh was visible through the dust sent up by their hooves. Soon the herdsman appeared and told him the whole astonishing story of how he had seen Rostam not only drive off the whole herd single-handed, but also kill many of the herdsman's companions besides.

It became a matter of urgent discussion among the Turks that Rostam had appeared there alone. They said, "This has gone beyond a joke; we must arm ourselves and respond. Or have we become so weak and contemptible that one man can come and kill whoever he wishes? We can't allow a solitary horseman to turn up and drive off our whole herd of horses."

Afrasyab Goes in Pursuit of Rostam

Afrasyab set off with four elephants and a detachment of soldiers in pursuit of Rostam. When they were close enough, Rostam unslung his bow from his shoulder and came riding toward them; he rained arrows down on them as thickly as the clouds rain down dew and then set about them with his steel sword. Having killed sixty of them, he exchanged the sword for his mace, and dispatched forty more. Afrasyab turned tail and fled. Rostam captured the four white elephants, and the Turanian soldiers despaired of life as he pursued them for two parasangs, raining down blows of his mace against their helmets and armor like a spring hail storm. Then he turned back and added the elephants to his plunder.

He returned to the stream in triumph, and once again met with the Akvan Div, who said,

"Don't you get tired of fighting constantly?
You fought the savage monsters of the sea,
Got back to land and, once you'd reached our plain,
It seems you couldn't wait to fight again!"

When Rostam heard him he roared like a warrior lion; he unhitched his lariat from his saddle and flung it toward the div, who was caught about the waist. Rostam twisted in the saddle and raised his mace, then brought it down with a blow like a blacksmith at his forge. The blow landed on the div's head and his skull and brains were smashed by its force. Rostam dismounted and with his glittering dagger severed the div's head. Then he gave thanks to God who had given him victory on the day of vengeance.

You should realize that the div represents evil people, those who are ungrateful to God. When a man leaves the ways of humanity consider him as a div, not as a person. If you don't appreciate this tale, it may be that you have not seen its real meaning.

Once Rostam had cut off the div's head, he remounted Rakhsh and, driving the herd of horses before him, together with whatever else he had looted from the Turks, he set off toward Khosrow's court. News reached the king that Rostam was returning in glory; he had set off to noose a wild ass, and now he had defeated a div and captured elephants besides. The king and his court went out to meet him, the courtiers wearing their crowns of office; the procession included elephants, trumpets, and the imperial banner. When Rostam saw the banner and realized that the king was coming to greet him, he dismounted and kissed the ground; the army shouted its approval and the drums and trumpets sounded. The nobles dismounted and only Khosrow remained in the saddle; he ordered Rostam to remount Rakhsh and the procession made its way cheerfully back to Khosrow's camp.

Rostam distributed the horses to the Iranian army, keeping none back for himself, as he considered only Rakhsh suitable to be his own mount. The elephants he gave to Kay Khosrow, as worthy of a lionlike king. The court spent a week rejoicing with wine and music and entertainers, and when Rostam was in his cups he told the king about the Akvan Div, saying, "I never saw such a majestic wild ass, of such a splendid color; but when my sword cut its hide, it was an enemy I saw, not a friend. It had a head like an elephant's, long hair, and a mouth full of boar's tusks; its two eyes were white and its lips black; its body didn't bear looking at. No animal is like him, and he'd turned that whole plain into a sea of blood; when I cut his head off with my dagger, blood spurted into the air like rain."

Kay Khosrow was astonished; he set down his wine cup and thanked God for creating such a hero, the equal of whom the world had never seen.

Two weeks passed with feasting, pleasure, and telling stories, and when the third began Rostam decided to return home in triumph. He said, "I long to see Zal, my father, and I can't hide this wish any longer. I shall make a quick journey home and return to court, and then we can plan our campaign. Capturing a few horses is too trivial to count as vengeance for the blood of Seyavash."

Kay Khosrow opened the doors of his treasury. He had a goblet filled with pearls brought, and five royal robes worked with gold, as well as Rumi slaves with golden belts, girls with gold torques about their necks, carpets and an ivory throne, brocade and coins and a crown studded with turquoise. All these he sent to Rostam saying, "Take them as a present for your journey. But stay today; tomorrow we can think about your leaving." Rostam stayed that day, drinking with the king, but when night came he was determined to leave. The king accompanied him two parasangs of the way, and then the two embraced and bade farewell to one another. Kay Khosrow took the way back to his court, and the world was filled with his justice and goodness, while Rostam continued on the journey to Zabol.

BIZHAN AND MANIZHEH

A night as black as coal bedaubed with pitch,
A night of ebony, a night on which
Mars, Mercury, and Saturn would not rise.
Even the moon seemed fearful of the skies:
Her face was three-fourths dimmed, and all the night
Looked gray and dusty in her pallid light.
On plain and mountainside dark henchmen laid
Night's raven carpet, shade on blacker shade;
The heavens seemed rusted iron, as if each star
Were blotted out by tenebrous, thick tar;
Dark Ahriman appeared on every side
Like a huge snake whose jaws gape open wide.
The garden and the stream by which I lay
Became a sea of pitch; it seemed that day
Would never come, the skies no longer turned,
The weakened sun no longer moved or burned.
Fear gripped the world and utter silence fell,
Stilling the clamor of the watchman's bell,
Silencing all the myriad cries and calls
Of everything that flies or walks or crawls.
I started up, bewildered, terrified;
My fear awoke the woman at my side.
I called for her to bring me torches, light;
She fetched bright candles to dispel the night
And laid a little feast on which to dine,
Red pomegranates, citrons, quinces, wine,
Together with a polished goblet fit
For kings or emperors to drink from it.

"But why do you need candles now?" she said.
"Has sleep refused to visit your soft bed?
Drink up your wine and—as you do so—I
Will tell a story from the days gone by,
A story full of love and trickery,
Whose hero lived for war and chivalry."
"Sweet moon," I said, "my cypress, my delight,
Tell me this tale to wile away the night."
"First listen well," she said, "and when you've heard
The story through, record it word for word."

The Story Begins

When Kay Khosrow decided on revenge for his father's death, he put the world's affairs on a new footing; the crown of Turan began to lose its luster, and the Persian throne gained in glory. The heavens smiled on Iran and its people; the world was renewed again, as in its early days, and Khosrow washed his face in the waters of loyalty and good faith, although no wise man will put his trust in this world where all things flow away like water.

One day Khosrow was sitting with his warrior chieftains at an entertainment. His throne was draped with brocade and he wore a jeweled crown; in his hand was a cup encrusted with rubies and filled with wine, and the heart-ravishing sound of harps echoed in his ears. Their wine cups filled with wine like rubies from the Yemen and white roses set out before each one, his loyal nobles surrounded him: Kavus's son Fariborz, Gostaham, Gudarz, Farhad, Giv, Gorgin, Shapur, Nozar's son Tus, Roham, and Bizhan. Serving girls stood before Khosrow, their hair like musk, their skin like jasmine; all the court was alive with color, perfumes, and beauty, and the king's chancellor presided over the feast.

A doorman entered and went over to the chancellor; he said that a delegation from the Ermani tribe, who inhabit the border region between Iran and Turan, were outside asking to see the king. They had traveled a long way and were demanding justice. The chancellor relayed their request to the king who granted them audience; they were brought in according to court protocol, their arms crossed over their chests, and when they had kissed the ground they presented their petition to the throne. In deep distress they said, "Great king, may you live victorious and forever. We have traveled a weary way from our country, Erman, which lies between Iran and Turan, and we bring you a sorrowful message. You are the scourge of evil in seven countries, the prop of the helpless, and long may you flourish! Our country borders Turan, from which great disasters have come to us. Within our marches, toward Iran, is a forest, parts of which we have cultivated. It's full of fruit trees and we also pasture our flocks there; in short, we depend on this area and we appeal to the king to help us. Innumerable wild boar have overrun this forest; their tusks are like an elephant's, they're of mountainous size, and they are destroying the land of Erman, killing our animals, trampling our crops, smashing with their tusks trees that have been there for longer than anyone can remember. Granite is not as tough as their tusks, and we fear that our good fortune is at an end."

When the king had heard them out he pitied their plight and he turned to his chieftains:

> "Who is ambitious for success and fame?
> Which warrior here is worthy of the name?
> Who'll chop these wild pigs' heads off with his sword?
> I won't be miserly with my reward!"

Then he ordered his treasurer to bring in a golden tray heaped high with jewels jumbled pell-mell together; near this was set a quantity of brocade, and ten horses branded with Kavus's mark and caparisoned with golden bridles were led in. Once again he turned to his nobles and said,

> "Who here will do the bidding of the throne,
> And with his efforts make my wealth his own?"

No one answered, except Bizhan, son of the great warrior Giv: he stood and said, "Long may your realm and clan flourish, and the world submit to your authority. I will undertake this mission, my body and soul are yours to command."

Giv glanced up and it was clear that he was worried by his son's remark. He made his obeisance to the king, then turned to Bizhan: "This is mere young man's talk. What makes you so sure of your strength? A youth might be knowledgeable and of good family but he won't manage anything without experience. He has to see the world first, both good and bad, and he has to taste life's bitterness. Don't go wandering off where you've never been before, and don't make such a fool of yourself in front of the king!"

Bizhan was a quick-witted young man whose star was rising; he was infuriated by his father's talk and he turned directly to the king: "Don't think I'm not capable of this; believe me, I have the strength of a young man and the wisdom of a graybeard: I'll cut these wild pigs' heads off or I am not Bizhan, the son of Giv, destroyer of armies." Khosrow responded, "You are full of talents, and may you always be our shield against evil; any king who has a subject like you would be a fool to fear his enemies." Then he turned to Gorgin, Milad's son, and said, "Bizhan is young and ignorant of the way: be his guide and companion to where the river marks the boundary of our domain."

Bizhan tightened his belt, placed his helmet on his head, and prepared to leave. He took Gorgin as a companion to turn to if anything should go wrong, and the two set off with hawks and cheetahs intending to hunt as they proceeded on their long journey.

Like an elephant foaming at the mouth, Bizhan gave chase to wild asses and gazelles, slicing off their heads; his cheetahs brought down mouflon, ripping their bellies open, the rest of the flock scattering in terror. With his bow Bizhan was like another Tahmures, the binder of demons, and his hawks' talons made such havoc among the pheasants that their blood spotted the jasmine plants by the wayside. Indeed, Bizhan and Gorgin went forward as if the plain were their private hunting park.

They reached the forest of wild boar; the animals were milling about with no knowledge that Bizhan had saddled his horse to deal with them, and the young warrior was enraged by their number and effrontery. He said to Gorgin, "Let's go in together, or, if you'd rather, you wait over by the lakeside there, while I attack them with my arrows. When you hear them squealing among the trees, have your mace ready for any that escape me."

But Gorgin said, "This is not what we agreed to before the king: you took all the jewels and gold and silver, and you agreed to do the fighting; all you could expect from me was that I show you the way here." Bizhan frowned in astonishment at this response; nevertheless,

he entered the forest like a lion and set about shooting arrows at the
herd of boar. His war cry was like a spring cloud's thunder, and the
trees' leaves came pattering down like rain. He went after the herd like
an enraged elephant, a glittering dagger in his hand; they turned to
charge him, tearing up the ground with their tusks, sparking fire where
their tusks struck rock, as if they would burn the world. One sprang at
Bizhan like a devil, ripping open his armor, then withdrew and rubbed
its tusks against a tree, as if it were an armorer honing a sword on stone.
But when it renewed its attack, the young warrior plunged his dagger
into its belly, splitting its mammoth body in two. Then the remaining
boar scattered like foxes, their bodies wounded, their hearts sick of
combat. Bizhan lopped off the heads of those he'd killed with his dag-
ger and fixed them to his saddlestraps. He intended to take the tusks
back to the king and to display the severed heads to the court as a
demonstration of his prowess; their combined weight would have
exhausted a buffalo.

Resentful and scheming, Gorgin emerged from where he had been
lurking; he was so filled with chagrin that the forest appeared like pitch
to him. He congratulated Bizhan and made a show of rejoicing at his
success, afraid of the shame that might come to him from this business.
Ahriman twisted his heart; forgetful of God, for the sake of his own rep-
utation, he began to plot against Bizhan and spread a snare before him.

He said, "My congratulations; you've a warrior's heart and a wise
man's soul; God and your good fortune have given you victory here.
There's something I wanted to tell you: I've been in these parts a few
times before, with Rostam, Giv, and Gostaham. Tus was here, too, and
Gazhdaham. What splendid deeds we did on this wide plain then; how
famous we became, and how dearly Khosrow loved us! But the heav-
ens have moved on since then. About two days' journey from here,
toward Turan, there's a place where people gather to hold festivals;
you'll see a wide pasture, all green and gold, a sight to rejoice any free
man's heart. The landscape is filled with copses of trees, flowers, flow-
ing streams; it's a place worthy of a hero. The ground's as soft as silk, the
air's scented like musk, the streams seem to flow with rosewater; jasmine
tendrils bow down to the ground with the weight of their flowers, and
the roses there are incomparably beautiful; pheasants strut among the
rosebushes, and nightingales sing from the cypress branches.

"In a few days from now the whole area will be like a paradise, the meadows and mountain slopes dotted with groups of angelic young women, all led by Manizheh, the daughter of Afrasyab. She and her attendants will be staying there; the Turkish girls are cypress-slender, smelling of musk, with faces like rose petals, languorous eyes, lips that taste of wine and rosewater. If we hurried we could be there in a day, and we could seize a few of these delectable girls and take them back in triumph to Khosrow."

When Bizhan heard this his young blood was roused; he agreed to the venture, partly from a thirst for fame, but partly too for the pleasure it promised. The two set off on the long journey, one urged on by desire, the other by malice. They traveled for a day between two forested areas, and then spent two cheerful days hunting in the Ermani grasslands. Gorgin knew that Manizheh was not far off, and that the whole plain was as bright as a pheasant's eye with her entourage, and so he repeated to Bizhan what he had said about the festival held there.

Bizhan said, "I'll go on ahead; I'll spy out the festival from a distance, to see how the Turanians manage these things. Then I'll ride back here and we can decide what to do. I'll be able to think better once I've seen them." Then he turned to his steward and said, "Bring me my golden diadem that looks so splendid at banquets, and the torque and earrings Kay Khosrow gave me, and the armbands covered in jewels that I have from my father." He also asked for a jeweled belt, then wrapped himself in a splendid Rumi cloak and fixed an eagle's feather to his diadem. His horse Shabrang was saddled and he set off for the festival, his ambitious heart filled with curiosity.

When he came in sight of the festivities, he stretched out beneath a cypress tree, to stay out of the sun. He was close to the princess's tent, and he felt his heart fill with longing. The whole plain echoed with the sound of music and singing, as if welcoming his soul. The princess peered from her tent and saw the stretched-out warrior, his cheeks as bright as Canopus in the skies above Yemen, or like jasmine petals encircled by dark violets, an imperial diadem on his head, a brocade cloak covering his body. Within her tent the princess felt the force of love, and she made no attempt to veil herself from the stranger. She said to her nurse,

> *"Go quickly over there; find out for me*
> *Who's lying underneath that cypress tree:*

I think it's Seyavash, or else he seems
More like the angels that we see in dreams.
Ask him, 'What brings you here? Won't you at least
Join in our festival and share our feast?
Are you Prince Seyavash, then? Or are you
An angel's child? Because whichever's true,
You've lit in me a fire that makes me fear
The world will end and Judgment Day is near.
I've come here every year to celebrate
The spring's arrival on this happy date,
But never saw a stranger here before:
Now I've seen you, and I shall see no more.'"

When the nurse reached Bizhan, she bowed to him and spoke as Manizheh had instructed her. Bizhan blushed like a rose, then said confidently enough, "Messenger of your beautiful mistress, I am not Seyavash, nor am I born of an angel; I'm from Iran, from the land of the free. I am Bizhan, Giv's son, and I traveled here from Iran to fight against wild boar. I cut their heads off and left them lying in the dirt; I'm going to take their tusks back to my king. When I heard about this festival, I put off returning to my father: I thought my good fortune might show me the face of Afrasyab's daughter in my dreams. And now I see this plain decked out like a Chinese temple with splendor and wealth. If you treat me well I'll give you a golden diadem, earrings, and a belt; take me to your beautiful mistress, and incline her heart favorably toward me."

The nurse returned to Manizheh and whispered in her ear, describing his face, his stature, and how God had made him. Straightaway Manizheh sent her back, with the message, "If you come over to me and brighten my dismal soul, you will find you have gained what you dreamed of." When Bizhan heard this, the time for talk was over; full of hope and curiosity, he walked from the tree's shade to the princess's tent.

He entered the tent, tall as a cypress; Manizheh embraced him and removed his gold-worked belt. She asked him about his journey, and which warriors had accompanied him on his expedition. "And why," she said, "should such a handsome and noble person be tiring himself out with a mace?" She washed his feet in rosewater and musk and had an elaborate meal set before the two of them; wine was brought and the tent was cleared of everyone except Manizheh's musicians, who stood before them with lutes and harps. The ground was spread with brocade sewn with gold coins and embroidered like a peacock, and the tent was filled with the scents of ambergris and musk. Old wine in crystal goblets overcame the warrior's defenses; for three days and nights the two were happy in each other's company, till finally drink and sleep defeated Bizhan.

The time for departure came, and Manizheh felt she could not bear to be separated from Bizhan; seeing his sad face she called her serving girls and had them prepare a soporific drug which they mingled with his drink. They fitted up a traveling litter, so that one side was for pleasure, the other for sleep; the sandalwood of the sleeping area was drenched in camphor and rosewater, and there they set the unconscious warrior. As they approached the town Manizheh covered him with a cloth; stealthily, at night, Bizhan was conveyed into the castle, and she mentioned her secret to no one.

After his long sleep Bizhan awoke to find his beloved in his arms; he was in Afrasyab's palace, and Manizheh's face was beside him on the pillow. He started up in alarm and cried out to God for protection against Ahriman: "How can I ever escape from this place? Listen to my sufferings, take revenge for me on Gorgin; he it was who led me into this, who deceived me with a thousand tricks."

But Manizheh said, "Live happily, my love, and reckon as wind what has not yet happened. All kinds of fate come to men, sometimes feasting, sometimes fighting." They prepared to eat, not knowing whether a gallows awaited them or a marriage ceremony. Manizheh called for musicians; each of the young women was dressed in Chinese brocade and, to the sound of their lutes, Bizhan and Manizheh passed the day in pleasure.

Afrasyab Learns of Bizhan's Presence

A few days passed in this way, and then gossip caused disaster's tree to tremble. A rumor reached the court chamberlain, and he secretly investigated the matter, tracing the reports back to their source. He inquired as to where the interloper was from and why he had come to Turan; when he found out, he feared for his own life and made all haste to save himself. He saw no choice but to tell the king and ran to him with the news: "Your daughter has taken a lover from Iran."

Outraged by Manizheh's behavior, the king shook like a willow tree
in a storm, called on God to aid him, and sent for his councilor Qara
Khan. "Give me," he said, "good advice as to what to do with this
shameless woman."

Qara Khan replied, "First enquire more closely into the accusation.
If the matter turns out to be as you say, then I have nothing to add.
But hearing about something is not the same as seeing it." Afrasyab
turned to Garsivaz and said, "How much we've endured at the hands
of Iran and will endure in the future! And now Fate has added a faith-
less daughter to my troubles from that country. Go with loyal horse-
men and watch the gates and roofs; tie up any stranger you find within
the palace and bring him here."

His men surrounded the inner palace, occupied the roofs, and kept
a watch on the exits while Garsivaz approached the main door. He
found it secured from the inside, and sounds of feasting and revelry
could be clearly heard. Garsivaz tore the door from its hinges and
leaped into the chamber beyond; immediately, he made his way to the
room where Bizhan was. When he saw Bizhan, his blood boiled with
rage; three hundred serving girls and musicians were there, singing to
lutes and serving wine. Bizhan sprang up in fear, his one thought being
how he could fight without his armor or his horse Shabrang. He was
alone and his father Giv could not help him now; God was his only
recourse.

He had always kept a glittering dagger inside one boot, and this he
now drew as he leaped toward the door, saying:

> "I am Bizhan, Giv's warlike son; I claim
> An ancient Persian family's noble name.
> No one skins me, unless he's sick of life
> And wants his head slashed open with this knife;
> And if the earth resounds with Judgment Day,
> No man will ever see me run away.
> If you insist on war, prepare for war—
> I'll soak my fists in your Turanian gore
> And hack your heads off. But if you agree
> To intercede before your king for me,
> I'll tell him why I'm here. You are a knight,
> Be chivalrous and we won't need to fight."

Garsivaz saw what Bizhan was about, but he also saw the sharp dagger in his hand and knew that he meant it when he said he would soak his fists in their blood. He swore a solemn oath that he would do as Bizhan suggested, and with his promises he managed to cajole the dagger from Bizhan's hand. He then talked him into allowing himself to be bound in fetters; they trussed him up like a caught cheetah.

> When Fortune turns her face away from you,
> What can your manly skills or virtues do?

And so Bizhan was haled before Afrasyab, bareheaded, and with his hands bound. He greeted the king and said, "If you want the truth from me, here it is: I had no desire to come to this court and no one is to blame for my being here. I came from Iran to destroy a herd of wild boar and found myself near your borders. I sent my people to search for a lost hawk, while I sheltered from the sun under a cypress tree and fell asleep there. A denizen of fairyland came and spread her wings over me and gathered me up, while I was still sleeping, to her bosom. She separated me from my horse and took me along the path where your daughter and her escort of soldiers were. The plain was filled with horsemen, and various litters and palanquins passed me by. In the distance an Indian parasol appeared, surrounded by Turanian cavalry, and as it came closer I saw that the parasol covered a splendid litter in which lay a beautiful young woman; a crown was on the pillow beside her. The being that held me repeated the name 'Ahriman' a few times and then like a mighty wind swooped down among the horsemen; suddenly she set me in the litter and whispered a spell over the woman there so that she remained asleep until we entered the castle. I wept to see her, but I've committed no sin, and Manizheh has suffered no stain or taint of guilt in all this. I think the being who did this to me must have been a fairy of ill omen."

But Afrasyab said, "Bad luck's caught up with you, and none too soon. You came from Iran with your bow, looking for a fight and hoping to make a name for yourself; now you stand in front of me defenseless as a woman and with your hands tied, prattling about dreams as if you were drunk. You think you can deceive me with your lies?"

Bizhan replied, "You majesty, listen to what I have to say for a moment, and realize its truth: a boar can fight anywhere with its tusks, as a lion can with its claws; warriors need a sword, a mace, a bow in order to fight against their enemies. You can't have on the one side a man naked and with his hands tied, and on the other a man armored in mail; no matter how brave it might be, how can a lion fight without its claws? If the king wishes me to show my prowess before his men, let him have a horse and a heavy mace brought here. Then he can set a thousand of his horsemen against me, and if I leave one of them alive, never call me a man again."

When he heard this, Afrasyab glared at Bizhan in fury and turned to Garsivaz. "You see how he's still plotting against me; the evil he's done already's not enough for him, he asks to be allowed to kill my men in combat! Take him bound as he is and get rid of him; have a gallows erected before my castle gates so that everyone who passes by will see him. String him up and never mention him to me again, so that the Persians will know not to come snooping around here any more."

As they dragged Bizhan to the door he wept in bitterness of heart, and said, "If God has written on my forehead that I am to die in an evil time, I fear neither death nor the gallows. I fear the warriors of Iran; I fear that my enemies among them will call me a coward because I was strung up unwounded; I fear that my noble ancestors will reproach me, and that my soul will linger here, having shamed my father."

The Arrival of Piran

God pitied his youth and confounded his enemies' plans. While the pit for the gallows was being dug, Piran appeared in the distance; as he approached he saw a gallows being erected with a noose swinging from it and called out, "Who is to be hanged here? And is the king's gateway a fitting place to raise a gibbet?"

Garsivaz answered, "This is for Bizhan, the king's enemy, who comes from Iran."

Piran urged his horse forward and came up to Bizhan; he saw he was in great distress, naked, dry-mouthed, and pale, with his hands tied tightly behind his back. He said, "How did you come to be here? Did you come to Turan looking for bloodshed?" Bizhan told him his tale of bad luck, and Piran wept to hear it. He ordered the soldiers to pause before hanging him, to wait until he had talked with the king and pointed out to him where his best interests lay.

He entered the court humbly, his arms folded across his chest, bowed before Afrasyab, and waited. The king realized he had some petition to make and laughed, saying:

> *"Out with it then! Tell me, what's your request?*
> *Noblest of all my chieftains, and the best,*
> *If you want gold or jewels or wealth from me,*
> *If you want troops, or arms, or sovereignty,*
> *You know my goods are yours, as payment for*
> *Your peerless services in peace and war."*

Loyal Piran kissed the ground, stood, and said, "May your auspicious reign never end; the world's kings praise you and your splendor is like the sun's. Whatever I have—be it people, wealth, or authority—is from you; my request is not for myself, since no subject of yours wants for anything. I have given the king advice on many matters many times before this, but my advice was not followed. I told you not to kill Kavus's son, Seyavash, who was of royal lineage and who was tireless on your behalf, as this would make Rostam and Tus your enemies, bringing them from Iran on their war elephants, tearing apart the bonds that unite us. And have you not seen the damage the Persians have done to our country, trampling two-thirds of it underfoot, making our lives bitter as brackish water? And Zal's sword is still not sheathed; his son Rostam is still lopping off heads with it and staining the sun with blood. Now that there's the chance of peace, you're looking to stir up new troubles, foolishly sniffing at the poisoned blossoms of hatred. If you spill Bizhan's blood, once again the dust of vengeance will rise up from Turan. The king is wise and I am his subject, but open your heart's eyes to the truth. Think how the king of Iran has profited from our enmity, and yet you're trying to provoke it further, to make disaster's tree bear fruit again. We cannot survive a second war against them; no one knows Giv, and that monster Rostam, or iron-fisted Gudarz better than you do."

Piran threw cold water on the raging fire, but Afrasyab replied, "And you don't know what Bizhan has done to me, embarrassing me before all Turan and Iran. Can't you see the humiliation that shameless daughter of mine has brought to my white hairs, destroying my women's reputation in the world? My whole country and army will make fun of my disgrace for ever. If he escapes from me with his life, everyone will reproach me; I'll spend the rest of my days weeping, disgraced, and despised."

Piran repeatedly called down heaven's blessing on the king and said, "My noble lord, favored by fortune, all is as you say, and it's your reputation that's at stake. But consider my suggestion carefully: chain him in heavy chains, such that he'd rather die on the gallows than suffer the pain they bring. This will teach the Persians a lesson, and they won't be in such a hurry to plot against us in the future. Any man who languishes in your dungeons is not going to be reckoned a useful warrior."

The king followed his advice and said to Garsivaz, "Prepare a dark pit and heavy chains: bind his arms tightly, shackle him hand and foot, and hang him head down within the pit so that he sees neither sun nor moon. Take elephants, and have them drag here the huge rock that the Akvan Div wrenched from the ocean depths; cover the pit's entrance with it, and let Bizhan suffer there till he loses his mind. Then go with your cavalry to that shameless hussy Manizheh's palace and destroy it; strip her of her crown and status and say to her, 'Wretched woman, you deserve neither crown nor throne; you have shamed the king before his ancestors and dragged their noble name in the dust.' Then hale her to the pit and say to her,

> 'See in this pit now, naked and alone,
> The man you set beside you on your throne;
> You were the springtime of his life; now be
> His friend and jailer in adversity.'"

Garsivaz strode from the king's presence to carry out his evil orders. Bizhan was dragged from beneath the gallows to a deep pit, loaded from head to foot with heavy chains, and lowered head down into its darkness. A stone was placed over the opening, and from there Garsivaz led his men to Manizheh's quarters; her wealth was plundered, and the crown torn from her head. Barefoot, clad only in her shift, her hair loose, her face smeared with blood and tears, Manizheh was dragged stumbling to the pit's edge. There Garsivaz said to her, "Here is your lord and household; you're to be this prisoner's jailer forever."

For a day and a night Manizheh wandered moaning about the wilderness. As dawn approached she came back to the pit's edge and scrabbled away the dirt beneath the stone till she could force her hand into the darkness. When the sun rose above the mountain tops she began to go from door to door, begging for bread. At the end of the day she brought the scraps she had collected and pushed them through the opening she'd made, offering them to Bizhan. And so, in grief and wretchedness, she passed her days.

Gorgin Returns to Iran Without Bizhan

After a week, Gorgin saw that Bizhan had not returned and he began to search for him everywhere, his face bathed in tears of shame. He regretted what he had done and wondered how he could have betrayed his companion like this. He hurried in the direction Bizhan had taken and went through the groves of trees looking for him, but he saw no one and heard not even so much as a bird's song. He scoured the meadows calling for his friend, and finally caught sight of Bizhan's horse in the distance. The reins were loose, the saddle had slipped down, and the horse's lower lip hung pendulous, as if the animal were consumed with rage. Gorgin gave Bizhan up for lost, certain that he would never return to Iran: either he had been strung up on a gallows or was languishing chained in a pit, but it was clear that Afrasyab had harmed him in some way. Gorgin flung down his lariat and turned aside his face in shame; he was sorry for what he had done and longed to see his friend. He led Bizhan's horse back to their camp and rested there for a day; then he set out for Iran, travelling day and night without stopping to sleep.

When the king learned that Gorgin was returning without Bizhan, he told Giv to ask Gorgin what had become of his son. Giv ran weeping into the street, his heart filled with anxiety, crying out, "Bizhan has not come back, and why should he stay with the Ermani?" He ordered that a horse he had used in crises before be saddled; inwardly raging like a leopard, he rode out to meet Gorgin, intending to ask him where Bizhan was, and what had happened. To himself he said, "This Gorgin has secretly and suddenly tricked him; if I find it's true that he's coming back without Bizhan, I'll cut his head off there and then."

Gorgin saw Giv approaching. He dismounted and ran forward, then groveled in the dust before him, his head bared and his cheeks scored by his nails. He said, "My lord, you are the king's elect, the leader of his armies, why have you come out to meet me, your eyes flowing with tears? I return sick at heart, and seeing you, my wretchedness increases; I look at you and my face is bathed in shame's hot tears. But don't fear for him; no harm has come to him, and I can give you proof of this."

When Giv heard the warrior's words and saw his son's dusty, desolate horse led by Gorgin, he fell from his own mount as if unconscious. His head sank into the dust; moaning, he tore at his clothes and hair and beard, and cried out, "God of the heavens, who has placed intelligence and love in my heart, now that I have lost my son it is right that the bonds of life dissolve in me; take me to where the blessed spirits live, you who know better than I do the extent of my heart's sorrow. In all the world he was all I had, as a companion and as a help in times of trouble; now that ill fortune has taken him from me, I am left here to grieve alone."

Again he turned to Gorgin. "Tell me what happened, from the beginning. Did Fate suddenly snatch him away, or did he leave you of his own accord? What disaster overtook him? Tell me what snare the heavens laid for him, what devil confronted him and destroyed him in the uplands there. Where did you find his abandoned horse? Where did you lose sight of Bizhan?"

Gorgin replied, "Calm yourself, and listen to my words carefully. Know, then, my lord—and may your presence always lend splendor to our court—what happened, and how it happened, while we were fighting the wild boar. We traveled from here to confront the herd and when we reached the borders of Erman we saw a once-wooded region that had been leveled as flat as the palm of a hand; all the trees had been torn down, and the whole area was full of boars' lairs. We seized our spears and went to work, yelling to drive the boar into the open and fighting like lions; the day ended and we still weren't tired of our task. Like charging elephants we drove them before us, and we hacked out their tusks with chisels. Then we set off on the return journey to Iran, rejoicing and hunting as we came. Suddenly a wild ass appeared, more beautiful than any ever seen before; its coat was like that of Gudarz's horse, it had Farhad's horse's muzzle, feet like the Simorgh's, but with steel hooves, and its head, ears, and tail were like those of Bizhan's horse, Shabrang. Its mane was like a lion's, and it was as swift as the wind; you'd think it had been sired by Rakhsh. It made for Bizhan like a towering elephant, and he noosed it with his lariat, but it charged off into the distance, dragging Bizhan out of sight. Their struggle sent a cloud of dust into the air and both the wild ass and his captor disappeared from view. I searched everywhere, until my mount was exhausted, but I found no trace of Bizhan: all I could discover was his horse, trailing its saddle in the dust. I stayed there for a long time calling Bizhan's name, but finally I gave up and decided that the wild ass must have been the White Demon. My heart burned with anxiety, wondering how his struggle with the Demon had turned out."

When Giv heard this speech he knew that something terrible had happened; he saw that Gorgin was talking at random, his eyes downcast, his fearful face the color of straw, his trembling voice indicative of his guilty heart. Giv thought that his son was lost to him, and he saw that Gorgin was lying; Ahriman plucked at his heart, and he longed to take revenge for his son's disappearance, no matter how shameful such a course might seem. But then he reflected that this would clarify nothing. "What good will it do me to kill him now?" he thought. "It will only make Ahriman glad and profit Bizhan nothing at all. I must look for another way forward. I'll tell Gorgin's tale to the king and see if that will clear matters up; I can easily take my revenge later, as he has no defense against my spear if I choose to use it."

Giv roared at Gorgin, "You devil's spawn, you've taken the sun and moon from my life, you've stolen away the king's chosen champion, you're forcing me to travel the world in search of relief for my sorrow—how can you sleep or rest enmeshed in such lies and deceit? But I shall go before the king, and after that I shall be revenged on you with my dagger."

And so he went to the king, and after greeting him respectfully and wishing him long life and good fortune, he said,

> "In all the world I had but one delight—
> My son, for whom I fretted day and night,
> For whose pure soul I wept paternal tears;
> To lose him was the worst of all my fears.
> And now Gorgin returns alone and tries
> To hide his guilty soul with specious lies;
> He brings bad news of my beloved son
> And has no sign of him to show but one—
> A riderless, led horse. Your majesty,
> Look closely at this matter and you'll see

That my demand for vengeance here is just;
Gorgin has brought my head down to the dust. "

The king was moved by Giv's grief; he turned pale and grew sick at heart thinking of Bizhan. He asked Giv, "What did Gorgin say about where Bizhan is?" Giv told him Gorgin's tale, and Khosrow answered, "Think no more of this, mourn no longer; Bizhan is alive and you should live in hopes of seeing your lost son again. I have agreed with my priests that I and my troops shall soon set out for Turan to fight in the war of vengeance for Seyavash: I and my elephants will overcome that country, and Bizhan will be there by my side, fighting like a devil on our behalf. Grieve no more; I am as eager as you are to see him again." Giv left his presence, his heart filled with pain and grief, his cheeks sallow, his eyes wet with tears.

When Gorgin arrived at Khosrow's court he found it empty; the courtiers had left with Giv to comfort him. Gorgin went forward, shamefaced and apprehensive, kissed the ground before Khosrow, and greeted him. He placed the boars' tusks, glittering like diamonds, before the king, and said, "May the king be victorious in all things, may all his days be springtime, and may the heads of all his enemies be cut off as I cut off these boars' heads!"

Khosrow looked at the tusks and questioned Gorgin about the expedition, asking how he had been separated from Bizhan and what disaster had befallen him. At first Gorgin was speechless, but then he began to tell his lying tale, trembling from fear of the king. But before he could finish, Khosrow, realizing that his confusion indicated his guilt, started up and pushed him away from the throne, reviling him: "Haven't you heard the old saying that even a lion who arouses the vengeance of Gudarz's clan will perish miserably? If you weren't such a wretch, and so certain to come to a bad end, I'd have your head twisted off like a chicken's!"

Khosrow gave orders that blacksmiths fashion heavy shackles for him, and that his feet be fettered, so that he could reflect on the evil he'd done. To Giv, Khosrow said, "Calm yourself, we must begin the search for Bizhan. I shall send out a thousand horsemen to see if they can find news of him, and if we hear nothing at first, do not despair. Wait until spring brings in the new year, and the sun renews the world;

then when the flowers reappear and the earth turns green again, and the breezes are laden with scent, I shall pray to Hormoz. I shall have the world-revealing cup that shows the seven climes brought to me, and I shall invoke God's blessings on our noble ancestors. Then I will tell you where Bizhan is, since the cup will answer my prayers."

Giv's heart was reassured, and he thanked the king and wished him long life and prosperity.

As soon as Giv had left the king's presence, he sent out horsemen in every direction to see if they could find some trace of his son. They covered all Iran and Turan but found nothing, so that when the spring came and the world was renewed the king turned to the world-revealing cup.

Hopeful for news of his son, Giv entered the court, and when Khosrow saw him bent over and withered away with worry, he put on the Rumi cloak he wore to pray. He cried out to God, calling down blessings on the sun as it inaugurated the new year, and asked for strength and help to defeat the power of Ahriman. Then he returned in solemn procession to his palace, replaced the crown on his head, and took the cup in his hands. He stared into it and saw the world's seven climes, the turnings of the heavens, all that happened there, and how and why things came to pass. He saw from the sign of Pisces to that of Aries, he saw Saturn, Mars, the sun, Leo, Venus, Mercury above, and the moon below. The royal magician saw all that was to be seen. Searching for some sign of Bizhan, his gaze traversed the seven climes until he reached the land of the Gorgsaran, and there he saw him, bound with chains in a pit, longing for death; beside him princess Manizheh stood, ready to serve him. The king turned toward Giv and his smile lit up the council chamber. "Rejoice, Bizhan is alive, rid yourself of your anxiety. He is imprisoned, but this is small cause for grief, because he is alive and a noble woman is attending him. He suffers terrible pains, and it hurts me to see him like this, weeping, despairing of help from his family, trembling like a willow tree. But who can go to his rescue, who is loyal enough to undertake this expedition, to save him from his sorrows? Only Rostam, who can pluck monsters from the sea's depths, is fit for this task. Go to Zavolestan and travel day and night without rest; take my letter but breathe not a word of it to anyone as you go."

Khosrow's Letter to Rostam

A scribe was called in and the king dictated a friendly letter to Rostam:

> "Great Rostam, noblest of our warriors,
> Whose deeds remind us of our ancestors,
> Leopards submit to you, sea-monsters roar
> In terror when you walk upon the shore,
> Persia's stout heart, prop of our sovereignty,
> Prompt with your help in all adversity:
> The demons of Mazanderan were slain
> By you, your mace destroyed their evil reign.
> How many kings, how many enemies
> You've conquered, and how many provinces!
> To pluck from darkness any mortal who
> In peril or affliction turns to you,
> The Lord has given you a mammoth's might
> And lionhearted courage when you fight.
> Gudarz and Giv in their despair now ask
> For your assistance in a worthy task;
> You know how close this clan remains to me,
> Never have they endured such agony.
> Giv has a single son, and all his joy,
> His hopes of life, are centered on this boy;
> To me he's been a loyal courtier who
> Will do whatever I command him to.
> Now, when you read this letter, don't delay,
> Return with Giv, hear what he has to say;
> In council we'll decide what must be done
> To save this noble warrior's captive son.
> I'll provide men and treasure, you're to free
> Bizhan from his Turanian misery."

Khosrow sealed the letter; Giv took it, made his obeisance to the king, and went home to prepare for the journey. He rode with his clansmen, quick as a hunted animal, covering two days' travel in each day, crossing the desert and heading for the River Hirmand. When he reached Gurabad a lookout saw him and shouted that a warrior and his entourage were approaching the riverbank; the leader carried a Kaboli sword in his fist, and they were followed by a banner flapping in the wind. Rostam's father, Zal, heard the lookout's cry and rode out to meet them, so that they would have no reason to act hostilely toward him. As he saw Giv coming, his face downcast and preoccupied, he said to himself, "Something has happened to the king, there's no other reason for Giv to come here." When he met up with them he asked after the king, and how the war with Turan was faring. Giv greeted him respectfully from Khosrow, and then unburdened his heart, telling him the tale of his lost son. He asked for Rostam, and Zal answered, "He's out hunting wild asses: when the sun goes down he'll be back." Giv said, "I'll go and find him, I have a letter from Khosrow I have to give him." But Zal answered, "Stay here, he'll be here soon; come to my house and spend the day feasting with me."

But as Giv entered the outer court Rostam was seen returning from the hunt. Giv went out to greet him and dismounted before him. Hope flared up in his heart and the color came back to his face, although his eyes were still filled with tears. When Rostam saw the anxiety in his expression and the marks of tears on his face, he said to himself, "Some disaster has happened to Iran and to the king." He dismounted and embraced Giv, asking after Khosrow, and then for news of Gudarz, Tus, Gazhdaham, and various other warriors at the Persian court such as Shapur, Farhad, Bizhan, Roham, and Gorgin. When Giv heard the name "Bizhan," a cry escaped from his lips and he said to Rostam, "My lord, all kings honor you, and I am happy to see you and to hear you speak so kindly; those you ask after are well, and they send their greetings to you. But you don't know the terrible calamity that has stricken me in my old age; the evil eye has lighted on Gudarz's clan and destroyed all our good fortune. I had one son in all the world; he was both my boy and my confidant, my councilor. He has disappeared from the face of the earth; no one in my clan has suffered such a calamity. I've ridden day and night searching the world for Bizhan. But now, at the turning of the year, our king has prayed to God and seen in the world-revealing cup that he is in Turan, loaded down with chains; seeing this, Khosrow sent me here to you. I stand before you, my heart filled with hope, my cheeks sallow with grief, my eyes blinded by tears: I look to you as my one recourse in all the world, as you are ready to help everyone in their time of need."

He wept and sighed, and as he handed over Khosrow's letter he told

Rostam of the business with Gorgin. Rostam too wept as he read the letter, and loathing for Afrasyab welled up in him. He cried out for Bizhan and said, "Think no more of this; Rostam will not remove the saddle from Rakhsh's back until he has taken Bizhan's hand in his and destroyed the chains and prison that hold him. By God's power and the king's good fortune, I shall bring your prince back from Turan."

They went to Rostam's castle, where Rostam went through Khosrow's letter and said to Giv, "I understand what's to be done, and I shall carry out the king's commands. I know what services you've rendered, to me and to the court, and though I rejoice to see you here, my heart grieves for Bizhan. But you should not despair; I shall act as the king orders me and do my best to rescue your son, even if God should separate my soul from my body in the attempt. I'm ready to sacrifice my soul, my men, and my wealth on Bizhan's behalf. With God's help and our victorious king's good fortune, I'll free him from his chains and the dark pit where he languishes and return him to the Persian court. But now, you must be my guest for three days, and we shall drink together and take our ease; there is no thine or mine between you and me. We'll feast here and tell tales of the heroes and kings of old, and on the fourth day we'll set out for Khosrow's court."

Impulsively Giv stepped forward and kissed the hero's hand, chest, and feet. He praised Rostam and wished him eternal strength and wisdom. When Rostam saw that Giv was reassured he said to his steward, "Set out a feast, call our councilors and chieftains." After the banquet, Zavareh, Faramarz, Zal, and Giv sat in a bejeweled hall where musicians and wine servers entertained them; their hands were stained with ruby wine, the goblets glittered, and the harps resounded. And so three days and nights passed in pleasure and happiness; on the fourth they prepared to set out. Rostam ordered the baggage train to be made ready, laid his ancestors' mace in the saddle, and mounted Rakhsh. Rakhsh pricked up his ears, Rostam's head seemed to overtop the sun, and he and Giv, together with a hundred selected Zavoli horsemen, set out impatiently on their journey to Iran.

As Rostam approached the Persian heartland, the pinnacles of Khosrow's castle could be seen in the distance and a welcoming wind came down to him from the heavens. Giv said, "I shall ride on ahead and announce your coming."

Giv reached the court and made his obeisance to Khosrow, who asked him about his journey and where Rostam was. Giv replied, "Great king, your good fortune makes all things turn out well; Rostam did not refuse your orders. When I gave him your letter he reverently placed it against his eyes, and he has come here as befits a loyal subject, his reins twisted with mine. I rode on ahead to announce his coming to you."

Khosrow's answer was, "And where is this prop of our nobility, this paragon of loyalty now?" He ordered Gudarz, Tus, and Farhad, together with two companies from the army, to go out and greet the approaching hero. The din of drums rang out and the welcoming party was drawn up; the world was darkened by their dust, and in the gloom their lances glittered and their banners fluttered. When they reached Rostam they dismounted and bowed before him, and he too descended from his horse and asked each one for news of the king. Then everyone remounted and the group made its way to the royal palace.

Rostam Addresses Kay Khosrow

When Rostam entered the audience hall he ran forward, invoking the blessings of Hormoz upon the king. He then called on the angel Bahman to protect his crown, the angel Ordibehesht to protect his person, the angel Shahrivar to give him victory, the angel Sepandarmez to watch over him, the angel Khordad to bring prosperity to his lands, and the angel Mordad to watch over his flocks.

Khosrow stood, motioned Rostam to sit beside him, and said, "You are the champion of the world's kings; what men conceal you know, and what you do not conceal is still unknown to them. The Keyanids have chosen you before all others; you are the support of their army, the guardian of Iran, the refuge of their troops. I rejoice to see you here, valiant and vigilant as ever. Now, are Zavareh, Faramarz, and Zal well? What news can you give me of them?" Rostam knelt and kissed the throne and replied, "Victorious king, all three are well and prosperous, thanks to your good fortune. Blessed are those whom the king remembers!"

Khosrow ordered his chamberlain to summon Gudarz, Tus, and other courtiers of the first rank. The steward had the royal gardens prepared; a golden crown and throne were placed beneath a tree whose blossoms were beginning to fall, royal brocades were spread on the grass, and the flower gardens glowed like lamps at night. Near where the king sat a tree was placed so that its shade covered him; its trunk was of silver, its branches of gold encrusted with rubies and other precious stones; its leaves and buds were made of emeralds and agates that hung like precious earrings. Golden oranges and quinces grew from the branches; they were hollow inside and filled with musk macerated in wine, and their surfaces were pierced like a flute's, so that the scent diffused through the air, delighting the king. The wine servers who stood before the guests had bejeweled crowns, and their cloaks were of brocade shot with gold; they wore torques and earrings, and the bodices of their clothes were worked with gems. The faces of the servants who burned sandalwood before the king and played on harps glowed like rich brocade. All hearts rejoiced to be there; the wine went round and even before it took effect the guests' faces shone like pomegranate blossoms.

Khosrow sat Rostam in the place of honor beneath the tree and said to him, "My noble friend, you are Iran's shield against all evil, protecting us as the Simorgh spreads out her wings. You have always been ready to serve Iran and her kings, and with your mace and the might of your royal *farr* you destroyed the demons of Mazanderan. You know how Gudarz's clan has served in good fortune and bad, always ready to do my bidding and to guide me toward the truth, and Giv especially has been my bulwark against all evils. Such a sorrow has never come to this clan before, for what sorrow is greater than the loss of a child? If you do not agree to help us now no other lion-warrior will; think what must be done to save Bizhan, who languishes a captive in Turan. Whatever horses or arms or men or treasure you need, take them, and give the matter no more thought!"

Rostam kissed the ground, rose quickly, and said,

> *"Your majesty, you're like the radiant sun*
> *Bestowing light and life on everyone:*
> *May greed and anger never touch your reign*
> *And may your enemies live wracked with pain.*
> *Monarch with whom no monarch can compete,*
> *All other kings are dust beneath your feet,*
> *Neither the sun nor moon has ever known*
> *A king like you to occupy the throne.*

My mother bore me so that you could live
Sure of the service that you knew I'd give;
I've heard the king's command and I agree
To go wherever he might order me.
The heavens can rain down fire but I won't leave
This mission that I undertake for Giv
Until success is mine—and I won't ask
For chiefs or troops to help me in this task."

Gudarz, Giv, Fariborz, Farhad, and Shapur, together with the other assembled chieftains, called down the world Creator's blessings on Rostam, and the company sat to their wine, as happy and radiant as the springtime.

Gorgin Sends a Letter to Rostam

When Gorgin heard of Rostam's presence at the court, he realized that here was the key to his deliverance. He sent him a message: "O sword of fortune, scabbard of loyalty, banner of greatness, treasury of faith, gateway of generosity, imprisoner of disaster, if it does not pain you to hear from me, let me tell you of my sorrows. The hunchbacked heavens have doused the torch of my heart and left me in darkness; what was fated to happen to me has happened. If the king will forgive me my sins and restore me my good name, I'm ready to throw myself into fire before him, I'll do anything to rid myself of this disaster that has come to me in my old age. If you will ask for me from the king, I will follow you with all the energy of a wild mountain sheep. I shall go to Bizhan and grovel before him, in hopes of getting back my good reputation."

When Gorgin's message reached Rostam, he sighed, troubled by Gorgin's sorrow and by his foolish request. He sent the messenger back and told him to say to Gorgin, "You fearless fool, haven't you heard of what the leopard said to the sea monster: 'When passion overcomes wisdom, no one can escape its clutches; but the wise man who overcomes passion will be renowned as a lion'? You talk like a cunning old fox, but you didn't see the trap set for you. How can I possibly mention your name before Khosrow for the sake of such a foolish request? But you're so wretched that I'll ask Khosrow to forgive your sin and brighten your life's darkened moon. If God wills that Bizhan be freed from his chains, you'll be set free, too, and no one will take any further revenge on you. But if the heavens will otherwise, you must despair of life. I shall go on this mission, armed with God's strength and the king's command, but if I don't return successfully, prepare yourself for Gudarz and Giv to wreak vengeance on you for their child's death."

Two days and nights passed and Rostam made no mention of the matter; on the third day, when Khosrow was seated on his ivory throne, the hero came to him. He began to talk about Gorgin's miseries, but the king cut him off: "You're my general, and you're asking me to break the oath I swore by my throne and crown, by the lord of the sun and moon, that Gorgin would see nothing from me but suffering until Bizhan was freed from his chains. Ask me for anything else, for thrones, seal-rings, swords or crowns!"

Rostam replied, "My noble lord, if he did wrong, he repents of it and is ready to sacrifice his life in a good cause; but if the king will not forgive him, his name and reputation are lost forever. Anyone who strays from wisdom's path sooner or later regrets the evil that he does. It would be right for you to remember his former deeds, how he was always there in every crisis, and how he fought steadfastly for your ancestors. If the king can grant me this man, it may be that fortune will smile on him again." Khosrow allowed his request, and Gorgin was released from the dark pit where he had been chained.

Then the king asked Rostam how he intended to go about his task, what he would need in the way of troops and treasure, and who he wanted to accompany him. He added, "I fear Afrasyab will kill Bizhan in a fit of impatience. He has a demon's nature and he's impulsive; he might well suddenly destroy our warrior." Rostam replied, "I shall prepare for this task in secret; the key to these chains is deceit, and we must not act too hastily. We must tug back on the reins, and this is no time for maces, swords, or spears. I'll need a quantity of jewels, gold, and silver; we'll go with high hopes, and when we're there, fear will make us cautious. We'll go as merchants, and this will give us a good excuse to linger in Turan for a while. I'll need carpets and clothes, and things to give as presents."

Khosrow gave orders that his ancient treasuries be opened; the king's treasurer brought brocades and jewels, and Rostam came and selected whatever he needed. He had a hundred camel-loads of gold coins made up, together with a hundred mule-loads of silver, and he had the court chamberlain choose a thousand lion hearted warriors.

Seven noblemen—Gorgin, Zangeh, Gostaham, Gorazeh, Farhad, Roham, and Ashkash—were to go with him as his companions and as guardians of the wealth. When these men were summoned, Zangeh asked, "Where is Khosrow, and what's happened that he has called for us like this?"

Rostam and the Seven Persian Heroes Enter Turkestan

At dawn the chamberlain appeared at the castle gates, and the seven heroes stood before the chosen troops, fully armed and ready to sacrifice their souls if need be. At cock crow, as the sky whitened, war drums were fastened on the elephants and Rostam, tall as a cypress tree, appeared in the gateway, mace in hand, his lariat hitched to his saddle. He called down God's blessings on his country, and the group set off.

They neared the border with Turan, and he called the army's leaders to him. He said, "You are to stay here, alert and on guard; you are not to leave this place unless God divides my body from my soul; be prepared for war, however, have your claws ready for blood."

The army stayed on the Persian side of the border while Rostam and his nobles pressed on to Turan. But first they disguised themselves as merchants, removing their silver sword belts and dressing in woolen garments. They entered Turan as a richly laden caravan, accompanied by seven horses, one of which was Rakhsh; there were a hundred camel-loads of jewels, and a hundred mule-loads of soldier's tunics and armor. The bells on the animals and the clatter of their progress made a noise like the trumpets of Tahmures; the whole plain was filled with their din until they reached the town where Piran lived. Piran was away hunting; when Rostam saw him returning, he had a goblet filled with jewels and covered with a fine brocade cloth and two horses with jeweled bridles and draped with brocade led forward. Servants took the gifts to Piran's palace, and Rostam accompanied them. He greeted Piran respectfully, as one whose virtues were known both in Iran and Turan. By God's grace Piran did not recognize Rostam; he said to him, "Where are you from, who are you, and why have you come here in such a hurry?" Rostam replied, "I am your servant, sir; God's led me to your town to refresh myself and rest. I've come the long and weary way from Iran to Turan as a merchant; I buy and sell all sorts of things. I've traveled here assured of your kindness, and hope has now conquered my heart's fears. If you will take me under your wing's protection, I shall stay here to sell jewels and buy horses. Your justice will ensure that no one harms me, and your benevolence will rain down blessings upon me." Then he set before Piran the goblet filled with jewels and had the splendid Arab horses, that had no trace of wind-blown dust on their immaculate coats, led forward. Invoking God's benediction, he handed the presents over, and the bargain was made.

When Piran saw the jewels glittering in the goblet he welcomed Rostam warmly and sat him on a turquoise throne, saying, "Be happy here, be sure you'll be safe in my city; I'll give you quarters near to my palace and you need have no fears for your goods, no one will give you any trouble. Bring everything you have of value here and then look for customers. Make my son's house your personal headquarters, and think of yourself as one of my family." Rostam replied, "My lord, I brought this caravan from Iran for you, and all that I have in it is yours. Wherever I stay will be suitable for me, but with my victorious lord's permission, I'll stay with the caravan; there are all kinds of people traveling with me, and I don't want any of my jewels to disappear." Piran said, "Go and choose any place you desire; I'll send guides to help you."

Rostam chose a house for his party to stay in, and a warehouse for his goods. News spread that a caravan had come to Piran's castle from Iran and customers began to arrive from all quarters, particularly when it became known that there were jewels for sale. Buyers for brocade, carpets, and gems converged on the castle, and Rostam and his companions decked out their warehouse so that it shone like the sun itself.

Manizheh Comes to Rostam

Manizheh heard about the caravan from Iran and hurried to Piran's city. Unveiled and weeping, Afrasyab's daughter came before Rostam; wiping her tears from her face with her sleeve, she said,

> "I wish you life and long prosperity,
> May God protect you from adversity!
> May heaven prosper all you say and do,
> May evil glances never injure you.
> Whatever purposes you hope to gain
> May all your efforts never bring you pain,
> May wisdom be your guide, may fortune bless
> Iran with prosperous days and happiness.

What news have you? What tidings can you bring
Of Persia's champions, or of their king?
Haven't they heard Bizhan is here, don't they
Desire to help their friend in any way?
Will he be left by Giv, by all his kin,
To perish in the pit he suffers in?
Fetters weigh down his legs, his arms and hands
Are fixed to stakes by heavy iron bands;
He hangs in chains, blood stains his clothes, I weep
To hear his groans, and never rest or sleep."

Rostam was afraid when he heard her, and he burst out as if in rage, pushing her toward the street: "Get away from me, I don't know any kings, I know nothing about Giv or that family, your words mean nothing to me!"

Manizheh stared at Rostam and sobbed pitifully. She said, "You're a great and wise man and your cold words don't suit you. Say nothing if you wish, but don't drive me from you, for my sufferings have worn away my life. Is this the way Persians treat people? Do they deny news to the poor and wretched?"

Rostam said, "What's the matter with you, woman? Has Ahriman told you the world's coming to an end? You disrupted my trade, and that's why I was angry with you. Don't let what I said upset you; I was worried about selling my goods. As for the king, I don't live in the city where he does, and I know nothing about Giv or his clan; I've never been to the area where they live."

Quickly, he had whatever food was available set in front of the poor woman, and then he questioned her as to what had made her unhappy, why she was so interested in the Persian king and nobility, and why she kept her eye on the road from Iran the whole time.

Manizheh said, "And why should you want to know about my sorrows and misfortunes? I left the pit with my heart filled with anguish and ran to you thinking you were a free and noble man, and you yelled at me like a warrior attacking an enemy. Have you no fear of God in you? I am Manizheh, Afrasyab's daughter; once the sun never saw me unveiled, but now my face is sallow with grief, my eyes are filled with bloody tears, and I wander from house to house seeking charity. I beg for bread; this is the fate God has visited upon me. Has any life ever been more wretched than mine? May God have mercy on me. And poor Bizhan in that pit never sees the sun or moon, but hangs in chains and fetters, begging God for death. His pain adds to my pain, and I have wept so much that my eyes can weep no more. But if you go to Iran again and hear news of Gudarz, or if you see Giv at Kay Khosrow's court or the hero Rostam, tell them that Bizhan lies here in deep distress and that if they delay it will be too late. If they wish to see him alive, they should hurry, for he is crushed between the stone above him and the iron that binds him."

Rostam wept tears of sympathy and said to her, "Dear lovely child, why don't you have the nobles of your country intercede for you with your father? Surely he would forgive you and feel remorse for what's happened?" Then he ordered his cooks to bring Manizheh all kinds of food, and especially he told them to prepare a roasted chicken folded round with soft bread; when they brought this, Rostam dexterously slipped a ring into it and gave it to Manizheh, saying, "Take this to the pit, and look after the poor prisoner who languishes there."

Manizheh hurried back to the pit, with the food wrapped in a cloth and clutched against her breast. She passed it down to Bizhan just as she'd received it. Bizhan peered at it in astonishment and called out to her, "Dearest Manizheh, you've suffered so much on my behalf. Where did you get this food you're in such a hurry to give me?" She said, "From a Persian merchant who's come with a caravan of goods to Turan; he seems like someone who's passed through many trials, a noble and splendid man. He has a great many jewels with him and has set up shop in a big warehouse in front of Piran's castle. He gave me the food wrapped in a cloth and told me to bring it to you, and said that I could return for more later."

Hopeful and apprehensive, Bizhan began to open the bread, and as he did so he came on the hidden ring. He peered at the stone set in it and made out a name, then he laughed in triumph and astonishment. It was a turquoise seal, with the word "Rostam" engraved on it with a steel point, as fine as a hair. Bizhan saw that the tree of loyalty had born fruit; he knew that the key that would release him from his suffering was at hand. He laughed long and loud and when Manizheh heard him laughing, chained in the darkness as he was, she was alarmed and feared that he had gone mad. She called down to him, "How can

you laugh when you can't tell night from day? What do you know that
I don't? Tell me. Has good fortune suddenly shown you her face?"

Bizhan replied, "I'm hopeful that fate will finally free me from this
pit. If you can swear to keep faith with me, I'll tell you the whole tale
from beginning to end, but only if you'll swear yourself to secrecy,
because a man can sew up a woman's mouth to prevent idle talk and
she'll still find some way to free her tongue."

Manizheh wept and wailed, "How wretched my fate is! Alas for the
days of my youth, for my broken heart and my weeping eyes. I've given
Bizhan my body, my soul, and my wealth, and now he cannot trust me.
My treasury and my jeweled crown were plundered, my father cast me
out, unveiled and humiliated, before his court, and now that Bizhan
sees hope he leaves me in despair. The world is dark to me, my eyes see
nothing, Bizhan hides his thoughts from me, and only God knows all
things."

Bizhan replied, "What you say is true. You lost everything for my
sake. I should not have said what I said. My kindest friend, my dearest
wife, you have to guide me now, the agony I've suffered has turned my
brains. Know then that the man selling jewels, whose cook gave you the
food you brought, has come to Turan looking for me; that's the only
reason he's here selling jewels. God has taken pity on me and I shall see
the broad earth once again. This jeweler will save me from my long
agony, and you from your grief and beggary on my behalf. Go to him
once again and say to him in secret, "Great hero of the worlds' kings,
tender-hearted and resourceful, tell me if you are Rakhsh's lord.""

Manizheh hurried to Rostam like the wind and spoke as Bizhan
had instructed her. When Rostam saw her come running like this and
heard what she said, he knew that Bizhan had entrusted her with their
secret. His heart melted and he said, "May God never withdraw his
kindness from you, my lovely child. Tell him, 'Yes, I am Rakhsh's lord,
sent by God to save you. I have traveled the long road from Zavol to
Iran and from Iran to Turan for your sake.' Tell him, but let no one else
know of this; in the darkest night listen for the least sound. Spend the
next day gathering firewood in the forest, and when night comes, light
a huge bonfire."

Overjoyed at his words and freed from all sorrow, Manizheh hur-
ried back to the pit where Bizhan lay bound. She said, "I gave the great

lord your message, and he confirmed that he was the man you said he was. He told me to wipe away my tears and to say to you that he had come here like a leopard to find you, and now that he had done so you would soon enough see his sword's work. He will tear up the ground and throw the stone that covers you to the stars. He told me that when the sun releases its grip on the world and night comes I'm to build a huge fire so that the stone and the pit's whereabouts shine like the daytime, and he will be able to use the glow as a guide to us."

Bizhan said, "Light the fire that will deliver us both from darkness," and he prayed to God, saying, "Pure, splendid, and just, release me from all sorrows and strike down my enemies with your arrows; give me justice, for you know the pains and grief I have suffered; allow me to see my native country again and to smash against this stone my evil star." Then he addressed Manizheh:

> "And you, who've suffered long and patiently,
> Who've given heart and soul and wealth for me,
> Who thought that, undergone for me, distress
> Was but another name for happiness,
> Who cast aside your kin, your noble name,
> Your parents, crown and land, to share my shame:
> If in my youth I find I'm free again,
> Delivered from this dragon and this pain,
> I'll bow before you like a man whose days
> Are passed before his God in prayer and praise;
> Prompt as a slave who waits before his lord,
> I'll find for you a glorious reward."

Manizheh set about gathering firewood, going from branch to branch like a bird, her eyes fixed on the sun to mark when it would drop behind the mountains. And when she saw the sun disappear and night draw its skirts over the mountain slopes, at that moment when the world finds peace and all that is visible fades from sight because night's army has veiled sunlight in darkness, Manizheh quickly lit the flames. Night's pitch-black eyes were seeled; Manizheh's heart pounded like a brass drum as she listened for the iron hooves of Rakhsh.

For his part, Rostam put on his armor and prayed to the God of the sun and moon, saying "May the eyes of the evil be blinded, give me strength to complete this business of Bizhan." He ordered his warriors to prepare for battle; poplar wood saddles were placed on their mounts, and they made ready to fight.

They set out toward the distant glow, and traveled expeditiously. When they reached the great stone of the Akvan Div and the pit of sorrow and grief, Rostam said to his seven companions, "You'll have to dismount and find some way to remove that stone from the mouth of the pit." But no matter how hard the warriors struggled, they could not shift the stone; when Rostam saw how they sweated to no avail, he too dismounted and hitched up his skirts about his waist. Praying to God for strength, he set his hands to the stone and lifted it; with a lion's power he flung it into the forest, and the ground shuddered as the stone landed.

He peered into the pit and, sighing in sympathy, addressed Bizhan: "How did such a misfortune happen to you? Your portion from the world was to have been one of delight, how is it that the goblet you took from her hands was filled with poison?" Bizhan answered from the darkness, "Your journey must have been long and hard; when I heard your war cry, all the world's poison turned to sweetness for me. You see how I have lived, with iron as my earth and a stone as my sky; I've suffered so much pain and grief that I gave up all hope of the world."

Rostam replied, "The shining Keeper of the World has had mercy on your soul, and now I have one request to ask of you: that you grant me Gorgin's life, and that you drive from your heart all thoughts of hatred for him." Bizhan said, "What do you know of my experiences with this companion of mine; my lionhearted friend, what do you know of how Gorgin treated me? If I ever set eyes on him again my vengeance will be like God's last judgment."

Rostam said, "If you persist in this hatred and refuse to listen to what I have to say, I shall leave you chained here in this pit; I shall mount Rakhsh and return whence I came." When he heard Rostam's words, a cry of grief rose up from the pit, and Bizhan said, "I am the most wretched of our clan's heroes. The evil that came to me was from Gorgin, and now I must suffer this, too: but I accept, and drive all thoughts of hatred for him from my heart."

Rostam lowered his lariat into the pit and brought Bizhan out of its depths, wasted away with pain and suffering, his legs still shackled, his head uncovered, his hair and nails grown long, all his body caked with blood where the chains had eaten into the flesh. Rostam gave a great cry when he saw him weighed down with iron and set about breaking the fetters and shackles. They made their way home, with Bizhan on one side of Rostam and the woman who had succored him on the other; the two young people recounted their sufferings to the hero, who had Bizhan's head washed and fresh clothes brought for him. Then Gorgin came forward and sank to the ground, striking his face against the dust; he asked pardon for his evil acts and for the foolish things he had said. Bizhan's heart forgave him, and he forgot all thoughts of punishment.

The camels were loaded with their goods, Rostam put on his armor once more, and the Persian warriors mounted, with drawn swords and maces at the ready. Ashkash, who was a wary fighter, always on the lookout for whatever might harm the army, led off the baggage train. Rostam said to Bizhan, "You and Manizheh should go with Ashkash. Afrasyab will be so enraged we can't rest tonight; I'm going to play a trick on him within his own walls, and his whole country will laugh at him tomorrow." But Bizhan's answer was, "If I'm the one who's being avenged, I should be at the head of this expedition."

Rostam and Bizhan Attack

Rostam and the seven warriors left the baggage train in Ashkash's capable hands and set out. Letting their reins hang slack on their saddles and drawing their swords, they arrived at Afrasyab's palace at the time when men turn to drunkenness, rest, and sleep. They attacked and confusion reigned: swords glittered, arrows poured down, heads fell severed from bodies, mouths were clogged with dust. Rostam stood in the portico of Afrasyab's palace and yelled, "So you sleep well, do you, you and your valiant warriors? You slept in state while Bizhan was in the pit, but did you dream of an iron wall confronting you? I am Rostam, the son of Zal; now is no time for sleep in soft beds. I have smashed your chains and removed the stone you set as Bizhan's keeper; he is free of his fetters, and rightly so, since this was no way to treat a son-in-law! Were Seyavash's sufferings, and the war that came from them, not enough for you? You had no right to seek Bizhan's life, but I see your heart's stupefied and your mind's asleep." And Bizhan cried out, "Misbegotten, evil-minded Turk, think how you dealt with me when you were on your throne and I stood chained before you; then, when

I was bound motionless as a stone, you were savage as a leopard, but now I walk freely on the face of the earth, and the ferocious lion slinks off."

Afrasyab struggled with his clothes and called out, "Are all my warriors asleep? Any man who wants jewels and a crown, block these enemies' advance!" Cries and a confused noise of combat resounded on all sides, and blood streamed beneath Afrasyab's door; every Turanian warrior who ventured forward was killed, and finally Afrasyab fled from his palace. Rostam entered the building and distributed among his men its cloth and carpets, the noble horses with their poplar wood saddles covered with leopard skins and jewels, and the king's womenfolk, who took the Persian heroes by the hand.

They left the palace and packed up their plunder, having no intention of staying any longer in Turan. Because of the baggage they carried and to avoid a bitter outcome to their expedition, they urged the horses forward as fast as they could. Rostam became so exhausted by their haste that even the weight of his helmet was a trouble to him, and his companions and their horses were so weak they had hardly a pulse left in their arteries. Rostam sent a messenger to the forces he had left when he crossed into Turan, saying "Draw your swords from their scabbards; I am certain that the earth will soon be black with an army's hooves. Afrasyab will muster an army of vengeance, and follow us here; their lances will darken the sunlight."

At last the returning group reached the waiting army; they made themselves ready for battle, their lances sharpened, their reins at the ready. A lookout saw horsemen approaching from Turan and Rostam went to Manizheh in her tent and said, "If the wine has been spilt, its scent still lingers: if our pleasures are past, the memory of them is still ours. But this is the way of the world, giving us now sweetness and pleasure, now bitterness and pain."

Rostam's Battle with Afrasyab

As soon as the sun rose above the mountain tops Turan's warriors had begun to prepare for their onslaught. The town was filled with a deafening clamor: horsemen mustered in their ranks before Afrasyab's palace, Turan's nobles bowed their heads to the ground before him, and all were eager to exact vengeance from Iran. They felt that the time had passed for words; a remedy had to be found, since what Bizhan had done had disgraced their king forever. "The Iranians do not call us men," they said. "They say we are women dressed as warriors."

Like a leopard, Afrasyab strode forward and gave the signal for war: he ordered Piran to have the war drums strapped on their elephants, saying, "These Persians will make fun of us no more." Brass trumpets, bugles, and Indian chimes rang out before the palace. Turan was in an uproar as the army set out for the Persian border, and the whole earth seemed like a moving ocean.

A lookout saw the earth heaving like the sea and ran to Rostam: "Prepare to fight, the world has turned black from the dust flung up by their horsemen." But Rostam replied, "There's no cause for fear; dust is what they'll come to if they fight with us." Leaving the baggage with Manizheh, he donned his armor and came out to inspect his troops, roaring like a lion, "What use is a fox when it's caught in a lion's claws?" Then he addressed his men:

> *"The day of battle's come: my noble lords,*
> *Where are your iron-piercing spears, your swords?*
> *Now is the time to show your bravery*
> *And turn our vengeance into victory."*

The trumpets blared and Rostam mounted Rakhsh. He led his men down from the mountainside as the enemy were passing through a defile to the plains. The two sides ranged themselves behind walls of iron-clad warriors. On the Persian side, Ashkash and Gostaham and their horsemen made up the right flank, the left was commanded by Farhad and Zangeh, while Rostam himself and Bizhan were in the center. Behind them towered Mount Bisitun, and before them was a wall of swords. When Afrasyab saw that the enemy forces were led by Rostam, he put on his armor uneasily and ordered his men to hold back. He had them form defensive ranks; the air darkened and the ground disappeared. He entrusted his left flank to Piran, and the right to Human; the center was held by Garsivaz and Shideh, while he himself kept an eye on all parts of the line.

Like a massive mountain, Rostam rode up and down between the armies and called out

"You miserable, wretched Turk—you shame
Your throne, your warriors, and your noble name.
Your heart's not in this fight: how many men
You've mustered in your army's ranks, but when
The battle's joined at last and I attack,
I'll see no more than your retreating back.
And did my father never say to you
The ancient proverbs that are always true?
'A herd of milling asses cannot fight
Against a single lion's savage might;
All heaven's stars will never equal one
In glory and in radiance—the sun;
Words won't give courage to a fox, no laws
Can make an ass develop lion's claws.'
Don't be a fool, and if you want to save
Your sovereignty, don't act as if you're brave;
If you attack this time, in all this plain
You won't escape alive from me again!"

When the Turkish king heard these words he trembled, heaved a bitter sigh, and cried out in fury, "Warriors of Turan! Is this a battle-field, or a banqueting hall?"

When they heard their commander's voice a great shout went up from the Turanian ranks; dust rose into the sky obscuring the sun, war drums were fastened on elephants, horns and trumpets sounded, and the line of armored warriors made a solid iron wall. The plain and mountain slopes re-echoed with cries from men on both sides, in the dusty air the glitter of swords flashed as if the world's end had come, and blows from steel maces rained down on armor and helmets like hail. Rostam's banner, with its dragon device, seemed to eclipse the sun; wherever he rode, sev-ered heads fell to the ground. With his ox-headed mace he was like a maddened dromedary that has slipped its tether, and from the center of the army he scattered his enemies like a wolf.

On the right flank Ashkash pressed on like the wind, eager for combat with Garsivaz; on the left Gorgin, Farhad, and Roham pushed back the Turkish warriors; and in the center Bizhan went tri-umphantly forward as if the battle were a celebratory feast. Warriors' heads fell like leaves from a tree, and the battlefield became a river of blood in which the Turkish banners lay overturned and abandoned.

When Afrasyab saw the day was lost and that his brave warriors had been slain, he threw away his Indian sword and mounted a fresh horse: he separated himself from the Turkish army and rode toward Turan, having achieved nothing by his attempt to ambush the Persians. Rostam sped after him, raining arrows and blows on the intervening Turks; like a fire-breathing dragon he followed him for two parasangs, but finally returned to camp, where a thousand Turkish prisoners were waiting. There he distributed to the army the wealth his men had captured, loaded up the elephant train with baggage, and set out in triumph to Kay Khosrow.

Rostam Returns with Bizhan from Turan to Iran

When news reached the king that the lion was returning victorious, that Bizhan had been released from the prison where he'd been held, that the army of Turan had been smashed and all their hopes had come to naught, he prayed to God for joy, striking his face and forehead against the dust.

Gudarz and Giv hurried to Khosrow. The noise of the approaching army's war drums and trumpets could be heard; then the ground in front of the king's palace was darkened by horses' hooves, the clamor of trumpets and horns resounded throughout the city, the banners of Gudarz and Giv were raised, chained leopards and lions were led out on one side and on the other were mounted warriors. In this fashion, as the king had commanded, the army went out to greet the returning victors.

When Rostam emerged from the approaching group, Gudarz and Giv dismounted, and all the Persian nobility followed suit. Rostam too dismounted and greeted those who had come to welcome him. Gudarz and Giv addressed him, "Great commander, may God hold you forever in his keeping, may the sun and moon turn as you would wish, may the heavens never tire of you; you have made us your slaves, for through you we have found our lost son; it is you who has delivered us from pain and sorrow, and all Persians long to serve you."

The nobles remounted and processed toward the king. When they were close to the city, Khosrow came out and welcomed Rostam as the guardian of all his heroes. Rostam saw that the king himself was coming to greet him and he dismounted once more, saying he was humbled that the king had put himself to this trouble. Khosrow embraced him and said, "You are a root stock of manliness and a mine of virtues; your deeds shine like the sun, for their goodness is seen everywhere." Quickly Rostam took Bizhan by the hand and handed him over to his father and his king. Then he brought the thousand Turanian prisoners bound before the king, and Khosrow called down heaven's blessings on him, praising Zal, who had such a son, and Zavol, that had nurtured such a hero.

Next the king addressed Giv: "The hidden purposes of God have looked kindly on you: through Rostam He has restored your son to you." Giv replied, "May you live happily and forever, and may Rostam's luck remain ever fresh and green, and may Zal rejoice in his son."

Khosrow gave a great feast for his nobles, after which the company went to a splendid hall where they were plied with wine and entertained by richly dressed musicians whose cheeks blushed like rich brocade, and who accompanied their songs with the bewitching sound of harps. There were golden trays heaped with musk, and to the front of the hall was an artificial pool filled with rosewater; in his glory, the king seemed like a cypress topped by the full moon, and when the nobles left his palace every one of them was drunk.

At dawn Rostam returned to the court, prompt to serve his prince and with not a care in his heart; he asked for permission to return home, and Khosrow discussed this with him for a while. He ordered his chamberlain to bring in a suit of clothes sewn with jewels, a cloak and crown, a goblet filled with royal gems, a hundred saddled horses, a hundred laden mules, a hundred servant girls, a hundred serving youths—all these he gave to Rostam, who kissed the ground in thanks. The hero then placed the crown on his head, girt himself in the cloak and belt, made his farewells to the king, and took the road to Sistan. And his noble companions, who had seen so much sorrow and joy and suffering at his side, were also given presents, and they too left the king's palace in good spirits.

When the king had said farewell to his champions, he settled contentedly on his throne and summoned Bizhan. He asked him about the pains and sorrows he had endured, the narrow pit where he'd languished, and the woman who had ministered to him. Bizhan talked at length, and as the king listened he was moved to pity, both for him and for the torments Afrasyab's poor daughter had endured. He had a hundred sets of clothes of cloth of gold worked with jewels brought in, as well as a crown, ten purses of gold coins, slaves, carpets, and all manner of goods and said to Bizhan, "Take these to your grieving Turkish friend: speak gently to her, see you don't make her sufferings worse, think what she has gone through for your sake!

"Live your life in happiness with her now, and consider the turnings of Fate, who lifts one to the high heavens so that he knows nothing of grief or pain, and then throws him weeping beneath the dust. It is fearful, terrible, to think on this. And while one is brought up with luxury and caresses, and is thrown bewildered and despairing into a dark pit, another is lifted from the pit and raised to a throne where a jeweled crown is placed on his head. The world has no shame in doing this; it is prompt to hand out both pleasure and pain and has no need of us and our doings. Such is the way of the world that guides us to both good and evil. Now you should never need for wealth, and I wish you a heart free from all sorrow."

*T*he war between Iran and Turan continued, but Turan's forces were inexorably driven back and defeated by Khosrow's army. In one encounter Piran was killed (by Gudarz) and his death was lamented by both Kay Khosrow and Rostam who remembered him as a noble, conciliatory counselor who had protected fugitive Persians in Turan, and tried when possible to make peace between the two peoples.

Piran died stoically, accepting his fate, but when Afrasyab was finally captured and brought before Kay Khosrow he pleaded for his life and was ignominiously executed.

Still alive, but living in retirement and far from the center of events, Kay Kavus felt that, with the death of his lifelong enemy, his life's last mission had been accomplished.

THE OCCULTATION OF KAY KHOSROW

Once Kavus felt that his land was safe, he opened his heart to God and said: "O thou who art the guide to every blessing and who art higher than all fate, through you I found *farr,* glory, good fortune, greatness, my crown and my throne. You have given no one else the treasure and fame that you gave to me; I asked you for a warrior who would avenge the blood of Seyavash, and I saw my farsighted grandson, ambitious, glorious and wise, a man who outshines all former kings. But now I have lived for a hundred and fifty years and my hair that was as black as musk has turned as white as camphor. My body that was as straight and elegant as a cypress is bent like a bow, and if my days are to come to an end I shall not see death as a misfortune."

A short while later he died; all that remained of him in the world was his name. The lord Kay Khosrow came from his palace and sat himself down on the black earth: dressed in black and dark blue, devoid of all glory, the Persian nobles walked before him on foot. They mourned their king for two weeks, and built him a palatial tomb, ten lariat-lengths high. His body was treated with a salve compounded of camphor and musk, and then wrapped in robes of silk and brocade. Attendants placed him on an ivory dais, and anointed his head with camphor and musk. Kay Khosrow left the chamber, and the door to the king's resting place was sealed. No one ever saw Kavus again: he rested from war and revenge forever.

> *Such is the passing world that you must leave,*
> *All men must die, and it is vain to grieve.*
> *No learning will suffice against Death's hand,*
> *Whose might no arms or helmet can withstand;*

And—king or prophet—in the end you must
Descend to dirt, and slumber in the dust.
Pursue desire, consider life a game
And, if you can, look out for luck and fame—
But know the world's your enemy; your head
Will lie in dust, the grave will be your bed.

The king mourned his grandfather for forty days, shunning the crown and throne and pleasure. Then he sat himself on the ivory throne and placed on his own head the heart-delighting crown. The army assembled and the nobility came before him in their golden diadems: they acclaimed him as king and scattered jewels over his crown. The victorious champion was enthroned, and from end to end the world rejoiced.

Kay Khosrow Becomes Sated with Kingship

Sixty years passed, and all the world was under the king's command. The king's great soul began to brood on his power and on the passing of time. He said, "I have cleansed all inhabited lands of malevolent souls, from India to China to Byzantium, from the east to the west; mountains and wastelands and deserts and fertile plains—all are under my command. The world has no fear now of evil beings, and I have lived for many days. Although it was revenge I sought, God granted me all that I wished. My soul must not become filled with hubris, with foul thoughts and the ways of Ahriman. I shall then be as evil as Zahhak, or like Jamshid who suffered the same fate as Tur and Salm. On the one side I'm descended from Kavus, and on the other from that wicked wizard Tur: my ancestors are Kavus and Afrasyab, who even when he slept dreamt only of crookedness and trickery. One day I shall become ungrateful to God, terror will touch my soul's radiance, the divine *farr* will leave me and I shall swerve toward crookedness and evil; I shall go forward into darkness until my head and crown are tumbled in the dust. I shall leave an evil name behind me, and my fate before God will be evil. My flesh will decay and my bones will lie scattered on the ground; virtue will fail, ingratitude will take its place, and in the other world my soul will dwell in darkness. When another has taken my crown and throne, and trampled on my fortune, all that will remain

of me will be an evil name; the rose that grew from my age-old strug-
gles will be a briar, no more.

"Now that I have sought vengeance, adorned the world with splen-
dor, killed those who rose against God and whom it was necessary to
kill, there is not a place on earth which does not recognize my author-
ity: however wealthy or strong they may be, the great of the earth are
my servants. I am grateful to God that he has given me this *farr*, and
that the heavens' revolutions have looked favorably on me. It is best
that I turn now toward God, that I seek him while I can still do so
honorably, as one who has prayed to him privately: he will take my
soul to the abode of the blessed, for this crown and throne will perish.
No one will ever have more fame or happiness or greatness or peace
of mind than I have enjoyed: I have reached life's bourn, I have seen
the world's secrets, its good and evil, what is plain and what is hidden,
and I have seen that whether a man tills the soil or reigns as a king he
must finally pass through death."

The king ordered his chamberlain to send away anyone who might
come seeking him, and to do this politely, with sweet words, avoiding
all harshness.

He shut the doors to his court, loosened his clothes, and began to
lament his state. He washed his head and body preparatory to praying:
with the torch of wisdom he sought out a path toward God. Then he
strode to the place where he prayed, and spoke to the Judge of all secrets:

> "O higher than all souls, of unmatched worth,
> Who makes fire spurt forth from the darkened earth,
> Look on me now, vouchsafe me wisdom here
> To know the truth, to know what I should fear.
> I'll pray to you incessantly and strive
> To do good deeds whilst I remain alive—
> Absolve me of the evil I have done,
> Let me not trespass against anyone.
> Drive sin out from my soul and keep me free
> From demons and their cunning sorcery:
> Let me control desire that won control
> Over Zahhak's, Kavus's, Jamshid's soul.
> If devils hide the road to what is right
> Evil will triumph when I come to fight—

Save me from demons' wiles, let me avoid
The snares by which my soul will be destroyed:
Lead me, protect me, be my constant guide
To where the just eternally abide."

The Persians Plead with Kay Khosrow

Day and night he stood in prayer; his body was in the palace but his soul was in another place. After a week his strength began to fail; he found he could stand no longer and on the eighth day he returned to his throne. The champions of the Persian army were bewildered by their king's behavior, each of them ascribing it to a different cause.

The king took his place on the throne, and the chamberlain drew back the curtain that separated him from his courtiers. The commanders entered, their arms crossed in humility over their chests; among them were Tus, Gudarz, brave Giv, Gorgin, Bizhan, and the lion-like Roham. When they saw the king they prostrated themselves before him and said: "O brave and just king, possessor of the world, noblest of the noble: no king like you has ever assumed the throne. All champions serve you, and we live only because you keep watch over us. You have laid all your enemies low, and there is no one left in the world for you to fear. We have no notion why the king's thoughts should be darkened at a time like this; now is the time for you to rejoice in your good fortune, not to grieve your life away in anxiety. Whether we have done something to upset the king, or whether it is another matter that is no fault of ours, may he tell us what troubles him, so that we can reassure him and bring fire back to his cheeks. And if some secret enemy disturbs his peace may the king inform us who it is: each king who has worn the crown has seen the value of his wealth and might in this, that he could cut off his enemies' heads, or sacrifice his own head when he put on a warrior's helmet and rode out to war. Tell us what you are hiding, and we will find a remedy for it."

The great king answered: "Set your minds at rest my champions: the world contains no enemy that troubles me, and my wealth is all intact; nothing the army has done has offended me, and none of you is guilty of sin. When I rode out in vengeance for my father's death I spread justice and righteousness throughout the world; there is no portion of the black earth that has not known my seal's imprint. Sheathe your swords, and grasp the winecup; drink, rejoice, and replace the noise of bowstrings with the sounds of flutes and harps. For a week now I've prayed before God: I have a hidden desire which I long for God to grant me. When he answers my prayer this will be a blessing for me and I shall tell you openly what it is. Meanwhile you too should pray to God on my behalf, for it is he who gives us strength for good and evil. Pray to him for guidance, then give yourselves to wine and cheerfulness, forgetful of all sorrow. Know that this unstable world makes no distinction between a king and his subject, that it snatches away both the old and the young, and that from it both justice and tyranny come to us."

Sadly and anxiously the nobles left his presence, and the king ordered his chamberlain to admit no one to him. That night he returned to the place of prayer and opened his lips to the Lord of Justice:

> "O higher than the highest, show to me
> The ways of righteousness and purity:
> Guide me to heaven, let me leave behind
> This fleeting habitation of mankind,
> And let my heart shun sin, so that I might
> Pass to the realms of everlasting light."

Giv Travels to Zabol

After a week had passed and Khosrow had still not reappeared, a confused murmuring could be heard: the nobles gathered together and there was much discussion of the ways of great kings, both those who were god-fearing and those who had lived as tyrants. Finally Gudarz, Giv's father, turned to his son and said, "Fortune has favored you and you've always given your support to the crown and throne; you've undergone many troubles for Iran's sake, putting your loyalty before your family and homeland. Now a crisis is before us, and we should not take it lightly: you must travel to Zabol and tell Zal and Rostam that the king has turned away from God and has lost his way. He has barred his court's door to the nobility, and takes council with demons. We've tried to reason with him, and our words were meant well, but though he heard us out he gave us no answer: we can see that his heart is confused, and his head is full of wind. We're afraid that he'll go astray as Kavus did, and that demons will lead him into evil paths. Tell

Rostam and Zal that they are heroes, that they are the wisest and most capable of men: have them assemble the astrologers and sages of Zabol and bring them here to Iran. Since Khosrow has hidden his face from us, the kingdom is full of rumors: we have tried every remedy and now all our hopes rest on Zal and his son."

Giv chose a number of warriors as his retinue and set off for Sistan. There he told Rostam and Zal what he had seen and heard: Zal was saddened by his words and said, "Truly, grief has become our companion." Then he ordered Rostam to call together the astrologers and priests of Sistan and Kabol, so that they could accompany them on the journey to Iran. Sages of all kinds gathered at Zal's court, and the group set out.

The king prayed for seven days and on the eighth, at daybreak, he returned to his throne and had the chamberlain draw back the curtain from the outer door. The chieftains and priests streamed into the audience hall, and Khosrow received them graciously as befits a king, motioning them to their places. But they stood before him, their hands crossed in reverence over their chests, and none sat in the place where he had been assigned. They said, "Immortal soul, just lord of all the world, might and the royal *farr* belong to you, and from the sun to the fish beneath the earth is yours. Your clear soul knows all beings: speak wisely to us. We stand before you as your slaves and champions: tell us what we have done that you forbid us access to you. Days have passed like this, and our hearts are filled with foreboding. Tell your secret to us, the guardians of your distant frontiers; if your sorrow is from the sea we shall dry it up, and spread it with a mantle of powdered musk; if it is from a mountain we shall level it and with our daggers spit your enemies' hearts; if wealth will cure your sorrow there will be no lack of cash. We are all guardians of your glory, and we weep in sympathy for your sorrows."

The world's lord answered: "I am not without need of my champions; but my heart has no anxiety about my might or men or wealth, and no country's produced an enemy for me to worry about. My heart has conceived a desire which I'll not relinquish: in the dark night and the bright day I have hopes of its fulfillment. When I achieve it I will tell you what my secret prayers have been. Go now, victorious and happy, and rid your minds of evil thoughts." All his nobility paid him homage, but their minds were clouded with sorrow. When they had left, the king ordered that the curtain be lowered; and he who had won so many victories sat weeping by the door, with despair in his heart.

Kay Khosrow Sees the Angel Sorush in a Dream

Again the world's lord stood in prayer, asking for guidance:

> *"Lord of the heavens, Lord of unmatched might,*
> *Of goodness, justice, and celestial light,*
> *What shall my kingdom profit me if you*
> *Remain unsatisfied with all I do?*
> *But, good or evil, may my deeds suffice*
> *To win for me a place in paradise."*

He prayed before God, wailing and groaning in his anguish, and after five weeks of prayer, one night, as the moon rose, he fell asleep. He slept, but his bright soul became wisdom's companion and did not sleep. In his dream he saw the angel Sorush whisper in his ear, "O king, good fortune and benevolent stars have guided you, and you have seen enough of torques and crowns and thrones. If you would leave this world you have found what you are seeking; you will find a home beside the Source of Righteousness, there is no need for you to sojourn in this darkness any longer. Give your treasures to those who are deserving; relinquish this fleeting world to another. When you enrich the poor, and your own people, you will be made stronger. You will not remain here long now; choose a king in whom all creatures, down to the smallest ant, can place their trust. And when you've given away the world, you cannot rest: you must prepare for your departure."

When the exhausted king woke he saw that the place where he had been praying was awash with water: he wept and placed his face against the ground, giving thanks to God. He said, "If I can soon move onward, God has given me all I desire." He dressed himself in clothes that had never been worn before and ascended his throne: there he sat, but wearing neither his torque, nor the royal jewels, nor his crown.

Zal and Rostam Reach Iran

At the week's end Rostam and Zal arrived in Iran full of apprehension as to what was afoot. Hearing of their approach a group of heavy-hearted Iranian nobles led by Tus and Gudarz hurried out to greet them.

They said: "The devil Eblis has led our king astray. What is his court but his army? And yet for days and nights now no one has seen him except during the brief moments when the court doors are opened to us. My lords, Khosrow has changed from that cheerful and glorious monarch you knew; his cypress stature is bent, and the roses of his cheeks have turned pale as a quince. I don't know what evil eye has struck him, and why he withers like a shriveled petal, unless it is that the Persians' luck is clouded and misfortune strikes him from an evil star."

Brave Zal said to them: "It may be that the king is sated with power; all seems well and then difficulties arise, pleasure and pain both come to us. Do not grieve over this, grief will only weaken your grip on life: we shall talk with him, our advice will make the stars favorable again."

The group traveled to the court, where immediately the curtain was drawn back and they entered in good spirits. Zal, Rostam, Tus, Gudarz, Gorgin, Bizhan, Gastahom, and a great many other nobles and their retainers crowded into the audience chamber. When Khosrow heard Rostam's voice from beyond the curtain, and saw Zal's face, he was puzzled and leapt up from the throne; he extended his hand to them and asked them why they had come. Then he questioned the sages of Zabol and its environs, and motioned them to seats in his court: the Iranian nobles too were assigned places according to their rank.

Zal greeted the king and wished him long life, listing the great monarchs of the past and saying that he had seen none who equaled Khosrow in stature and possession of the Divine *farr*, in chivalry, victory, and benevolence: he hoped that the king would reign forever, continuing to bestow justice on the world and enjoying the fruits of conquest, for there was no noble who was not as dirt beneath the king's feet, no poison for which the king's mere name was not a remedy. Then he continued: "We have heard unwelcome news, and hearing it we hurried to your court: we have consulted astrologers with their Indian charts, seeking to know the heaven's secrets and why it has exiled Iran from its benevolence. A messenger came saying that the victorious king has ordered that the curtain that guards his court not be drawn back, and that the king hides his face from his people. Sympathy for the Persians has made me fly here like an eagle, like a skiff over water, so that I might ask the world's lord what secret anxiety is troubling him. Three things cure all ills, and make the throne wholly secure. These three are wealth, effort, and chivalrous men:

without these no battles can be fought. And the fourth is that we praise God, praying before him day and night, for it is he who helps his slaves, and saves them from harm. We shall give great wealth to the poor, in hopes that God will clarify your soul, and that wisdom will course through your brain again."

Kay Khosrow's Answer to Zal

When Khosrow had heard Zal out he gave him a wise answer. He said: "Old man, your words and thoughts are always welcome; from the time of Manuchehr until now you have advised the court well. And your mammoth-bodied son Rostam has been a prop to the Kayanid kings, the cynosure of the court: it was he who brought up Seyavash and taught him virtue. When an army caught sight of his massive mace, his helmet and mighty stature, many would flee without fighting, abandoning their bows and arrows on the battlefield. He guided my ancestors in their wars of vengeance. If I list all your exploits I will be talking for a hundred generations, and if my words seem flattery they will, if examined truly, be seen to underestimate you. But as to your question about why I have not granted audience; the world has become contemptible to me, and for five weeks now I have stood in prayer before God, the Just Guide, asking that he absolve me of past sins and illuminate the darkened moon of my life; asking that he take me from this fleeting world and that I suffer here no longer. I have been close to abandoning the ways of righteousness, to twisting my head aside as other kings before me have done; now that I have achieved all I sought I must prepare to leave this world, and good news has reached me. Last night at dawn I slept and an angel came to me from God, saying 'Rise, the time for your departure has come, your sleepless sorrow is over.' My reign, and all my concern for the army, crown, and throne, are drawing to an end."

Zal Advises Kay Khosrow

The courtiers listened to him in bewilderment, and sorrow filled their hearts. But Zal was angered, and heaved a cold sigh. He said to the assembled Persians: "This is not right, wisdom has no place in his mind. I have never seen a king who talked in this way, and since he has spoken his mind so must we. When he says such things we are under no obligation to agree with him. It's as if a demon has been advising him; he's abandoned the path of God. Feraydun and the god-fearing

Hushang never grasped at such straws: I shall tell him the truth even if it means I shall suffer for it." The Persians answered him: "No Kayanid has ever talked like this: we are all behind you in what you tell the king."

Zal stood and addressed Kay Khosrow: "Just king, listen to the words of an old and experienced man, and if my advice seems crooked to you make me no answer. Speech in support of what is right is bitter, and this bitterness closes the door against injury and loss. You should not be offended by the true words that I say here, in this company. Your mother bore you in Turan, and you grew up there; you're the grandson on one side of Afrasyab, who practiced black magic even in his sleep. Your other grandfather was that malevolent king Kavus whose dissembling face hid a heart filled with trickery and cunning. He ruled from the east to the west but he wanted to fly up to the heavens and count the stars there. I advised him at length not to try this, and my words were bitter: he heard my advice but it did him no good and I left him with a heart full of sorrow and pain. He rose into the air and tumbled to earth; God granted him his life but he felt no gratitude, his head was filled with dust, his mind with terror. You led a hundred thousand armed warriors to battle on the Chorasmian plain, and before the armies you fought on foot with Pashang. If he had conquered you, Iran would have been open to Afrasyab's forces, but God delivered him into your hands. You were able to kill whoever men feared, whoever gave no thought to God's law. I told you to cease your wars then, that the time for forgiveness and rejoicing had arrived. But now worse times than ever have come to Iran, and men's hearts are filled with a more terrible fear; you've abandoned God's ways, and strayed into an evil path. You'll get no profit from this, and it will not please God. My king, if this is what you want no one will support you; you'll regret these words, think of what you're doing and don't follow demons' orders. If you persist in this devilish plan God will cut you off from his *farr*; you will live a life of pain and sin and no one will call you king again. If you ignore my advice you are following Ahriman; pain will be yours, and you will lose good fortune, the homage due to a king, and the throne itself. May wisdom guide your soul, may your mind remain pure and steadfast!"

Zal fell silent and the whole company spoke in his support, saying: "We agree with all that this old man has said: the doorway to truth should not be concealed!"

Kay Khosrow's Answer to Zal

When Khosrow had heard him out he said nothing for a while, and remained lost in thought. Then he spoke quietly, weighing his words. "You have seen the world's ways Zal, and you have lived long years chivalrously and well. If I spoke coldly to you here before this assembly, God would not approve of such an evil act. Also, Rostam would be upset, and when he is upset Iran suffers; his efforts on Iran's behalf far outweigh the wealth he has received as a reward. The heavens made him my shield, the scourge of evildoers, leaving them time for neither sleep nor food. I shall answer you mildly, my words won't break your heart." Then in a voice that all could hear he said, "My victorious lords, I have heard everything that Zal has said before this assembly. I swear by God himself that I am far from obeying demons: it is to God that my soul inclines, for I see him as the cure to my suffering. In clarity of heart I have looked on the world, and wisdom has become my armor against evil." Turning to Zal he said, "There's no need for such anger; speak as is fitting. First, you said no wise or perspicacious person was ever born of Turanian stock: I am the son of the great Seyavash, the scion of an invincible Kayanid king, the grandson of Kavus who was a wise, fortunate, and well-loved monarch. On my mother's side I am descended from Afrasyab, whose hatred deprived me of rest and food; his forebear was Feraydun and there is no shame in such an ancestry, for Iran's lion-like warriors fled to the sea in terror before Afrasyab. Then you said that Kavus built himself a flying chariot, and tried to go beyond what is fitting for a king: but you should know that ambition is not a fault in a king. Next, I sought revenge for my father's death and won victory in all the world: I killed my enemies who had spread injustice throughout the land. My task in the world is complete; no trace remains of the evildoers against whom I fought. Whenever I think deeply about prosperity and enduring royal power I see the examples of Kavus and Jamshid before me; I fear that I'll forget my status as they did, that I'll become corrupt like Zahhak and Tur, whose evil sickened the world. I fear that when the thread of my days draws to an end I, like them, shall be headed for hell.

"For these five weeks in which I have prayed day and night, know that the great God has freed me from the sorrows of this dark earth. I am sated with my army, the crown, and the throne: I am unencumbered now, and ready to depart. You Zal, with all the experience of your advanced age, say that I have fallen into a demon's trap, that I am wandering far from the right road in darkness and sin: but I cannot see how I have done evil, or where you can find God's punishment in all this."

Zal Asks for Forgiveness

When Zal heard these words he turned aside in shame; a cry came from his lips and he addressed Khosrow:

> *"Great king, my words were hasty and unwise,*
> *Wisdom is yours, and I apologize;*
> *If demons have deluded anyone*
> *I am that person—forgive what I have done.*
> *I've lived for countless years, and always shown*
> *Unswerving loyalty to Persia's throne,*
> *Till now I've never seen a monarch pray*
> *For heaven's holy guidance in this way,*
> *But Kay Khosrow is now my sapient guide,*
> *And may I stay forever at his side.*
> *Throughout Iran all virtuous men will grieve*
> *To learn the king we've served now longs to leave,*
> *How can we hope for this? But what he chooses*
> *No loyal subject of the king refuses."*

When Khosrow heard Zal's words he accepted his apology, knowing that all he said came only from his love for him: he took Zal by the hand and sat him next to himself on the throne. Then he said: "Go now with Rostam, Tus, Gudarz, Giv, and the rest of our nobility, and pitch tents and pavilions on the plain outside the city. Display our banners, assemble our troops and elephants there as if for a splendid celebration." Rostam did as the king ordered: the nobles brought tents and pavilions out of storage and filled the valley from mountain side to mountain side with white, black, purple, and blue tents; flags of red, yellow, and purple fluttered there, and in the midst of all stood the Kaviani banner. Zal's tent, with its black flag, was pitched next to the king's and on its left was Rostam's tent, where the dignitaries he had brought from Kabol were gathered. In the foreground were the tents of Tus, Gudarz, Giv, Gorgin, Kherrad, and Shapur; immediately behind them those of Bizhan, Gastahom, and the other important chieftains.

Kay Khosrow Addresses the Persians

The king sat on his golden throne and took the ox-headed mace in his hand. On one side, like a great mammoth and a savage lion, were Zal and Rostam and on the other Tus, Gudarz, Giv, Roham, Shapur, and Gorgin. All stared at the king, waiting to hear what he would say. He addressed them in a loud voice: "My champions, favored by Fortune, each of you with sense and wisdom knows that both good and evil pass away: we too, and the world itself, are ephemeral. Why then do we suffer such pain and sorrow and grief? We build with our hands and what we build we leave to our enemies, while we ourselves must depart: but the ox of our sorrows is still not skinned, since rewards and punishments are with God. Fear God then, and do not rejoice in this dark earth, for this day passes from everyone, and time counts every breath we breathe. From Hushang to Kavus there have been kings possessed of *farr*, the crown, and the throne; nothing remains of them but their names. No one can compute the number of those who have gone before us. Many turned against God, and in their last days they feared the evil they had done. I am a slave like them, and though I have striven and suffered I see that no one remains on this earth. Now that I have torn my heart and soul from this fleeting world, I have brought my grief and pain to an end. I have gained all I sought, and I have turned my face aside from the royal throne. I give to anyone I have offended whatever wealth he desires. I shall tell God, who knows all that is good, of the actions of those heroes who have helped me. I donate my possessions, my weapons, my treasuries, to the nobility of Iran. I have listed and hand over my cash and slaves and flocks, for I am setting out on a journey and have separated my heart from this earthly darkness. Rejoice now for a week, give yourself to pleasure and food and drink: wish me well, pray for my safe passage from this world, and that I may depart without suffering."

When the king finished speaking the heroes of Iran were bewildered and uncertain what to make of his words. One said, "This king is mad: wisdom and his heart are utter strangers to one another. Who knows what will become of him, or of the crown and throne?"

The plain and mountain slopes were filled with warriors; they formed groups and began to feast. The valley re-echoed with the sounds of flutes and singing and drunken shouts: the revels went on for a week, and no one gave a thought to pain or sorrow.

Kay Khosrow's Words to Gudarz

On the eighth day Kay Khosrow sat on his throne, but he wore neither the royal crown nor torque, and the royal mace was nowhere in evidence. Since he felt that the time for his departure was at hand he opened one of his treasuries and said to Gudarz: "Consider how the world passes, and take note of what is hidden as well as what is plain. There is a day for amassing treasure and a day for distributing it: look at our ruined frontier forts and bridges, at our crumbling reservoirs, destroyed by Afrasyab; look at our motherless children, at our widowed wives who sit alone and desolate, at our indigent old people, at those who harbor secret sorrows. Don't hold back the contents of our treasuries from those in need; distribute wealth to them, in fear of future bad fortune. And I have a treasury called 'Badavar' which is filled with jewels and diadems: use this for our ruined cities that have become lairs for leopards and tigers, for our smashed fire temples left without officiating priests, for those who are old and poor because they gave away their wealth when they were young, for our dried up wells left waterless for years. In the city of Sus there is another treasury built up by my grandfather; its name is 'Arus'; give its contents to Zal, Giv, and Rostam."

He then consigned the contents of his wardrobe to Rostam, together with his torques, royal jewels, corselet, and heavy maces. His flocks of horses he gave to Tus; his orchards and gardens to Gudarz; tired now of war, he gave his armor, in which he had endured so much, to brave Giv. To Fariborz, Kavus's son, he gave his castles, tents, pavilions, and stables, as well as his helmet and diadem. He gave to Bizhan a torque brighter than the planet Jupiter, and two famous rings set with rubies, with his name engraved on them, saying as he did so, "Take these in memory of me, and see that you sow only seeds of righteousness in this world."

The Persians Remonstrate with Kay Khosrow

The king said, "My life draws to an end, and I long for another dispensation. Ask from me what you will; the time has come for this assembly to disperse." All the nobles wept at the prospect of losing their sovereign lord, and said, "Who will inherit the king's crown?"

Zal, who had always been loyal to the Persian throne, kissed the ground and stood to speak: "Lord of the world, it is right that I express my desires openly. You know what Rostam has done for Iran; the pains he has taken, the labors he has undergone, the battles he has fought. When Kavus went to distant Mazanderan and was captured by demons, along with Gudarz and Tus, Rostam went there alone on a journey that pitted him against deserts, darkness, demons, a lion, a dragon, and a sorceress. He won through to the king in Mazanderan; he cut the White Demon in pieces and did the same to other demons there too, and he severed the head of Sanjeh, whose screams re-echoed to the heavens. Because of Kavus's enmity, he killed his son Sohrab, whose like the world had never seen, and wept for him for months and years. If I were to describe all the tales of his prowess I would never finish. If the king is tired of his crown and throne what will he leave to this loyal, lionhearted warrior?"

Khosrow replied, "Who but God himself, the lord of justice and love, can know all that Rostam has done on my behalf, the struggles he has undertaken, the sorrows he has suffered? His valor is no secret, and no one has seen his equal in all the world."

He ordered that a scribe bring paper, musk, and ambergris, and a document was written, by Khosrow's command, conferring on Rostam, the mammoth-bodied warrior who was praised by all men, the lordship of Sistan. The document was affixed with the royal seal and Khosrow handed it to Rostam, saying, "May this land remain forever under Rostam's sovereignty." He then gave robes, gold, silver, and a goblet filled with jewels to the astrologers who had come to court with Zal.

Then Gudarz rose and addressed the king: "Victorious king, I have seen no occupant of the throne to equal you. From the time of Manuchehr to that of Kay Qobad, and throughout noble Kavus's reign, I stood ready and vigilant in our kings' service. I had seventy-eight sons and grandsons; eight are left to me and the others have perished. My son Giv lived as a fugitive in Turan for seven years; wild asses were his food, and he clothed himself in their skins. When the king reached Iran he saw all that Giv had endured on his behalf. And now that the lord of all the world is tired of the throne and crown, Giv hopes for a reward for his labors."

The king replied: "He did far more than this, and may he be blessed a thousand times! May God protect him, and may his enemies' hearts be lacerated with thorns! All I have is yours; I pray that you survive in health and glory!" He ordered that a charter be written on silk, conferring sovereignty of Qom and Esfahan, the cradle of champions, on Gudarz; a gold seal was attached to it, and Khosrow pronounced his benediction saying, "May God be pleased with Gudarz, and may his enemies' hearts be filled with confusion." To the Persian nobility he said, "My hope is that Giv will never tire of his noble deeds: know that he will be a remembrance of me in the world, the defender whom I leave to you. Obey him, and do not slight either his or his father's commands."

When Gudarz had taken his seat again, Tus rose and kissed the ground before Khosrow. He said: "Long live the king, and may evil never touch him! I alone of those here am descended from Feraydun, and I headed this clan until Kay Qobad came. I have led the Persians in battle, and have never relaxed my vigilance, not for a single day. In the mountains of Hamavan I endured the wounds my armor inflicted on my shirtless body; in the battle of revenge for Seyavash I kept watch every night; when Kavus was imprisoned in Mazanderan, Tus was imprisoned with him: I have never deserted our troops and no one has ever complained of my conduct. Now that the king, who knows all my abilities and faults, has grown tired of his crown and throne and prepares to leave this fleeting world, what orders does he give me? What authority does he leave me?"

Khosrow replied, "You have striven and suffered beyond measure; be lord of the Kaviani banner, commander of my armies, and the sovereign of Khorasan." This too was recorded before the nobles, written on a royal charter, and sealed with gold.

Kay Khosrow Confers the Crown on Lohrasp

When the king had dealt with his nobles' affairs, he sank back, exhausted and weak. One who had not been mentioned yet as a beneficiary of the king's bequests was Lohrasp, and Khosrow ordered Bizhan to bring this chieftain before him. As he entered, the king rose and opened his arms in welcome. Descending from the throne, he lifted the crown from his own head and gave it to Lohrasp saying, "I bestow on you sovereignty over the land of Iran: may this crown that is new to you bring you good fortune, and may all the world be as your

slave. I hand over to you here the sovereignty and treasure which I have
built up with such struggle and pain. Henceforth see that only justice
issues from your mouth, since it is justice that will bring you victory
and prosperity; if you would have your luck remain ever young and

fresh, allow no demons access to your soul. Be wise, harm no one, and
always guard your tongue." Then he turned to the Persians assembled
there and said, "Rejoice in his throne and good fortune!"

The Persians were astonished by this turn of events, and bridled
like angry lions; none could accept that they would have to call
Lohrasp their king. Zal strode forward and said aloud what he felt in
his heart: "My lord, is it right for you to dignify such dirt in this way?

My curses on anyone who calls Lohrasp his king, no one here will submit to such injustice! I saw Lohrasp when he arrived in Iran; he was a wretch with one horse to his name. You sent him off to fight against the Alans, and gave him soldiers, a banner, and a sword belt. How many wellborn Persians has the king passed over for this man, whose family I've never set eyes on, whose ancestry's all unknown? No one has ever heard of such a man becoming a king."

As soon as Zal finished speaking a roar of agreement came from the courtiers there, and voices cried out, "We'll serve no longer! If Lohrasp is to be king he can count on us for neither his banquets nor his battles." When Khosrow heard Zal's words he said to him, "Not so fast, and calm your rage: a man who speaks unjustly is more interested in smoke than fire. God does not approve of our doing evil, and the wicked will tremble before the revolutions of Fate. When God makes a man fortunate, deserving of sovereignty, an ornament to the throne, that man has wisdom then, as well as *farr*, dignity, and royal ancestry; he will be just and victorious, and his justice will bring him prosperity. As God is my witness, Lohrasp is possessed of these qualities. He is descended from the pure-souled Hushang, who was lord of all the world; he will cleanse the earth of evil magicians and establish the ways of God; the world will be renewed through his guidance, and his son will continue his legacy. Greet him as your king, and as you love me do not turn aside from my advice. Any man who ignores my words has destroyed whatever credit he may have built up fighting for me; he is ungrateful before God and his soul will be assailed from every side by terror."

When Zal had heard him out he touched the earth with his fingers and smeared black dirt on his lips. Loudly, he greeted Lohrasp as king, and said to Khosrow, "Live in happiness my lord, and may evil never touch you. Who but the king of victory and justice could have known that Lohrasp was of royal descent? I have sworn repentance for what I said, blackening my lips with dirt; may my sin be cancelled." The chieftains scattered jewels over Lohrasp, hailing him as king.

Kay Khosrow Bids Farewell

The great king said to his people, "The road I take now is the one you will take tomorrow: when I have left this wretched earth behind me I shall commend you to God." His eyelashes were wet with tears as he kissed each of them farewell: weeping openly, he embraced the heroes one by one. He said, "Would that I could take all of this company with me." Such a cry went up from the army that the sun lost its way in the heavens: women and little children wept for him in the streets and bazaars, and the houses were filled with groans and lamentation for the king's passing. The king said:

> *"Glorious for your deeds, and glorious in descent,*
> *Rejoice in God's commands and be content.*
> *Now I prepare my soul for death; my name*
> *Shall live henceforth with undiminished fame,*
> *Sorush has come to guide me, and my heart*
> *Withdraws from life: I'm ready to depart."*

He called for a horse, and as his soldiers lamented, he rode toward the royal apartments, his cypress-stature bent with age and weakness over the pommel. He had four women who were as beautiful as the sun, such that no man had ever seen except in dreams: he summoned them and told them what was in his heart. He said: "It is time for me to leave this fleeting world; I am tired of the earth's injustice, and you will never see me alive again. Keep your hearts free of pain and grief."

But the four fainted, and when they revived they wailed aloud for love and sorrow: they scored their cheeks and tore out their hair, they ripped their fine clothes and destroyed their jewelry, and cried out to him, "Take us with you from this hateful world, be our guide to the happiness you seek." The king answered, "The road I take now is the one you will take tomorrow: there Jamshid's sisters live, and great kings in their pomp and glory; my mother, Afrasyab's daughter, is there, who fled across the Oxus with me, and Tur's incomparable daughter Mah Afarid. The bed and pillow of them all is dust, and I do not know whether they dwell in hell or heaven. Don't try to deflect me from my journey; it will be easy enough to find me." He wept and called Lohrasp to him and said to him, "These are my womenfolk, the glory of my bedchamber: while you are king, grant them the same privileges and quarters they have always had. See that they are no cause of shame to you when God summons you to His presence: remember, you will see me there, next to Seyavash. Do nothing that will humiliate you when you stand before us in the other world." Lohrasp agreed to all he said, promising to maintain the king's women in respectable privacy.

Then the king bound on his sword belt and went out to address his men, to whom he said: "Have no pain or fear in your hearts because of me. Do not rush to embrace this world, for its depths are but darkness: live in justice and happiness, and think only well of me." Iran's chieftains bowed their heads to the ground and said that they would remember his advice as long as they lived. He told Lohrasp to take up residence in the palace, saying that his own days were now at an end. "Maintain the royal throne in glory, sow only seeds of righteousness in the world: when nothing threatens or troubles you, see that the crown and luxury and wealth do not corrupt your soul. Remember that your departure will not be delayed for long, and that the days of your life narrow toward their end. Seek justice, act with justice, free those who are just from evil."

Lohrasp wept and dismounted from his horse and kissed the ground. Kay Khosrow said to him, "Farewell, be the warp and woof of justice in this world."

Zal, Rostam, Gudarz, Giv, Bizhan, and Gastahom, together with Kavus's son Fariborz who made a seventh and Tus who made an eighth, accompanied by their separate bands of troops, went with Kay Khosrow as he made his way from the plain to the mountain foothills. There they rested for a week, moistening their dry lips, wailing and weeping at the king's decision: no man could reconcile himself to such sorrow, and the priests said in secret that no one had ever heard of a king acting in this way.

When the sun rose over the mountain peaks, groups came from every direction, a hundred thousand Persian men and women, weeping before the king; all the mountain side was filled with the sounds of mourning, and the granite slopes re-echoed with their cries. They said: "Great king, what has filled your bright soul with such pain and confusion? If you are angry with the army, or if you're tired of the crown, tell us why, but do not quit the Persian throne, or hold the crown in contempt. Stay, and we shall be the dust beneath your horse's hooves, the slaves of your eternal flame. But where is your knowledge, your judgment, your wisdom? The angel Sorush never appeared to a king before, not even to Feraydun: we pray before God and in our fire-temples that God will grant our desire, and that the priests' hearts will look favorably on us."

The king was astonished at this outpouring and called his priests to him. He said, "What happens from now on is a blessing, and why should men weep at a blessing? Be grateful to God, be pure and Godfearing: do not grieve at my departure for we shall all be reunited soon enough." Then he turned to his chieftains and said, "Descend this mountain side without your king: the road ahead is long, hard, and waterless, without vegetation or shade. No one can traverse these slopes unless he has the divine *farr* to help him." Three of the heroes, Zal, Rostam, and Gudarz, heard him and obeyed: but Tus, Giv, Fariborz, Bizhan, and Gastahom did not turn back.

The group went forward for a day and into the night, weakened by the wilderness and lack of water. Then they came on a stream, where they refreshed themselves and rested. The king said to his followers, "We'll stay the night here and talk over the past: you won't see me for much longer now. When the shining sun unfurls its banner and turns the purple land a liquid gold, the time for me to part from you will have come. Then I shall meet Sorush: if my heart trembles at this last journey I shall tear its darkness from my side."

Kay Khosrow Disappears

When part of the night had passed, Khosrow bent over the stream and washed his head and body in its clear water, murmuring the words of the Zend Avesta as he did so. Then he addressed his companions:

> *"Farewell forever. When the sun's first beams*
> *Appear, henceforth I'll come to you in dreams*
> *But you will never see me here again.*
> *Go back tomorrow to the Persian plain—*
> *Even if musk should rain down far and wide*
> *Don't linger on this lonely mountain side;*
> *A wind will blow here soon, a wind to freeze*
> *The mountain slopes and uproot stalwart trees,*
> *From dark clouds snow will fall, you'll lose your way*
> *Back to your Persian home if you delay."*
> *Weary and saddened by his words they wept,*
> *Uneasily, at last, the heroes slept:*

And when the dawn's light touched their resting place
The king had gone, leaving no earthly trace.

They searched the desolate mountain slopes, but as they found no sign of him they returned to the stream like men insensible with grief, and in their hearts they bade a last farewell to the world's king.

Fariborz said, "I can't believe that Khosrow's words were wise: the earth is warm and soft, and the weather's clear; given what we've suffered I don't think it's reasonable for us to set off immediately. We should rest and eat, and after we've slept we can leave this stream and go back." They camped by the stream and went over what Khosrow had done, saying that no one had ever seen or heard of such a wonder (nor would he even if he remained in the world for a long time) as this departure of the king which they had witnessed. They lamented his good fortune and wisdom, his greatness and nobility; but they added that the wise would laugh at the notion that a man could go before God while he was still alive. Who knew what had befallen Khosrow, and what could they say when people refused to believe them? Giv said, "No hero has ever heard of a man who was his equal, not for manliness, generosity, wisdom, valor, appearance, stature, glory, or lineage: leading his troops in battle he was massive as a mammoth, and presiding crowned at his banquets he was radiant as the full moon."

Tus, Fariborz, Giv, Bizhan, and Gastahom Die in the Snow

They ate the provisions they had with them and soon fell asleep. But a wind sprang up and black clouds amassed; the air became as dark as a lion's maw, a blizzard began to blow, and the snow piled higher than the heroes' lances. One by one they were buried in the snow; for a while they struggled beneath its canopy, trying to clear a space to survive, but finally their strength gave out and their sweet souls sought release.

Rostam, Zal, and Gudarz had waited for three days further down the mountain side. As the fourth day dawned they said, "This has gone on too long, how long must we wait here on these stony slopes? If the king has disappeared from the world, like a wind that blows through a group of heroes and is gone, what has happened to our chieftains? Didn't they follow Khosrow's advice?" They waited for a week on the

mountainside, but when the week was over they despaired of seeing
their companions again. They mourned for them, and Gudarz tore out
his hair and scored his cheeks with his nails. He said: "No man has ever
seen such evil as has come to me from the seed of Kavus: I had an army
of sons and grandsons, ambitious and noble youths all of them, and all
were slain in the wars of revenge for Seyavash, so that our tribe was
broken and lost its luster. And now another has disappeared from my
sight; who has seen such sorrows as I have endured?"

Zal counseled him at length: "To be wise is to accept God's justice:
they may yet find a way through the snow and return. But we should not
stay on this mountain side and lamentation will not help us. We can send
footsoldiers out to look for some trace of them." Weeping, they made
their way down the mountain side, each thinking of one or another of
the lost heroes, of his son or relative or friend, and of the king who had
been like a cypress overtopping all the orchard.

> So turns the world; her favors are soon passed,
> All whom she nourishes must die at last.
> One she will raise from earth to heights unknown,
> One she will cast down from a royal throne;
> But there's no cause to triumph or complain,
> Such is the way she turns, and turns again:
> Where are those heroes now, those champions, where?
> Drive out such mortal thoughts, that bring despair.

*L*ohrasp became king of Iran, as Khosrow had directed. He had two sons Goshtasp and Zarir, and while still a young man Goshtasp demanded that his father name him as heir to the throne. His father refused to do this, and Goshtasp left the court in high dudgeon and traveled to India. His brother Zarir was sent to fetch him home again, but no sooner was he back in Iran than he quarreled with his father and set off on his travels again, this time to Rum, where he lived in disguise. There he tried his hand at various occupations but his royal qualities rendered him unfit for all of them. He was seen by Katayun, the King of Rum's daughter and she fell in love with him. Reluctantly the king allowed his daughter to marry the stranger, who then ingratiated himself with the court by killing a wolf and a dragon. Once established as his father-in-law's favorite, he began to threaten Iran. When he finally returned to Iran accompanied by his Rumi bride Katayun, Lohrasp ceded him the throne and went into religious retirement at Balkh.

At this point Ferdowsi includes in his text an account, by the poet Daqiqi, of the coming of the prophet Zoroaster to Goshtasp's court, and the acceptance by the court of the new religion promulgated by him.

A new king, Arjasp, now reigned in Turan, and at the prompting of Zoroaster Goshtasp demanded tribute from him. In response Arjasp attacked Iran. Goshtasp's brother Zarir was killed in the ensuing war, and it was only the valor of Goshtasp's son, Esfandyar, that was able to drive the Turanian army back. Esfandyar is presented as ambitious, but also righteous, chivalrous, and an invincible warrior: he embraced the court's new faith of Zoroastrianism with great zeal, and propagated the faith by the sword. But his enemies at court made his father suspicious of his ambitions for the throne: Goshtasp believed the calumny and imprisoned Esfandyar.

Hearing of this Arjasp sent an army against Balkh: the city was sacked, the aged Lohrasp killed, and many Persian prisoners, including Esfandyar's sisters, were taken back to Turan. Goshtasp appealed for help to Rostam, but the now aged hero made his excuses and refused to have anything to do with the situation. Goshtasp himself led the counter attack and was defeated, barely escaping from the battlefield with his life. His counselor Jamasp advised him that only

Esfandyar could save the situation: Esfandyar was released from prison and drive back the Turanian army.

Goshtasp then asked Esfandyar to travel deep into Turanian territory to rescue his sisters, who were being held in a fortress made of brass. Esfandyar's journey to the brass fortress involved him in a series of seven trials, which closely parallel the trials undergone by Rostam when he traveled to Mazanderan to rescue Kavus from captivity. During the rescue, Arjasp was killed, and Esfandyar then returned in triumph to Iran, fully expecting to be given royal honors by his father. But Goshtasp had one more task in store for him.

ROSTAM AND ESFANDYAR

I heard a story from a nightingale, repeating words come down to us from ancient times.

One night, drunk and dejected, Esfandyar came from his father's palace and went to see his mother Katayun, the daughter of the king of Rum. He embraced her, called for more wine, and said: "The king treats me badly; he told me that once I'd avenged the death of his father by killing king Arjasp, freed my sisters from captivity, cleansed the world of evildoers and promoted our new faith of Zoroastrianism, then he would hand over to me the throne and crown; I'd be king and leader of our armies. When the sun rises and he wakes up I'm going to remind him of his own words: he shouldn't keep from me what's rightfully mine. By God who guides the heavens, I swear that if I see any hesitation in his face I'll place the crown on my own head and distribute the country to its local lords; I'll be as strong and fierce as a lion, and make you queen of Iran."

His mother's heart was saddened at his words; her silk clothes pricked like thorns against her skin. She knew that the king was in no hurry to hand over his crown, throne, country, and royal authority to his son. She said: "Brave boy, don't be so angry with your fate. The army and treasury are yours already, don't over-reach yourself. What's finer in all the world than a young lion-like warrior, girded for war, standing ready to serve his father? When Goshtasp dies, his crown, throne, greatness, and splendor will all be yours."

Esfandyar replied: "It was a wise man who said a man should never tell his secrets to women, because as soon as he opens his mouth he finds his words on everyone's lips. And he also said a man shouldn't do what a woman tells him to, because none of them have any sense." His mother's face clouded with pain and shame, and she regretted having spoken to him.

Esfandyar went back to his father's palace and spent two days and nights there drinking, surrounded by musicians and his womenfolk. Goshtasp brooded on his son's ambitions for the crown and throne, and on the third day he summoned his councilor Jamasp, and had Esfandyar's horoscope cast. He asked whether the prince would have a long and happy life, reigning in safety and splendor, and whether he would die at another's hand or greet the angel Sorush from a peaceful deathbed.

When Jamasp consulted the astrological tables, frowns furrowed his forehead and his eyes filled with tears. He said: "Evil is mine, and my knowledge brings me only evil; would that I had died before your brother Zarir, and not seen his body weltering in blood and dust, or that my father had killed me and this evil fate had not been mine. Esfandyar subdues lions, he has cleared Iran of its enemies, he is fearless in war, he has driven your foes from the face of the earth, he tears the dragon's body in two. But will not sorrow come from this, and the taste of bitterness and grief?"

The king replied, "I trust you to tell me what you know, and not to deviate from wisdom's ways. If he is to die as Zarir did, my life will be a misery to me. You frowned at my question, but tell me what you see: at whose hand will he die, bringing me tears and sorrow?"

Jamasp said, "My lord, misfortune will not hold back because of me. He will die in Zabolestan, fighting with Zal's son, Rostam."

Then the king said, "Take seriously what I'm about to say: if I give him my treasury, the throne and sovereignty, and if he never travels to Zabolestan, will he be safe from the turnings of Fate, will fortunate stars watch over him?" But the astrologer replied, "The heaven's turnings cannot be evaded; neither strength nor valor will save you from the dragon's claws. What is fated will surely come to pass, and a wise man does not ask when." The king grew pensive, and his thoughts made his soul like a tangled thicket. He brooded on the turnings of Fate, and his speculations turned him toward evil.

At dawn the next day the king sat on his throne, and Esfandyar stood humbly before him, his arms crossed on his chest. The court was filled with famous warriors, and the priests stood ranged before the king. Then the mighty champion Esfandyar spoke, and suffering was evident in his voice. He said: "Great king, may you live forever, blessed by the divine *farr*. Justice and love emanate from you, and the crown and throne are made more splendid by you. Father, I am your slave, prompt to carry out all you desire. You know that in the wars of religion with Arjasp, who attacked us with his Chinese cavalry, I swore before God that I would destroy any idolater who threatened our faith, that I would slash his trunk in two with my dagger and feel no fear. And when Arjasp came I did not flee from the leopard's lair. But drinking at your banquet you believed Gorazm's slander, and had me hung with heavy chains and fettered in the fortress of Gonbadan, despised among strangers. You abandoned Balkh and traveled to Zavol, thinking all battles were banquets, and forgetting the sight of your father Lohrasp pierced by Arjasp's sword, lying prone in his blood. When your councilor Jamasp came and saw me worn away by captivity, he tried to persuade me to accept the throne and sovereignty. I answered that I would show my heavy chains to God on the Day of Judgment. He told me of the chieftains who'd been killed, of my imprisoned sisters, of our king fleeing before the Turkish hordes, and asked me if such things did not wring my heart. He said much more besides, and all his words were filled with sorrow and pain. Then I smashed my chains and ran to the king's court: I slaughtered his enemies and rejoiced the king's heart. If I were to describe my seven trials the account would never end. I severed Arjasp's head from his body and avenged the name of Lohrasp. I brought here their treasure, their crown, their throne, and their women and children. I did all you had commanded me, kept to all your orders, never swerved from your advice. You'd said that if you ever saw me alive again you would cherish me more than your own wellbeing; that you would bestow the crown and ivory throne on me, because I would be worthy of both. And now when our nobles ask me where my treasure and army are, I blush for shame. What excuse do you have now? What's the point of my life? What has all my suffering been for?"

The king answered his son: "There's no way forward but the truth. You have acted as you say, and may God favor you for it. I see no enemy in all the world, neither open nor secret, who does not shudder at the mention of your name: shudder I say, he gives up his soul there and then. No one in all the world is your equal, unless it be that foolish son of Zal. His valor lifts him above the skies, and he thinks of himself as no king's subject. He was a slave before Kavus, and he lived by the grace of Khosrow; but about me, Goshtasp, he says, 'His crown is new, mine is ancient; no man anywhere is my equal in battle, not in Rum nor Turan nor Iran.' Now, you must travel to Sistan and there use all your skill, all your ruses and devices. Draw your sword and your mace, bind Rostam in chains; do the same with Zavareh and Faramarz, and forbid them to ride in the saddle. I swear by the Judge of all the world, by Him who lights the sun and moon and stars, that when you do what I have commanded, you shall hear no more opposition from me. I shall hand over to you my treasury and crown, and I myself will seat you on the throne."

This was Esfandyar's response: "O noble and resourceful king, you are straying from the ancient ways; you should speak as is appropriate. Fight with the king of China, destroy the lords of the steppe, but what are you doing fighting against an old man whom Kavus called a conqueror of lions? From the time of Manuchehr and Kay Qobad all the kings of Iran have delighted in him, calling him Rakhsh's master, world-conqueror, lion-slayer, crown-bestower. He's not some young stripling making his way in the world; he is a great man, one who entered into a pact with Kay Khosrow. If such pacts are wrong then he shouldn't be seeking one with you, Goshtasp."

His father said: "My lionhearted prince, you've heard that Kavus was led astray by the devil, that he attempted to fly into the skies on the wings of eagles and fell wretchedly into the sea at Sari; that he brought a devil-born wife back from Hamaveran and gave her command of the royal harem; that Seyavash was destroyed by her wiles and the whole royal clan put in peril. When a man has broken his promise before God, it's wrong even to pass by his doorway. If you want the throne and crown, gather your troops and take the road for Sistan. When you arrive bind Rostam's arms, and lead him here. Watch that Zavareh, Faramarz, and Sam don't trick you: drag them all on foot to this court. And then no one, no matter how rich or illustrious he might be, will disobey my commands again."

> The young prince answered: as he spoke he frowned,
> "Enough! It isn't them you're circling round,
> You're not pursuing Zal and Rostam—I,
> Your son, am singled out by you to die;
> Your jealous passion for your sovereignty
> Has made you want to rid the world of me.

So be it! Keep your royal crown and throne,
Give me a corner to live in alone.
I'm one of many slaves, no more; my task
Is to perform whatever you may ask."

Goshtasp replied: "Don't be too impetuous, but if you're to achieve greatness don't hold back either. Choose experienced cavalry from our army; weapons, troops, and cash are all at your disposal, and any holding back will be because of your own suspicious mind. What would treasure, an army, the crown, and throne be to me without you?"

Esfandyar said, "An army will be of no use to me in this situation. If the time to die has come, a commander can't ward it off with troops." Troubled by thoughts of the crown, and by his father's words, he left the court and made his way to his own palace; there were sighs on his lips, and sadness filled his heart.

Katayun's Advice to Esfandyar

Weeping and in a turmoil of emotion, the beautiful Katayun came before her son, to whom she said: "You remind us of the ancient heroes, and I have heard from Bahman that you mean to leave our gardens and journey to the wastes of Zabolestan. You are to capture Zal's son, Rostam, the master of sword and mace. Listen to your mother's advice; don't be in a hurry either to suffer evil or commit it. Rostam is a horseman with a mammoth's strength, a river's force is nothing against him; he ripped out the guts of the White Demon, the sun is turned aside in its path by his sword. When he sought revenge for the death of Seyavash, and made war on Afrasyab, he turned the world to a sea of blood. Don't throw your life away for the sake of a crown; no king was ever born crowned. My curses on this throne and this crown, on all this slaughter and havoc and plundering. Your father's grown old, and you are young, strong, and capable; all the army looks to you, don't let this anger of yours put you in harm's way. There are other places in the world besides Sistan; there's no need to be so headstrong, so eager for combat. Don't make me the most wretched woman both here and in the world to come; pay attention to my words, they come from a mother's love."

Esfandyar replied: "Dear mother, listen to me: you know what Rostam is, you're always talking about his greatness. It would be wrong to kill him, and no good can come of the king's plan: there's no one in Iran who's finer or more noble than Rostam. All this is true, but don't break my heart, because if you do I shall tear it from my body. How can I ignore the king's orders, how can I refuse such a mission? If heaven wills it I shall die in Zabol, but if Rostam accepts my orders he'll hear no harsh words from me."

His mother said, "My mammoth warrior, your strength makes you careless of your soul, but you won't be strong enough to defeat Rostam. Don't leave here without warriors to help you, offering your life up to Rostam like this. If you're determined to go, this mission is the work of Ahriman; at least don't take your children to this hell, because the wise will not think well of you if you do," and as she spoke she wept bloody tears and tore at her hair.

Esfandyar replied, "It's wrong to keep youngsters away from battle. If a boy stays shut up with women he becomes weak and sullen; he should be present on the battlefield and learn what fighting means. I don't need to take an army with me: men from my own family and a few noblemen will suffice."

At cock-crow the next morning the din of drums rang out; Esfandyar mounted his horse and set off like the wind at the head of a band of warriors. They went forward until they came to a place where the road forked; one track led to the fortress of Gonbadan and the other toward Zabol. The camel that was in the lead lay down on the earth as if it never meant to rise again, and though its driver beat it with a stick it refused to budge, and the caravan halted. Esfandyar took this as a bad omen, and gave orders that the beast's head be severed, hoping to deflect the bad luck he foresaw. This was done, and although Esfandyar was alarmed he made light of it, saying:

> "A noble warrior whose audacity
> Lights up the world and brings him victory
> Laughs at both good and evil, since he knows
> Both come from God, whom no one can oppose."

Inwardly afraid of what lay ahead, he reached the River Hirmand, the border of Rostam's territory. A suitable place was selected, and the group pitched camp in the customary fashion. In Esfandyar's pavilion a throne was placed, and his warriors assembled before him. The prince called for wine and musicians, Pashutan sat opposite him, and as he drank and relaxed Esfandyar's face opened like a blossom in spring. He said to his companions: "I haven't carried out my father's orders; he told me to capture Rostam quickly, and not to hold back in humiliating him. I haven't done what he ordered me to, because this Rostam is a lionhearted warrior, who has undergone many trials, whose mace has set the world in order, and in whose debt all Persians live whether they are princes or slaves. I must send him a messenger, someone who's wise and sensible, a horseman who has some dignity and presence, someone whom Rostam can't deceive. If he'll come to me and dispel this darkness in my soul, if he'll let me bind his arms and in so doing bind the evil that haunts me, and if he has no malevolence against me, I will treat him with nothing but kindness."

Pashutan said, "This is the right path; stick to it, and try to bring peace between men."

Esfandyar ordered his son Bahman to come before him, and said to him: "Saddle your black horse, and dress yourself in a robe of Chinese brocade; put a royal diadem studded with fine jewels on your head, so that whoever sees you will single you out as the most splendid of all warriors and know that you are of royal blood. Take with you ten reputable priests and five horses with golden bridles. Make your way to Rostam's palace, but do so at a leisurely pace. Greet him from me, be polite, flatter him with eloquent words, and then say to him: 'No one with any sense ignores a king's commands. A man must be grateful before God, who knows eternally what is good. If a man augments what is good and holds his heart back from evil, God will fulfill his desires and he will live happily in this fleeting world. If he abstains from evil he will find paradise in the other world; a wise man knows that in the end his bed will be the dark earth and his soul will fly up toward God. One who can distinguish between the good and evil of this world will be loyal to his king.

" 'Now we wish to reckon up what you have done, neither adding to nor diminishing your achievements. You've lived for many years and seen many kings come and go in the world, and if you follow the way of wisdom you know that it was not right for someone who has received so much in the way of wealth and glory from my family to have refused to visit Lohrasp's court. When he passed on sovereignty over the land of Iran to his son, Goshtasp, you paid no attention. You wrote no congratulatory letter to him, you ignored the duties of a subject, you didn't travel to his court to pay homage: you call no one king. Since the time of Hushang, Jamshid, and Feraydun, who wrested sovereignty from Zahhak, to the time of Kay Qobad, there never was such a king as Goshtasp, not for fighting or feasting or hunting. He has adopted the pure faith, and injustice and error have hidden themselves away: the way of God shines out like the sun, and the way of demons is destroyed. When Arjasp attacked with an innumerable army, Goshtasp confronted him and made the battlefield a graveyard for his dead: great men will talk about this exploit until the end of the world. He breaks the back of every lion, and all the east and west are his: travel from Turan to China to Byzantium and you'll see that the world is like wax in his hands. The desert Arabs brandishing their lances send him tribute, because they have no heart or strength to fight against him. I tell you all this because the king is offended by your behavior. You haven't gone to his palace or seen his noble courtiers; instead, you've hidden yourself away in this remote province. But how can our leaders forget you, unless they have neither brains nor hearts remaining to them? You always strove for the good, and held yourself ready to do your kings' bidding. If your pains are reckoned up they exceed the treasure you've accumulated, but no king has ever accepted that his subject could act in this contemptuous way. Goshtasp has said to me that Rostam is so wealthy now that he sits drunk in Zavolestan and gives no thought to us. One day in his fury he swore an oath by the shining day and darkness of the night that no one would ever see you at his court unless it were in chains. Now, I have come from Iran for this purpose, and the king ordered me not to delay in carrying it out. Draw back now, and fear his anger. If you will go along with this and give up your contemptuous ways, I swear by the sun, by the spirit of Zarir, by my lion-like father's soul, that I will make the king take back his words, and that your glory will shine with splendor once again. Pashutan is my guide and witness that I have tried to fathom the king's purposes in this, and see no fault in him. My father is my king and I am his subject; I can never refuse his orders. Your whole clan—Zavareh, Faramarz, Zal, and all the rest of your tried and true chieftains—should hear my words and take my advice. This house must not be left a prey to Persian warriors and destroyed. When I take you bound before the king, and then go over your faults with him, I'll calm his anger and make him forget all thoughts of vengeance. I am a prince, and I give you my word that I will not let even the wind touch you.'"

Bahman Goes as a Messenger to Rostam

Bahman dressed himself in cloth of gold, placed a princely crown on his head, and set out from the encampment, his banner fluttering behind him. A proud young man, on a splendid horse, he made his way toward the River Hirmand, and as soon as the lookout saw him he shouted out to his companions in Zabolestan, "A fine warrior on a black horse is coming our way; his harness tinkles with golden bells, and he's followed by a group of mounted soldiers; he's already crossed the river with no difficulty."

As soon as he heard this Zal rode to the lookout post, his lariat coiled at his saddle and his mace at the ready. When he caught sight of Bahman he sighed and said, "This lordly young man with his royal clothes must be someone from Lohrasp's clan; may his coming here be auspicious for us." Pensively, his heart filled with foreboding, he rode back toward his castle. Radiating princely pride, Bahman approached; he did not recognize Zal, and raising his arm he called out, "My noble friend, where can I find great Rostam, the prop of our times? Esfandyar has camped by the river, and is looking for him."

Zal replied, "There's no need for such hurry, young man! Dismount, and call for wine, and calm yourself. Rostam is out hunting with Faramarz and a few friends; they'll be back soon enough. Rest here with your retinue, and drink a little wine."

But Bahman answered, "Esfandyar said nothing to us about wine and rest: find someone to guide us to the hunting grounds."

Zal said, "What's your name? Whose clan do you belong to, and what have you come here for? I think you're kin to Lohrasp, and descended from Goshtasp too."

Bahman said, "I am Bahman, son to invincible Esfandyar, lord of the world."

When he heard this Zal dismounted and made his obeisance before him. Bahman laughed and dismounted as well, and the two embraced and kissed. Zal urged him to stay, saying that his haste was unnecessary, but Bahman replied that Esfandyar's message could not be treated so lightly. And so Zal chose a warrior who knew the lie of the land and sent him with Bahman to where Rostam was hunting. He was an experienced man called Shirkhun, and after he had led him a fair distance he pointed out the way and went back, leaving Bahman to go on ahead.

Bahman urged his horse up a mountain slope, and when he reached the summit he gazed at the hunting grounds spread out below. He saw there a mighty warrior, a man massive as the cliff of Bisitun, who had uprooted a tree and was using it as a spit on which to roast a wild ass, which he handled as easily as if it weighed no more than an ant. In his other hand he held a goblet full of wine, and in front of him a young man was standing ready to serve him. Nearby, close to a stream and a clump of trees, Rakhsh stood cropping grass. Bahman said, "This is either Rostam, or the sun itself. No one has ever seen such a man in all the world, or heard of his like among the ancient heroes. I fear that Esfandyar will be no match for him, and will flinch from him in battle. I'll kill him here and now with a rock, and so break Zal's heart." He tore a granite boulder from the mountain side and sent it tumbling down the slope. Zavareh heard the rumble of its descent and saw it plunging toward them; he shouted out, "Rostam, a great rock is rolling down the mountain." Rostam made no move; he didn't even put down the wild ass he was roasting. As Zavareh hung back in alarm, Rostam waited until the boulder was almost on him, and the dust it sent up had obscured the mountain above; then he kicked it contemptuously aside. Zavareh and Rostam's son Faramarz cheered, but Bahman was horrified at the exploit, and said, "If Esfandyar fights with such a warrior he'll be humiliated by him; it'll be better if he treats him politely and circum-spectly. If Rostam gets the better of Esfandyar in combat he will be able to conquer all Iran." Bahman remounted his horse, and with his heart full of foreboding descended the mountain slope.

He told a priest of the wonder he had seen, and made his way by an easier path at the foot of the mountain toward Rostam. As he approached, Rostam turned to a companion and said, "Who is this? I think it's someone from Goshtasp's clan." Then he caught sight of Bahman's retinue waiting on the mountain side, and he grew suspi-cious. He and Zavareh, and the rest of the hunting party, went forward to greet their guest. Bahman quickly dismounted and greeted Rostam civilly. Rostam said, "You'll get nothing from me until you tell me who you are." Bahman replied, "I am Esfandyar's son, chief of the Persians; I am Bahman." Rostam immediately embraced him and apol-ogized for his tardy welcome.

Together they made their way back to Rostam's camp and when
Bahman had sat himself down he greeted Rostam formally, and con-
veyed to him the greetings of the king and his nobility. Then he went
on: "Esfandyar has come here and pitched camp by the River
Hirmand, as the king ordered him to. If you will hear me out, I bring
you a message from him."

Rostam replied: "Prince, you've taken a great deal of trouble and
traversed a great deal of ground; first we should eat, and then the world
is at your disposal." A cloth was spread on the ground, and soft bread
was placed on it; then Rostam set a roasted wild ass, its flesh still hot,
before Bahman. He called for his brother Zavareh to sit with them, but
not the rest of his companions. He had another wild ass brought, since
it was his custom to eat a whole animal himself. He sprinkled it with
salt, cut the meat, and set to. Bahman watched him, and ate a little of
the wild ass's meat, but less than a hundredth of the amount Rostam
consumed. Rostam laughed and said:

> *"A prince who's so abstemious surely needs*
> *An army to assist him in his deeds:*
> *I've heard that in your father's battles you*
> *Fought with him: what exactly did you do?*
> *You eat so little you're too weak to wield*
> *A warrior's weapons on the battlefield."*

Bahman replied:

> *"A noble prince will neither talk at length*
> *Nor eat too much: he'd rather save his strength*
> *For battles than for banquets, since it's war*
> *That shows a warrior's worth, not who eats more."*

Rostam laughed long and loud and said, "A fighting spirit won't stay
hidden long!" He called for enough wine to sink a ship: filling a
golden goblet, he toasted the memory of noble heroes, then handed
another to Bahman and said, "Toast whoever you want to!" Seeing the
proffered goblet Bahman hesitated, so Faramarz drank first, saying,
"You're a princely child, we hope you enjoy the wine, and our drink-
ing together." Bahman took the goblet and reluctantly drank a little; he

was as astonished by Rostam's capacity for food and drink as he was by
his massive body, arms, and shoulders. When they had finished their
meal, the two heroes rode together for a while, side by side, and
Bahman told Rostam the details of Esfandyar's message.

Rostam's Answer to Esfandyar

As he listened to Bahman's words, the old man grew pensive. He said,
"I've heard your message through and I'm pleased to see you. Now,
take my answer back to Esfandyar: 'Great, lionhearted warrior, any
man who is wise considers the realities of a situation. A man like you
who's rich, brave, and successful in war, who has authority and a good
name among other chieftains, should not give his heart to malice and
suspicion. You and I should act justly toward one another; we should
fear God and not make evil welcome. Words that have no meaning are
like a tree without leaves or scent, and if your heart's given over to
greed and ambition, you will toil long and hard and see no profit for
your pains. When a nobleman speaks he should weigh his words well
and avoid idle talk. I've always been happy to hear you praised, to hear
people say that no mother ever bore a son like you, that you surpass
your ancestors in bravery, chivalry, and wisdom. Your name is known
in India and Rum, and in the realms of wizards and witches; I praise
God for your glory day and night and I have always longed to set eyes
on you, to see for myself your splendor and graciousness. I welcome
your arrival, and I ask that we sit together and drink to the king's
health. I'll come to you alone, without my men, and listen to what the
king has commanded. I'll bring you the charters past kings, from Kay
Qobad to Kay Khosrow, have granted my family, and I'll make known
to you the pains I've suffered, the difficulties I've endured, the good
I've done for past princes, from ancient times up to the present day. If
the right reward for all I have undergone is to be led in chains, would
that I had never been born, or that once born I had soon died. Am I,
who broke elephants' backs and flung their carcasses in the ocean, to
come to court and publish all my secrets to the world, my arms tied,
my feet hobbled in leather bonds? If it becomes known that I've com-
mitted any sin, may my head be severed from my body. May I never
speak unseemly words, and you should keep yours for cursing devils;
don't say these things that no one has ever said, and don't think your
valor will enable you to catch the wind in a cage. No matter how great

a man is, he can't pass through fire, or survive the seas if he can't swim, or dim the moon's light, or make a fox a lion's equal. Don't provoke me to a fight, because fighting with me will be no trivial matter: no man has ever seen fetters on my ankles, and no savage lion has ever made me give ground.

"'Act as becomes a king; don't let yourself be guided by devils and demons. Be a man, drive anger and malice out of your heart, don't see the world through a young man's eyes. May God keep you happy and prosperous; cross the river, honor my house with your presence, don't refuse to see someone who offers you his allegiance. As I was Kay Qobad's subject, so I will serve you, willingly and cheerfully. Come to me without your armed companions, stay with me for two months; there's good hunting here, the waterways are full of fowl, and if you tire of this you can watch my swordsmen in combat with lions. When you want to return to the Persian court I'll load you with gifts from my treasury and travel side by side with you. I'll enter the king's presence and gently ask his pardon: when I've kissed his head and eyes and feet in sign of submission, I'll ask him why my feet should be shackled.' Now, remember everything I've said and repeat it to noble Esfandyar."

Bahman went back with his retinue of priests: Rostam remained in the roadway for a while, and called Zavareh and Faramarz to him. He said, "Go to Zal and tell him that Esfandyar has arrived, and that he's full of ambitious plans. Have a fine welcome prepared, something even more splendid than was customary in Kay Kavus's time: place a golden throne in the audience hall and have royal carpets spread before it. The king's son has come here and he's bent on war; tell Zal that this prince is a famous fighter and that he'd feel no fear confronted by a whole plain filled with lions. I'll go to him, and if he'll accept to be our guest we can hope for a good outcome; if I see that he's a well-disposed young man I'll give him a golden crown set with rubies, and I won't stint him jewels or fine cloth or weapons either. But if he turns me away and I come back here with no hope of a peaceful resolution, then you know that my looped lariat, which has caught wild elephants' heads in its coils, is always ready."

Zavareh said, "Give the matter no thought: a man who has no quarrel with someone doesn't go looking for a fight. I know of no stronger or more chivalrous warrior in all the world than Esfandyar. Wise men don't act in evil ways, and we've done him no harm."

Zavareh made his way to Zal's court, and Rostam rode to the shore of the River Hirmand, fearful of the harm he foresaw. At the river's edge he tugged on the reins, halting his horse, and prayed to God.

Bahman Takes His Father Rostam's Message

When Bahman reached camp, his father was standing before the royal pavilion, waiting for him, and he called out "What did the hero tell you then?" Bahman went over all he'd heard. He began by giving Rostam's message and then he described Rostam himself. He told everything he'd seen, and much that he'd inferred, and ended by saying, "There's no one like Rostam anywhere. He has a lion's heart and a mammoth's body, he could snatch a sea monster from the waves. He's coming unarmed, with no corselet, helmet, mace, or lariat, to the banks of the Hirmand: he wants to see the king, and he has some private business I don't know about with you."

But Esfandyar angrily turned on Bahman and humiliated him before their companions saying,

> "No self-respecting warrior would ask
> Advice from women for a warrior's task,
> And no one who is soldierly or wise
> Would send a boy on such an enterprise.
> Just where have you seen champions, that you praise
> This Rostam for his fine courageous ways?
> He's like a mammoth in the wars you say—
> D'you want my men to fight or run away!"

Then he said in an undertone to brave Pashutan, "This Rostam still acts like a young man, age hasn't broken him yet."

He gave orders that a black horse be saddled in gold, and then he led his men toward the bank of the Hirmand, his lariat coiled at his side.

Rostam Comes to Greet Esfandyar

Rakhsh neighed on one side of the river, and on the other the Persian prince's horse answered. Rostam urged Rakhsh from dry land into the water: when he had crossed he dismounted and greeted Esfandyar. He said: "I have asked God continually to guide you here as you have now come, in good health and accompanied by your army. Now, let us sit together and discuss things courteously and kindly. As God is my witness, wisdom will guide me in what I say; I will not try to snatch any advantage from our conversation, nor will I lie to you. If I had seen Seyavash himself I would not rejoice as I do now seeing you; indeed, you resemble no one so much as that noble and unfortunate prince. Happy is the king who has a son like you; happy are the people of Iran who see your throne and your good fortune: and woe to whoever fights against you, since dust will overwhelm both his throne and his luck. May all your enemies be filled with fear, may the hearts of those who are against you be cut in two, may you remain victorious forever, and may your dark nights be as bright as the days of spring!"

When he heard him Esfandyar too dismounted, embraced Rostam, and greeted him warmly and respectfully, saying "I thank God to see you cheerful and confident like this: you deserve all men's praise, and our heroes are like your slaves. Happy is the man who has a son like you, who sees the branch he has put forth bear fruit: happy is the man who has you as his support, since he need fear nothing from Fate's harshness. When I saw you I thought of Zarir, that lionlike warrior and tamer of horses."

Rostam replied, "I have one request, and if you grant it to me my desires are fulfilled: delight my soul by coming to my house. It is unworthy of you, but we can make do with what there is and so confirm our friendship."

Esfandyar answered, "You are like the heroes of old, and any man who has your reputation rejoices the land of Iran. It would be wrong to ignore your wishes, but I cannot turn aside from the king's orders. He gave me no permission to stay in Zavol with its chieftains. You should quickly do what the king has ordered; place the fetters on your own feet, because a king's fetters are no cause for shame. When I take you before him, bound like this, all the guilt will redound on him. I must bind you, but my soul is grieved by it, and I would rather serve you: I won't let you stay in chains beyond nightfall, and I won't let the least harm come to you. Believe me, the king will not injure you, and when I place the crown on my own head I will give the world into your safekeeping. This will not be a sin before God, and there is no shame in doing what a king demands; and when the blossoms and roses open, and you return to your Zavolestan, you'll find that I'll be generous, and load you down with gifts to beautify your land."

Rostam replied, "I have prayed God that I might see you and rejoice, and now I've heard what you have to say. We are two noble warriors, one old, one young, both wise and alert; but I fear the evil eye has struck, and that I'll never know sweet sleep again. Some demon has pushed in between us, ambition for a crown and glory has perverted your soul. It will be an eternal shame to me if a great chieftain like yourself refuses to come to my house and be my guest while he is in this country. If you can expel this hatred from your mind, and undo this demon's work, I'll agree to anything you wish, except to be chained: chains will bring shame, the ruin of my greatness, and an ugly aftermath. No one will ever see me in chains alive; my mind's made up and there's nothing more to be said."

Esfandyar answered: "The heroes of the past are met in you, all you have said is true, and perverse paths bring no man glory. But Pashutan knows the orders the king gave me when I set out: if I come now to your home, and stay there enjoying myself as your guest, and you then refuse to accept the king's orders, I shall burn in hell's flames when I pass to the other world. If you wish, we can drink together for a day and swear friendship to one another; who knows what tomorrow will bring or what will be said of this later?"

Rostam replied: "I must go and rid myself of these clothes. I've been hunting for a week, eating wild ass instead of lamb; call for me when you're seated with your people, ready to eat." He mounted Rakhsh and deep in thought galloped back to his castle. He saw his father's face and said, "I've visited this Esfandyar: I saw him mounted, tall as a cypress tree, wise and splendid, as if the great Feraydun himself had given him strength and knowledge. He exceeds the reports about him; the royal *farr* radiates from his face."

When Rostam rode away from the river Hirmand, Esfandyar was filled with foreboding. At that moment, Pashutan, who was his councilor, came into his tent, and Esfandyar addressed him:

> "We thought this would be easy, but we've found
> Our way's unsure, and over rocky ground;
> I shouldn't visit Rostam's home, and he
> For his part ought to stay away from me.
> If he neglects to come I won't complain
> Or summon him to sit with me again.

If one of us should die in this affair
The other will be vanquished by despair."

Pashutan said, "My lord, who has a brother to equal Esfandyar? When I saw that you two were not looking to fight with one another, my heart opened like the blossoms in springtime, both for Rostam and for Esfandyar. I look at what you're doing here and I see that some demon has blocked off wisdom's way forward. You're a religious and honorable man, one who obeys God and his father: hold back, don't give your soul over to violence; my brother, listen to what I'm telling you. I heard all Rostam said: he is a great man, your chains will never bind his feet and he will not lightly take your advice. The son of Zal will not walk into your trap so easily; I fear that this will be a long drawn out contest between two haughty warriors, and one with an ugly ending to it. You are a great man too, and wiser than the king; you're a better soldier and a finer man than he is. One of you wants rejoicing and reconciliation, and the other wants battles and vengeance. Consider for yourself, which of you is more praiseworthy?"

Esfandyar replied,

"But if I turn away from what my king
Commands there's no excuse that I can bring,
I'll be reproached in this world, and I fear
God's probing of my life when death draws near;
For Rostam's sake I cannot throw away
My life both here and after Judgment Day—
There is no needle that can sew the eyes
Of Faith tight shut, no matter how one tries."

Pashutan said, "I've given my advice, and it will benefit you physically and morally. I've said all I can; now, choose the right way, but remember that princes' hearts are not inclined to vengeance."

Esfandyar ordered his cooks to prepare supper, but he sent no one to summon Rostam. When the food had been eaten he lifted his winecup and began to boast of his past exploits, toasting the king occasionally as he did so. Rostam was in his castle all this while, waiting for Esfandyar's invitation. But as time passed and no one came, and then supper time was over and he was still staring at the empty road, fury took possession of his mind. He laughed and said to his brother, "Have the meal prepared and call our men to eat. So this is our famous hero's way of behaving, is it? See that you never forget his splendid manners!" Then he ordered that Rakhsh be saddled and richly caparisoned after the Chinese fashion, and said,

> *"I'm going to tell this noble prince that he*
> *Has now deliberately insulted me."*

Rostam and Esfandyar Meet for the Second Time

The mammoth warrior mounted Rakhsh, whose neigh resounded for two miles, and made his way quickly to the river's edge. The Persian troops there were astonished by his massive frame and martial bearing, and said to one another "He resembles no one but Esfandyar himself, and would be the victor in combat with an elephant. The king's unwise obsession with his throne has made him send a splendid hero to his death; as he grows older all the king thinks of is wealth and his royal authority."

Esfandyar welcomed him, and Rostam replied, "My fine young warrior, it seems you've developed new customs, new ways of behaving. Why am I unworthy to drink with you? Is this how you keep your promises? Now, take seriously what I tell you, and don't be so foolish as to get angry with an old man. You think you're greater than everyone else and you take pride in your chieftains: you consider me a lightweight, someone whose opinions don't matter. But know that the world knows I am Rostam, scion of the great Nariman; black demons bite their hands in horror at my approach, and I fling wizards into the pit of death. When chieftains see my armor and my Rakhsh like a raging lion they flee in terror; I have caught in my lariat's coils warriors like Kamus and the Khaqan of China, I have dragged them from their saddles and bound their feet. I am the keeper of Iran and its lionlike chieftains, the support of its warriors on every side. Don't slight my overtures to you, don't think of yourself as higher than the heavens. I'm seeking a pact with you, and I respect your royal *farr* and glory. I have no desire for a prince like you to die at my hands. I am descended from Sam, before whom lions fled from their lairs, and you are the son of a king. For a long time now I have been the world's first warrior,

and I have never stooped to evil: I have cleared the world of my ene-
mies, and I have suffered countless pains and sorrows. I thank God that
in my old age I have met with a fine strong warrior willing to fight
with a man of the pure faith, one whom all the world praises."

Esfandyar laughed, and said, "And all this anger is simply because
no invitation came? The weather's so hot and it's such a long way that
I didn't want to put you to the effort of coming back. I said to myself
that I'd go to you at dawn tomorrow and offer my apologies: I'd be
happy to see Zal and I'd spend time drinking with you both. But now
that you've taken the trouble to leave your house and cross the plain to
get here, calm yourself, sit down, take the winecup in your hand, and
put aside your anger and irritation." And he moved over so that there
was a place for Rostam to his left. But Rostam's response was, "That's
no place for me, I'll sit where I wish to." Esfandyar ordered Bahman to
vacate the space to the right, but Rostam retorted in fury, "Open your
eyes and look at me: look at my greatness and at my noble ancestry,
I'm of the seed of Sam, and if there's no place worthy of me in your
company I still have my victories and fame." Then the prince ordered
that a golden throne be brought and placed opposite his own: still
enraged Rostam sat himself down on the throne, and toyed with a
scented orange in his hand.

Esfandyar addressed Rostam, "You're a powerful and well-intentioned
hero, but I've heard from priests, chieftains, and other wise men that Zal
was nothing but demon-spawn, and can boast of no better lineage. They
hid him from Sam for a long time, and the court was in an uproar
because he was so ugly, with a black body and white hair and face; when
Sam finally saw him he was in despair and gave orders that he be exposed
on the seashore as a prey for the birds and fish. The Simorgh came down,
flapping its wings, and seeing no signs of grandeur or glory in the child
to deter him, he snatched him up and took him to his nest, but even
though he was hungry Zal's puny body didn't seem worth eating. So he
flung him naked in a corner of the nest, where the child lived off scraps.
Finally the Simorgh took pity on him, and after he'd subsisted on the
Simorgh's leavings for a number of years he set off, naked as he was, for
Sistan. Now because Sam had no other children, and was old and stupid
as well, he welcomed him back. My great ancestors, who were noble and
generous men, gave him wealth and position, and when many years had
passed he grew to be a fine tall cypress of a man. And a branch of this

same cypress is Rostam, who by his valor and splendid appearance and fine deeds outreached the heavens, until his ambition and excesses have procured a kingdom for him."

Rostam replied; "Calm yourself; why are you saying such offensive things? Your heart's filled with perversity and your soul's puffed up with demonic pride. Speak as becomes a royal personage; kings say nothing but the truth. The lord of the world knows that Sam's son Zal is a great, wise, and renowned man. And Sam was the son of Nariman, who was descended from Kariman, whose father was Hushang, the crowned king of all the earth. Haven't you heard of Sam's incomparable fame? There was a dragon in Tus, a monster that terrorized the beasts of the sea and the birds of the air; and then there was a wicked demon so huge that the sea of China reached only to its waist while its head towered into the sky and obscured the sun; it would snatch fish up from the ocean depths and store them beyond the sphere of the moon, and cook them by holding them against the sun; the turning heavens wept to see such a monster. These two hideous beings trembled before Sam's courage and his sword, and perished by his hand.

"My mother was the daughter of Mehrab, under whose rule India flourished, and who was descended, through five generations, from Zahhak, a monarch who lifted his head higher than all the kings of the world. Who has a more noble lineage than this? A wise man does not try to deny the truth. Any man who makes claims to heroism has to test himself against me. I hold my fiefdom by irreproachable treaty from Kavus, and it was renewed by the greatest of warrior-kings, Khosrow. I have traveled the world, and slain many unjust kings: when I crossed the Oxus Afrasyab fled from Turan to China; I fought for Kavus in Hamaveran and when I journeyed alone to Mazanderan, neither Arzhang, nor the white demon, nor Sanjeh, nor Kulad Ghandi hindered me. For that king's sake I killed my own son, and there never was such a strong, chivalrous, war-tried hero as Sohrab. It is more than six hundred years since I was born of Zal's seed: in all that time I have been the world's heroic champion, and my thoughts and deeds have always been one. I'm like the noble Feraydun, who crowned himself, and dragged Zahhak from the throne and laid him in the dust. And then Sam, whose wisdom and knowledge of magic are unmatched in the world, is my grandfather. Thirdly, when I have girded on my sword our kings have lived free from all anxieties: there's never been such pleasure at the court, or such security from evil's inroads. The world was as I willed it to be, ordered by my sword and mace.

> *I've told you this so that you'll understand*
> *That though you govern with a princely hand,*
> *You're new to this world's ancient ways, in spite*
> *Of all your splendor and imperial might.*
> *You look out on the earth and all you see*
> *Is your own image and ability,*
> *But gazing at yourself you're unaware*
> *Of all the hidden dangers lurking there.*
> *I've talked enough; let's drink, and may the wine*
> *Dispel all your anxieties, and mine."*

Hearing him, Esfandyar laughed, and his heart lightened. He said, "I've listened to the tale of your exploits and sufferings, now hear how I've distinguished myself. First, I have fought for the true faith, clearing the land of idol-worshippers, and no one's seen any warrior slaughter them in such numbers as I have, covering the ground with their corpses. I'm Goshtasp's child, and he was the child of Lohrasp, who was the child of Orandshah, a descendant of the Kayanid kings. My mother's the daughter of Caesar, who rules in Rum and is descended from Salm, the son of Feraydun, the king who established the ways of faith and fair-dealing, and without whose glory there would be little enough justice in the world, as no one can deny. You're a man who stood as a slave before my royal ancestors, you and your forebears too. I'm not saying this to cause dissension between us, but you received sovereignty as a gift from my family, even though you're now trying to kick over the traces. Wait now, and let me tell you how things are, and if there's one lie in what I say, show it to me.

"Since Goshtasp has been king my chivalry and good fortune have been at his service. I was the man who was praised for spreading the faith, even though I was then imprisoned because of Gorazm's slanders. Because I couldn't help him Lohrasp was defeated, and our land was overrun by enemies, until Jamasp came to release me from my chains. The blacksmiths tried to free me, but my impatient heart was the sword that finally broke my fetters: I roared at their delay, and it was my own strength that smashed the shackles binding me. Arjasp, our enemy, fled before me, and so did all his chieftains, and I harried their routed army like a savage lion. You've heard how lions and Ahriman beset me during my seven trials, how I entered the Brass Fortress by a trick, and destroyed everything there; how I sought revenge for our nobles' deaths, how I took war to Turan and China and suffered hardships and privations there more terrible than a leopard inflicts on a wild ass, or than the sailor's hook that torments a great fish's gullet. There was a dark castle high on a distant ridge, shunned for its evil reputation and filled with depraved idol-worshippers: I took that castle, smashed its images against the ground, and lit the sacred flame of Zoroaster in their place. I came home with my God-given victory, and not an enemy of ours survived; not a temple or an idol-worshipper remained.

> These battles that I fought, I fought alone,
> No man has shown the valor I have shown.
> But we have talked enough: if you agree,
> Take up your wine, and slake your thirst with me."

Rostam replied: "Our deeds will be our memorial in the world. Now, in fairness to me, listen to the tale of an old warrior's exploits. If I had not taken my heavy mace to Mazanderan where Kavus, Giv, Gudarz, and Tus were imprisoned, their hearing shattered by the din of wardrums, who would have disemboweled the White Demon? Who could have hoped to accomplish such a deed by his own strength? I took Kavus from his chains back to the throne, and Iran rejoiced to receive him. I cut off their wizards' heads, and left their bodies unburied and unlamented. And my only companions were my courage, my horse Rakhsh, and my world-conquering sword. And then when Kavus went to Hamaveran and was imprisoned, I led a Persian army there and killed their kings in war. King Kavus was a prisoner, heart sick and wretched, and Afrasyab was harrying Iran. I freed Kavus, Giv, Gudarz, and Tus, and brought them and our army back to Iran. Eager for fame, careless of my own ease, I went on ahead in the darkness of the night, and when Afrasyab saw my fluttering banner and heard Rakhsh neigh, he fled from Iran toward China; the world was filled with justice and my praises. If Kavus's blood had flowed then, how could he have sired Seyavash, who in turn fathered Kay Khosrow, who placed the crown on Lohrasp's head? My father is a great warrior, and he swallowed the dust

of shame when he had to call your insignificant Lohrasp his king. Why
do you boast of Goshtasp's crown and Lohrasp's throne?

> *Who says, 'Go now, and shackle Rostam's hands?'*
> *The heavens themselves don't issue such commands.*
> *I've never seen, not since I was a child,*
> *A man as headstrong, obstinate, and wild*
> *As you: my courtesy is your excuse*
> *To treat me with contemptuous abuse!"*

Esfandyar laughed with delight at his rage and grasped him firmly by
the hand, saying: "Great, mammoth bodied warrior, you're just as I've
heard you described: your arm's as massive as a lion's thigh, your chest
and shoulders like a dragon's, your waist lean as a leopard's." As he
spoke he squeezed Rostam's hand, and the old man laughed at the
young man's efforts: lymph dripped from his finger nails, but he didn't
wince at the pain. Then he in turn gripped Esfandyar's hand, and said,
"My God-fearing prince, I congratulate king Goshtasp on having such
a son as you, and your mother, whose glory is increased by bearing
you." He spoke and, as his grip tightened, Esfandyar's cheeks turned
crimson; bloody liquid spurted from beneath his nails, and the pain
showed in his face. Nevertheless he laughed and said, "Enjoy your
wine today, because tomorrow when we meet in combat you won't be
thinking of pleasure. I'll saddle my black horse, put on my princely
helmet, and unseat you with a lance; that'll put an end to your wran-
gling and rebellion. I'll bind your arms together and take you to the
king. But I'll tell him that I've found no fault in you; I'll go before him
as a suppliant, and clear up all this quarrel. I'll free you from sorrow and
pain, and in their place you'll find treasure and kindness."

Rostam too laughed and said, "You'll tire of battle soon enough.
Where have you ever seen real warriors fight, or felt the wind a mace
makes as it whistles by you? If the heavens will that no love's lost
between us, we'll drink down vengeance, not red wine; our fate will
be ambush, the bow and lariat, the din of drums instead of the sound
of lutes, and our farewells will be said with sword and mace. When we
meet man to man on the battlefield tomorrow, you'll see which way
the fight will go. I'll pluck you from your saddle, and bear you off to
noble Zal. There I'll sit you on an ivory throne and place on your head

a splendid crown that I had from Kay Qobad, and may his soul rejoice in heaven! I'll open our treasury's gates and lay our wealth before you: I'll give you troops, and raise your head up to the skies. Then, laughing and lighthearted, we'll make our way to the king: I'll crown you there, and that's how I'll show my loyalty to Goshtasp. Only then will I agree to serve him, as I served the Kayanid kings before. My heart will grow young again with joy, like a garden cleared of weeds: and when you're king and I'm your champion, a universal happiness will come."

Rostam Drinks with Esfandyar

Esfandyar answered: "Too much talk is pointless: our stomachs are empty, the day's half over, and we've said enough about battles. Bring whatever you have to our supper, and don't invite those who talk the whole time." When Rostam began to eat the others were astonished at his appetite; they sat opposite him watching him feast. Then Esfandyar gave orders that Rostam be served with red wine, saying "We'll see what he wants when the wine affects him, and he talks about King Kavus." A servant brought old wine in a goblet, and Rostam toasted Goshtasp and drank it off. The boy refilled it with a royal vintage, and Rostam said to him quietly, "There's no need to dilute it with water, it takes the edge off an old wine. Why do you put water in it?" Pashutan said to the serving boy, "Bring him a goblet filled with undiluted wine." Wine was brought, musicians were summoned, and the group watched in wonder as Rostam drank. When it was time for Rostam to return to Zal, Esfandyar said to him: "May you live happily and forever, may the food and wine you've consumed here nourish you, and may righteousness sustain your soul!"

Rostam replied: "Prince, may wisdom always be your guide! The wine I've drunk with you has nourished me, and my wise mind wants for nothing. If you can be intelligent enough, and man enough, to lay aside this desire for combat, come out of the desert to my home and take your ease as my guest: I'll do everything I promised, and I'll give you good advice. Rest for a while, turn aside from evil, be civil, and come back to your senses."

Esfandyar replied: "Don't sow seeds that will never grow. Tomorrow when I bind on my sword belt for combat you'll see what a warrior is. Stop praising yourself: get back to your palace and prepare yourself for the morning. A battle is as of little account to me as a drinking party. But my advice is that you don't try to fight with me: do what I say, accept the king's command that you be bound in chains, and when we go from Zabol to Goshtasp's court you'll see that I'll be even more chivalrous than I have promised. Don't try to cause me any more sorrow."

> *Then grief filled Rostam's heart, and in his sight*
> *The world seemed like a wood bereft of light.*
> *He thought: "Either I let him bind my hands,*
> *And in so doing bow to his commands,*
> *Or I must fight against him face to face*
> *And bring on him destruction and disgrace.*
> *No good can come of either course, and I*
> *Shall be despised and cursed until I die:*
> *His chains will be the symbol of my shame,*
> *Goshtasp will kill me and destroy my fame—*
> *The world will laugh at me, and men will say*
> *'Rostam was hung with chains and led away,*
> *A stripling conquered him.' And all I've done*
> *Will be forgotten then by everyone.*
> *But if we fight each other and he's slain*
> *I cannot show my face at court again;*
> *They'll say I left a fine young prince for dead*
> *Because of one or two harsh words he'd said;*
> *In death I'll be reviled, my name will be*
> *A byword for disgrace and infamy.*
> *And then if I'm to perish at his hand*
> *My clan will lose Zabol, our native land—*
> *One thing would still survive though, since my name*
> *Would be remembered and not lose its fame."*

Then he spoke to his haughty companion, saying: "Anxiety robs my skin of its color; you talk so much about chains and binding me, and everything you do alarms me. What the heavens will is sovereign over us, and who knows how they will turn? You're following a demon's advice, and refusing to listen to reason. You haven't lived many years in this world, and you don't know how deceptive and evil it is, my prince. You're a simple, straightforward man, and you know nothing about life: you should realize that evil men are trying to destroy you. Goshtasp will never tire of his crown and throne, and he will drive you throughout the world, make you face every danger, to keep you away from them. In his mind he searched the world, his intelligence hacking away like an axe, to find some hero who would not refuse to fight with you, so that such a man would destroy you, and the crown and throne would remain his. You blame my motives, but why don't you examine your own heart? Prince, don't act like some thoughtless youth, don't persist in this disastrous course. Be ashamed before God and before my face, don't betray yourself, and don't think that combat with me would be a game. If Fate has driven you and your men here, you will be destroyed by me: I shall leave an evil name behind me in the world, and may the same fate be Goshtasp's!"

Esfandyar replied: "Great Rostam, think of what a wise sage once said, 'A man in his dotage is a fool, no matter how wise or victorious or knowledgeable he's been.' You want to trick me and slip out of this, you want to convince people by your smooth talk, so that they'll say 'Rostam welcomed him warmly' and call you a wise benevolent man, while they'll say that I was unrighteous—I, who always act from righteous motives! You want them to say, 'The prince refused to listen to him, so that he had no choice but to fight. All his pleas were treated with contempt, and bitter words passed between them.' But I shall not swerve aside from the king's commands, not for the crown itself: all the good and evil of the world I find in him, and in him lie both heaven and hell. May what you've eaten here nourish you and confound your enemies: now, go home and tell Zal everything you have seen here. Prepare your armor for battle, and bandy no more words with me. Come back at dawn ready to fight, and don't draw this business out any further. Tomorrow on the battlefield you'll see the world grow dark before your eyes: you'll see what combat with a real warrior is."

Rostam replied: "If this is what you want I'll return your hospitality with Rakhsh's hooves, and my mace will be a medicine for your head. You've listened to your own court telling you that no one can match his sword against Esfandyar's; but tomorrow you'll see me grasping Rakhsh's reins, with my lance couched, and after that you'll never look to fight again."

The young man's lips broke into bewitching laughter, and he said:

"For a fighting man you've let our conversation anger you too easily! Tomorrow you'll see how a man fights on the battlefield: I'm no mountain, and my horse beneath me's no mountain either, I'm one man like any other. If you run from me with your head still on your shoulders your mother will weep for your humiliation; and if you're killed I'll tie you to my saddle and bear you off to the king, so that no vassal of his will ever challenge him again."

Rostam Addresses Esfandyar's Tent
When Rostam left Esfandyar's pavilion he paused for a moment, and spoke to it:

> *"O tent of hope, what glorious days you've known!*
> *Once you were shelter to great Jamshid's throne,*
> *In you Khosrow's and King Kavus's days*
> *Were passed in splendor, pageantry, and praise—*
> *Closed is that glorious gate that once you knew,*
> *A man unworthy of you reigns in you."*

Esfandyar heard him, planted himself in front of Rostam, and said: "Why should you speak to our pavilion so intemperately? This Zabolestan of yours should be called 'Lout-estan,' because when a guest has eaten his fill here he starts loutishly insulting his host!" Then he too addressed the royal tent:

> *"You sheltered Jamshid once, who erred and strayed,*
> *Who heard God's heavenly laws and disobeyed;*
> *Then came Kavus, whose blasphemous desires*
> *Sought to control the skies' celestial fires—*
> *Tumult and plunder, plots, perfidy, pain*
> *Filled all the land throughout his wretched reign,*
> *But now your walls encompass King Goshtasp*
> *Who rules with his wise councillor Jamasp;*
> *The prophet Zoroaster, who has brought*
> *Heaven's scriptures to us, shares his noble court,*
> *Good Pashutan is here, and so am I*
> *His prince, watched over by the turning sky,*

Protector of the good, scourge of the horde
Of evildoers, who bow before my sword."

When Rostam had left, Esfandyar turned to Pashutan and said, "There's no hiding such heroism: I've never seen such a horseman, and I don't know what will happen tomorrow on the battlefield. When he comes armored to battle he must be like a raging elephant; his stature's a marvel to gaze upon. Nevertheless, I fear that tomorrow he will face defeat. My heart aches for his kindness and glory, but I can't evade God's commands: tomorrow when he faces me in combat I'll turn his shining days to darkness."

Pashutan replied: "Listen to what I have to say. Brother, do not do this. I have said it before and I will say it again, because I will not wash my hands of what is right. Don't harry him like this; a free man will never willingly submit to another's tyranny. Sleep tonight and, when dawn comes, we'll go to his castle, without an escort, and there we'll be his guests and answer his every anxiety. Everything he has done in the world has been for the good, benefiting the nobility and the general populace alike. He won't refuse your orders, I can see that he'll be loyal to you. How long are you going to go on with all this rage and anger and malice? Drive them out of your heart!"

Esfandyar answered him: "Thorns have appeared among the roses then: a man of pure faith shouldn't talk as you're doing. You're the first councilor to Persia's king, the heart, eyes, and ears of its chieftains, and yet you think it right and wise to disobey the king like this? Then all my pains and struggles were pointless, and Zoroaster's faith's to be forgotten, because he has said that hell will be the home of whoever turns aside from his king's command. How long are you going to tell me to disobey Goshtasp? You can say this, but how can I agree to it? If you're afraid for my life, I'll rid you of that fear today: no man ever died except at his appointed time, and a man whose reputation lives on never dies. Tomorrow you'll see how I'll fight against this fearsome warrior."

Pashutan said: "And for how long are you going to talk about fighting? Since you first took up arms, Eblis has had no control over your thoughts: but now you're opening your heart to demons, and refusing to hear good advice. How can I drive fear from my heart when I see that two great warriors, two lions in battle, are to face one another, and what will come of this is all unknown?"

The hero made no answer: his heart was filled with pain, and a sigh escaped his lips.

Rostam Returns to His Castle

By the time Rostam reached his castle he could see no remedy but warfare. Zavareh came out to greet him and saw his pallor, and that his heart was filled with darkness. Rostam said to him, "Prepare my Indian sword, my lance and helmet, my bow and the barding for Rakhsh: bring me my tiger skin, and my heavy mace." Zavareh had the steward bring what Rostam had asked for, and when Rostam saw his weapons and armor he heaved a cold sigh and said,

> "My armor, for a while you've been at peace,
> But now this indolence of yours must cease—
> A hard fight lies ahead, and I shall need
> All of the luck you bring me to succeed:
> Two warriors who have never known defeat
> Like two enraged and roaring lions will meet,
> And in that struggle on the battlefield
> Who knows what tricks he'll try to make me yield!"

Zal Advises Rostam

When Zal heard from Rostam what had happened, his aged mind was troubled. He said, "What are you telling me? You're filling my mind with darkness. Since first you sat in the saddle you've been a chivalrous and righteous warrior, proud to serve your kings and contemptuous of hardships. But I fear your days are drawing to an end, that your lucky stars are in decline, that the seed of Zal will be eradicated from this land, and our women and children hurled to the ground as slaves. If you're killed in combat by a young stripling like Esfandyar, Zabolestan will be laid waste and all our glory will be razed and cast into a pit. And if he's hurt in this encounter your good name will be destroyed: everyone will tell the tale of how you killed a young prince because of a few harsh words he'd said. Go to him, stand before him as his subject: and if you can't do that then leave, go and hide yourself in some corner where no one will hear of you. You can buy the world with treasure and trouble, but you can't cut Chinese silk with an axe. Give his retinue robes of honor, get back your independence with gifts. When he leaves the banks of the Hirmand, saddle Rakhsh and go with him: as you travel to the court swear fealty to him. And when Goshtasp sees you, there's no danger he'll harm you: it would be an act unworthy of a monarch."

Rostam replied: "Old man, don't take what I've said so lightly. I've fought for years and have experienced the world's good and evil. I encountered the demons of Mazanderan and the horsemen of Hamaveran, I fought against Kamus and the Emperor of China whose armies were so mighty the earth trembled beneath their horses' hooves. But if I now flee from Esfandyar there will be no castles or gardens for you in Zabolestan. I may be old, but when I put on my tiger skin for battle it makes no difference whether I face a hundred maddened elephants or a plain filled with warriors. I've done all that you're asking me to, I read the book of loyalty to him; he treats my words with contempt and ignores my wisdom and advice. If he could bring his head down from the heavens and welcome me in his heart, there's no wealth in my treasury, no weapon or armor, that I wouldn't give him. But he took no notice of all my talk and left me empty-handed.

"If we were to fight tomorrow, you could despair of his life. But I won't take my sharp sword in hand, I'll bear him off to a banquet: he'll see no mace or lance from me, and I won't oppose him man to man. I'll simply lift him from the saddle and acknowledge him as king in Goshtasp's place. I'll bring him here and seat him on an ivory throne, load him with presents, keep him as my guest for three days, and on the fourth when the sun's red ruby splits the darkness I'll set off with him for Goshtasp's court. When I enthrone him and crown him I'll stand before him as his loyal subject, concerned only for Esfandyar's commands. You remember how I acted with Qobad, and you know how it's my quarrelsome, passionate nature that's made my reputation in the world. And now you're telling me either to run off and hide, or to submit to his chains!"

Zal broke into laughter, shaking his head in wonder at his son's words. He said, "Don't say such things, even demons couldn't put up with such foolish talk. You chatter about what we did with Qobad, but he was living obscurely in the mountains then, he wasn't a great king with a throne, crown, treasure, and cash at his disposal. You're talking about Esfandyar, who counts the emperor of China among his subjects, and you say you'll lift him from the saddle and bear him off to Zal's palace! An old, experienced man doesn't talk like this. Don't court bad luck by setting yourself up as the Persian king's equal. You're the best of all our chieftains, but I've given you my advice, and may you follow it!"

Having spoken, he bent his forehead to the ground in prayer: "Just judge, I pray you to preserve us from an evil Fate." And so he prayed throughout the night, his tongue untiring until the sun rose above the mountains.

When day broke Rostam put on his mail and tigerskin, hitched his lariat to his saddle, and mounted Rakhsh. He summoned Zavareh and told him to have their army's ranks drawn up in the foothills. Zavareh saw that this was done, and Rostam couched his lance and rode out from the palace. His soldiers called out encouragement as he went forward, followed by Zavareh who was acting as his lieutenant. Privately Rostam said to him, "Somehow, I'll put paid to this evil devil's spawn, and get my soul back into the light again. But I fear I shall have to harm him, and I don't know what good can come out of all this. You stay with our troops, while I go to see what Fate has in store for me. If I find he's still the same hothead, spoiling for a fight, let me face him alone, I don't want any of our warriors hurt in this. Victory favors the just."

He crossed the river and began to climb the opposite bank, and wonder at the world's ways filled his mind.

He faced Esfandyar and shouted, "Your enemy has come: prepare yourself."

When Esfandyar heard the old lion's words he laughed and shouted back, "I've been prepared since I woke." He gave orders that his armor, helmet, lance, and mace be brought, and when he was accoutered he had his black horse saddled and brought before him. Then, glorying in his strength and agility, he thrust his lance point into the ground and, like a leopard leaping on a wild ass and striking terror into its heart, he vaulted into the saddle. The soldiers were delighted, and roared their approval.

Esfandyar rode toward Rostam and when he saw his opponent had come alone, he turned to Pashutan and said, "I need no companions in this: he is alone, and I shall be too: we'll move off to higher ground."

Pashutan withdrew to where the Persian soldiers waited, and the two combatants went forward to battle, as grimly as if all pleasure had

been driven from the world. When the old man and his young oppo-
nent faced each other, both their horses neighed violently, and the
noise was as though the ground beneath them split open.

Rostam's voice was serious when he spoke: "Young man, you're
fortune's favorite, and your heart's filled with the joys of youth; don't
go forward with this, don't give yourself up to anger. For once, listen
to wisdom's words. If you're set on bloodshed say so, and I'll have my
Zaboli warriors come here, and you can send Persians against them,
and the two groups can show their mettle. We'll watch from the side-
lines, and your desire for blood and combat will be satisfied."

Esfandyar answered him: "How long are you going to go on with
this pointless talk? You got up at dawn and summoned me to this hill-
side. Was that simply deception? Or is it that now you foresee your own
defeat? What could a battle between your warriors and mine mean to
me? God forbid I should agree to send my Persians into battle while I
held back and crowned myself king. For a man of my faith, such an act
would be contemptible. I lead my warriors into battle, and am the first
to face the foe even if it is a leopard. If you need companions to fight
with you summon them, but I shall never call on anyone's aid. God is
my companion in battle, and Good Fortune smiles on me. You're look-
ing for a fight, and I'm ready for one: let's face each other man to man,
without our armies. And let's see whether Esfandyar's horse returns rid-
erless to its stable, or Rostam's turns masterless toward his palace."

The Combat Between Rostam and Esfandyar

They swore that no one would come to their aid while they fought.
Again and again they rode against one another with couched lances;
blood poured from their armor, and their lances' heads were shattered,
so that the combatants were forced to draw their swords. Weaving and
dodging to right and left, they attacked one another, and their horses'
maneuvers flung them against one another with such violence that their
swords too were shattered. They drew their maces then, and the blows
they dealt resounded like a blacksmith's hammer striking steel. Their
bodies wounded and exhausted, they fought like enraged lions until the
handles of their maces splintered; then they leant forward and grasped
each other by the belt, each struggling to throw the other, while their
horses reared and pranced. But though they strained against one another,
exerting all their strength and massive weight, neither warrior was

shifted from his saddle. And so they separated, sick at heart, their mouths smeared with dust and blood, their armor and barding dented and pierced, their horses wearied by their struggle.

Zavareh and Nushazar Quarrel

When the combat had gone on for some time, Zavareh grew impatient at the delay and shouted to the Persian soldiers: "Where is Rostam? Why should we hang back on a day like this? You came to fight against Rostam, but you're never going to be able to bind his hands, and we won't sit here while a battle's going on." Then he began cursing his opponents, and Esfandyar's son Nushazar, who was a fiery ambitious youth, was enraged at the insults this provincial from Sistan was heaping upon them, and responded in kind. "Is it right for a noble warrior to make fun of a king's commands? Our leader Esfandyar gave us no orders to fight with dogs like you, and who would ignore or override his wishes? But if you want to challenge us, you'll see how real warriors can fight with swords and spears and maces."

In response, Zavareh gave the signal for Sistan's warcry to ring out, and for his men to attack: he himself rushed forward from the rear of his troops, and a tumultuous noise of fighting began. Countless Persians were slaughtered, and when Nushazar saw this he mounted his horse, grasped his Indian sword in his hand, and headed for the fray. Among the Sistani troops one of their best warriors was a wild tamer of horses, a man named Alvad, who was Rostam's spear bearer and always accompanied him into battle. Nushazar caught sight of him, wheeled toward him, and struck him a mighty blow with his sword: his head was severed and his body slid lifeless from its saddle into the dirt. Zavareh urged his horse forward and called out, "You've laid him low, but stand your ground and fight, because Alvad is not what I'd call a horseman." With that Zavareh flung his lance, which pierced Nushazar's chest, and a moment later the Persian warrior's head lay in the dirt.

Nushazar and Mehrnush Are Killed by Faramarz and Zavareh

When the great Nushazar was killed, good fortune deserted the Persian army. His brother, Mehrnush, saw Nushazar's death; at once weeping and enraged he urged his great horse forward to the fray, and the froth of fury stood on his lips. Faramarz stood before him like a massive maddened elephant, and attacked him with his Indian sword: a huge cry went up from both armies as the two noble fighters closed, the one a prince, the other a mighty champion. They fell on one another like enraged lions, but Mehrnush's eagerness for combat was not sufficient to prevail against Faramarz: thinking to sever his opponent's head with a sword blow, he brought his weapon down on his own horse's neck, and his mount sank to the ground beneath him. Once he was on foot Faramarz was able to overcome him, and his red blood stained the dust of the battlefield.

When Bahman saw his brother killed, and the dirt beneath him mired with his blood, he made his way to where Esfandyar had been in combat with Rostam, and said, "Lion-warrior, an army has come up from Sistan, and your two sons Nushazar and Mehrnush have been pitifully slain by them. While you're here in combat, two of our princes lie prone in the dust, and the sorrow and shame of this will live forever." Esfandyar's heart clouded with rage, sighs escaped his lips, and tears stood in his eyes: he turned to Rostam and said, "Devil's spawn, why have you forsaken the path of justice and good custom? Didn't you say that you would not bring your troops into this conflict? You don't deserve your fame: have you no shame before me, no fear of what God will demand of you on the Day of Judgment? Don't you know that no one praises a man who goes back on his word? Two of your Sistani troops have killed two of my sons, and your men are still wreaking havoc."

When Rostam heard this, sorrow seized him and he trembled like a bough in the wind. He swore by the soul and head of the king, by the sun and his sword and the battlefield, by the fire that Kavus had lit and through which Seyavash had passed unscathed, by the Kayanid throne and the Zend Avesta, by the soul and head of Esfandyar himself: "I did not give the orders for this attack, and I've no praise for whoever carried it out. I shall bind my own brother's hands if he has been responsible for this evil, and I shall bind my son Faramarz's arms too, and bring him here to you. If they are guilty, kill them both in vengeance for your sons' split blood. But don't let your judgment be clouded by what has happened."

Esfandyar replied,

> "To avenge a peacock's death, no king would take
> The worthless life of an ignoble snake:
> Look to your weapons now, you wretch, defend
> Yourself, your days on earth are at an end:

I'll stake your thighs against your horse's hide,
My arrows will transfix you to his side
And you and he shall be like water when
It's mixed with milk and can't be found again.
From now on no base slave shall ever strive
To spill a prince's blood: if you survive
I'll bind your arms—without delay I'll bring
You as my captive to our court and king,
And if my arrows leave you here for dead
Think of my sons, whose blood your warriors shed."

Rostam replied: "What good is all this talk, which only increases our shame? Turn toward God and trust in Him, who guides us to both good and evil ends."

Rostam and Esfandyar Renew the Battle

They turned then to their bows and poplar wood arrows; the sun turned pale and fire flashed from Esfandyar's armor where the arrow heads struck. He frowned with shame, since he was a man whose arrows no one escaped: he notched diamond headed shafts to his bow, bolts that pierced armor as if it were paper, and sorely wounded both Rostam and Rakhsh. Esfandyar wheeled round, circling Rostam, whose arrows had no effect, and who felt that he faced defeat. He said to himself, "This Esfandyar is invincible," and he knew that both he and Rakhsh were growing weaker. In desperation he dismounted and began to climb the mountain side, while Rakhsh returned home riderless and wounded. Blood poured from Rostam's body, and as his strength ebbed from him this great mountain of a man began to tremble and shake. Esfandyar laughed to see this, and called out:

"Where is your mammoth strength, your warrior's pride?
Have arrows pierced that iron mountain side?
Where is your mace now and your martial might,
That glorious strength with which you used to fight?
What are you running from, or did you hear
A lion's roar that filled your heart with fear?
Are you the man before whom demons wept?
Whose sword killed everything that flew or crept?

Why has the mammoth turned into a fox
That tries to hide among these mountain rocks?"

Zavareh saw Rakhsh in the distance, wounded, returning home: the world darkened before his eyes, and he cried aloud and hurried to the place where Rostam and Esfandyar had fought. He saw his brother there, covered in unstanched wounds, and said to him, "Get up, use my horse, and I shall buckle on my armor to avenge you." But Rostam replied, "Go, tell our father that the tribe of Sam has lost its power and glory, and that he must seek out some remedy. My wounds are more terrible than any disaster I've survived, but I know that, if I live through this night, tomorrow I shall be like a man reborn again. See that you look after Rakhsh, and even if I stay here for a long time I'll rejoin you eventually." Zavareh left his brother and went in search of Rakhsh.

Esfandyar waited a while, and then shouted: "How long are you going to stay up there: who do you think is going to come and guide you now? Throw your bow down, strip off your tiger skin, undo your sword belt. Submit, and let me bind your arms, and you'll never see any harm from me again. I'll take you, wounded as you are, to the king, and there I'll have all your sins forgiven. But if you want to continue fighting, make your will and appoint someone else to rule these marches. Ask pardon for your sins from God, since God forgives those who repent, and it would be right for Him to guide you from this fleeting world when you must leave it."

Rostam replied: "It's too late to go on fighting: who wages war in the dark? Go back to your encampment and spend the night there; I shall make my way to my palace and rest, and sleep awhile. I'll bind my wounds up, then I'll call the chieftains of my tribe to me, Zavareh, Faramarz, and Zal, and I'll set out to them whatever you command: we'll accept your guarantee of justice."

Esfandyar answered him: "Old man, you're infinitely clever, a great man, tempered by time, knowing many tricks and wiles and stratagems. I've seen your deceit, but even so I don't want to see your destruction. I'll give you quarter tonight, but don't be thinking up some new dishonest ploy. Stick to what you've agreed to, and don't bandy words with me any more!"

Rostam's only reply was: "Now I must seek help for my wounds."

Esfandyar watched him make his way back to his own territory.

Once Rostam had crossed the river he congratulated himself on his narrow escape and prayed: "O Lord of Justice, if I die from these wounds, who of our heroes will avenge me, and who has the courage and wisdom to take my place?"

Esfandyar saw him gain dry land and murmured to himself, "This is no man, this is a mammoth of unmatched might." In wonder he said, "O God of all desires, time and place are in your hands, and you have created him as you willed. He has crossed the river with ease, despite the terrible wounds he's suffered from my weapons."

As Esfandyar approached his encampment, he heard the noise of lamentation for Nushazar and Mehrnush. The royal tent was filled with dust, and his chieftains had rent their clothes: Esfandyar dismounted and, embracing the heads of his two dead sons, spoke quietly to them:

> *"Brave warriors, whose bodies here lie dead,*
> *Who knows to what abode your souls have fled?"*

Then he turned to Pashutan who knelt lamenting before him and said: "Don't weep for the dead any longer: I see no profit in such tears, and it is wrong to trouble one's soul in this way. Young and old, we are all destined for death, and may wisdom guide us when we depart."

They sent the two bodies in golden coffins, on teakwood litters, to the court, and Esfandyar sent with them a letter to his father: "The tree you planted has borne fruit. You launched this boat on the water: it was you that wanted Rostam as a slave, so now when you see the coffins of Nushazar and Mehrnush, do not lament overmuch. My own future is still uncertain, and I don't know what evil Fate has in store for me."

He sat on the throne, grieving for his sons, and then began to talk about Rostam. He said to Pashutan: "The lion has evaded the warrior's grasp. Today I saw Rostam, the massive height and strength of him, and I praised God, from whom come all hope and fear, that such a man existed. He has done such things in his time: he has fished in the Sea of China and drawn forth monsters, and on the plains he has trapped leopards. And I hurt him so severely that his blood turned the earth to mud; his body was a mass of arrow wounds but he made his way on foot up that mountain side, and then, still encumbered with his sword and armor, he hurried across the river. I know that as soon as he reaches his palace his soul will fly up to the heavens."

Rostam Consults with His Family

When Rostam reached the palace his kinsfolk clustered around him: Zavareh and Faramarz wept to see his wounds, and his mother Rudabeh tore at her hair and scored her cheeks in her grief. Zavareh removed his armor and tiger skin, and the leaders of the tribe gathered before him. Rostam asked that Rakhsh be brought to him, and that farriers be found to treat his wounds. Zal tore at his hair and pressed his aged face against Rostam's wounds, saying "Woe that I with my white hairs should ever see my noble son in this state!"

But Rostam said to him: "What use are tears, if heaven has decreed this? There is a harder task ahead of me, one that fills my soul with fear. I have never seen a warrior on the battlefield like this invincible Esfandyar, although I have traveled the world and have knowledge of what is plain and what is hidden. I lifted the White Demon by the waist and flung him against the ground like a willow branch. My arrows have pierced anvils and rendered shields futile, but no matter how many blows I rained on Esfandyar's armor my strength was useless against him. When leopards saw my mace they would hide themselves among the rocks, but it made no impression on his armor, or even so much as damaged the silk pennant on his helmet. But how much more can I plead with him and offer him friendship? He is stubborn in all he does and says, and wants only enmity from me. I thank God that night came on, and that our eyes grew dim in the darkness so that I was able to escape this dragon's claws. I don't know whether I'll be able to survive these wounds: I see nothing for it but to leave Rakhsh tomorrow, and seek out some obscure corner where Esfandyar will never hear of me, even if this means that he'll sack Zabolestan. He'll get tired of that eventually, although his nature rejoices in the evils of conquest."

Zal said to him: "My son, listen to me, and think carefully about what I'm going to say. There is one way out of all this world's troubles, and that is the way of death. But I know of a remedy, and you should seize on it. I shall summon the Simorgh, and if he will help us we may yet save our tribe and country. If not, then our land will be destroyed by this malevolent Esfandyar, who rejoices in the evil he does."

The Simorgh Appears Before Zal

They agreed to the plan. Zal filled three braziers with fire, and with three wise companions set out from the palace. They climbed to a high peak, and there the magician drew a feather from its brocade wrapping; fanning the flames in one of the braziers he burnt a portion of the feather in the fire. One watch of the night passed, and suddenly the air turned much darker. Zal peered into the night, and it seemed as if the fire and the Simorgh's flight were liquefying the air: then he caught sight of the Simorgh and the flames flared up. Fearful, with anguish in his heart, Zal sat and watched as the bird drew closer: next, he threw sandalwood on the braziers and went forward, making his obeisance to the Simorgh. Perfume rose up from the fires, and the sweat of fear shone on Zal's face. The Simorgh said to him:

> "O king, explain to me what you desire
> That you have summoned me in smoke and fire."

Zal answered: "May all the evils that have come to me from this baseborn wretch light on my enemies! The lionhearted Rostam lies grievously wounded, and my feet feel as though shackled by his sorrows. No man has ever seen such wounds and we despair of his life. And it seems that Rakhsh too will die from the arrow heads that torment him. Esfandyar came to our country, and the only gate he knocked at was the gate of war. He will not be content with taking our land and wealth and throne from us, he wants to uproot our family, to extirpate us from the face of the earth."

The Simorgh said:

> "Great hero, put away all grief and fear,
> Bring Rakhsh and noble Rostam to me here."

Zal sent one of his companions to Rostam who, together with Rakhsh, was brought up the mountainside. When Rostam reached the summit, the Simorgh saw him and said:

> "O mammoth-bodied warrior, tell me who
> Has laid you low like this and wounded you.
> Why did you fight with Persia's prince, and face
> The fire of mortal combat and disgrace?"

Zal said: "Now that you have vouchsafed us the sight of your pure face, tell me, if Rostam is not cured, where can my people go in all the

world? Our tribe will be uprooted, and this is no time to be question-
ing him."

The bird examined Rostam's wounds, looking for how they could
be healed. With his beak he sucked blood from the lesions, and drew
out eight arrow heads. Then he pressed one of his feathers against
the wounds, and immediately Rostam's spirits began to return. The
Simorgh said: "Bind up your wounds and keep them safe from further
injury for seven days: then soak one of my feathers in milk and place it
on the scars to help them heal." He treated Rakhsh in the same manner,
using his beak to draw six arrow heads from the horse's neck, and imme-
diately Rakhsh neighed loudly, and Rostam laughed for joy. The
Simorgh then turned to Rostam and said: "Why did you choose to fight
against Esfandyar, who is famous for being invincible in battle?"

Rostam replied: "He talked incessantly of chains, despite all the
advice I gave him. Death is easier for me than shame."

The Simorgh said: "To bow your head down to the ground before
Esfandyar would be no shame: he is a prince and a fine warrior, he lives
purely and possesses the divine *farr*. If you swear to me that you will
renounce this war and not try to overcome Esfandyar, if you will speak
humbly to him tomorrow and offer to submit to him (and if in fact his
time has come, he will ignore your overtures of peace) then I will assist
you, and raise your head to the sun's sphere."

Rostam was overjoyed to hear this, and was freed of the fear of
killing Esfandyar. He said: "Even if heaven should rain swords on my
head I shall keep faith with what you say to me."

The Simorgh said: "Out of my love for you, I shall tell you a secret
from heaven: Fate will harry whoever spills Esfandyar's blood, he will
live in sorrow, and his wealth will be taken from him; his life in this
world will be one of suffering, and torment will be his after death. If
you agree to what I say, and overcome your enmity, I shall show you
wonders tonight and seal your lips against all evil words. Choose a glit-
tering dagger, and mount Rakhsh."

Rostam prepared himself, mounted Rakhsh, and followed the
Simorgh as it flew until they reached a seashore. The air turned dark
from the Simorgh's shadow as it descended and came to rest on the
beach. He showed Rostam a pathway that led over dry land, over
which the air seemed impregnated with musk. He touched Rostam's
forehead with one of his feathers, and indicated that they should fol-

low the pathway. They reached a tamarisk tree rooted deep in the earth, its branches reaching into the sky, and the Simorgh alighted on one of the branches. He said to Rostam: "Choose the straightest branch you can find, one that tapers to a point: do not despise this piece of wood, for it holds Esfandyar's Fate. Temper it in fire, place an ancient arrow head at its tip, and fix feathers to the shaft. Now I have told you how to wound Esfandyar."

Rostam cut the tamarisk branch and returned to his castle, and as he came the Simorgh guided him, its talons clutching his helmet. The Simorgh said: "Now, when Esfandyar tries to fight with you, plead with him and try to guide him toward righteousness, and don't attempt to trick him in any way. Your sweet words might remind him of the ancient days, and of how you have fought and suffered throughout the world for Persia's cause. But if you speak fairly to him and he rejects your words, treating you with contempt, take this arrow, having steeped it in wine, and aim it for his eyes, as is the custom of those who worship the tamarisk. Fate will guide the arrow to his eyes, where his *farr* resides, and his death."

The Simorgh took its farewell of Zal, embracing him as if they were warp and weft of one cloth. Filled with hope and joy, Rostam lit the fire and watched the Simorgh fly serenely up into the air. Then he fitted the arrow head and feathers, as he had been instructed.

Rostam Kills Esfandyar

Dawn touched the mountain tops and dispersed the darkness of the night. Rostam put on his armor, prayed to the world's creator, and, eager for combat, made his way toward the Persian army. As he rode he called out exultantly: "Brave lion-heart, how long will you sleep? Rostam has saddled Rakhsh: rise from your sweet sleep and face Rostam's vengeance."

When Esfandyar heard his voice, all worldly weapons seemed useless to him. He said to Pashutan: "A lion cannot fight with a magician. I didn't think that Rostam would be able even to drag his armor and helmet back to his palace, and now he comes here riding Rakhsh, whose body yesterday was a mass of wounds. I have heard that Zal is a magician, that he stretches out his hands toward the sun, and that in his mantic fury he surpasses all other magicians: it would be unwise for me to face his son."

Pashutan said: "Why are you so hesitant today? Didn't you sleep through the night? What is it between you and Rostam, that you must both suffer so much in this business? I think your luck is abandoning you; all it does is lead you from one war to another."

Esfandyar dressed himself in his armor and went out to Rostam. When he saw his face he cried out: "May your name disappear from the surface of the earth! Aren't you the man who fled from me yesterday, shorn of heart, soul, courage, life itself? Have you forgotten then, you Sistani wretch, the power of my bow? It's only through the magic you've practiced that you're able to stand before me again: Zal's magic cured you, otherwise you'd be food for wild cats by now. But this time I shall fill you so full of arrows that all Zal's magic will be useless: I shall so batter your body that Zal shall never see you alive again."

Rostam replied: "Will you never tire of combat? I have not come to fight against you today, I have come humbly offering an honorable reconciliation. Fear God, and do not drive wisdom from your heart. Constantly you try to treat me unjustly, blinding yourself to wisdom's ways. By God Himself, by Zoroaster and the pure faith, by the sacred fire and the divine *farr*, by the sun and moon and the Zend Avesta, I swear to you that the road you are following is one of harm and evil. Forget the harsh words that have passed between us. I shall open to you my ancient treasuries, filled with marvels I have gathered over many years: I shall load my own horses with wealth and you can give them to your treasurer to drive before you. I shall ride with you, and if you so command me I shall come into the king's presence, and if the king then kills me or enslaves me I accept this as my due. Remember what an ancient sage once said, 'Never seek to have shame as your companion.' I am doing everything in my power to make you give up your thirst for combat."

Esfandyar said: "I'm not a fraud who looks one day for battle and the next day skulks in fear. Why do you talk so much about your wealth and possessions, washing your face with the waters of friendship? If you want to stay alive, submit your body to my chains."

Once more Rostam spoke: "Forget this injustice, prince. Don't sully my name and make your own soul contemptible; only evil will come of this struggle. I shall give you a thousand royal gems, along with torques and pearls and ear-rings. I shall give you a thousand sweet lipped boys to serve you day and night, and a thousand girls, all from Khallokhi whose women are famous for their charm, to make your court splendid with their beauty. My lord, I shall open the treasuries of

Sam and Zal before you and give you all they contain; I shall bring men from Kabolestan for you, fit companions for your feasting and fearless in war. And then I shall go before you like a servant, accompanying you to your vengeful king's court. But you, my prince, should drive vengeance from your heart, and keep devils from dwelling in your body. You are a king, one who fears God, and you have other ways of binding men to you than by chains; your chains will disgrace my name forever, how can such an evil be worthy of you?"

Esfandyar replied:

> "How long will you tell me to turn away
> From God and from my king? To disobey
> My sovereign lord and king is to rebel
> Against God's justice and to merit hell.
> Accept my chains, or enmity and war—
> But bandy pointless words with me no more."

When Rostam saw that his offers of friendship had no effect on Esfandyar, he notched the wine-soaked tamarisk arrow to his bow and lifted his eyes to the heavens, saying:

> "Just Lord, who gives us knowledge, strength, and life,
> You know how I have sought to end this strife;

Creator of the moon and Mercury
You see my weakness and humility,
And his unjust demands: I pray that you
See nothing sinful in what I must do."

Rostam hung back for a moment, and Esfandyar taunted him: "Well, famous Rostam, it seems your soul's grown tired of combat, now that you're faced with the arrows of Goshtasp, the lion heart and spear points of Lohrasp."

Then, as the Simorgh had ordered him, Rostam drew back his bow. Aiming at Esfandyar's eyes he released the arrow, and for the Persian prince the world was turned to darkness. The tall cypress swayed and bent, knowledge and glory fled from him; the God-fearing prince bowed his head and slumped forward, and his Chinese bow slipped from his hand. He grasped at his black horse's mane as his blood soaked into the earth beneath him.

Rostam addressed Esfandyar: "Your harshness has borne fruit. You were the man who said, 'I am invincible, I can bow the heavens down to the earth.' Yesterday I was wounded by eight arrows, and bore this silently: one arrow has removed you from combat and left you slumped over your horse. In another moment your head will be on the ground, and your mother will mourn for you."

Esfandyar lost consciousness and fell to the ground. Slowly he came to himself, and grasped the arrow: when he withdrew it, its head and feathers were soaked in blood. The news immediately reached Bahman that the royal glory was shrouded in darkness: he ran to Pashutan and said: "Our expedition here has ended in disaster: his mammoth body lies in the dirt, and the world is a dark pit to him."

They ran to him, and saw him lying soaked in his blood, a bloody arrow in his hand. Pashutan said: "Who of our great men can understand the world's ways? Only God who guides our souls and the heavens, and the planets in their courses, knows its truth. One like Esfandyar who fought for the pure faith, who cleared the world of the evils of idol-worship and never stretched out his hand to evil deeds, dies in the prime of youth, and his royal head lies in the dirt; while one who spreads strife in the world, who torments the souls of free men, lives for many years unharmed by Fate."

The young men cradled the fallen hero's head, wiping away the blood. With sorrow in his heart, his face smeared with blood, Pashutan lamented over him: "O Esfandyar, prince and world conqueror, who has toppled this mountain, who has trampled underfoot this raging lion? Who has torn out the elephant's tusks, who has held back the torrent of the Nile? Where have your heart and soul and courage fled, and your strength and fortune and faith? Where now are your weapons of war, where now is your sweet voice at our banquets? You cleansed the world of malevolence, you were fearless before lions and demons, and all your reward is to reign in the earth. My curses on the crown and throne: may they and your faithless father king Goshtasp be forgotten forever!"

Esfandyar said: "Do not torment yourself for me. This came to me from the crown and court: the killed body goes into the earth, and you should not distress yourself at my death. Where now are Feraydun, Hushang, and Jamshid? They came on the wind and were gone with a breath. My noble ancestors too departed and ceded their place to me: no one remains in this fleeting world. I have traveled the earth and known its wonders, both those that are clear and those that are hidden, trying to establish the ways of God, taking wisdom as my guide; and now that my words have gone forth and the hands of Ahriman are tied, Fate stretches out its lion claws for me. My hope is that I shall reap the reward of my efforts in Paradise. Zal's son did not kill me by chivalrous means. Look at this tamarisk wood grasped in my fist: it was this wood that ended my days, directed by the Simorgh and by that wily cheat Rostam. Zal, who knows all the world's sorcery, cast this spell."

Hearing his words, Rostam turned aside, his heart wrung with anguish. He said: "Some evil demon has brought this suffering to you. It's as he said; he acted honorably. Since I have been a warrior in the world I have seen no armed horseman like Esfandyar, and because in myself I was helpless against his bow and strength I sought for help rather than yield to him. It was his death that I notched to my bow, and released, since his time had come. If Fate had meant him to live, how could I have found the tamarisk? Man must leave this dark earth, and cannot prolong his life by so much as a breath beyond his appointed time. I was the means by which the tamarisk arrow struck him down."

Esfandyar said: "Now my life draws to an end. Come closer, don't leave me. My thoughts are different now from what they were. Listen to my advice, and what I ask of you concerning my son, who is the center of my life. Take him under your wing, show him the path to greatness."

Hearing his words, Rostam came weeping to his side, lamenting loudly, with tears of shame flowing from his eyes. News reached the palace: Zal came like the wind, and Zavareh and Faramarz approached, bewildered with sorrow. Zal addressed Rostam: "My son, I weep heart's blood for you, because I have heard from our priests and astrologers that whoever spills Esfandyar's blood will be harried by Fate: his life in this world will be harsh, and when he dies he will inherit torment."

Esfandyar's Last Words to Rostam

Esfandyar spoke to Rostam:

> "All that has happened happened as Fate willed.
> Not you, your arrow, or the Simorgh killed
> Me here: Goshtasp's, my father's, enmity
> Made you the means by which to murder me.
> He ordered me to sack Sistan, to turn
> It to a wilderness, to slay and burn,
> To suffer war's travails, while he alone
> Enjoyed the glory of his crown and throne.
> I ask you to accept my son, to raise
> Him in Sistan, to teach him manhood's ways:
> He is a wise and willing youth: from you
> He'll learn the skills of war, what he must do
> At courtly banquets when the wine goes round,
> How to negotiate or stand his ground,
> Hunting, the game of polo—everything
> That suits the education of a king.
> As for Jamasp, may his accursed name
> Perish, and may he waste away in shame!"

When Rostam had heard him out he stood and laid his hand on his chest and said: "If you die I swear to fulfill what you have said: I shall seat him on the ivory throne and place the royal crown upon his head myself. I shall stand before him as his servant, and call him my lord and king."

Esfandyar answered: "You are an old man, a champion of many wars, but, as God is my witness, and by the Faith that guides me, all this good that you have done for the world's kings will avail you nothing: your good name has turned to evil and the earth is filled with mourning for my death. This deed will bring sorrow to your soul, as God willed should happen." Then he addressed Pashutan: "I expect now nothing but my shroud. When I have left this fleeting world, lead our army back to Iran, and there tell my father that I say to him: 'As you have achieved what you desire, don't look for excuses. The world has turned out entirely as you wished, and all authority is yours now. With my just sword I spread righteousness in the world and no one dared oppose you, and when the true Faith had been established in Iran I was ready for greatness. Before our courtiers you praised me, and behind their backs you sent me to my death. You have gained what you sought; rejoice and put your anxieties to rest. Forget about death, let your palace be filled with celebration. The throne is yours; sorrow and a harsh fate are mine: the crown is yours; a coffin and a shroud are mine. But what have the wise said? "No arrow can defeat Death." Put no faith in your wealth and crown and court: I shall be watching for you when you come to that other place, and when you do we shall go together before the world's Judge to speak before him and to hear his verdict.' When you leave him go to my mother, and tell her that death has taken her brave ambitious son; that against death's arrow his helmet was like air, and that not even a mountain of steel could have withstood it. Tell her that she shall come soon after me, and that she should not grieve her soul for my sake, or unveil her face before the court, or look on my face in its shroud. To see me would make her weep, and no wise man would praise her grief. And bid my sisters and my wife an eternal farewell from me. Evil came to me from my father's crown; the key to his treasury was my life. Tell my womenfolk that I have sent you to the court to shame his dark soul." He paused, and caught his breath, and said, "It was Goshtasp, my father, who destroyed me," and at that moment his pure soul left his wounded body, which lay dead in the dust.

Rostam tore his clothes and in an agony of grief smeared dust upon his head. Weeping he said: "Great knight, son and grandson of a king, famed throughout the world, Goshtasp brought you to an evil end." When he had wept copiously he addressed the corpse again:

> *"To the high heavens your pure soul has flown,*
> *May your detractors reap what they have sown!"*

Zavareh said to him: "You should not accept this trust. An ancient saying says that, if you rear a lion cub, when it cuts its teeth and the instinct for hunting grows in it, the first person it will turn on is its keeper. Our two countries have an evil history: evil has come to Iran with the death of Esfandyar, and Bahman will bring evil to Zabolestan. Mark my words, when he becomes king he will seek vengeance for his father's death."

Rostam replied: "No one, good or evil, can deflect what the heavens will. I shall do what is wise and honorable: if he turns to evil, Fate will answer him. Don't provoke disaster by your prophecies."

Pashutan Takes Esfandyar's Corpse to the Court of Goshtasp

They made an iron coffin lined with Chinese silk, and wrapped him in a shroud of gold brocade. His chieftains lamented for him as his body was clothed and his turquoise crown placed upon his head. Then the coffin was closed, and the royal tree that had borne so much fruit was hidden from men's sight. The coffin was sealed with pitch and smeared with musk and sweet smelling oils.

Rostam brought forty camels caparisoned in Chinese brocade, one of which bore the coffin, while the rest formed columns to right and left of the army. All who were there scored their faces and plucked out their hair, calling out the prince's name as they did so. At the head of the army Pashutan led Esfandyar's black horse, which had had its mane and tail docked: the saddle on the horse's back was reversed, and Esfandyar's mace, armor, helmet, and spear hung from it. The army made its way back to Persia, but Bahman stayed weeping and mourning in Zabolestan.

Rostam took him to his palace, and looked after him there as if he were his own soul.

Goshtasp Learns That Esfandyar Has Been Killed

News reached Goshtasp that the young prince's head had been brought low in death. The king rent his clothes, and poured dust on his head and crown: the palace resounded with the noise of lamentation, and the world was filled with Esfandyar's name.

Goshtasp said: "O pure of Faith, our land and time will never see your like again! Since Manuchehr reigned there has been no warrior to equal you: your sword was always at the service of our Faith, and you maintained our chieftains in their glory."

But the Persian nobles were angered by his words, and washed their eyes of all sympathy for the king. With one voice they said: "Accursed king, to keep your throne and crown you sent Esfandyar to his death in Zabolestan: may the Kayanid crown shame your head, may the star of your good fortune falter in its course!"

When the news came to the women's quarters his mother and sisters, together with their daughters, went out to meet the returning army: their heads were unveiled, and they went barefoot in the dust, tearing their clothes as they walked. They saw the weeping Pashutan approach, and behind him Esfandyar's black horse, and the coffin. The women clung to Pashutan, weeping and wailing, begging him to open the coffin and let them see the slaughtered prince. Grief-stricken and hemmed in by the lamenting women who tore at their flesh in their anguish, Pashutan called to the army's blacksmiths to bring tools to open the coffin. The lid was lifted and a new wave of lamentation broke out as his mother and sisters saw the prince's face, and his black beard anointed with musk. The women fainted, and their black curls were clotted with blood. When they revived, they turned to Esfandyar's horse, caressing its neck and back: Katayun wept to think that this horse had carried her son when he was killed, and said, "What hero can you carry off to war now? Who can you deliver to the dragon's claws?" They clung to its shorn mane and heaped dust on its head, and all the while the soldiers' lamentations rose into the sky.

When Pashutan reached the king's audience hall he neither paused at the door, nor made his obeisance, nor came forward to the throne. He shouted out: "Most arrogant of men, the signs of your downfall are there for all to see. You have destroyed Iran and yourself with this deed: wisdom and the divine *farr* have deserted you, and God will repay you for what you have done. The back of your power is broken, and all you will hold in your grasp from now on is wind. For the sake of your throne you imbrued your son in blood, and may your eyes never see the throne or good fortune again! The world is filled with evil, and you will lose your throne forever: in this world you will be despised and in the world to come you will be judged." Then he turned to Jamasp and said:

"And you, you worthless evil councilor, who knows no speech in all the world but lies, who turns all splendor to crooked deceit, who stirs up enmity between princes, setting one against another, all you know how to do is to teach men to desert virtue and cleave to evil. But as you have sown so shall you reap. With your talk you destroyed a great man, saying that Esfandyar's life was in the palm of Rostam's hand."

Pashutan paused, and then he told the king plainly what had passed between Rostam and Bahman. When he had heard him out the king regretted what he had done. The court was cleared and his daughters, Beh Afarid and Homay, came before their father, their cheeks scored and their hair torn out in their sorrow for their dead brother.

They said: "Great king, haven't you considered what Esfandyar's death means? He was the first to avenge Zarir's death, he led the attack against the Turks, it was he who stabilized your kingdom. Then on the words of some slanderer you imprisoned him, and immediately our army was defeated and our grandfather was killed. When Arjasp reached Balkh he struck terror into the land, and we who live veiled from men's eyes were driven naked from the palace into the common highway. Arjasp extinguished the sacred fire of Zoroaster and seized the kingdom. And then you saw what your son did: he utterly destroyed our enemies and brought us back safely from the Brass Fortress where we'd been imprisoned. He was the savior of our country and of your throne. And so you sent him to Sistan, filling him with specious talk so that he'd give up his life for the sake of your crown, and the world would lament his death. Neither the Simorgh nor Rostam nor Zal killed him: you killed him, and as you killed him you have no right to weep and complain. Shame on your white beard, that you killed your son for the sake of greed. Before you, there have been many kings worthy of the throne; none killed his own son or turned against his own family."

The king turned to Pashutan and said: "Bestir yourself, and pour water on these children's fiery rage." Pashutan led the women from the court, saying to Esfandyar's mother Katayun, "How long will you rage and grieve like this? He sleeps happily, and his bright soul rests from the strife and sorrow of this world. Why should you grieve for him, since he is now in heaven?"

Katayun took his wise advice, and accepted God's justice. For a year, in every house and in the palace, there was mourning throughout the country, and for many years men wept to think of the tamarisk arrow, and the Simorgh's trick, and Zal.

Meanwhile Bahman lived in Zabolestan, hunting, drinking, taking his ease in the country's gardens. Rostam taught this vengeful youth how to ride, to drink wine, and the customs of a royal court. He treated him more warmly than if he'd been his own son, and rejoiced in his company day and night. When he had fulfilled his promise, the door of Goshtasp's revenge was closed.

Rostam's Letter to King Goshtasp

Rostam wrote a sorrowful letter, setting out his kindness to the king's son. He began by invoking Zoroaster and then went on: "As God is my witness, and Pashutan can testify, I said many times to Esfandyar that he should lay aside all enmity and desire for war. I told him I would give him land and wealth, but he chose otherwise; Fate willed that he ignored my pleas, and who can oppose what the heavens bring about? His son Bahman has lived with me, and is more splendid in my eyes than shining Jupiter: I have taught him how to be a king, instructing him in the elements of wisdom. If the king will promise to forget the tamarisk arrow and accept my repentance, all I have is at his disposal— my body, soul, wealth, crown, my very flesh and bones are his."

When the letter arrived at Goshtasp's court his courtiers soon learned of it. Pashutan came and confirmed everything Rostam had said: he recalled Rostam's grief at having to face Esfandyar, and the way that he had counseled him. He spoke too of Rostam's wealth, and of the land he ruled over. Pashutan's remarks pleased the king and had a good effect. The king's heart warmed toward Rostam, and he put aside his sorrow. Immediately he wrote a magnanimous answer to Rostam's letter: "When the heavens will someone an injury, who has the wisdom to prevent this? Pashutan has told me of what you tried to do, and this has filled my heart with kindness toward you. Who can withstand the heavens' turning? A wise man does not linger on the past. You are as you have always been, and more than this: you are the lord of Hend and Qannuj, and whatever more you desire, be it a throne or authority or arms, ask for it from me." As his master had ordered him, Rostam's messenger quickly took back the king's answer.

Time passed, and Prince Bahman grew to be a man. He was wise, knowledgeable, authoritative, every inch a king. Jamasp, with his understanding of good and evil, knew that the kingdom would one day be Bahman's, and he said to Goshtasp: "My lord, you should consider Bahman's situation. He is mature in knowledge, and an honorable man. But he's lived in a foreign land for too long, and no one has ever read him a letter from you. A letter should be written to him, something as splendid as a tree in Paradise. Who have you but Bahman to cleanse the sorrow of Esfandyar's fate from your mind?"

Goshtasp was pleased by this suggestion and answered: "Write him a letter, and write one also to Rostam, saying: 'God be thanked, great champion, that I am pleased with you, and my mind is at rest. My grandson Bahman, who is dearer to me than our own soul and is wiser than my councilor Jamasp, has learned all kingly skills from you: now you should send him back to me.' To Bahman write: 'As soon as you read this letter stay in Zabol no longer: I have a great desire to see you. Put your affairs in order and come as quickly as you can.'"

When the letter was read to him, Rostam was pleased, and he prepared a parting gift for Bahman. He opened his treasury and brought out armor, shining daggers, barding for horses, bows, arrows, maces, Indian swords, camphor, musk, sandalwood, jewels, gold, silver, horses, uncut cloth, servants and young boys, gold belts and saddles, and two golden goblets filled with rubies. All these he handed over to Bahman.

Bahman Returns to King Goshtasp

Rostam came two stages of the road with the prince, and then sent him on his way to the king. When Goshtasp saw his grandson's face, tears covered his cheeks and he said: "You are another Esfandyar, you resemble no one but him." Bahman was intelligent and quick witted, and from then on he was called Ardeshir. He was a strong, fine warrior: wise, knowledgeable, and God-fearing. When he stood, his finger tips came to below his knees. In all things he was like his father, whether fighting or feasting or hunting. Goshtasp could not be separated from him, and made him his drinking companion. He would say:

> *"Now, since my noble, warlike son has died,*
> *May Bahman live forever at my side."*

THE DEATH OF ROSTAM

Zal had a female slave who was a musician and storyteller. She gave birth to a son whose beauty eclipsed the moon's: in appearance he resembled Sam, and the whole family rejoiced at his birth. Astrologers and wise men from Kabol and Kashmir came with their astronomical charts to cast the boy's horoscope, and to see whether the heavens would smile on him. But when they had done so they looked at one another in alarm and dismay, and said to Zal: "You and your family have been favored by the stars, but when we searched the secrets of the heavens we saw that this boy's fortune is not an auspicious one. When this handsome lad reaches manhood and becomes a warrior he will destroy the seed of Sam and Nariman, he will break your family's power. Because of him Sistan will be filled with lamentation and the land of Iran will be thrown into confusion: he will bring bitter days to everyone, and few enough of you will survive his onslaught."

Zal was saddened by these words and turned to God in his anxiety: "Lord of the heavens, my refuge and support, my guide in all my actions, creator of the heavens and the stars: may we hope for good fortune, and may nothing but goodness and peace come to us." Then he named the boy Shaghad.

His mother kept him by her until he was weaned; he was a talkative, charming, and quick witted child. When his strength had begun to develop, Zal sent him to the king of Kabol. There he grew into a fine young man, cypress statured, a good horseman, and skillful with mace and lariat. The king of Kabol looked on him with favor, and considered him worthy of the throne: he bestowed his own daughter on him in marriage and provided her with a splendid dowry. Shaghad was the apple of his eye, and he thought nothing of the stars and the astrologers' predictions.

The chieftains of Persia and India told Rostam that every year the kingdom of Kabol was required to hand over as tribute the hide of a cow. But the king of Kabol was sure that, now his son-in-law was Rostam's brother, no one would be concerned about a cow skin worth a few coins.

But when the time came for the tribute to be paid it was demanded, and the people of Kabol took offense at this. Shaghad was disgusted by his brother's behavior, but he told no one, except the king to whom he said, in secret: "I am tired of the world's ways: my brother treats me with disrespect, he has no time for me. He's more like a stranger to me than an older brother, more like a fool than a wise man. You and I should work together to entrap him, and this will win us fame in the world." The two confabulated together, and in their own eyes they overtopped the moon: but listen to what the wise have said, "Whoever does evil will be repaid in kind."

All night, until the sun rose above the mountains, the two evaded sleep, plotting how to wipe Rostam's name from the world, and make Zal's eyes wet with tears of grief. Shaghad said to the king: "If we're going to turn our words into actions, I suggest you give a banquet with wine, musicians, and entertainers, and invite our chieftains. Whilst we're drinking wine, in front of all the courtiers and guests, speak coldly and slightingly to me. Then I'll go to my brother, and to my father, and curse the lord of Kabol for a lowborn wretch, and complain about how he has treated me. Meanwhile, you should go to the plain where we hunt, and have pits dug there. Make them deep enough to swallow up both Rostam and Rakhsh, and in the base of the pits plant sharpened stakes, spears, javelins, swords, and so on. If you can dig a hundred pits rather than just five, so much the better. Get a hundred men together, dig the pits, and don't breathe a word even to the wind. Then cover over the pits' surface, and see that you mention what you've done to no one at all."

The king's good sense deserted him, and he gave orders for a banquet to be prepared, as this fool had suggested to him. He summoned the chieftains of his kingdom to a splendid feast and, when they had eaten, they settled to their wine, watching entertainers and listening to musicians. When his head was well-filled with royal wine, Shaghad suddenly sprang up and bragged to the king:

"I am the first in any company—
What noble chieftain can compare with me?
Rostam's my brother, Zal's my father, can
Such boasts be made by any other man?"

Then the king too sprang up and retorted:

"This is your constant boast, but it's not true,
The tribe of Sam has turned its back on you:
Rostam is not your brother, when has he
So much as mentioned your base name to me?
You're a slave's son, not Zal's. And Rostam's mother
Has never said that you're that hero's brother."

Shaghad was infuriated by his words, and with a few Kaboli warriors he immediately set out for Zabolestan, revolving thoughts of vengeance in his heart. He entered his noble father's court in a rage, and when Zal saw his son's stature and splendor he made much of him, questioned him closely, and sent him to Rostam.

Rostam was delighted to see him, thinking of him as a wise and pure hearted man, and greeted him warmly: "Sam is a lion, and his progeny produce only strong, courageous warriors. How is your life now in Kabol, and what do they say about Rostam there?"

Shaghad's answer was: "Don't mention the king of Kabol to me. He treated me well before, addressing me with respect, but now as soon as he drinks a little wine he becomes quarrelsome, thinking he's superior to everyone else: he humiliated me in front of his courtiers, and talked publicly about my low origins. Then he said, 'How long do we have to pay this tribute? Don't we have the strength to defy Sistan? Don't tell me, "But it's Rostam you're dealing with." He's no more of a man than I am, and no more nobly born either.' Then he said that I wasn't Zal's son; or that, if I was, Zal didn't care about me. I was ashamed to be spoken to like this in front of his chieftains, and when I left Kabol my cheeks were pale with fury."

Rostam was enraged, and said: "Such talk won't stay private for long. Don't bother yourself with his army: my curses on his army and on his crown too. I'll destroy him for these words of his, I'll make him and his whole tribe tremble for what he's said. I'll place you on his throne, and I'll drag his luck down into the dust."

He entertained Shaghad royally for a few days, putting a splendid residence at his disposal; then he picked his best warriors and ordered them to get ready to travel to Kabol. When the preparations for departure had been made, Shaghad came to Rostam and said, "Don't think of going to war against the king of Kabol. I'd only have to trace the letters of your name in water for everyone in Kabol to be sleepless with anxiety. Who would dare to stand against you in war, and if you set out who is going to wait for you to confront them? I think that by now the king must regret what he's done, that he's searching for some way to neutralize the effects of my departure, and that he'll send some of his chieftains here to apologize."

Rostam replied: "Here's what we should do: there's no need for me to lead my army against Kabol, Zavareh and about a hundred horsemen, together with a hundred infantry, should be sufficient."

The King of Kabol Prepares the Pits

As soon as the malignant Shaghad had left Kabol the king hurried off to his hunting grounds. He took sappers renowned for their ability from his army, and had them excavate pits at various places on the road that led through the area. At the bottom of each pit javelins, spears, and sharp swords were stuck into the ground. Then the pits were covered over with straw and brush so that neither men nor their mounts could see them.

When Rostam was ready to set out, Shaghad rode on ahead of him and told the king of Kabol that Rostam and his men were approaching, and that the king should go to meet them and apologize for what he had done. The king came out of the city, his tongue ready with glozing talk, his heart filled with poison and the longing for vengeance.

As soon as he saw Rostam he dismounted. He removed his Indian turban and placed his hands on his forehead: then he removed his boots, began to weep, and bowed his face down to the ground, asking pardon for what he had done to Shaghad, saying that if he had spoken intemperately it was because he was drunk, and that Rostam should forgive him. He came forward, barefoot, but his mind was filled with thoughts of vengeance.

Rostam forgave him, awarding him new honors, and told him to replace his turban and boots, and to remount his horse.

There was a green, delightful garden in Kabol, filled with streams and trees. Seats were set there, and the king ordered that a banquet be brought; then he called for wine and musicians to entertain his chieftains and courtiers. Whilst the festivities were in progress he turned to Rostam and said: "What would you say to a hunting expedition? I have a place near here which includes both open country and mountain landscape, and it's filled with game. There are mountain sheep, deer, and wild asses: a man with a good horse can run down any number of prey: it's a pleasure no one should miss."

His description of the landscape with its streams and wild asses filled Rostam with enthusiasm:

> For when a man's days reach their end, his mind
> And heart grow undiscerning, dim, and blind:
> The world has no desire that we should see
> The hidden secrets of our destiny.
> The crocodile, the lion, the elephant
> Are one with the mosquito and the ant
> Within the grip of Death: no beast or man
> Lives longer than his life's allotted span.

Rostam gave orders that Rakhsh be saddled, and that hunting hawks be made ready: he took up his bow, and rode out on the plain with Shaghad. Zavareh and a few of their retinue accompanied them. The group dispersed, some going toward solid ground, others to where the earth had been excavated; as Fate would have it, Zavareh and Rostam went to the area where the pits had been dug. But Rakhsh smelt the freshly dug earth: his muscles tensed and he reared up in fright, his hooves pawing at the ground. He went forward, placing his hooves with care, until he was between two of the pits. Rostam was irritated by his caution, and Fate blinded the hero's wisdom. He lightly touched Rakhsh with his whip, and the horse bounded forward, searching for firm ground. But his forelegs struck where one of the pits had been dug, and there was nowhere for him to find a hold. The base of the pit was lined with spears and sharp swords: courage was of no

avail, and there was no means of escape. Rakhsh's flanks were lacerated
by the weapons, and Rostam's legs and trunk were pierced by them:
exerting all his strength, he pulled himself from their points, and raised
his head above the pit's edge.

When in his agony he opened his eyes, he saw the malignant face
of Shaghad before him. He knew then that Shaghad had tricked him,
and that this evil was his doing. He said:

> *"Ill-fated wretch, what you have done will leave*
> *Our land a desert where men curse and grieve:*
> *You will regret your evil, senseless rage;*
> *Tormented, you will never see old age."*

Shaghad replied: "The turning heavens have dealt justly with you.
How often you've boasted of the blood you've spilt, of your devasta-
tion of Iran, and of your battles. You won't be demanding tribute from
Kabol any more, and no kings will tremble before you now. Your days
are at an end, and you shall perish in the snare of Ahriman."

At that moment the king of Kabol reached them: he saw Rostam's
open, bleeding wounds and said, "My lord, what has happened to you

here in our hunting grounds? I shall hurry to bring doctors to heal your wounds, and to dry my tears of sympathy for your suffering."

Rostam replied: "Devious and lowborn wretch, the days when doctors could help me are over, and you need weep no tears for me. You too will not live long; no one passes to the heavens while still alive. I possess no more glory than Jamshid, who was hacked in two by Zahhak; and Gerui slit Seyavash's throat when his time had come. All the great kings of Iran, all those who were lions in battle, have departed, and we are left here like lions at the wayside. My son Faramarz will demand vengeance from you for my death." Then he turned to Shaghad and said: "Now that this evil has come to me, take my bow from its case: don't refuse me this last request. String my bow and put it in front of me, together with two arrows: a lion may come looking for prey, and if it sees me helpless here it will attack me; my bow will defend me then. And if no lion tears my flesh, my body will lie beneath the earth soon enough."

Shaghad came forward and took out the bow; he strung it, and pulled back the string to test it. Then he laughed and placed it in front of Rostam, filled with joy at the thought of his brother's death. With a mighty effort, Rostam picked up the bow, and notched an arrow to the string. His brother was filled with fear at the sight of the arrow, and to shield himself he went behind a huge, ancient plane tree, the trunk of which was hollow, although it still bore leaves.

Rostam watched him go, and then, summoning his last strength, he drew back the bowstring and released the arrow. The shaft pierced the tree and his brother, pinning them to one another, and the dying Rostam's heart rejoiced to see this. Shaghad cried out with the pain of his wound, but Rostam soon put him out of his misery. Then he said:

> "Thanks be to God, to whom for all my days
> I've offered worship and unceasing praise
> That now, as night comes on, with my last breath,
> Vengeance and power are mine before my death."

With these words his soul left his body, and those who stood nearby lamented and wept.

In another pit Zavareh too died, as did those who had ridden with Rostam, both his chieftains and their followers.

Zal Learns of Rostam's Death

But one of his retinue survived and, sometimes riding, sometimes on foot, made his way back to Zabolestan, where he said: "Our mammoth warrior is made one with the dust; Zavareh too, and all their men, are dead, and only I have escaped from the evil that befell them."

The noise of mourning was heard throughout Zabolestan, and execrations against Shaghad and the king of Kabol. Zal strewed his body with dust, and clawed at his face and chest in his grief.

> Then in his agony he cried aloud:
> "All I can bring you, Rostam, is your shroud;
> And Zavareh, that lion chief in war,
> That dragon in close combat, is no more:
> My curses on Shaghad, whose treachery
> Has ripped up by the roots our royal tree.
> Who would have thought a cunning fox could leave
> Our mammoth heroes dead, and me to grieve?
> Why could I not have died before them? Why
> Should I endure the world whilst they must die?
> What's life to me that I should breathe and live,
> What comfort can my throne or glory give?"

And he wept bitterly, lamenting Rostam's departed greatness. His lion courage and bravery, his chivalry and good council, his mighty weapons and valor in war—all were gone, now that he was one with the earth.

Then Zal cursed his son's enemies and summoned Faramarz: he sent him to make war on the king of Kabol, to retrieve the dead bodies from the pits, and to give the world there cause for lamentation.

But when Faramarz reached Kabol he found none of the nobility there: they had all fled from the town, weeping and terrified by the world-conqueror's death. He made his way to the hunting grounds, where the pits had been dug, and when he saw his father's face, and his body lying on the ground, soaked in blood, he roared like a lion in pain. He said: "Great warrior, who has done this evil to you? My curses on his boldness, and may dust cover his head in place of his crown! I swear by God and by your soul, by the dust of Nariman and

Sam, that I shall not remove my armor until I have wreaked revenge upon this treacherous people for your death. I shall not leave one of those who were any part of this plot alive."

He removed his father's armor, and the clothes beneath it, and gently washed the blood from his body and beard. The company burnt ambergris and saffron, and with it sealed his wounds. Faramarz poured rosewater on his father's brow, and smeared camphor over the body. Then they wrapped him in brocade, over which they sprinkled rosewater, musk, and wine. Two great boards were necessary to carry his corpse, which seemed more like the trunk of a huge shade-giving tree, than the body of a man. A magnificent coffin was made of teak, with a design inlaid in ivory, and the nails were of gold: the joints were sealed with pitch that had been mixed with musk and ambergris.

Then Rakhsh's body was drawn up from the pit and washed, and draped in fine brocade: carpenters spent two days making a litter from heavy boards for the body, and this was loaded onto an elephant. From Kabol to Zabol the land was filled with lamentation. Men and women stood crowded at the wayside to see the procession, and the crowds passed the coffins of Rostam and Zavareh from hand to hand; so great was the number who did this that the burden seemed light as air. The journey took ten days and ten nights, and not once were the coffins set down. The world was filled with mourning for Rostam, and the plain seemed to seethe with sorrow; so great was the noise that no individual's voice could be heard within the roar of sound.

In a garden they built a great tomb whose roof reached to the clouds. Within, two golden daises were built, on which were laid the dead heroes: freemen and slaves came together and poured rosewater mixed with musk over the heroes' feet, and addressed Rostam:

> *"Why is it grief and musk that we must bring*
> *And not the glory that attends a king?*
> *You have no need for sovereignty, no need*
> *For armor, weapons, or your warlike steed,*
> *Never again will your largesse reward*
> *Courtiers with gifts from your rich treasure hoard.*
> *Justice was yours, and truth, and chivalry,*
> *May joy be yours for all eternity."*

Then they sealed the tomb and went on their way: so ended the lion hero who had lifted up his head in the world with such pride and valor.

Faramarz Marches on Kabol

When his father's obsequies were completed, Faramarz gathered an army on the plain and equipped it from Rostam's treasury. At dawn the tucket sounded, and was answered by the din of drums and Indian bells. The army set out for Kabol, the sun obscured by its dust.

News reached Kabol's king of their approach: he gathered his scattered army together and the ground became a mass of iron armor, while the air was darkened with dust. He marched his men out to confront Faramarz, and the sun and moon were dimmed. The armies met and the world was filled with the sounds of battle. A wind sprang up, and a dust cloud hid the earth and sky: but Faramarz at the head of his army never took his eyes from the enemy king. The din of drums rang out on each side, and Faramarz together with a small escort forced his way into the center of the Kaboli troops. There in the dusty darkness stirred up by the cavalry he closed in on the king and captured him. That great army scattered, and the warriors of Zabol fell on the retreating men like wolves: they ambushed them from every side, and pursued them as they fled. They killed so many Indian soldiers, so many warriors from Sind, that the dust of the battlefield was turned to mud with their gore: their hearts forgot their country and their homes, their wives and little children were left unprotected.

Kabol's king, his body covered in blood, was flung into a chest hoisted on an elephant's back. Faramarz led his men to the hunting grounds where the pits had been dug. Then the king was dragged forward, with his hands bound, together with forty members of his tribe. They trussed the king so tightly that his bones showed through his skin, and he was suspended upside down in one of the pits, his body covered in filth, his mouth filled with blood. Next Faramarz had a fire lit in which the forty members of the king's family were burnt; then he turned to where Shaghad was still pinned to the plane tree. Shaghad's body, the tree, and the surrounding countryside were consumed by flames, that flared up like a great mountain of fire. When he set out again for Zabol, he brought the ashes of Shaghad to give them to Zal.

Having killed those who had committed evil, Faramarz appointed a new king for Kabol, as the old king's family had been annihilated. He returned from Kabol still filled with fury and grief; the brilliance of his days had turned to darkness. All Zabolestan shared his grief, and there was no man who had not rent his clothes in mourning. All of Sistan lamented for a year, and all its inhabitants wore the black and dark blue clothes of mourning.

Rudabeh's Madness

One day Rudabeh said to Zal: "Weep for Rostam in bitterness of heart, for since the world has existed no one has ever seen a darker day than this." Zal turned on her and said, "Foolish woman, the pain of hunger is far worse than this sorrow." Rudabeh was offended and swore an oath, saying: "I shall neither eat nor sleep in the hopes that my soul will join Rostam, and see him in that blessed company."

In her heart she communicated with Rostam's soul, and for a week she kept herself from eating anything. Weakened by hunger, her eyes darkened, and her slender body became frail and feeble. Everywhere she went, her serving maids followed her, afraid that she would harm herself. By the week's end her reason had deserted her, and she was expected to die.

When the world was asleep she went into the palace kitchen garden, and there she saw a dead snake lying in the pool. She reached down and picked it up by the head, intending to eat it, but a serving girl snatched the snake from her hand, and the girl's companions led Rudabeh away to her apartments. They made her comfortable, and prepared food for her. She ate whatever they brought, until she was full, and then her servants laid her gently on her bed.

When she woke her reason had returned, and she said to Zal: "What you told me was wise: the sorrow of death is like a festival to someone who has neither eaten nor slept. He has gone, and we shall follow after him: we trust in the world creator's justice. Then she distributed her secret wealth to the poor, and prayed to God:

> "O Thou, who art above all name and place,
> Wash guilt and worldly sin from Rostam's face:
> Give him his place in Heaven: let him be shown
> The fruitful harvest of the seeds he's sown."

Bahman and Faramarz

Goshtasp's fortunes declined, and he summoned his councilor, Jamasp. He said to him: "My heart is seared with such sorrow for this business of Esfandyar that not one day of my life passes in pleasure: malignant stars have destroyed me. After me, Bahman will be king, and Pashutan will be his confidant. Keep faith with Bahman, and obey him: guide him in his duties, point by point, and he will add luster to the throne and crown."

He handed Bahman the keys to his treasury, and heaved a cold and bitter sigh. Then he said: "My work is over; the waters overtop my head. I have reigned for a hundred and twenty years, and I have seen no one else with my power in all the world. Strive to act justly, and if you do you will escape from sorrow. Keep wise men near you and treat them well, darken the world of those who wish you ill: act righteously, and you will avoid both deviousness and failure. I give you my throne, my diadem, and my wealth: I have experienced enough sorrow and grief." He spoke, and his days on the earth came to an end. They built a tomb for him of ebony and ivory, and his crown was suspended over the coffin.

When Bahman ascended his grandfather's throne he acted with decision and generosity, giving his army cash, and distributing land among them. He called a council of the wise, the noble, and those experienced in the ways of the world.

He said to them: "All of you, old and young, who have gracious souls, surely remember Esfandyar's life and the good and evil that Fate dealt him: and you recall what Rostam and that old wizard Zal did to him in the prime of his life. Openly and covertly Faramarz does nothing but plot vengeance against us. My head is filled with pain, my heart with blood, and my brain is empty of everything but thoughts of revenge: revenge for our two warriors Nushazar and Mehrnush, whose agonies caused such sorrow, and revenge for Esfandyar who had revived the fortunes of our nobility, who was slain in Zabolestan, for whose death the very beasts were maddened with grief, and the frescoed portraits in our palaces wept.

"Our ancestors, when they were brave young warriors, did not hide their valor in obscurity, but acted as the glorious king Feraydun did, who destroyed Zahhak in revenge for the blood of Jamshid. And Manuchehr brought an army from Amol and marched against Salm and the barbarous Tur, pursuing them to China in pursuit of vengeance for his grandfather's death. I too shall leave such a tale behind me. When Kay Khosrow escaped from Afrasyab's clutches he made the world like a lake of blood: my father demanded vengeance for Lohrasp, and piled the earth with a mountain of dead. And Faramarz, who exalts himself above the shining sun, went to Kabol pursuing vengeance for his father's blood, and razed the whole province to the ground: blood obscured all the land, and men rode their horses over the bodies of the dead. I, who ride out against raging lions, am more worthy than anyone to take revenge, since my vengeance will be for the peerless Esfandyar. Tell me how this matter appears to you; what answer can you give me? Try to give me wise advice."

When they heard Bahman's words everyone who wished him well said with one voice: "We are your slaves, our hearts are filled with goodwill toward you. You know more about what has happened in the past than we do, and you are more capable than any other warrior: do what you will in the world, and may you win praise and glory for your deeds. No one will refuse your orders, or break faith with you."

Hearing this answer Bahman became more intent on vengeance than ever, and prepared to invade Sistan. At daybreak the din of drums resounded, and the air was darkened by his armies' dust: a hundred thousand mounted warriors set out.

When he reached the banks of the River Hirmand he sent a messenger to Zal. He was to say on behalf of Bahman: "My days have been turned to bitterness because of what happened to Esfandyar, and to the two worthy princes Nushazar and Mehrnush. I will fill all the land of Sistan with blood, to slake my longing for vengeance."

The messenger arrived in Zabol and spoke as he had been instructed: Zal's heart was wrung with sorrow, and he said: "If the prince will consider what happened to Esfandyar, he will see that this was a fated event, and that I too suffered because of it. You were here, and saw all that happened, both the good and the evil, but from me you have only seen profit, and no loss. Rostam did not ignore your father's orders, and his fealty to him was heartfelt. But Esfandyar, who was a great king, in his last days became overbearing toward Rostam: even the lion in his thicket, and the savage dragon cannot escape the claws of Fate.

"And you have heard of Sam's chivalrous deeds, which he continued until Rostam, in his turn, drew his sharp sword from its scabbard. Rostam's heroism in battle was witnessed by your forebears, and he acted as your servant, your nurse, your guide in the ways of warfare. Day and night I weep and mourn for my dead son, my heart is filled with pain, my two cheeks have turned sallow with grief, and my lips are blue with my sufferings: my curses on the one who overthrew him, and on the man who guided him to do so. If you can consider the sorrow we now endure, and think well of us, if you can drive these thoughts of vengeance from your heart, and brighten our land with your mercy, I shall lay before you golden belts and golden bridles, and all my son's treasures and Sam's cash: you are our king, and our chieftains are your flock."

He gave the messenger a horse and money, and many other presents. But when the messenger reached Bahman and told him what he had seen and heard, the king refused to accept Zal's words, and flew into a rage. He entered the city with pain in his heart, and still revolving thoughts of vengeance. Zal and the nobility of Sistan rode out to welcome him: when he drew near to Bahman, Zal dismounted, made his obeisance before him, and said: "This is a time for forgiveness, to put aside suffering and the desire for vengeance. I, Zal, stand before you, wretched and supported by a staff: remember how good I was to you when you were young. Forgive the past and speak of it no more: seek honor, rather than revenge for those who have been killed."

But Bahman so despised Zal that his words enraged the king: without further ado he had Zal's legs shackled and, ignoring the protests of both councilor and treasurer, he gave orders for camels to be loaded with the goods in the castle. Cash, uncut gems, thrones and fine cloth, silver and golden vessels, golden crowns, earrings, and belts, Arab horses with bridles worked in gold, Indian swords in golden scabbards, slaves, bags of coins, musk, camphor—all the wealth that Rostam had accumulated with such effort, or received as presents from kings and chieftains, was collected and taken. Purses and crowns were distributed to Bahman's nobility, and Zabolestan was given over to plunder.

Faramarz Makes War on Bahman

Faramarz was in the marches of Bost when he heard this; outraged by the treatment meted out to his grandfather, he prepared to take his revenge. His chieftains gathered about him and he said: "Zavareh would often sigh and say to my father that Bahman would seek revenge for the death of Esfandyar, and that this threat should not be taken lightly. But, for all his experience of the world, my father wouldn't listen to him, and this is the reason that his territories are now laid waste. When his grandfather died Bahman ascended the throne, and raised his crown to the moon's sphere; now that he's king he's once again intent on revenge for Esfandyar, and for Mehrnush and Nushazar too. He wants to destroy us as vengeance for their deaths, and he's led here from Iran an army like a black cloud. He's arrested and bound in chains my revered grandfather, who was a shield to the Persians in their wars, and always held himself ready to serve them. What will happen to our people now, what disasters will close in from every side? My father has been slain, my grandfather languishes in chains, all our land has been given over to plunder, and I am half mad with the grief of all this: well, my noble warriors, what have you to say about our situation?"

They answered him: "O bright souled hero, whose leadership has been passed down from father to father, we are all your slaves, and live only for your orders."

When he heard this, Faramarz's heart was filled with longing for vengeance, his head with thoughts of how to save his family's honor: he put on his armor and led his army against Bahman, and as he marched he rehearsed in his mind Rostam's battles.

When the news reached Bahman he acted immediately: he had the baggage trains loaded up, and then led his army toward Ghur, where he stayed for two weeks. Faramarz pursued him, and his cavalry turned the world black with their dust. For his part Bahman drew up his battle lines, and the shining sun could no longer see the ground. The mountains rang with the squeal of trumpets and the clanging of Indian bells. The sky seemed to soak the world in pitch, arrows rained down from the clouds like dew, and the earth seemed to shudder with the din of battleaxe blows, the humming of released bowstrings. For three days and nights, by sunlight and moonlight, maces and arrows rained down and the sky was filled with clouds of dust. On the fourth day a wind sprang up, and it was as if day had turned to night: the wind blew against Faramarz and his troops, and king Bahman rejoiced to see this. His sword drawn, he charged forward, following the billowing dust clouds, and raised such a hue and cry it seemed that the Last Judgment had come. The men of Bost, the army from Zabol, the warriors of Kabol, all were slaughtered

or fled, and not one of their chieftains remained. All turned tail and for-
got their allegiance to Faramarz: all the battlefield was strewn with
mountainous piles of bodies of men from both sides.

With a few remaining warriors, his body covered in sword wounds,
Faramarz fought on, for he was a lion fighter, descended from a race of
lions. Finally, the long arm of Bahman's might caught him, and he was
dragged before the king. Bahman glared at him in fury, and denied him
all mercy. While still alive, Faramarz's body was hoisted upside down on
a gibbet; and Bahman gave orders that he be killed in a storm of arrows.

Bahman Frees Zal and Returns to Iran

Pashutan was the king's trusted advisor, and he was very troubled by
this execution. Humbly he stood before his royal master and said:
"Lord of Justice and Righteousness, if you desired vengeance you have
achieved it. You would do well to give no more orders for plunder,
killing, and warfare, and you should not take pleasure in such tumult.
Fear God, and show shame before us: look at the turnings of the heav-
ens, how they raise one to greatness, and cast another down to
wretchedness and grief. Did not your great father, who brought the
world beneath his command, find his coffin in Sistan? Was not Rostam
lured to the hunting grounds in Kabol, and there destroyed in a pit?
While you live my noble lord you should not harass those of exalted
birth. You should tremble that Sam's son Zal complains of his fetters,
since his stars will advocate his cause before God who keeps us all. And
think of Rostam, who protected the Persian throne, and who was
prompt to undergo all hardships for Persia's sake: it is because of him
that this crown has come down to you, not because of Goshtasp and
Esfandyar. Consider, from the time of Kay Qobad to that of Kay
Khosrow, it was because of his sword that the kings were able to reign.
If you are wise you will free Zal from his chains, and turn your heart
away from evil paths."

When the king heard Pashutan's advice, he regretted the pain he
had caused, and his old longing for revenge. A cry went up from the
royal pavilion: "My noble chieftains, prepare for our return to Iran
and stop this rampage of plunder and killing." He gave orders that
Zal's legs were to be freed from their fetters, and, as Pashutan sug-
gested, he had a tomb built for the slain Faramarz. Zal was brought

from the prison to his palace, and there his wife Rudabeh wept bit-
terly when she saw him, saying:

> *"Alas for Rostam, for his noble race,*
> *Our hero lies in his last resting place,*
> *And when he lived, who could have guessed or known*
> *That Goshtasp would ascend the royal throne?*
> *His wealth is gone, his father's now a slave,*
> *His noble son lies murdered in the grave.*
> *May no one ever know such grief, or see*
> *The fateful sorrows that have come to me!*
> *My curses on them: may the earth be freed*
> *From Bahman and his evil father's seed!"*

News of her rage reached Bahman and Pashutan, and Pashutan
grieved to hear of Rudabeh's pain: his cheeks turned sallow with grief
and he said to Bahman, "O king, when the moon has passed her zenith
tonight, as dawn comes on, lead your army away from here. This busi-
ness has grown weighty and serious: I pray that those who wish you
evil cannot harm your crown, and that all your days may be passed in
joy and festivities. My lord, it would be better if you remained in Zal's
palace no longer."

When the mountain tops turned red in the rising sun, the din of
drums rang out from the court, and Bahman, who had looked for
vengeance for so long, commanded that the army be drawn up in
marching order. Drums, trumpets, and Indian bells sounded in the
royal pavilion, and the army set out for home, as Pashutan had sug-
gested. When they reached Iran Bahman rested at last, and sat himself
on the imperial throne. He gave himself to the business of govern-
ment, distributing money to the poor; and some were pleased with his
reign, while others lived in grief and sorrow.

*B*ahman, now also referred to as Ardeshir, had a son called Sasan. He also had a beautiful daughter named Homay, with whom he fell in love, and he slept with her, "according to the custom called Pahlavi." When Homay was six months pregnant, Bahman became ill, and, realizing he was going to die, he resigned his throne to Homay and her heirs.

> But when Sasan heard this, in rage and shame,
> He fled to Nayshapour, forsook his fame,
> And inconspicuously lived out his life.
> A well-born local girl became his wife
> And she in time bore him a son, whom he
> Named Sasan too. Then, unexpectedly,
> The elder Sasan died. The son was wise
> But poverty obscured him from men's eyes
> And as a shepherd he was forced to keep
> The King of Nayshapour's rich flocks of sheep.

From this lowly shepherd would come the last of the great pre-Islamic dynasties of Iran, the Sasanians.

THE STORY OF
DARAB AND THE FULLER

Homay Entrusts Her Son to the Euphrates

Bahman, also called Ardeshir, fell sick and died, and the throne became vacant. Homay, his daughter, who was pregnant by him, placed the crown on her own head and began a new reign. She reviewed the army and distributed wealth from her treasury, and as she inaugurated her rule she announced to the world her justice and generosity. Calling down blessings on the crown and throne, she cursed any who wished her ill, promised that she would act benevolently and harm no one, that she would help the poor, and that the rich and powerful had nothing to fear from her. Her wisdom and justice surpassed her father's, and the world flourished beneath her righteous reign.

When the time came for her to give birth, she hid herself away from the army and townsfolk. She enjoyed the fact that the throne was hers, and that the world was in her hands. Her son was born in secret, and she told no one, keeping the boy hidden. Secretly she entrusted the prince to a nobly born wet nurse and told anyone who had got wind of his birth that the boy had died. And so she kept the crown on her own head, victorious and happy in her occupancy of the throne. She sent her armies against powerful enemies wherever they sprang up, and nothing good or bad that happened in the world remained hidden from her. Everywhere, she pursued justice and righteousness and ruled well. The world became safe under her care, and the people of every country praised her.

So eight months passed, but then the young prince began to resemble the dead king. Homay ordered a trustworthy carpenter to choose wood that could be delicately carved. She had him make a small chest, which was smeared outside with pitch, musk, and wax, and lined with soft brocade from Greece. A little mattress sewn with precious pearls

was placed inside, and red gold together with rubies and emeralds were
lavishly scattered there. A jeweled clasp was fastened to the still
unweaned prince's arm.

> Then while the unsuspecting baby slept
> His nurse embraced him and profusely wept;
> She laid the boy to whom she'd fed her milk
> Within the chest, beneath a shawl of silk.
> The lid was fastened down with pitch and musk;
> Now, silently, as night succeeded dusk,
> They took the casket to the riverside
> And launched it on the quickly flowing tide.
> Two men detailed to watch it through the night
> Were forced to run to keep the chest in sight—
> It bobbed along as if it were a boat.
> The broad Euphrates kept the craft afloat
> And bore it downstream on its watery way
> Until the sunrise brought another day.

A Fuller Brings Up Homay's Son

At dawn the chest bumped against the riverbank. It had reached a
place where the river had been deliberately narrowed, and stones had
been placed in the channel; fullers worked there, washing and bleach-
ing clothes. One of them caught sight of the little craft and ran over
to free it from where it had stuck. When he opened the chest, and
drew aside the rich cloths within, he was astonished at what he saw.
He wrapped the chest in the clothes he'd been washing and ran home
with it, full of hopes that this would mean a change in his fortunes.
Meanwhile, the men detailed to watch what happened to the chest
quickly went back to the palace and reported to Homay all that had
occurred. The queen told them that they must not reveal to anyone
else what they had seen.

When the man who had found the chest arrived at his house unex-
pectedly, his wife said, "What brings you home at this time, with the
clothes all wet still? Who's going to pay you for work like that?"

It happened that the couple had had a fine baby boy who had
recently died, and the fuller's heart was still grieving for his lost child;

his wife too was still weeping and groaning, and had scratched her face with her nails in her grief. The man said to her, "Come on now, pull yourself together, all this crying and moaning isn't doing you any good. Now, promise you'll keep a secret, my dear, and I'll tell you something worth hearing. Next to the boulder where I beat the clothes, where I throw the clean clothes into the water to rinse them, I saw a little chest stuck in the channel, and hidden inside it was a baby. When I opened the lid and saw the little mite inside I could scarcely believe my eyes. Our own little one died after a short life, but now you've found another son, and there's money with him and all manner of finery."

Then he set the clothes down on the floor, unwrapped them, and opened the chest; his wife stared in astonishment and called down God's blessings on the baby over and over again. She stared at the infant's shining face, which looked like Ardeshir's, nestled in the silk, and at the pearls sewn into the mattress, the rubies and emeralds by his feet, the red gold piled on his left, and the royal jewels to his right. Quickly, overwhelmed with joy, she set the baby to her milk-filled breast; the little child and the wealth that was with him made her forget all her sorrows. Her husband said to her, "We must always protect this child, even at the risk of our own lives. He must be the son of someone important; perhaps he's one of the world's princes." The fuller's wife cared for the child as if he were her own. On the third day they named the child, and because he had been plucked from flowing water [ab], they called him Darab.

One day the fuller's wife, who was a sensible woman, said to him, "What are you going to do about the jewels? What do you think would be the wisest course?" He answered, "My dear, hidden jewels are no more use to me than dirt is. It's better that we leave this town and all our past poverty and difficulties behind. We should go to a town where people don't know whether we're rich or poor." The next morning they packed up their household and quitted their home, and they gave their country no further thought. They carried Darab in their arms and took with them the jewels and gold, and that was all. They traveled for about two hundred miles, and then settled in a town where they were strangers. Here they lived as relatively well-to-do people, being careful to placate the local lord with gifts of jewels, and he sent them cloth and cash in return. The wife, who was always giving her husband advice, said to him, "We don't need to work any more: you're a rich man now, and you needn't worry about looking for a trade to follow." But the fuller answered, "My dear, you're a sensible woman and you give good advice, but what's better than what you call a 'trade'? A trade is the best thing a man can have. And yours is to bring up Darab properly and well, until we see what fate has in store for him." They brought up the child with such care and tenderness that no harsh wind ever harmed him.

In a few years he grew into a fine boy, strong, and with the royal *farr* visible in him. He'd challenge older boys in the street to wrestling matches and none of them were his equals in strength; then they'd rush at him in a group, but he would defeat them all. The fuller became exasperated with him. His own fortunes had declined, and he ordered the boy to beat clothes against the rocks with him, saying there was no shame in this. And when Darab ran away from the work, the man wept tears of rage and grief. He had to spend a good part of each day looking for the boy, either in the town or out on the plain. Once he found him with a bow in his hand and a thumbstall to protect his thumb as he loosed the arrows. He took the bow from him and coldly said, "You're acting like a vicious, uncontrollable wolf: what business can you have with a bow and arrow? Why have you become such a troublesome young man?"

> And Darab answered, "Father, why must you
> Muddy the stream of everything I do?
> Send me to someone learnèd, one who teaches
> The customs that the Zend-Avesta preaches;
> Then you can put me to a trade. But don't
> Think I'll be settled yet, because I won't."

The fuller remonstrated with him for a long time but finally sent him to a group of teachers, where he learned to be a cultivated young man and stopped being so abusive and stubborn. Nevertheless he told his father, "I'm not cut out to wash clothes; stop worrying about me. The one thing I want in the world is to be a horseman." His father found a fine horseman, a man with a good reputation as a horse-tamer who was also skillful with the bridle. He sent his son to him, and there Darab learned all that pertained to horsemanship: the use of the bridle, lance, and shield, how to control a horse in battle, how to play polo, how to shoot with a bow from the saddle, how to seek honor, and how to evade the enemy's reach.

Darab Questions the Fuller's Wife About Himself and Becomes a Knight

One day Darab said to his father, "There's something I've kept hidden. I don't feel any instinctive love for you, and your face doesn't resemble mine at all. It always surprises me when you call me 'son' and when you make me sit with you at your work." The fuller answered, "These words of yours bring back old sorrows. If you feel your nature is above mine, then go and find your father. Your mother knows the secret of all that business." And when the fuller left one day for the river, Darab locked the house door and came before his mother with a sword in his hand. He said to her, "Don't try any tricks or lies; give me an honest answer to everything I'm going to ask you. How am I related to you? Whose family do I belong to? And why am I living here with someone who washes clothes?"

The man's wife was terrified and begged Darab not to harm her. Invoking God to protect her, she said, "Don't spill my blood; I'll tell you everything you've asked." And then she described without prevarication all that had occurred, telling him about the chest containing the unweaned baby and about the coins and royal jewels. She went on, "We were folk who worked with our hands; we weren't from a wealthy family. All we have in the way of fine clothes and wealth is from you. We served you and brought you up, but it's for you to give the orders. We are yours body and soul, and you must decide what's to be done."

Darab was amazed when he heard all this, and he brooded for a while before saying anything. Then he asked, "Is there any of the wealth left, or has your husband spent it all? We live wretchedly enough these days, but is there enough left to buy me a horse?" The woman answered, "There's more than enough left for that, and besides we've bought profitable woodland, orchards, and pasture." She gave him some money and showed him the jeweled clasp. Darab used the money to buy a fine horse, a cheap saddle, and a lariat.

There was a great lord of the marches living in the neighborhood, a dignified and wise man able to give good guidance. His soul trou-

bled by dark thoughts, Darab presented himself before this man, who
took him into his service and saw that he came to no harm. It so hap-
pened that an army from the west attacked and began plundering the
area. The lord was killed in battle, and his troops were left leaderless.
When Homay heard this she sent her general, Reshnavad, to drive the
enemy back and to destroy their strongholds. Reshnavad gathered an
army and inspected and provisioned it. Darab was overjoyed at the
news of the expedition and hurried to register his name as a warrior.
Troops poured in from all sides, and when they were amassed Homay
and her military chiefs came out of the palace to watch the troops pass
by and be counted and to have their names checked. She caught sight
of Darab and the *farr* radiating from him. With his great strength and
the massive mace on his shoulders, it seemed as though only he were
on the plain, and that the ground was there merely to bear his
warhorse. And as she stared at his chest and his handsome face, her
maternal breasts flowed with milk. She said to one of her entourage,
"Where is that knight from? The one who seems to be such a strong,
splendid young man? He looks like a nobleman, like a knight who's
experienced in warfare, brave, proud, and dignified, but his weapons
aren't worthy of him."

The army met with her approval, and she selected an auspicious day
for them to begin the campaign. The leaders agreed on their strategy and
led the army away. Homay sent her agents with them, so that nothing
that transpired would be hidden from her and she would know every-
thing that went on in the army, whether of good or evil, and her wor-
ries would be laid to rest. The army set out, filling the plain, marching
by stages beneath the moon.

Reshnavad Learns the Truth About Darab

One day a violent wind began to blow; thunder crashed and the sky
was filled with rain and lightning. The land was awash with water, and
the army fled in all directions, trying to get out of the rain and look-
ing for places to pitch their tents. The commander Reshnavad was
worried by this turn of events. Darab too was bewildered by what was
happening and tried to escape from the heavy rain. He saw a mass of
ruins with an archway that was still standing. High, ancient, and crum-
bling, it looked as if it had once been part of a royal edifice. Darab had
no palace hall or women's quarters at his disposal, not even a tent or a

companion or pack animals; he was alone and friendless, and he had no choice but to sleep beneath the crumbling archway.

While Reshnavad was trying to round up his scattered troops he happened to pass by the archway, and he heard a roaring sound coming from the ruins that seemed to say,

> "O ruined arch, be on your guard and keep
> The Persian king you shelter safe in sleep;
> He had no tent or friend, and so he lies
> Beneath you, sheltering from the stormy skies."

Reshnavad said to himself, "Is that the noise of thunder, or is it the howling wind?" And then he heard the roar again,

> "O arch, keep wisdom's eyes awake, take care,
> King Ardeshir's young son lies sleeping there."

And the roar sounded for a third time, at which he turned in astonishment to an advisor and said, "What can this mean? Someone should go and investigate who is sleeping under that arch." A group went and saw a young man lying there; he looked both wise and warrior-like, but his clothes and horse were soaking wet and filthy, and his bed was the black earth. When Reshnavad was told what they had seen, the commander's heart beat faster and he said, "Call him here quickly: who could endure to hear such a roar as we heard?" They went back and called out, "Hey, you lying asleep on the ground, wake up, get on your feet!" As Darab mounted his horse, the arch collapsed. Reshnavad fixed his eyes on Darab, scanning him from head to toe, and said, "This is a marvel among marvels, nothing more wonderful could be imagined." Then he hurried the young man to his pavilion, praising God as they went. He ordered clothes to be brought and a place to be set aside for Darab. They lit a large fire on which they burned sandalwood, musk, and ambergris.

When the sun rose above the mountain top, Reshnavad took a complete set of clothes, a saddled horse with a golden bridle, a bow, and a sword in a golden sheath to Darab. As he presented them, he said to the young man, "You're lionhearted, a fine young man eager for fame, but who are you, what's your lineage, and what country are you from? It would be best for you to tell me the truth." Darab told Reshnavad everything, just as the woman he had thought was his mother had explained it to him. He told him about the chest and the rubies, the jeweled clasp on his arm, the gold coins, the brocade in which he had been wrapped, and his sleep in the casket where he had been concealed. At once Reshnavad said to a messenger, "Go like the wind and bring the fuller and his wife here; bring me this Mars and Venus, both of them."

The army then marched to the frontier with Greece, and Darab was made leader of the advance guard, the tips of whose spears had been dipped in poison. They met with the vanguard of a Greek force patrolling the borderlands. Suddenly the two armies were face to face, and the dust of battle rose into the sky. They fought hand to hand, and blood flowed like a river. Quick as wind-blown dust, Darab urged his horse into the melée and killed so many of the enemy soldiers that it seemed as if heaven itself wielded his sword. It was as if a lion attacked, a lion grasping a monster as a weapon and with a dragon for his mount. The lion pressed on to the Greek camp, guided by his sword's search for victims, till the earth was awash with a sea of Greek blood. Having routed the enemy forces Darab returned in triumph to his commander. Reshnavad showered him with praise and said, "May the royal army never lack your presence. When we get back to civilization from this Greek expedition, you'll be richly rewarded by the queen; she'll give you horses, seal rings, swords, and diadems." All night the army prepared its armor and horses for the coming day, and when the sun rose, illuminating the land like a lamp, the two armies met again and the dust of their encounter darkened the sun. Darab launched his attack, releasing the reins of his charger. He slew all the champions who rode forward from the Greek ranks and like a wolf made for their army's heart, scattering the huge force before him. From there he turned against their right flank, plundering weapons and baggage as he went, with their troops fleeing from him pell-mell. The Persian warriors followed in his wake like lions, killing so many of the Greek troops that the ground turned to a quagmire with their blood. Darab killed forty of their priests and returned to his own lines with a captured cross in his fist. When Reshnavad saw the wonders Darab performed, his heart bounded with joy; again he showered Darab with praise, adding words of affection as well. Then night came on, the world turned black as pitch, and everyone turned back from the battlefield.

Reshnavad made his headquarters in the captured Greek camp; there he rested and loosened his sword belt. When it came to the distribution of plunder, he first sent someone to Darab, telling him to take what he would like and to distribute the rest as he saw fit, as he was a finer warrior than even the great Rostam. Darab chose a fine lance and passed everything else back to Reshnavad, wishing him victory and joy in the days to come.

After sunset, as darkness spread, it was as if a cloth of black brocade had covered the army. The commander made the rounds of the camp guards, and their shouts re-echoed in the darkness like the rumbling of an earthquake, or the roar of a wild lion. When the sun lifted its golden shield again, the sleeping warriors woke, donned their armor once more, and set off in pursuit of the Greek forces. They torched the towns they came on, and the name of Greece was obliterated from the land. Lamenting was heard throughout Greece for the loss of territory: its king felt himself hemmed in by the world's fury, and his noblemen turned pale with shame and fear. His messenger arrived before Reshnavad, saying, "May your queen be just to us: we who desired war are exhausted by it, and Greece's fortunes have declined. If you desire us to pay taxes, we will pay them; let us renew the peace treaty between us." The Greek king also sent gifts of many kinds, in addition to numerous slaves bearing purses of cash. Reshnavad accepted whatever was sent, which included gold coins and uncut jewels.

Homay Recognizes Her Son

Darab and Reshnavad returned in triumph to the ruined arch where Darab had been found sleeping. Filled with fear and foreboding, the man who had found him in the chest, together with his wife, who had brought the jeweled clasp, were waiting for them, and as the two of them were called forward, they entrusted themselves to God's protection. Reshnavad questioned them closely, and they told him all they could remember about the chest and the uncut jewel. Reshnavad said to them,

> *"May you be prosperous now and live in glory,*
> *For no one's ever heard so strange a story,*
> *No priest or chronicler has ever told*
> *A tale like this the two of you unfold."*

Immediately he wrote to Homay, telling her of Darab's sleep in the
ruin and of his valor on the battlefield, of how the moment he
mounted his horse the arch collapsed, of how a voice had resounded
from the arch, and of the dread that he, Reshnavad, had felt on hear-
ing it. Then he added all that the fuller had said concerning the chest,
the baby it contained, and the riches. Next, he summoned a messen-
ger, gave him the red jeweled clasp, and said, "Make the wind your
partner as you travel." The man brought the jewel to Homay, handed
over the letter, and told the queen what he had heard from
Reshnavad's lips. And when she saw the jewel and read the letter, tears
spilled from her eyelashes. She knew that the tall, splendid young man
with a face as fresh as the springtime, the man she had seen that day
she reviewed the troops drawn up on the plain, was none other than
her own son, a noble shoot of her own stock. Weeping, she said to
the messenger, "A master has come to the world. My mind has never
been free from care; I have been filled with anxiety for the empire,
fearing God and brooding on my ingratitude to him."

Coins were liberally distributed, wine, musk, and jewels were
mixed together, and for a week the doors of Homay's treasury stood
open to relieve the poor. Wealth was given to all her provinces, and on
the tenth day her army commander, together with his officers and
Darab, entered the court. But nothing had been divulged concerning
Darab's identity.

For a week, by the queen's order, the curtain signifying that the court
was closed to outsiders remained in place. She had a golden dais pre-
pared, as well as two thrones studded with turquoise and lapis lazuli, a
crown encrusted with royal jewels, two armbands, a jeweled torque, and
royal clothes woven with gold and jewels. An astrologer sat before the
queen, calculating the most propitious day for what she planned. Then,
on the fourth day of the month of Bahman, the queen gave audience to
Darab. She filled a bowl with rubies and another with topaz stones. As
Darab approached she came forward and made her obeisance before
him; she scattered the precious stones before him and, turning aside,
wept bitterly. She clasped her son tightly to her breast, kissing him and
running her fingers over his face; then she led him to the golden dais and
stared at him in wonder. When he had taken his place on the throne,
Homay brought the royal crown and placed it on his head, and in this

way proclaimed his coronation to the world. As light flashed from the crown, Homay begged forgiveness for the past, asking him to consider all that had happened as the wind that passes by: her youth and sudden wealth and woman's wiles, his father dead, and her position as a queen bereft of good counsel. She hoped he would pardon her evil deed, and from now on occupy no seat but the throne.

The young prince answered his mother, "You are descended from champions, and it's no surprise that ambition bubbled up in your heart. Why should you weep and wail so much for one bad act? May the Creator be pleased with you, and may the hearts of those who wish you ill be filled with smoke and dust. The things you talk about will ensure that I'm remembered, and my story will never grow old." Then Homay in her splendor called down blessings on his head and said, "May you endure as long as the world endures!"

Then the chief priest was called, and the wise men of every province, together with the army's warlike chieftains: all were commanded to hail Darab as their sovereign, and as they did so, jewels were scattered over the throne. Homay confessed to what she had done in secret, and to the terrible suffering this had caused her. "Know," she said, "that in all the world this prince is the sole heir to King Bahman: everyone must obey him, for he is the shepherd and his warriors are his sheep. Greatness, sovereignty and military might belong to him, and it is your duty to support him." A shout of joy went up from the palace, and men said that they had seen a new shoot of the royal stock. So many gifts were brought from all sides that the young king was almost smothered by them: the world was filled with rejoicing and justice, and old sufferings were forgotten. Homay said to the priests, "I have handed over the empire and all its wealth to him, these things that have caused me such sorrow for thirty-two years. Rejoice and obey him, and take no breath without his advice."

Darab took his place on the throne with pleasure and wore the crown in contentment. Then the fuller and his wife appeared, and cried out, "Young prince, may the royal throne bring you good luck, and may your enemies' heads be severed at the neck!" Darab ordered that ten purses of gold and a goblet of jewels, together with five bolts of various cloths, be given to them for all they had done and suffered. He said to the man, "Keep to your trade, and stay always alert: it may be that you'll find a chest with a little prince in it!" The couple left the court calling down blessings on the king; the fuller's fate was fulfilled, and he returned to his trade and the alkali ashes with which he cleaned clothes.

The Reign of Darab

When Darab was crowned he prepared himself to be a warrior and a generous benefactor to his people. He addressed his priests, counselors, and chieftains: "I did not scheme and struggle to rule the earth; God placed the crown on my head. No one in the world has ever heard a more remarkable tale than mine, and I know of no greater reward for justice than to be praised after my death. No one must suffer because of my ambition, or because I accumulate wealth. May the land prosper through my justice, and my subjects live in happiness." Representatives came from India and Greece and from every inhabited country, bringing gifts and wishing the new king health and prosperity.

Darab Defeats Sho'ayb

And then a hundred thousand warlike Arabs attacked, under the leadership of a chieftain from the Qotayb tribe, called Sho'ayb. The king of Iran mustered innumerable troops, and when the two armies met, the world was filled with terror and destruction. The earth could hardly bear the weight of such forces, and such was the press of troops that no one could find a way through them. The land was awash with blood from the rain of javelins and arrows; cries resounded from all sides, and everywhere heaps of dead bodies could be seen. The battle lasted for three days and nights, and both sides were hard pressed, but on the fourth night the Arabs turned tail, abandoning the battlefield. Sho'ayb had been killed in the fighting, and the tide of battle had turned against the Arabs. In their flight they left behind many Arab horses with their poplar wood saddles, as well as lances, swords, and helmets. Homay's son distributed the plunder to his soldiers and chose a man from the army who understood Arabic to be lord of the marches. He sent this man to the plains where the Arabs lived, to demand that year's and the previous year's tribute.

Darab Fights Against Filqus and Marries His Daughter

After Darab had defeated the Arabs, he marched his army against Greece. The king there was a man called Filqus, who was in league with the king of Susa. This man wrote to Filqus, saying that Homay's son was attacking with an enormous army. When the Greek king heard this, he remembered the ancient feud between the two countries and gathered together an army of experienced warriors from the district of Amourieh. As Darab approached, the Greek nobles abandoned the border areas, while Filqus led his army down from Amourieh. Two fierce battles were fought during three days, but as the sun rose on the fourth day Filqus's army broke ranks and fled, leaving behind even their helmets and Greek headgear. Their women and children were taken prisoner, and a number of men were put to the sword or killed with arrows. Filqus's retreating army had been reduced by a third and the remnant traveled with their lances strapped on their backs. They took refuge in the fortress at Amourieh, and most of them were ready to sue for peace.

A messenger from Filqus arrived before Darab. He was a wise, intelligent man, with the airs and graces of a courtier. He brought slaves, purses of coins, two chests filled with jewels, and the following message:

> "I ask one thing from God, who is my guide,
> That we should look for peace, and put aside
> Our ruinous deceit and enmity;
> Come, let us promise mutual amity.
> But if you think that in some covert way
> You'll take my capital, Amourieh,
> There'll be no banquet to confirm our pact.
> Honor will make me fight if I'm attacked.
> Do what befits a king: your father knew
> How kings conduct themselves, and so do you."

When Darab had heard him out he summoned his nobles and laid the matter before them, asking them what they thought of such talk, by which Filqus hoped to save face. They answered, "O perspicacious and pure-hearted king, lord of all lords, whose choice is to do that which is best: this chieftain has a daughter, elegant as a cypress tree, her face as fresh as springtime. No one has ever seen any idol in China as lovely as she is, she outshines all others in her beauty. If the king sees her, she will please him: this cypress would be well placed in his garden."

The king called in the Greek messenger, repeated what he had

heard from his advisors, and said, "Go to your king and tell him this:
'There is a young woman in your palace, who is the crown of all
princesses; you call her Nahid, and you have assigned her a golden
throne. If you want to preserve your honor and keep your country
untroubled, give her to me, along with the tribute that Greece owes.'"
The messenger traveled like the wind and repeated the message to the
Greek king, who was overjoyed that his son-in-law would be the
Persian king. There was some discussion about the tribute to be paid,
but finally it was agreed that each year Greece would hand over a hun-
dred thousand eggs made of gold, each weighing forty *mesqal*s, and
studded with jewels.

Filqus gave orders that the roads to the borders of Greece be dec-
orated, and then a magnificent escort bearing gifts set out with his
daughter. They had prepared a golden litter and gathered together a
group of noble attendants for her. There were ten camels carrying
Greek brocade embroidered with jewels and gold, together with three
hundred camel loads of carpets and necessities for the journey. The
princess remained in her litter, guided by a bishop and a monk. Behind
her came sixty maidservants, each of them adorned with a diadem and
earrings and carrying a golden goblet filled with jewels. The bishop
handed the beautiful princess over to Darab, and the jewels were
counted out to his treasurer. After this Darab quit the military camp
where he had been waiting and led his army back to Persia. He placed
a crown on the princess's head, and they set out happily for Pars.

The Birth of Sekandar

One night this lovely moon, arrayed in jewels and scents, lay sleeping
beside the king. Suddenly she sighed deeply, and the king turned his
head away, offended by the smell of her breath. This bad odor sickened
him, and he frowned, wondering what could be done about it. He sent
knowledgeable doctors to her; one who was especially expert was able
to find a remedy. There is an herb that burns the palate, which they call
"Sekandar" in Greece, and he rubbed this against the roof of her
mouth. She wept a few tears and her face turned as red as brocade,
because it burned her mouth, but the ugly smell was gone. But
although this beautiful woman's breath was now as sweet as musk, the
king no longer felt any love for her. His heart had grown cold toward

his bride, and he sent her back to Filqus. The princess grieved, because she was pregnant, but she told no one of this.

When nine months had gone by she gave birth to a boy as splendid as the sun. Because of his stature and splendor, and the sweet smell that his flesh exhaled, she named him Sekandar, after the herb that had cured her of her malady. Her father the king told everyone that the boy was his and made no mention of Darab, because he was ashamed to tell people that Darab had rejected his daughter. The same night that Sekandar was born, a cream-colored mare in the royal stables, a huge warlike horse, gave birth to a gray foal with a lion-like chest and short pasterns. Filqus took this as a good omen, raising his hands to the heavens in gratitude. At dawn the next day he had both the newborn child and the mare and her foal brought to him and passed his hands over the foal's eyes and chest, because he was exactly the same age as Sekandar.

So the heavens turned and the years passed. Sekandar grew to have a princely heart, and his speech was that of a warrior. Filqus treated him even more attentively than a son and loved to dress him as a champion. In a little while the boy gained in wisdom; he became adroit, intelligent, grave in his manner, and knowledgeable. He was made the kingdom's crown prince, and Filqus delighted in his presence. Sekandar learned the arts of kingship from his teachers, and it seemed he was born to administer justice, to occupy a throne, and to found an empire.

In Persia, after Nahid had returned to her father, Darab took another wife. She gave birth to a fine, princely son who was a year younger than Sekandar. On the day he was born he was named Dara, and it was hoped that his good fortune would be greater than his father's. Then, after twelve years, Darab's star declined: he grew sick and wasted away and knew he would be called to another place. He summoned his nobles and counselors and spoke to them at length about the business of government and kingship. Then he added: "Dara, my son, will guide you well. Listen to him and obey him, and may your souls know peace in obedience to his commands. This royal throne is no one's for long, and in the midst of pleasure we are called away. Strive to be kind and just, and rejoice when you remember me." Having said this he heaved a sigh from the depths of his being, and the rosy pomegranate petal turned as pale as fenugreek.

SEKANDAR'S CONQUEST OF PERSIA

The Reign of Dara

Dara grieved for his father's death, and exalted the royal crown of Persia above the sun. He was young, fiery-tempered, quick to take offense, and his heart and tongue were hard enough to blunt a sword. From the throne he addressed his court: "Noblemen and warriors, I do not want my head to be brought down into the pit of servitude, and I will summon no one who is in that pit to approach my throne. Any man who ignores my commands can consider his head as no longer attached to his body, and if anyone so much as murmurs in his heart against me, my sword shall deal with him. No rich man is to use his wealth contrary to my wishes. I need no counselors: I am my own counselor and responsible for my own well-being. The pleasure, treaties, greatness, and sovereignty of the world are mine." He summoned a learned scribe and after some discussion had him write a letter as trenchant as a dagger, in the name of Dara, the son of Darab, the son of Ardeshir, to every other king and independent ruler. The letter read: "Whoever opposes my policies or orders will learn how I can lop off heads. Whether you command souls or your soul is commanded by others, see that you obey my edicts."

Then he opened his father's treasuries, summoned his warriors, and distributed their pay. He raised the stipend of those who had received four coins to eight, paying one man with a goblet full of coins, another with a bowlful. He gave experienced commanders border provinces as gifts and saw that everyone in his army received something of value. Representatives bearing presents and tribute came from all countries and kings, from India, China, Greece, and other lands, since no one felt able to stand against him. He built a city called Noshad—New

Happiness—and the province of Ahvaz rejoiced in his reign. He was just to the poor, and he distributed wealth to whoever asked him.

The Death of Filqus: Sekandar Becomes King

It was at about this time that Filqus died, and Greece mourned for him. Sekandar ascended his grandfather's throne and was a man who sought good and impeded the reach of evil. There was a famous man named Arestalis in Greece, in whom the whole country rejoiced: he was a wise, intelligent, and resourceful person. This man came before Sekandar and said, "Fortune smiles on you now my lord, but even you can lose your fame. The royal throne has seen so many kings like you, and it belongs to no one forever. Whenever you say to yourself, 'I have reached my goal, I need no one to guide me in this world,' know that at that moment, when you will not listen to a wise counselor's words, you are the stupidest of men. We are made and born from dust, and we have no choice but to return to dust. If you act well, your name will survive you and you will prosper during your reign; and if you sow evil, you will reap evil, and not sleep easily in this world for a single night."

> *King Sekandar approved of what he said*
> *And instantly decided he'd be led*
> *In banquets and in battles by this guide,*
> *And see that he was always at his side.*

Then one day an eloquent and courteous messenger arrived from Dara, asking that Greece's tribute be paid. But Sekandar became angry at the thought of this tax he'd inherited and said, "Go and tell Dara that the time for tribute from us is over. The hen that laid those golden eggs has died and there's no more tribute to be had." When he heard such language, the messenger was terrified and scuttled away from Greece. Sekandar, meanwhile, gathered an army together, told them of what had happened, and said, "Not even a good man can escape the turning of the heavens. I must travel the face of the earth, and reckon up what there is of good and evil in the world. And now you must prepare yourselves to bid your country farewell." He opened the doors of his grandfather's treasury and had his army equipped. At dawn an uproar could be heard outside the young king's court: he set out followed by his ban-

ner, on which images of the bird of royal fortune, the homa, and the
beloved cross were embroidered in red on a turquoise ground.

The Greek army bore down on Egypt, and so thick were their
ranks that not a mosquito or an ant could find a way through them.
For a week the armies fought, and on the eighth day Sekandar defeated
the Egyptian forces. So many prisoners and so much plunder were
taken that the victors were at a loss as to what to do with everything:
there were maces and horses, warriors' armor and horse armor, Indian
swords in golden scabbards, golden belts and golden saddles, brocade
and more coins than their pack horses could carry; as well as the innu-
merable chieftains and horsemen who surrendered to them.

From there this lionhearted warrior stretched out his claws toward
Persia. When Dara heard that the Greek army was threatening his coun-
try's frontiers he set out toward Greece with an army from Estakhr, and
so numerous were its lances that they impeded the winds as they blew.
When his men reached the Euphrates, their number was greater than
the blades of grass on its shores; the river's water was invisible beyond
the press of their armor.

Sekandar Acts as His Own Envoy

Sekandar heard of the Persian troops' approach and set out to meet
them. When there were about two parasangs' distance between the two
armies, he summoned his counselors. But after a while he tired of their
talk and said,

> *"There's only one way forward in this case:*
> *I'll go myself and meet him face to face.*
> *I'll be my own ambassador, and see*
> *The strengths and weakness of my enemy."*

He put on a jeweled belt and a royal cloak worked with gold figures;
his mount had a golden saddle, from which hung a golden scabbard.
He picked ten Greek advisors who were skilled in languages to accom-
pany him, and he and his chieftains and interpreters set off at dawn.

As he approached Dara he dismounted and greeted the Persian
king respectfully. Dara called him forward and motioned him to a seat
at a lower level than the throne. Dara's nobles were astonished by the
handsome young man's stature and splendor and by his courteous

behavior. Silently, to themselves, they called down blessings on his head. He sat where Dara had indicated, then he rose and, as if he were a mere envoy, produced a letter from Sekandar. He began by wishing the king an eternal reign and then continued:

> "I have no wish to seize your country, nor
> To fight against you on the plains of war;
> My aim's to travel round the earth, to see
> The spacious world in its entirety.
> I look for justice, and I understand
> That you are sovereign over Persia's land,
> But if my progress here is not allowed
> I can't go forward like an airborne cloud.
> You've come here with an army, unaware
> Of Sekandar's intentions: but beware,
> If you desire to fight with me, I'll fight—
> I won't retreat in ignominious flight.
> Say when you're ready then: you name the day
> And see you don't forget or run away:
> No overwhelming force will make me yield
> When once my army's on the battlefield."

Dara heard him out, and it seemed to him as if this young man were Dara himself, seated on the ivory throne, with the royal torque and armbands, resplendent with *farr*, and with the crown on his head. Dara answered him, "What's your name and lineage? The royal *farr* shines from your forehead as if you were a Kayanid prince. You're too fine a man to be anyone's subject: I think that you are Sekandar himself! With this *farr* and stature and eloquence of yours you seem born to sit on a throne." Sekandar answered, "Neither in peace nor in war has a king ever done what you're suggesting. There are plenty of fine talkers in my monarch's court; they're the crown of all wise men. Sekandar is wise enough to follow his ancestors and not to act as his own envoy. My commander gave me the message as I have delivered it to you, your majesty."

A suitable pavilion was prepared for his stay, and when the evening meal was served Dara had the Greek envoy summoned to eat with him. Once they had eaten, musicians were called and wine was served.

As soon as he had drunk his wine, Sekandar secreted the goblet beneath his clothes, and he did this a number of times. The cupbearer went to Dara and said, "Your Greek guest can't be separated from the goblets I serve him." Dara told him to ask why he kept the goblets in this way. "Why, my lion lord," said the cupbearer, "are you keeping the goblets I give you?" Sekandar answered, "And isn't his goblet the envoy's reward? But if the custom is different in Persia, then take them back and place them in your king's treasury." Dara laughed to hear of such a custom, and had a goblet filled with jewels, surmounted by a splendid ruby, handed to him.

Just at that moment the men who had gone to Greece to demand tribute arrived at the gathering. Their leader saw Sekandar's face and as soon as he had made his obeisance before the king he said, "That man is the great Sekandar, whom I saw seated on his throne, crowned and holding the royal mace. As the king had ordered, we went to him and asked for our tribute: he humiliated me and talked insultingly about your majesty. We fled from his realm on horseback, by night. I saw no one like him in all of Greece, and now he has had the audacity to come to this country. He means to deprive you of your army, wealth, throne, and crown." As he listened to the man's words, Dara stared intently at Sekandar, who knew very well what was passing between them. As the sun set in the west he made his way to the tent he had been assigned, then, quickly mounting his horse, he said to his entourage, "Our lives depend on our horses: if they falter, we are finished." The group galloped away and were lost to sight in the darkness. Dara sent someone to Sekandar's tent, and as soon as it became clear that his guest had fled, he sent a thousand warriors after him. They rode like the wind, but in the darkness they lost their way, and when they caught sight of the Greek advance guards they turned back, having achieved nothing for all their pains.

Sekandar reached his own camp, and the Greek nobles crowded round to see their prince return under cover of darkness. He showed them four goblets and the jewels he'd been given, and said, "Give thanks for my good fortune: I earned these cups at the risk of my life, and the stars seconded my attempt. I reckoned up the number of their troops, who are far more numerous than we had heard. Draw your swords for combat. We must march forward across this plain, and if you suffer in the battle, think of the kingdoms and wealth you will win.

God is with me, and the stars are favorable to my plans." The nobles congratulated him and wished for world prosperity beneath his reign. They said, "We are ready to sacrifice our lives for you, and we shall never break this promise. Who of all kings could claim to be your equal in manliness, stature, or glory?"

Dara Makes War on Sekandar and Is Defeated

The sun rose over the mountains, and the land glowed like a golden lamp. Dara mustered the ranks of his army, which covered the earth like a pitch-black cloak. He led his men, more numerous than blades of grass, across the Euphrates, and when Sekandar heard of their approach, he had the war drums sounded and his troops prepared. The two hosts could not be counted, but in all the world there was only one Sekandar. Dust loomed over the scene like a mountain, and the whole plain seemed a seething sea of weapons and warriors, of armor and Indian daggers, of war horses and barding. On each side the troops were drawn up, and the sun flashed on their swords. In the vanguard were the war elephants, and behind them the cavalry, men who had renounced all love of life. The very air seemed to cry out for blood, the land to groan with the warriors' battle cries, the mountains to shake with the din of trumpets and Indian chimes. The horses' neighing and the combatants' shouts, the crashing of heavy maces on armor, all seemed to transform the plain to a mountain of warfare, and the air turned black with dust. For seven days the battle raged, and on the eighth a dust storm obscured the sun and blew against the blinded Persians, who fled from the battlefield. Sekandar's men pursued them—the one host full of sorrow, the other of joy—back to the banks of the Euphrates, where innumerable Persians were killed. At first the Greek troops turned back from the river, but Sekandar ordered them across, and they entered the abandoned Persian camp in triumph.

Dara's Second Battle Against Sekandar

When Dara fled from Sekandar, he sent mounted messengers in all directions, summoning Iran's chieftains and lords. He distributed money and had the army's quartermasters prepare to provision new troops. By the end of the month he had gathered a new army and renewed his commanders' warlike ambition. Once more he crossed the river and drew up his troops on the wide plain. As soon as Sekandar heard of this, he left his army's impedimenta in their camp and set out to face him. The two armies met and again the land was filled with the din of warfare. For three days they joined battle, until the heaped-up dead hemmed them in. Numberless Persians were slain, and the great king's good fortune deserted him. Full of sorrow, he turned back from the battle, since the lord of the moon gave him no help, but Sekandar pursued him as quickly as wind-blown dust, praising the world creator as he came. He had his heralds cry out to the Persians, "You are subjects who have been misled, but you have no need to fear me, and my army has no desire to meddle with you. Go home safely to your houses and live God-fearing lives. Even though you have washed your hands in Greek blood, you have escaped safe and sound from the Greek army." When the Persians heard they were being granted quarter, they submitted. Sekandar had the plunder heaped up on the battlefield and distributed to his troops, who now found themselves well equipped. He and his army rested in that area for four months.

Dara meanwhile reached Jahrom, where he had access to treasure. Filled with grief and sorrow, his nobles came before him; sons wept for their lost fathers, and fathers for their lost sons. All the land of Iran was filled with the sounds of mourning, and tears stood in all eyes like dew. From Jahrom Dara made his way to the pride of Persian cities, Estakhr. Again messengers were sent out to all quarters, and an army gathered before the king's palace. Dara sat there on a golden throne and his loyal troops paraded before him; then he addressed them:

> "My wise and warlike warriors, you see
> The straits we're in, you know our enemy."
> And as he spoke grief overwhelmed his voice.
> He wept, then said, "It is a better choice
> To die today as men, than to remain
> Alive and subject to an alien reign.
> The ancient kings who came before us here
> Were paid with foreign tribute every year.
> Once we were mighty, and in everything
> The Greek realm bowed before the Persian king.
> Our luck has turned, and Sekandar alone
> Will rule this land, and seize our crown and throne.

Soon he'll be here, too soon, and Persia then
Will be a sea of blood, this country's men,
Its women and its children, will be made
The captives of this conquering renegade.
But if you'll now make common cause with me
We can drive back this pain and misery.
These warriors were our prey once—filled with dread,
When Persia threatened, they turned tail and fled.
Now they're the leopard, we've become the prey,
When battle's joined it's we who run away.
But if we stand together we can still
Crush them and bend their country to our will.
Whoever falters in this war and tries
To save his selfish soul should realize
It is the world that will be lost or freed—
They are Zahhak, and we are now Jamshid."

He wept as he spoke; his heart was filled with pain, his cheeks were yellow, and his lips blue with suffering. His wise, grief-stricken nobles rose and shouted in answer, "We have no desire to live without the king; we are ready for battle, and we shall make the world a harsh place for those who wish you ill. We shall fight together, whether we conquer lands and provinces, or find only the earth of the grave." Dara distributed weapons and money to his army and to his country's chieftains.

The Third Battle Between Sekandar and Dara and Dara's Flight to Kerman

When Sekandar heard of Dara's renewed bid for sovereignty, he led his army out from Iraq, and as he marched he prayed to God in Greek. Sekandar's army had neither center nor limit, and Dara's good fortune had deserted him. Nevertheless Dara led his army out from Estakhr and his troops were so numerous that they seemed to block the turning of the stars in the sky. The armies of the two countries were drawn up in ranks, the men clutching their lances, maces, and daggers. Such a cry went up from both hosts that it seemed to split the ears of the heavens; the warriors' blood transformed the earth to a sea, and headless bodies lay strewn about the battlefield. For the third time Dara suffered defeat; Sekandar pressed forward with his attack, and in fear for his life Dara led his army toward Kerman. Sekandar meanwhile took up residence in Estakhr, the noblest of Persian cities, and from his court a bold proclamation was made:

> *"Whoever seeks out God's forgiveness for*
> *The deeds that he's committed in this war,*
> *Or looks for my protection, will soon find*
> *That I've a merciful and generous mind.*
> *I'll help the wounded, and I will not shed*
> *The blood of enemies who were misled.*
> *Since I'm aware the God of victory*
> *Has given this imperial crown to me,*
> *My hand won't touch what isn't mine; my soul*
> *Has chosen light and wisdom as its goal.*
> *But as for those who'd thwart my wishes, they*
> *Will find a dragon standing in their way."*

Then he distributed the plunder to his army.

By the time Dara reached Kerman, two-thirds of his forces were nowhere to be seen, and wailing was heard among his troops, who were helmetless and dejected. He called together the chieftains who had been with him in battle, all of whom were weeping and bemoaning their fate. Dara addressed them, "There can be no doubt that the heavens have turned against us because of me. No one in the world has ever seen such a defeat, nor have we heard of one like this from those who know the past. Our royal women and children are captives, or they have been murdered with lances and arrows. What can you see that might save us, or that might make those who hate us turn back from their course? No country, no army, no throne or crown, no sovereignty, no heirs, no treasure or forces remain to us. If God does not have pity on us now we are ruined forever."

The nobles wept before the king and said, "Your majesty, we have all been wounded by fate's malevolence. The army is beyond rallying, we are like men over whose helmets floodwaters are rising. Fathers have lost their sons and sons their fathers, and this is now the way of the turning heavens toward us. Our mothers, sisters, and daughters are in Sekandar's hands, and the veiled women of your court who trembled for your life, together with the ancestral treasures you inherited—the noble women of our people and the wealth of our kings—are all in the palm of the Greek conquerors. Your one hope is to conciliate him, for the crown does not stay always with one man. You will have to truckle to him and speak fair words to him, and then we shall see whether all this will end with fate looking more favorably on us. Write him a letter, and try to enlighten his dark soul. The heavens turn above him too, and a wise man will understand this." When he had heard them out, Dara did what seemed best to him and summoned a scribe.

Dara's Letter, Suing for Peace

This is the grief-filled letter he wrote, beginning: "From Dara, the son of Darab, the son of Ardeshir, to the conqueror, Sekandar." His cheeks gaunt with suffering, his eyes filled with tears, first Dara praised God, from whom come the good and evil of our days, then continued, "Certainly a wise man cannot escape the heavens' revolutions, since it is from them that we are fortunate or wretched, that we are sometimes lifted up and sometimes cast down. It wasn't human agency that decided this battle between us, but the dealings of the sun and the moon. Now what was fated has happened, and my heart is left in pain. What is it we can hope for from the blue vault above? Now if you will agree to sign a treaty with me, and repent of your war against Persia, I shall convey from my treasury to yours Goshtasp's and Esfandyar's treasures, including their royal torques and jewel-encrusted crowns, and also the treasures that I have accumulated by my own efforts. I shall be your ally in war, and day and night I shall be prompt in your service. If you will, send me my family members whom you now hold, my women and children—this is what I would expect of you, since a world conqueror is not a man to indulge in petty revenge, and great kings who enslave women receive nothing but reproaches. When my lord reads this letter, may he in his wisdom vouchsafe me an answer."

Quickly a messenger took the letter from Kerman to Sekandar, who was still hostile to Dara. But when he read it he said in answer, "May wisdom always be the companion of Dara's soul! Anyone who stretches out his hand toward your family, either against your women-folk or your children, will find that the only throne he will see will be his bier as he is laid in the grave, or he will be hanged from a tree limb. Your family is safe and comfortable in Esfahan, and God forbid that I should demand their wealth from them. If you come to Pars, all the sovereignty of this land is yours; I shall never swerve aside from what you say, and I shall not so much as breathe without asking your advice." Like a skiff over the waves the messenger sped back to his king, whose eyes were filled with tears, his heart with grief.

Dara Is Killed by His Entourage

When Dara read this answer he saw the straits that the world had brought him to and was struck dumb. At last he said, "This is worse than death, that I should stand before Sekandar as his servant; a tomb will be better for me than such shame. Everyone turned to me for help in warfare, but now that it is I who need help, I see that I have no friend in all the world. God is now my only hope." Since there was no one to come to his aid he wrote a humble letter begging for help to the Indian prince, Foor. He began by praising God, and then continued, "Lord of the Indian peoples, wise, knowledgeable, and clear-spirited, you will have heard of the calamity the stars have dealt me: Sekandar brought his army from Greece and has taken from me my country, family, children, throne, crown, treasuries, and army. If you can help me now, I shall send you from what I have left enough jewels and treasure that you shall never want for wealth in the future, and by this act you will also find fame in the world, and noble men will praise you." He dispatched his messenger, who rode as quickly as the wind to Foor.

But Sekandar learned of his plan and had the tucket sounded, and the noise of kettle drums and Indian chimes filled the camp. His army set out from Estakhr, and their dust was so thick that the sun in the heavens lost its way. A great cry went up when the two armies met, and the Greek warriors were impatient for the battle to begin. Sekandar drew up his army's ranks, the air turned black with dust, and the earth could not be seen beneath the mass of men. But when Dara led out his men, they had no longing for battle: their hearts were weary and they were sick of warfare. Fortune had deserted the Persians. They hardly resisted the Greek onslaught; the once-savage lions fled like foxes. Dara's commanders surrendered, and the crest of their glory was humbled in the dust. Seeing this, Dara turned tail and fled, lamenting as he did so, and about three hundred of his cavalry followed him. Two of his closest advisors were also with him on the battlefield that day;

one was a Zoroastrian priest called Mahyar, and the other's name was Janushyar. When these two saw that Dara's situation was hopeless, one said to the other,

> *"This wretch is now deserted and alone,*
> *He's lost the glory of his crown and throne.*
> *A dagger in his chest and he'll be dead,*
> *A single sword blow could cut off his head,*
> *Then Sekandar will honor us and we*
> *Shall have a share in Persia's sovereignty."*

The two rode with him, one on each side: Janushyar, who was his chief counselor, on the left, and Mahyar, who was his treasurer, on the right. And as they did so Janushyar plunged a dagger into the king's chest. Dara slumped forward and his head hung down; as one man his remaining warriors fled from him.

Dara's Dying Words to Sekandar

Dara's counselors made their way to Sekandar and said, "Wise and victorious lord, we have killed your enemy: his days as king are over." When Sekandar heard Janushyar's words, he said to him and to Mahyar, "Where is this enemy of mine whom you've cast aside in this way? Take me to him." The two led Sekandar, whose heart was bursting with rage, to where Dara lay with his chest covered in gore, and his face as pale as fenugreek. Sekandar gave orders that no one else should approach, and that Dara's two counselors be detained. Quick as the wind he dismounted and laid the wounded man's head on his thigh. He rubbed both his hands against Dara's face until he began to revive and speak. Then Sekandar removed the royal diadem from Dara's head and loosened his armor. No doctor was nearby, and when he saw Dara's wounds, a few tears dropped from Sekandar's eyes. "May this pass easily from you," he said, "and may the hearts of those who wish you ill tremble in terror! Get up, and let me lay you in a golden litter, or if you have the strength, sit yourself in the saddle. I will bring doctors from India and Greece, and I shall weep tears of blood for your pain. I shall restore your kingdom to you, and when you have recovered, we shall swear friendship. This instant I shall hang from a gibbet those who have injured you. When I heard last night what had happened, my heart filled with sorrow, my soul with anger. We are from the same stock, the same root, the same people: why should we destroy one another for ambition's sake?"

When he heard Sekandar, Dara said, "May wisdom always be your companion! I think that you will find the reward for what you have said from God himself. You said that Iran is mine, and that the crown and the throne of the brave are mine; but death is closer to me than the throne. The throne is over for me, and my luck has run out. So the high heavens revolve; their turning is toward sorrow, and their profit is pain. Look at me before you say 'I am exalted above all this great company of heroes.' Know that evil and good both come from God, and see that you remain grateful to him for as long as you live. My own state shows you the truth of what I say. Look how I, who had such sovereignty and glory and wealth, am now despised by everyone. I who never injured anyone, who had such armor and such armies, such splendid horses, such crowns and thrones, who had such sons and relatives, and so many allies whose hearts bore my brand. Earth and time were my slaves, and remained so while my luck held. But now I am separated from good fortune, and have fallen into the hands of murderers. I despair of my sons and family; the earth has turned dark for me, and my eyes are white like the eyes of a blind man. Our own people cannot help us; my one hope is in God the Creator. I lie here wounded on the earth, fallen into the trap of death, but this is the way of the heavens whether we are kings or heroes. Greatness too must pass: it is the prey, and its hunter is death."

Sekandar's pity made his face turn pale, and he wept for the wounded king, lying there stretched out on the earth. Dara said to him, "Do not weep, there is no profit in it. My part in the fires of life is now merely smoke. This was my fate from him who apportions our fates. This is the goal toward which the splendor of my earthly days has led me. Listen to the advice I shall give you, accept it into your heart, and remember it." Sekandar said, "It is for you to order me: I give you my word." Then Dara spoke quickly, going over his wishes and omitting nothing. He began by saying, "You have achieved fame, but see that you fear the world's Creator, who has made the heavens and the earth and time, and the strong and the weak. Look after my children and my family, and my veiled wise women. Ask for my daughter's hand in marriage, and keep her gently and in comfort in the court. Her mother named her Roshanak and saw that the world was always a place of happiness and delight for her. Do not despise my daughter, or let malevolent men speak badly of her. She has been brought up as a princess, and at our feasts she has always been the loveliest person present. It may be that you shall have a son with her, and that the name of Esfandyar will be renewed in him, that he will preserve the fires of Zoroastrianism and live by the Zend-Avesta, keeping the Feasts of Sadeh and No-Ruz and preserving our fire temples. Such a son will honor Hormozd and the sun and moon, and wash his soul and face in the waters of wisdom; he will renew the ways of Lohrasp and Goshtasp, treating men according to their station whether it be high or low; he will make our faith flourish and his days will be fortunate."

Sekandar answered him, "Your heart is pure and your words are wise, O king. I accept all that you have said, and I shall not stray from your words while I am within the borders of your kingdom. I shall accomplish the good deeds you recommend, and your wisdom will be my guide." The master of the world grasped Sekandar's hand and began to weep bitterly.

> He kissed Sekandar's palm and said, "I pray
> That God will keep and guide you on your way.
> I give my flesh to dust, to God my spirit,
> My sovereignty is yours now to inherit."

He spoke, and his soul rose up from his body. All those gathered nearby began to weep, and Sekandar rent his clothes and poured dust on the royal diadem. Sekandar made a splendid tomb for him according to local custom and, now that the time for Dara's eternal sleep had come, the blood was washed from his body with clear rosewater. His body was wrapped in brocade woven with gold and sewn with jewels; it was then covered with camphor, even his face, so that no one could see it. As Dara's corpse was placed within its golden coffin the bystanders wept, and then it was carried in procession, passed hand to hand by the mourners, with Sekandar leading the cortege on foot, and as he approached the tomb, it seemed as if his skin would split with sorrow. The king's coffin was placed within the tomb according to the ancient royal rites, and the huge doors of the building were sealed. Then Sekandar had two gibbets built, one bearing the name Janushyar and the other Mahyar, and the two regicides were strung up on them. The soldiers who were there took rocks in their fists and stoned them to death, as a warning to those who would kill a king. When the Persians saw how Sekandar honored Dara and mourned for him, they offered the young king their homage and loyalty.

Sekandar Writes Letters to the Persians

From Kerman a noble messenger traveled to Esfahan, bringing Sekandar's good wishes to Dara's womenfolk. He described Dara's last days to them and said in Sekandar's name, "It is not right for either friends or enemies to rejoice when just kings die. You are to consider me as Dara now; if he has gone from the earth I have appeared before you. The privileges and pleasures of your life will be increased, and there is no need to claw your faces in fear and grief. King and soldier, we are all destined for death, though to some it comes soon and to others later. Go to the city of Estakhr and prepare to celebrate our alliance with all pomp and splendor. Persia is as she always was, and you should rejoice and keep body and soul in good spirits."

Then a letter was sent, from Sekandar the Great, the son of Filqus, world conqueror and destroyer of those who would oppose him, to every province of Persia, and to every nobleman and chieftain, saying, "May the good will of the Creator who made the world and all things visible and invisible, who turns the heavens above us and who alone can be called mighty and wise, who is able to do all things and whose slaves we are, bless our nobles and augment their prosperity! In victory I have known grief, and sorrow came to me in the midst of rejoicing. I swear by the lord of the sun that I intended no harm to Dara: the man who killed him was from his own household, his slave and not a foreigner. Now that man has received God's punishment; he acted evilly and evil came to him. But you must follow justice and swear allegiance to me, if you desire the blessings of heaven and to receive riches, slaves and high office from my hand. My heart is filled with grief for Dara, and I shall try not to stray from his advice. Whoever comes to my court will receive cash, ivory, and the confirmation of his crown and throne. If he prefers to remain in his own castle, as long as he does not go back on his word, he too will receive the treasures he desires from me. Mint coins in the name of Sekandar and see that you remain faithful to your treaties with me. Maintain your palaces as they have always been, and have the markets overseen as is proper, for such things reflect on my sovereignty. Show me your value by keeping watch on the frontiers so that thieves cannot despoil the countryside, and maintain yourselves in joy and prosperity. From every city send a slave girl, someone who is beautiful, modest, and intelligent, to serve in my women's quarters, but send only those who are willing to come, as slaves should not be forced or abused. See that you treat travelers well, especially those who behave appropriately and speak soberly, who are pure in heart and content with poverty, whom men call Sufis; place them at the head of those to whom you give charity. But if you find that people are oppressed by their overlords, break the hearts and backs of those who are troubling them, destroy them root and branch. I shall seek out those who do evil and have them strung up on a gibbet, and those who ignore my commands will pay dearly in the end for their crimes."

Sekandar presided over his court, welcoming the world in peace. From Kerman he made his way to Estakhr, where he placed the Kayanid crown on his own head.

> *Don't ask the world her secrets: she will hide*
> *Them from your gaze, and turn her face aside.*

THE REIGN OF SEKANDAR

Sekandar took his place on the throne and said, "Kings' souls should be imbued with wisdom, since it is God who gives victory in the world, and any king who does not fear him is evil. It is certain that both good and evil will pass, and that there is no escaping the clutches of fate. Whoever comes to my court seeking justice, even if it is against myself, and whether it is during a royal audience or in the middle of the night, will be answered as soon as he speaks. Since he who bestows sovereignty has given me glory and opened the gates of victory to me, I shall collect no taxes from any of my subjects for five years, whether they live in the mountains, the plains, by the sea, or in cities. I will distribute wealth to the poor and ask for nothing from the wealthy." With this fine speech Sekandar showed that he was disposed to rule justly, and a cry of homage went up from his palace. Then the crowd dispersed and the world's ruler sat closeted with his advisors.

Sekandar's Letter to Delaray, the Mother of Roshanak

Sekandar summoned a scribe, who brought a Chinese pen and silk. The scribe dipped his pen in the ink, and Sekandar dictated a letter to Roshanak's mother, Delaray, saying, "May God grant you grace and destroy your enemies. I have already written to you concerning your sorrows. When your husband's good fortune deserted him and he was murdered by one of his own slaves, I buried him according to the royal rites and bade him God speed from this world. Before we fought I tried to make peace with him, but his days were numbered and he refused. Even his enemies felt sorrow when his blood was spilled, and may God conduct him to the blue vault of heaven. None of us can escape the claws of death, which is like the winds of autumn before which we are blown like leaves. The world now waits for your response to Dara's dying wishes, which many witnessed: he gave Roshanak to me, saying that she was a suitable bride. Send her quickly to me, accompanied by serving girls, nurses, and Persian noblewomen, so that she may brighten my darkened soul. Keep Esfahan as your own, as it has been in the past, and see that it is looked after by the same wise, experienced, just, and humble administrators whom Dara appointed. And if you do not wish to reign there, all of Persia is yours to choose from. Fill your heart with civility toward me, and proclaim me before the world as the new Dara."

He sent a similar letter to Roshanak. It began with an invocation to the all-knowing God who maintains the world, and continued, "From royal stock none but noble offspring can come, delightful, wise and modest, well-spoken and soft-voiced. Shortly before he died, taking his glorious name to the grave, your father gave you to me. When you enter my apartments, you will be my chief desire, the first among my women: you will make the crown more splendid, the royal torque and ivory throne more glittering. I have written to your mother, asking her to send you to me in a manner fitting for your station, as a princess, preceded by the chief priest of Esfahan, in a splendid litter, and accompanied by your maidservants and the women who brought you up. Come to me with peace of mind, knowing you will be the first of my women, and may you always live securely and safely in my royal apartments."

When Delaray heard the messenger's words she heaved a cold sigh from the depths of her being and wept bitter tears for Dara, who had been hurried ignominiously beneath the dust. Still weeping, she called in her scribe and dictated a shrewd and dignified reply. She began by invoking the world's Creator, then said, "It was Dara's glory that I sought from heaven, from which come war and peace and mercy, but since his time has passed and he has exchanged the throne for a wooden coffin, I wish you well in the world. I wish you greatness, victory, and sovereignty, and that the world's affairs unfold as you desire, and I hide no secret meaning beneath my words. I have heard your offer of clemency, and may the heavens rejoice in the kindness of your soul. I have heard too of the tomb you made for Dara and the gibbets you made for Mahyar and that malignant slave Janushyar (when someone spills a king's blood, he is not long for this world). I know too that you have desired peace and reconciliation, and that you have spent many days with your counselors pondering this matter. But kings do not beg, and no one expects a crowned head to act as a slave. You are now our sovereign, and since the sun has set, you are the moon for us. May the world know only your happiness, and may your name resound forever in its palaces! And it has made our hearts happy that you have thought in this way of Roshanak. She is your handmaid; we are your slaves, and our heads are bowed awaiting your commands. She sends you greetings and has written you a letter, an answer as lovely as paradise. The Lord of the world has chosen you, and no one can turn aside from his commands. I have written to my nobles and warlike chieftains, telling them that Dara's sovereignty is now yours, and that no one should disobey you." Then she gave the messenger robes of honor, a purse of gold, and all manner of precious objects. He returned to Sekandar's camp and told the king all he had seen and heard concerning the court's pomp and majesty, which was as splendid as when its former king still reigned there.

Sekandar Marries Roshanak

Sekandar sent for his mother, who was then at Amourieh, and told her of Dara's dying words. "Go to Delaray," he said, "and win her over with sweet conversation. See that you meet Roshanak, who lives in purdah there, and convey to her my regards. Take torques, bracelets, and earrings, and a royal throne studded with jewels. Take a hundred camels laden with carpets, and a hundred more laden with gold-worked brocade. Take thirty thousand dinars from my treasury, packed in purses, to be scattered before the bride. Take a hundred thousand Greek serving girls, each one reverently carrying a golden goblet, as is proper before a princess. Take slaves to look after you along the way, and see that your progress is carried out with royal splendor."

The king's mother set out with ten wise and eloquent translators, and as she approached Esfahan the nobles of the city came forward in a throng to meet her. Delaray too came out from her palace, accompanied by her retinue of courtiers, and so many gold coins were scattered in the courtyard that men thought of silver as so much dirt. They sat within the palace, the nobles of the court crowded around them, and Delaray brought out such a dowry that it seemed the markets of the world had been emptied for the purpose. For parasangs there was camel after camel laden with gold, sliver, and colored cloths; there were clothes and carpets, cloths to spread and cloths to drape, Arab horses with golden bridles, Indian swords with golden scabbards, armor, and helmets and barding for horses, maces and Indian daggers; so much uncut cloth and so much cloth cut for clothes that no one had ever seen more in all the world.

Slaves were summoned from the palace and forty golden litters were prepared; her heart filled with happiness, Roshanak took her place in a litter shaded by a parasol and surrounded by servants. The road was a mass of gold and silver and horses and escorts; the streets of the city were hung with banners, and there was laughter on everyone's lips, excitement in everyone's heart. They poured coins on the brocade parasol as it passed, and scattered musk in the procession's path.

> Then, lovely as the moon, the princess dazed
> Sekandar's wondering sight—he stared amazed
> At her as though she were compounded of
> Intelligence and beauty mixed with love:
> Her stature and her soul-bewitching face
> Made his apartments an enchanting place.
> He sat his mother on a golden throne,
> Then fixed his eyes on Roshanak alone.
> For seven days they sat there side by side,
> Sekandar talking always to his bride,
> And all his manner showed his sovereignty,
> His grace and wisdom, charm, and modesty.

Gifts of gold and silver were distributed throughout Iran, and the whole country, together with the cities of China and Turan, sent their congratulations. All the world was filled with justice, and the places that had lain waste flourished again.

Sekandar Leads His Army Against Kayd

Mehran, the vizier of Kayd, the king of Qanuj, counseled his royal master, "Sekandar will come here with an army of chieftains chosen from Greece and Persia: if you wish to preserve your status be wise and do not look for war with him. You have four things the like of which no noble or commoner has ever seen in all the world. The first, which gives such luster to your crown, is your daughter, who is as lovely as paradise itself; the second is the philosopher you keep hidden, who tells you all the world's secrets; the third is your physician, who is renowned for his skill; the fourth is the goblet you possess that can never be emptied whether by fire or the sun, or when someone drinks from it. With these four things you can save your position. When Sekandar comes, rely on these and, if you don't want him to stay here a long time, don't think of resistance; you have not the might to withstand his army, wealth, and glory. Now is the age of Sekandar, who is the crown of all nobles. When he comes, give him these four things, and I think he will ask for nothing else from you. If you satisfy him in this manner he will go on his way, because he is wise and seeks after knowledge." When Kayd had heard Mehran's words, he felt that the ancient days of his splendor had been renewed.

Having secured Persia Sekandar led out his army, by roads and pathless wastes, toward India and King Kayd. As he went forward the cities opened their gates to welcome him. When his army reached the border city known locally as Milad, Sekandar, as eager as a lion that scents its prey, summoned a scribe and dictated a letter to Kayd. The letter began by praising those who wash their hearts in wisdom, who choose the ways of ease and look to enjoy their wealth, who turn to God for aid, placing their hopes and fears in him. It continued, "They are men who know that the throne derives from my power and that I, Sekandar, am the shadow of the world's victorious Lord. I have written this letter to enlighten your dark soul; when your scribe reads it to you, do not put it aside, thinking to deal with it later. If it comes at night, do not wait till dawn; prepare immediately to obey me. And if you disregard what I say I shall trample your head, crown, and throne beneath my feet."

Kayd welcomed Sekandar's envoy warmly and said, "I am filled with joy at his commands and will not turn aside from them for a moment. But before God, it isn't right to hurry things along in this fashion, and for me to go before him with no preparation." He summoned a scribe, who wrote at his dictation with an Indian pen on Chinese silk. First he praised the God of victory and fate, who is generous and just, and who rules over manliness, wisdom, and human skill, and then said, "Noble men will not ignore the king's commands, and we should hold nothing back from the master of armies, the crown, and the sword. I have four things that no one else in all the world has, either openly or in secret, and no one else ever will have possessions like them. If the king commands me, I shall send them to him, and his heart will delight in them. And then, when the king orders me to, I shall come like a slave to pay homage to him."

When the messenger told Sekandar what he had heard, and handed over Kayd's letter, Sekandar sent him back again, to ask what these four things were that no one else had. Kayd cleared his court and sat with his advisors. They called Sekandar's envoy in and made much of him, and then Kayd said to him,

> *"I have a daughter here whose lovely face*
> *Would make the sun dark if he glimpsed her grace;*
> *Her lips still smell of milk; her hair, pitch-black,*
> *Hangs like a woven lariat down her back;*
> *The cypress bows before her elegance,*
> *Roses are scattered by her eloquence;*
> *Her speech exceeds her beauty, all she says*
> *Seems taught by wisdom and beyond all praise,*
> *And when she chooses to be silent she*
> *Becomes the soul of gentle modesty:*
> *God-fearing and a princess, chaste and wise,*
> *Her like has not been seen by human eyes.*
> *Then there's the wondrous goblet that is mine*
> *Which, when it's filled with water or with wine,*
> *Stays always full. You and your chosen friends*
> *Could drink ten years, the liquid never ends.*
> *Next there is my physician, who can tell*
> *From one small drop of urine if you're well*
> *And, if not, what is wrong: there's no disease*
> *That can escape his cunning expertise;*
> *With him at court you could dismiss all fears*
> *Of sickness, and survive for countless years.*
> *And lastly there's my court philosopher*
> *Who from the turning heavens can infer*
> *All that will come to pass, and everything*
> *He learns he's prompt to pass on to his king."*

The envoy returned, riding his horse as quickly as the wind, and when he told Sekandar what he had heard, the world conqueror's heart opened like a flower in bloom. He said, "If all he claims is true, the world itself is hardly enough to pay for such things. When he sends these wonders to me, my dark soul will glow with light, and I shall not trample on him as I threatened, but leave his country as his friend."

Sekandar Sends Nine Knowledgeable Men
to See the Four Wonders

He chose a number of his advisors, all percipient and knowledgeable men, and sent a letter filled with honorifics and flattery to accompany them. "I am sending nine of my own trusted savants, all wise and reverend men who will not make any difficulties for you. Let the four wonders you mention stay where they are: show them to my envoys, and as soon as I receive a letter from these experienced graybeards saying they have seen these things with their own eyes, and that the world cannot show their like, I shall write a charter such as your heart would desire, confirming you as the king of India."

The nine Greek advisors made their way from Sekandar to Kayd, and the chancellor of Kayd's court made them welcome with questions about their journey and had a suitable place set aside for their stay. On the next day, as the sky turned yellow with dawn and the sun drew its sword for battle, Kayd's daughter was prepared for her audience, although the full moon needs no adornment. A golden throne was placed within the castle, and the room was decorated in the Chinese fashion. Her face as splendid as the sun, the princess sat on the throne, shining more brightly than Venus in the night sky. The nine sages came in, chattering pleasantries and ready to observe carefully. When they saw the princess's face, and the light flashing from her bracelets and throne, they were so astonished that they couldn't move, and their legs felt weak beneath them. The nine of them stood rooted to the spot, giving thanks to God for such loveliness; none of them could tear his eyes from her, or think how to turn away. They stayed so long that the king sent someone to fetch them, and he said, "What kept you so long? She has a lovely face, but she is human, endowed with her beauty by the stars." The sages answered, "No palace contains a portrait as lovely as she is: each of us will write to our king saying how incomparably beautiful she is."

Then they took pen, ink, and paper and wrote to Sekandar. A messenger took their letters to the king, who was amazed by what he read: each letter described her in the same fashion. The king's answer congratulated them on having seen the loveliness of paradise and continued, "There's no need to inquire any further: return at once and bring these four wonders to me. Assure Kayd that his daughter will be well looked after, and set off with this marvel immediately. Kayd has treated me justly, and from now on no one will be able to harm him."

The Nine Sages Bring Kayd's Four Wonders to Sekandar

The messenger made his way back to the nine sages, who returned to Kayd's audience hall with Sekandar's answers. The Indian king was overjoyed that the threat of an invasion by Sekandar had been lifted. He chose a hundred wise, eloquent Indians as an escort, and from his treasury generously selected bracelets, crowns, jewels, uncut cloth, and other suitable gifts, which were then loaded onto three hundred camels. Another hundred camels carried silver coins, and a hundred more gold. A litter was fashioned from sweet-smelling aloes wood and hung with cloth of gold on which jewels were sewn; ten elephants carried golden howdahs, and the finest of them bore a splendid saddle. The princess wept bitter tears of farewell and set off together with the philosopher and the doctor. A nobleman carried the famous goblet, and the wine in it kept the accompanying courtiers drunk.

When this beautiful princess, crowned with her musky hair, as elegant as a cypress topped by the moon, entered the inner apartments of Sekandar's castle, no one there felt worthy to look at her. She wore her hair plaited on the top of her head, her eyebrows were arched like a bow, her eyes like paradisal narcissi; she seemed to be fashioned wholly from charm and loveliness. Sekandar took in her stature, her hair, face, head, and feet, and under his breath he praised God that he had created such beauty, saying, "This is indeed the light of the world." He summoned all the wise men and priests of his entourage, and in their presence he asked for her hand in marriage, according to Christian custom. Then he poured over her so many gold coins from his treasury that it was only with difficulty that she could walk through them.

Sekandar Tests the Philosopher, the Physician, and the Goblet

When the lovely cypress had been taken care of and a place fitted out that was suitable for her, Sekandar turned his attention to the philosopher, to see how he would fare in a battle of wits. He sent him a large goblet filled with cow's fat, saying he should rub all his trunk and limbs with it, until his fatigue was quite gone, and then he could come and fill Sekandar's soul and mind with knowledge. But the philosopher looked at the fat and said, "I'm not fooled by this ploy," and he poured a thousand needles into the goblet and sent it back to the king. Sekandar looked at the needles and then had blacksmiths melt them down and make an iron disk from them, which he sent to the philosopher. He in turn looked at the disk and rubbed it for a while, until he transformed the dark metal into a bright mirror. This was taken to Sekandar at night, who kept his own counsel. He placed the mirror outside, so that the dew turned it black, then he sent it back to the philosopher, and so the duel of wits continued. The sage for his part polished the metal again, making it as bright as water, and sent it back to the king, but this time he smeared an unguent on it, so that humidity wouldn't quickly turn it black again.

Sekandar summoned him and had him seated below the throne. He questioned him, beginning with the goblet of fat, to see if the philosopher had understood what was meant. The sage said to the king, "Fat penetrates deeply into the body, and you were saying that your knowledge goes deeper than that of any philosopher. In answer I said, 'O king, the hearts of wise men are like needles that can penetrate feet and bones and split stones open.' You in turn asked, 'How can the subtle arguments of a wise man penetrate a heart that's been darkened by feasting, warfare, bloodshed, and constant fighting against enemies?' And I replied, 'My wise soul and heart know secrets subtler than a hair, but your heart is not darker than iron.' You said that in the passing of the years your heart had rusted with spilled blood, and how was it possible for this to be righted, and for you to frame words in such darkness? I answered that I would work on your heart with divine knowledge, until it became as bright as water and certain of truth."

Sekandar was delighted by the man's ready answers, and he ordered that his treasurer bring him a set of clothes, gold and silver, and a goblet filled with jewels. But when these were given to the sage, he said, "I have a hidden jewel that brings me whatever I wish and provokes no enemies, and unlike wealth, does not bring Ahriman in its train. It has no guards to demand a salary from me, and I fear no bandits when I'm traveling. Wisdom, knowledge, and righteousness are what's needed, and going astray from these will lead a man to knock at ruin's door. The

Lord of all that is visible and invisible can provide me with sufficient food and clothing; knowledge is my guardian at night, and wisdom is the crown of my active soul. Why should I rejoice in more than this and worry about guarding such wealth? Tell your servants to take these things somewhere else, and may wisdom be my soul's guide." Sekandar wondered at the sage and thought the matter over. He said, "From now on the Lord of the sun and moon will find no sin in me: I will follow your advice and pay attention to the profitable things you have said."

Sekandar Tests the Indian Physician

Sekandar summoned the Indian physician, who could diagnose a man's health from a drop of urine. He questioned him as to the cause of illnesses that make one weep with pain, and the physician answered, "Whoever overeats, and does not watch what he consumes during meals, will grow ill; a healthy person will not eat too much, and a great man is one who seeks to be healthy. Now I will prepare an ointment for you, from herbs gathered in various places, and by using this you will stay in good health. Your appetites will increase, but if you overeat there will be no harmful results. If you do as I instruct you, your blood and marrow will grow strong and your body more energetic, your heart will feel the happiness of springtime, your cheeks will flush with health, and you will be eager to do noble deeds. And your hair will not turn white (white hair makes one despair of the world)."

Sekandar said, "I have never heard of such a thing, or observed it of any sovereign. If you can bring me this ointment, you will be my guide through this world; my soul will be at your service and your enemies will be unable to harm you." He had a robe of honor and other fine gifts prepared for the physician, and made him the chief of all his doctors.

This eloquent physician then made his way into the mountains, with a few of his own companions. His knowledge of plants was extensive, and he knew both poisons and their antidotes. He gathered a great many mountain herbs, throwing away the useless ones and choosing those that were beneficial; these he used to prepare the ointment. He rubbed Sekandar's body with this concoction, and for years the king's body remained healthy.

Then the king began to devote his nights to carousing rather than to sleep. His mind was filled with the desire for women, and he sought out soft, enticing places to be with them. This way of life weakened the king, but he gave no thought to the harm he was doing his body. One day the physician noted signs of weakness in the king's urine and said to him, "There's no doubt that a young man grows old quickly by sleeping with women. It looks to me as though you haven't slept properly for three nights. Tell me, am I right?" Sekandar answered, "I'm perfectly well, my body has not a trace of weakness in it." But the Indian doctor did not agree with him, and that night he searched his books and prepared a remedy against bodily infirmities. That same night Sekandar slept alone, unaccompanied by any of his beautiful womenfolk. At sunrise the doctor came to examine his urine, and he found that there were no telltale signs in it this time. He threw away the remedy he'd mixed and ordered wine, a feast, and musicians. The king asked him, "Why did you throw away that medicine you'd taken such trouble to prepare?" He replied, "Last night the king of the world gave no thought to finding a companion; he slept through the darkness alone. And since you slept alone, my lord, you need no medicine." Sekandar laughed, pleased to be free of the threat of illness, and said, "May the world never be without India! All the astronomers and great savants of the world seem to live there." Giving the doctor a purse of gold, and a black horse with golden bells attached to its bridle, Sekandar said to him, "May wisdom always guide your noble soul!"

Sekandar Tests Kayd's Goblet
Next he gave orders that the golden goblet be filled with cold water and brought to him. Then everyone drank from the goblet, from dawn to dusk, but the water in it did not decrease. The king said to the wisest philosopher of his time, "You mustn't conceal from me what's happening here: how is it that the water in this cup is always replenished? Is it something to do with the stars, or is it a skill the Indians possess?"

The philosopher replied, "Your majesty, this goblet is not something to make light of. It took the makers many years and a great deal of toil to fashion this. Astrologers from every country gathered at Kayd's court to produce this cup and worked on it through bright days and dark nights, consulting their tables for days on end. Think of what happens here as analogous to magnetism, which attracts iron. In a similar way this cup attracts moisture from the turning heavens, but it does so in such a subtle fashion that human eyes cannot see the process." Sekandar was delighted with the answer, and he said to the elders of

Milad, "I shall never break my treaty with Kayd; he is a man whom one must respect, and as he has given me these four wonders I shall demand nothing further from him."

Then Sekandar gathered together two hundred camel loads of precious goods, to which he added a hundred jeweled crowns, as well as uncut jewels and gold coins, and had all this hidden in the mountains.

> *Once all this wealth had been concealed, the men*
> *Who'd done the deed were never seen again—*
> *Only the massive treasure's sovereign lord*
> *Knew where the mountains hid this glittering hoard.*

Sekandar's Letter to Foor

Having hidden his treasure in this way, Sekandar led his army out from Milad and bore down on Qanuj like the wind. He wrote a threatening, bellicose letter, "From Sekandar, the son of Filqus, who lights the flames of prosperity and adversity, to Foor, the lord of India, favored by the heavens, commander of the armies of Sind." The letter opened with praise of God the Creator who is eternal, saying that those to whom he gives victory never want for countries, crowns, and thrones, while those from whom he turns away become wretched, and the sun never shines on them. "You will have heard how God has given me *farr*, victory, good fortune, crowns, thrones, and sovereignty over this dark earth. But none of this will last, and my days draw on; another will come after me to enjoy my conquests. My only ambition is to leave a good name and no disgrace behind me on this sublunar earth. When they bring this letter to you, free your dark soul from sorrow; descend from your throne, do not consult with your priests or advisors, but mount your horse and come to me asking for my protection. Those who try to trick me only prolong matters, and if for one moment you disobey me by choosing arrogance and warfare, I shall descend on your country like a fire, bringing an army of picked warriors, and once you see my cavalry you will regret your delay in submitting to me." The letter was sealed with Sekandar's mark, and a soldier who was eager for fame was chosen to take it. The messenger arrived at the court, and when Foor was told of his arrival he was summoned into the royal presence.

When Foor read Sekandar's letter he started up in rage and immediately wrote a furious reply, planting a tree in the garden of vengeance. "We should fear God, and not use such presumptuous language, because a boastful man will find himself friendless and with no resources. Have you no shame that you summon me like this? Isn't your wisdom disturbed by this kind of talk? If it were Filqus writing thus to Foor, that would be something, but you? You dare to stir up trouble in this way? Your victory over Dara has gone to your head, but the heavens had had enough of him, and fate deals in this way with people who won't listen to good advice. And you found your quarrel with Kayd was like a feast, so now you think all kings are your prey to hunt down. The ancient kings of Iran never addressed us in this way. I am Foor, descended from the family of Foor, and we have never paid any attention to Caesars from the west. When Dara asked for my help, I sent him war elephants to buy time, although I saw that neither his heart nor his fortune were as they should be. When he was murdered by a slave, good fortune deserted the Persians. If evil came to him from an evil counselor, is that any reason for you to lose your good sense? Don't be so eager for battle and so disrespectful toward me; soon enough you'll see my war elephants and armies crowding the way before you. All you think of is your own glory, but inside you are the color of Ahriman. Don't sow these seeds of strife throughout the world; fear misfortune and the harm that will come to you. I mean well by this letter, and may it gratify your heart."

Sekandar Leads His Army Against Foor

After reading this letter, Sekandar immediately selected chieftains from his army, men who were worthy of command: old in their understanding but young in years. Then he led his men against Foor, and they were so numerous that the earth was like a heaving sea. They traveled by every pathway, so that there seemed to be no track that they didn't take, over mountains, along the seashores, and through the most difficult terrain. The army grew weary of harsh traveling and fierce battles, and one evening when they pitched camp, a group of them came before the king. They said,

> "Sovereign of Greece and of all Asia too,
> Earth cannot hold the massive armies you

Lead out against the world: Foor will not fight,
And China's emperor quails before your might.
Why should your army's valiant soldiers die
For worthless lands beneath an alien sky?
In all our ranks we cannot find one horse
That's fit for war; if we reverse our course
The infantry and cavalry will stray
By unfamiliar paths and lose their way.
Before, we fought and gained our victories
Against the strength of human enemies,
But none of us desires to die in wars
With mountains and the sea's infertile shores;
Men do not fight with rocks and ocean tides,
With barren plains and rugged mountain sides.
Do not convert the glory of our fame
To ignominious and ignoble shame."

Sekandar was angered by their words, and he made short work of their complaints. He said, "In the war with the Persians, no Greek soldier was injured; Dara was killed by his own slaves, and none of you suffered. I shall continue on my way without you, and place my foot on the dragon's heart alone. You will see that the wretched Foor will have no desire for either battles or banquets when I have dealt with him. My help comes from God and the Persian army, and I have no need of Greek goodwill." Frightened by his anger, the army begged him to pardon them and said, "We are all our Caesar's slaves, and we tread the earth only as he wills us to. We shall go on, and when there are no horses left, we shall fight on foot. If the earth becomes a sea with our blood, and the low places become hills of corpses, even if the heavens rain down mountainous rocks, no enemy will ever see our backs in battle. We are your slaves, here for you to command, and how could you suffer any injury from us?"

Sekandar then formed a new battle plan. He chose thirty thousand Persian warriors headed by experienced, well-armored chieftains. Behind them he placed forty thousand Greek cavalry, and behind them his warlike Egyptian cavalry, who fought with swords. Forty thousand of Dara's troops and men from the Persian royal family accompanied them. Sekandar picked out twelve thousand Greek and Egyptian cavalry to bring up the rear and scour the plains and valleys. With his army

Sekandar had sixty astrologers and sages to advise him on the most aus-
picious days for combat.

When Foor became aware of the enemy's approach, he chose a
place suitable for battle, and his troops crowded the plain for four
miles, with elephants in the van and his warriors behind them.
Meanwhile Sekandar's spies told him of the war elephants in Foor's
army, and how with their overpowering trunks (that were under the
protection of Saturn) they could destroy two miles of cavalry, who
would be unable either to defeat them or to get back to their own
ranks. The spies drew a picture of an elephant on a piece of paper and
showed it to the king, who had a model of the animal made from wax.
Then he turned to his advisors and said, "Who can think of some way
to defeat this?" The wise men of his court pondered the problem and
then gathered together, from Greece, Egypt, and Persia, a group of
more than forty times thirty blacksmiths, all of whom were expert at
their trade. They made a horse of iron, with an iron saddle and an iron
rider; its joints were held together with nails and solder, and then they
polished both the rider and his steed. It was mounted on wheels and
filled with black oil. They pushed it in front of Sekandar, who was
pleased by the device and saw that it would be very useful. He ordered
that more than a thousand of these iron horses and riders be made.
What king had ever seen an army of dappled, gray, bay, and black
horses, all of them made of iron? The devices went forward on wheels,
and looked exactly like cavalry prepared for war.

Sekandar's Battle Against the Indian Troops; He Kills Foor

As Sekandar approached Foor's forces, the two armies caught sight of
each other; amid clouds of dust a great cry went up from each side,
and the warriors advanced on each other eager for battle. Then
Sekandar's men set fire to oil in the iron horses and routed Foor's
forces. Flames flared out from the iron steeds, and as soon as the ele-
phants saw this they plunged precipitately this way and that. Foor's
army was in turmoil, and when the elephants wrapped their trunks
around the burning horses, they were maddened by their wounds, and
their mahouts were bewildered as to what to do. The whole Indian
army, including its mighty elephants, began to flee, and Sekandar pur-
sued his malicious enemies like the wind. As the air darkened at night-

fall there was nowhere left for the army to fight. Sekandar and the Greeks halted at a place between two mountains and sent out scouts to keep their camp safe from the enemy.

When the sun rose like a gold ingot, making the world as bright as clear crystal, the din of trumpets, bugles, and fifes rang out, and the two armies, thrusting their lances into the heavens, prepared to fight again. Clutching his Greek sword, Sekandar came between the hosts and sent a horseman to shout from a distance to Foor,

> *"Sekandar stands before his troops and seeks*
> *To talk with Foor, and hear the words he speaks."*

When Foor heard this he hurried to the head of his troops. Sekandar said,

> *"Two armies have been shattered on these plains*
> *Where feral scavengers eat human brains,*
> *And horses tread on bones. We're brave and young,*
> *Each of us is a noble champion—*
> *Our warriors have been killed, or they have fled:*
> *Why should they flee, or be left here for dead?*
> *Why should two countries fight when combat can*
> *Decide who is the victor, man to man?*
> *Prepare to face me, one of us alone*
> *Will live to claim these armies and this throne."*

Foor agreed to his proposal, thinking that his own body was like a lion's and that his horse was the equal of any fierce dragon, while Sekandar was as thin as a reed, wore light armor, and rode an exhausted mount. He said,

> *"This is a noble custom: hand to hand*
> *We will decide who's ruler of this land."*

Grasping their swords, they advanced on one another in the space between the two hosts. When Sekandar saw his massive opponent, his fearsome sword in hand and mounted on a huge horse, he was astonished and almost despaired of his life. Nevertheless he went forward, and as he did so Foor was distracted by a cry that went up from the rear of his army and turned toward it. Like the wind then Sekandar bore down on him, and struck the lion-like warrior with a mighty sword blow. The blade sliced through Foor's neck and trunk, and he fell from his horse to the earth.

The Greek commander was overjoyed and his warriors rushed forward; the earth and clouds re-echoed with the thunder of a lion-skin drum, and the blare of trumpets. The Indian warriors looked on Sekandar with fury and were ready to fight, but a voice rang out from the Greek ranks: "Foor's head lies here in the dust, his mammoth body is hacked and torn, who is it you wish to fight for, who will benefit from more sword blows and destruction? Sekandar has become to you as Foor was; it is he you must look to now for battles and banquets." With a roar the Indian warriors called out their agreement, and they came forward to gaze at Foor's hacked and bloody body. A wail of sorrow went up from their ranks, and they threw down their weapons. Fearfully they went before Sekandar, groaning and heaping dust on their heads, but Sekandar returned their weapons, and his words were welcoming: "One Indian has died here, but you should not grieve. I shall cherish you more than he did and try to drive sorrow from your lives. I will distribute his wealth among you, and make the Indians powerful with crowns and throne." Then he mounted Foor's throne; on the one side there was mourning and on the other feasting. But this is the way of the passing world, which brings sorrow to those who dwell in it.

For two months Sekandar sat on the Indian throne, distributing wealth to the army; then he placed there as his regent an Indian noble-man called Savorg, saying to him, "Don't hide your gold away. Dis-tribute and consume whatever comes to you, and put no faith in this passing world, which sometimes favors Sekandar, sometimes Foor, and sometimes gives us pain and rage, sometimes joy and feasting." Savorg too distributed gold and silver to the Indian warriors.

Sekandar's Pilgrimage to the Ka'abeh

Not long after Sekandar's army had become wealthy in this way, the clatter of drums rang out as dawn broke, and the air became as bril-liant as a rooster's eye from the throng of red, yellow, and purple silken banners. Sekandar set out for Mecca, and some of his entourage were pleased by this, some alarmed. With drums rolling and trumpets blar-

ing, he came to the house made with such toil by Abraham, the son
of Azar. God named the site the House of Holiness, the goal of all
God's roads. He named it his own house, and called you to worship
there: the world's God has no need for food or pleasure or rest or com-
fort, but this has always been his place of worship since any place at all
has existed, a place to remember God.

Sekandar approached Qadesiya, laying claim to the land from Jahrom
in Pars as he went. Nasr, the son of Qotayb, heard of his approach and
went out to welcome him with a group of noble horseman bearing
lances. A horseman hurried from Mecca to Sekandar telling him that
the man who was coming to greet him had no desire for wealth or
power and was a descendant of Esmail, the son of Abraham. When
Nasr arrived Sekandar welcomed him, and assigned him a splendid
place in his entourage; Nasr was overjoyed, and recounted to Sekandar
the secrets of his lineage. The king answered him, "My honest and
pure-hearted lord, tell me who is the noblest of your tribe, after your-
self?" Nasr replied, "O ruler of the world, Jaza' is the greatest man in
this place. When Esmail departed this life, the world conqueror Qahtab
appeared from the deserts with a host of savage swordsmen, and by
main force took the land of Yemen. Many innocent men were killed at
that time, and the fortunes of our tribe declined. But God was not
pleased with Qahtab, and the heavens darkened for him. When he died
Jaza' took his place, an unjust and troublesome man. From the shrine
here to the Yemen is all under his control, and his men fish the Red
Sea. He has turned away from justice and gives no thought to the one
God; he holds the lands here in his fist, and the tribe of Esmail welters
in blood because of him."

When Sekandar heard these words he sought out everyone he could
find from the family of Jaza' and had them killed: the children's souls were
parted from their bodies, and not one of his race was left alive. With the
help of his warriors he freed the Hejaz and the Yemen from their unjust
rulers, and exalted the tribe of Esmail. Then he went on foot to the
shrine, and the people of Esmail were so overjoyed at his presence that
wherever he trod the king's treasurer scattered gold coins before him.

Sekandar Leads His Army to Egypt

When he returned from his pilgrimage he bestowed gold on Nasr,
enriching those who had been poor and obliged to find food by their

own labors. Then he led his army to Jeddah, where he didn't stay long. The soldiers were set to work making ships and a number of boats, in which the world conqueror and his army set off for Egypt. The Egyptian king at that time was named Qaytun, and he possessed an unimaginably large army; when he heard that a victorious world conqueror was coming with a following wind from the shrine at Mecca, he set out with a large company of soldiers to welcome him and took coins, slaves, and crowns as presents. Sekandar was pleased to see him and stayed in Egypt for a year, until he and his troops were well rested.

Andalusia was ruled over by a woman; she was wise, had innumerable troops at her disposal, and ruled in prosperity and happiness. The name of this generous and ambitious woman was Qaydafeh. She sought out a painter from the ranks of her soldiers, someone who could make an accurate likeness, and said to him, "Go to Sekandar, and see that you make no mention of my country or of me. Look carefully at him, see what his complexion is, examine his face and stature, and then paint me a full-length portrait of him." The painter heard her and immediately mounted his horse, ready to carry out his sovereign's orders. As quick as a royal courier he made his way from Andalusia to Egypt and into the presence of Sekandar. He observed him when he gave audience and when he was in the saddle; then he took paper and Chinese ink, drew his portrait exactly as he was in real life, and returned to Andalusia. Qaydafeh was moved when she saw Sekandar's face and sighed to herself, then hid the portrait away.

Sekandar asked Qaytun, "Who is Qaydafeh's equal in the world?"

> And King Qaytun replied, "In all the earth
> There's no one of her glory and her worth;
> Unless he were to read the muster rolls
> No one could count the soldiers she controls.
> You won't find anyone in any land
> Who has the wealth she's able to command,
> Who has her dignity, her eloquence,
> Her wisdom, goodness, and magnificence.
> She's built from stone a wide and wondrous town
> So strong no leopard's claws could tear it down—
> Four parasangs in length, no man can measure
> Its endless width. And if you ask for treasure,

Hers is uncountable; for years there's been
Talk in the world of this exalted queen."

Sekandar's Letter to Qaydafeh

Sekandar summoned a scribe and had a letter written on silk, from
Sekandar, the slayer of lions and conqueror of cities, to Qaydafeh the
wise, whose name is unequalled in glory. The letter opened by invok-
ing God, who is generous and just and who bestows prosperity on
those who merit it, and continued: "I have not rushed into war with
you; rather, I have been weighing the reports of the splendor of your
court. When they bring you this letter, may it enlighten your dark soul.
Send tribute to me, and understand that you do not have the strength
to oppose me. You are wise, so act with foresight, as a powerful and
religious sovereign should. If you attempt any kind of trick against me,
you will see nothing but adverse fortune come your way. You don't
have to look far to learn this lesson: consider what happened to Dara
and Foor." As soon as the ink had dried the letter was sealed with
musk.

A quick messenger took the letter at Sekandar's command, and when
Qaydafeh read it she was astonished at its language. Her answer was as fol-
lows: "Praise be to him who created the earth, who has made you victo-
rious over Foor of India, over Dara, and over the nobles of Sind. Your
victory over these warriors has made you willful. You have crowned
yourself in victory, but how can you put me on their level? I am far
greater than they were, in *farr* and in glory, in my armies, and in my royal
wealth. How can I submit to a Greek overlord, and how can you expect
me to tremble with fear because of your threats? My armies number
more than a thousand thousand men, and princes command every one of
those armies. Who are you that you should boast in this way? Your defeat
of Dara has made you the prince of braggarts!" She placed her gold seal
on the letter and dispatched the messenger, who rode like the wind.

The Greeks Capture Qaydafeh's Son

Sekandar read her letter and then he had the trumpets sounded and his
army led out. They marched for a month until they reached the borders
of Qaydafeh's lands. A king called Faryan reigned there, a man possessed
of an army and wealth, and successful in his life. His city was built to
withstand war, and its walls were so high that cranes could not overfly

them. He and his army occupied this fortress, and Sekandar ordered that balistas and catapults be brought up to batter the walls. After a week of fighting his army entered the town, and the victor gave orders that no blood was to be spilled.

One of Qaydafeh's sons, named Qaydrus, was married to Faryan's daughter, and was in the city, as his father-in-law delighted in his company. Qaydrus and his wife, however, had been captured by a man named Shahrgir; Sekandar knew of this and looked for some way to free them. He summoned his vizier, a wise and reasonable man named Bitqun, and showed him his crown and throne, saying, "Qaydrus and his bride will come before you, and I shall call you Sekandar, the son of Filqus. You will be seated on the throne here like a king, and I will stand ready to serve you. You will give orders that Qaydrus's head is to be severed from his shoulders by the executioner. I will humble myself before you and plead for them; you will clear the audience hall of courtiers, and when I redouble my pleas, you will grant my request." The vizier was very troubled by all this, as he was unsure what it meant. Sekandar continued, "This business must remain secret. Call me in as an envoy and talk a little about Qaydafeh; then cordially send me off to her with ten horsemen, saying, 'Hurry and take this letter and bring me the answer.'" Bitqun replied, "I will do it: I'll carry out this deception according to your orders."

Dawn came, the sun drew its glittering dagger, and night fled away in fear. Bitqun sat on the royal throne, but there was shame in his face and anxiety in his heart. Sekandar stood before him as a servant: he had closed the doors to the court and opened the doors to deception. When Shahrgir led in Qaydafeh's weeping son as a captive, together with his young and beautiful wife, who was wringing her hands in grief, Bitqun quickly said, "Who is this man, who has cause to weep so much?" The young man answered, "Come to your senses! I am Qaydrus, Qaydafeh's son, and this is Faryan's daughter, my sole wife. I wish to take her home and cherish her like my own soul, but I am a prisoner in Shahrgir's hands, my soul wounded by the stars, my body by arrows." When Bitqun heard him he was distressed and angry. He started up and said to the executioner, "These two must be buried beneath the dust! Cut off their heads with your Indian sword: now, just as they are, in chains here."

Sekandar came forward and kissed the ground, and said, "Great king of royal lineage, if you will free them for my sake, I shall be able to hold my head up in any company. Why should you vengefully cut off the heads of innocent people? The world's Creator will not look well on us for this." Wise Bitqun answered him, "You have freed these two from death," and to Qaydrus he added, "You've kept your head, which was already leaving your shoulders! Now I shall send you and this man who has interceded for you to your mother, and he can explain what has happened. It would be good if she would then send us tribute: this would mean that no one will lose his skin in this quarrel. Look after this vizier of mine, who will offer your mother war with me or prosperity; act well toward him as he has done toward you, since a noble man's heart is moved to repay kindness. When he has received the queen's answer, send him safely back to me." Qaydrus replied,

> "I will not take my heart or ears or eyes
> From him: how could I treat him otherwise
> Since he has here restored to me my wife,
> My soul, the living sweetness of my life?"

Sekandar Goes as an Envoy to Qaydafeh

Sekandar selected ten suitable companions from among the Greeks: they were all privy to his identity and willing to keep his secret. He said to them, "On this journey address me as Bitqun." Qaydrus led the group, and Sekandar watched him and listened to him attentively. Their splendid horses galloped forward like fire, until the travelers came to a mountain made all of crystal, yet with fruit trees and many plants growing on its slopes. They continued into the queen's realm, and when Qaydafeh heard that her son, about whom she had been anxiously seeking news, was approaching, she went out to welcome him with a large escort of nobles. As soon as Qaydrus saw his mother he dismounted and made his obeisance before her. She told him to remount, and as they rode on together, she grasped his hand in hers. Qaydrus told her all that he had seen and heard, and he turned pale as he described his sufferings in Faryan's city, and how he was now bereft of his crown, throne, army, and wealth. And he added, "This man who has come with us saved my and my bride's lives; if he hadn't intervened, Sekandar would have ordered that my head be cut off and my body burned. Treat him well, and don't hold back with excuses that would make me break my promise to him."

Hearing her son's words, Qaydafeh was distraught with grief. She had the messenger summoned from her palace where he had been installed and motioned him to a fine throne. She questioned him closely and made much of him and saw that a special residence was set aside for his stay. There she sent fine foods, clothes, and carpets.

At dawn the next morning Sekandar made his way to the court to talk with the queen. Servants drew the curtain aside and let his horse enter. He stared in wonder at Qaydafeh on her ivory throne, with her crown studded with rubies and turquoise, wearing a Chinese cloak woven with gold, her many serving girls with their necklaces and earrings standing around her, her face shining like the sun, her throne supported on crystal columns, her gold dress woven with jewels and clasped with a precious black and white Yemeni stone. Under his breath he called on God repeatedly. He saw that her throne alone surpassed anything that Greece or Persia could provide. He came forward and kissed the ground, like a man anxious to make a good impression. Qaydafeh encouraged him by asking a number of questions; then, like the sun passing from the dome of the sky she declared that the audience for strangers was over, and summoned a meal, wine, and musicians. Tables made of teak and inlaid with gold on an ivory ground were brought in; various kinds of food were served, and wine was set out for when they had finished eating. Gold and silver trays were put before them; first they drank to Qaydafeh herself, and then, as she drank more deeply, the queen began to look closely at Sekandar. She said to her steward, "Bring me that shining silk with the charming face painted on it; bring it quickly, just as it is. Don't stand there wringing your hands, go!"

The steward brought the cloth and laid it before her. She stared at it for a long time and then looked at Sekandar's face: she saw no difference between them. Qaydafeh knew that her guest was the Greek king and the commander of his armies, that he had made himself his own messenger and bravely come into her presence. She said to him, "You seem a man well favored by fortune. Tell me, what message did Sekandar give to you?" And he replied, "The world's king spoke to me in the presence of our nobles. He said to tell the pure-hearted Qaydafeh, 'Pursue only honesty, pay attention to what I say, and do not turn your head aside from my orders. If your heart harbors any rebellion, I shall bring an army against you that will break it in pieces. I have found evidence of your greatness, and I have not hurried to declare war on you. Wisdom and modesty are yours, and your subtle policies maintain the world in safety. If you willingly pay me tribute, you need have no fear of me; if you refuse to go the way of rebellion and disaster, you will see from me nothing but kindness and righteousness.'"

Qaydafeh was infuriated when she heard this, but she thought that silence was the best policy. She said, "Go to your quarters now, and rest with your companions. When you come to me tomorrow, I shall give you my answer and some good advice for your return journey." Sekandar went to the building that had been assigned to him and spent the night considering what he should do. When the world's lamp appeared above the mountaintops, and the plains and foothills took on the appearance of glittering brocade, Sekandar made his way back to Qaydafeh's court; his lips were full of smiles, his heart of grief and anxiety. The chancellor recognized him as the foreign envoy and, after questioning him, led him into the queen's presence. The audience hall was full of strangers. The queen's throne was crystal patterned with agates and emeralds surrounding gems of royal worth; its base was sandal and aloes wood and it rested on pillars studded with turquoise. Sekandar was astonished at the splendor and glory he saw, and he thought, "This is indeed a throne room, and no God-fearing man ever saw its like." He came forward to the queen and was directed to a subsidiary golden throne. Qaydafeh said to him, "Well, Bitqun, why are you staring in this way? Is it that Greece can't produce the like of what you see here, in my humble country?"

Sekandar replied, "Your majesty, you should not speak contemptuously of this palace. It is far more glorious than the palaces of other kings and seems like a mine of precious stones." Qaydafeh laughed at his reaction, and she felt delight in her heart that she was able to tease him in this way. Then she cleared the court and motioned the envoy to come closer to her. She said to him,

> *"Filqus's son, I see you're fashioned for*
> *Battles and royal banquets, peace and war!"*

Sekandar turned pale at her words, and then blushed violently; his soul was filled with distress. He said, "Wise queen, such words are not worthy of you. I am Bitqun, don't say that I am a son of Filqus. I give thanks to God that there is no one of noble lineage here, because if he

reported what you have said to my king my soul would soon be sepa-
rated from my body." Qaydafeh replied,

> *"Enough excuses! If with your own eyes*
> *You see yourself, then you must recognize*
> *The truth of what I say, and don't attempt*
> *Either to lie or treat me with contempt."*

Then she produced the silk with the charming face painted upon it
and laid it before him; if the painted face had moved at all you would
have said that it was Sekandar himself. Sekandar saw it and he ner-
vously chewed his lower lip; the day had suddenly turned as dark as
night for him. He said, "A man should never go out in the world with-
out a hidden dagger!" Qaydafeh answered, "If you had your sword belt
on and stood before me with a dagger, you'd have neither the strength
nor an adequate sword nor a place to fight nor a means of escape."
Sekandar said, "A noble and ambitious man should not flinch at dan-
ger; a low-minded person will never rise in the world. If I had my arms
and armor here, all your palace would be a sea of blood; I'd have killed
you, or ripped open my own belly in front of those who hate me!"

Qaydafeh Gives Sekandar Some Advice
Qaydafeh laughed at his blustering manliness and his angry words. She
said, "O lion-like king, don't let yourself be led astray by your male
pride! The Indian king Foor wasn't killed because of your glory, and
neither were Dara and the heroes of Sind. Their good fortune was at
an end, and yours was in the ascendant; and now you're so full of your
manly valor because you've become the greatest man on earth at the
moment. But you should know that all good things come from God,
and while you live you should be grateful to him. You say the world is
yours because of your knowledge, but what you say does not seem true
to me. What will knowledge avail you when you go into the maw of
the dragon death? Acting as your own envoy is sewing your shroud
while you are still young. I am not in the habit of shedding blood, nor
of attacking rulers. When a monarch has power and is merciful and
just, that is when he becomes knowledgeable. Know that whoever
spills a king's blood will see nothing but fire as his reward. Be assured
of your safety, and leave here with joy. But when you have gone

change your habits: don't go acting as your own messenger again, because even the dust knows that you are Sekandar. And I'm not aware of any great hero whose portrait I don't possess, stored away with a reliable courtier. While you remain here I will call you Bitqun and seat you at court accordingly, so that no one will guess your secret or hear you name. I will send you on your way in safety, but you, my lord, must be reasonable and swear that you will never plot against my son, my country, or any of my people or allies, and that you will refer to me only as your equal, as the ruler of my own country."

Freed from the threat of being killed, Sekandar rejoiced to hear her words. He swore by the just God, by the Christian faith, and by the dust of battle that he would act only kindly and righteously toward her land, her son, and her noble allies, and that he would never plot their destruction. When she had heard his oath, Qaydafeh said, "There is one other piece of advice that should not be kept from you: know then that my son Taynush has little sense and pays scant attention to my knowledge and advice. He is Foor's son-in-law and he must not in any way suspect that you and Sekandar occupy the same skin, or even that you are friends. He is eager to avenge Foor, and to confound the earth and sky in war. Now, go joyfully and safely to your own quarters, and have no fear of the world's sorrows."

Sekandar Takes Precautions Against Taynush

When Sekandar left the wise queen Qaydafeh, his grateful heart seemed huge as a mountain; his brow was cleared of furrows, and he had no intention of going back on his promise. At dawn the next morning he went to her again when she was seated on an ivory throne with her commanders ranged about her. On the front of the throne was a design in gold, precious black and white Yemeni stones, surrounded by jewels, and before her there were bunches of musk-scented roses. Her sons Taynush, the breaker of horses, and Qaydrus stood in front of her, listening to her words. Her younger son said to his mother, "Just and fortunate queen, see that Bitqun leaves you well satisfied and with a guide to ensure that no one troubles him along the way or thinks of him as our enemy. I say this because he saved my life, and I think of him as my own soul." His mother said, "I will see that his honors are augmented." Then she turned to Sekandar and said, "Tell us what is hidden; what is it you desire, and what has Sekandar said? What message have you brought us from him?" Sekandar replied, "Noble queen, my stay with you has been lengthy. Sekandar told me to ask for tribute and said that if I delayed my return he would lead his army here and destroy this country together with its crown, its throne, its sovereign, its wealth, and its good fortune."

When Taynush heard Sekandar's words he started up like a wild gust of wind and burst out,

> "You fool, you nobody, whom no one who
> Has sense considers human, who are you?
> And don't you realize where it is you're sitting?
> Stand, and hide your hands! Don't you know what's fitting
> Before a queen? Your stubborn head is full
> Of harebrained speeches—you're contemptible!
> Who is this king of yours? If you don't bow
> Respectfully before our sovereign now
> I'll lop your head off here as easily
> As I might pick an orange from a tree.
> Before our armies I'll display your head
> And Foor will be avenged when you are dead!"

Seeing his bellicose rage, his mother shouted, "These are not his words, his friend sent him to our court and he speaks as his representative!" And she ordered that Taynush be taken out of the court. Then she turned to Sekandar and said to him privately, "This ignorant devil's spawn must not be allowed to think up some plot against you in secret. You're a wise and understanding man, what do you think should be done with him?" Sekandar answered, "This is not how he should be treated; it would be right to call him back." The queen recalled her son and motioned him to his throne again, and Sekandar addressed him, "My lord, if you would accomplish your desires, you should act more calmly. I accept whatever you say and feel no resentment against you. My unfortunate position here is because of Sekandar, who rejoices in his throne and crown. It was he who sent me here to ask for tribute from Queen Qaydafeh, so that I could bear whatever unfortunate consequences there might be. I will soon give him his answer, and I suggest a plan that should have splendid consequences. If I take his hand in

mine and bring him to where you're sitting in such a way that you'll see
no army with him, and no sword or crown or throne either, what will
you give me from your kingdom, if indeed you think well of my
friendly offer?"

Taynush responded, "These words of yours should be acted on now.
If you're being truthful and can do what you've described, I shall give
you treasure and money, horses and faithful retainers, whatever you
wish. I shall always be grateful to you and will make you a great lord.
You'll be my counselor and treasurer, here in this country." Sekandar
stood up and took Taynush's hand in his, to seal the pact. Taynush asked,
"But how can you manage this, what magic are you going to use?"

Sekandar said, "When I leave this court you must accompany me,
together with a thousand cavalry worthy of warfare. I saw a wooded
area on the way here, and I'll hide you and your army there and you
can wait in ambush. I'll go on ahead to sound out Sekandar's malevo-
lent soul, and I'll say to him, 'Qaydafeh has sent you so much tribute
that you'll never want for wealth again, but their envoy says he's afraid
to meet you while you're surrounded by your army. If you and your
advisors will come to see Taynush, you will be able to receive the won-
derful treasures he has brought. He'll come forward if he sees you
without your army, but if he decides to go back, the road is open and
we can't stop him.' When he hears these flattering words of mine, it
won't cross his mind that I'm deceiving him; he'll come into the shade
beneath the trees, asking his treasurer to bring along wine, and his
crown and throne. Then you will surround him with your troops and
his days will be at an end. My vengeance and your heart's desire will
be accomplished together, an enormous amount of wealth will come
into your hands, as well as slaves and caparisoned horses, and from then
on no one will seek to disturb your peace."

Taynush was overjoyed when he heard all this and lifted up his head
like a noble cypress tree. He said, "My hope is that his day will darken
while mine grows bright. He will fall suddenly into my trap and pay
for the blood he has spilled in the world, the blood of Dara, and of
Sind's nobility, and of brave Foor, the king of India." When Qaydafeh
heard Sekandar's words, she saw well enough what his plan was; she
smiled secretly, hiding her coral lips beneath her muslin veil. As Sekandar
left her presence, his darkened soul was filled with anxiety.

Sekandar's Treaty with Qaydafeh and His Return

All the long night he sought for some solution. When the sun showed the fringe of its Chinese royal robe, raising its golden banner above the mountains, and the purple silken banner of night dipped in submission, Sekandar made his way to the queen. A servant stood to greet him, and the world conqueror dismounted, as was customary, and walked into her presence. He was ushered forward, and the queen cleared the court of strangers. Seeing Qaydafeh on her throne, Sekandar said, "May the planet Jupiter accompany your deliberations. I swear by the Messiah's faith, by his just commands, by God who is a witness to my tongue, by our rites and by our great cross, by the head and soul of your majesty, by our vestments, our clergy, and the Holy Ghost, that the soil of Andalusia will never see me again; that I shall send no army here, that I shall not seek to deceive you, that I shall do no harm to your loved son, neither through my commands or by my own hand. I shall remember in my soul how you kept faith with me and I shall not seek your harm in any way. Anyone who wishes you well is my brother, and your court is as sacred as the cross to me."

Qaydafeh considered his oath, his sincere heart, and his promise. She had golden thrones placed throughout her audience hall, and the front of the hall was hung with splendid Chinese cloths. She summoned her chieftains and assigned them thrones, and then had her two noble sons, as well as her extended family and her allies, called in. She said, "In this fleeting world it is right to avoid sorrow when we can, and I have no desire that the turning heavens should send me vengeance and warfare as my fate. Sekandar's longing for wealth will never be sated, not if he brings the heavens down to the earth. For the sake of wealth he is seeking to harm us, but all the wealth in the world is not worth such pain and sorrow. I have no wish to make war on him, or to bring hardship on this realm. I shall send him a letter full of good advice; I will honor him and offer him good counsel. If then he still looks for war, he will find my advice will be followed by his defeat and imprisonment; if I lead my armies against him, the heavens and the moon will pity his plight. There is no harm in trying this, and it may be that we can remain friends. What do you say to my proposal? Answer me, and give me your counsel."

The assembly raised their heads and spoke in response. They said, "O just and righteous queen, whose like no one can remember having seen before, you say only what is best, and the land over which you rule is indeed fortunate! If this king does become your friend, this is an outcome that all good men would desire: your wealth will not be substantially diminished, and no wealth is worth your distress. If a man like Sekandar, who comes from Greece and turns countries into seas of blood with his sword, can be turned back from your door with a few gifts, we say that all the wealth in the world is not worth one coin if this can be achieved. We too desire only peace between you, and a man who seeks war is unworthy of respect."

Hearing her wise counselors' words, she had her treasury opened and her father's throne, together with his golden armbands and torques, brought out. There was also a crown, inlaid with jewels so splendid that no one in that country could put a value on them. She said to Sekandar's supposed envoy, "This crown is priceless, and it would be wrong for anyone else but your king to have it. Since I see that he is worthy of such a crown I choose him to own it rather than my own sons." The throne had been made in seventy sections, and it could be put together only by the man who had taken it apart, so cunningly were the pieces fitted to one another. Its feet were carved like dragons' heads, and no one could compute the value of the jewels with which it was studded: there were four hundred rubies the color of pomegranate seeds, each weighing two mesqals, and four hundred uncut emeralds, the color of the green in a rainbow. Besides this she gave four hundred huge elephant tusks; the skins of four hundred Barbary leopards; a thousand dappled deer skins, colorfully embroidered with various pictures; a hundred hunting dogs and cheetahs that could see a gazelle quicker than the arrow flies; two hundred water buffalo led by slaves; four hundred ebony stools upholstered in silk brocade; and four hundred more of aloes wood with gold designs on them. A hundred noble and richly caparisoned horses bearing precious goods were led in, besides which there were a thousand Indian and Greek swords to which the queen added suits of armor and twelve hundred helmets. Then she said to her treasurer, "This is the greater part of what I wish to give. Count it out to Bitqun, and tell him that he must be ready to leave at dawn."

Dawn lifted its banner and turned the purple sky as white as camphor; the earth was renewed, the mountains glowed red as juniper dye, and from the royal court the din of drums rang out. Sekandar mounted his horse, ready for the departure Qaydafeh had commanded. Taynush prepared his escort of warriors and made his way to the queen's palace. Those who were to leave bade her farewell, saying, "May your soul and the heavens be as the warp and weft of one cloth."

They traveled stage by stage until they had almost reached the Greek camp. Sekandar made a stop at the place in the woods that he had mentioned, where there was a flowing stream. He said to Taynush, "Rest here, and refresh yourself with wine. I shall go and do as I promised: I'll keep my word in every way." Sekandar traveled on with his men until they reached his army; a great shout of joy went up when he rejoined his troops, since they had despaired of ever seeing his face again. They prepared him a royal crown, congratulating him, and bowing their heads down to the ground in homage. Sekandar selected a thousand armored soldiers bearing ox-headed maces, and in battle order the men surrounded the wood where Taynush and his companions were. Then Sekandar cried out,

> "My headstrong lord, consider now and say
> Whether you want to fight or run away!"

Taynush trembled in his encampment and regretted his former plans. He said, "Great king, choose kindness over contempt. Act toward me as you did toward my brother, Qaydrus: be magnanimous and just to me. This is not what you promised my mother; didn't you tell her you wouldn't go back on your word?"

> And Sekandar replied to him, "What's made
> You turn so weak, and why are you afraid?
> Your heart should have no fear; you're safe with me,
> As are all members of your family.
> I shall not break my word to Qaydafeh—
> My promise will be kept in every way:
> There is no good in lying kings who make
> Fair promises they then proceed to break."

Taynush quickly dismounted, kissed the ground, and began to weep. The king took his hand in his, just as he had done when they sealed their pact, and said, "Calm yourself, and think no more of this, I bear no grudge against you in my heart. Before your mother on the throne

I put my hand in yours and said that in just such a fashion I would place the hand of the king of the world in yours. Now I fulfill my promise, since it is not right for kings to utter empty words. I am Sekandar, and I was Sekandar then, when I spun such tales at your court. Qaydafeh knew on that day that the hand in yours was a king's." Then he said to a servant, "Place a throne beneath that blossoming tree." He commanded that a meal, music, and wine be provided, and gave Greek, Chinese, and Persian robes of honor to Taynush. He gave the prince's companions gold and silver, and to those of appropriate rank he gave crowns and belts. Then he said to Taynush, "You should not stay here, this wood is far from your homeland. Say to Qaydafeh from me, 'Wise, far-sighted, and accomplished queen, while I live I shall keep faith with you, and my soul is filled with kindness toward you.'"

Sekandar Travels to the Land of the Brahmins

Sekandar led his army quickly from that place to the land of the Brahmins, as he wished to learn from the ascetics who lived there of the land's ancient practices. When the Brahmins heard that the king was approaching with his army, these God-fearing men made their way down the mountains and gathered together. They wrote a letter to Sekandar, which began by invoking God's blessings on him, and wishing him victory and increasing knowledge and power. It continued, "O warlike king, God has given you the great world, so why do you come to this worthless land, the dwelling place of those who live in worship? If you have come here looking for wealth, you must be sorely lacking in wisdom: we have only patience and knowledge, and this knowledge fills our souls with contentment. Patience cannot be taken from us, and knowledge never harms anyone. You will see nothing in this place but a troupe of naked ascetics, living scattered here and there in the wind and snow; and if you stay here for long, you will have to live off the seeds of herbs."

A messenger, clothed only in a covering of roots and vegetation about his loins, came to Sekandar, who read their letter and decided to treat the man kindly and well. He left the army where they had halted, while he himself went forward with his Greek philosophers. The ascetics heard of the king's approach and one by one they traveled to greet him. Since they possessed no wealth and had no produce or harvested grain to offer, they brought him small valueless things. One by one they greeted the magnanimous lord of the earth. Sekandar saw their faces, heard their chants, and saw them running with naked feet, bodies, and heads; he saw that their bodies were unprovided for but their souls were filled with the fruits of knowledge; their clothes were of leaves, their diet of seeds, they lived withdrawn from all fighting and warfare, and their food, sleep, and repose were in the plains and mountains.

He questioned them about their food and repose, and their peace in the midst of war. One replied, "We have small need of clothes, carpets, and food: because a man is born naked from his mother and returns naked to the earth, it is wrong for him to fuss about what he should wear. Every place is a place of fear, despair, and terror. The earth is our mattress, the sky our covering, and we watch the road for death to come. An ambitious man struggles to gain something that is not worth the effort he has put forth, and then he passes from the world while his gold and treasure and crown remain here. Only his good deeds will accompany him, and his head and glory will both return to dust."

Sekandar questioned him: "Who is the king of our souls? Who always accompanies us toward evil?" The ascetic answered, "Greed is the king, the ground of vengeance and the place of sin." Sekandar asked, "What is the reality of this thing that makes us weep with longing?" The sage replied, "Greed and need are two demons, wretched and malevolent; one is dry-lipped from longing, the other passes sleepless nights from excess. Time passing hunts down both, and blessed is the man whose mind accepts wisdom." When Sekandar heard these words, his face turned pale as fenugreek; his cheeks became sallow, his eyes filled with tears, and furrows filled his once-smiling face. The great king asked, "What do you need that I can provide? I will not hesitate to give you my wealth, or to undergo suffering for you." The ascetics answered, "Great king, close the door of death and old age for us." The king answered, "But there is no pleading with death: no matter how one hangs back from this sharp-clawed dragon, even if one is made of iron, one cannot escape him. And no matter how long our youth lasts, we cannot evade old age." The Brahmin said, "Wise and puissant king, since you know that there is no recourse against death, and that there is no disaster worse than old age, why do you long for the world in this way, why do you breathe in the scent of this poisonous flower so eagerly? All you will receive is suffering, while your enemies will inherit the wealth you acquire; to make oneself suffer for another's profit is the act of an ignorant man or a fool. White hairs are a message from death, and what makes you hope that you can stay in the world?"

The wise king replied, "Just as by God's will a slave must die, this is my fate too, as the turning heavens direct; neither wise men nor warriors can struggle against fate. And the star of those who were killed fighting against me had declined: they deserved their grief and to have their blood shed, since an unjust man cannot escape his end. They experienced divine punishment, because they had strayed from the way of wisdom. No man can evade the will of God, or explain what fate brings."

Sekandar offered many gifts to the ascetics, but none of them took anything from him: greed was not a part of their natures. He did no harm in that place, and set off toward the west.

Sekandar Reaches the Western Sea and Abyssinia

The army journeyed on, stage by stage, exhausted by their travels, but still determined. After he left the land of the Brahmins, Sekandar saw a deep and boundless ocean. On its shores lived men who veiled themselves like women and dressed in colorful splendid clothes. Their language was not Arabic, Turkish, Chinese, or Persian. Their diet consisted of fish, and their land was cut off from the outside world. Sekandar was astonished to meet such folk, and when he saw the ocean he invoked the name of God. Just at that moment a mountain rose up out of the water; it was in two sections and glittered yellow like the sun. Immediately Sekandar asked for a boat so that he could look at it more closely, but one of his Greek philosophers advised him not to cross the ocean's depths: he said Sekandar should send someone of less importance to look at it. Thirty Greeks and Persians manned the boat, but the yellow mountain was a huge fish and, as soon as the boat approached, it dived quickly beneath the surface, dragging the boat with it. Sekandar's army watched in horror and called on God to protect them. The Greek philosopher said, "Knowledge is the best of all things, and a knowledgeable man is greater than all others. If the king had gone in that boat and been destroyed, all this army would have suffered in their hearts."

Sekandar led his army forward and came to another body of water, surrounded by reeds that were like plane trees, more than fifty cubits high with trunks forty cubits in circumference. All the houses there were made of wood and reeds, and the ground seemed to give beneath their weight. It was inadvisable to stay there long, and the water was so brackish that no one drank it. When they left this place they came to a deep lake. The land there seemed inviting, the soil smelled of musk, and the water was as sweet as honey. They ate and drank and lay down to sleep, but as they did so countless snakes came slithering out of the water, and from the bushes flame-colored scorpions appeared. The world darkened for the sleepers, and many died, both warriors and wise men. Boars attacked them from one side, their tusks glittering like diamonds, and from the other came lions larger than oxen that the soldiers had not the strength to fight against. The army retreated to the reedbeds, which they set fire to, and so killed the lions that made their escape so difficult.

From there Sekandar went to Abyssinia, the land of the Habash. The country was crowded with men whose skin was as black as a raven's feather, and their eyes as bright as lamps. They fielded a redoubtable army of tall, naked soldiers, and when they saw Sekandar's army approaching, their war cries ascended to the clouds. The king's eyes darkened when he saw them advancing in their thousands: they killed many men as they attacked, hurling bones instead of lances. Sekandar ordered his men to prepare their weapons for battle. The naked Habash pressed on with their attack, and many were killed by Sekandar's lion-like forces, until those who survived fled from the battlefield. So much blood was spilled that the land from end to end was like the sea of China, with here and there mounds of the dead piled up. Straw was packed around these heaps of corpses, and Sekandar ordered that they be set on fire.

That night a rhinoceros could be heard, and Sekandar donned his armor and helmet. Then the animal came into view, more massive than an elephant, with a dark horn on his head. He killed a number of soldiers and did not retreat even though he was attacked repeatedly. Finally he was killed by the attackers' arrows, and this conqueror of lions lay there like a huge iron mountain. Sekandar left the area in haste, giving thanks to God as he went.

Sekandar Reaches a Land Where the Men Have Soft Feet and Kills a Dragon

They reached a land where men have soft feet; the host of inhabitants was beyond numbering, and each man was as tall as a cypress tree, but they had neither horses nor armor nor swords nor maces. Their war cry was like the roll of thunder, and they attacked naked, as if they were devils. Against Sekandar's army they hurled a hail of rocks, which rained down like an autumn wind bowing trees before it. But the army advanced with arrows and swords, and the day seemed to turn to night with the dust. When there were only a few of the soft-footed warriors remaining, Sekandar rested, and then led his army forward again.

They quickly reached a city that seemed limitless; the inhabitants courteously and kindly came out to welcome them, bringing with them carpets, clothes, and food as gifts. Sekandar questioned them and treated them respectfully, and a sufficient area for his army's camp was set aside. Tents were set up on the plain, and the army made no attempt to enter the city. Nearby there was an enormous mountain, which seemed almost to touch the skies. The few people on the mountain's slopes didn't stay there at night. Sekandar asked them the best way forward and by which paths he should lead his army. They made their obeisance before him and greeted him as the world's king, and then said:

> "A path exists around this mountainside
> But first you'll have to find a willing guide;
> Beyond the crest there lies a dragon's lair,
> His poison sickens birds that venture there.
> The noxious vapors reach the moon, there's no
> Safe route by which your warriors could go.
> His massive maw breathes fire, and he could snare
> An elephant with his two locks of hair;
> Our city doesn't have the strength to fight.
> We have to take up five cows, every night,
> For him to feed on; and how fearfully
> We place them on the rocks for him to see,
> Afraid that if he finds us he'll come down
> And, piece by piece, destroy us and our town."

Sekandar said, "Tomorrow, see that no one takes him any food." When the time for his meal had passed, the dragon stood on the mountain slope breathing fire, and Sekandar ordered his troops to shoot a storm of arrows against him. The foul dragon exhaled fire and caught a few

men in the blast. Sekandar had the war drums beaten, and the dragon
drew back in fear from the echoing drums.

The sun rose in Taurus, and the meadows resounded with the song
of larks. When it was again time for the dragon to be fed, the king chose
a number of men from his army and gave them money to buy five cows.
He killed the cows and skinned them, leaving the hide attached to their
heads. The hides were then filled with poison and oil and inflated;
prayers were said and the cows were passed from hand to hand up the
mountainside. The king approached the dragon and saw that he was like
a huge dark cloud: his tongue purple, his eyes blood red, and fire issuing
continuously from his maw. The soldiers rolled the cows down toward
the dragon, their hearts anxious to see what he would do. Immediately,
the dragon descended on the carcasses like the wind. He ate them,
and the poison spread throughout his body, bursting his intestines and
forcing its way even into his brain and feet. For a long time he beat his
head against the rocks in desperation, and the army released a hail of
arrows against him. The mountainous monster sank to his feet, and his
body finally succumbed to the arrows. Leaving the creature's body where
it lay, Sekandar quickly led his troops out of that area.

The adventurous hero led his men to another mountainous area,
where he saw an astonishing sight. Perched on a summit sharp as a
sword blade, far removed from all humanity, was a golden throne. On
the throne was a dead man, and even after death he radiated *farr* and
glory. He was wrapped in a brocade cloak, and on his head was a crown
encrusted with jewels. So much gold and silver was scattered around
him that no one could approach the throne, and anyone who went up
the mountain hoping to take some of the dead man's wealth would
tremble in terror and die, and eventually rot there. Sekandar ascended
the mountain and, as he stared at the man, and at the gold and silver,
he heard a great voice that said, "O king, you have lived long enough
in the world. You have destroyed so many thrones and raised your head
up to the heavens, and you have laid low so many friends and enemies,
but now the way of the world has changed." Sekandar's face glowed
like a lamp, and he descended the mountain sick at heart.

Sekandar Sees the Marvels of Harum

Sekandar pressed on with his Greek chieftains and reached a city called
Harum, a town inhabited only by women, to which no stranger was

granted entrance. The right breast of these women was as that of all women, like a pomegranate resting on silk, but on the left their bodies were like that of a warrior who wears armor on the day of battle. As Sekandar drew near the city, he wrote a polite letter to the inhabitants, as was fitting for a wellborn man to do, addressing it from the king of Iran and the West to the sovereign of Harum. He began his letter in the name of the Creator of the heavens, from whom come blessings, justice, and benevolence, and continued, "Whoever possesses wisdom in his soul and lives wisely has heard what I have done in the world, how high I have raised the banner of glory, and how those who oppose my will find that their only resting place is the black earth. I desire that no site in the world be forbidden to my eyes. My coming here is not to make war on you; I wish for only peace and friendship between us. If there is anyone among you who is knowledgeable and wise and able to read this letter, send a person who is honored by you to meet me, and no one will be hurt by such an encounter." He added some more eloquent phrases, and gave the letter to a Greek philosopher to deliver to the city.

When the sage drew near he saw that the city was populated by women, and that no men were there. All those who had the right to express their opinions came out in a body on to the plain, to see the Greek visitor and to hear his message. Once the city scribe had read the letter aloud and they had some notion of Sekandar's intentions, they sat and wrote an answer, as follows: "May you live forever, proud king. We have received your messenger and read through your letter. You speak about kings, victories, and your former battles; if you attack the city of Harum with your army, you will not see the earth for horses' hooves. There are innumerable streets within our town, and a thousand women live within each street. We sleep each night in our armor, cramped together since there are so many of us. And of all these women not one of us has a husband, because we are all veiled virgins. Whichever way you approach our country you will see a deep lake. If a woman decides she wants a husband, she must leave us; in fair weather or foul, she has to cross this deep lake. After taking a husband, if she gives birth to a daughter and the girl is feminine by nature and interested in pretty colors and scents, then she will remain where she was born and breathe the air of that sky. But if she is a manly, confident child, she is sent to Harum. If she gives birth to a son he stays where he is and has nothing to do with us.

"When on the day of battle any of us brings a warrior down from his horse, a golden crown is placed on her head, and she is given a throne more exalted than Gemini. There are thirty thousand women among us who possess a golden crown and earrings, because of such success in battle. You are a great and famous man; don't slam the door on your own reputation, so that men say of you,

> 'He fought with women on the battlefield,
> And when he fought them, he was forced to yield.'

Such a taunt will be shameful for you, and it will last for as long as the world does. If you wish to come with your Greek chieftains and go around our country, and if you act with honesty and chivalry, you will see nothing but kindness and festivities from us. We'll bring so many of our warriors to greet you that you won't see the sun or the moon for the dust."

A woman was chosen to deliver this reply; she wore a crown and royal clothes and was accompanied by ten beautiful outriders. As she approached the king's camp, he sent an escort out a little way to greet her; she handed over the letter to Sekandar and repeated her fellow warriors' message. When Sekandar saw their reply he chose a wise, understanding envoy and sent them an answer: "May men live with wisdom. In all the world there is no king or chieftain who is not my inferior, no matter how great or favored by the heavens he might be. White camphor dust and black earth are as one to me, and so are fighting and feasting. I have not come here to fight with elephants and war drums, and with an army whose horses' hooves trample the mountains and plains to dust. My intention was to see your city, but if you come to me this will be sufficient. When I have seen you I will lead off my army; I shall not stay here for long. I want to find out about your customs and glory, your horsemanship, your beauty, everything about you. I shall ask discreetly about your births here, since how can there be women without men? When death comes, how are your numbers kept up? I want to know what the solution to this problem is."

The envoy delivered his message, and the nobles of the city gathered to give their response: "We have chosen two thousand wise, eloquent women. Each hundred of them will take ten jeweled crowns, making two hundred crowns in all, each of them worthy of a king; with its jewels each crown weighs three *ratl*. When we hear that the king has arrived, we shall go out to meet him one by one, since we have heard of his knowledge and glory." The envoy returned and gave their reply; everyone spoke wisely in this business.

Two thousand women crossed the lake, all of them crowned and wearing earrings. There was a delightful area nearby, filled with trees and streams, and there they spread colorful carpets on the grass and laid out a feast. When Sekandar reached Harum the women ceremoniously welcomed him with the crowns, together with clothes and jewels. Sekandar accepted their presents and made much of them, entertaining them royally. When night gave way to day he entered the city and looked closely at parts of it, searching out information about both big and small things, and staying there till his questions were resolved.

Sekandar Leads His Army to the West

Having asked his fill of questions, and seen the lake, Sekandar led his army toward the western lands. He came to a large town inhabited by a savage population: they had red faces and blond hair, and all of them were fine warriors. Ordered to appear before Sekandar they came in pairs, striking their hands against their heads. When their leaders were asked what marvels there were in that country, one answered, "O king favored by fortune and conqueror of cities, on the other side of our town there is a unique body of water; when the shining sun reaches that place it plunges into the water's depths. Beyond the water the world is dark and the things of the world become hidden. We have heard endless tales about that darkness. A God-fearing and wise man says there is a source of water there, and he calls it the water of life. This wise man says, 'How can anyone die, if he drinks the water of life? The water there comes from heaven, and the man who bathes there washes away all his sins.'"

The king asked, "How can a horse get to this dark place?" The pious man answered, "A man must ride on a young mount to get there." Sekandar ordered that the local herdsmen bring their herds of horses to his camp. He chose ten thousand of them, all four years old and capable of work.

Sekandar Seeks the Water of Life

With happiness in his heart, Sekandar set out, calling his shrewdest chieftains about him. He traveled until he reached a town that seemed to have no center or limit and that was well appointed with gardens, open spaces, palaces, and public buildings. He dismounted, and at dawn he went without his army to the water's edge. He stayed there until the yellow sun descended into the dark blue waters, and saw God's marvel, the sun disappearing from the world. His mind filled with endless speculation, he returned to his camp. In the dark night he was mindful of God, and thought too of the water of life. He chose his most patient warriors to accompany him, packed provisions sufficient for forty days, and then set out impatient to see this wonder.

> He lodged his men within the town, then tried
> To find a capable and willing guide:
> Khezr was preeminent in all that land.
> Sekandar placed himself at his command
> And said to him, "I ask that you incline
> Your heart to this high enterprise of mine;
> If we can find life's water we shall stay
> A long while in the world to watch and pray—
> The man who nourishes his soul, who gives
> His mind to God's laws, does not die but lives.
> I have two seals that in the darkest night,
> When water's near, will shine with brilliant light:
> Take one, go on ahead of us, and you
> Will guide and guard us there in all we do:
> The other seal I'll keep with me, to show
> My soldiers where it's safe and wise to go,
> And so we'll see what God has hidden here."
> Then, as the soldiers gradually drew near
> The stream of life, the plains rang with a cry
> Of "God is Great" that echoed in the sky.
> Then, for the next stage, Khezr said that they ought
> To leave behind them all the food they'd brought,
> And for two days and nights the soldiers went
> With mouths that never tasted nourishment;
> The road split into two the following day
> And in the dark Sekandar lost his way.
> Khezr journeyed on; his head reached Saturn's sphere
> And when he saw life's glittering stream appear

He bathed his head and body there, and prayed
To God, the only guardian he obeyed:
He drank and rested, then went back again,
And praised God as he crossed the empty plain.

Sekandar Talks with the Birds

But Sekandar emerged into light, and saw a great shining mountain before him, near the top of which were two columns of ebony that reached into the clouds. Each column supported a large nest, on which sat a fierce green bird. The birds spoke in Greek and addressed him as the victorious ruler of the world. When he heard them Sekandar hurried to the foot of the pillars, and one of the birds said to him, "You take pleasure in your pain, but what is it you seek from this fleeting world? If you raise your head to the high heavens, you must return in despair. But now that you are here, tell me, have you ever seen a house made of reeds, or one made of golden bricks?" Sekandar said, "Both these exist." Hearing this reply the bird sat a little lower, and Sekandar, who was a God-fearing man, stared at it in wonder. The bird asked, "Have you heard the sound of lutes in this world, or the noise of drunkenness and singing?" The king answered, "People do not call any man happy who has not had some share of pleasure in the world, no matter how much he pours his heart and soul out to them." The bird hopped down from its ebony column onto the ground and asked, "Is there more knowledge and honesty, or ignorance and lies in the world?" He answered, "Anyone who seeks knowledge raises his head above both groups." The bird hopped back onto its column and cleaned its claws with its beak, then asked the king, "In your country, do God-fearing men live in the mountains?" Sekandar replied, "When a man becomes pure in thought, he goes into the mountains." At that the bird, with an air of authority and independence, sat on its nest again and sharpened its beak with its claws. It told the king that he should climb, without any companions, up to the summit of the mountain, where he would see something that would make any happy man weep.

Sekandar Sees Esrafil

Sekandar made his way to the mountain summit alone. There he saw Esrafil, the angel of death, with a trumpet in his hand, his head raised at the ready, his cheeks filled with breath, his eyes brimming with tears, as he waited for God to order him to blow. Seeing Sekandar on the mountain Esrafil roared with a voice like thunder,

> *"Stop struggling, slave of greed! One day, at last,*
> *Your ears will hear the mighty trumpet's blast—*
> *Don't worry about crowns and thrones! Prepare*
> *To pack your bags and journey on elsewhere!"*
> *Sekandar said, "I see that I'm to be*
> *Hurried about the world perpetually,*
> *And that I'll never know another fate*
> *Than this incessant, wandering, restless state!"*

He descended the mountain, weeping and praising God, then set out on the dark road again, following his guides.

Going forward in the darkness, the army heard a voice from a black mountain nearby, which said, "Whoever takes stones from this mountain will be sorry for what he holds in his hand, and whoever takes nothing will be sorry and look for a balm to ease his heart's pain." The soldiers listened to the voice, and wondered what the words could mean, since whether they took stones or didn't, they couldn't see what their future sufferings would be. One said, "The pain will be because of sin, that's the regret for taking stones along the way." Another said, "We should take a little; everyone has to suffer some pain." Some took stones, some took none, some out of laziness took only a few. When they left the land where the water of life was, and found themselves on the plain once more, the road was no longer dark and each man looked at what he'd tucked in his sleeves or his tunic, and so the deceiving riddle was revealed. One found his clothes filled with rubies, another with uncut gems, and they were sorry they had taken so few and hadn't taken emeralds as well. But those who had ignored the precious stones and taken nothing were even more sorry. Sekandar stayed in that area for two weeks, and when he was less fatigued he led his army forward again.

Sekandar Constructs a Wall to Defeat Yajuj and Majuj

Having seen the west, Sekandar turned his attention to the east, choosing to continue his wanderings in the world. He came to a town that seemed as if wind and dust had never blown against it, and when the trumpets were sounded from his elephants' backs and the town's nobility came out to welcome him, the procession stretched for two miles. The world wanderer greeted them warmly and asked, "What is the most astonishing thing about this place?" They began to weep and wail about the revolutions of fate, saying, "We face a difficult task, which we will tell to the victorious king. That mountain, whose summit is in the clouds, has made our hearts grieve and mourn: we cannot sleep because of Yajuj and Majuj, who live there and whom we have not the strength to resist. When a mob of them comes against our city, we know only pain and sorrow. They have faces like animals, with black tongues and bloodshot eyes; they have black skin and teeth like a boar's. How can anyone stand up to them? Their bodies including the chest are covered with dark hair, and they have huge ears like an elephant's; when they sleep they can fold an ear under them as a pillow, or spread it over them as a coverlet. All their females give birth to thousands of little brats, so that no one can count how many they are. They flock together like animals, running like wild asses. In spring when the clouds thunder and the green sea churns, the clouds suck up serpents from the waves and the air growls like a lion; then the clouds drop the serpents, and herds of these monsters come to feed on them. They eat them year after year till their chests and shoulders grow big and strong. After that they eat plants, which they collect from everywhere. When it's cold they get very thin, and then their voices are like a dove's, but if you see them in the spring they're like wolves, and they roar like trumpeting elephants. If the king can find some remedy against them, so that our hearts can be freed from this sorrow, all of us will praise him, and our praise will resound in the world for a long time. We ask that you be magnanimous and rid us of our grief, for you too need God's blessings."

Sekandar marveled at what they had told him. He was pensive for a while, then said, "I will provide treasure, your city must provide the labor and effort. With the help of God I will bring them under control." All the townsmen said, "O king, may bad luck never be yours! We are your slaves while we live, ready to offer whatever is necessary. We'll bring whatever you require, as nothing is more important to us than this." Sekandar went out and inspected the mountain and then summoned his sages to him. He called for blacksmiths, together with huge quantities of copper, brass, heavy hammers, plaster, stone, and an immeasurable amount of firewood, as much as would be necessary for the job in hand. When the plans had been well thought out, masons, blacksmiths, and all manner of artisans came from throughout the world to help Sekandar with this project. Craftsmen from every country gathered there, and two walls were constructed on the opposite sides of the mountain, a hundred fathoms wide and stretching from the mountain's base to its summit. One cubit was of charcoal and the next of iron with a little copper mixed into it, then sulfur was poured over it, following the method of the Kayanid craftsmen. Course was laid above course in this way, and then holes were drilled in it from its base to the summit. Next, oil and turpentine were mixed together and poured over the materials. Finally a mass of charcoal was placed on the top of the walls, and the whole construction was set alight. At the king's command a hundred thousand blacksmiths fed the flames with air from bellows; a great roar went up from the mountain, and the stars seemed eclipsed by the fire. The result of all the blacksmiths' labor, the bellows fanning the flames, the materials laid one above another and then melting in the flames, was that the world was freed from Yajuj and Majuj, and the earth was once again a place of peace and pleasure: the famous barrier of Sekandar had delivered the world from strife. The city's nobles thanked him and wished him eternal life; they brought him many presents, but to their astonishment he accepted none of them.

Sekandar Sees a Corpse in the Palace of Topazes

The king and his army marched onward for a month and were sorely tried by their journey. They came to a mountain, where they saw no sign of either wild or domestic animals. The mountain's crest was of lapis lazuli, and a palace stood there, made of topazes. It was filled with crystal chandeliers, and in its midst was a fountain of salt water. Next to this fountain was a throne for two people, on which was stretched a wretched corpse. He had a man's body, but his head was like that of a boar; there was a pillow of camphor beneath his head, and a brocade covering had been drawn up over his body. Instead of a lamp a brilliant red jewel shone there, illuminating the whole area; its rays twinkled like stars in the water, and all the chamber glowed as if in sunlight. Whoever went there to take something, or even simply set foot within the palace, found himself rooted to the spot; his whole body began to tremble, and he started to waste away.

A cry came from the salt water, saying, "O king, still filled with longing and desire, don't play the fool much longer! You have seen many things that no man ever saw, but now it's time to draw rein. Your life has shortened now, and the royal throne is without its king." Sekandar was afraid and hurried back to his camp as fast as wind-blown smoke. Quickly he led his army away, weeping and calling on God's name. From that mountain he headed toward the desert, afflicted with sorrow and concerned for his soul. And so he went forward, at the head of his troops, weeping and in pain.

Sekandar Sees the Speaking Tree

The desert road led to a city, and Sekandar was relieved when he heard human voices there. The whole area was one of gardens and fine buildings and was a place to delight any man. The city's noblemen welcomed him, calling out greetings and showering him with gold and jewels. "It is wonderful that you have come to visit us," they said. "No army has ever entered this town, and no one in it has ever heard the name of 'king.' Now that you have come our souls are yours, and may you live with bodily health and spiritual serenity." Sekandar was pleased by their welcome and rested from the journey across the desert. He said to them, "What is there here that's astonishing, that should be inquired into?" A guide said to him, "Victorious king, there is a marvel here, a tree that has two separate trunks together, one of which is female and the other male, and these splendid tree limbs can speak. At night the female trunk becomes sweet smelling and speaks, and when the daylight comes, the male speaks." Sekandar and his Greek cavalry, with the nobles of the town gathered around, listened and said, "When is it you say that the tree speaks in a loud voice?" The translator replied, "A little after day has disappeared one of the trunks begins to speak, and a lucky man will hear its voice; in the dark night the female speaks, and its leaves then smell like musk."

Sekandar answered, "When we go beyond the tree, what wonders are there on the other side?" The reply was, "When you pass the tree there is little argument about which way to take, as there is no place beyond there; guides say it is the world's end. A dark desert lies ahead of you, but no man is so weary of his own soul as to go there. None of us have ever seen or heard that there are any animals there, or that birds fly there." Sekandar and his troops went forward, and when they came near the speaking tree the ground throbbed with heat and the soil there was covered with the pelts of wild beasts. He asked his guide what the pelts were, and who it was that had skinned so many animals in this way. The man answered, "The tree has many worshippers, and when they come here to worship, they feed on the flesh of wild animals."

When the sun reached its zenith Sekandar heard a voice above him, coming from the leaves of the tree; it was a voice to strike terror and foreboding in a man. He was afraid and said to the interpreter, "You are wise and mean well, tell me what the leaves are saying, which makes my heart dissolve within me." "O king, favored by fortune, the leaves say, 'However much Sekandar wanders in the world, he has already seen his share of blessings: when he has reigned for fourteen years, he must quit the royal throne.'" At the guide's words Sekandar's heart filled with pain, and he wept bitterly. He was sad and silent then, speaking to no one, until midnight. Then the leaves of the other trunk began to speak, and Sekandar again asked the interpreter what they said. He replied, "The female tree says, 'Do not puff yourself up with greed; why torment your soul in this way? Greed makes you wander the wide world, harass mankind, and kill kings. But you are not long for this earth now; do not darken and deaden your days like this.'" Then the king said to the interpreter, "Pure of heart and noble as you are, ask them one question: Will this fateful day come in Greece; will my mother see me alive again, before someone covers my face in death?"

> The speaking tree replied, "Few days remain;
> You must prepare your final baggage train.
> Neither your mother, nor your family,
> Nor the veiled women of your land will see
> Your face again. Death will come soon: you'll die
> In a strange land, with strangers standing by.
> The stars and crown and throne and worldly glory
> Are sated with Sekandar and his story."

Sekandar left the tree, his heart wounded as if by a sword. When he returned to his camp, his chieftains went into the town to collect the gifts from the town's nobility. Among these was a cuirass that shone like the waters of the Nile and was as huge as an elephant skin: it had two long tusks attached to it and was so heavy it was hard to lift. There was other armor, as well as fine brocade, a hundred golden eggs each weigh-

ing sixty *man*, and a rhinoceros made of gold and jewels. Sekandar
accepted the gifts and led off his army, weeping bitter tears as he went.

Sekandar Visits the Emperor of China

Now Sekandar led his army toward China. For forty days they traveled,
until they reached the sea. There the army made camp and the king
pitched his brocade pavilion. He summoned a scribe to write a letter to
the Chinese emperor from Sekandar, the seizer of cities. The message
was filled with promises and threats, and when it was completed
Sekandar himself went as the envoy, taking with him an intelligent
companion who was one with him in heart and speech and who could
advise him as to what to do and what not to do. He entrusted his troops
to the army's commander and chose five Greeks as his escort.

When news reached the Chinese emperor that an envoy was
approaching his country, he sent troops out to meet him. Sekandar
reached the court and the emperor came forward in welcome, but his
heart was filled with suspicious thoughts. Sekandar ran forward and made
his obeisance to him, and then was seated in the palace for a long while.
The emperor questioned him and made much of him and assigned him
noble sleeping quarters. As the sun rose over the mountains, dying their
summits gold, the envoy was summoned to court. Sekandar spoke at
length, saying what was appropriate, and then handed over the letter. It
was addressed from the king of Greece, possessor of the world, lord of
every country, on whom other kings call down God's blessings. It con-
tinued, "My orders for China are that she remain prosperous, and that
she should not prepare for war against me; it was war against me that
destroyed Foor, and Dara, who was the lord of the world, and Faryan
the Arab, and other sovereigns. From the east to the west no one ignores
my commands, the heavens themselves do not know the number of my
troops, and Venus and the sun could not count them. If you disobey any
command of mine you will bring distress on yourself and your country.
When you read my letter, bring me tribute; do not trouble yourself
about this, or look for evil allies to make war on me. If you come you
will see me in the midst of my troops, and when I see that you are hon-
est and mean well I shall confirm you in the possession of your crown
and throne, and no misfortune will come to you. If, however, you are
reluctant to come before your king, send me things that are peculiar to

China—your country's gold work, horses, swords, seal rings, clothes, cloth, ivory thrones, fine brocade, necklaces, crowns—that is, if you have no wish to be harmed by me. Send my soldiers back to me, and rest assured that your wealth, throne, and crown are safe."

When the emperor of China saw what was in the letter, he started up in fury, but then chose silence as a better course. He laughed and said to the envoy, "May your king be a partner to the heavens! Tell me what you know about him. Tell me about his conversation, his height and appearance, and what kind of a man he is." The envoy said, "Great lord of China, you should understand that there is no one else in the world like Sekandar. In his manliness, policy, good fortune, and wisdom he surpasses all that anyone could imagine. He is as tall as a cypress tree, has an elephant's strength, and is as generous as the waters of the Nile; his tongue can be as cutting as a sword, but he can charm an eagle down from the clouds." When he heard all this, the emperor changed his mind. He ordered that wine and a banquet be laid out in the palace gardens. He drank till evening brought darkness to the world, and the company became tipsy. Then he said to the envoy, "May your king be Jupiter's partner. At first light I'll compose an answer to his letter, and what I write will make the day seem splendid to your eyes." Sekandar was half drunk, and he staggered from the garden to his quarters with an orange in his hand.

When the sun rose in Leo and the heavens dispelled the darkness, Sekandar went to the emperor, and all suspicious thoughts were far from his heart. The emperor asked him, "How did you spend the night? When you left you were quite overcome with wine." Then he summoned a scribe, who brought paper, musk, and ambergris, and dictated a letter. He began with praise of God, the lord of chivalry, justice, and ability, of cultivated behavior, abstinence, and piety, and called down his blessings on the Greek king. Then he continued, "Your eloquent envoy has arrived, bringing the king's letter. I have read through the royal words and discussed its contents with my nobles. As for your claims concerning the wars against Dara, Faryan, and Foor, in which you were victorious, so that you became a shepherd whose flock consists of kings, you should not consider what comes about through the will of the Lord of the Sun and Moon as the result of your own valor and the might of your army. When a great man's days are numbered, what difference does it make whether he dies in battle or at a banquet? If they died in battle with you this is because their fate was fixed for that day, and fate is not to be hurried or delayed. You should not pride yourself so much on your victories over them, because even if you are made of iron there is no doubt that you too will die. Where now are Feraydun, Zahhak, and Jamshid, who came like the wind and left like a breath? I am not afraid of you and I will not make war against you, neither shall I puff myself up with pride as you are doing. It is not my habit to shed blood, and besides it would be unworthy of my faith for me to do evil in this way. You summon me, but to no purpose; I serve God, not kings. I send with this more riches than you have dreamed of, so that there shall be no doubting my munificence."

These words were an arrow in Sekandar's vital organs, and he blushed with shame. In his heart he said, "Never again shall I go somewhere disguised as my own envoy." He returned to his quarters and prepared to leave the Chinese court.

The proud emperor opened his treasuries' doors, since he was not a man who found generosity difficult. First he ordered that fifty crowns and ten ivory thrones encrusted with jewels be brought; then a thousand camel loads of gold and silver goods, and a thousand more of Chinese brocades and silks, of camphor, musk, perfumes, and ambergris. He had little regard for wealth, and it eased his heart to be bountiful in this way. He had ten thousand each of the pelts of gray squirrel, ermine, and sable brought, and as many carpets and crystal goblets, and his wise treasurer saw to their being loaded on pack animals. Then he added three hundred silver saddles and fifty golden ones, together with three hundred red-haired camels loaded with Chinese rarities. He chose as envoy an eloquent and dignified Chinese sage and told him to take his message to the Greek king with all goodwill and splendor, and to say that Sekandar would be warmly welcomed at the Chinese court for as long as he wished to stay there.

The envoy traveled with Sekandar, unaware that he was the Greek king. But when Sekandar's regent came forward and the king told him of his adventures, and the army congratulated him on his safe return and bowed to the ground before him, the envoy realized that he was indeed the Greek king and dismounted in consternation. Sekandar said to him, "There is no need for apologies, but do not tell your emperor of this!" They rested for a night, and the next morning Sekandar sat on the royal throne. He gave gifts to the envoy and said to him, "Go to your emperor and tell him that I say 'You have found honor and respect with me. If you wish to stay where you are, all China is yours, and if you wish to go elsewhere, that too is open to you. I shall rest here for a while, because such a large army as mine cannot be mobilized quickly.'" The envoy returned like the wind, and gave Sekandar's message to the emperor.

Sekandar Leads His Army to Babylon

Sekandar camped there for a month, and then led his army toward Babylon, and the air was darkened with the dust of their march. They pressed on for a month, and no one had any rest during this time. They came to a mountain range so high that its summit was hidden by dark clouds, as if it reached to Saturn. The king and his army could see no way forward but over the mountains and so with difficulty they climbed up toward the crest. The climb exhausted them, but once there they saw a deep lake lying below them. Joyfully and praising God, they began their descent; there was game of all kinds on every side, and for a while the soldiers lived off what they hunted.

Then in the distance a wild man appeared. He was covered in hair, and his body beneath the hair was a dark blue color, and he had huge ears, as big as an elephant's. The soldiers captured him and dragged him to Sekandar, who called on God in his astonishment at being confronted by such a creature. He said, "What kind of a man are you? What is your name? What can you find to live off in this lake, and what do you want from life?" The man replied, "O king, my mother and father call me Pillow-Ears." Then the king asked what it was that he could see in the middle of the lake, over toward where the sun rises. The man answered, "O king, and may you always be renowned in the world, that's a town that is like heaven; you'd say that earth had no part in its making. You won't see a single building there that isn't covered with fish skins and fish bones. On the walls they've painted the face of Afrasyab, and he looks more splendid than the sun itself; and warlike Khosrow's face is there too, and you can see his greatness and generosity by looking at it. They're painted on bones; you won't see one bit of soil in the whole city! The people eat fish there; that's the only thing they have to nourish them. If the king orders me to, I'll go there, but without any of your soldiers." Sekandar said to the man with huge ears, "Go, and bring back someone from the town, so that we can see something new."

Pillow-Ears hurried off to the town and soon came back with some of its inhabitants. Seventy men crossed the water with him; some were young and some old, and they were dressed in various kinds of silks. The older, more dignified men each carried a golden goblet filled with pearls, and the young ones each carried a crown; they came before Sekandar with their heads reverently bowed. They made their obeisance to him, and he talked with them for a long time. The army stayed there that night, and at cockcrow next morning the din of drums rang out from the king's pavilion. Sekandar continued the march to Babylon, and the air was dark with the dust sent up by his soldiers.

Sekandar's Letter to Arestalis and Arestalis's Reply

The king knew that death was close, and that his days were darkening, and he decided that no one of royal lineage should be left alive in the world: he wanted to ensure that no man would be able to lead an army against Greece. With his mind fixed on this arrogant scheme, he wrote a letter to Arestalis, saying he would invite everyone of royal lineage to his court, where they were to come unsuspecting of what was in store for them. When this letter was delivered to the Greek sage, his heart seemed to break in two. Immediately he wrote a reply, weeping as if his ink were tears. "The king of the world's missive arrived, and he should give up this evil design of his. As for the evil you have already done, think no more of it but distribute goods to the poor. For the future, abstain from evil and give your soul to God; sow nothing but seeds of goodness in the world. From birth we are all marked for death, and we have no choice but to submit. No one who dies takes his sovereignty with him; he leaves, and hands on his greatness to another. Live within limits and do not shed the blood of the great families, which will make you cursed until the resurrection. And if there is no army or king in Persia, armies will sweep in from Turkestan, India, Scythia, and China, and it would be no surprise if whoever took Persia then marched on the west. The descendants of the Persian kings should not be harmed so much as by a breath of wind. Summon them to your court, but be generous to them, feast them, and consult with them. Treat each according to his rank and see that their names are listed in your pension rolls, since it is from them that you took the world, paying nothing for it. Do not give any of them power over another, or refer to any of them as king of the world, but make these royal nobles a shield to protect the west against foreign invasion."

Sekandar changed his mind when he read this letter. He summoned the world's nobly born, all who were chivalrous by nature, to his court, and assigned them suitable places there. He wrote a charter, which designated the portion of each, with the stipulation that none was to encroach on another's power: these nobles he called "kings of the peoples."

That night Sekandar reached Babylon, where he was joyfully greeted by the local nobility. During the same night a woman gave birth to an astonishing child that had a lion's head, a human chest and human shoulders, a cow's tail, and hooves. The baby was stillborn, and it would have been better if the woman had had no offspring at all rather than such a monster. Immediately they brought the child to Sekandar, who took it as an omen, and ordered that it be buried. He told his astrologers of the child, who grew pensive and silent. He demanded their opinion, saying, "If you keep anything back from me I'll cut your heads from your bodies this minute, and your shroud will be a lion's maw." When the king stormed in this way, they said:

> *"First then, as scribes have written, at your birth*
> *The lion's emblem, Leo, ruled the earth.*
> *You saw the dead child had a lion's head,*
> *Which means your majesty will soon be dead.*
> *The world will be a place of strife until*
> *A new king bends its peoples to his will."*
> *The king grew pensive, then replied, "I see*
> *Death comes, for which there is no remedy.*
> *I'm not long for this world, I know, but I*
> *Refuse to brood on this until I die.*
> *Death comes to us on the appointed day—*
> *We cannot make fate hurry, or delay."*

Sekandar's Letter to His Mother

That day, in Babylon, he fell sick, and he knew that his end was approaching. He summoned an experienced scribe and dictated what was in his heart, in a letter to his mother. He said, "The signs of death cannot be hidden; I have lived the life allotted to me in this world, and we cannot hurry or delay our fate. Do not grieve at my death, for this is not a new thing in the world: all who are born must die, be they kings or paupers. I shall tell our chieftains that when they return from this land to Greece they must obey you alone. I have established those

Persians who fought against our armies as lords over their realm, so that
they shall have no desire to attack Greece; our country will be secure
and at peace. See that my body is buried in Egypt, and that you fulfill
all that I say here. Every year distribute ten thousand gold coins of my
wealth to the peasantry. If Roshanak bears a son, then my name will
surely survive; no one but he must become king of Greece, and he will
renew the country's prosperity. But if, when her labor pains come to
her, she bears a daughter, marry the child to one of Filqus's sons and
call him my son, not my son-in-law, so that my name shall be remem-
bered in the world. As for Kayd's innocent daughter, send her back to
her father in India, together with the crowns and silver and gold and
all the dowry she brought. Now I have completed my affairs and have
no choice but to prepare my heart for death. First, see that my coffin
is of gold and that my body's shroud is worthy of me; let it be of
Chinese silk impregnated with sweet scents, and see that no one neg-
lects the offices due to me. The joints of my coffin should be sealed
with pitch, as well as camphor, musk, and ambergris. Honey should be
poured into the coffin, then a layer of brocade placed there, on which
my body is to be laid; when my face has been covered there is no more
to be said. When I have gone, wise mother, remember my words. As
for the things that I have sent from India, China, Turan, Iran, and
Makran, keep what you need and distribute the surplus. Dear mother,
my desire is that you be sensible and serene in your soul; do not tor-
ment yourself on my behalf, since no one who lives in the world lives
forever. When your days too draw to a close, my soul shall surely see
yours again; patience is a greater virtue than love, and a person blown
hither and thither by emotion is contemptible. For months and years
you lovingly cared for my body; now pray to God for my soul; with
these prayers you will still care for me. And consider, who is there in
all the world whose soul is not cast down by death?"

He sealed the letter and ordered that it be taken with all speed
from Babylon to Greece, to give news there that the imperial glory
had been eclipsed.

Sekandar Dies in Babylon

When the army learned of the king's illness, the world grew dark before
them. Their eyes turned toward the throne, and the world was filled with
rumors. Knowing that he had few days left to live and hearing of his

army's concern, Sekandar gave orders that his sickbed be taken from the palace out to the open plain. His saddened troops saw his face devoid of color, and the plain rang from end to end with lamentations, as if the soldiers were burning in flames; they cried, "It is an evil day when the Greeks lose their king: misfortune triumphs, and now our country will be destroyed. Our enemies have reached their hearts' desire, while for us the world has turned bitter, and we shall mourn publicly and in secret."

> Then in a failing voice their king replied,
> "Live humbly, fearfully, when I have died,
> And if you'd grow and prosper see that you
> Keep my advice henceforth, in all you do.
> This is your duty to me when I'm gone
> Lest time undo the work that I have done."
> He spoke, and then his soul rose from his breast:
> The king who'd shattered armies was at rest.

An earsplitting wail went up from his troops as they heaped dust on their heads and wept bitter tears. They set fire to the royal pavilion, and the very earth seemed to cry out in sorrow. They cut the tails of a thousand horses and set their saddles on them back to front, as a sign of mourning. As they brought the golden coffin their cries resounded in the heavens; a bishop washed the corpse in clear rosewater and scattered pure camphor over it. They shrouded their king in golden brocade, lamenting as they did so, then placed him beneath a covering of Chinese silk, his body soaked from head to toe in honey. The coffin lid was fastened, and the noble tree whose shade had spread so widely was no more.

They passed the coffin from hand to hand across the plain, and as they went forward, two opinions began to be heard. The Persians said, "He should not be buried anywhere but here: this is the land of emperors, what are they doing carrying the coffin about the world like this?" But a Greek guide said, "It would not be right to bury him here; if you hear my view you'll see that I'm right. Sekandar should be buried in the soil that nourished him." A Persian interrupted, "No matter how much you continue this conversation it won't get to the root of the matter. I'll show you a meadow near here that's been preserved since the time of our ancient kings: old folk call it Jorm. There is a wooded area there, and a lake; if you ask it a question, an answer will come from the mountain nearby. Take an old man there, together with the coffin, and ask your question; if the mountain answers, it will give you the best advice." As quickly as mountain sheep they made their way to the thicket called Jorm. And when they asked their question, the answer came, "What are you doing with this royal coffin? The dust of Sekandar belongs in Alexandria, the town he founded while he was alive." As soon as they heard this, the soldiers hurried from the area.

The Mourning for Sekandar

When Sekandar's body reached Alexandria the world was beset with new disputes. The coffin was set down on the plain, and the land was filled with rumor and gossip. As many as a hundred thousand children, men, and women flocked there. The philosopher Arestalis was there, his eyes filled with bitter tears; the world watched as he stretched out his hand to the coffin and said, "Where are your intelligence, knowledge, and foresight, now that a narrow coffin is your resting place? Why in the days of your youth did you choose the earth as your couch?"

The Greek sages crowded round, each speaking in turn, lamenting Sekandar's death. And then his mother came running, and placed her face on his chest, and said,

> "O noble king, world-conqueror, whose state
> Was princely, and whose stars were fortunate,

You're far away from me and seem so near,
Far from your kin, far from your soldiers here.
Would that my soul were your soul's slave, that I
Might see the hearts of those who hate you die."
Then Roshanak ran grieving to his side,
Crying, "Where are those kings now, and their pride?
Where's Dara, who once ruled the world? Where's Foor?
Where's Ashk? Faryan? The sovereign of Sharzoor,
And all those other lords who put their trust
In battle and were dragged down to the dust?
You seemed a storm cloud charged with hail: I said
That you could never die, that you had shed
So much blood, fought so many wars, that there
Must be some secret you would not declare,
Some talisman that fate had given you
To keep you safe whatever you might do.
You cleared the world of petty kings, brought down
Into the dirt an empire's ancient crown,
And when the tree you'd planted was to bear
Its fruits you died, and left me in despair."

When the sky's golden shield descended, the nobles were exhausted by
their grief, and they placed the coffin in the ground. There is nothing
in the world so terrible and fearful as the fact that one comes like the
wind and departs as a breath, and that neither justice nor oppression
are apparent in this. Whether you are a king or a pauper you will dis-
cover no rhyme or reason to it. But one must act well, with valor and
chivalry, and one must eat well and rejoice: I see no other fate for you,
whether you are a subject or a prince. This is the way of the ancient
world: Sekandar departed, and what remains of him now is the words
we say about him. He killed thirty-six kings, but look how much of
the world remained in his grasp when he died. He founded ten pros-
perous cities, and those cities are now reed beds. He sought things that
no man has ever sought, and what remains of him within the circle of
the horizon is words, nothing more. Words are the better portion,
since they do not decay as an old building decays in the snow and rain.
I have finished with Sekandar now, and with the barrier that he built;
may our days be fortunate and prosperous.

THE ASHKANIANS

What was said in that *Book of the Righteous,* concerning ancient times? What does it say about the period after Sekandar had gone? Who occupied the throne then? A knowledgeable landowner from Chach put it like this: no one occupied the ivory throne. The chieftains who claimed descent from Arash, who were a valiant, impulsive, and stubborn clan, were scattered about in different corners of the world, each of them cheerfully ruling a petty kingdom. Collectively they were called the "kings of the peoples."

> *And so two hundred years went by: you'd say*
> *That monarchy itself had passed away.*
> *The local chiefs were happy to ignore*
> *Each other, and the earth was cleansed of war.*
> *Sekandar had foreseen and planned this peace*
> *To safeguard the prosperity of Greece.*

The first among the new kings was Ashk, of the family of Qobad; others included Shapur who was of equally noble birth, the Ashkanian prince Gudarz, the Kayanid prince Bizhan, Nersi, the mighty Hormozd, and Arash, who was a fearsome warrior. After him there was Ardavan, a wise, clear-sighted man. When the Ashkanian Bahram became king he distributed wealth among the deserving and was called Ardavan the Great because he was a man who protected his flock from the wolves' claws. He held the area from Shiraz to Esfahan, which discerning men have called the seat of nobility, and by his authority Estakhr was ruled by Babak, a man whose snares terrified dragons. But all these ruled for such a short time and had so little influence that the chronicler did not record their lives in detail; I have heard nothing but their names, and seen nothing about them in royal records. All this was as the dying Sekandar had planned: Greece would remain safe and prosperous while the Eastern princes were preoccupied with local affairs, and so paid no attention to her. When a wise man becomes king, his knowledge ensures that such plans come to fruition.

Babak Sees Sasan in a Dream

When Dara was killed in battle and his family fell upon dark times, a wise, brave son, who was called Sasan, survived him. When he saw that his father had been murdered, and that the Persians' fortunes were in ruins, he fled before the Greek army and escaped from the general disaster. He died obscurely in India, but left behind him a son who bore his name, which continued in the family for four generations. They lived as shepherds, sometimes as camel drivers, and all their years passed in poverty and hard labor. The last, while still a child, presented himself before Babak's chief shepherd and said, "Do you need a laborer, someone who can live out his wretched life here?" The shepherd hired Sasan, who worked hard day and night and pleased his masters, so that when he grew up he became chief shepherd in his turn. He was a man who lived in sadness, by the sweat of his brow.

One night as Babak slept, his bright soul dreamt that Sasan was riding a war elephant, and in his hand was an Indian sword. Everyone who came before him bowed down to him; he made the earth flourish, and drove sorrow from men's hearts. The next night Babak dreamed that a fire worshipper lit three fires on the plain; they were just like the fires in the temples of Azar-Goshasp, Khorad, and Mehr, and they shone like the turning heavens. All three burned before Sasan, who fed them with aloes wood. Babak woke in consternation from his dream and summoned oneiromancers. They gathered at his court and when Babak told them what he'd seen, they grew pensive. Finally the most senior among them said, "Great king, we must consider what this means. Anyone who is seen in this way by others, in a dream, is destined to raise his head above the sun in sovereignty: and if the dream does not refer to him it will be fulfilled by his son."

Babak was overjoyed when he heard this, and rewarded each of those present according to his rank. Then he gave orders for his chief shepherd to appear before him. It was a bitterly cold day, and the man appeared dressed in coarse clothes, his sheepskin coat covered in snow, and his heart almost split in two with anxiety. Babak commanded that the court be cleared, and the servants and counselors left the two alone. He questioned Sasan, and was cordial to him, seating him beside himself. He asked him about his family and lineage, but the shepherd was terrified at first and made no answer. Finally Sasan said, "Your majesty, if you will take pity on your shepherd, swear with your hand in mine that no matter what my lineage might be you will not seek to harm me, either openly or in secret." Babak swore by merciful God that he would not harm him in any way; his intention was only to make him happy and treat him with respect.

Then the young man said, "I am the son of Sasan, a descendant of King Ardeshir, who is remembered under the name Bahman, and who was the son of the great Esfandyar, the son of Goshtasp." When he heard this, Babak wept that he had seen such dreams. He had splendid clothes and a royally accoutered horse assigned to Sasan and said to him, "Go to the hot baths while they prepare your court clothes." He had a palace built for this man who had once been his chief shepherd, and when he was installed there Babak gave him slaves and attendants and every kind of necessity for life. He gave him more wealth than he could need, and lastly Babak gave him in marriage the crown of his life, his lovely daughter.

The Birth of Ardeshir Babakan

When nine months had gone by, this beautiful princess gave birth to a boy as splendid as the sun. He looked like Ardeshir, and he grew quickly into a brave, formidable child. His father called him Ardeshir, and his grandfather rejoiced to see him and was always cradling him in his arms. So time passed, and perceptive men referred to the boy as Ardeshir Babakan. He was taught all the skills a prince should acquire, and they made his kingly nature even more splendid: his face and manner were such that you'd say the heavens themselves shone with their borrowed light.

News of the knowledge and courtly accomplishments of this young man, who was said to be a raging lion in battle and as gracious as the goddess Nahid at banquets, came to Ardavan, who wrote a letter to Babak. It said, "Wise, prudent, eloquent, and renowned chieftain, I have heard that your grandson Ardeshir is a fine horseman, an eloquent boy, and a quick study. As soon as you read this letter, send him to me and I shall treat him well. I'll give him all that he requires, and make him the first of my warriors. When he is with my sons I shall make no distinction between him and them."

Babak wept when he read this letter, and had Ardeshir and a scribe brought to him. He said to the young man, "Read Ardavan's message and pay close attention to it. I shall write an answer to the king now and send it with a trusted servant. I shall say, 'I send you this brave, fine, young man who is my heart, the apple of my eye; I have advised him on how to act when he reaches your exalted court. Act toward him as befits a king, and do not let even the winds of heaven blow against him.'" Then Babak quickly opened his treasury doors and made the young man's heart happy with his gifts. He presented him with golden saddles, maces and swords, gold coins and brocade, horses and slaves, Chinese cloths and imperial textiles. He laid his wealth before him, holding back nothing from the boy who was to serve Ardavan. He also sent gifts with Ardeshir for the king—brocade and gold coins, musk and ambergris. And so the promising young man left his grandfather and set off for Ardavan's court at Rey.

Ardeshir Arrives at Ardavan's Court

Word was sent to the king as soon as Ardeshir arrived at the court, and Ardavan had him brought in. He talked with him for a while about Babak, seated him near the throne, and had quarters in the palace assigned to him. He also saw that food, clothes, and furnishings were provided for the young man. Ardeshir, and his companions, who had made the journey with him, went to the lodgings they had been given.

When the sun placed its throne in the heavens, and the world turned as pale as a Greek's face, Ardeshir called one of his servants and had him take to King Ardavan the presents that Babak had sent. Ardavan was delighted by them, and the young man who had brought them seemed to him to be a fine addition to the court. He treated him as his child and for a while saw that nothing disturbed the youth's happiness. Whether they were drinking wine or at banquets or out hunting, Ardavan kept him always nearby, and there was no difference between Ardeshir and Ardavan's own sons.

And so it was that one day a group of courtiers and the king's four sons, all fine young princes, had scattered across the plain in a hunting expedition; Ardeshir rode next to Ardavan, who was delighted to have the young man with him. Then in the distance a wild ass appeared, and cries went up from the hunters; everyone gave chase, and the company was covered in dust and sweat. Ardeshir outstripped the rest, and as he neared the prey he notched an arrow to his bow. When he loosed the shaft, it struck the animal in the flank, and the whole arrow, head, feathers, and all, passed right through the body. Just at that moment King Ardavan rode up; he saw the arrow fly and the wild ass lying dead, and exclaimed, "Bravo, whoever shot that arrow!" Ardeshir said, "I killed this wild ass, with my arrow." But one of Ardavan's sons said, "I killed this beast, and I'd like to see anyone else manage such a feat!" Ardeshir turned to him and said, "The plain is wide, and there are asses and arrows in abundance; let's see you bring another one down in the same way. To a man with any pride, a lie is a sin!" But Ardavan was enraged by this remark and shouted, "This is my fault, since it was me who brought you up. Why should I have you at my banquets and take you hunting with me if you're going to push ahead of my sons and lord it over everyone? Go and look after my Arab horses, and sleep in the stables with them. You can act the master there and be everyone's boy for every job that's to be done!"

Ardeshir's eyes filled with tears, but he had no choice other than to go and live in the stables. He wrote a letter to his grandfather Babak, and as he did so his heart was filled with sorrow, his head with wild schemes. He wrote of how Ardavan had acted toward him and added that he hoped the man would endure bodily pains and mental distress. He went over everything that had happened, and where and why Ardavan had erupted in rage. When this message reached Babak, he kept its contents to himself. He was upset, and he sent the young man ten thousand dinars from his treasury. Then he called in a scribe and dictated a letter to Ardeshir: "You're a callow young man, and you haven't much wisdom as yet. When you went hunting with Ardavan, what business had you attacking his son like that? You're a servant there, not one of the family! You are your own worst enemy, and you've grown used to acting foolishly. Now you must try to please him and keep him satisfied with you: don't deviate from his orders even for a moment. I've sent you some money, and here I'm sending you some advice. When you use the one remember the other, until this business is over."

An old experienced messenger quickly brought the letter to Ardeshir, who was pleased when he read it. His heart began to weave plots and plans. He chose a house near the stables and filled it with carpets, fine clothes, and good food, so that it was hardly suitable for the work he was supposed to be doing. He spent his days and nights eating and drinking; wine and entertainers were his companions.

Golnar Sees Ardeshir; the Death of Babak

> *King Ardavan possessed a slave whose face*
> *Lit up his palace with bewitching grace:*
> *She seemed a painting, lovely and bejeweled.*
> *Her name was Golnar, and this slave girl ruled*
> *The palace as her monarch's counselor—*
> *His first advisor, and his treasurer.*
> *He loved her more than life itself: the sight*
> *Of Golnar filled the king's heart with delight.*

One day Golnar went up onto the palace roof and glimpsed the merrymaking in Ardeshir's courtyard. She was charmed by it, and when she saw Ardeshir's smiling face, the young man slipped into her heart. That night, toward dawn, she knotted a rope and let it down from the battlements. Boldly, invoking God's benevolence as she did so, she made her way to the ground. Wearing her jewels and scented with musk, she appeared before Ardeshir; he raised his head from his brocade pillow, emerging from sleep, and took her in his arms. The young man stared at the beautiful girl before him, at her hair and face and splendor, and said, "Where have you come from, to delight my sorrow-stricken heart in this way?" She answered, "I am a slave, and I live to see you alone, in all the world: I am King Ardavan's treasurer, and the chief pleasure and solace of his soul. But if you accept me, I shall be your slave and fill my heart and soul with adoration for you. I shall come to you whenever you wish, and change the darkness of your days to splendor."

A little later Babak, who had brought up Ardeshir, died, and left his place in this world to others. When news of this reached Ardeshir his soul was darkened and he grieved for his protector. All the nobles vied to be appointed governor of Pars, but the king entrusted the post to his eldest son: he gave orders that the drums were to be sounded, and the army set off across the plain. Ardeshir's heart was dark with grief for the benevolent old man who had guided and cherished him, and he took no pleasure in Ardavan's rule or his army. The news made him look for another course; his heart was filled with resentment, and he looked for some means of escape.

At that time King Ardavan, seeking to know who would be favored by the heavens, summoned astrologers to his court. He sent them up to Golnar's quarters, whence they could observe the stars. For three days they worked there, casting the king's horoscope. The treasurer overheard their conversation about the stars, and for three days and nights, through the third watch of each night, she eavesdropped on them, her heart filled with hope, her lips with sighs. On the fourth day the sages took their astrological tables from Golnar's quarters to the king, and put before him what they had discovered. They told him in detail how the secrets of high heaven affected him, and said that in the near future something would happen that would bring anguish to the king's heart. A servant who was valiant and of noble birth would flee from his court, and this man would become a great king, a ruler of the world, powerful and blessed by the stars. Ardavan's heart was deeply troubled by their words.

Ardeshir Flees with Golnar

The land turned pitch black and the slave girl made her way to Ardeshir. He was a sea of anger and resentment, unable to have a single day's peace because of his preoccupation with Ardavan. Golnar told him what the astrologers had told the king, and when he heard this he calmed down and was silent for a while. Her words concentrated his mind, and he decided on flight. He said to her,

> "If I'm to get to Pars, if I'm to see
> That land again where men are brave and free,
> I must know if you'll come with me, or stay
> Behind here with King Ardavan in Rey.
> If you accompany me you'll be the crown
> Of Persia, which will fill with your renown."
> And she replied, between expressive sighs
> While flowing tears fell from her lovely eyes,
> "I am your slave, I have one life to give
> And it is yours entirely, while I live."

Ardeshir said to the beautiful girl, "We have no choice but to do this tomorrow." She returned to her own quarters, determined to take her life in her hands and risk everything.

When dark night withdrew and the world turned gold with the rising sun, Golnar opened the treasury doors and began to choose among the jewels there. She selected rubies and other royal gems, as well as a sufficient number of gold coins for their purposes, then returned to her room. There she waited till night came up over the mountains, and Ardavan's sleeping palace was deserted. Quick as an arrow then, clutching the jewels and cash she had taken, she came to the valiant Ardeshir; he stood with a wine goblet in his hand, the stable guards asleep at his feet. He had made them drunk so that they would not impede the escape, and he'd picked out and saddled two fine horses. When he saw Golnar's face and the jewels and red gold she'd brought, he immediately set down the goblet and put the bridles over the horses' heads. Armored, and with a glittering sword in his hand, he mounted one horse and helped Golnar on to the other; together they fled from the palace buildings and took the road to Pars, their hearts filled with joy and ambition.

Ardavan Learns of What Golnar and Ardeshir Have Done

It was Ardavan's habit never to rise from his brocade bed, until he had first seen Golnar's face as a good omen for the day. But when the time came for him to get up and to have his throne spread with brocade, and the slave girl still had not come to his pillow, he exploded with fury against her. The guards stood before his door; his throne, crown, and audience hall were ready for him, and his chamberlain came in saying, "Your warriors and the country's nobility are waiting at the door." The king said to his servants, "See what is the matter with Golnar; it never happens that she doesn't come to my pillow; she knows what my habits are." At that moment the chief scribe came in and said, "Some time last night Ardeshir fled; he's taken from the stables a black horse and a gray, both of them mounts favored by the king. And at the same time the king lost his beloved companion, since it is clear that your treasurer has fled with Ardeshir."

Ardavan's warlike heart was enraged and he set off with a large group of horsemen in pursuit of the fugitives. You'd have said that their horses trod on fire, so swiftly did they gallop. At the roadside they saw a well-populated settlement with a number of animals and asked if before sunrise anyone had heard the sound of galloping. A man volunteered that two figures on two horses, one gray and the other black, had galloped across the plain, closely followed by a pristine mountain sheep, which kicked up as much dust as the horses did. Ardavan asked his advisor why a mountain sheep should be running behind them, and the man replied, "That is his *farr*, an earnest of his good fortune and sovereignty. If this sheep sticks with him, do not struggle against the fact, or this will turn into a lengthy business for us." Ardavan dismounted at the settlement, ate, and rested for a while, and then renewed the chase. With Ardavan and his advisor leading them, the group pressed on in pursuit of Ardeshir.

Meanwhile the young man and the slave girl rode like the wind, without resting for a moment; whoever is favored by the high heavens cannot be harmed by enemies. When they were tired out by their efforts, Ardeshir caught sight of a lake beneath them as they crested a hill, and he turned to Golnar and said, "Now that we are both exhausted by the journey, we should ride down to that water; both we and our horses are weak and worn out. We can stay by the water and eat something, and ride on when we've rested." But as they approached the lake, with their faces as yellow and sickly as the sun, Ardeshir saw two young men standing there, who shouted to him,

> *"Stay in your stirrups now, shake out your reins,*
> *Continue on your ride across the plains—*
> *You have escaped the dragon's deadly breath*
> *But if you drink here you'll encounter death."*

Ardeshir said to Golnar, "Remember their words." Their stirrups became heavy, their reins light; Ardeshir lifted his glittering lance to his shoulders and on they rode.

Tired and with darkness in his soul, Ardavan still rode after them like the wind, until at midday, when the sun had traversed half the sky, he saw a fine town. A number of its inhabitants came out to meet him, and he called out to their priests, "When did you last see a young man ride this way?" One of them answered, "Your majesty, benevolent and blessed by heaven, at the time when the sun sets and night spreads its dark veil over the land, two people rode through this town; they were covered in dust and their lips were dry with thirst. A mountain sheep followed one of them, and she was more splendid than any I've ever seen in a painting on a palace wall." Ardavan's advisor said to him, "The situation has changed; you should turn back here, muster an army, and prepare for war. His good fortune follows him, and our chasing after him like this is mere clutching at the wind. Write a letter to your son, telling him of the whole business; perhaps he can find some trace of Ardeshir. He must not be allowed to drink this sheep's milk!" When Ardavan heard these words, he knew that his days were numbered and that his glory was fading. He dismounted at the town, and prayed to God from whom all blessings come.

At dawn the following morning he gave orders for the return journey. He entered Rey at nightfall, his cheeks as pale as reeds. There he wrote a letter to his son, saying, "In our orchard, a twisted root has born fruit. Ardeshir has fled from my hearth quicker than any arrow. He has gone to Pars; find him, but do it discreetly, and tell no one in the world of this."

Ardeshir Gathers an Army

For his part, Ardeshir reached the shore of a wide body of water, where he prayed, "Sole source of help, who has made me safe from my malevolent enemy, I pray that his body may never know health again." Then he rested and talked with a ferryman there for a long time about the past. The ferryman, who was a wise old man, stared at Ardeshir's face and stature and realized that he must be descended from the Kayanid kings; the prince's *farr* and glory delighted him. Quickly he ferried Ardeshir across the water, and when the young man reached the other side and news of his coming spread, an army of supporters gathered there. Babak's men from Estakhr came, overjoyed at the news of their new king, and all of Dara's descendants came to him from the various provinces where they ruled. Joy at King Ardeshir's presence made old men's hearts young again, and band by band men poured in from the river valleys and mountains. Wise counselors came from every city and gathered about the ambitious youth. He addressed his followers: "Illustrious and righteous as you are, there is no one here who has not heard what the malevolent Sekandar, out of the baseness of his heart, did on this earth. One by one he killed my ancestors and unjustly grasped the world in his fist. Since I am descended from Esfandyar, it is right that I cannot recognize Ardavan as king here. If you are with me in this, I shall not let anyone usurp the title and throne that should be mine. What do you say? What's your answer? Tell me clearly!"

Everyone there, whether a warrior or a counselor, rose to his feet, and together they spoke from their hearts: "Those of us who are from Babak's tribe rejoice to see your face, and those of us who are Sasanians will bind on our sword belts to serve you in war. Our souls and bodies belong to you, our joys and sorrows depend on you. Your lineage on both sides is nobler than anyone's; kingship and heroism are your birthright. If you give the order, we shall make mountains level with the plains, and with our swords we shall make the ocean's water into blood." At such an answer Ardeshir's mind out-soared the spheres of Venus and Mercury. He thanked the nobles gathered there and meditated war in his heart.

At the edge of the water he built a city, which became the site of his preparations for war. A priest there said to him, "O fortunate and inspiring king, renewer of the monarchy, you must cleanse the province of Pars and then make war on Ardavan, because you are a young king and your star is still young. Of all those they call the 'kings of the peoples,' he is the richest, and besides, he has harassed and harried you. Once you have removed him from power, no one will have the strength to offer you any resistance." This was what had to be said, and Ardeshir was happy to hear such words. As the sun rose above the mountain peak he left the shore and set off toward Estakhr. But when the news reached Bahman, Ardavan's son, his soul darkened and his heart filled with pain; he did not sit idly on the royal throne but at once mustered his troops and prepared for war.

Ardeshir's Victory over Bahman

There was a nobleman called Sabak, a just and well-meaning man in charge of armaments and troops, who ruled over the town of Jahrom. He had seven fine sons. When he heard what was afoot he defected from Bahman's side and ceremoniously brought his army, with its war drums beating, to join forces with Ardeshir. As was customary, he dismounted and ran forward to kiss Ardeshir's feet. The ambitious young king made much of him and acknowledged the value of his prompt defection. But he was suspicious of Sabak, and in his heart he feared him. He was guarded with him as they marched, aware of the might of Sabak's large army. But Sabak was old and experienced, and he realized what Ardeshir was thinking. He came to the commander with the Zend-Avesta in his hand and said, "I swear by almighty God that Sabak's life is worthless if my heart is not blameless toward you. When I learned King Ardeshir was gathering troops on that shore, I became disgusted with Ardavan, just as a young man will be disgusted by an old woman. Consider me as a kind, patient, trustworthy slave, who will bring you good luck." Hearing this, Ardeshir changed his mind about Sabak; he thought of him henceforth as his father, and placed him in command of his other officers.

With his heart freed from this anxiety, Ardeshir paused at the fire-temple of Ram-Khorad; there he prayed earnestly for God to guide him, to give him victory in all his undertakings, and to allow the tree of greatness to flourish for him. Then he returned to his pavilion, where his officers and men awaited him. He distributed cash to his troops, invoking God as he did so. His army was now like a valiant leopard, and he advanced against Bahman, the son of Ardavan, to give battle.

As the two armies approached one another, each side formed ranks ready for battle, with lances and Indian swords grasped in their hands. Then they fell on one another like warring lions, and blood was spilled in rivers. So they fought until the sun turned pale, and the air was filled with dust, the ground with corpses. At dawn the next morning, when the sky's veil turned the color of turquoise, Sabak's troops entered the fray. A wind sprang up, and the dust made the air like pitch. Ardeshir attacked from the center, and such was his might and the strength of his *farr* that he slew many men with his mace. Bahman fled before him, his body wounded with arrows and his soul shrouded in darkness. King Ardeshir pursued him relentlessly, with trumpets sounding and arrows raining down, until they reached the city of Estakhr, the seat of Bahman's power. At the the sound of Ardeshir's voice a vast number of troops defected to him. He distributed to them the wealth that Bahman had toiled to accumulate, scattering the hoarded coins. Strong and confident, he led his armies out of Pars.

Ardeshir's War Against Ardavan; Ardavan Is Killed

The news of Bahman's defeat brought terror to Ardavan's heart and his soul darkened. He said, "A man who knew the secrets of the turning heavens once said to me that whenever an evil surpasses our imagination, our efforts can have no effect on our fate. I would not have thought that Ardeshir could become so ambitious or turn into a conqueror of cities." He opened his treasury's doors, distributed provisions, mustered his army, and set off. He led his men through Gilan and Daylam, and the dust they sent up ascended to the moon. On the other side, Ardeshir too pressed forward; his men were so numerous that they stopped the wind in its tracks, and the columns resounded with the blare of trumpets and bugles, the jangling of bells, and the clashing of Indian cymbals. The armies were now two bowshots from one another, and the very snakes in the ground cowered away in terror. With a roar the columns attacked, their banners bravely fluttering, their swords lopping off heads, empurpled with blood.

The fighting lasted for forty days. The common soldiers were hard pressed, their provisions ran out, and it was difficult to resupply them. So many corpses were piled there that the plain seemed like a mountain, and the wounded despaired of life. Finally a fierce wind sprang up, and a black cloud that made it impossible to fight spread over the armies; the mountainside groaned, the ground shook, and the noise re-echoed in the heavens. Ardavan's army was terrified; they all believed that this was a sign from God against their king, and that there was nothing to do for their forces now but weep. On that day, the tide of battle turned against them and they all surrendered. Ardeshir advanced from the center of his troops, through the clash of weapons and a hail of arrows. Ardavan, who had devoted his sweet soul to the crown, was captured by a man named Kharrad who seized his bridle and dragged him before the king. Ardavan dismounted before Ardeshir, wounded and in despair. Ardeshir turned to his executioner and said, "Take that enemy of the king and split him open with a sword: fill the hearts of those who plot against us with terror." The man came forward and did as he had been ordered, and so this illustrious ruler was lost to the world.

> *The ancient heavens turn; kings disappear,*
> *Now Ardavan is gone, now Ardeshir,*
> *And though their heads reach to the stars they must*
> *At last be humbled in the lowly dust.*

The humiliation of the family of Arash was increased by the capture of two of Ardavan's sons. Their legs were bound, and the king gave orders that they be imprisoned. The two eldest sons fled from the battlefield and escaped capture; weeping they fled to India, and theirs is a story worth recounting. The whole battlefield was strewn with horse gear, baldrics, weapons, and gold and silver objects; the king had all this collected, and then distributed it to his soldiers. Sabak left the other chieftains and cleansed Ardavan's body of blood. Weeping, he wiped away the grime of battle, and made him a tomb suitable for a king. He wrapped the wounded body in brocade and placed a pillow of camphor beneath his head. But when the soldiers went on to Rey they trampled the dust of Ardavan's palace beneath their feet.

Then Sabak came before Ardeshir and said, "Wise king, demand Ardavan's daughter in marriage: she has splendor and beauty and the dignity of her station. The crown and wealth that Ardavan took such trouble to accumulate will be in your hands." Ardeshir accepted this advice, and immediately demanded the girl in marriage. He stayed two months in her apartments; he was now a mighty commander, and a mighty king. Then he made his way from Rey to Pars, having rested from battle and the world's strife. He built a town there filled with palaces and gardens, streams, open spaces, and mountain slopes: a wise old local dignitary still refers to that place as Khurreh-ye Ardeshir— "The Glory of Ardeshir." From an inexhaustible spring of water within the town, he led off streams and irrigation channels. Near the spring he built a fire-temple, and there he celebrated the Zoroastrian festivals of Mehregan and Sadeh. Around the temple there were gardens, open spaces, and palaces; he made it into a splendid place. When later this wise and powerful king had died, the lord of the marches there called the place the city of Gur. Ardeshir built villages around it and settled the area. Although there was a deep lake nearby, it was separated from the town by a mountain. Ardeshir had laborers hack a hundred channels through the rock with picks, so that the water from the lake irrigated Gur, which became filled with buildings and livestock.

Ardeshir's War with the Kurds

Ardeshir led a huge army out from Estakhr, to fight against the Kurds. He sought aid from God in his expedition to spill the blood of these thieves, but when he entered Kurdish territory, a numberless host welcomed him with war. An expedition that should have been a minor matter became difficult, because the whole countryside supported the Kurds, so that they outnumbered the king's men thirty to one. They fought a whole day till nightfall, when the king's army fled and the battlefield was crowded with so many corpses that one could hardly move. Only a few soldiers remained behind with their king, and they were tormented with thirst because of the dust and the heat of the sun. Then night spread its banner and put an end to the fighting and tumult.

Ardeshir saw a fire on the mountainside; he and his companions made their way up to it, and as they drew nearer they saw a few shepherds there, watching their sheep and goats. He and his soldiers dismounted, and as their mouths were filled with the dust of battle, Ardeshir immediately asked for water, which the shepherds gave him, together with some yogurt. He rested and ate a little of what was before him: then he spread out his armor to sleep on, and his pillow was his royal helmet.

Dawn broke over the lake, and the king of Persia lifted his head from sleep. The chief of the shepherds came to his pillow saying, "I wish you lucky days and nights. How is it that you've come here, as this is no place for someone like you to sleep?" The king questioned him about the way, and where he could find a place to rest. The shepherd answered, "You won't find any houses unless you have a guide. But about four parasangs from here there is a place where you could rest, and from there you could go from village to village until you reach the one where the local headman lives." Ardeshir took a few of the older men there as guides and made his way to the village where the headman was. From there he sent horsemen, young and old, to Khurreh-ye Ardeshir, and when the army heard of his escape, they were overjoyed and set out to come to his aid. Meanwhile Ardeshir posted spies, who quickly reported back that the Kurds were reveling in their success and giving no thought at all to the king. They thought that his luck had grown old and feeble, and that he had gone back to Estakhr. The king was happy to hear this, and soon forgot his recent reverses. He selected thirty thousand cavalry from the army that had joined him, as well as a thousand archers.

As the sun grew yellow in the west he led his army out, leaving behind those unfit for the march. By the time half the night had passed, and it was pitch dark, Ardeshir was close to the Kurds. The whole plain was filled with sleeping men, lying here and there, careless of their safety. He drew his sword, slackened his grip on the reins, and charged the Kurds' camp. The grass was crowned with their blood, the plain was filled with their severed heads and limbs, and the heaps of dead were dreadful to see. A huge number of them were taken prisoner: their violence and stupidity had been humbled. Ardeshir turned the country over to his soldiers for plunder, and distributed purses of gold and crowns to them. The countryside there became so secure because of Ardeshir's rule that an old man could have walked across the plain with a salver of gold coins on his head, and no one would have so much as looked at him. Ardeshir did not stay to enjoy the fruits of war but hurried back to Estakhr, where he gave orders that the men's horses were to be tended to and their armor was to be repaired. He told his soldiers to rest and enjoy themselves, since the time for warfare would come again quickly enough. His warriors feasted and rested, while Ardeshir's thoughts were of war.

The Story of the Worm of Haftvad

Consider this strange story, revealed by a local dignitary, telling old obscure tales. There was a poor but populous town called Kajaran near the Persian Gulf, where all the inhabitants lived by their own efforts. A number of girls who had to work for their livelihood lived there. To one side of the town was a mountain, where the girls would go together, taking cotton and spindles made of poplar wood. Traveling in a group through the main town gate, they would make their way to the mountain slopes, taking just enough food with them. But there was very little talk of eating or resting, since their sole concern was the cotton they'd brought to spin. Then they would return to their homes at nightfall, bringing the yarn they had spun. In this needy but cheerful place there also lived a man called Haftvad, who had seven sons, as his name indicates. He had a fine daughter, too, but he took no notice of her. One day the group of girls was sitting on the mountainside with their spindles, which they had put aside for a moment while they were eating.

> Just at that moment Haftvad's daughter found
> A windfall apple lying on the ground

And picked it up—now listen carefully
Because this story's quite extraordinary:
She bit the apple then, but as she tried it
She saw a little worm there, coiled inside it;
She scooped it out, and gently found a place
For this small worm inside her spindlecase.
And as she took her cotton up she said,
"By God I swear, today I'll spin such thread,
Helped by this apple's lucky worm, that you
Will be amazed at all that I can do!"
The girls began to laugh—in their delight,
Their faces glowed, their teeth shone silver-white.

But that day she spun twice as much as she normally did; she marked the amount on the ground and ran like wind-borne smoke to show her mother how much she had completed. He mother smiled and congratulated her and said, "You've done well by your mother, my pretty one." The next morning the girl took twice as much cotton as usual, and when she had joined her friends she put her heart into her work and said, "I'm going to spin so much thread, by the grace of this worm, that I'll never be poor again!" She spun what she had brought, and if she had had more with her, she could have spun that, too. She took the thread home, and her mother was so pleased with her daughter that she felt she was in heaven. Every morning the girl fed the worm a piece of apple, and however much cotton there was, the girl magically spun it into thread.

This went on until one day her mother and father said to their clever daughter, "You spin so much that it seems as though you've taken a fairy as your sister!" But the lovely child quickly answered her mother, "It's from the apple, and the little worm that was hidden in it." Then she showed her parents the marvelous worm and explained everything to them. Haftvad took all this as a good omen, and as his prospects seemed to brighten every day, he stopped worrying about his own work. He talked only about the good fortune brought by the worm, and how the worm had renewed his luck. They didn't neglect to look after the worm but gave it good, nourishing food. The worm grew plump and strong, its head and its back became splendid and formidable. The spindlecase was now too small for its body, and from one end to the other its skin was like black musk with a saffron-colored pattern on it. Haftvad made it a fine black chest to live in.

Now no discussion about civic affairs could go forward in the town without Haftvad: he and his seven sons became powerful, respected citizens. But there was a nobleman in the town, a proud man who had his own followers, and he looked for some excuse to take this commoner's wealth away from him. Haftvad was afraid and stole out of the town, leaving his seven sons there. Wherever he went he complained of their situation, and soon a group of men, young and old, had gathered around them. Haftvad was liberal with his gold, and soon he had an army, which made its way to his sons, determined to fight on their behalf.

The noise of trumpets was heard throughout Kajaran, and the army attacked with lances, swords, and arrows. Haftvad fought bravely at the head of his men, took the town, and killed the nobleman who had been harassing him; a great deal of wealth and jewels came into his possession. Men flocked to him, and he left Kajaran and went into the mountains. There, on a summit, he built a fortress with an iron door for his followers: it was a place of pleasure and repose, but also a place that could withstand a siege. A stream there flowed into the fortress, and around the whole area he built a wall so high that its summit was invisible.

Meanwhile the worm had grown too big for its chest, and so they made a stone cistern inside the fortress, and when the air had sufficiently warmed the stone and mortar, they very gently placed the worm inside it. Every morning the worm's keeper ran from Haftvad and fed the worm with rice, which its swollen body soon disposed of. After five years of this the worm was as massive as an elephant. The fortunate girl still looked after the worm, while Haftvad commanded their armies. A vizier and a scribe waited on the worm, and now it was fed on milk and honey. Haftvad was in charge of the fortress and decided all matters that came before him. He now had an army, a counselor, a chancellor for his court, everything in fact that pertained to a king, and his armies controlled the land from Kerman to the sea of China. Haftvad's seven sons each commanded ten thousand men, and they had wealth and arms at their disposal. If any king marched against them, as soon as his soldiers heard the tale of the worm they lost heart and the army broke up. Haftvad's fortress became so renowned that even the winds of heaven did not dare blow about it.

Ardeshir Fights Against Haftvad and Is Defeated

Ardeshir was not pleased when he heard about Haftvad, and he sent a commander against him, with a fine body of men ready for battle. But Haftvad was not at all alarmed: he set up an ambush in a defile of the mountains and then went against the approaching army at the head of his troops. When the two armies had joined battle and were laying about one another with maces and battleaxes, the hidden soldiers burst out from the ambush, and the earth became a dark place for the invaders. They were so hemmed in that no one knew his hands from his feet, and so many were killed that the victors were stupefied by the number of dead. Anyone from Ardeshir's forces who remained alive quickly fled back to the king.

Ardeshir was angered when he heard about the way his troops had been killed and their baggage plundered. He quickly mustered an army, to whom he distributed arms and cash, and set out against Haftvad immediately, while this commoner was still exalting in his triumph. Haftvad brought treasure and weapons from his fortress and was not at all troubled by Ardeshir's approach. His eldest son was living far away, but when he heard of his father's battles, he gave up his life of lazing and feasting and took ship to return. This ambitious youth was called Shahuy, and he was an ill-made, ill-spoken man. When he disembarked, Haftvad's heart rejoiced to see his son, and he put him in charge of the right wing of the army, while he himself remained the overall commander.

Now face to face, the two armies were both well equipped, eager for war, and backed up by considerable wealth. King Ardeshir looked at them, and his young heart grew old with anxiety. The columns faced one another, and the sun glinted on their swords. Then the din of drums resounded from the elephants' backs, and men two miles away quailed at the noise: the blaring of trumpets began, and the squeal of brazen bugles. The earth quaked beneath the horses' hooves, the air was crimson with chieftains' banners, and so great was the racket of maces against helmets that the sky seemed to bid the earth farewell. Galloping horses tore up the earth, the plain was filled with trunkless heads, and Haftvad's army fought with such fury they seemed like a lake whipped up by the wind. So thick was the press of men on each side that not an ant or a mosquito could have found room there. So the battle went on until the day paled into evening, and then night spread its purple cloak. Ardeshir summoned his scattered soldiers and made camp beside a brackish lake. When the rust-colored waters turned black, each army sent out its scouts and guards. The king's army was badly fed that night, because their malevolent enemy had cut off the road by which they'd been supplied.

Mehrak, the Son of Nushzad, Sacks Ardeshir's Palace

In Jahrom there was a low-born man called Mehrak, the son of Nushzad. When he heard that Ardeshir had left the area and was camped by a lake after a hard-fought battle, and that the army's supply route had been interrupted, he set off for the king's palace with a large group of followers. He looted its treasures and distributed crowns and cash to his men. Ardeshir received news of this at the lakeside and grew pensive, saying to himself, "Why am I fighting against strangers when I haven't secured my own palace?"

He summoned his chieftains and told them at length about Mehrak, and then said, "You are my army commanders, what do you think we should do in this desperate situation? Fate has sent us sorrows enough, and we overlooked Mehrak and his potential for trouble." They answered, "Your majesty, may your eyes never see ill fortune. Since Mehrak has revealed himself as your covert enemy, why should you endure these hardships to conquer the world? But you have greatness and the earth is yours; we are your slaves and you our master."

Ardeshir ordered that a meal be prepared, and asked for wine and entertainers. A few spitted lambs were placed before the men, and they began to eat. Ardeshir had a piece of bread in his hand when an arrow plunged right into the lamb carcass in front of him. Alarmed, the chieftains drew back from the food, while one of them took the arrow out of the meat. There was writing on it, and an officer who was also a scribe read it aloud. The inscription was in Pahlavi, and it said,

> "Listen, wise king: this arrow's from the fort
> Where peace reigns, and the mighty worm holds court:
> If I had aimed the shaft at Ardeshir
> It would have passed right through you. It is clear

No king like you can hope for victory
Against the worm's all-powerful sovereignty."

It was two parasangs from the fortress to their camp, and when the inscription was read the chieftains' hearts were horrified; all of them invoked God's blessings on their king and his glory.

Ardeshir brooded on these events all night, and when the sun rose the next morning he struck camp and led the army back from the lake, toward Pars. They marched quickly but the enemy forces harassed them from behind, raiding the columns constantly and killing many of their leaders. The cry pursued them:

"The worm's good fortune shines, and he alone
Illuminates the splendor of the throne."

The soldiers said to one another, "This is a wonder, which everyone should marvel at." They rode on across uneven ground, their hearts filled with anxiety, until they saw a large city, and they bore down on it with the speed of wolves. Nearby, they saw two young men standing in front of a house. The king and his men paused for a moment, and the strangers questioned them, asking how they came to be there so unexpectedly, and where they had arrived from, covered in the dust of the road. The king said, "Ardeshir fled this way, and we were left behind in his flight; he's running from the worm, and from Haftvad, and from their rabble of an army." The two young men started forward, filled with concern on the fugitives' behalf. They had them dismount, welcoming them and making them a place to rest and sleep. The two sat with the king at his meal and entertained him well, saying, "My lord, neither sorrow nor joy last for long. Look at the unjust Zahhak and all he took from the royal throne, and at the malevolent Afrasyab, who tormented the Persian kings, and at Sekandar, who in recent times killed the world's kings; they have all departed. All that remains of them is an evil name, and they will not taste the joys of paradise. This Haftvad will end in the same way; he too will at last writhe in his death agony."

At their words, the king's heart opened like a flower in springtime. He was so comforted by their remarks that he decided to tell them the truth, and said, "I am Ardeshir, the son of Sasan, and I need your advice. How can I fight against this accursed worm, and against Haftvad?" The two young men bowed before him, and both said, "May you always thrive, and may the reach of evil be far from you. Our bodies and souls are your slaves; may your spirit endure forever. As for the worm, some kind of stratagem must be employed against it. You won't be able to defeat it unless you resort to underhand tactics. The worm and his treasure and followers are ensconced on that mountaintop, with a city on one side and the lake on the other, and the way up their fastness is a difficult one. In his essence that worm is Ahriman, the enemy of the Creator of the world. You say he's a worm, but inside that leathery skin he's a devil thirsty for blood."

Ardeshir felt reassured by their kind words and said, "All this is true, and I leave it to you to come up with something against him." They answered, "We are your slaves and will always recommend what is right to you." Cheered by their talk the king went forward, once more assured of victory, taking the two young men with him. And so they proceeded, with clear consciences and confidence, to Khurreh-ye Ardeshir.

There, with his courtiers assembled about him, he rested from war, re-provisioned his army, and then turned to the problem of Mehrak, the son of Nushzad. Mehrak was terrified to learn of his approach, and as Ardeshir drew near Jahrom, the traitor hid from him. But the king was determined to hunt him down, and when Mehrak was taken prisoner Ardeshir cut off his head with an Indian sword, and had his headless trunk burned. Then he stabbed to death every member of Mehrak's family who fell into his hands, apart from one of the daughters, who managed to keep herself hidden, even though she was sought for throughout the whole town.

Ardeshir Kills Haftvad's Worm

His next concern was to make war on the worm, and he mustered an army for this purpose. Assembling twelve thousand experienced cavalry, he reunited his scattered troops and brought his reconstituted forces to an area between two mountains. He appointed a shrewd man named Shahrgir as his commander and said to him, "Stay here, and be on your guard; send scouts out day and night, and let them be good, capable horsemen; likewise have sentries and watchmen posted to safeguard the army. Meanwhile I'm going to resort to a trick—Esfandyar's an ancestor of mine, after all. If the watchman sees smoke rise up in the daytime, and then fire at night as bright as the sun, you're to understand that the worm's power is at an end; that I've turned his luck, and rid the world of him."

He chose seven of his best warriors, all brave as lions and men whom he could trust. Not a word was said to anyone else as to what was afoot. He picked out a large number of jewels from his treasury, as well as brocade, gold coins, and other kinds of wealth, his wise eyes carefully selecting the best items. Then he filled two chests with lead and included a brass cauldron, an item that would be crucial for the success of his venture. He wrapped everything in cloth, procured ten large donkeys from the head of his stables, loaded up his goods, and covered them over with coarse kilims. Impatient to put their plan into action, the little group set off for the worm's fastness. The two young men who had entertained Ardeshir during his flight went with them: they had become friends with Ardeshir, and he valued their advice. The caravan was disguised to look like a merchant's.

When they could see the castle and its city in the distance, a lookout called to them, "What have you got in those chests?" The king shouted back, "All sorts of things for sale: cloth and clothes, gold and silver, gold coins, brocade, pearls and jewels. We're merchants from Khorasan, always traveling, never resting. I've accumulated a fine amount of goods, thanks to the worm's good fortune, so now I've come to pay my respects before his throne. It's his luck that has helped me, and if it is allowable I will offer my homage to him." The worm's servant opened the gates to the castle, and the caravan went inside.

Ardeshir quickly opened up his packages and handed over things worthy of the man's station. He set out a stall before the servants, opened the chests, and filled a goblet with wine. Those whose turn it was to feed the worm with milk and rice turned away from the wine, not wanting to get drunk at this time. Realizing this, Ardeshir stood up and said, "I have a huge amount of rice and milk, and if his keeper will allow it I shall be pleased to feed the worm for three days. This will give me a name in the world, and the worm's lucky star might look kindly on me. Drink wine with me for three days, and on the fourth, when the sun rises to illuminate the world, I'll make a fine shop here, even higher than your palace, and I'll ply my trade of buying and selling. In this way I'll increase my honor in the worm's eyes." With these words he got his wish; the keepers responded, "You can serve the wine." The donkey driver placed everything at their service, and began to serve the wine. Gradually they became drunk; those whom the worm had commanded were now commanded by wine. As soon as their tongues were fuddled, the king and the two young men brought out the cauldron and lead and made a fire. When it was time for the worm to be fed, its food was boiling lead. They saw its vermilion tongue, waiting to lap up the rice as it usually did. The young men poured the lead down its throat, and when its bowels split, its strength oozed away. A loud crack came from its throat, and the cistern where it lived and the whole town round about shook with the force of it. Ardeshir and the two young men attacked like the wind; they snatched up their maces, swords, and bows, and not one of the drunken servitors escaped from them alive. From the roof of the castle they sent up a column of smoke, as a signal to the army commander. Seeing it, a watchman ran to Shahrgir saying, "King Ardeshir is victorious." Immediately he led the army forward to join their king.

Ardeshir Kills Haftvad

When Haftvad heard what had happened he was frightened and confused. He hurried to the castle to retake it, but the king was already on its ramparts. All his efforts were useless: a lion stood on his city's walls. Shahrgir brought up the army like a mighty mountain, but his men hesitated and hung back. Ardeshir shouted down to them, "Come forward and fight, Shahrgir. If Haftvad escapes us, for all your efforts you'll have nothing in your fist but air. I fed the worm hot lead; his power is gone, his anger has melted away." When they heard the king's voice the Persian troops took heart, put on their metal helmets, and prepared for battle. The wind of war turned against the worm's forces: Haftvad was captured, and so was Shahuy, his eldest son and the commander of his troops. King Ardeshir came down from the battlements, and Shahrgir came forward to greet him on foot. He brought a horse caparisoned in gold, on which the triumphant king sat. He gave orders that two gibbets were to be set up on the lake shore, where the two malefactors were strung up alive; the sight of them broke the hearts of Ardeshir's enemies. Then Shahrgir stepped forward from the ranks of soldiers, and Haftvad and his son were killed in a rain of arrows. Ardeshir gave the town over to plunder, and the troops enriched themselves. Servants brought out whatever was valuable in the fortress and took everything to Khurreh-ye Ardeshir. A fire-temple was built in the province, and the festivals of Mehregan and Sadeh were celebrated there; the land was handed over to the two young men who had been Ardeshir's hosts when he fled from the area.

Ardeshir returned in triumph to Pars, and when the populace and flocks were settled again, he led his army to Khurreh-ye Ardeshir. He sent an army to Kerman to keep order in the area, under a man who was worthy to rule. And now that his enemies had been defeated, he took up residence in Ctesiphon.

THE REIGN OF ARDESHIR

Ardeshir assumed the ivory throne in Baghdad and crowned himself there; with his sword belt, royal mace, and splendid palace, he was indistinguishable from Goshtasp, and from that time on people called him the King of Kings. After he had placed the crown on his head, he gave an address from the throne: "In this world my treasure is justice, and the world prospers through my efforts and good fortune. No one can take this treasure from me, since evil comes to those who do evil; if the world's God approves of my actions, he will not begrudge me mastery of this dark earth. From end to end the world is in my keeping, and my way is the path of justice. No one, whether he be a slave or a free man, must sleep uneasily because of my subordinates, or captains, or cavalry: my court is open to everyone, whether they wish me good or ill." The court called down blessings on him, saying, "May the earth prosper beneath your righteousness!" Then he sent armies in each direction, to persuade whatever chieftains who might oppose him to submit, or face conquest by the sword.

Ardeshir and the Daughter of Ardavan

When Ardeshir killed Ardavan and grasped the world in his fist, everyone, young and old, rejoiced, since Ardavan had acted tyrannically, and Ardeshir's justice would make the world flourish once again. Ardeshir married the dead king's daughter, hoping that she would reveal to him where her father's treasure was hidden. Two of Ardavan's sons were in India, enduring both good and bad fortune together. Two more were in Ardeshir's prisons, their hearts filled with grief, their eyes with tears. The oldest, who was in India, was called Bahman. When he saw that he had lost the whole kingdom, he found a young persuasive messenger, and gave him a package filled with poison. He said, "Go to my sister and say,

'Don't look for kindness from an enemy;
You have two brothers suffering grievously
In India, and two more brothers here
Chained in the dungeons of King Ardeshir—
And can you think that heaven will approve
Of how you're now denying them your love?
But if you would be Persia's queen, and live
Admired by all brave men, contrive to give
—In one dose—this fell poison that I bring
From India, to your husband and your king.'"

The envoy arrived at nightfall and gave his message to the princess. She felt pity for her brothers, and her face glowed with sympathy for their

plight. Anxiously she took the precious poison, planning to do what her brother desired.

And so it happened that, when Ardeshir had spent half of one day hunting wild asses with his arrows, he returned to the palace and Ardavan's daughter ran to his side. She brought him a goblet encrusted with topazes in which she had mixed cold water with sugar and wheatmeal and the poison, hoping to bring about the end her brother Bahman desired. But as Ardeshir took the cup from her, it fell from his hand and smashed on the ground. The princess trembled apprehensively and felt her heart fail within her. Her agitation aroused the king's suspicions, and he wondered what fate the turning heavens had in store for him. He had a servant bring four domestic hens and watched them carefully as they pecked up the wheatmeal. When he saw that as soon as they ate the food they fell down dead his suspicions were confirmed. He summoned his chief priest and asked him, "If you were to assign a throne to your enemy, and he became so intoxicated by your kindness that he gratuitously made an attempt on your life, what punishment would you impose on him? What would be the medicine to cure such folly?" The man's answer was, "If a subject stretches out his hand against the king, his head must be severed for this sin; and anyone who advises otherwise should be ignored." The king said, "Take Ardavan's daughter and divide her body from her soul."

Trembling and with guilt in her heart, Ardavan's daughter left the audience chamber with the priest. She said to him, "You are a wise man and know that your days and mine will both come to an end. If you must kill me, know that I am carrying Ardeshir's child. If indeed I'm worthy of the gallows and deserve to have my blood spilled, wait until this child is born, and then do as the king has ordered." The shrewd priest retraced his steps and told Ardeshir what she had said. But the king's answer was, "Don't listen to anything she has to say; take a rope and hang her for her crime."

The Birth of Ardeshir's Son, Shapur

The priest said in his heart, "It's an evil day when the king gives such an order: young and old, we are all destined for death, and Ardeshir has no son to his name. So that even if he lives for many years, when he dies his throne will be inherited by his enemies. It would be best if I were to act chivalrously and make something good come from this sad state of affairs. I will deliver this woman from death, and it may be that I can make the king regret his order. And if not, when her child is born will be the time to attend to his commands. This is not a matter to take lightly, and it is better that I act prudently rather than rashly."

He had a place set aside for the princess in his palace and looked after her as if she were his own flesh and blood. He told his wife, "I shall not be content if even so much as a breath of wind touches her." Then he reflected that there are enemies everywhere, and that all men are thought well of by some and badly by others. He said to himself, "I must arrange matters so that those who'd like to slander me won't be able to pour filthy water into my stream." He went into his house and there cut off his testicles; he then cauterized the wound, applied a salve to it, and bound it up. Pallid and groaning with pain, he quickly put the testicles in salt and placed them in a round jeweler's box, which he immediately sealed. He came into the throne room, carrying the sealed box, and said, "I ask that the king entrust this to his treasurer." The date was written on the box, so that there could be no argument about when this had occurred.

When the time for the princess's confinement came, the priest kept everything secret, so that even the winds of heaven knew nothing of what was happening. Ardavan's daughter gave birth to a splendid son who seemed every inch a royal child. The priest kept visitors away from his house and had the boy named Shapur. He hid him away for seven years, and the boy grew into a fine young prince, endowed with *farr* and a noble stature.

Then one day the priest, who was also Ardeshir's vizier, saw tears in his sovereign's eyes, and said to him, "May the king prosper, and his thoughts nourish his soul! You have achieved your heart's desire in this world and driven your enemies back from the throne: now is a time for rejoicing and to drink wine, not for troublesome thoughts. The seven climes of the earth are yours, and the world flourishes because of your justice." The king answered, "My priest, your heart is sincere and you are privy to all my secrets. My sword has civilized the world; sorrow, pain, and evil have been driven away: But I am now fifty-one years old, my musky hair has turned white as camphor, and the roses of my cheeks are faded. I need a son, standing here in front of me, someone who charms the world, who is strong and a leader of men. A father without a son is like a son without a father: no stranger will embrace him as his own. After I am gone, my crown and treasure will belong to my enemies; my life's profit will be only dust and sorrow."

The old priest said in his heart, "The day to speak has come," and he addressed the king, "Your majesty, protector of the weak, chivalrous, enlightened, and mighty, if you will now guarantee that my life is safe, I will take this sorrow away from you." The king replied, "You are a wise man; why should you fear for your life? Tell me what you know, speak as much as you wish, what is finer than a wise man's words?" The vizier answered, "You have a jeweler's box in your treasurer's keeping; have it brought to us." The king ordered his treasurer to bring the box and said, "Give it back to him so that we can see what is in it, and whether it will enable me to live freed from anxiety."

The treasurer brought the box and handed it over. The king asked what was hidden under its seal, and the vizier answered, "My own warm blood is there, and my shameful parts, cut cleanly from my body. You gave Ardavan's daughter into my keeping, saying that you wanted her to be a lifeless corpse. I didn't kill her, because she was pregnant, and I feared God's judgment on me if I did. I disobeyed your orders, but at the same time I castrated myself so that no one could speak evilly of me and soak me in a sea of infamy. Now your son Shapur is seven years old: no other king has had such a son, he resembles the moon in the heavens. I named him Shapur, and may the heavens smile on your good fortune. His mother is with him and has brought the young prince up."

The king was astonished and brooded on this child. Finally he said to his vizier, "You have a good heart and pure thoughts; you have suffered much over this, and I would not have your suffering continue. Find a hundred boys of his age, and of the same stature, bearing, and appearance. Dress them all alike, and see there's no difference between them; then send them to the playing fields and have them play polo there. When the plain is filled with these handsome children, we'll see if my soul responds at the sight of my own boy: my heart will bear witness to the truth of what you've said, and acquaint me with my son."

Shapur Plays Polo and His Father Recognizes Him

At dawn the following day the vizier had a bevy of boys assembled on the playing fields, all dressed in the same way, and so similar in face and stature that one could not be told from another. The field was like a festival, and somewhere among the participants was the prince, Shapur.

The ball was thrown down, and each of the children strove to outdo the others. As dawn broke Ardeshir arrived at the field, accompanied by his favorite courtiers. He stared at the scene before him and sighed, then pointed to the boys and said, "Is there an Ardeshir among them?" His vizier answered, "Your heart will tell you which is your son." The king said to one of his servants, "Go and get possession of the ball with your polo stick; stay with the children and hit the ball toward me. Then we'll see which of them is no respecter of persons, which one is brave enough to come forward and strike the ball before my eyes, outrunning the others like a lion surrounded by horsemen. That one will certainly be my son, born of my line and loins."

The servant did as he was told and hit the ball so that it flew in front of the mounted children. They galloped after it as swiftly as arrows, but when it came close to Ardeshir, they hung back, hesitating; all except Shapur, who swept forward and struck the ball away from his father toward the waiting boys. Ardeshir felt his heart fill with happiness, like that of an old man who has regained his youth. The participants lifted Shapur up and passed him from hand to hand till he reached the king, who folded him in his embrace and called down blessings on him, kissing his head and eyes and face and saying,

> "A marvel such as you are cannot stay
> Concealed: I'd never hoped to see this day,
> Since in my heart I thought Shapur was dead
> But even if a man should lift his head
> Above the sun, he cannot turn aside
> The will of God, who humbles all our pride:
> And God has added to my sovereignty
> By giving my young son, Shapur, to me."

He called for jewels, coins, and rubies, and scattered gold, gems, musk, and ambergris over the boy till gold covered the crown of his head and his face was hidden by jewels. Ardeshir also scattered jewels over his vizier, seated him on a golden throne, and gave him beautiful artifacts to adorn his castle. He had Ardavan's daughter come before him, happily and serenely; he pardoned all her past sins and cleansed the stain of guilt from her lovely face. He summoned teachers skilled in the various branches of knowledge to his city, where they taught Shapur how to write in Pahlavi, how to hold a royal audience, how to ride into battle and confront his enemies, the protocols of wine drinking, banquets, and kingly generosity, and how to draw up his army and conduct himself on the day of battle. Ardeshir then had the design of his coins changed, both the gold coins and those of lesser value: on one side was inscribed King Ardeshir, and on the other the name of his vizier, who was honored in this way. The king's letters were signed in the same manner, and the vizier was given the king's seal and authority. Ardeshir distributed wealth to the poor who lived by the labor of their hands, and in a waste place he built the city of Jondeshapur, by which name he always referred to the area.

Ardeshir Asks the Indian Kayd to Predict His Future

When Shapur had grown into a youth as elegant as a tall cypress tree, Ardeshir feared that someone might cast the evil eye on him; the two were never separated, and Shapur was like another advisor and vizier to his father. But Ardeshir was constantly harassed by wars; he could not spend his time in pleasure because as soon as he had dealt with one enemy another would raise his head elsewhere. He said, "I ask God to tell me what is hidden and what is plain, and whether I can rid the world of my enemies." His wise vizier said to him, "I will send someone to Kayd, who is a seeker after knowledge and a help in such matters. He knows the stars in the high heavens, the way to sovereignty, and the path to ruin. If you are to rule the seven climes with no rival, he will be able to foresee this. He can explain things to you one by one, without any difficulty, and he will not ask you for payment for his answers."

Ardeshir chose a fine, intelligent young man as a messenger. He prepared a gift of horses, cash, and silk for the Indian sage, and said to the young envoy, "Go to this knowledgeable man and say to him, 'Fortunate and inquiring as you are, look at the stars and tell me when I can rest from war and bring these provinces under my control. If this is to happen, show me how to plan for such a day, and if it is not to be, I'll give up the struggle and stop spending my wealth needlessly.'" The envoy took the gifts to Kayd and told him the secrets of Ardeshir's heart. Kayd questioned him and grew pensive; then he applied himself to his science, consulting the stars, his astronomical tables, and his astrolabe, to see what the heavens held of comfort and profit, and of pain and loss.

He said to the envoy, "I have consulted the stars, as they affect Iran and the king. If he will join his line to that of Mehrak-e Nushzad, he will rule in peace and there will be no need for him to send out armies everywhere. His wealth will increase and his troubles will decrease. Go now, and ignore the enmity between these families. If he does as I have suggested, Iran will flourish and he will achieve all that he desires." Then Kayd gave the envoy a gift and added, "Don't keep back anything I've said. If he follows what I've said the high heavens will smile on him."

The envoy returned to Ardeshir and reported what he had been told. But Ardeshir heard his words with pain in his heart and his face turned sallow with grief. He said to the envoy, "May I never set eyes on any of Mehrak's family. It would be bringing an enemy off the street into my house, someone intent on destroying me and my people. And then what would my profit be from all the wealth I have spent, all the armies I have dispatched, all the trials I have undergone? Mehrak has one daughter, no more, though no one has ever seen her. I'll have her sought for in Rome, China, India, and Taraz, and when I find her I'll have her burned alive; I'll make the dust itself weep for her sorrows."

He sent horsemen, under the command of an ambitious warrior, to Jahrom, where Mehrak's daughter was living, but when she heard of their approach she escaped from her father's house and hid herself away in a village. There the local headman treated her with respect.

> Now like a lovely cypress tree she grew;
> Wisdom was hers, and royal glory too—
> Her wondrous beauty was beyond compare,
> Unrivaled in that land, or anywhere.

Shapur Marries Mehrak's Daughter

Listen now to what happened between Mehrak's daughter and the valiant warrior Shapur. The king's prosperity flourished, and one day as dawn broke he set out to hunt, taking his son Shapur with him. The horsemen rode forward, clearing the plain of game, and then there came into view a distant village filled with gardens, open spaces, villas, and fine buildings. Shapur rode to the village and dismounted before the headman's house. There was a lovely garden there, and a young woman, splendid as the moon, came into that green courtyard. She let a bucket down into the well and then caught sight of Shapur. She greeted him respectfully, saying, "May the prince live happily for many years, with laughter on his lips, and safe from the world's harm. Your mount must be thirsty, and generally the water in this village is brackish, but the water from this well is cold and sweet; let me draw some for you."

Shapur replied, "Your face is so radiant, why should you be put to such trouble? I have servants enough with me to draw the water." The young woman turned away and sat at a distance, beside the garden's watercourse. Shapur ordered one of his attendants to draw the bucket up from the well; the man ran forward and strained at the rope, but the full bucket was too heavy to raise, and the man's face frowned with the effort. Shapur came forward and muttered impatiently at him, "You haven't half the strength of a woman! Wasn't a woman letting this bucket down into the well and drawing it up, and you're struggling and straining and begging for help?" He snatched the rope from the man's hand and started to raise the bucket himself, but when he saw what an effort it required he congratulated the girl, and said, "Anyone who can lift a bucket this heavy must come from a noble background!" When he had raised the bucket, she came forward and said, "May you live forever, prosperous and guided by wisdom. By the grace of Ardeshir's son, Shapur, the water in this well will surely turn to milk."

Shapur said to this courteous girl, "And how do you know that I'm Shapur?" She replied, "I have heard righteous men say often enough,

> 'Prince Shapur is a noble cypress tree,
> A River Nile of generosity,
> A mammoth in his strength—in everything
> The image of his father and his king.'"

Shapur said to her, "You are a beautiful young woman, now answer my questions truthfully. Tell me what your lineage is, because there are signs of royalty in your face." She replied, "I'm the headman's child, that's why I'm so pretty and so strong." He answered, "A lie to a prince never prospers. No peasant ever had a daughter as lovely and as bewitching as you are." She said, "O prince, when I have a guarantee that my life is not in danger from the anger of the King of Kings, I shall tell you about my lineage." The prince replied, "In a garden like this, anger between friends doesn't spring up from the grass. Tell me what you have to say, and have no fear of me in your heart, nor of our king, who is a just man." She answered, "In all honesty then, I am the daughter of Mehrak-e Nushzad. A wise courtier of his brought me here and gave me to the headman for safekeeping. He is a good man, and out of fear of the king I became his servant and draw water for him."

Shapur scoured the village until the headman stood before him, and said: "Give this beautiful young woman to me in marriage, and may you be our witness." The man did as he was ordered and married them according to the fire worshippers' rites.

Mehrak's Daughter Gives Birth to Hormozd, the Son of Shapur

After nine months this beautiful woman gave birth to a fine son. From his appearance you would have said that he was Esfandyar, or Ardeshir. Shapur named him Hormozd, and the boy stood out like a cypress emerging from a swamp. After seven years Hormozd had no equal, but he was kept hidden from everyone and was not allowed out to play.

King Ardeshir went for a week's hunting, and Shapur accompanied him. Hormozd was tired of his lessons, and he rode out onto the king's main square, a bow in one hand and two arrows in the other, and met up with a group of children who were playing polo there. Just at that moment Ardeshir and his entourage returned from the hunt, and a child struck the ball so hard that it came to rest close to the king; the children hung back, and none of them ran forward to retrieve it. But Hormozd dashed out of the group and snatched up the ball from in front of his grandfather, so that all the soldiers and courtiers began gossiping about him. Then the boy let out a great shout of triumph, which astonished the king, who turned to his chief priest and said, "Find out which family that boy belongs to."

The priest made inquiries, but no one knew anything, or if they did they preferred to remain silent. So the king said, "Pick him up out of the dirt and bring him to me." The priest went and lifted the boy up and brought him to the king, who said, "You're a fine little man, and who are we to say your family is?" The boy felt no fear and said loudly, "My name and family should not be hidden. I'm Shapur's son, as he is your son, and my mother is from Mehrak's family."

The king was astonished at the workings of the world; he laughed and then grew pensive. He gave orders that Shapur appear before him, and he questioned him thoroughly. Shapur was afraid; his heart quaked and his face turned pale. But Ardeshir smiled at his fear and said, "Don't hide your boy away; see that he has everything he's entitled to, so that men say 'He is the prince's son.'" Shapur replied, "May your reign be long and prosperous. He is my child, his name is Hormozd, and he is like a tulip among weeds. I was hiding him from your majesty only until he could show his mettle. He is Mehrak's daughter's boy, and I'm quite certain that he is my son." Then he described the meeting at the well and what had happened there, and during his account the king asked him various questions. The king was happy to hear the tale and went off contentedly to his palace, accompanied by his vizier. He took Hormozd along with him, carrying him in his arms, and in the throne room he had a place prepared for the boy, and gave him a royal torque and a golden crown. They poured gold coins and jewels over the little boy until the pile mounted over his head, and then his grandfather plucked him from the heap, which was distributed to the poor. Ardeshir gave his grandson other valuables, and the fire temple and the rooms in the palace where the New Year's and Sadeh celebrations were held were hung with brocade.

A hall was prepared for festivities; the country's nobility gathered there, and they were entertained by musicians. Then Ardeshir addressed them: "The words of a wise astrologer cannot be gainsaid. The Indian Kayd told me that neither I, nor this country, nor my crown, throne, or army would enjoy good fortune unless my lineage were joined to that of Mehrak-e Nushzad. Now eight years have passed and the heavens have turned as we would wish: that is, since Shapur sought his happiness with Mehrak's daughter, he has seen nothing but what he desires from the world. The world's seven climes are under my command, and my heart has received from the heavens all it has desired." From this time on the king's functionaries referred to him as the King of Kings.

Ardeshir's Reforms

Listen now to Ardeshir's wisdom, and learn of all his reforms one by one. His efforts resulted in new laws, and he made everyone the beneficiary of his benevolence and justice. To assure that the court had sufficient warriors, he sent messengers everywhere to proclaim that whoever had a son should not allow him to grow up without military training: young men should learn how to ride in battle, and how to use the mace and bow. When a young man acquired manliness by such exercises and was skillful in all areas of warfare, he was to come to the king's court, where his name would be inscribed in a muster roll, and he would be assigned quarters. When war was declared the young warriors would ride out with a seasoned champion, and each thousand of them would be accompanied by someone who would report back to the king on who fought weakly and unsatisfactorily, as well as on who distinguished himself in battle. Then their sovereign would prepare robes of honor and presents for those who had fought well, while those who had been unskillful in battle were dismissed from his service. These reforms increased the size of his army until it was greater than any the stars had ever looked down on. He raised above the mass of men those who were skilled in strategy, and proclaimed, "Let anyone who seeks to satisfy the king, who has soaked the ground in his enemies' blood, come forward and receive a royal robe from me, and his name will be remembered in the world." So his armies subdued the earth; he was the shepherd, and his warriors were his flock.

For the functioning of his government he chose able men and did not entrust work to the ignorant. He chose scribes who paid attention to words and writing and who were skillful in the smallest details of their profession, and when one of them distinguished himself, the king increased his salary. Anyone who was not such a good scribe, or who was lacking in intelligence, could not become a member of Ardeshir's administration. Such men were employed by underlings, while the best scribes were reserved for the king's divan. Ardeshir knew the value of his civil servants, and when he saw a scribe at the court he would say, "A scribe who gathers revenue and diminishes trouble by his efforts is the means by which the country, its needy subjects, and its army prosper; scribes are like the sinews of my soul, they are the unseen rulers of the kingdom."

When an administrator set out for a province, the king advised him, "Despise wealth, and see that you do not sell men for its sake; remember that this fleeting world passes for all men. Seek justice and honor always, and may greed and folly stay far away from you. Take none of your family and dependents with you: the entourage I provide you with will be sufficient. Give money to the poor every month, but give nothing to those who harbor malevolent thoughts. If your justice makes the province flourish, you can remain there and rejoice in your just rule. But if a single poor man sleeps in fear, this means that you have sold a soul for the sake of gold and silver."

Whoever came to the king's court, either on official business or to demand justice, was questioned by the king's officers about the governor of his province. He was asked whether the man administered the province justly or whether he was greedy for wealth, and who lay down in fear because of him. He was also asked about who the wise men of his district were, and whether there were men there who were kept in obscurity by their poverty. He was questioned too as to who was worthy of the king's notice, whether they were old, experienced men, or men distinguished by their honorable behavior. The king would say, "No one should profit from my labors and wealth unless they are knowledgeable men who are willing to learn; what is finer than an old man filled with wisdom?"

When his army set out for war, Ardeshir made wisdom his companion and acted with caution and foresight. He selected a wise and knowledgeable scribe as an envoy and entrusted him with a letter that was polite and conciliatory, so that war would not be declared unjustly. The messenger would go to the enemy to find out his secret intentions, and if the opposing leader seemed to be a wise man who was contemptuous of evil's efforts, he would be rewarded with a royal robe of honor, as well as with a charter and earrings as a sign of his authority. But if his head was filled with rebellion, his heart with hatred, and his entrails with bloodlust, Ardeshir would distribute money to the army, so that there were no malcontents in the ranks. Then he chose a renowned warrior, someone sagacious, alert, and calm, as their commander. He also sent a scribe with his own entourage to accompany the army, to keep an eye on any injustices the soldiers might commit. He had someone whose voice could carry for two miles mounted on an elephant, and this herald would proclaim, "Warriors ready for war, all of you who have any heart, or reputation, or sense of shame: know that neither the poor nor the rich must suffer because of you. At every stage of your journey you must pay for what you eat and show respect to those who serve you; anyone who fears God will not steal others' property. Any man who turns his back on the enemy will suffer a harsh fate: either he will dig his own grave with his nails or chains will wear away his body. His name will be stricken from the muster roll; his food will be dirt and he will crawl in the dust."

To the commander he said, "Do not act feebly, but don't be precipitate and rash either. Keep your elephants in the army's vanguard, and send out scouts to a distance of four miles. When the day for battle comes you must go around the whole army explaining to your soldiers why they are fighting, and tell them that if they can bring down a hundred of the enemy's horses for every one of ours (and even a hundred for one is too few), then they will all, young and old, receive robes of honor from Ardeshir for their service. When the battle begins in earnest and the cavalry charges from both sides, no matter how many men you have, see that the center of the army is not abandoned. Try to manage things so that your left and right flanks attack together, but the center is to remain firm and no one there is to leave his post. After you are victorious, shed no one's blood, because if men have to flee from you, they will hate you the more. If anyone from the enemy's ranks asks for quarter, grant it to him, and put aside any desires for vengeance.

"If you see the enemies' backs, don't dash after them but stay where you are; you shouldn't disregard the possibility of ambush, and your army should remain on the battlefield. When you are safe from the enemy, don't listen to anyone's advice, but distribute booty to those who fought well and who bravely risked their sweet lives. Immediately bring any prisoners you take to my court, and I shall build a town for them in the provinces, on what was formerly thorny wasteland. If you wish to live without pain and trouble, do not deviate from this advice, and in victory see that you turn to God, for he is your only true guide."

If an envoy came from another land, whether from the Turks, the Romans, or other peoples, the lord of the marches there was informed of his approach and he did not treat this as an unimportant matter. He had places prepared along the envoy's route, and these were stocked with provisions, clothes, and carpets. Once the local governor was apprised of why the envoy was coming to see the king, he dispatched a scribe on a noble mount to Ardeshir, so that an escort could be sent to welcome the envoy. The king prepared a throne for his arrival, and servants stood on either side of the approachway, with their garments embroidered in gold. The king summoned the envoy into his presence

and seated him on a throne close by, then he questioned him about
himself, the good and bad of his life, and his name and title. He asked
him also about the justice and injustice he had witnessed, and about his
country, its customs, king, and army. He had the envoy conducted to
his quarters with due ceremony, and everything he could need was
provided for. The visitor feasted and drank wine with the king, and he
was seated on a golden throne, and the king took him hunting, together
with an innumerable entourage. At his departure he was given a fitting
farewell, and was presented with a royal robe of honor.

Ardeshir sent wise and benevolent priests about his kingdom, so that
they could establish cities and distribute wealth by providing food and
shelter for those who had no houses, or were destitute and had fallen
on hard times; and in this way the number of his subjects increased.

> *In public and in private his good name*
> *Filled all the world with its illustrious fame;*
> *No king like him had ever ruled, and when*
> *He died his like was never seen again.*
> *I seek to make his name live on—may he*
> *Know happiness for all eternity.*

He talked in secret with many men, and men reported back to him
from everywhere. When he heard of someone worthy who had lost his
wealth, he helped him as was appropriate, so that the man's days did
not remain dark for long: he gave him land and a place to live, servants
and subjects, and everything that was fitting. All this was done in secret,
without anyone else being aware of it. He gave goods to those who
were indigent, and placed children with teachers, caring for them as if
they were from his own family; in every street there was a school and
a fire-temple. He let no one remain in want, and he kept all this gen-
erosity carefully hidden. At dawn he walked in the open spaces of the
town, and people came to him asking for justice; in his judgments he
tried to harm no one and made no distinction between the least of his
subjects and the children of his allies. His justice made the world flour-
ish and rejoiced his subjects' hearts.

Where there were ruins, or where drought had dried up the water-
courses, he remitted the taxes of that area; where the peasants were

impoverished and faced death, his treasury provided them with animals and tools; he would not allow them to be swept away by disaster.

Ardeshir Bestows the Kingdom on Shapur

When Ardeshir had lived for seventy-eight years he grew sick. He summoned Shapur and gave him extensive advice on how to rule. He knew that he was close to death, and that the green leaves of his life would soon turn yellow. He said to his son, "Pay close attention to what I have to say, and as for those who would oppose you consider their words as so much wind. Act according to my words, since I assume you can distinguish what is valuable from what is worthless. I have ordered the world with the sword of justice, and respected the rank of those who are wellborn. When I had put the world on a sound footing, my territories increased, but my life drew toward its close. And as I have endured countless sorrows, and in the midst of them accumulated my wealth, so there is sorrow and happiness facing you, times of retrenchment and times of triumph. This is the way of the turning world, bringing you sometimes pain and sometimes pleasure. Fortune is sometimes like an unbroken horse, suddenly giving you a harsh ride when you are enjoying yourself; and sometimes she is a well-trained mount, lifting her head proudly, trotting forward as she should. But you should know, my son, that this deceitful world will not give you pleasure without pain, and if you wish your days not to end badly look after both your body and your spirit.

"When a king respects religion, religion and royalty become as brothers: religion has no stability without the royal throne, royalty cannot survive without religion. They are two brocades interwoven with one another by wisdom. Religion cannot do without the king, and the king will not be respected without religion; they are guardians of one another, and you could say that they live together beneath one tent. The former cannot function without the latter, nor the latter without the former; we see them as two companions united in doing good. A religious man is lord of wisdom and sense, and he inherits this world and the world to come; when a king is religion's guardian, you can only call these two brothers. But if a religious man is resentful of the king, you should beware of calling him righteous: any man who speaks against a just king should not be considered as truly religious. As a praiseworthy sage once said, 'When we look closely we see that religion is the pith of justice.'

"The throne is threatened by three things. First if the king is unjust; next, if he promotes worthless men over those who are accomplished; third, if he uses his wealth for his own glory and is always trying to increase his income. Turn toward generosity, and follow religion and wisdom so that no lie can make any headway with you. A lie blackens a king's face, so that his sovereignty lacks all luster. See that you don't hoard your wealth, because this only brings trouble: if a king is greedy for gold, he harms his subjects, since no matter how hard the peasant works, his wealth becomes the king's, whereas a good king is the guardian of his subjects' wealth, so that their efforts bear fruit. Try to control your anger, and when men transgress, be generous and close your eyes. If you are angry, you will regret it; if men repent, have the balm of mercy ready. Whenever a king is quick tempered wise men think of him as a lightweight. It is ugly for a king to have malevolent desires, and you should fill your heart with kindness; and if you ever let fear into your heart, those who wish you ill will confuse all your intentions.

"Don't hold back from being generous, and as far as you can, my son, know what things are worth. You should realize that sovereignty belongs to the king whose generosity encompasses the cosmos. Sometimes the royal office brings sorrow, and then the king should turn to his counselors and priests, asking them what is just and what is unjust, and preserving their answers in his heart. On the days when you go out with your hunting cheetahs, see that you don't play two games at once: riding out and hunting don't mix with wine drinking and banquets, since the body becomes heavy when you drink wine. The nobility know this nostrum. And if an enemy should appear, then both drinking and hunting must be set aside in favor of distributing money, preparing arms, and summoning troops from the provinces. Don't put off until tomorrow what must be done today, and don't promote bad advisors to high office.

"Don't look for righteousness in the hearts of vulgar folk, your search will be a waste of time; and if they speak ill of someone, ignore their calumnies. There's no making head nor tail of someone who loves neither his God nor his king. This is how the common people are, but may you be endowed with wisdom. Beware of those who have an evil nature, and pass your secrets on to no one, for your confidant will have his own friends and confidants, and your words will soon be everywhere. When your secrets are known to the nation, wise men's hearts will lose all respect for you. You'll be angry then, and even if they thought you wise before, people will say you have a trivial nature.

"Don't pay attention to reports of faults in other people, since the person who finds fault in this way will find fault with you too, and if passion overcomes reason, the wise will not think of you as human. A king should be wise and benevolent toward everyone, and God forbid that a quarrelsome man who delights in arguments and confrontation should have any place near you or be your guide. If you wish those who have noble minds to praise you, you must put aside all anger and thoughts of vengeance when you become king. You should not talk too much, and you should not make a show of your goodness. Listen to others' words, consider which you find pleasing, and remember the best of them. Weigh your words well when you speak to educated men, and welcome them politely and with smiles. Don't despise the petitions of the poor, and don't promote to high rank people who have an evil nature. If a man repents of his sins, forgive him and put aside your anger against him. Always be someone who dispenses justice, and who looks after his subjects, since a man who is generous and patient is blessed.

"When your enemies are afraid of you they will flatter you, but you should prepare your army and have the kettle drums made ready. Attack when your enemy is trying to avoid a fight and comes weak to the battlefield. But when he sues for peace and you can see no deceit in his heart, then demand tribute from him and give up your desire for vengeance: act toward him in such a way that he saves face and honor is satisfied. Adorn your heart with knowledge and act on it as far as you are able to, since a man's value is measured by his knowledge. If you are generous, you will be loved, and your knowledge and justice will make your name illustrious.

"Keep your father's advice in mind, and pass it on to your own son. When I hand over power to my son I do so having injured no one in the world; see that you do not ignore my words or dismiss what I have to say to you. Follow your father's advice, act well, and then you can think of evil as so much wind. Do not make my soul distraught, or plunge my lifeless body into the fire, and do not harm others, my son; do not seek out ways to torment people.

"*The realm that your descendants build will last*
Unharmed until five centuries have passed;
But then the members of your clan will spurn
My testament to you; proudly they'll turn
Their heads away from knowledge, and despise
The teachings of the just, preferring lies,
Injustice, exploitation, cruelty
To wise benevolence and loyalty.
They will oppress their subjects and condemn
As foolish simpletons God-fearing men:
They'll wear the shirt of evil, and exult
As worshippers of Ahriman's foul cult.
Whatever I have bound they will release,
The faith that I have purified will cease.
My testament will be as naught, and all
Our sovereignty will crumble then, and fall.

"I pray to God who knows all things visible and invisible that he protect you from all evil, and that all men of good repute be your allies. God and I both bless that man whose warp is justice and whose weft is wisdom, who will not break the testament I give, or try to convert my honey to bitter colocynth. Now forty years and two months have passed since I placed the royal crown on my head. I have founded six cities, which have pleasant air and are well-watered. One I call Khurreh-ye Ardeshir, and its winds would make an old man young again: Khuzestan was revived by founding this city. Now it is a well-watered province, filled with men and business. The name of the next town is Jondeshapur, a place that delights my chief priest. The next is Maysan by the Euphrates, a town filled with streams, livestock, and vegetation. Another is Barkeh-ye Ardeshir, a place of orchards, flower gardens and pools. Another is Ram-e Ardeshir, which I have joined by road to the province of Pars. The last is Hormozd-e Ardeshir, whose air is like musk and whose streams run with milk.

"Keep my soul happy by acting justly, and may your reign be a victorious one. I have borne many sorrows in this world, some known to others some unknown. Now I am ready for the tomb, and you must order my coffin and prepare my bier."

When he finished speaking, his good fortune darkened: alas now for his mind, his crown, and his throne. Happy is he who has not known greatness, and who does not have to leave a throne. You struggle and accumulate all kinds of goods, but neither men nor goods remain. Finally we are partners with the dust, and our cheeks are covered by a shroud.

Come, let us do good with our hands, and not give this unstable world over to evil.

> *That man who lifts a wine glass in his hand*
> *In memory of the kings who ruled this land*
> *Knows happiness: the toasts come thick and fast*
> *Until, content and tired, he sleeps at last.*
> *Tell us of Shapur's banquets now, explain*
> *The story of this noble prince's reign.*

THE REIGN OF SHAPUR,
SON OF ARDESHIR

When Shapur sat on the throne of justice and placed the royal crown on his head, the priests and nobles of the country gathered before him, and he addressed them: "My wise counselors, I am the son of the illustrious King Ardeshir, hear my commands and do not swerve aside from loyalty to me. Live content with your good name and have nothing to do with malevolent troublemakers. Only those who are lacking in sense will covet others' wealth. My benevolence toward you exceeds that radiated by the stars. I shall keep Ardeshir's ordinances in effect with you, asking for no more than a thirtieth of landowners' incomes, and that only so that I can provide in some small way for my army. Goodness is my eternal treasure, bravery and chivalry are the foundations of my kingdom; I have no need of others' possessions, since this desire is what turns men into enemies. All of you are free to visit me at any time, and I shall treat all who wish me well with affection."

His nobles and subjects stood and acclaimed Shapur as king: they poured emeralds over his crown and called down blessings on his head.

Shapur's War Against Rome
News spread that the throne was left idle, that the wise King Ardeshir had died, leaving his wealth and crown to Shapur. Lamentation arose from every quarter, and Qaydafeh, in the Roman provinces, ceased to send tribute. When Shapur heard of this he readied his army, with its drums and banners, for war. Under the leadership of a brave and capable commander they made a quick march, with virtually no baggage, as far as Altouyaneh. The dust of the army that marched out to oppose them from Qaydafeh obscured the sun, and it was joined by a force from Altouyaneh under the leadership of Baranush, a fine horseman who was highly regarded by the Romans.

When the din of drums arose from the opposing camps, Baranush advanced to lead the Roman forces, and from the Persian side a brave warrior called Gorzasp took the offensive. Drums and trumpets were sounded on each side, and the new Persian king, stationed in the center of his troops, felt the thrill of battle. There was such a wailing of trumpets and clashing of Indian bells that the moon and the vault of the heavens shook; there were war drums strapped to the elephants, and their thundering noise carried for two miles. The earth trembled, dust swirled, lances glittered like fire, and the sky seemed to rain down stars. Sick at heart and sorely wounded, Baranush was captured in the midst of his men; three thousand Romans were killed at the Battle of Altouyaneh, and one thousand six hundred were taken prisoner. Their warriors' hearts were filled with despair.

The Roman emperor sent an envoy to Shapur, saying "How much blood will you shed before God, for the sake of money? What excuse can you bring for such behavior on the Day of Judgment? We will send the tribute as before, so that no further ills befall us, and along with the tribute I will also send you a number of hostages, people of my own family. But you should then evacuate Altouyaneh, and if you do I will send whatever further gifts you desire."

Shapur waited until the tribute had been delivered in ten ox skins, together with a thousand Roman young men and women as slaves and innumerable valuable brocades. He stayed for seven days in Altouyaneh, then left Roman territory and returned to Ahvaz. He built a city, with a great deal of effort and at great expense, completing it on the auspicious twenty-fifth of the month. The city was named Shapurgerd; it was a fine flourishing place, and the Roman captives were settled there. It formed the entryway to Khuzestan, and everyone entering the province from that direction had to pass through it. In addition, he built a splendid city in Pars, and another in Sistan, where there are abundant groves of date palms. This latter city had been begun by Ardeshir, and Shapur completed it. He also made the area around Kohandezh into a city, and to this day men say the town was built by Shapur's justice.

Wherever he went he took Baranush with him and paid attention to what he said. There was a river near Shushtar that was so wide no fish could swim across it. Shapur said to Baranush, "If you're an engineer, build a bridge here, so strong that when we pass away it will remain, as a sign to the wise. Make it a thousand cubits long. When you have done this, ask me for whatever treasure you desire. Use the knowledge of Roman savants to build monuments in this country; when you have made the bridge, which will lead to my palace, you can live as my guest, in happiness and safety, secure from evil and the wiles of Ahriman." Baranush set to work and completed the bridge, which was a thousand paces long, and Shapur hastened to cross it in state, passing from Shushtar to his palace.

Shapur's Advice to His Son, Hormozd

After thirty years and two months, the king's splendor and *farr* began to fade. He summoned Hormozd, and said to him,

> *"Now you will blossom like an opening flower;*
> *Be wary as you wield imperial power,*
> *And pay attention to the words of those*
> *Who know how worldly fortune comes and goes.*
> *Don't hope for much from sovereignty; take heed*
> *Of all the ancient precepts of Jamshid:*
> *Be just in all your deeds—to nobles be*
> *Their splendor, to the poor their sanctuary.*
> *Be kind and openhanded, do not make*
> *A great noise for a minor setback's sake.*
> *These are the words I learned from Ardeshir,*
> *Remember all that I have told you here."*

When he had finished speaking his face turned pale in death, and the young man grieved in his heart.

*F*erdowsi gives brief accounts, omitted here, of the relatively uneventful reigns of Hormozd, Bahram Hormozd, Bahram Bahram, Bahram Bahramian, Nersi Bahram, Hormozd Nersi.

THE REIGN OF SHAPUR ZU'L AKTAF

After Hormozd the son of Nersi had reigned for nine years, the pome-
granate color of his cheeks became like a yellow flower. His kingly
mind felt the sorrows of death, and he died, leaving behind no son.
This exalted and eloquent man passed from the fleeting world with a
cry of anguish on his lips.

He was mourned for forty days; during this time the throne remained
empty and lost its power and prestige, and the country's nobility were
filled with anxiety. Then a priest discovered a beautiful young woman
in the king's private quarters: her face was as splendid as the new moon,
her cheeks glowed like tulips, her eyelashes were like daggers from
Kabol, and her braided hair, gathered in a knot on the top of her head,
was as curled and wavy as the script the Mongols use. This lovely young
woman was pregnant, and the world rejoiced as soon as this became
known. The celebrations, with feasting and music, lasted for forty days,
and a royal couch was prepared for her. The crown was suspended above
her belly, and gold coins were poured over it. Forty days passed, and a
baby as splendid as the sun was born to her. The chief priest named him
Shapur, and held festivities in his honor. The boy seemed blessed with
wisdom and the royal *farr*. The gold-belted nobility poured gold over
the boy's crown; he was suckled till he was satisfied and then wrapped
in silk swaddling clothes. For forty days the baby lay on his father's royal
throne, beneath the suspended crown.

A learned priest acted as regent; he was humble in his manner and
ruled wisely and well. He managed the army and the king's wealth, and
was an adornment to the throne and palace. This continued until the
little prince was five years old. One evening the boy was sitting in
Ctesiphon, and his wise regent was with him. As the sun set and night
began to spread its purple cloak, a confused noise rose up from the

direction of the river, and the prince asked his regent, "What's that shouting?" The man answered, "Blessed and fortunate king, this is the time when men who have shops or go out to work return home. The bridge over the Tigris is narrow, and the men crossing over it are so cramped for space that they're afraid of being jostled and squeezed, and that's why they shout out as loudly as a drum being beaten." Shapur said to his advisors, "My wise counselors, now you must build another bridge, so that there will be one for coming and one for going, and my subjects and soldiers will be able to pass back and forth without trouble. We must spend a lot of money from the treasury on this." The king's advisors were pleased that the young sapling had so soon produced green leaves. The regent had another bridge built, as the young prince had ordered, and his mother was overjoyed and arranged for tutors to begin teaching him. He learned so quickly that he soon surpassed his teachers in knowledge. When he was seven he learned to ride, both as a warrior and a polo player: at eight he learned the ceremonies of kingship, and he was careful to make his body and appearance worthy of his rank. He fixed his capital at Estakhr, following the example of his illustrious ancestors.

The Arab Tayer Captures Nersi's Daughter and Shapur Attacks

When Shapur had been king for some time, the lionhearted warrior Tayer, a chieftain of the Ghassanid tribe, gathered a huge army together from Roman territories, Qadesiya, Bahrain, Kurdistan, and Pars, and attacked the outskirts of Ctesiphon. No one could resist his forces, and they plundered the whole area. A daughter of King Nersi, named Nobahar, was living there, and Tayer attacked her palace, while the whole of Ctesiphon waited apprehensively. His ignorant, barbarous troops took her from the palace as a captive. For a year Nobahar lived, wretched and heartsick, with Tayer and then gave birth to his daughter, a lovely child who was the image of her grandfather, King Nersi, and indeed she seemed so worthy to rule that her father named her Malekeh [Queen].

Years passed and Shapur reached the age of twenty-six; he was a noble king, as splendid as the sun. He came out onto the plain, inspected his army, and chose twelve thousand warriors mounted on swift camels. The group set off, led by a hundred guides, with each man riding on a camel and leading a horse, in search of that ravening lion, the Ghassanid

chief. When they found the enemy, they killed many of them, and seeing this, Tayer himself turned tail and fled. The din of blows and counterblows rose up; the Persians captured innumerable prisoners, and the remnant of Tayer's people made their way to the Yemen. There they took refuge in a fortress, which soon filled with the wailing of men, women, and children. Shapur besieged them with such a mass of men that not an ant or a mosquito could have passed between them. The siege lasted for a month, and provisions began to run low in the fortress.

Tayer's Daughter, Malekeh, Falls in Love with Shapur

At dawn Shapur mounted his horse, wearing his black royal armor, and a shining black sash was tied about his helmet; he grasped his bow and rode forward impetuously. Malekeh looked down from the fortress walls and saw the warrior's sash and helmet: his cheeks were as pink as rose petals, his hair as black as musk, his face as ruddy as the sweet smelling blossoms of the Hyrcanian willow tree. All rest and sleep deserted that lovely young woman, and with her heart overflowing with love, she came to her nurse and said:

> *"This king who's come against us here to fight*
> *Shines like the sun itself; how could his might,*
> *His power, be something that I'd fail to see?*
> *I name him World, since he's the world to me.*
> *Take him a message now, and tell Shapur*
> *I welcome him, although he comes for war,*
> *And tell him that through Nersi we are kin,*
> *Descended from a common origin.*
> *Say that my promise to him is, 'If you*
> *Desire me you will have this fortress too.'"*

The nurse said, "I shall do as you have ordered, and bring you news of him."

When night took possession of the world, and its army spread from sea to sea, when the plains darkened and the mountains seemed like indigo, and in the empyrean the stars flickered like thirty thousand suspended candles, the nurse set out, trembling with apprehension, her heart filled with anxiety lest Tayer learn of her movements. When she reached the entrance to Shapur's royal pavilion she said to one of the guards, "If you take me to the king I'll reward you with a diadem and a ring." The chamberlain ushered her into the king's presence. She prostrated herself, touching the ground with her eyelashes, and told him the words Malekeh had said to her. The king laughed in response, and in his joy gave the nurse a thousand gold coins, two armbands, a torque, a ring, and brocades from China and Barbary. Then he said,

"Speak gently and at length to your lovely mistress. Tell her that I swear by the sun and moon, by the belt our priests wear, by Zoroaster himself, and by the royal crown, that she can have whatever she desires from me, even if to give it will harm my kingdom. Her ears will never hear harsh words from me, and I shall never try to escape her embraces. I swear by God that I will bestow treasures and troops and a crown and throne on her."

As soon as she had heard him out the nurse ran back to the fortress. There she told her mistress, who was as lovely as a silver cypress tree and whose face was as splendid as the shining moon, all she had heard. She said that now Venus would mate with the sun itself, and she described Shapur's stature and appearance, and how the meeting had gone.

Malekeh Delivers Tayer's Fortress to Shapur; Tayer Is Killed

When the sun showed its crown in the east and turned the ground that had been as dark as teak the color of yellow roses, Malekeh took from the castle's treasurer the keys to where the victuals and amphorae of wine were kept. She sent food and wine, together with scents made from narcissi and fenugreek, to the nobles and warriors in the fortress. Then she called the wine steward to her and spoke to him kindly and carefully: "Tonight see that you serve Tayer unmixed wine: keep him and his men plied with wine till they are drunk and fall asleep." The steward replied: "I am your slave; it is by your commands that I live in this world."

When the sun turned yellow in the west, and night was hard on its heels urging it onward, Tayer asked for a bowl of royal wine. First he toasted his Ghassanid kinsfolk and, by the time the first watch of the night was over Tayer was oblivious to the tumult around him. Then the castle's inhabitants made their way to their sleeping quarters, and Malekeh ordered her servants not to speak above a whisper. Secretly they opened the great door to the fortress.

King Shapur was watching, filled with impatience at the sounds of drunkenness that he could hear. Then seeing a candle glimmer through the open door, he said, "Good fortune is with us!" The beautiful Malekeh was spirited away to his tents, where he'd had a fine space prepared for her. A force of picked warriors was ready, together with a few horsemen. They entered the fortress and set about killing the

defenders and looting its ancient treasures. More than a thousand sleep-
ing, drunken soldiers were with Tayer in that fortress. Some woke in
bewilderment, and in every part of the building they fought back;
none turned tail out of fear, and the Persian king killed a number of
them. Tayer was caught and pushed before the king, running and
naked, as a captive. The whole fortress and all its goods were now in
Shapur's hands, and his enemies were his prisoners.

Night passed, and when the sun raised its golden crown above the
horizon, a turquoise studded throne was ceremonially installed in the
fortress, and Shapur held court there. Once the formal audience was
over, Malekeh, as lovely as a flower that blossoms in the spring, came
before him. She wore a crown of red rubies, and her glittering robes
were made from Chinese cloth of gold. Then Tayer understood that
the trick that had been played on him was her doing, and that his evil
fortune was because of her. He said,

> "You are a noble king, your majesty,
> Consider what my child has done to me!
> Be careful of her kindness—you should fear her,
> And watch for any strangers who come near her."

But Shapur said to this contemptible man, "When you stole the king's
daughter from her apartments, and shamed and humiliated her people,
you rekindled old enmities that had died down." He gave orders that the
executioner cut off Tayer's head, and that his body be burned. He for-
bade the Arab prisoners to speak to anyone; he removed their shoulder
blades from their bodies, an act which astonished the world. From this
time on the Arabs called him Shapur Zu'l Aktaf, which means Shapur,
Lord of the Shoulders.

Then he returned to Pars, and all the world bowed down before
him. So the heavens smiled on Shapur for a while, but then they
showed him a quite different face.

Shapur Travels to Rome and the Emperor of Rome Has Him Sewn in an Ass's Skin

One day, despite his crown and wealth, Shapur felt oppressed by his exis-
tence. When three watches of the night had passed, he called for his
astrologer, and asked him what would become of the royal throne, and

to describe the good and evil days that lay ahead. The man shook off his sleep and brought an astrolabe; he looked in the house of Leo, the harbinger of victory and glory, to see whether misfortune threatened the king, or whether his favor with God would increase. When he had examined the signs he said, "O noble king, who rules the world and is pure of heart, a difficult and painful business lies ahead, and no one has dared warn you of this."

Shapur replied, "You are a knowledgeable man, and able to search out secrets. What can I do so that this will pass from me, and evil stars will not bring me to my knees?" The astrologer answered, "My lord, bravery and knowledge will not enable a man to evade the revolution of the heavens, no matter how wise or warlike he is. What is fated will surely happen, and we cannot fight against the turning of the sky." The king said, "May God be our refuge from all evil, for it is he who created the turning heavens, and all that is powerful or weak."

For a while Shapur ruled justly, and he remained prosperous and without troubles. Under his care all the provinces flourished, and seeing this he conceived a wish to travel to the west, to see whether the Roman emperor was worthy of the position he occupied, and to find out about his armies and wealth. He disclosed this secret plan to his vizier, who was a fine, sensible warrior, but told no one else, and added, "Rule this realm justly in my absence; your justice will bring you happiness."

Then he asked for ten camel caravans, each with its own leader, and loaded up thirty camels with jewels and gold coins. Carefully, he made his way toward Roman territory. Near Rome there was a small town, and he stopped there, at the house of a landowner, and asked for shelter. The owner warmly welcomed him, saying he had never had such a distinguished guest. The king ate and slept there for one night, and when he gave the owner a present, he again received the man's blessings. At dawn he loaded up his camels and set out quickly for the emperor's palace. There he greeted the chamberlain respectfully and gave him a present of cash. The man said, "Tell me who you are. You have the stature and air of a king." Shapur replied, "I'm a free Persian, my lord, and I've come from Jez as a merchant, bringing a caravan of silks and fine textiles. I've come to see if I can gain entrance to the emperor, so that I can present him with something valuable from my merchandise—jewels, or weapons for his army. If he'll accept some token from me, I'll be very happy and hand it over willingly. Then I can sell the rest of my goods for gold and silver, and I'll be under the emperor's protection, so I'll have nothing to fear. And I can buy what I need in Rome and then make my way back to Persia."

The old man got up from his seat by the palace doorway and went and told the emperor what he had heard. The emperor had the curtains drawn aside, and Shapur was brought into his presence. He made a fitting obeisance, and the emperor scrutinized him carefully, taking in his fine appearance and manner. He had wine and food brought, and the court was cleared of all but his counselors. But there was an Iranian there, a cruel, unjust man, who said to the emperor, "My lord, I've some news to tell you, in confidence. Listen: this fine merchant who's here selling silks for cash, I tell you he's none other than Shapur, the Persian King of Kings: he has the king's way of talking, he looks like him, and he has that aura of glory the Persian kings have."

When the emperor heard this, his mind darkened and his eyes clouded over: he signed to a guard to watch Shapur, but told no one else. Shapur became drunk; he stood up, and the emperor continued to stare at him. Then the guard strode forward and seized hold of him, saying, "You are Shapur, Nersi's son; it's a wonder you show yourself here." They took him to the women's quarters, and bound his arms. They lit a candle in front of the drunk king, and by its light they sewed him into an ass's skin, saying as they did so, "This luckless fool gave up his throne for an ass's skin."

There was a small dark room nearby, and they threw the unfortunate man into that tiny space and locked the door. The emperor gave the key to the mistress of the palace and said to her, "Give him a little bread and water, and that should cool his greed. If he lives for a while, he'll realize what my throne and crown are worth, and he'll see that the Roman emperor's throne is no concern of anyone who is not of the imperial family." The emperor's wife locked the doors and retired to her own part of the palace. There was a beautiful serving woman whom she had chosen as her subordinate and treasurer, who was Persian by descent and who remembered her family's former generations, from father to father. To this woman the empress gave the key to the chamber where Shapur was kept. That same day the emperor led his troops across the border with Persia, while Shapur languished in the ass's skin.

As the Roman troops approached the frontier with Iran, they drew their swords for battle. The Persians had no one to lead them, and the Romans carried off numerous captives. Iran became depopulated and bereft of wealth: neither men, women nor children remained, and the Persian army had no news of whether Shapur was dead or alive. The population fled before the Roman armies, and the land emptied of its inhabitants. Innumerable Persians became Christians, and the land surrendered itself to their bishops.

The Empress's Servant Frees Shapur from the Ass's Skin

So conditions continued for a while, with Persia's army in disarray, and Shapur imprisoned and watched constantly. Because she was of Persian descent, the empress's servant was not happy to see Shapur still sewed in the ass's skin, and day and night she wept for him.

> One day she said to him, "O handsome youth,
> Who are you? Have no fear now, tell the truth.
> Sewn in that skin your slender form can find
> No bodily content or peace of mind:
> You were a cypress in your elegance,
> Your face the full moon in its radiance,
> Your hair a musky crown—and now you've grown
> So bent and thin you seem mere skin and bone.
> My heart's tormented for you, day and night
> My eyes weep tears for your horrific plight.
> What can you hope for now? Why keep from me
> The secret hiding your identity?"

Shapur said to her, "If you feel any love for me, I ask that you will remember my sufferings and hardships, and that you swear that never will the least of what I say to you reach my enemies; then I will tell you truthfully what you have asked." The maidservant swore by the seventy twists in a priest's belt, by the soul of Jesus and his sufferings on the cross, and by the lord of Iran that she would neither tell anyone his secret, nor seek to worsen his situation in any way. Then Shapur told her all that he'd kept from her and added, "If you do what I say and keep my secret in your heart, your head will be lifted above that of all other women, and the world will be at your feet. When it's

time to bring me bread, stealthily bring warm milk, and with it mac-
erate this ass's hide, which is going to be notorious throughout the
world and will be remembered by the wise long after I'm dead."

Quietly, undetected, the serving girl procured milk and heated it
over a fire in a large dish shaped like a ship. Telling no one of what she
was up to, she took the milk to Shapur. Two weeks passed, and finally
the ass's skin became pliable enough for Shapur to emerge from it, his
body covered in blood, his heart filled with pain. He said to the serv-
ing girl, "You are a pure-hearted and resourceful woman; now we
must think hard and find some way to get away from this accursed city
of Rome." She answered, "Tomorrow at dawn all the nobles here are
going to gather together for a festival; there's a celebration going on,
and everyone will be there—men, women, and children. When the
empress leaves the city for the festivities, the palace will be empty and
I'll find a way to save us; I'm not afraid of rumormongers. I'll gladly
bring you two horses, two maces, a bow, and arrows."

The maid put her mind to the task and chose two fine horses from
the stables; then she provided herself with a sword, maces, barding for
the horses, armor, and an Indian helmet. She'd thought long and hard
and prepared her heart for what had to be done, taking wisdom as her
guide. When the sun set in the west, and night drew its dark veil over
its head, King Shapur's soul was filled with anxiety, wondering what
the maidservant would do the next morning.

Shapur Flees from Rome to Iran

The sun rose in the house of Leo, day dawned, and sleep fled. As the
people of the city went to enjoy their festival, the resourceful maidser-
vant put her plan into action. The palace was now empty and in her
hands, and she felt her heart was like a lion's, her grip like a leopard's.
She brought two noble horses from the stables, fine armor for a knight,
as well as a number of gold coins, pearls, rubies, and other valuables. By
the time she had everything ready for their flight, night had fallen again.
Then the two of them set out joyfully for Iran, riding day and night
without pausing either to eat or sleep. When they reached Khuzestan
their bodies and horses were weak with exhaustion, and they looked for
somewhere they could dismount and rest. They saw a beautiful village
before them; it was filled with gardens and open spaces for the inhabi-
tants to gather and enjoy themselves. Tired out by their flight, they

knocked at the door of an orchard. The owner, a kindhearted and hos-
pitable man, came running, and as soon as he caught sight of the two,
dressed in armor, helmeted, and holding lances, he said, "What kind of
a greeting is this? Where have you sprung from at such an hour, and
why are you all dressed up for a military expedition?"

Shapur replied, "You seem a good man, but how many questions are
you going to ask someone who's lost his way? I'm a Persian, and I've
come here fleeing from the Roman emperor and his army, and may I
never see his head or crown again! If you can give me shelter tonight and
treat me well, as a lord of the marches would, I think this will stand you
in good stead one day; the tree you plant will bear you fine fruit." The
man answered, "My house is yours and I am at your service; I'll try to
provide whatever I can for you, and I'll mention your presence here to
no one." King Shapur dismounted from his horse, and the maidservant
followed suit. The orchard owner's wife made them a little meal from
whatever was available to her, and when they had eaten, they were
shown to a place where they could relax and drink wine. Their host
passed the wine to Shapur and said, "Drink to whoever is in your mind
now!" Shapur replied, "My fine and eloquent host, the man who brings
the wine should drink first, especially if he is older and wiser. You seem
a little older than I am, and as you brought the wine, you should drink
first." The owner replied, "A sober answer! The man who is more cul-
tivated should drink first, which means you should, as you are old in the
grace of your manner, even though you are still a young man. The scent
of the crown comes from your hair, and your face glows like ivory."

Shapur laughed and took the wine, and a cold sigh rose from his
vitals. He said to his host, "You're a man of the pure faith: what news
have you of the fortunes of Iran?" His host answered, "My lord,
may evil never touch you, and may our enemies suffer as the Roman
emperor has made Iran suffer. Persia's population has scattered, and
agriculture here has gone to rack and ruin. There has been so much
looting, and so many men and women have been killed, that this
great people has hidden itself away. And many have turned Christian
and gone over to their bishops." Shapur said, "And where is King
Shapur, whose splendor was like that of the full moon, that the
Roman emperor has grown so powerful, darkening the bright fortune
of Iran?"

The orchard owner said, "My lord, may you be always mighty and prosperous: Iran's nobles have no notion where he is, or whether he's alive or dead; everyone who was of any consequence here is now a prisoner in Rome." And the man began to weep bitterly. He said, "Stay here for three days, and make my house shine like the sun with your presence, for a sage has said that whoever acts inhospitably has no wisdom and will suffer a harsh fate. Stay, rest, drink wine to your heart's content, and then, when it seems appropriate to you, tell me your name." Shapur replied, "I accept, and for now my host is as my king."

The Persians Recognize Shapur and Come to Welcome Him

That night passed in drinking and the back and forth of conversation. When the first light of dawn touched the mountain peaks and spread its golden banner over the foothills, the owner of the orchard came to his guest and said, "May your day be happy, and your head reach higher than the rainy clouds. My house is unworthy of you, it's not a fit place for you to stay. You have to eat like a poor man here, and I have neither clothes to offer you, nor the means to make you comfortable." Shapur said, "You are a lucky man, and I would rather be in your house than crowned and seated on a throne. Bring me the Zend-Avesta, and the barsom, and as we pray I wish to ask you something."

The man brought all the king commanded, and when everything was ready the king asked him in the murmur of prayer, "Tell me truly, where is the chief priest now?" And the answer came, "From where I am sitting now I can see the house of the chief priest." Then quietly the king said to him, "Ask the headman of this village for clay to make a seal." No sooner had he heard these words than the man ran to bring clay, musk, and wine. The king set his seal ring in the clay, handed the impression over to his host, and said, "Give this clay seal to the chief priest, and pay attention to what he says."

At first light, the man took the impression made by the king's seal to the chief priest. The door to the audience hall was closed and guarded by a number of men, and he shouted out asking to be admitted. When they let him in, the orchard owner went straight to the chief priest, showed him the clay, and made his obeisance. When he looked at the seal's impression, the priest's heart leaped for joy; he wept over the name he saw, and said, "Whose seal is this?" The orchard owner said, "The knight who owns it is sitting in my house; there is a lovely young woman with him, as slender as a cypress tree; she is beautiful, wise, and has a royal dignity about her." The priest said, "Describe this man's face and stature to me."

> *The man replied, "In springtime, when you see,*
> *Beside a stream, a single cypress tree—*
> *That's how this knight is: he has arms the size*
> *Of some great horse's noble thighs,*
> *His chest is like a lion's, and his face*
> *Is ruddy: there you see such kindly grace*
> *It makes you blush bright red: it is as though*
> *His face gave off a crown's imperial glow."*

As the orchard owner spoke the priest realized that this lionhearted man could be none other than the king, and that such a face belonged only in the royal court. He sent an envoy to the army's commander saying that the glory of Shapur had been found, and that he should gather forces from every quarter. The priest's messenger hurried to his destination and said, "In the garden of happiness and good fortune, the royal tree has blossomed!" The commander was overjoyed at these words: his lips were filled with sighs, his heart with the longing for warfare. He prayed to God, saying, "O you who holds the world, only you are worthy of praise! Who could have known that Shapur would see the army again, or that the army would see him?"

When night displayed its black flag and the stars appeared around the moon, from every quarter an army of men gathered in the place where the lord of the world was living. Joyfully they crowded about the house belonging to the orchard owner, who came to Shapur and said, "An army has collected outside our door, what do you think we should do?" Although the place was small and humble, Shapur ordered that they be admitted; as they entered one by one, they bowed their faces down to the dust. Shapur embraced each of the nobles and wept to tell them of the evils he had endured. He told them of what he had suffered in the ass's skin, and of the words he had heard from the emperor; he described the beautiful serving girl's nobility of spirit, and all she had done for him, and added,

> *"To her and God I owe my life: may she*
> *Be blessed with happiness eternally!*

> *A mighty king's the slave of those slaves who*
> *Show magnanimity in all they do:*
> *I am the slave of this true-hearted slave*
> *Who's been so selfless, generous, and brave.*

"Now that I resume my kingship and the command of my armies, send messengers and set advance guards on the roads; in particular close the roads to Ctesiphon, as I want no news of this to reach the Roman emperor. If he realizes the glory of Persian sovereignty has awoken again, he will lead an army against us and break the backs of our forces. At the moment we can't equal him in military might, and we shouldn't engage in a struggle with his flourishing good fortune. When our priests have gathered an army so dense that not a mosquito can pass through the ranks, then we shall revise our plans and secretly rid our garden of these noxious weeds. For now we need guards everywhere, watching day and night: no one should take off his armor and lie down to sleep while the Roman threat hangs over us."

Shapur Attacks by Night and Takes the Roman Emperor Prisoner

Not many days passed before the Persian army had grown to six thousand men. Shapur sent spies to Ctesiphon, which had been occupied by the Romans, to report on the emperor and his court there. Stealthily and secretly the spies collected information; they reported to the king and said, "The emperor spends all his time drinking and hunting, and gives no thought to warfare. His army is scattered about the countryside plundering what they can find. They send out no scouts by day, they set no guards at night, they're like a flock without a shepherd. The emperor has no thought of any enemy attacking from anywhere, and is content to live following his fancies."

Shapur was overjoyed to hear this, and his past sorrows dispersed like the wind. He chose three thousand Persian warriors, well equipped and with barding for their horses. They put on their armor in the night's darkness and set off toward Ctesiphon, riding quickly by night and hiding during the day. The king and his men rode through deserts and mountains, by trackless ways, with scouts sent two parasangs ahead of the main body of men. So they went forward, until the scouts came within sight of Ctesiphon. At this time two watches of the night had passed, and the emperor had no suspicion that anything was amiss, until he heard the din of drums and the cries of sentries ringing out like a cockcrow. The whole plain was filled with the Roman tents, but who in all that encampment was aware of the impending attack? The emperor was drunk in his pavilion, and his soldiers were crowded around in disorder. When Shapur saw how things stood, he gave his horse its head, and his men charged the Roman camp, with the king laying about him with a huge mace. The blare of trumpets, the clash of maces, the clanging of Indian bells rose up to the clouds. Cries of combat and the noise of arms crashing against armor came from every side: you'd have said the sky had split open, and that the sun dripped blood down through the air. In the darkness the Kaviani banner glittered and swords flashed, and it seemed that the earth was covered with clouds that rained down weapons. The dust of battle hid the mountains, and the stars veiled their light. Shapur flattened the evil emperor's pavilion; his men set fires on all sides throughout the Roman camp, and the skies seem to come down to the earth. Finally the emperor was taken prisoner, and his fortunate star deserted him. Many of his brave nobles and commanders were hauled from their tents and put in chains.

At dawn, when night drew in her skirts and the sun's banner appeared on the mountain tops, Shapur asked for a scribe to come, bringing a pen, inks, musk, and silk. A letter was written to every chieftain, every king, and every country. The letter began with praise of God, whose slaves we are, since it is he who aids the virtuous and has no need of human aid, who created the world and guides us to righteousness. It continued, "Since the Roman emperor did not take wisdom as his soul's guide, but instead ignored God's commands and sowed nothing but seeds of evil in Iran, he now languishes weeping in chains. God entrusted him with the crown of Iran, but he will take nothing from this world but an evil name. By the power of God who guided us, his court and army have been broken, and any Romans found in the city will be put to the sword. Pursue justice, obey my commands, and willingly renew your oaths of loyalty to me." Swift messengers took the king's letter to every quarter.

Shapur moved his court from the camp to Ctesiphon, and when he placed his ancestors' crown upon his head again, he gave thanks to God. He sent a scribe to the prisons, to write down the names of their captives; the number of Roman nobles held there came to one thousand one hundred and ten, all of whom were relatives or allies of the emperor, and among the first men of their country. The king had the hands and feet of those who had been involved in oppression cut off, then he ordered that the Roman emperor be brought before him. The executioner dragged him by the arm from the prison, and he was like a man who has lost consciousness. When this tyrannical man saw Shapur's face, he wept and prostrated himself, rubbing his face in the dust, and calling down blessings on the throne and crown. His tears soaked the ground, and his face and hair were coated with dust.

The king said to him, "You are entirely evil, a Christian, and an enemy of God. You say that he who has no partner, whose realm has no beginning or end, has a son. You don't know how to speak except in lies, and lies are an evil fire that gives no light. If you are an emperor, where are your shame and good sense, where is your conscience to guide you? Why did you imprison me in an ass's skin and bring my greatness down into the dust? I came as a merchant looking for a fair, I didn't come with drums and an army looking for war. But you shut your guest up in an ass's skin and led your army against Iran. Now you know what war with brave men means, and you won't be looking to fight with Iran again."

The emperor replied, "Who can evade God's will? My royal fortune made wisdom a stranger to me, and my soul became a devil's mercenary. But if you return good for evil, you will be a legend in the world, your name will never grow old, and your chivalry will bring you all that you desire. If I receive my life at your hands, all wealth and gold will be contemptible to me, I shall be a slave at your court, seeking nothing but how to augment its splendor." Shapur answered, "You are an evil, ignorant man. Why did you plunder this country? I want back immediately all the prisoners you took from here to Rome; then you must return all the wealth you took to Rome too, and may you never see that shameful city again! You must provide money to rebuild the parts of Persia you have ruined, where lions and leopards now build their lairs. Further, you must have ten noble Romans handed over for every Persian you killed; I want only members of the imperial family, and they will live here with me as hostages in this happy land. For every tree you cut down in Persia—and a good man does not cut down trees—you must plant another and build walls to protect it, and in this way you may lessen the rage that people feel against you. I have you in chains now, but how can I ever forgive you that ass's skin? If you do not do as I have ordered, your own skin will be cut open from head to foot." They split his ears with a knife, and bored a hole through his nose, in which they put a piece of wood of the kind by which a camel is led; this was done because Shapur remembered the ass's skin. Two heavy shackles were placed on his feet, and the executioner returned him to prison.

Shapur Leads His Army into Roman Territory: His Battle with the Emperor's Brother

Shapur drew up his troops for review, and as the treasuries were opened and he provided his men with provisions and payment, his head filled with thoughts of revenge, his heart with ambition. He led his army into Roman territory; they killed whomever they found there and burned all the buildings, making the world glow with fire.

When news reached Rome from Persia that their land had been devastated and the emperor taken prisoner while fighting at night, all Rome wept and trembled at the name of Shapur. They said, "Who but our emperor, that unchivalrous man, brought this evil on us?" The emperor had a younger brother; their father was dead, but their mother was still alive. This brother's name was Yanus, and he was an ambitious, generous, open-hearted man. The army gathered at the imperial court, and Yanus's mother, who was a bellicose woman, distributed cash to them and said to Yanus, "You must avenge your brother, since you can see an army is attacking us from Iran." Yanus was swept away by anger when he heard this and said, "Revenge for a brother is not something to push aside and forget!" He had the drums sounded and brought a large cross out before his formidable army.

When the armies came face to face, the men on each side were eager for battle. Their ranks were drawn up, the din of battle began, and Yanus led his troops in an attack. But such clouds of dust sprang up that his men lost their way. On one side they were hemmed in by mountains, and on the other by a wide river, and the dust continued until the sun turned yellow in the sunset. So many men were killed that the ground seemed paved with the iron armor of the dead. Shapur was in the center of his forces, calling out to his officers on the right and left; he and his nobles urged their horses forward, the ground shook, and their troops engaged the enemy. They launched an all-out attack against the Romans in which officers and foot soldiers became indistinguishable. Yanus saw that his forces couldn't withstand the king's, and he and his army fled. Shapur pursued them, and the dust dimmed the shining air. Heaps of corpses lay everywhere, and the plants that grew there were smeared with men's brains. The whole plain was filled with trunkless, limbless heads of slaughtered Romans. No army or cross remained on that plain, and no bishops or crosses remained in the castles. The army was astonished at the amount of booty that was gathered on all sides. The king distributed everything to his troops, reserving only the emperor's personal treasure for himself, a treasure that had caused him such pain in the past and that was not enough to cancel that pain. The Roman soldiers gathered round and spoke against their emperor, saying, "May we never have another ruler like him, may the name of emperor disappear from Rome! Away with altars and crosses and vestments; now our priests' belts and crosses have been burned, Rome is like pagan Qanuj for us, and the fame of the Messiah's faith grows weaker."

Baranush Is Crowned Emperor of Rome: His Letter to Shapur

There was a noble Roman, of the emperors' line, called Baranush: he was a wise man, knowledgeable and able to give good advice. The army said to him, "You should be emperor, and the leader of this country and people." They prepared an ivory throne for him, and Baranush placed the crown on his own head. The Romans sat him in the center of power and all of them called down blessings on him.

Baranush sat on his throne and thought of Rome and her battles. He knew that she would be harmed by further confrontations with the great king, and he selected a messenger, a man who was sensible and humble, who could speak wisely and eloquently, and was both a great scribe and someone experienced in the ways of the world. He summoned this man and conferred with him, then dictated a letter to Shapur, beginning with praise of God, who rules the world. It continued:

> "May all the chieftains of the world bow down
> As slaves before your everlasting crown:

You know that our nobility condemn
Oppression visited on guiltless men.
Whether performed in Rome's or Persia's name,
Rapine and murder are a source of shame.
If we may trace this warfare to the time
Iraj died, Manuchehr avenged that crime—
Both Tur and Salm are dust now. And if you're
Remembering Dara's and Sekandar's war,
Dara was murdered by his ministers
And plucked from power by his opposing stars.
And if you hate our emperor, he remains
A captive in your dungeons, bound in chains.
But Rome, which has no equal anywhere,
Should not be prey to ruin and despair.
If you attack us we cannot withstand
The force of your assault against our land,
Our wives and children are already yours,
Made captive, or left wounded by your wars.
It's time to close your eyes to what is past,
To lay aside your warlike plans at last.
Day follows day, and every day in turn
Sees yet another of our cities burn!
Let joy into your heart—it cannot be
That God looks kindly on such tyranny.
God keep Your Highness—may your star arise,
And crown the moon, and dominate the skies."

The letter was sealed with the emperor's seal, and the messenger set off for Shapur's court. When the letter with its fine sentiments was read to Shapur, he frowned, his eyes filled with tears, and he forgave the Romans. He immediately wrote an answer, going over the good and bad of the past, and adding, "Who was it who sewed his guest in an ass's skin and rekindled ancient enmities? But if you are wise come before me, bringing philosophers from your country. Since I have decided on peace, I shall not prepare for war. I shall let you go free from this narrow pass in which you find yourself." The messenger returned and took the king's answer; word by word he reported everything that had been said.

Baranush Visits Shapur and They Conclude a Treaty

Baranush was overjoyed when he saw the answer to his letter. He ordered that a hundred Roman nobles travel with him to Shapur's court, and took sixty donkey loads of silver, together with jewels and textiles, and thirty thousand gold coins as a present. The nobles entered Shapur's presence bareheaded and scattered the gold before him. Shapur welcomed them warmly, then turned to Baranush and said, "Many shameless, unjust men came here from Rome and turned our cities into waste reed beds. I want compensation for these ruined places that are now the haunts of lions and leopards." Baranush replied, "Tell us what must be done; do not turn your face from us now that you have granted us peace." The great king answered, "If you wish me to cancel your sins against us, three times a year Rome must send us a million gold coins; and if you wish to curtail my anger you will grant me the town of Nasibin, in Mesopotamia." Baranush replied, "Iran is yours, and Nasibin and its plains and warriors are yours; we accept your terms and the tribute we must pay, since we have not the power to oppose your anger." In the treaty between them, Shapur promised never to lead an army into Roman territory, unless it was done in a fitting, ceremonial manner that did nothing to diminish Rome's dignity. Then Shapur made much of his guests, treating them more kindly than his own nobles.

When the embassy had gone, Shapur gave many thanks to the world's Creator and set off joyfully for Estakhr, the most splendid site in Pars. But when news of the treaty reached Nasibin, its inhabitants prepared for war, saying, "Shapur should not own Nasibin or bring an army here, since he has no respect for Christianity; all his concern is for the Zend-Avesta and the faith of Zoroaster. He won't listen to us when he comes, and we have no interest in his scriptures or his faith." The common people took over the city, and its citizens sat in the saddle ready for war. When news arrived that the way to Nasibin had been blocked, Shapur burst out in rage against the Christian faith and sent a huge army against the town. He said, "It's ridiculous to respect a religion whose prophet was killed by the Jews." The army traveled as quickly as wind-borne dust; for a week its cavalry and lionhearted warriors fought, and the city's inhabitants were hard pressed. The Persians killed many of their leaders and put those who remained alive in chains. Then the citizens sued for quarter, sending a letter to Shapur, who granted their request and ordered his army home.

Shapur was now famous throughout the world, and his power was acknowledged everywhere; he was referred to as "the victorious king." As for the young serving girl who had released him from captivity, and helped him to this power, he named her Delafruz-e Farrokhpay—the heart's delight who brings good luck—and she was his favorite among his womenfolk. He gave the orchard owner considerable wealth and sent him happy on his way. The Roman emperor remained in his prison, wretched and in chains, with his flesh eaten away by shackles. His wealth in Rome was gathered together and sent to Persia, and he lived a little longer, with sighs always on his lips. Finally he died while still chained and imprisoned, and his crown passed to another man. Shapur sent his corpse to Rome, in a coffin, with his head crowned with musk, and said, "This is the end of all of us, and I do not know where our peace is to be found. One man acts with cruelty and stupidity, another with wisdom and glory; but for each of them his time here passes in the same way. Blessed is the man who commits no evil in the world!"

Then Shapur built a city for the prisoners he'd taken, in Khuzestan, which he called Khorramabad—The City of Joy—and he settled there the men whose hands he'd cut off; the whole area was given over to them and each New Year they received a robe of honor from the king. He built another city in Syria, which he named Piruz-e Shapur—Shapur's Victory—and he built a third city, which had a castle and a hospital in it, near Ahvaz. He called this city Kenam-e Asiran—The Captives' Dwelling—and his prisoners found peace and contentment there.

The Coming of Mani: His Claim to Be a Prophet

Shapur had reigned for fifty years, and there was no one to equal him at that time. An eloquent man arrived from China, and the world will never see his like again. His abilities had stood him in good stead, and he had become a powerful man: his name was Mani. He said, "I am a prophet and a painter, and I am the first of those who introduce new religions into the world." He asked for an audience with Shapur, hoping to persuade the king to support his claim to be a prophet. He spoke fluently, but the king remained unconvinced by his talk. Shapur's mind was troubled by his words, and he summoned his priests and spoke to them at length about Mani. He said, "This man from China talks very well, but I have doubts about the religion he proposes. Talk to him and listen to what he has to say; it may be you'll be won over by him." They answered, "This painter will be no match for the chief priest. Listen to Mani by all means, but summon our chief priest, and when Mani sees him he won't be in such a hurry to talk."

Shapur sent for the chief priest, who spoke for a long time with Mani, and Mani was left speechless in the middle of his discourse, unable to answer the chief priest's remarks about the ancient faith of Zoroaster. The chief priest said to him, "You love images; why do you foolishly strive with God in this way, God who created the high heavens and made time and space in which darkness and light are manifest, whose essence is beyond all other essences, and who fashioned the heavens to turn by night and day? Your refuge is with him, all you suffer is from him. Why do you put such trust in images, ignoring the advice of the prophets? Images are multiple, but God is one, and you have no choice but to submit to him. If you could make your images move, then you could say that this is a demonstration of the truth of what you say. But don't you see that such a demonstration would fail? No one is going to believe your claims. If Ahriman were God's equal, dark night would be like smiling daylight; in all the years that have gone by, night and day have kept their places, and the heavens' turning has neither increased nor diminished. God cannot be contained by our thoughts, for he is beyond all time and place. You talk as madmen do, and that is all there is to it: no one should support you." He said much more beside this, and Mani was unable to answer his words. Mani's credibility, which had seemed so flourishing, withered away. The turning of the heavens was against Mani. The king was enraged by him and had him ignominiously dragged from the court. He said, "The world is no place for this image maker; he has disturbed the peace long enough. Let him be flayed and his skin stuffed with straw so that no one will be tempted to follow his example." They hung his body from the city gates, and then later from the wall in front of the hospital. The world praised Shapur, and men flung dirt on Mani's corpse.

Shapur Makes His Brother, Ardeshir, His Regent

Shapur's life became a garden within which grew roses without thorns. His justice and good sense, his actions, his wars and his policies were such that he had no enemies anywhere, and evil had no refuge in all the world. When he was more than seventy years old and had little hope of living longer, he summoned a scribe, together with the chief priest, Ardeshir, a wise and just man who was Shapur's own younger brother. Shapur had a son who was still very young and had little experience of the world.

The king said to Ardeshir, "You are a champion among men, and a fine, brave horseman. If you will swear truthfully to me, giving your word, that when my son reaches his majority and has grown into a brave youth, you will hand over to him the throne, the royal treasuries, and command of the army, and that you will be his benevolent guide until then, I shall hand over this royal crown to you, together with our treasuries and the army." Before the scribe and the nobles who were there, Ardeshir accepted Shapur's words, promising that when the boy reached manhood and was worthy of the royal crown, he would hand over the authority of kingship to him and would strive only to advance his interests.

Then Shapur handed him the crown and royal seal, in front of the nobles, and gave him lengthy advice on the duties of a just king. When he had heard Shapur out, his brother wept. The king lived for one more year after he made Ardeshir his regent.

F̶erdowsi's accounts of the brief reigns of Ardeshir Niku Kar, Shapur III and Bahram Shapur are omitted.

THE REIGN OF YAZDEGERD
THE UNJUST

Yazdegerd rejoiced at his brother's unhappy death, taking his crown and placing it on his own head. All those who had lived by the sword and mace trembled like willow trees; Yazdegerd's rule over the world became more secure, and his benevolence faded away as his authority increased. Wise men meant nothing to him, and his royal obligations were forgotten; lords of the marches, champions, scholars, and learned priests—all were like so much wind to him, and his dark soul gave itself over to tyranny. Justice and kindness were cancelled from his heart, and he granted no man his requests. He respected no one's rank, and faults were elaborately punished. His ministers, whose task was to increase his power and glory, agreed among themselves never to tell the king of the country's true condition; they all shrank from him in terror and lived in fear for their lives. As soon as the chamberlain heard that envoys had come to see the king, or that subordinates had arrived at court seeking help, he hurried to reassure them with kind and gentle words. Later he said, "The king is not in the mood for work, and you cannot have an audience with him. I have told him of your requests, and he will act appropriately."

The Birth of Yazdegerd's Son, Bahram

Seven years went by, during which time the country's priests lived in fear and torment because of Yazdegerd's cruelty. Then, at the beginning of the eighth year of his reign, at the spring equinox, a son was born to him under an auspicious star. Delighted with his little son, Yazdegerd named him Bahram. Two renowned astrologers were summoned before the king: Sorush was the best of Indian astrologers, a man of great glory and intelligence; Hoshyar was a Persian, and his knowledge was such that he could put a bridle on the heavens. They used their astrolabes and Greek astrological tables to uncover the happy fortune that Bahram would be a great prince in the world, and that he would rule over the seven climes. Still grasping their instruments and tables, they ran into the king's presence and said, "We have brought together all we know, and it is clear from the stars that the heavens look kindly on this baby: he will rule the seven climes, and be a great and glorious king." Yazdegerd was overjoyed to hear this and rewarded them with royal jewels.

Once the astrologers had left the court, the priests and ministers sat together and discussed what should be done. They believed that if the new prince did not take after his father he could be a great and just king, but if his character turned out like his father's, he would ruin the whole country, and neither the priests, nor the country's warriors, nor the young prince himself would have an auspicious future. With good intentions in their hearts, they went to the king and said, "This splendid child is beyond any reproach or blame; all the world is his to rule, every country will pay him tribute. Look for a place where wisdom has ensured the country's peace and prosperity, and choose someone noble from there to bring him up. Then this fine prince will learn the skills he needs, and the world will rejoice in his rule."

Accordingly, the king summoned envoys from every country, and at the same time he sent his own men to Rome, India, China, and other civilized regions. One man went among the Arabs to study the nature of their life, and he searched for someone eloquent and wise who could bring Bahram up. Experienced sages came from every country and gathered at the Persian court. The king questioned them at length, made much of them, and assigned them living quarters. One night two Arab princes, No'man and his father Monzer, arrived with their entourage. When all these visitors had assembled in Pars, they presented themselves before Yazdegerd and said, "We are your slaves and will the obey the words we hear from you. Who among us will be fortunate enough to take the king's son in his arms, to teach him the ways of knowledge and to cleanse his heart of darkness?" Then each of these eloquent, experienced men, whether he was from Rome or India or Persia, whether an astrologer, a mathematician, or a philosopher, said humbly, "O just, wise, and honorable king, we are all as the dust beneath your feet, and stand ready to act as your guide to knowledge. Look at us, and decide which of us pleases you, which of us will be useful to you." But Monzer said,

"We are your slaves, and our lives in this world are the king's. The king knows of our qualities, since he is as a shepherd to us and we are his flock. We are riders, warriors, tamers of horses, and we have no tolerance of so-called wise men. We are not astrologers or mathematicians: our souls are filled with love of the king, and we trust in the quick Arab horses we ride. We are all your son's slaves, and we laud his glory."

Yazdegerd Entrusts His Son Bahram to Monzer and No'man

When Yazdegerd heard these words, he gathered his thoughts together, came to a decision, and handed over Bahram into Monzer's keeping. He had a robe of honor made for Monzer and exalted his head to the skies; the king of the Yemen's horse was called for at the door to the court, and all the plain in front of the palace was filled with camels, horses, litters, servants, and nurses for the baby. The whole area from the city gates to the court was decorated in royal fashion for the prince's departure.

When Monzer arrived back in the Yemen, all the men and women of the country came out to greet him, and as soon as he reached his home he began to search for worthy, wellborn women to suckle the child. From among the noble Persians and Arabs there he chose four accomplished women: two were Arabs, and two were Persians of royal descent, and these four prepared themselves to act as the baby's wet nurses.

They suckled him for four years, and he grew satisfied and stout on their milk; they weaned him with difficulty, but still they continued to cuddle and caress him. When he was seven the wise child said to Monzer, "My lord, don't treat me like a baby at the breast! Send me to teachers; there's work to be done, don't leave me idle and useless like this!" Monzer replied, "You don't need teachers yet, my lord. When it's time for you to be taught your lessons, I won't leave you to play in the palace and boast about your games." But Bahram answered him, "Stop thinking of me as an idle good-for-nothing. It's true I'm young in years, and my chest and shoulders aren't like a hero's, but I have some knowledge. You're old in years, but you don't have much wisdom, and my nature isn't what you think it is. Don't you know that when someone is ready to seek things out, he chooses what he has to do first and concentrates on that? If you're going to be always waiting for the right time, your heart will lose everything good, everything will be out of place, and nothing will come out right. It's the head that matters for a human being! Teach me everything that a king should know: the beginning of righteousness is a knowledge of God, and blessed is the man who is wise and has knowledge!"

Monzer stared at him in astonishment and murmured the name of God to himself. He immediately sent a messenger to Shurestan, who sought out three teachers who were highly respected there. One was to teach the boy how to write, and so to cleanse his heart of darkness. Another was to instruct him in the management of hawks and hunting cheetahs, which delights the heart. Another would teach him how to play polo, shoot with a bow, fight in combat against enemies, and tug his reins to right and left and so control his horse on the battlefield. These learned men presented themselves to Monzer and described to him the things they could teach. Monzer handed the young prince over to them for instruction, and he learned so quickly that his abilities were soon those of a grown man. His intellect grasped whatever they said to him, and by the time he was eighteen he had grown into a brave youth as splendid as the sun. He no longer needed his instructors to tell him anything about hunting with hawks and cheetahs, or about how to ride and attack on the battlefield. He said to Monzer, "My pure-hearted protector, you can send these teachers back to where they came from." Each of the men was given a number of presents, and they left Monzer's court in good spirits.

Later Bahram said to Monzer, "Have the Arabs bring their horses before me, and make them tug on the reins and flourish their lances. Then they can put a price on whichever horse pleases me, and I'll pay more for it than they ask." Monzer replied, "You're an ambitious young prince, and the herder of my horses is at your service, as his lord is too. I have no objection if you want to buy an Arab horse." Bahram said, "You have a noble reputation, and may you live prosperously for many years. I'll choose a horse I don't have to rein in when going down a slope, one I can make sure-footed at a gallop, and then I'll have him outstrip the winds of spring. But before he's properly trained, it's not right to force a horse to gallop too fast."

Monzer said to No'man, "Choose a number of horses, and as they're driven across the plain, watch out for a good mount for a warrior." No'man quickly brought a hundred horses, of which he chose a number suitable to be ridden in battle. Bahram wandered among them, but whenever he mounted one that had the speed of the wind, it could not bear his weight. This continued until finally he settled on a chestnut horse that was both swift and broad chested. He also chose a bay horse with a black mane and tail that was as big as a sea monster, and Monzer paid a just price for the two of them. They were both from the woods near Kufah. Bahram accepted the horses as a gift from him, and they glowed like the fires of Azar-Goshasp. Monzer looked after the young prince as if he were the apple of his eye, and did not let even the wind disturb him.

One day Bahram said to Monzer, "You are a noble, well-intentioned man, but you hem me in with your excessive care and constant worry. Everyone we see has some secret sorrow that turns his face yellow with grief, and a free man's health is revived by pleasure, so allow me this one further pleasure then, the pleasure that cures all pains. Whether he's a prince or a warrior, a young man finds comfort and happiness with women. They are the foundation of our faith, and they guide young men toward goodness. Have five or six beautiful slave girls, as splendid as the sun, brought here, so that I can pick one or two of them. I've been thinking too that I should have children: if I had a child that would bring me some comfort. The king would be pleased, and men would praise me for it."

The old man congratulated the young prince on his words and had a broker hurry to the slave-seller's depot.

> He brought back forty western slaves, each one
> A heart-delighting girl, a radiant sun.
> Bahram chose two of them, who seemed to be
> Fashioned from roses and pale ivory;
> Tall in their elegance, and cypress slim,
> Their grace and loveliness delighted him.
> One played the harp, one seemed to Bahram's eyes
> Bright as Canopus in the Yemen's skies.

Monzer bought both of them and Bahram laughed, then blushed like a ruby from Badakhshan.

The Story of Bahram and the Harp-Player
For a while Bahram occupied himself solely with playing polo and hunting. And so it was that one day he went out hunting without any of his companions, taking with him only his harp-playing slave girl. Her name

was Azadeh, and her cheeks were as red as wine: she sat with him on his mount, her harp in her hand. She was his heart's delight and desire, and his name was always on her lips. That day, Bahram had asked for a brocade cloth to be draped across his camel's back, and that it be provided with four gem-studded stirrups, two of which were silver and two of gold. Beneath his quiver he had a slingshot, as he was adept at all forms of hunting. Two pairs of deer appeared in front of them and the young prince turned smiling to Azadeh and said, "When I draw back the bowstring, which of these two do you want my arrow to strike? There is a young female, and she has an old male companion." Azadeh replied, "You are a lion of a man, and a warrior doesn't fight against deer! But turn that doe to a buck with an arrow, and with another arrow make the buck into a doe. Then urge your camel forward, and as they flee from you, use your slingshot, and strike one of the deer on the ear, so that she will rub it against her shoulder and lift up her foot to scratch the spot, and when she does that—if you want me to call you the light of the world—pin her foot, ear and head together with one shaft."

Bahram readied his bow and broke the silence of the plain with his cry. He had a double-headed arrow in his quiver, and as the buck fled before him, he shot this arrow so that it severed the buck's antlers; instantly, now that its antlers were gone, the buck looked like a doe, and Azadeh stared at Bahram in astonishment. Then he shot two arrows into the doe's head, so that they protruded like antlers, while the blood ran down over her muzzle. Next he urged his camel toward the other pair; he fitted a pellet in the fold of his slingshot and loosed it at the ear of one of them. He was rightly pleased with his skill, because the deer immediately scratched at its ear, and Bahram notched an arrow to his bow. The shaft pinned foot, ear, and head together, and Azadeh's heart was wrung for the animal. Bahram pushed her from the saddle and she fell headlong to the ground. He said, "You're nothing but a stupid harp-player. What do you mean by setting me such a task? If I had missed, I'd have brought shame on my lineage." He trampled her beneath his camel's hooves, and blood spurted from her breast and arms. After this, he never took a slave girl hunting with him again.

Bahram Shows His Prowess as a Hunter

Another time, Bahram went out to the hunting grounds with a large group of companions, taking his hawks and hunting cheetahs with him. On a mountainside he saw a lion clawing apart the back of a wild ass. He notched an arrow with three raven plumes to his bow string and pinned the wild ass's heart and the lion's back to one another. The lion lay drenched in blood atop the ass, and their hunter returned in triumph to the palace, his sword in his fist. Another time he went hunting with No'man and Monzer, together with a number of noble Arabs who had been his advisors for good and ill, and Monzer was eager for Bahram Gur to display his horsemanship and hunting skills to them. They saw a flock of ostriches running about like a herd of camels, and Bahram Gur sped forward like the wind. He laughed as he took his bow in hand and thrust four poplar wood arrows into his belt. One by one he notched them to the bowstring, and as each found its mark each one split the feathers of the former arrow; there was not a needle's width between where they struck. The nobles went forward and examined the prey and found not a hair's breadth of space from arrow to arrow. Monzer cried out his congratulations to him, as did their companions. Monzer continued,

> *"You fill my heart with such intense delight,*
> *You're like a rosebush blossoming in my sight—*
> *And may your moonlike glory never wane,*
> *Your back remain unbent and free from pain!"*

And as soon as they reached the palace Monzer, whose thoughts elevated Bahram to Saturn's sphere, sought out painters from the Yemen. A number of them gathered at the court, and Monzer gave orders that they were to represent Bahram mounted on a camel, together with the ostrich wounded by his arrows. His slingshot was also to be there, as well as the lions, deer, and wild asses he'd brought down by his massive strength and skill. The ostrich's wound, Bahram's arrows, and the surrounding plain all lived again in black ink brushed on silk. The picture was sent by a mounted messenger to King Yazdegerd, and there the whole court crowded around to see his missive. They were astonished at what they saw and called down blessings on Bahram and his skill.

Bahram Returns with No'man to His Father, Yazdegerd

His father longed to see Bahram again, who seemed less a man than the glorious sun itself. The lion prince said to Monzer, "The longer I stay with you the more I wish to see my father. My heart tells me that I'll be safe with him." Monzer collected together appropriate royal presents from his country: Arab horses with gold-worked bridles, valuable objects, Yemeni textiles and swords, as well as whatever precious stones the mines of Aden could provide. Bahram traveled with No'man, who was highly regarded by the king, until they reached the city of Estakhr. As soon as the king learned that his son and No'man were approaching, he and his courtiers went out to meet them, and when he saw his son's glory, his fine body and shoulders, his stature and noble bearing, he was sunk in amazement. He questioned him closely and made much of him, and kept him nearby. He chose lodgings for No'man and an appropriate palace for Bahram. Day and night Bahram was with his father, and he was treated with such attentive kindness that he scarcely had to lift a finger.

After No'man had been with the king for a month, he was ready to return home. Yazdegerd summoned him one night, sat him down beside him on the royal dais, and said, "Monzer took great pains to bring Bahram up, and I shall reward him well: he has been like an angel of good fortune to me. I delight in his intelligence and opinions, and I see his aim has always been wisdom. You have been with us for some time now, and your father must be watching the roads for your return." From the treasury he was given fifty thousand gold dinars, together with royal clothes; from the stables ten fine horses with gold and silver trappings. To these were added beautiful carpets, as well as other splendid gifts that were brought one by one and handed over to No'man. Yazdegerd was happy to open the doors of generosity and to reward No'man's entourage with gifts too, according to their rank. He then wrote a letter worthy of his royal state to Monzer, thanking him for the guidance and friendship he had shown to Bahram, and saying that he now lifted up his head in pride because of his son and would attempt to repay the debt he owed.

Bahram Gur also wrote a letter to Monzer, saying, "My life here is hard and bitter: I didn't expect my father to treat his inferiors in the way he does. I'm not like a son here or a servant, and I'm not like one of his subjects who's happy simply to be at the court." He told No'man what he had seen in private of the king's evil ways. No'man returned to Monzer and gave him the king's letter. Monzer kissed it and touched it to his forehead: he was overjoyed to see the gifts that had been sent and repeatedly expressed his wonder and gratitude.

Then in private No'man told Monzer of Bahram's complaints, and when a scribe read out his letter, Monzer's face turned pale. He immediately wrote Bahram a careful answer, saying, "My noble lord, see that you don't oppose your father. Be content with what he does, whether for good or ill; obey him and be prudent. Noble men escape evils through patience, and a man must be wise in such cases. To some the heavens send a heart filled with kindness, to others a vengeful heart and a frowning face: this is how God has made the world, and we must walk as he directs us to walk. I'm sending you whatever you might need by way of gold and royal jewels; my wealth is not worth your suffering. See that you keep your heart free from pain. I'm sending ten thousand dinars as a gift, and also the slave girl who delighted you so much and who was like a guide to you, so that she may lighten your soul's darkness. Whenever you need money, don't burden the king with your requests; I can send you much more than I have done, and other kinds of wealth from our kingdom too. Strive to be ever more obedient and humble: you can't privately separate the king from his evil ways." Monzer sent ten eloquent and loyal Arab horsemen, and they reached Bahram with the money and Bahram's favorite slave. Bahram was pleased at this, and his sorrows disappeared; wisely he followed the Arab king's advice and served his father obediently by night and day.

Yazdegerd Has Bahram Confined in His Palace; Bahram Returns to Monzer

One day, when Bahram had been standing before the king at a banquet, for a long time, he was overcome by the need for sleep. When his father saw Bahram's eyes closing, he shouted in his fury,

> *"Take him away! He can't act as he ought,*
> *Never again will he appear at court.*
> *Lock him in his palace. He's unfit for*
> *The royal throne and leadership in war."*

For a year Bahram stayed in his palace sick at heart, and never saw his father's face, except during the festivals of No-Ruz and Sadeh, when he was simply one of the crush of people who appeared before the throne. This was the situation when the Roman envoy Taynush arrived at court with the cash and slaves that had been sent as tribute. The King of Kings welcomed him and assigned him suitable living quarters. Bahram sent him a message: "You are a noble and successful man; something has made the king angry with me, and I've been excluded from his presence, even though I've done nothing wrong. If you intercede on my behalf, the king might look kindly on me, so that my fortunes will flourish again. He might send me to the people who brought me up, because Monzer means much more to me than my own mother and father do."

Taynush agreed to help him, and Bahram, whose heart had been so troubled, was overjoyed. He was freed from his miserable confinement and, after distributing many goods to the poor, made preparations to leave. He gathered his people together and in the darkness of the night they set off like the wind. He said to his friends, "Thanks be to God that we've managed to get away, and are safe from fear." When he arrived in the Yemen, men, women, and children came to greet him. No'man and Monzer and an escort of riders bearing lances set out, and the crush of people around Bahram was so great that the world grew dark with the dust they sent up. The two of them dismounted, and Bahram told them of his sorrows and hardships. Monzer wept to hear his words, and then asked after the fortunes of the king. Bahram replied, "May he never realize how evil his star is!" They took him to his former quarters and added new kindnesses to the old. Bahram spent his time in festivities and on the playing field, in largess and training for combat.

Yazdegerd Travels to Tus and Is Killed by a White Horse

And so for a time the father was in Iran while his splendid son lived in the desert. Yazdegerd grew concerned for his sovereignty and summoned advisors from every province. He told his astrologers to look at the stars and tell him when his death would come, and where his head and helmet would be darkened, how and when the flower of his life would wither. The astrologers said, "It is wrong for the king to think on the day of his death. When the fortune of the King of Kings declines, he will travel from here to the fountain of Su; he will gather his men together and go accompanied by the noise of drums and trumpets to Tus, and it is there that death will come to him." The king swore an oath by the fire-temple of Khorad-Borzin and by the golden sun, saying, "My eyes will never see the fountain of Su, neither in times of joy nor in distress."

So three months passed, and then the world was thrown into turmoil by a rumor about the king's blood, causing men to say that he had been an unjust shepherd to his flock, and now all his sins were returning to him. Blood began to flow from Yazdegerd's nose one day, and doctors came to him from every quarter. They stopped the flow for a week with their medicines, but then it began again, coursing down like tears. His priest said to him, "Your majesty, you strayed from God's path when you said you would escape the clutch of death, which is like the autumn wind that tears the leaves from the tree. You must go in a litter, by way of Shahd, to the fountain of Su. Pray to God and make your way, weeping and penitent, to that scorching land. Say 'I am a helpless slave who trapped his own soul by an oath, and now I come before you, O just and righteous Lord, to know when my time will be fulfilled.'"

The king accepted his advice, and with a caravan of three hundred litters he set off for Shahd. He stayed in his litter day and night, and still from time to time blood flowed from his nose. When he reached the fountain of Su, he came out of his litter and saw the lake there. He dabbed a little of its water on his head and prayed for God's benevolence. In a short time the flow of blood from his nose stopped, and he and his advisors rested in relief. But then his pride and complacence took over and he said, "I've done what I was supposed to, so why should we sit here any longer?" Because of the king's arrogance in ascribing everything good to himself, a white horse emerged from the lake. He had a round rump, like a wild ass, and short pasterns. He was tall and had black testicles and eyes like a crow's; his tail reached to his black hooves, and he had a full mane. He galloped forward, raging like an angry lion, with foam flying from his mouth. Yazdegerd told his courtiers to have the horse brought to him. A herdsman and ten men experienced at breaking horses set off with a saddle and a long looped lariat. But what did Yazdegerd know of the secrets of God, who had set this monster in his path? The herdsman and his assistants were helpless to control the animal, and in his fury the king snatched the lariat and saddle from them and confidently approached the horse, who then stopped stock still, and stirred neither his forelegs nor his hind legs. He let the king fasten the bridle on him and stayed quiet as the saddle was put in place. The king pulled the saddle straps tight, and still the horse did not stir. Then the king went behind him to loop the crupper under his tail, and the stony-hoofed horse neighed loudly and kicked him so hard in the chest that his head and crown struck the dust. Yazdegerd had come from dust, and now he returned to the dust. When the king was dead, the horse galloped to the lake, which was the color of lapis lazuli, and he disappeared beneath its surface; in all the world no one had ever seen such a marvel.

A cry like a roll of drums went up from the army: "O king, it was your fate that brought you to Tus." Everyone present ripped their clothes and heaped dust on their bodies. Then a priest removed the dead king's brain and the vital organs from the body cavity; filling the space with camphor and musk, he wrapped the body in brocade to keep it dry. The king's corpse was conveyed to Pars in a golden coffin within a litter made of teak. So turns this world, and it is when you feel secure that you should fear its evil. Though you might rest, the world will not, and when you eat your bread, wine is the best comfort. While a man lives in this world, it is better to follow the faith than to act sinfully.

The Nobles Set Khosrow on the Throne

After the king of the world had been placed in his tomb, the Persian nobles gathered together and wept. The lords of the marches, the priests and great warriors, the wise counselors, all came to Pars and gathered at Yazdegerd's tomb. Gostahm who had killed an elephant while he was mounted on a horse; Qaren, who was Goshasp's son; Milad, the lord of Pars and a breaker of horses; Piruz, famous for his exploits with his mace; and all the other great lords whom Yazdegerd had treated with such contempt came together in Pars. Goshasp, an eloquent and literate man, addressed them:

> *"My noble lords, no man has ever seen*
> *A king as wicked as this king has been:*
> *He hoarded all he'd stolen from the poor,*
> *His reign was murder, rapine, grief, and war.*
> *No one has heard of any former reign*
> *That was so evil, or that caused such pain.*
> *We do not want his seed here on the throne*
> *And from his dust we turn to God alone.*

> *Proud Bahram is his son, and we'll soon find*
> *He has his father's heart, and will, and mind;*
> *Besides, he talks of Monzer all the time.*
> *We can't accept a king who's steeped in crime!"*

All the Persian lords swore a solemn oath that they did not want any-
one of the seed of Yazdegerd to assume the crown and throne. Then
they rose, determined to find some other king.

When news of Yazdegerd's death spread among the nobility, various
chieftains, such as Alan Shah, Bivard, and Shegnan with his golden dia-
dem, each thought, "Sovereignty is now mine, from the earth to the
moon's sphere." And since there was no king occupying the throne, the
world was filled with discord. The priests and champions of Iran gath-
ered in Pars and discussed the situation, wondering who was worthy of
the throne and of such a task. They wanted a just and generous man to
quell the disorder in the land, since without a king the world was like
an uncultivated meadow. There was an old, chivalrous man from a
wealthy and noble family, who lived in the borderlands. His name was
Khosrow; he was benevolent and had been successful in his life. Iran's
chieftains bestowed the crown and throne on him, and an army of men
from every quarter came to him.

Bahram Gur Learns of His Father's Death

They told Bahram Gur of the bitter fortune that had come to the
throne, saying, "Your father, illustrious among kings, has died, and
in dying he took the good name of the kings with him. An assembly
of nobles has sworn that they want no seed of his to be king, that
Bahram, his son, is as he was, and that in both appearance and substance
he takes after his father. They have placed a man named Khosrow on
the throne."

Bahram scored his cheeks with his nails; he seemed desperate with
sorrow at his father's death, and for two weeks the wailing of men,
women, and children could be heard throughout the Yemen. At the
new moon, after he had mourned for his father for a month, he gave
audience again. Monzer and No'man and a crowd of Arabs came weep-
ing into his presence, burned by their sorrow. Monzer spoke: "Great
prince, all of us arrive in this world destined for dust, and we come

with no hope of a remedy for this. Whoever is born from his mother dies; I see man's life as injustice, and it is death that is justice."

Bahram Gur said, "If the name of king passes from my family, a great glory will depart. These usurpers will attack your plains, and the land of the Arabs will become like a pit of death. Mourn for my father, then think how you can help me." Monzer chivalrously replied, "This land is mine, and I pass my days hunting in these plains. You should mount the throne and govern the land, and may your reign last forever!" All the nobles supported what he had said and rose up before the young ambitious prince, ready for war. Monzer said to No'man, "Bring together an army of ten thousand young lions from the Shayban and Qaysian tribes, then I will show these Persians who is king!"

No'man gathered together a mighty army of warriors armed with swords and lances and ordered them to begin their attacks and to subdue the land. They trampled all the marshy country beneath their horses' hooves, as far as Ctesiphon; the people had no protector, and men, women, and children were taken captive. The throne was powerless and the world became a place of plunder and burning; news reached Rome, China, India, Makran, and the land of the Turks that there was no worthy candidate to be king. All these peoples prepared to attack, stretching out their hands toward Iran, and each thinking to make their own lord the King of Kings.

The Persians Write to Monzer: His Response

When the Persians became aware of this, they scrambled to find some remedy for their plight. They chose an eloquent and perceptive priest named Javanui as their messenger; he was to go to Monzer and say to him, "Protector of Iran and support of the valiant; when our throne became vacant our country turned as red with blood as a francolin's wing, and we asked you to be our lord, since we thought our land worthy of you. But now you are plundering us, shedding our blood, and spreading rapine and warfare through our land, although previously you were not an evil ruler. Fear men's curses and reproaches. You are an old man—take heed of what we say, and may it please and benefit you. There is another judge besides you, one who is above the understanding of the highest of men."

Javanui traveled to the land of the Arabs, where he spoke to Monzer and gave him the letter with which he had been entrusted, repeating all the Persians had said to him. The Arab king heard him out but did not reply to the charges. Instead he said, "You are a wise man, seeking a way out of misfortune; tell the King of Kings what you have said. If you want a response, tell King Bahram what you have told me; he will show you what must be done." He sent a courtier to take Javanui to the prince. When he saw him, Javanui was astonished at the might of Bahram's chest and shoulders, at his strength and stature, and called down God's blessings on his head. The prince's cheeks were the color of red wine, and his hair exhaled the scent of musk. The learned messenger lost all his dignity of rank; he became confused, and his message went completely out of his head. Bahram saw that the man was bewildered, and questioned him at length, gently and kindly, and sat him on a throne. When Javanui had come back to himself, Bahram asked him why he had made the arduous journey from Persia.

He sent Javanui back to Monzer, with a courtier, saying that Monzer was to write a suitable answer to the letter. Monzer smiled, his face opening like a blossoming flower when he heard this reply. He set about writing his answer, and said to Javanui, "You're a wise man, and you know that whoever does evil will suffer punishment. I heard your message and the greetings you brought from Iran's chieftains. Say to them, 'Who began this? Who was senseless enough to start this war? Bahram Gur, the King of Kings, is here, splendid, powerful, and possessed of an army, and if you drag a serpent from its hole, you're likely to see your skirts dragged through blood. If I had been the Persians' advisor, they wouldn't have been overrun in this way.'" Javanui had seen Bahram's face and talked with him, and he pondered whether Bahram was worthy of the throne. As he listened to Monzer, he had an idea and said: "You are a noble lord who needs no one else's advice. Since the Persians lost their wisdom, many of their leaders have been killed. I'm an old man looking to save my reputation, and if you will hear me out, I will put a plan to you. You and Bahram Gur, as King of Kings, must come to Iran without warfare or strife. Come with your hawks and hunting cheetahs, as befits a splendid king. You have heard what the Persians said, and no harm will come to you there. You are a sensible man, far from all foolishness, and you will know what must be said in such circumstances." Monzer gave him gifts and sent him happily on his way back to Iran.

Bahram Gur Travels to Jahrom, and the Persians Come to Meet Him

Monzer, Bahram, and an advisor discussed the situation in private. They agreed that, together with a group of warriors, they would travel to Iran. Monzer chose thirty thousand Arabs armed with lances and daggers, paid them in gold, and filled their leaders' heads with ambitious hopes for the expedition. News of this reached the Persians as Javanui arrived at the assembly of their chieftains. The leaders were apprehensive as to what would happen, and they gathered in the fire-temple of Borzin to pray, asking God to convert their state of warfare to one of peace and happiness.

Monzer approached Jahrom, traveling across the waterless plain. King Bahram pitched his pavilion and the army gathered about him. He said to Monzer, "You've traveled from the Yemen to Jahrom, and now their armies and ours are face to face. What should we do now? Fight, or negotiate?" Monzer replied, "Call their chieftains here and prepare a table for them. Talk with them and listen to what they have to say, and if anyone gets angry, you must stay calm. We shall see what they are hiding and who they want to nominate as the world's king. When we know what they intend, we can take appropriate measures. If things go easily, we can put aside thoughts of war, and if they want to fight, if they won't fall in with our plans and show themselves like leopards eager for prey, then I'll convert this plain of Jahrom into a sea of blood. But I think that when they see your face and stature and goodness, and how wise, cultivated, patient, knowledgeable and dignified you are, they won't want anyone else for their crown and throne but you. And if they make a mistake and think they can deprive you of your position, then I and these cavalry will use our swords to bring the Day of Judgment down on their heads. When they see our innumerable army and our dignity and discipline, and when they reflect that kingship is your inheritance, passed down from father to son as is right, and when they consider that bloodshed is our trade and that God is our support, then they are not going to want anyone but you as their king." Bahram's heart was filled with joy at these words, and he laughed aloud.

As the sun rose above the mountain peaks the Persian nobles prepared to welcome Bahram. Meanwhile, Bahram was seated on an ivory throne, and he wore a crown of great value. He held court according to the protocol of a King of Kings: on one side of him Monzer sat, and on the other No'man, his sword in his hand. Around his pavilion, circle upon circle, stood Arab chieftains. A number of the noblest of the Iranians approached the pavilion threshold; Bahram gave orders that the flap be drawn back, and their arrival was announced in a loud voice. They called down blessings on the king's head and wept as they did so. When they came into King Bahram's presence and saw the splendor of his crown and throne, they said with one voice, "May you prosper, and may evil be far from you!" The king of kings questioned them kindly, then motioned them to places according to their rank.

He said, "My noble lords, you have seen the world and are experienced in its ways; from father to son, sovereignty has passed to me; why then is the choice now up to you?" The Persians answered, "Do not prolong our sufferings. None of us want you as king; even if you have an army to back up your claim, this land is ours. The seed you're from has brought us grief and sorrow, filling our days and nights with sighs and torment." Bahram answered, "It is true that everyone will wish to be a king. But even if you did not want me, why did you put someone in my place without consulting me?" A priest replied, "If you will join us in choosing a king, everyone will praise the process."

Three days passed while they searched for a king among the Persians. Then they wrote down the names of a hundred nobles worthy of the crown, throne, and royal belt. One of these hundred was Bahram, whose royal charm won many hearts. The hundred were reduced to fifty, and the debate grew long and earnest. Bahram was the first contender among the fifty, and this was so irrespective of the fact that it was his father's place he was seeking. From fifty they came to thirty, and from this thirty the wise priest reduced the number to four, of whom Bahram was still the first. But when the discussion seemed close to a conclusion, all the older Persians said, "We don't want Bahram; he is brave, foolhardy, and arrogant." Shouting broke out among the chieftains, and men's hearts seethed with anger.

Monzer said to the Iranians, "I want to know for good or ill why you are so troubled about this young prince." In answer the nobles summoned many Persians who had suffered under Yazdegerd. One by one they presented themselves: one had had both his hands and feet cut off; another's body was in one place but his mind in another; one had lost both hands, both ears, and his tongue, and he was like a body that had no soul; another had had his shoulder blades removed; another his

eyes gouged out. Monzer stared at these men in bewilderment, and
rage swept through him. Bahram was deeply affected by what he saw,
and he cried out to his father's dust, "If you shut your eyes to human
happiness, did you have to steep your soul in the fires of hell as well?"
Monzer said to Bahram, "This evil is not something that can be pushed
aside for them. You heard what they had to say, now you must give
your answer. Anger does not become a prince."

Bahram Speaks to the Persians About His Qualifications to Be King

Bahram said, "My noble lords, you know the world's ways, and you
have spoken truly. There are even worse things still unsaid, and it is
right that I reproach my father. All this is bitter in my mouth and has
darkened my soul. His palace was my prison, and it was God who saved
me; Taynush freed me from his snare. I fled to Monzer for refuge
because the king had never shown me any kindness. May men never
have his nature; if that were to happen, all trace of humanity would
disappear. I thank God that I have wisdom, and that my soul is nour-
ished on wisdom. I have prayed to God that he guide me, so that I can
cleanse men's souls and hearts of all the evil this king did. I am a God-
fearing man, and I live for my subjects' well-being: I shall be a shep-
herd and my subjects my flock. I will seek only peace and justice. I am
magnanimous, cultivated, and careful in my judgments. An unjust king
has no sound judgment: his wretchedness makes him vile and perverse,
and one should weep for such a tyrant. Sovereignty passes to me from
father to son, and I am wise and benevolent. On my mother's side I am
descended from King Shemiran, and my wisdom equals that of my
ancestors. I have wisdom, good judgment and greatness; I ride well, I
am humane, and I am strong. I consider no one my equal in manliness,
not in fighting or feasting or any other matter. I have a hidden trea-
sure, which is those illustrious men who are loyal to their sovereign. I
will make the world flourish from end to end with justice, and may all
of you flourish and live happily! I will rebuild those lands the king's
injustice destroyed, and make them prosperous again.

"Now I will make a pact with you, which I will swear before God
to keep. Let us bring the ivory throne of the King of Kings and set the
crown upon it. And then bring two savage lions from the wilderness
and set them on either side of the crown. We'll tie them one on each

side, and whoever desires to be king will go between them, take the crown, and place it on his own head. Then he will sit as king between the two lions: the king in the middle, the crown above him, the throne beneath him. We'll have no one but that man as our king, even if other candidates are just and nobly born. And if you reject my plan and choose some ambitious contender in place of me as your king, you will have horsemen's spears to prick and goad you. I and Monzer and our maces and swords will be there; Arab warriors have never learned how to flee from the battlefield, and we'll raise the dust of warfare over your kingdom and its provinces. Now, reply to what I have said, and use your best judgment as you decide." Then he retreated into his tent, and the world was astonished by his words.

The Persian priests and nobles who heard his speech said, "He possesses the divine *farr;* this is not said out of perversity or folly. He speaks about nothing but justice and we should rejoice in this. And as for his talk of wild lions and placing the crown and throne between them, God will not question us if the lions tear him in pieces, because it was his idea. Not that we would be pleased if he were to die; and if he does gain the crown, his glory will surpass Feraydun's. We want only him as our king and agree to what he has proposed."

Bahram Takes the Crown from Between the Lions

The next day at dawn Bahram sat on his throne and summoned the Persians to him. They talked about the previous day's discussions and then the priests said:

> *"We see you are the wisest of the wise:*
> *If, by your skill and bravery, you rise*
> *To be the King of Kings, what will you do*
> *To further justice? How will you renew*
> *The ways of righteousness, and set us free*
> *From fears of theft and royal tyranny?"*

Bahram replied, "My actions will be greater than my words. I shall avoid injustice and ambition, and I shall distribute territories to those who are fit to rule. I will hold the world by justice, and this will be my happiness and security. I will relieve the sufferings of the poor. If a man sins I shall admonish him, and if he sins again, I shall imprison him. I shall pay the army at the appointed times and make the wise rejoice. My heart is as I speak, and I will turn my soul aside from all perversity and darkness. If a man dies without heirs, I shall distribute his goods to the poor, keeping nothing for my own treasury, since my heart is not set on the pleasures of this fleeting world. I will consult with the wise, and by their advice break the back of foolish desires. If I want to embark on any new venture I'll consult the priests first. If a man comes to me seeking justice, I shall not dismiss the assembly, but dispense justice to whoever desires it, saying nothing but what is right, and punishing evil, as a king must. All this I swear by God, as wisdom guides my tongue."

When the assembled nobles and priests heard his answer, they regretted what they had said before. Those who had sinned sought to remedy their wrongdoing and said, "Who is more worthy to rule than he is? In chivalry, eloquence, wisdom, and lineage, no one has ever been born who equals him. God has created him from justice, and may evil never touch him!" They addressed Bahram, "You possess the divine *farr,* and our souls accept you as our king. None of us knew of your abilities and knowledge, or of your soul's purity. But Persia has sworn allegiance to Khosrow, who is descended from Pashin; we are bound by our oath to him, and you could say we are at his mercy. If he were to remain as Persia's king, all our country will be rent apart by lions' claws, with one side supporting Bahram and the other rallying to Khosrow. But it would be just for you to be king and for the world from now on to be beneath your command. We could use your proposed combat with lions as a pretext, and then no one would put himself forward as a candidate." Bahram agreed to this, as it was he who had originally suggested it.

The custom of that time was that when a new king was to be crowned the chief priest and three wise advisors went before him and placed him on the throne. They called down blessings on the crown, which was placed on his head in the name of the Kayanid kings; then the chief priest placed his cheeks in joy against the king's chest. Lastly the king distributed largess to the needy, using the goods that had been brought to him in homage, and a throne and crown were presented to the chief priest, who returned to his home in the plains.

The warrior Gostahm kept two savage lions in chains, and handed

these over to a priest. They dragged the animals to the foot of the ivory
throne and secured them there: the men who handled the chains almost
fainted from fear. Placed on the throne, in one corner, was the royal
crown. The world watched, wondering what would happen to the
prince, who seemed so blessed by fortune.

Bahram and Khosrow, their hearts filled with apprehension con-
fronted the lions. When Khosrow saw the two savage beasts and the
crown placed between them, he turned to the priests and said,

> *"Only a prince ambitious for renown*
> *Deserves to reign and to possess the crown;*
> *And then I'm old, while he is young and strong—*
> *I can't fight lions' claws, I've lived too long.*
> *Let him display his prowess, let us see*
> *His youth and health enjoy their victory."*

Bahram said, "What you say is true, and there is no reason to hide the
truth." At that, he seized his ox-headed mace while the world looked
on in wonder. A priest said to him, "My lord, you are wise, knowl-
edgeable, and nobly born; who has ordered you into this combat against
lions? What more can you desire than the crown? Don't lose your life
seeking sovereignty and pointlessly feed your body to the fishes. We are

innocent of this, it is your doing; there's no need for it, all the world is with you." Bahram replied, "You're a seeker of religious truth, and you and everyone else are innocent in this affair. I will face these lions in combat, and it is I who desire to fight against them!" The priest said, "Before you go further in this, cleanse your soul of sin, before God." Bahram did as he advised, repenting of his sins and purifying his heart.

Then he strode forward with his mace. As soon as they saw him the lions were eager to attack, and one of them broke free of his chains and bounded toward the prince, who struck him on the head with his mace, so that the light faded from the animal's eyes. Then he turned to the other one and struck him too a mighty blow on the head, so that the blood flowed down from his eyes onto his chest.

The world conqueror sat on the ivory throne, placed the splendid crown on his head, and prayed to God, who shows the right way to the lost, as his refuge. Khosrow came before him and paid homage to him, saying, "Great king, may your reign be glorious, and may the world's heroes stand before you as your slaves. You are our king, and we are your slaves who wish you well." The nobles poured jewels over him and called down blessings on the new wearer of the crown. The world rang with acclamations, and all this happened in the month of Azar, on the day called Sorush.

*W*hen Bahram became king he rewarded Monzer and No'man with splendid gifts, and at Monzer's intercession forgave those who had opposed his becoming king. He also treated the interim king Khosrow well and compensated everyone who had suffered under Yazdegerd. He made his own younger brother, Nersi, the commander of his armies. Then he declared a tax amnesty and burned the tax records, an act which caused rejoicing throughout the country.

THE REIGN OF BAHRAM GUR

Once Bahram was established in his reign
Grief fled, and pleasure flourished once again;
Horses were his delight, and he would play
At polo or go hunting every day.

The Story of Bahram Gur and Mehrbandad

Bahram enjoyed hunting with cheetahs, and one day when he was occupied in this manner, with a swift horse under him and with his hawk on his wrist, he came on a well-wooded place that looked like the home of people who'd been blessed by good fortune. The green pastures and foliage were like a paradise, but Bahram could see neither men nor flocks there. He said, "There must be lions around: this is somewhere for brave men to show their mettle." He readied his bow, and as he did so a male lion appeared and gave a mighty roar. The king's arrow pierced its side and entered its heart. Seeing this, the female lion's heart was wrung, and she roared and sprang at Bahram, so that her claws scored his body. He struck at her with his sword, and the valiant beast sank back defeated.

An old man emerged from the trees and spoke sweetly to Bahram. His name was Mehrbandad, and he was overjoyed at the king's sword-stroke. He was a farmer, a God-fearing man, and the wooded area was his home. He came forward and congratulated the king and bowed before him.

He said, "My lord, may heaven favor you
And make you prosperous in all you do!
My noble lord, I farm these fields—I own
The land here, both the waste tracts and the sown,

As well as donkeys, cows, and flocks of sheep.
These lions' attacks have made me curse and weep,
But now through you I'm free of them—God sent
Your strength and prowess as their punishment!
Stay with me for a while, and when you dine
I'll set before you honey, milk, and wine:
I've plenty of good lamb, and there's a glade
Whose trees will give us fruit and ample shade."

Bahram dismounted and saw that the green landscape filled with streams was a delightful place for a young man to spend time. Mehrbandad went to the nearby village and returned with the village elders and a group of musicians. He slaughtered a number of plump sheep and came to Bahram with a golden goblet in his hand. After their meal, cups were placed before them, surrounded by roses and wild saffron flowers. When Mehrbandad had grown tipsy with the wine, he said to Bahram, "You're a fine, fortunate fighter, and you should know that you look just like a king and deserve a golden throne and all its pomp and ceremony!" Bahram replied, "You're right, and he who limns our faces has created them as he wishes them to be, and chooses whomever he wishes to choose. If I look just like a king, I bestow on you as a gift all the area here, the forest and the surrounding land."

Then he mounted his horse, rode back to his beautiful palace quite drunk, and slept that night in his orchard.

The Story of Kebrui; Bahram Forbids the Drinking of Wine

At dawn the next morning Bahram called for wine, and his courtiers began another round of merry-making. At that moment the headman of a village entered with a present of fruit: he brought camel-loads of pomegranates, apples and quinces, and also bouquets of flowers fit for the royal presence. The king welcomed this man, who had the ancient, noble name of Kebrui, and motioned him to a place among the young men there. He handed him a large goblet of wine, that held two maund. The visitor was pleased at the king's and his courtiers' atten-tion, and when he had drained the cup, he caught sight of another and felt a craving for it in his heart. In front of all the nobles there he reached out and seized it. He stood and toasted the king, and said, "I'm a wine-drinker, and Kebrui is my name. This goblet holds five maund of wine, and I'm going to drain it seven times in front of this assembly. Then I'll go back to my village, and no one will hear any drunken shouts from me." And to the astonishment of the other drinkers there he drained the huge cup seven times.

With the king's permission he left the court, to see how the wine would work in him. As he started back on his journey across the plain, the wine began to take effect. He urged his horse forward, leaving the crowd who were accompanying him behind, and rode to the foothills of a mountain. He dismounted in a sheltered place and went to sleep in the mountain's shadow. A black raven flew down from the mountain and pecked out his eyes as he slept. The group that had been following along behind found him lying dead at the foot of the mountain, with his eyes pecked away and his horse standing nearby at the roadside. His servants, who were part of the group, began wailing and cursed the assembly and the wine.

When Bahram awoke from sleep, one of his companions came to him and said, "Kebrui's bright eyes were pecked out by a raven while he was drunk at the foot of a mountain." The king's face turned pale, and he grieved for Kebrui's fate. Immediately he sent a herald to the palace door to announce: "My lords, all who have glory and intelligence! Wine is forbidden to everyone throughout the world, both noblemen and commoners alike."

The Story of the Cobbler's Son and the Lion: Wine Is Declared Permissible

A year passed, and wine remained forbidden. No wine was drunk when Bahram assembled his court, or when he asked for readings from the books that told of ancient times. And so it was, until a shoemaker's son married a rich, wellborn, and respectable woman. But the shoemaker's boy's awl was not hard enough for its task, and his mother wept bitterly. She had a little wine hidden away; she brought her son back to her house and said to him,

> "Drink seven glasses of this wine, and when
> You feel you're ready, go to her again:
> You'll break her seal once you two are alone—
> A pickax made of felt can't split a stone."

The boy drank seven glasses down, and then an eighth, and the fire of passion flared up in him immediately. The glasses made him bold, and he went home and was able to open the recalcitrant door; then he went back to his parents' house well pleased with himself. It happened that a lion had escaped from the king's lion-house and was wandering in the roads. The cobbler's son was so drunk that he couldn't distinguish one thing properly from another; he ran out and sat himself on the roaring lion's back, and hung on by grasping hold of the animal's ears. The lion keeper came running with a chain in one hand and a lariat in the other and saw the cobbler's son sitting on the lion as unconcernedly as if he were astride a donkey. He ran to the court and told the king what he had seen, which was a sight no one had ever heard of before. The king was astonished and summoned his advisors. He said to them, "Inquire as to what kind of a man this cobbler is." While they were talking, the boy's mother ran in and told the king what had happened.

> She said to him, "May you live happily
> As long as time endures, your majesty!
> This boy of mine's just starting out on life—
> He'd found himself a satisfactory wife.
> But when the time came . . . well, his implement
> Was just too soft, and he was impotent.
> So then I gave the boy (but privately,
> To make him father of a family)
> Three glasses of good wine; at once his face
> Shone with a splendid ruby's radiant grace,
> The floppy felt stirred, lifted up its head,
> And turned into a strong, hard bone instead.
> Three drafts of wine gave him his strength and glory
> Who would have thought the king would hear the story?"

The king laughed at the old woman's words and said, "This story is not one to hide!" He turned to his chief priest and said, "From now on wine is allowed again. When a man drinks he must choose to drink enough so that he can sit astride a lion without the lion trampling him, but not so much that when he leaves the king's presence a raven will peck his eyes out." Immediately a herald announced at the palace door, "My lords who wear belts made of gold! A man may drink wine as long as he looks to how the matter will end and is aware of his own capacity. When wine leads you to pleasure, see that it does not leave your body weak and incapable."

Bahram Gur's Priest Ruins and Revives a Village

Another day Bahram went out hunting at dawn with a group of companions. His vizier Hormozd rode on his left, and a priest on his right, and the two told him tales of Jamshid and Feraydun. They took dogs, cheetahs, and hawks with them and searched through the morning, but by noon they'd found no trace of either onager or deer, and when the sun shone in the heavens like a bright coin, Bahram irritatedly made his way back from his expedition. A green area, filled with men and flocks, appeared, and many people gathered round to stare at the hunters. Bahram was weary and feeling short-tempered; he'd hoped to dismount and rest in the village, but no one came forward to greet him, and the place seemed inhabited by donkeys. He grew angry with the people there and looked askance at them, saying to his priest,

> "May this green, prosperous village be a den
> Of beasts—a wild, uncultivated fen—
> And may the water dry in every ditch
> And turn to stagnant mud as black as pitch!"

The priest knew how to fulfill Bahram's command and he turned aside from the road and entered the village. He said, "This green area, filled with houses, people, and flocks, has pleased King Bahram and he has a new plan for you. Rejoice in your hearts, you are all masters now and can make this a splendid place. Here women and children are masters too, and no one has to obey anyone else. Laborer and headman are equal: men, women, and children, you are all headmen of the village!" A cry of joy went up from the inhabitants; in their minds men and women were the same, and laborers and servants were equal to the village headman. Since the young men now felt no fear of authority, they cut off the heads of the village elders: everyone became muddled up with everyone else, and bloodshed became commonplace. The area became as confused and horrifying as the Day of Judgment, and the inhabitants fled. A few weak, old men stayed there, but every sign of activity or prosperity had gone. The whole village took on a rundown look: trees withered, irrigation ditches dried up, houses were in ruins, fields were uncultivated, men and their flocks were nowhere to be seen.

A year passed, and the following spring Bahram again went hunting in that area. He reached the place that had seemed so pleasant and prosperous, but the village he remembered was not there. All the trees were dead, the houses in ruins, the fields empty of flocks and people. Bahram's heart was wrung to see this; he feared God and wished to act justly. He said to his priest, "Ruzbeh, it hurts me to see this lovely place in ruins: go quickly and provide them with money from my treasury, so that they won't suffer any more."

The priest left his king's side and rode into the ruins. He went from house to house and finally found an old man who had no work. He dismounted, greeted him politely, and invited the man to sit with him. He said, "Old man, who ruined this prosperous place?"

> *The old man answered him, "By chance one day*
> *The king and his companions came this way.*
> *A foolish priest with no sense in his head,*
> *One of those noble idiots, born and bred,*
> *Declared to us, 'You're all the masters here,*
> *Social distinctions are to disappear.*
> *The ranks of those who rule and those who serve*
> *Are niceties that no one need observe.'*
> *As soon as he'd said that our little village*
> *Was filled with fights and plundering and pillage:*
> *May God reward that man's stupidity*
> *And fill his days with grief and misery!"*

Grieved to hear this, Ruzbeh asked, "Who is your village headman?" The man replied,

> *"A headman's for a place where grain is grown,*
> *And men can reap the harvest they have sown."*

Ruzbeh said, "You are to be the headman here, you're to rule over these ruins. Ask the king for cash, seed, cows, and donkeys, and bring back to your village whomever you can find who is destitute. You are to be the headman and they're to do as you tell them. And don't curse that priest who came here before, as he didn't want to say what he did. If you need help from the king's court, I'll send you whatever you need. All you have to do is ask."

The old man was pleased to hear this and forgot his former sorrows. He immediately went from house to house to find men to work on the irrigation channels and to start cultivating the land again. They asked neighboring villages for donkeys and cows and set to work making the plain productive. The headman and his villagers worked hard at planting trees everywhere, and their hearts were filled with happiness each time they saw a house had been rebuilt. All those who had fled from the place weeping and wailing came back one by one when they heard of the success of the old headman's efforts. The watercourses in the streets were rebuilt, the stocks of hens, cows, donkeys, and sheep multiplied in the pastures, and the trees that people planted everywhere made the former ruins look like a paradise.

By the following year the village had responded to the old man's efforts and was as he wished. Once again, at spring time, the king went hunting with his priest, Ruzbeh, and for a third time they came to the village. Bahram Gur saw the land under cultivation, the herds of animals, the fine buildings, the plains and mountain slopes covered with sheep and lambs, the water courses coming down from the foothills, and the village filled with handsome men. He turned to his priest and said, "Ruzbeh, what have you done? This fine village was in ruins, its people and animals had fled. What did you give them so that they were able to make it flourish again?"

Ruzbeh answered, "One speech was enough to bring this ancient village to its knees, and one idea was enough to make it prosperous again, and so rejoice the heart of Persia's king. You had ordered me to destroy the village using money from your treasury, but I was afraid of God's judgment and the reproaches of noblemen and commoners. I saw the strife that results when one heart has two thoughts, and knew that when a town has two masters it cannot survive. I told the village elders that there was no master over them, that women were masters now, and children too, as were servants and laborers. When the commoners became masters, the masters' heads were brought down to the dust. This lovely place was destroyed by a speech, and I escaped reproach and did not fear God's judgment. But then the king forgave them, so I went to them and suggested another course of action. I set a wise old man over them as their headman, someone who was eloquent and knowledgeable. Through his efforts he restored the village's prosperity and made his inferiors' hearts happy. Once one man was put in charge of the rest, things went well again: goodness increased and evil decreased. I showed them the way of evil and then I opened the door to God for them. If a man uses speech in the right place, it is worth more than fine jewels. If you want your soul to have no troubles, wisdom must be your king, and language your champion. May the king's heart be eternally happy, triumphing over all evil and ruin."

The king responded, "Ruzbeh, you are worthy of a crown!" He gave this clever and perspicacious man a purse of gold coins and a royal robe of honor, raising his head to the clouds in glory.

The Story of Bahram Gur and the Four Sisters

One week the king went out hunting with his priests and advisors, and they stayed for a month drinking wine and hunting game in the mountains and plains. When they had had their fill of this, the king set off in good spirits to the city again, but night overtook them on the way and the world turned black before them. The group pushed on through the darkness, telling stories of the ancient kings. Then Bahram saw a fire in the distance, like those the king lights during the winter festival. He stared at the fire and made out a pleasant village to one side of it. In front of the village there was a mill, where the village elders were sitting, scattered in little groups. On the other side of the fire were some young women wearing chaplets of flowers in their hair, and musicians were sitting all round them. They were singing songs about the king's exploits, and as one song ended they started another. Their faces shone like the moon, their musky hair was arranged in ringlets, and there were jewels sewn onto their clothes. They were lined up on the grass in front of the mill door: each of them held a bouquet of flowers, and they were half-drunk with wine and happiness. Loudly their song rang out:

> "Long live King Bahram, glorious and brave,
> To whom the turning heavens are a slave,
> Whose hair is musky, and whose handsome face
> Is red as wine and filled with kindly grace—

They call him Bahram Gur, and every day
Wild onagers and lions are his prey!"

Hearing their song, the king tugged on his rein and went over toward them. As he approached he saw that the plain was filled from end to end with young women, each of whom was as lovely as the full moon, and he realized that he was in no hurry to reach the city. He ordered the wine servers to bring him some wine and invite a few of the women who were drinking there to come to him. A servant put a crystal goblet in Bahram's hand, and the four leaders of the young women stepped forward. There names were Moshk, Sisanak, Naz, and Susanak. Tall, and as lovely as the spring, they held hands as they approached the king. They sang a song to Bahram, the wise and famous King of Kings, and his heart was charmed by them. He said to the four of them, "Your faces are like roses; whose daughters are you, and why have you lit this fire?" One answered him, "And you, a horseman tall as a cypress tree, the image of a king in every way, know that our father is an old miller who is out hunting in these mountains with his bow. He should return soon, now the night has grown dark and he finds it hard to see in the darkness."

And at that moment the miller returned from the mountain, bringing the game he had killed. When he saw Bahram, the good old man bowed his face down to the dust, and Bahram ordered that a golden goblet be handed to him. He said, "Why do you keep these four, whose faces are as lovely as the sun? It's time they were married." The old man called down blessings on him and said, "There are no husbands for these four girls of mine. They've reached the right age, and they have lived modestly, but they have no wealth; I don't want to say any more than this now." Bahram said to him, "Give these four to me, and see you don't have any more daughters!" The old man replied, "My lord, don't say such things. We've no land or income, no gold, no house, no cows or donkeys." Bahram replied, "Then they will suit me; I must have them just as they are, with no dowry." The old man said, "All four are your wives then, to serve you in the privacy of your home: you've seen their good and bad qualities, and you liked what you saw." Bahram answered him, "I accept all four, from the hand of the good man who raised them."

Having said this he jumped up, and the sound of his escort's galloping horses was heard on the plain. He had his eunuchs take the four young women to the king's harem. One by one his escort came forward, and it took the whole night for them all to pass by. The miller was astonished at this and spent the night brooding on what it could mean. He said to his wife, "How did this nobleman, a man as radiant as the moon, and with such an entourage, come to our mill in the darkness of the night?" His wife replied, "He saw the fire from far away and heard the girls singing." Then the miller said, "Tell me wife, is this going to end well or badly?" She answered, "It's God's doing; when he saw them he didn't ask about their family, and he wasn't concerned about their wealth. He was searching the world for a woman as lovely as the moon, and he didn't care about money or royal rank. If idol worshippers in China saw girls as lovely as ours, they'd forget about their idols!" And so the two talked all night about evil men and good, until the sun shone on the mountain slopes and the world glowed like a lamp.

When night had turned to day, a local landowner came to the old miller and said, "Luck came to your pillow in the dark night, and the green branch of your tree has borne fruit. In last night's darkness King Bahram was returning from a hunting trip. He saw your celebration and the fire, tugged at his reins, and came to this spot. Now your daughters are his wives and live in comfort and security in his harem. Their faces, hair, and elegance made them fit for a king; Bahram, the King of Kings, is your son-in-law, and in every country from now on men will remember you. He has given you this entire province; grieve no more, you can live free from sorrow and fear. Give us your orders, we are all yours to command. We are your subjects; no, more, we are your slaves!"

The miller and his wife stared at him in wonder, repeating the name of God over and over again. The landowner said, "Those faces and that hair brought a husband down from the sun's sphere."

Bahram Gur Finds Jamshid's Treasure

Bahram Gur was out hunting with his priests and companions another time when one of his devoted subjects approached the group, running like the wind and carrying a spade. He asked where he could find King Bahram. Everyone said to him, "What do you want the king for? Can't you tell us?" He answered, "I'm saying nothing until I see the king's face." A priest said, "What do you know about the king's face? Tell me what you have to say." When finally they took him to the king, the man said, "I have something to tell you in private." Bahram gave a tug to his reins and rode apart from his companions, and then the man told him, "You're a king who's seen the world, but listen to what I have to say. I'm the landowner here; the crops this area produces and its buildings are all mine. I was channeling water to irrigate the land so that I could get the best yield from it, and at one point the force of the water undermined the earth and a hole appeared. Then I heard a terrifying cry, followed by the clash of cymbals; that noise indicates there's a treasure there." Bahram rode over to the area the man indicated and saw a green landscape with irrigation channels in it. He summoned a number of workmen with spades who had to be brought from far away; then he dismounted, and a tent was pitched for him in the pastures. Night fell, the soldiers in his entourage lit candles, and fires burned throughout the camp.

When the sun rose above the sea and its blue surface glittered with light, workmen gathered from every quarter. They started to dig, and soon the whole plain was covered with ditches. Just as they were getting tired a structure like a mountain appeared in the ground. It was a building made of baked brick and covered with splendid plaster work. The workmen excavated all round it, until a door appeared. A priest and a companion entered and saw a long, wide room several cubits high. Two bulls made of gold were standing in front of a feeding trough, also made of gold, in which there were emeralds mixed with rubies. The bulls were like two signs of Taurus; their bellies were hollowed out and filled with artificial pomegranates, apples, and quinces. In the midst of the quinces were splendid pearls, each as clear as a drop of water. The bulls were represented as old, with wrinkled foreheads, and their eyes were made of rubies. All around them were lions and wild asses with eyes made of rubies or crystal, and there were golden pheasants and peacocks whose breasts and eyes were made of jewels.

The priest returned to the king, and said to him politely, "Come, your majesty; we have found a treasure to eclipse all others. There is a room full of jewels, to which the heavens hid the key." Bahram replied, "See if anyone has written his name on this treasure, saying it is his. See whose it is, or in whose reign it was collected here." The priest went back and saw the seal of Jamshid on the bulls. He reported to the king, "I looked, and on the bulls there is written 'King Jamshid.'"

"O wisest of the wise," King Bahram said,
"Why should I claim the treasures of the dead?
As Jamshid put together this rich hoard,
I'll win my wealth with justice and my sword.
God keep me from defeat and poverty!
Distribute all you've found in charity,
Don't give it to my soldiers, I have land
And gold enough for those whom I command.
Sell all the jewels for cash, and so relieve
Our widows and our orphans, those who grieve
Because they're poor despite a noble name,
Living their lives in indigence and shame.
Bring them from every ruin, every town,
And one by one write all their details down;
Give them this wealth, and may your actions bring
Peace to the soul of Persia's ancient king.
That man the soldiers tried to keep from me,
Who showed us where the treasure ought to be,
Should get a tenth of everything we found.
But I'm still young, my body's strong and sound,
So why should I have Jamshid's gold? I'll fight
With China and with Rome—my army's might,
My horse Shabdiz, my sword will win me fame,
And royal treasure, and a glorious name."

Then he went to his own treasury, whose contents he had accumulated by the sweat of his brow, and summoned all the country's warriors and gave them a year's pay. He decreed festivities, like those held at spring, and his audience hall, encrusted with gems, was prepared for this. Bahram Gur held a crystal goblet filled with ruby wine, and in his happiness he said to his companions, "My noble lords, who have heard tell of the great men who have reigned here, from Hushang to the famous Nozar, who was a descendant of Feraydun, and so to Kay Qobad who placed the crown of Feraydun on his head; you see what has remained of these great men, who speaks anything but good of them? When their days were cut short, speech remained to remind us of them, saying that this one had magnanimity and that one did not, that one was reproached and another praised. One by one we too shall depart, and it would be well for us not to act evilly in the world. Why should we covet the wealth of the dead, or give our hearts to the greed for gold? I shall not tie my heart to this fleeting world, or glory in the crown, or seek for treasure. If our days can pass in happiness, why should a wise man grieve? I want neither the crown nor my wealth if any of my subjects, any farmer or courtier, complains of being harmed by me."

Bahram Gur and the Jeweler's Daughter

Bahram, Ruzbeh, and a thousand horsemen went hunting and came on a plain filled with wild asses. It was spring and the males were searching for females and fighting with one another; they bit one another's hides so viciously that the ground was stained ruby red with their blood. Bahram watched one such combat, until the animals separated in their fury, and the victorious male mounted a female. Bahram smiled to see the animal's pleasure and drew back his bow. The arrow entered the male's back and the whole shaft sank in, up to the feathers, pinning the male and female together. Those in his entourage who had seen the shot congratulated the king and said, "May the evil eye be far from you, and all your days be like a festival: you have no equal in the world, you are a king, an emperor, and a hero!"

Bahram was riding Shabrang and urged him forward to a thicket, where he saw a pair of lions. He drew back his bow, and the arrow entered the male lion's chest, which it passed right through, and then plunged into the ground. He then loosed an arrow at the female, which pinned her thigh to the earth. He said, "That last arrow had no feathers, and its point was blunt." His soldiers all congratulated him and said, "No one has ever seen a king like you; if you can subdue a lion with a flightless arrow, you can overturn a granite mountain."

Bahram and his companions rode in the meadows. They saw a grove of trees where there were many sheep, but the shepherds were fleeing as if in fear of some danger. The head shepherd ran toward Bahram, who asked, "Who has brought these sheep to such a dangerous place?" The man replied, "In all the world I'm the only man brave enough to come here. These sheep belong to a jeweler, and I brought them down from the mountain yesterday. The owner of the flock is rich, and he's always worried about danger. He has donkey loads of fine jewels, as well as gold and silver. He has just one daughter, who plays the harp and whose hair is a mass of ringlets. He'll only take his wine from her hand: no one's ever seen an old man like him. And if it weren't for King Bahram's just rule, how would he be able to keep his wealth? The King of Kings isn't greedy for gold, and his chief priest isn't an unjust man either. Won't you tell me who killed these two savage beasts, may God preserve him?"

Bahram replied, "These two lions were killed by a brave warrior, and then he left; he rode away with seven companions. But where's this jeweler's house? Tell me how to get there, don't hide anything." The head shepherd answered him, "Go straight ahead and you'll come to a recently built village. The fame of this place has reached the town and even King Bahram's palace. When the heavens spread their black silk over the world, the jeweler starts his merry-making. If you wait there a while, you'll hear toasts and the sound of a harp." Bahram asked for a pack horse and royal clothes: then he left his vizier and the soldiers and went off with his head full of high hopes.

Ruzbeh said to the priests and courtiers, "Now the king is going to that village. He'll sit down in the jeweler's house, and you mark my words, he'll ask her father for that young woman's hand. There's no doubt he'll put a golden crown on her head. He can never get enough of sleeping with women, and in the darkness of the night his sleeping partners run away from him. He keeps more than a hundred at a time there; whoever heard of such a king? The chief eunuch has counted nine hundred and thirty nobly born women in his harem, and all of them have their diadems and jewels and crowns and bracelets and golden thrones and bejeweled Byzantine brocade. None of them are left without their own wealth. He keeps demanding tribute from every country and province, and every year the tribute from Rome is spent on them. I grieve for our king's strength and stature, for that face of his with which he commands the court: no one's ever seen a man who could pin two wild asses together with one arrow. All this sleeping with women will destroy him; he'll soon be as soft as silk. His eyes will darken, his cheeks turn yellow, his body will become weak, his lips will turn blue; his hair will turn white from the scent of women, and white hair means you must despair of the world. His back will become bent while he's still young. So many evils come from associating with women! Once a month is sufficient for sex; if it's more often than that a man is just pouring his blood away. A wise young man should stick to once a month, and that's for the sake of having children. If you do it more often it weakens you, and when a man gets soft like that his body becomes bloodless." And so the conversation went on as they made their way back to the palace till one man said, "The sun has lost its way."

Meanwhile Bahram rode through the darkness, accompanied only by a groom. Hearing the sound of a harp, he directed his horse toward it and quickly reached the jeweler's house. He lifted the knocker on the door and asked for hospitality. One of the jeweler's maids, a kind woman, said, "Who's knocking at our door in the darkness of the night, and why?" Bahram answered, "This morning the king went hunting, and my horse was lamed under me and I had no choice but to turn back. With a horse like this, and with its gold-worked bridle, I'm afraid I'll be set on by thieves, so I'm looking for shelter." The maid told her master, "There's a man who wants to stay with us. He says that people will steal his fine horse and its golden trappings, and that if he goes any further he'll be in difficulties." Her master said, "Open the door," and to Bahram he called out, "Come on in, boy!"

When Bahram entered he saw a fine hallway with servants standing ready. He said to himself, "O God of justice, guide me now. May all my acts be just, and may I not follow the ways of pride and greed. Make me just, so that my subjects rejoice in my existence. If my justice and knowledge increase, my memory will remain bright after my death. May all my subjects live as this jeweler does, with wine and the sound of the harp." As he went further he saw his host's daughter through a doorway. When the jeweler saw Bahram he stood, came forward, and bowed his tall, straight body before him. He said, "May this night bring you good fortune and make those who wish you ill your slaves." He spread a carpet and placed a cushion on it, and then quickly had a table laden with various kinds of food brought in. He told a servant to see to Bahram's horse, and Bahram's groom was given a separate table and a place to sleep. They brought a seat for the host and he sat himself down next to the king. Then he made excuses for his hospitality and said, "You seem to be a lord of the marches; while you are a guest in my house, my body and soul are at your service."

Bahram replied, "Who can find such a welcoming host in the darkness of the night? When we've eaten, we must drink wine and refresh ourselves with sleep. And we must not be ungrateful to God, because a man who forgets God lives in fear." A maid brought water in a bowl for them to wash their hands, and she stared at their guest in astonishment. The host called for the comforts of wine and music, and the maid brought red wine, roses, and wild saffron flowers. The host drank first, then he washed the cup, which was very beautiful, in musk and rosewater, passed it to Bahram, and said, "And what's our wine-drinker's name? I want to make a pact of friendship with you now, and seal it in the name of King Bahram." The king laughed long and loud and said, "My name is Goshasp, and I'm a knight; I came here because I heard the sounds of a harp, not for somewhere to rest."

His host replied, "This daughter of mine makes me so proud I feel my head's in the heavens! She serves wine, plays the harp, and sings better than anyone. Her name is Arezu." Then he called to Arezu, who was as elegant as a cypress tree, "Bring your harp and show Goshasp what you can do." The harp-player came before Bahram, moving as beautifully as if she were a Hindu idol, and said to him, "You are a fine knight, and in everything you are like a prince. You should understand that this house is here for your pleasure, and that my father is both your host and your treasurer. May the dark nights bring you good fortune and lift your head above the clouds!" Bahram replied, "Sit down, and take your harp: I want a song now."

Arezu lifted her harp and sang first a song in praise of the Zoroastrian priests. Then she sang in praise of her father; the harp itself seemed to weep in her hands, and as the silken strings began to speak, all her house was filled with the scent of jasmine. This was the song she sang for her father:

> "Mahyar, a noble cypress tree that grows
> Beside a bank where limpid water flows,
> Your musky hair's grown camphor-white, your mind
> Is gentle and your voice is warm and kind—
> May wisdom nourish your good soul, and may
> Confusion sweep your enemies away!
> You are like Feraydun, that noble king
> Who valued freedom above everything,
> And your obedient daughter Arezu
> Lives only to devote her life to you.
> Now you've a guest, I'm like a king who sees
> His armies conquer all his enemies."

When she had finished her song she turned toward their guest; again she took up her harp and sang to him:

> *"And you are like a prince, whose heart's sincere,*
> *Who's fortunate in war, who knows no fear,*
> *And any man who hasn't seen our king,*
> *Great Bahram of whom all musicians sing,*
> *Should look upon your face without delay,*
> *Since you resemble him in every way.*
> *You're cypress-tall, reed-slim, your walk's a stride*
> *That's like a strutting pheasant's in its pride;*
> *Your heart is like a lion's, and your face*
> *Shines with a pomegranate blossom's grace,*
> *As though a rose were washed in wine. You stand,*
> *And like a mountain dominate the land:*
> *No one has seen, no one will ever see,*
> *A man like you for war and victory.*
> *May Arezu live all her years for you,*
> *The dust beneath your feet in all you do!"*

The king was so overcome by her song and her playing, by her beauty, her bearing, and her voice that his heart was thrown into a tumult. When the wine had begun to affect Mahyar, Bahram said to him, "If you want to be well thought of, give me your daughter in marriage." Mahyar turned to Arezu and said, "Do you want this lionhearted guest to pay court to you? Look at him well and see if he pleases you, and if you think you would like to live with him." Arezu said, "My kind and noble father, if you wish to give me to anyone, let if be to none but this knight Goshasp, who so resembles Bahram: simply to sit with him for a while is like life itself." But Mahyar did not accept his daughter's words, and he said to Bahram, "Look at her carefully, from head to foot; consider her knowledge, diligence, and intelligence. See if she pleases you, and if she measures up to her reputation. She is a fine woman, and she is not poor. I'm not one to compare my wealth with others', but if you count up Mahyar's jewels, they come to more than you'd find in a king's purse. Even if you still want her, drink another cup of wine; there's no hurry, you should rest tonight. Men of standing don't enter into agreements when they're drunk, especially if they have any sense.

Stay here till sunrise and our elders have woken up, and then we can call together those who have patient hearts and are literate. It's against our customs to do these things in the darkness of the night; King Feraydun would not have done it like this. And it's not auspicious to ask for a woman's hand, or to start on any new undertaking, when one is drunk."

Bahram replied, "There's no point in saying this, and it's a bad idea to start predicting what might happen. This harp-player pleases me tonight, so you should stop all this talk about the future." Mahyar turned to his daughter Arezu and said, "Does his character please you, and what he says?" She answered, "Yes, they please me; my heart and soul have been his since I set eyes on him. Do it, and leave the rest to God; the heavens are not at war with Mahyar." Her father replied, "Then you are now his wife, and you should understand that you now live for him." And he gave her to Bahram, who took her as his wife.

As night began to turn to day all had happened as it should, and Arezu went through the sleeping household to her own room. In another part of the house Mahyar was preparing everything for his guest, the knight Goshasp. He said to a servant, "Lock the doors, and send someone quickly to the shepherds: we can't have a meal without lamb, and it must be the best lamb too. When he wakes up take him some beer and some ice, and see that someone is there to serve him. And set a bowl of camphor mixed with rosewater in his bedchamber, so that it smells sweet. Despite the wine I drank, I feel as fresh as I did yesterday: wine's not going to overcome this old jeweler!" Having said this he pulled the coverlet over his head and sank into an untroubled sleep.

When the sun lifted its glowing crown into the sky and the world glowed like a sea of ivory, Bahram's servant hung his master's whip on the door at the front of Mahyar's house. The king's men were looking for some sign of their master, and as soon as they saw the whip they began to gather in front of the house, as they would in front of the king's court, and everyone who recognized the whip went forward and greeted it respectfully. When Mahyar's doorman saw this huge crowd, with so many of them wearing nobles' belts and boots, he ran to his sleeping master and woke the old man. He said, "Get up and quickly, this is no time for sleep or rest. Your guest is the king of the world, and he's staying in this humble little house of yours!" Bit by bit the old jeweler took in what his doorman was saying, and then his heart was in a turmoil. He said to him, "What are you telling me? What's this about the king?" He was still drunk, but when at last he realized what he was being told, he leaped up and shouted, "A wise old man like you doesn't say things like this." To which his doorman responded, "Since you're so experienced, tell me who has made you the king of Iran? At dawn, before the sun came up, your guest's groom hung a golden whip covered in jewels on our door, right where people pass by our house."

When he had heard his doorman out, the old man woke up completely and said, "And I got drunk last night in front of the King of Kings, and had my daughter serve him wine?" He went to Arezu's room and said to her, "My dear, you've always loved your freedom: well, that was Bahram, the King of Kings, who came to our house last night. He had been hunting and turned aside from the road to Kohandezh. Now get up and put on your Chinese silk gown, and put on that diadem you were wearing last night. Make him a present of some of our best jewels, give him three red rubies worthy of a king. When you see his sun-like face, bow before him and cross your hands over your breast, and don't look him in the eye. You're to think of him as your own body and soul. If he questions you, speak gently, humbly, and respectfully. I won't put in an appearance unless he calls me and places me among his servants. To think that I sat at the table with him last night as an equal, it makes me want to smash every bone in my body! How could I be so forward with the king? Wine leads young and old alike astray!" At that moment a slave ran in and said, "His serene highness the king has woken up."

Bahram woke feeling healthy and happy and went into the garden where he washed his head and body. He prayed before the sun, and his heart was filled with hopes of God's favor. Then he went and sat down and called for someone to serve him wine. When he heard about his subjects gathered at the door waiting for him, he ordered them to go back to the court. He asked that Arezu be sent to him, as he had a strong desire to see her. Arezu went to him with wine and her gifts, wearing her diadem and earrings. She bowed low and kissed the ground before him: the king smiled at her and said, "You made me drunk and then disappeared. Where have you been keeping these? But taking gifts from a woman is for others; all I want from you is your songs. Sing me those songs you told me about, the ones about hunting and battles and lances and the king's blows." Then he added, "Where's the jeweler I got drunk with last night?" The young woman called her father; she was astonished at the king's kindly manner. The jeweler came in, his arms crossed over his chest, and stood before his sun-like king. He said, "Your majesty, how wise, how noble, how great, how brave, how heroic, and how learned you are. Before you, a person with any sense can only choose to be silent. My sin came from ignorance: you must think I am crazy. It would be fitting for you to forgive my sin, because I am a foolish slave at your door, and the King of Kings cannot consider me as someone possessed of intelligence."

The king replied, "Wise men don't take offense at anything done by someone who is drunk. If a man is made surly by drinking wine, then he should leave it alone, but I saw nothing bad in you when you were drunk. But now we'll listen to Arezu, and you can consider her song about tulips and jasmine as your excuse. As she sings we'll have some wine and give no thought to the days that are to come." Mahyar kissed the ground, brought in a table, and made everything ready, and then invited in the nobles who were standing outside the door. Arezu went to her own room, frowning at the appearance of these strangers, and stayed there until the heavens put on their black veil and stars came out around the moon.

When they had eaten, Arezu was summoned and seated on a throne worked in gold. Mahyar told her to take up her harp and sing the song that the king had mentioned. Arezu sang:

> "Brave king, at whose name lions disappear,
> Leaving their dens to slink away in fear;
> Destroyer of your foes, victorious king,
> Whose face is like a tulip in the spring:
> No king is tall like you, the moon at night
> Does not possess your beauty or your light,
> When your victorious armies take the field
> Your enemies disperse, their forces yield,
> Their hearts break with despair, in headlong flight
> Their ranks are broken and they cannot fight."

As they grew happy and tipsy with the wine, they progressed from small cups to large. Ruzbeh joined them and lodgings were found for him in the village. Bahram summoned forty charming servants; their Byzantine faces were as beautiful as Byzantine brocade and they escorted Arezu to the king's harem, where they placed a jeweled crown on her head. The King of Kings and Ruzbeh returned cheerfully to the palace, and Bahram made his way to his jasmine-scented beloved.

Bahram Gur, the Landowner Farshidvard, and the Gatherer of Thorns

The next morning Bahram returned to his hunting grounds, and for a month he and his entourage stayed on the plain, both following the paths and going by unfamiliar ways. They camped in tents and pavilions and emptied the area of game. There was no sleeping on that plain while they were there, only hunting, wine, and the sounds of music, and fires burning both dry and green wood lit up the landscape. People looking for a profit came out of the city to trade with the hunters; a lively market was set up and the waste places bustled with activity. Anyone could find game and ducks to buy, to take home to their children and guests by the donkey-load.

After a month Bahram was overcome with a desire to sleep in his harem again; he and his men began their return, and the dust they sent up obscured the roads. They rode quickly until the day turned purple with dusk, when they saw a little town filled with houses, streets, and shops ahead of them. Bahram ordered his men to continue on their way with the baggage, while he would stay there alone that night. He asked who the local landowner was and made straight for his house. He saw a wide, deep, broken-down doorway; the owner appeared and bowed before him. Bahram said, "Whose is this ruin, and what is a ruin doing in the middle of the village?" The owner replied, "This house is mine, and you can see what a pass bad luck has brought me to. I've no cows, no clothes, no donkeys, no knowledge, no courage, and no strength. You've seen me, now come and see my house, which is more deserving of curses than praise."

Bahram's limbs were weak with fatigue; he dismounted and looked about the house. The floors were covered in sheep droppings, but it was a fine building, large and spacious. Bahram said, "You seem a hospitable man; bring me something to rest on."

The man replied, "Why are you mocking me?
There are no carpets here, as you can see,
And there's no food here either—you had best
Look for another place to eat and rest."

Bahram said, "At least bring me a cushion, so that I can sit for a while."

The man replied, "A cushion! That's absurd,
You might as well expect milk from a bird!"

"Well," Bahram said, "just bring me some warm milk then; and, if you can find it, some bread that's not stale."

"Pretend I gave it you," the man replied,
"And that you ate it and felt satisfied:
If there was bread to eat, then I assure you
You'd see a much more healthy host before you."

Bahram asked, "If you have no sheep, how is it your house is full of their droppings?"

"It's dark already, look!" the owner said,
"This talk of yours has muddled up my head.
Go choose a house where they can entertain you
And where the owner will be happy to detain you:
Why stay with some unhappy wretch who grieves
For his bad luck, and has to sleep on leaves?
You have a gold sword, and gold stirrups too,
You don't want thieves to come and frighten you.
A house like this attracts such dangerous men,
And lions might well choose it as their den."

Bahram said, "If thieves take my sword, I won't hold you responsible."

The man replied, "Enough of all this chatter;
No one stays in this house; that ends the matter!"

But Bahram persisted, "Why should a wise old man like you be so troubled by my presence? But I think you will have the magnanimity at least to give me a drink of cold water."

> He said, "Go back two bow shots and you'll see
> A pond—drink all you want. Stop bothering me,
> It's obvious I'm old, worn out, and poor,
> Too weak to earn my living anymore."

Bahram replied, "If you've no nobility about you, at least don't quarrel with people. What's your name?"

> He said, "My name is Farshidvard, and I've
> No clothes or food to keep myself alive."

Bahram asked, "Why don't you make some effort to earn your daily bread?"

> He said, "I pray for my release; I pray
> You'll leave my ruin and be on your way.
> What's brought you to this empty house? It's clear
> There's never any wealth or welcome here!"

And as soon as he'd finished talking he began to weep and wail so loudly that the king fled from the noise. Laughing at the old man, he left the town, and his entourage rejoined him. They came to a waste area covered with thorn bushes, which a man was chopping down with an ax. Bahram left his men and said to him, "You're a real enemy to those thorns! Who would you say is the most powerful man in these parts?" He answered, "That's Farshidvard, a man who for years has hardly let himself eat or sleep, even though he owns a hundred thousand sheep and about as many horses and camels. The ground is full of the gold he's hidden there, and may he have neither marrow in his bones nor skin on his body! His belly's hungry, his body's naked, he's no children, relatives, or friends. If he sold the farmland he owns, he could fill his house with jewels. His shepherds boil their meat in milk, while he eats a measly bit of bread and cheese. He's never owned two sets of clothes at the same time; he's his body's own worst enemy."

Bahram said to the thorn cutter, "If you don't know how many sheep he has, is there someone who does know?" The man replied, "My lord, no one knows how rich he is." Bahram gave the man some gold coins and said to him, "Now you've become someone to reckon with." He ordered one of his entourage to come forward, a man also named Bahram: he was a brave knight who charmed those who met him. The king also chose thirty horsemen, selected for their suitability for the work he planned for them, together with a scribe who was a good accountant. Then he said to the thorn cutter, "Off you go now; you've cut thorns and now you're going to harvest gold. Show these men the way to Farshidvard's wealth, and you will get to keep a tenth of it."

The thorn cutter's name was Delafruz; he was strong, and a fine figure of a man. Giving him a splendid horse, Bahram said, "You must make the wind your partner." Delafruz took the group to the mountains and plains, and there they found innumerable sheep. In the mountains were ten caravans of camels, each one with its own camel driver. There were draft oxen and milk cows, as well as wool, oil, buttermilk, and cheese; the whole plain was churned up with hoof prints. They found jars of butter kept in caves, and three hundred thousand cheeses stored in camel-loads next to a stream. Bahram the knight wrote to Bahram the king, beginning his letter with praise of God, who rules and nourishes all things, and invoking blessings on the king, who makes evil customs wither away. Then he continued, "King of the world, nobles and commoners rejoice in your reign. This Farshidvard, whom no one's ever seen at either a banquet or a battle, whose name is unknown to both nobles and commoners, who is loyal neither to his king nor his God, and who does not know what gratitude is, has untold wealth scattered throughout the world, while he sits hidden away, empty-handed and bent with grief. His injustice is—and do not take what I am saying as a sin—as extensive as the king's justice. You can make a great treasury of his wealth, and three years will not be enough to reckon it all up. I've summoned scribes and installed them in the mountains here; their backs are bent with the work, but I've been told that he has hidden under the earth more gold and jewels than we have already found, and the extent of his riches is not apparent yet. I wait in the mountains for your orders. Greetings from me to the king of Iran, and may his fame live forever!" He sent a swift messenger to the king with his letter.

When Bahram Gur read this missive through, he was saddened; his eyes were wet with tears and his warlike eyebrows frowned. He summoned a scribe, who brought a Byzantine pen and Chinese silk, and began his letter with praise of God, who confers victory and well-being, who is the Lord of knowledge and glory and of the imperial crown. Then he wrote: "If I am to be just, I should not harass this man. He didn't amass his wealth by theft and bloodshed, nor did he lead anyone else into evil ways. His sin is his ingratitude, the lack of any fear of God in his heart. He has been a guardian of this wealth, and the more he accumulated, the more his heart and soul withered away. What's the difference between having wolves or sheep on the plain if his sheep are not to be used for anything? What does it matter if one has jewels or gravel hidden underground if the jewels are not to procure anyone food and clothing? I won't make a treasury of my own out of his wealth, because I won't tie my heart to this fleeting world. Feraydun has disappeared from the world, and Iraj, Salm, and Tur have gone from our nobility, as have Jamshid, Kavus, Kay Qobad, and the other great men whom we remember. My father too, who grieved so many hearts and who was neither just nor chivalrous, has gone from this earth. None of these great men are here now, and we cannot quarrel with God because of this. Gather Farshidvard's wealth together, distribute it, and don't keep back one item from it. Give it to those who have concealed their needs and who are unable to escape their poverty, to those who are old and unable to work and are despised by the powerful, to those who have consumed their wealth and who are now left only with sorrow and heavy sighs, to those who still have a reputation but no money and who have no one to help them among the merchants, to orphans whose fathers have died and left them without money, to women who have no husbands or no clothes and who have no skill or energy to earn their living. Give these people all this wealth, and rejoice the hearts and souls of those who have suffered. Although you have gone in search of Farshidvard's riches, be just and temperate. Leave him the money and jewels he has hidden away, so that he won't live in want, even though they are like so much dirt to him that he has buried them in the earth. May the turning heavens be favorable to you, and may you act with justice and sobriety." They placed the king's seal on the letter, and the messenger returned with it.

The Emperor of China Invades Persia

Word reached India, the western kingdoms, the Turks, and China that Bahram was a pleasure-loving king who gave no thought to anyone or anything, who sent out no lookouts or spies, and who did not trouble to place good warriors at his frontiers. It was said that he passed his time in entertainments and had no notion of what was going on, either openly or covertly.

When the emperor of China heard this, he gathered an army from China and Khotan, distributed gold, and set off for Iran, believing that no one paid any attention to Bahram. And on the western frontier the Byzantine emperor also raised an army to threaten the country. Hearing that the Byzantine and Chinese emperors had mobilized armies against their country, the Persian nobles, both old and young, came before Bahram Gur. They were angry and filled with bitterness and spoke harshly to him, saying, "Your splendid good fortune has abandoned you. A military leader spends his time fighting with his army, but your heart is taken up with pleasure and banquets. In your eyes the army and treasury are of no account, and neither are the crown and throne of Iran." The king replied to them, "The just God of this world, who is beyond the knowledge of the greatest of men, is my support, and I shall preserve Iran from the wolf's claws. With my fortune, army, sword, and wealth I shall drive this threat back from Iran."

He went on with the pleasures of his life as before, and the country's leaders wept bitter tears. Each of them said, "The hearts of honorable men are abandoning this king." Bahram was aware of this, and troubled by it. In secret he built up his army, and no one knew of his preparations. The whole country was afraid because of the way he was living, and men's hearts were riven with anxiety. Everyone despaired of the king, despising both him and his rule. When news reached the king that the emperor of China's forces were menacing the frontier, he summoned Gostahm, who was a wise counselor and a fine warrior, and discussed the situation with him. He also summoned Behzad's son Mehr-Piruz, and Khorad's son Mehr-Borzin, as well as Bahram Piruz, Khazravan, Andian, the king of Gilan, the king of Rey, Dad-Borzin who governed Zavolestan, and Borzmehr's son Qaren. He gathered a force of thirty thousand Persian warriors, men who were prudent and ready for combat. Next he handed over the crown and throne to his brother Nersi, a wise man, just, God-fearing, and possessed of the divine *farr*, enjoining him to watch over the country's wealth and army. Then he led the forces he had gathered to Azerbaijan. Because he was taking so many troops from Pars, everyone, nobles and commoners alike, believed that he was fleeing from the war.

While Bahram was on the march, a messenger arrived from the emperor of Rome, and Nersi assigned him suitable quarters in the palace. Advisors sat with Nersi and their talk was all concerning the king. They said, "He has given all he has achieved to the wind." Meanwhile representatives of the army came to the chief priest and said, "He has scattered gold everywhere and doesn't know what behavior is appropriate for a youth. The country and the army are in turmoil, and everyone is trying to push his way to the top. Now we have no news of him, and we don't know whether to expect good or evil." After a long discussion, they agreed to send someone to the emperor of China to try to prevent an attack, so that the land of Iran would survive, even though its leader had fled. But Nersi said, "This is not what we should do, there's no channel in all the world for such waters to flow in! We have arms, wealth, and fine warriors who are able to fight with fire and sword. Bahram has left with a few soldiers; is that any reason for despair? If you think evil, evil will come to you; why have your thoughts become so gloomy?"

The Persians heard him out but disagreed: "Bahram has taken his army, and it is right that our hearts are filled with melancholy. If the emperor of China makes war on Iran, this country will forfeit all its splendor and glory; neither the army nor Nersi will survive, and the invaders will trample us beneath their feet." The Persians chose a wise and knowledgeable priest called Homay as the man best suited to represent them. Then they wrote a letter from Iran to the emperor. Saying that they were his slaves, and that their heads were bowed awaiting his commands, they wrote, "We will send what we can in the way of gifts and tribute from Iran to the emperor of China, since we do not have the strength to resist the armies of central Asia." Homay and a group of noble companions took the Persian nobles' letter and presented it to the emperor, whose heart rejoiced to see it. Homay also told him of Bahram's hasty flight with his army, and the emperor's heart and soul opened like a blossoming flower. He said to his Turkish companions,

"What sovereign has subdued Iran before,
By policy and plans, without a war?"

He showered gifts on the Persian envoy and gave him Chinese gold and silver coins. He composed his answer: "May wisdom be the companion of well-meaning men. I agree with all the messenger has said. I shall travel with my army as far as Marv and make the countryside there as resplendent as a pheasant's feathers. We shall wait for the Persian tribute, and the gifts from her warriors. I shall halt at Marv and go no further, since I do not wish to inflict suffering on you with my armies." The messenger hurried back to Iran and reported all he had seen and heard.

The emperor came to Marv, and the world turned black with the dust sent up by his cavalry. When he had rested he occupied himself with feasting, and no one there gave any thought to Bahram. So loud were the sounds of harps and lutes in Marv that no one could sleep, and the army wandered across the plain in no order, without posting sentries or sending out bands of scouts. The emperor's time, day and night, was taken up with hunting, drinking wine, feasting, and the music of harps, and he gave no thought to war. He was watching for the tribute from Iran to arrive, and his heart grew angry that it was taking so long.

Bahram Gur Attacks the Emperor of China

But for his part Bahram stayed alert and preserved his army from the enemy. Day and night he sent out spies, and his own troops' whereabouts remained unknown. When he learned that the emperor and his forces were in Marv, he brought his men from the environs of Azar-Goshasp; each soldier traveled with two horses, his armor, and a Byzantine helmet. Like a flood rushing down a mountain, they marched from Ardebil to Amol and thence to Gorgan, and as their leader, Bahram bore all the expedition's anxieties. They pushed on to Nisa, following a skillful guide through trackless mountains and deserts, traveling by both day and night. In the daytime they sent out scouts, and at night posted sentries. And so they came to Marv more swiftly than a pheasant can fly. His spies informed Bahram that the emperor spent his days and nights carelessly hunting at Keshmihan, or closeted with his advisor, who was of the spawn of Ahriman. Bahram rejoiced to hear this, and the pain of all his efforts dispersed like the wind.

He rested for a day, and when both he and his army were refreshed, Bahram made his way to Keshmihan as the sun rose above the mountains. Suddenly all ears were filled with the blare of trumpets, all eyes with the colors of banners. The sounds of men's cries and the clash of arms rose up from the hunting grounds, splitting the ears of the king and his men. The emperor had been asleep, worn out by the hunt, and he woke to find that he had been captured by Khazravan. The earth of the battlefield was so soaked in blood that it seemed to have rained down from the moon. Three hundred Chinese noblemen were captured and slung across saddles, and the captured emperor's dream was shattered. Bahram marched from Keshmihan to Marv; he had ridden so long and so hard that he was as thin as a reed. Few of the Chinese troops had remained in the city; those who were still there were killed, and Bahram went in pursuit of those who had fled. He followed them for thirty leagues, with Qaren bringing up the rear. When he returned, he went to the hunting grounds and distributed plunder to his men. He lifted up his head in pride at his victory over China and acknowledged that all power comes from God, who gives strength to both the good and the evil, and who is Lord of the Sun and Moon.

Bahram Gur Erects a Column to Mark the Border Between Iran and Turan

Bahram Gur rested for a week, and when he and his horses were refreshed he decided to make war on Bokhara. Princely ambition, rather than hunting and pleasure, preoccupied him, and in a day and a night he reached Amui. From there, in one watch of the night, he reached the sands of the River Oxus and crossed at the town of Farab. When the sun turned the air yellow and cast aside night's black cloak, the dust of his armies made the world as dark as a black hawk's feathers. He pressed on through Mai and Margh, overwhelming the Turkish forces and setting fire to the countryside as he went. The stars clung to the moon's skirts for comfort, and fathers fled to their children for safety. The leaders of the Turks, both the elders and young warriors, came to Bahram on foot, as abject suppliants, saying,

> *"Great king, whose star has brought you victory,*
> *Lord of the earth and its nobility,*

If China's mighty emperor betrayed you
And went back on the promises he'd made you,
You conquered him in war; the renegade
Is now your prisoner and his debt is paid.
Do not then shed the blood of innocents,
Such cruelty mars a king's magnificence;
If you want tribute, this is just—but why
Should guiltless people be condemned to die?
Our men and women are your slaves, we bow—
Defeated by your strength—before you now."

Bahram's heart was wrung for them, and with the hand of wisdom he sewed shut the eyes of anger. The God-fearing king became thoughtful and forbade his warriors to shed any more blood. When it was clear that mercy had prevailed with the king, the suppliants' hearts grew calm again. Their leader agreed to send a large tribute, to be paid annually, and Bahram also imposed a fine on them. Smiling and content, he then made his way back to Farab, where he rested for a week. He summoned the Chinese nobles and erected a column of stones and mortar. He said that no one from the land of the Turks was to pass this column into Persia except with the king's permission, and that the River Oxus was to be the frontier between the two peoples.

There was a man in the army named Shemr, who was wise, powerful, and from a fine family. Bahram made him king over Turan. A gold crown was placed on his head, and all the land of Turan rejoiced in his reign.

*B*ahram Gur wrote to his brother Nersi describing his victory over the emperor. The nobles who had been in touch with the emperor asked Nersi to write to Bahram and intercede for them. Nersi did this, and Bahram forgave them. Before returning to his capital Ctesiphon, he went to Azerbaijan, where he prayed in the great fire-temple there and refurbished it, and distributed wealth to the poor. In Ctesiphon he made a proclamation to his people remitting taxes for seven years and promising to relieve the sufferings of the poor. He sent his brother Nersi to rule Khorasan.

The Ambassador from Byzantium

One day Bahram said to his chief priest, "That messenger the emperor of Byzantium sent has been here a long time now; what kind of a man is he, and how wise is he?" The chief priest answered, "May the king of the world flourish, blessed by divine glory. He is an old man, intelligent, and humble; he's a persuasive speaker and has a soft voice. He was a student of Plato; he's wise, knowledgeable, and from a good family. When he came he was very confident, but now he seems lost in our country, withered away like a tulip in winter; his body has grown emaciated and his face has turned the color of dry reeds. His entourage are like sheep when a hunting dog confronts them. He regards us with neither anger nor lethargy; he takes no account of anyone in this country."

Bahram said, "God has made me victorious and turned night to day for me, and I should remember that Feraydun placed a crown on the head of Salm, from whom the present Byzantine emperor is descended. He has acted with nobility and chivalry and has not taken leave of his senses like the emperor of China. I will summon his ambassador when I give audience, and see if he has anything useful to say. Then I will send him back in a friendly manner, since I'm not someone who doesn't care what others in the world think of him. Some seek for war and muster armies, others bring a golden crown and look for peace; I must distinguish the one from the other. It takes greatness to deal with these leaders." The priest blessed him and said, "May you enjoy happiness for as long as the heavens continue to turn."

The Ambassador's Questions

Bahram summoned the messenger to his court, and the old man, who had seen the world and was eloquent and wise, entered the audience hall. His arms were crossed over his chest, and his head bowed: he knelt before the throne. Bahram questioned him kindly and motioned him to a turquoise-studded seat. "You have been here a long time," he said, "and must be tired of this country. My war with China was like a constant companion and kept me away from you. Seeing you now has refreshed my life, but your stay here has gone on for too long. Whatever you say we will respond to, and your voice will distinguish this day for us."

The old man praised the king, saying, "May time and place never be without you. You are the most magnificent of the world's kings, because you have greatness as well as sovereignty; you have knowledge, good sense, justice, and glory, and you act as a victorious king should act. You have wisdom and morality, and you are the lord of the learned. I wish long life to your body and noble soul; may the heavens never see you grow weak. Your speech is as balanced as a scale, and your words are like jewels, jewels that can never be weighed in gold. Although I am the Byzantine emperor's messenger, I am also the servant of your majesty's servants. I bring greetings from the emperor to the king, who wishes long life to you, your crown, and your authority. He has also commanded me to ask your wise men seven things."

The king said, "Say what these seven things are: a fine speaker is highly honored." He called the chief priest forward, together with other distinguished advisors, and the messenger revealed what the emperor had told him to say. Addressing the chief priest, he said, "Guide us then: what is that thing which you call 'within,' and then what is that thing which you call 'outside,' because you know no other name for it? What is 'above' and what is 'below,' what is 'limitless,' and what is 'contemptible'? What is that thing which has many names and which rules everywhere?" The chief priest answered him, "Be in no hurry, and do not turn aside from the path of knowledge. There is one answer to each of your questions; that concerning 'within' and 'outside' is a small matter. 'Outside' is the sky, and 'within' is the air, by the glory of God who orders all things. That which is 'limitless' in the world is God, and it is evil to turn from him. 'Above' is paradise, and hell is 'below'; and anyone who opposes God, he too is evil. That which has many names and rules everywhere is wisdom that, old man, has many names; it is wisdom that enables a king to fulfill his desires. Some call it 'kindness,' others 'fidelity'; when wisdom leaves, pain remains, and oppression. The eloquent call it 'righteousness,' the fortunate call it 'cleverness.' Sometimes it is called 'the patient one,' sometimes 'the keeper of secrets,' since speech is safe with it. Wisdom has innumerable names; you know nothing that is higher than wisdom, since it is the best of everything that is good. Wisdom seeks out the secrets that the world contains, those hidden things our eyes cannot see. As for what is 'contemptible,' this refers to a branch of knowledge of the works of God. The man who sees the shining stars in the high heavens and claims to know their number, who says he can distinguish the rays of Mercury, when the heavens cannot be measured in leagues and no one has access to their depths—such a man will astonish those with understanding. What is more contemptible than someone who numbers the stars in the heavens?"

When the emperor's representative heard these answers, he kissed the ground and acknowledged defeat. He turned to Bahram and said, "You rule the earth, your majesty; ask for no more than you already have from God, since all the world is under your command and the heads of the haughty obey your orders. The world cannot recall another king like you, and your priestly advisor is more knowledgeable than other wise men. Philosophers are his slaves and bow their heads before his knowledge." Bahram's heart lit up at these words, and he showed his pleasure. He rewarded his chief priest with gold, fine clothes, a horse, and other goods. Having demonstrated his wisdom, the chief priest left the court in state, and the ambassador returned to his quarters.

Bahram Gur Bids Farewell to the Byzantine Ambassador
When the sun touched the heavens the king sat on his golden throne, and the ambassador and chief priest presented themselves at court again. They talked happily about various matters, and then the priest said to the

ambassador, "You are unique in your intelligence; tell me, what is the most harmful thing in the world, whose actions make one weep; and what is the most profitable, whose actions raise a man up to glory?" The ambassador said, "A man who is knowledgeable will always be great and powerful, while the body of an ignorant man is more contemptible than mud and suitable for nothing good. Your question refers to ignorance and knowledge, and you have received, I think, a just answer. It is good to talk about knowledge. If you would put the matter differently, tell me, since knowledge increases honor." The priest answered, "Think, then, for speech grows beautiful from thought. The less a man hurts others, the greater an evil you should consider his death to be; but it's right to rejoice in the death of evil men, since both the good and evil are born for death. One is profitable, the other harmful, and you must make your wisdom distinguish between them."

The ambassador approved of this answer; he smiled and congratulated the king, saying, "Happy the land of Iran, that has such a king and such a chief priest! It is right that you demand tribute from the emperor of Byzantium, since your advisor is a king of the world." Bahram was pleased by his words, and his heart opened like a rose in springtime. The ambassador left the court. Night came with its black banner and its musky cloak, darkening the face of the sun. But the turning heavens did not pause and soon roused the sleepers again. The sun raised its banner, and the world's king woke lightly from sleep. His chamberlain opened the door to the audience hall, and Bahram seated himself on his throne. He ordered that a robe of honor be prepared and delivered to the ambassador, and to this he added unimaginable quantities of silver, gold, horses and their trappings, gold coins stamped with kings' names, jewels, musk, and ambergris.

Bahram Addresses His Court

After Bahram had dealt with Byzantium, he became concerned for his armies. Calling his chief priest and the leaders of the country before him, he gave his warriors grants of land, together with cash, horses, seal rings, and diadems; to the greatest of them he gave provinces and crowns. He filled the world with justice, and both nobles and commoners rejoiced in his reign. He sent away the unjust, without gifts and with cold words, and then he addressed his priestly advisors: "You are wise, capable, and pure of heart; you know all the ways of the world, and the acts of just and unjust kings. How many kings were left empty-handed and worn out for lack of rest, because of greed and injustice! The world lived in fear because of their malevolence, and good men's hearts were broken; everyone strove to do evil and no one battled for God. Women and children had no king as their protector, and the hearts of the righteous were filled with grief. Demons stretched out their hands everywhere, and men's hearts forgot the fear of God. The source of good, the hand of evil, the door to knowledge, the struggle for wisdom—all these come from the king, from whom all things come, whether righteous or perverse. If my father stretched out his hand toward injustice, if he was neither pure, knowledgeable, nor God-fearing, if the colors of fire overcame his bright heart, this should not surprise you. Look at what Jamshid and King Kavus did when they followed demons' ways. My father sought the same ways they had sought and did not wash his dark soul in the waters of wisdom. All his subjects trembled for their lives, and many lost their lives because of his anger. Now he has gone and left an evil name behind him, and there is no more to say: no one blesses his memory. But I bless his memory, for I would not have his soul be tormented by our rancor. Now that I am seated on his throne, surely he travels toward the celestial regions.

"I ask the Creator to give me strength to act with probity toward my subjects, in private and in public, and to turn the common earth into pure musk for them, so that when I become one with the dust again, the oppressed will not grasp at my skirts in reproach. May you veil yourselves in righteousness, and wash all evil from your hearts; for all men—Persian, Arab and Roman alike—are born from their mothers marked for death, whose attack is like a lion's, and from whose claws no man can turn aside his neck. The ravening lion himself is death's prey, and death humbles the dragon in the dust. Where are the heads and crowns of our kings, the nobles and splendid courtiers? Where are the proud knights, of whom we see no trace in the world? Where are the women, whose beautiful faces delighted the hearts of our nobles? Know that all those who once veiled their faces are now partnered with the dust."

Bahram Gur Writes a Letter to Shangal,
the King of India

One day the king's vizier rose and said, "King of justice and righteousness, the world has no fear of malevolence now, and within our borders suffering and hardship have disappeared; but the soul of Shangal, the lord of India, turns away from justice. From India to the border with China the land is overrun with bandits. He has designs on Iran, and it would be appropriate to do something about this. You are the king, and Shangal is only the guardian of India, so why does he demand tribute from China and Sind? Consider this, and look for a way to remedy the situation; evil should not be allowed to flourish."

The king became thoughtful, and the world appeared as a thicket before his eyes. He said,

> "I'll act in secret; I shall go alone
> To see this Indian Shangal on his throne.
> I'll see the customs of his court, his land,
> And all the forces under his command.
> I'll be my own ambassador—no one
> In Persia is to know where I have gone."

His vizier, a scribe, and other indispensable courtiers discussed the matter, then wrote a letter to Shangal. Beginning with praise of God, of wisdom, and of those who act wisely, it continued, "But you do not know your own limits, and your soul wallows in blood. Since I, Bahram, am now king, and good and evil emanate from me, how is it right for you to act as a king? Discord springs up on all sides, and it is not a kingly custom to attack others, or to consort with troublemakers. Your grandfather was our subject, your father stood as a slave before our kings, and none of us ever allowed the tribute from India to come late. Look at what happened to the emperor of China when he marched on Iran: all he had brought was looted, and he regretted the evil he had done. I see your preparations, your distribution of largess, and your glory. But I am ready for war; I have wealth and a united and determined army. You don't have the strength to resist my warriors, and there is no one in India who knows how to lead an army. You're mistaken in your assessment of your power; you're opposing your little stream against an ocean. I am sending you an eloquent, knowledgeable, and noble envoy;

remit to us the tribute you owe, or if you ignorantly decide on war, see that you are well prepared for our response. I give my greetings to any man whose warp and weft are justice and wisdom." When the ink had dried, they scattered musk on the letter, which was addressed, "In the name of Bahram, whose justice resolves all evils, who received the Kayanid crown from Yazdegerd on the day of Ard in the month of Khordad, lord of the marches and protector of his country, to whom the Romans and Slavs pay tribute, to Shangal, guardian of India from the Lake of Qanuj to the frontier with Sind."

Bahram Gur Travels to India with His Own Letter

When the royal seal had been placed on the letter, Bahram made preparations as if for a hunting expedition. None of his courtiers knew where he was going, except the nobles who accompanied him as an escort. He traveled to India, crossed the magicians' river, and saw before him Shangal's palace. Its roof reached into the sky, and in front of it there were armed men, cavalry, and elephants, and the air rang with the din of bells and trumpets. Bahram was astonished at the sight and grew thoughtful. He said to the doorkeepers and other servants there, "A messenger has come to this court from the victorious king Bahram." Immediately the chamberlain went behind the curtain to the king, ordered that the curtain be drawn back and that Bahram be conducted to the audience hall with appropriate ceremony.

The ceiling of the room Bahram entered was made of crystal, and there he saw Shangal seated on a throne of crystal and gold, wearing his crown, and dressed in cloth of silver embroidered with gold and sewn with jewels. His advisor stood behind him, and his brother was seated on another throne and wore a crown studded with precious stones. Bahram approached Shangal's throne and made his obeisance; he waited for a long time, and then said, "I bring a letter, written in Pahlavi on silk, to the king of India, from the great King Bahram, lord of the world and servant of God." When the king heard Bahram speak, he had a golden seat brought for him, and his companions were invited forward from the doorway. As soon as he was seated, Bahram began his speech: "Great king, as you command me, I shall speak, and may virtue and power never forsake you." King Shangal said, "Well, speak then; the heavens look well on a good speaker."

Bahram said, "I bring a letter to the king of India, written in

Pahlavi on silk, from my king, born of kings, the like of whom no mother ever bore, who lifts up his head in glory, whose justice turns poison to its antidote; to whom the great of the world pay tribute, whose prey is lions, whose sword in battle turns the desert to a sea of blood, whose generosity is like a cloud that rains down pearls, and who has contempt for gold treasures."

Shangal's Answer to Bahram's Letter

Shangal asked for the letter and looked at the envoy in astonishment. When his scribe read the letter aloud, Shangal's face turned as yellow as bile. He said to Bahram, "You speak well, but don't be in a hurry to talk now, and control your emotions. Your king has shown us his greatness, and so have you by coming here. But I cannot agree with anyone who asks for tribute from India. This letter talks about armies and treasure and trampling countries underfoot, but you must understand that kings are like herons, and I am an eagle compared to them; or they are like dust, and I am the ocean. A man does not attack the stars, or vie with the heavens in glory. Virtue is a finer thing than vain talk, which will only make knowledgeable men contemptuous of you. You have no courage, no knowledge, no country, no city; your sovereignty is all in your tongue. My land is filled with hidden treasures untouched by my ancestors, and there is so much barding and armor hidden away that if my treasurer wanted to access it all, he would need elephants simply to bring the keys to the places where it's stored. If you reckoned up my swords and breastplates, they would outnumber the stars. The earth cannot support my armies and war elephants. Multiply thousands upon thousands, and that is the number of people in India who call me their king. Mountains and seas of jewels are mine, and it is I who sustain the world. I own the sources of amber, aloes wood, and musk, unexhausted stores of camphor, medicines enough for everyone in the world who falls sick; my country is filled with all these things, as well as with gold, silver, and jewels. Eighty crowned kings stand ready to serve me, seas and rivers enclose my country, and no devil can conquer our land. From Qanuj to the sea of China, from the land of the Slavs to Iran, all the chieftains are under my control and have no choice but to serve me, and only my name is on the lips of those who guard the borders of India, China, and Khotan. The daughter of the emperor of China lives in my harem and calls down blessings on my head; I have a son by her, a lion-

hearted boy whose sword can cleave mountains. From the time of Kay
Qobad and Kavus, no one has ever thought to demand tribute from this
country. Three hundred thousand warriors call me their king; one
thousand two hundred allies, each of them related to me by blood, pro-
tect me and give no one access to me, and lions bite their nails in ter-
ror when they attack. If it were permissible for a nobleman to kill an
envoy in anger, I would have severed your head from your body."
Bahram replied, "Great king, if you are a nobleman, don't stir up unjust
desires. My king told me to say, 'If you are wise, don't follow unjust
ways. Produce two knowledgeable and eloquent men from your court
and if either of them shows himself superior in wisdom to one of my
men I have no claims on your country, because a wise man does not
despise language. Or, if you would rather, choose a hundred of your
mace-wielding cavalry and let them fight against one of our men. If
they can show their worth and courage, I shall not ask for tribute.'"

Bahram Wrestles Before Shangal
and Shows His Prowess

Shangal heard him out and said, "You don't think in a chivalrous way.
Come down from your arrogance for a while, and be more at ease;
there is no point in saying such foolish things." Bahram rested in his
quarters until midday, while a splendid banquet was prepared. When the
food was set before Shangal, he said to one of his servants, "Bring that
envoy of the Persian king. He talks well and he's a novelty for us. Bring
his companions too, and sit them with the other envoys." Bahram came
quickly; he sat down, reached for the food, and said nothing. Once the
main course was over, musicians were called in while the guests reclined
on gold-worked embroideries, and the scent of musk rose up from the
wine. The courtiers became cheerful from the wine and forgot their
anxieties over all that was yet to come.

Shangal summoned two wrestlers, men who could stand against a
devil. They put on their wrestling breeches and began their bout,
straining and struggling against one another. The wine had taken effect
in Bahram's brain; he picked up a crystal goblet, and said to Shangal,

> "Let me put on those breeches! When I fight
> Against a man of comparable might,

The wine I've drunk has no effect on me—
I'm not unmanned by feasts and luxury!"

Shangal laughed and said, "Go on then, and if you bring one of them down, shed his blood!" Bahram stood and bent his tall body, crouching in the wrestler's stance. He grasped one of the two around the waist, like a lion leaping on a wild ass, and threw him against the ground with such force that the man's bones were broken, and his face turned pale. Shangal gazed in astonishment at Bahram's stature, his broad shoulders, and his strong body. In his own language he said the name of God to himself and reflected that Bahram had the strength of more than forty men. When the assembly was drunk, the party broke up and left the jewel-encrusted hall. The sky put on its cloak of Chinese silk, and everyone, young and old, rested from drinking.

When night's musky tent turned gold again, and the sun showed its face in the heavens, the Indian king rode out with a polo stick in his hand. His men had brought his bow and some arrows, and he amused himself with these for a while. Then he ordered Bahram to mount and to take the royal bow in his hand. Bahram said, "Your majesty, I have a number of horsemen with me who would dearly like to play at polo, or to shoot at the target. What are your orders for them?" Shangal replied, "Skill with the bow is certainly praiseworthy in a knight. You, with your strength and stature, draw this bow back and show us your skill." Bahram gave his horse its head, and as it galloped forward he shot an arrow that shattered the target. All the knights and warriors who were there cried out their congratulations together.

Shangal Is Suspicious of Bahram and Prevents Him from Returning to Persia

Shangal became suspicious of Bahram and thought, "No envoy—neither Indian, Turkish nor Persian—has his strength and glory, or his skill with a bow. If he is himself the king, or a great nobleman, it would be best for me to refer to him as the king's brother." He smiled, and said to Bahram, "You are skilled and have the qualities of a man of authority. With such strength and abilities you must be your king's brother. You have the royal *farr*, and a lion's might, you must be more than just a brave warrior." Bahram replied, "Your majesty, do not mock a simple messenger. I am not of Yazdegerd's family, nor am I the king, and it would be a sin for me to refer to the king as my brother. I am just a stranger from Iran, neither a scholar nor a nobleman. Allow me to return now, since the road is long, and I do not want to incur my king's wrath." Shangal said, "Not so fast; you and I still have things to discuss. You should not be in any hurry to leave; a quick departure would not be appropriate. Stay with us, and put your heart at rest, and if you don't want our strong wines, drink new wine."

Then he called his vizier and talked with him about Bahram for a while. He said, "This is either Bahram, or at least someone more important than a simple warrior. Tell him kindly that he should stay here and not try to leave Qanuj. If I tell him, he will be afraid; you can say whatever's appropriate. Tell him that the best thing he can do is ingratiate himself with the king of India. Say, 'If you stay near the king and follow his advice, he'll give you the choicest province, you'll be the army commander there and recipient of the taxes in a place where it's always spring and the streams give off the scent of spring, where there are jewels and cash enough to keep a man's heart from sorrow. You have won favor with the king and he smiles whenever he sees your face. A man who is fortune's favorite will not leave Qanuj, where the trees bear fruit twice a year.' When you've talked to him in this way, ask him his name, because I'd dearly like to know it. If he is happy to stay here in our country, our glory will be increased by his. I'll quickly make him the leader of our armies and equal to myself in this land."

The vizier said all this to Bahram, and then asked him his name, indicating that his answer would not be complete if he didn't give it. The color in Bahram's face changed, and he wondered how he should respond. Then he said,

> "Don't shame me in two countries in this way!
> For treasure, or from need, I won't betray
> My country's king—our faith says that to rise
> Against our kings is neither good nor wise:
> Since good and evil, all we meet with here,
> Will pass away from us and disappear,
> A wise man does not let ambition lead
> His soul astray, or give his heart to greed.

Great Feraydun, and Kay Khosrow, and all
The mighty kings who held the world in thrall,
Where are they now? And Bahram is a king
Who won't be disobeyed in anything.
If I should go against his orders he
Won't be content when once he's punished me;
He'll conquer India, and bring this land
Of ancient magic under his command.
It's better I return to see once more
My valiant king, victorious in war.
As for my name, they call me Borzui,
This is the name my parents gave to me.
Tell Shangal all I've said, so that he'll know
That I've been here too long now and must go."

The vizier went over all he had been told with his king, who frowned and said, "This is pointless chatter; I'm going to arrange something that will bring this splendid warrior's life to its close."

Bahram Fights Against a Rhinoceros and Kills It

Roaming in Shangal's territories was a rhinoceros so huge that even lions and vultures fled from it, and the whole country was in a deafening uproar. Shangal said to Bahram, "All men respect you, and this is a task for you: you must approach this rhinoceros and pierce his hide with your arrows. If your glory can rid our land of this danger, I shall seat you next to myself, and your name will live forever in India!" Bahram said, "I shall need a guide, and when I catch sight of this animal, by the strength that God has given me, you'll see his hide soaked in blood."

Shangal gave him a guide who knew the area where the rhinoceros was lurking. As they approached the place the guide described the animal's lair, and the great size of its body. He pointed out the thicket where the rhinoceros was and withdrew, while Bahram strode forward. A few Persians were following him, thinking they too would fight against the rhinoceros. But when they saw its huge snout in the distance, and all the vegetation there flattened by its weight, they said as one man to Bahram, "Your majesty, this is beyond any man's courage;

no matter how valiant a prince you are, people don't fight with mountains and rocks. Tell Shangal that this can't be done, and that you don't have your king's permission for such a battle." But Bahram replied, "If God has given me a grave in India, how can my death occur somewhere else? It is impossible even to think such a thing!" The young man grasped his bow, as if careless of his life. He ran forward until he was close to the rhinoceros, his brain full of fury, his heart ready for death, and snatched a poplar wood arrow from his quiver. He rained down arrows like a hail storm, until the rhinoceros started to weaken, and when he saw that the animal's time had come, he exchanged his bow for a dagger. He severed the rhinoceros's head and cried, "I do this in the name of the one God, who has given me this strength and glory, and at whose command the sun shines in the heavens!"

He ordered that an oxcart be brought, to take the rhinoceros's head out of the thicket. When Shangal saw them in the distance, bringing the head, he had his audience hall hung with brocade, and as the great king sat on his throne, Bahram was ushered into his presence. All the nobles of India and the Chinese knights who were there called down blessings on him, and chieftains went forward with gifts, exclaiming, "No one's feats of bravery can compare with yours." Shangal showed joy outwardly, but his heart was troubled; at times his face was full of smiles, and then a frown would cross his features.

Bahram Gur Kills a Dragon

Also in that country was a dragon that lived both in the water and on dry land, sometimes wallowing in a lake, sometimes sunning itself on land. Its long tail could encompass an elephant, and it made great waves in the lake's waters. Shangal said to his intimate advisors, "This lion-like envoy sometimes delights me and sometimes fills me with anxiety. If he stays here, he'll be a great support to me, and he can lead the armies of Qanuj; but if he goes back to Iran, I fear that Bahram will destroy Qanuj. With a subject like this envoy and a king like Bahram, nothing of value will be safe here. I've pondered this all night, and I've thought of another stratagem: tomorrow I'll send him against that dragon, from which he certainly won't escape unharmed. I won't be blamed for this because he'll be only too eager to fight it."

He summoned Bahram and talked with him at length about the deeds of brave warriors. Then he said, "God brought you from Persia to India so that you could cleanse our country of evil, as is the custom of great men. There's something that has to be done, and it is a difficult and dangerous task, but it could end with your becoming wealthy. When you have completed this task you are free to go with my blessings." Bahram replied, "The heavens will change their courses before I disobey your orders." Shangal continued, "The disaster we're faced with is a dragon; he lives both on dry land and in the water, and he can kill a gaping crocodile. If you can rid India of this monster, then you can take India's tribute back to Iran, and everyone in our country will agree to this. You will also take presents from India, like aloes wood and ambergris and all sorts of other things." Bahram said, "Your majesty, great lord of India, as God is my witness I will eradicate all trace of this dragon. But I don't know where he lives, someone must show me the way to him."

Shangal sent a guide with him to point out the dragon. Thirty Persian knights rode with him too, as far as the lake. They saw the dragon looming in the darkness, and the Persian nobles were so alarmed at the sight that they cried to Bahram, "My lord, you shouldn't think of this monster as being like the rhinoceros." Bahram replied, "We must leave the outcome to God. If I am to die fighting this dragon that will neither increase nor decrease my courage." He readied his bow and selected arrows whose tips had been dipped in poison and milk; then he showered the dragon with arrows, shooting on horseback, striking it right and left. The steel arrowheads pinned its mouth shut, and the surrounding thorns were burned by the poison it shed. Then Bahram struck its head, and mingled blood and poison coursed down its chest. The dragon's body was weakening, and the ground was awash with blood and poison; Bahram drew his glittering sword and split open the monster's heart. With his sword and an ax he hacked off the head and flung the lifeless body to the ground.

He had the head dragged to Shangal on a cart, and when Shangal saw it all India called down God's blessings on Persia that had produced such a strong and splendid knight who was worthy of combat with a dragon, and whose only equal was his own king.

Bahram Marries the Daughter of the King of India
But Shangal's heart was heavy with worry, and his face turned yellow at the thought of Bahram's feats. When night fell he called his advisors to

him, men of his own family and others to whom he was not related, and said to them, "This man of King Bahram's, with that strength and power and authority he has, says that nothing will keep him here, although I have offered him all kinds of glory and splendor. But if he returns to Iran and goes to his courageous king, he'll say our army is weak and that there are no knights in India. My enemy will be contemptuous of me. To prevent this I shall cut off his envoy's head. I want to do away with him in secret; what do you say to my plan, and how should I proceed?"

His advisors said, "Your majesty, do not torment yourself in this fashion. To kill a king's messenger would be a foolish act; no one has ever thought like this or followed such a path. Your name would be despised, and a king should be dear to his people. And then an army would come from Iran, and a king like Bahram wouldn't leave a single one of us alive; you must not wash your hands of righteousness in this way. He delivered us from the dragon, and his reward for his troubles should not be that he is killed. In our land he killed both the dragon and the rhinoceros, and he deserves a long life, not death." Shangal's soul was darkened, and he was unsure what to do.

At dawn the following morning he sent for Bahram and talked with him alone, with neither his vizier nor his advisors present. He said, "You charm everyone, and you've become very powerful, but don't be too ambitious. I'm going to give you my daughter in marriage, and I shall do more than I have promised. But when I have done this, you must forget about leaving here. I shall make you commander of the army, and you will rule over India." Bahram was silent, and he thought of his throne, his lineage, and his battles. To himself he said, "There's no arguing with him. It would not be shameful to be related to Shangal, and besides I shall save my life in this way, and perhaps one day see Persia again. I have been here a long time now: the lion has fallen into the fox's trap." He answered, "I shall do as you say, and your words will be my soul's guide. Choose one of your three daughters, and when I see her I shall call God's blessings down on her."

The king was delighted at his response and had his audience hall decorated in Chinese silk. His three daughters came forward in their gorgeous clothes, their scent, and their beauty. Shangal said to Bahram, "Go, and delight your heart with something you've never seen before."

Bahram hurried to them, and chose one, as lovely as the spring. Her name was Sepinoud, and she seemed compounded of modesty and grace, good sense and desire. Shangal gave him Sepinoud, who was as elegant as a cypress, and as pure as a candle that burns without smoke. He then selected a rich treasury and gave his daughter the key to it. Next he gave gold and silver coins and other goods such as aloes wood, ambergris, and camphor to the splendid knights in Bahram's entourage. His jewel-studded chamber was decorated for a feast, and all the nobility of Qanuj came to the festivities, which were presided over by the king. For a week they sat there, carousing happily with wine, and Sepinoud, as lovely as wine in a crystal goblet, was seated at Bahram's side.

Bahram Gur Flees from India with Shangal's Daughter

When Bahram had lived with Shangal's daughter for a while, she realized that he was the king of the world. Day and night she wept with love for him, and her eyes were always fixed on his face. And when Shangal learned of their mutual love, he ceased to be suspicious of Bahram.

Bahram and Sepinoud were seated together one day happily talking of this and that, when he said to her, "I know that you want what is best for me. I want to tell you a secret, but you must see that it remains unknown to anyone else. I want to leave India: can you agree to this? I'm telling only you about it, and nobody else must know. My situation in Persia, where I am under God's protection, is much better than here. If you wish to go too, your good sense will guide us and you will be recognized as a queen everywhere; your father will kneel before your throne."

Sepinoud said, "You are a proud man; see that you don't wander from wisdom's path. But the best of all women in the world is the one who makes her husband smile continually; my soul will deserve your contempt if it deviates from your intentions." Bahram said to her, "Then find some way to carry out this plan, and speak not a word to anyone." Sepinoud replied, "Truly you are worthy of the throne: I will find a way, if luck helps me. There is a place in the forest not far from here, where my father holds religious festivals. It's about twenty leagues away, and is believed to be sacred; it's customary to weep in front of the idols there. Good hunting for wild asses can be found there, and aloes wood for burning in Qanuj grows in that area. The king and his entourage are going, and there will be such a crush the roads will be blocked. If you want to leave for Iran, wait for five days, and be ready to set off when the king leaves the city."

Bahram was overjoyed to hear her suggestion, and that night he did not sleep till dawn for thinking about it. The next day, when the sun touched the morning sky, and like a stranger night prepared to depart, Bahram went out hunting for wild asses. As he left he said to his wife, "Make everything ready for our departure, but tell no one." All the Persians in his escort went with him, and they reached the shores of a river, where they saw merchants' baggage piled up. They were Persian merchants, men who braved the seas and the deserts, and when they saw Bahram's face the king bit his lip and ordered them not to bow down before him. Wanting to keep his identity hidden, he said to the merchants, "Keep your mouths shut; this situation can be profitable but also dangerous. If the secret of who I am is known in India, Persia's soil will be drenched in blood. A man who can keep his mouth shut can help me; he needs his lips closed and his hands ready for action. Swear silence, till Fortune favors us. Swear that if you ever betray King Bahram, you have broken with God and made a pact with the devil!" When they had sworn to this, Bahram's heart ceased to worry about their loyalty. He said, "If you would turn my words to diadems, guard my secret as you guard your souls. If the throne loses me, armies will attack Iran from all sides, and there will be no merchants or king there, no landowners, no army, no throne, and no crown."

They wept at his words and said, "May our merchants' souls be sacrificed for you, and youth and sovereignty be yours!" The king called down blessings on them, and then, entrusting his soul to God, he returned anxiously to his quarters. There he said to his wife, "When King Shangal goes to the sacred grove, a messenger is sure to come from him asking for me. Arrange things with your mother, but in such a way that she doesn't realize your secret. Tell her that Borzui is sick, and may the king excuse his absence." Sepinoud told her mother this, and when Shangal was ready to set out for the grove his wife said to him, "Borzui is ill; he asks to be excused, your majesty, and says that you are not to worry about him. A sick man will only be depressed by such observances, as the king knows." Shangal agreed: "A sick man should not be thinking of ceremonies."

At dawn the following day Shangal set off from Qanuj with his

entourage. When night came Bahram said to his wife, "My dearest partner, it's time for us to leave." Invoking God's name, he placed Sepinoud in the saddle; then he put on his armor and mounted his horse. His lariat was tied to the saddle, and he grasped his mace in his fist. They rode until they came to the river, where they saw the group of Persians asleep. Bahram commandeered a boat for his companions and placed Sepinoud in a little skiff; they reached the far shore just as dawn was breaking.

Shangal Pursues Bahram and Learns Who He Is

A horseman rode out from Qanuj with the news that Borzui and his Persian entourage had left, taking the king's daughter with them. When Shangal heard this, he came from the hunting grounds like a raging fire. With a group of soldiers he pursued Bahram until he reached the banks of the river and saw Bahram and Sepinoud on the other shore. In his fury, he crossed the river in the twinkling of an eye. He said to his daughter,

> "May no king ever have a child like you!
> This man deceived you, and away you flew
> To cross this river without telling me—
> You're leaving our celestial sanctuary
> For what? A ruined and impoverished land!
> You'll know the force of this spear in my hand

If you think you can simply leave my side
And, without warning, run away and hide!"

Bahram said to him, "You wretch, why have you ridden here like a fool? You've put me to the test and you know that I'm as much of a man on the battlefield as I am at banquets and wine drinking. You know that a hundred thousand Indians against me count for less than one knight. If I and my thirty companions are armored and have our Persian swords, we can fill the land of India with blood, and leave not one person alive."

Shangal knew that he spoke the truth, because there was no denying his courage and fighting ability. Shangal said to him, "You were dearer to me than my own eyes, I preferred you to my children and to all my family. I put a crown on your head and gave you the bride you wanted. I acted justly toward you, and you acted deceitfully. You chose treachery instead of loyalty, and when has it ever been right to return loyalty with treachery? What can I say of a man whom I treated as my own son, whom I believed to be wise, and who now acts like a belligerent knight, or as though he were the king himself? When was a Persian ever loyal? When a Persian says 'yes' he's thinking 'no.' This is just how a lion cub acts; its keeper cares for it and soaks it in tears, but when it cuts its teeth and its claws become sharp, all it wants is to fight with whoever brought it up."

Bahram replied,

"When you know who I am, you will not blame
Me for my acts, or slander my good name.
I am the King of Kings, and my commands
Are absolute throughout the warlike lands
Of Persia and Turan. From now on you
Will reap the benefits of all I do.
You'll be my father here, and I won't say
'Where is the tax your country has to pay?'
Your daughter is the eastern candle flame
Who crowns all other women with her fame."

Shangal was astonished at his words. He tore his Indian turban from his head and urged his horse forward, so that he left his troops and stood before the king. In his happiness he embraced Bahram, asked pardon for what he had said, and commanded that a meal and wine be prepared. Bahram explained everything that had been hidden from him, telling him all the details of what had happened. They drank a quantity of wine and then rose; each asked pardon of the other, and the two brave, God-fearing kings clasped hands in promises of mutual devotion, saying,

> *"Our hearts will never break this loyalty,*
> *And we'll uproot the tree of treachery;*
> *The friendship that we swear to will abide*
> *Forever now, with wisdom as our guide."*

Shangal bade farewell to Sepinoud, embracing her as though his own chest were the warp and hers the weft of one cloth. Then the two kings quickly turned from one another, having abandoned all the rancor that was in their hearts. Happily and in haste they set out, one over dry land and the other over water.

The Persians Come to Welcome Bahram Gur

When news reached Iran that the king and his entourage had returned from Qanuj, all the streets and towns along the way were decorated to welcome him, and everyone took part in this, scattering gold and silver coins, musk and saffron. Bahram's son Yazdegerd called the scattered troops together to form a welcoming party, and Nersi and the chief priest accompanied him. When Bahram's son saw his father, he went forward and pressed his face against the dust, as did Bahram's brother Nersi and the chief priest, and though their faces were dusty, their hearts were filled with happiness. And so the king progressed toward his palace, entrusting his body and soul to God. The world turned dark, and he rested; the moon was like a silver shield in the sky.

When day tore night's dark shirt, and the candle that lights the world appeared in the sky, the King of Kings sat on his golden throne. The doors to his audience hall were opened, and his lips were closed. The nobles, wise men, and client rulers of his realm came before him. Bahram rose and addressed them with words of advice and wisdom: his nobles responded with congratulations, and by calling down blessings on his head.

Then the king mounted his horse, and he and his courtiers rode to the fire-temple of Azar-Goshasp. There he distributed a great quantity of gold and silver to the poor, giving more to those who tried to conceal their need from him. The keepers of the flame of Zarathustra came to him with gifts and the sacred barsom, and Bahram presented Sepinoud to them. They taught her the principles of the faith and bathed her in pure water, so that she was cleansed of all corruption, dust, and dirt. Bahram opened the prison gates, freeing the prisoners, and gave money liberally to the needy.

Shangal and Seven Kings Visit Bahram

After Sepinoud had been Bahram's wife for some time and had told her father of Bahram's exploits, Shangal desired to go to Iran. He sent an eloquent and noble Indian messenger to request that a new treaty be drawn up between him and Bahram, one that he could keep in his palace as evidence of their friendship. Bahram responded with a new treaty that was as fair as the sun shining over a celestial garden. He also wrote a letter in Pahlavi script that the messenger took to Shangal. The king of India then made preparations to travel to Iran, but hid all this from his Chinese father-in-law.

Seven kings came to Shangal's court to accompany him on his journey, including the king of Kabol; Sandal who came with his entourage; the noble Mandal; and the powerful Jandal. All were great kings, eager for fame; they wore torques and earrings and were resplendent in jewels, gold, and silver. Parasols of peacocks' feathers were held over their heads, and their elephants were draped in brocade. The caravan's splendor could be seen for miles as they traveled taking gifts for Bahram, even though he despised such wealth. They went forward, stage by stage, and when Bahram heard of their approach, nobles from every town went out to welcome them. The King of Kings traveled as far as Nahravan, and there the two great monarchs met and dismounted, each offering greetings and apologies for the trouble the other had taken. These two crowned, glorious kings embraced one another, while their escorts dismounted and the world was filled with the hubbub of greetings. The two kings traveled on horseback, side by side, gossiping of this and that, until they reached Bahram's palace, where a golden throne was placed ready for Shangal, and imperial robes were given to him. The tables spread for the feast stretched for a bowshot and were piled with lamb and spit-roasted chicken. Musicians sang and wine was brought, so that from one end of the feast to the other all the glasses were full. A splendid space for talk and relaxation, with attentive servants, had been prepared for after the meal, and the whole palace and its grounds seemed like a paradise. The wine flasks were all of crystal and set out on golden trays, and other trays were piled with musk, while the stewards wore golden diadems and jewel-encrusted slippers.

Shangal was astonished by the palace, and as he drank his wine he thought to himself, "Is this paradise, or a garden where all one's companions exhale the scent of musk?" In private he said to Bahram that he would like to see his daughter, and the king gave orders that eunuchs from his entourage escort him to her. As Shangal went with them he saw other parts of the palace that were as beautiful as the spring. And then

> He saw his daughter, gloriously gowned,
> Calm on her ivory throne, and nobly crowned;
> He kissed her forehead then, and bent to place
> His face against her radiant, moonlike face:
> They wept in one another's arms, and he
> Caressed her hands with his continually.
> He said, "You live in paradise, my dear;
> The palace that you left, compared to here,
> Is ugliness itself—a noisome lair,
> Impoverished, idolatrous, and bare!"

He gave her the presents he had brought—purses of gold, crowns, and slaves—and they made her apartments look like a garden in springtime. Then he returned to Bahram but saw that the festivities were breaking up; the nobles were tipsy with wine and calling for all kinds of bedding, ready to go to their sleeping quarters. Shangal too decided to sleep. The musky cloak of night, spotted with stars like a leopard's hide, was spread, and all the wine drinkers slept until that golden goblet that we call the sun appeared. Night's cloak was pushed aside, and the plains glistened like yellow topaz. Bahram took the king of India hunting, and when they returned they sat to feasting again. Whether they were engaged in conversation, hunting, or feasting, Shangal was almost never absent from Bahram's side.

Shangal Returns to India

Shangal went to his daughter and there asked for a pen, paper, and ink made from black musk. He wrote a proclamation, beginning with blessings on him who had cleansed the world of sorrow, spreading righteousness and justice so that evil and vice had become only the devil's portion. Then, "I gave Sepinoud to the famous King Bahram as his bride; may the King of Kings live forever, with all other nobles as his slaves. When I leave this fleeting world I entrust Qanuj to King Bahram. Commit my dead body to the flames, and do not disobey Bahram. Hand my treasures over to him, and hand over to him too our country, its crown, its throne, and its armies." He gave this proclamation, written in Devanagari script on silk, to Sepinoud.

Shangal stayed for two months in Persia; then he sent a messenger to Bahram, asking that he and his entourage be allowed to return home. Bahram agreed to his return to India and ordered his chief priest to select some Persian goods as presents: there were gold coins and royal jewels, innumerable swords, helmets and belts, and more brocades and uncut cloth than one could reckon. According to their rank, the men of his entourage were given horses caparisoned in Chinese brocades. Then the king cheerfully bade them farewell and went with them for three stages of the journey. Not content with what he had already bestowed on them, he gave them enough fodder for their animals to last until they reached the border with India.

Bahram Remits the Taxes Paid by Landowners

When Bahram returned, he sat quietly on his throne and thought of the evil day of death; his heart was filled with pain, and his face turned pale. He summoned his vizier and commanded him to inspect his treasuries and count the gold, jewels, and cloth he possessed. He did this because the words of his astrologer were troubling him. He had said, "You will live for three score years, and during the fourth must weep for death." Bahram had replied, "I shall enjoy myself for twenty years, with partners for my journey through the world; during the next twenty I shall act righteously and justly in private and in public; and during the third

twenty I shall stand before God asking for his guidance." The astrologer
had said sixty-three years, but the number three was obscure. It was his
words that had made him think of his treasury, even though he usually
paid little attention to wealth. Blessed is the man who lives without
trouble or self-indulgence, especially if he is a king.

His vizier spent many difficult days reckoning up his wealth, and
when he arrived at a figure he returned thoughtfully to the king. He
said, "You have sufficient wealth to last for twenty-three years. I have
taken into account provisions, the pay for your splendid army, and the
expenses of messengers who come to your court from client kings and
the provinces. Your treasury is full of gold and silver and other wealth,
and will last for twenty-three years." When Bahram heard this and
reflected on it, he stopped worrying about those things that were to
come.

> He said, "My reign is coming to a close.
> Consider: we've three days here, and of those
> Tomorrow has not come, while yesterday
> Has gone forever now, and passed away:
> I won't be bent down by anxiety
> During the one day that is left to me."

He gave orders that taxes, on both the nobility and the commoners,
were to be remitted throughout the world. Then he established a priest
in each town to wake up those who were asleep and act as a mediator
in all disputes. He gave these men a stipend for food, clothes, and fur-
nishings and said to them, "Neither good nor evil must be hidden from
me; arbitrate among men and tell me of both the good and the bad so
that I can lay my fears of evil to rest."

The priests went out into the world, and nothing, whether good or
evil, remained hidden from them. They did as they were ordered, but
letters came in from every province saying that wisdom was deserting
men's minds, that the world was full of battles and bloodshed. The
young did not respect their elders; their hearts were puffed up with
wealth and they had no regard for the king or his priests. As the letters
arrived, one after another, the king's heart became tired of bloodshed.
He chose an administrator for each province, a man who was just,
knowledgeable, and well qualified. These functionaries were given a

stipend from the treasury and told to collect silver in the form of taxes from the area's subjects for six months. They sat in state and were crowned; for six months they collected taxes, and for six months distributed revenue, but they themselves were not to profit from the silver they collected. The intention was to stop the bloodshed caused by men being led astray, but the king's agents wrote to him that justice and security were disappearing from the world: the rich paid no taxes, but in their arrogance thought only of squabbles and arguments.

When Bahram read these letters, his heart became bitter. He chose lords of the marches, righteous men such as the situation required, gave them financial support for a year, and ordered them to apply God's law against those who were shedding blood, so that men should be at peace again. When some days had passed he wrote to his agents, who were scattered throughout the country, asking them to identify those things that were harmful to his kingdom. They answered, "The king's liberality has meant that no one cares for the old and true ways. Agriculture is neglected, we see draft oxen wandering at will, and plants are growing indiscriminately in the fields and plains." He answered, "Men are not to rest from agricultural labor till midday, when the sun is high in the sky. But don't expect to get anything out of men who have nothing. When men don't work, it's from ignorance, and ignorance is something we should weep over. A man in that condition should be given a few coins to stave off hunger. If a man has neither seed nor livestock, don't act harshly with him; help him with money, to relieve his sufferings. Do likewise when disaster strikes from the sky, since no man can rule the sky; if the ground is covered with locusts that eat all the crops, give the farmers a grant from the treasury, and have this proclaimed throughout the province. And if there is an uncultivable or sterile area, as there is in all provinces, on the lands of both nobles and commoners, if any man tries to collect taxes on such an area, even if he were my own guardian, I'll bury him alive and curse his house!" They set the king's seal on this letter, and a messenger took it to all quarters of the land.

Bahram Gur Brings the Luris from India

Where there were poor men he clothed them, and he wrote a letter to the provinces asking who lived well, and who were destitute. "Tell me," he wrote, "what is happening in the world, and lead my heart toward the light." Answers came from the nobles in all provinces saying, "We see that the land is flourishing, and everywhere blessings are called down upon you, but the poor complain about the king and about their bad luck. They say, 'When the rich drink their wine they have chaplets of flowers on their heads, and they drink to the accompaniment of musicians' songs. They don't consider us as people at all, which is unwise of them: we have to drink our wine without music and without any flowers.'"

The king laughed aloud at this letter, and he sent a hard-riding messenger to Shangal saying, "You must help me out now: choose ten thousand of those Luris, men and women both, who know how to play the lute. Send them to Persia so that they can entertain the poor here." Shangal read the letter, chose the Luris, and sent them to the king, just as he had asked. When the Luris arrived at court, the king admitted them and gave an ox and a donkey to each of them, hoping to make farmers of them. He also donated a thousand ass-loads of wheat, so that they could use the animals to plough the land, sow the wheat, and so bring it to harvest. They were also to be musicians for the poor, so that commoners would be like the nobility. Off the Luris went, but they ate the oxen and the wheat, and by the end of the year their faces were pale with hunger. The king said to them, "You weren't supposed to waste the seed like this, and forget about seed time and harvest! Well, you still have the donkeys; load up your goods and put silk strings on your lutes!" And now, because of his words, the Luris wander the world trying to make a living, traveling and stealing by day and night.

Bahram Gur's Life Comes to an End

And so sixty-three years passed, and the king was unequaled in the world. At the new year, the wise priest who was his vizier came to him and said, "The great king's treasury is empty, and I have come to hear your commands." The king replied, "Do not trouble yourself, we no longer need such things. Abandon the world to its Creator, who established the turning heavens. The heavens turn and God remains, guiding both you and me toward the good." He slept that night and at dawn the following morning a large crowd came to the court. All who should be there had come, among them the king's son Yazdegerd. In front of the assembled nobles Bahram gave him the crown, the royal torque, the diadem, and the ivory throne. He wished to devote his thoughts to God, and so gave away the crown and throne. He was tired of the world's affairs, and when the dark night came he tried to sleep.

When the sun raised its hand in the sky, the king's vizier became anxious because the king had not risen, and he was afraid that Bahram had fled from the world. Yazdegerd went to his father's side, and when he saw him the saliva froze in his mouth. The king's cheeks had the withered color of death; wrapped in golden brocade, he had given up his soul. So this world is, and always has been. Do not torment your soul with greed and ambition: even a heart of stone or iron fears death, and there is nothing you can do against it. You must act with humanity, troubling no one, if you want your past not to harm you. Here I remind men of Bahram's justice and generosity, and may no one think ill of his memory!

They made him a royal tomb, and his people mourned his death.

*B*ahram Gur was succeeded by his son Yazdegerd, who ruled for eighteen years. He was succeeded by two of his sons—Hormozd, who reigned for only a year, and Piruz, who ruled for eleven years. Piruz was succeeded by his sons Balash, who ruled for five years, and Qobad. During Qobad's reign a man called Mazdak, who claimed to be a prophet, appeared.

THE STORY OF MAZDAK

A man named Mazdak, who was eloquent and knowledgeable and possessed of great abilities, came to the court. Qobad listened to his wise words and made him the king's chief minister and treasurer.

There was a drought, and food became scarce throughout the world, for both the common people and the nobility. No clouds appeared in the sky, and throughout Iran no one saw either rain or snow. The great men of the land appeared at Qobad's door, demanding bread and water, and Mazdak said to them, "The king will be able to give you hope." Then he ran to the king and said, "Your majesty, there is one question I wish to ask you, in hopes that you will give me an answer." Qobad replied, "Speak, refresh my mind with your words." Mazdak said,

> *"Suppose there's someone who's been bitten by*
> *A poisonous snake, and he's about to die:*
> *What do you say, my lord, should happen to*
> *A man who has the antidote but who*
> *Insists on hoarding it, and will not give*
> *The bitten man the means to help him live?"*

The king replied, "The man who has the antidote is a murderer. He should be hanged at the gates as punishment for the dead man's blood, as one hangs an enemy one has captured." Mazdak left the king's presence and returned to the crowd that was seeking relief. He said to them, "I have talked with the king about your demands. Wait until dawn tomorrow, and then I shall show you the path of justice."

The crowd came back the next morning, weeping and with their faces gaunt with sorrow. When Mazdak saw them from the doorway, he hurried to the king and said, "You majesty, victorious, eloquent,

and wise, I asked you a question and you answered, opening a door
that had been closed to me. If you will allow it, your councilor wishes
to ask you one more thing." The king said, "Speak, don't hesitate; let
me profit from your conversation." Mazdak said,

> *"Picture a man in chains; for want of bread*
> *He wastes away and soon he will be dead:*
> *Now he's denied bread by a passerby*
> *Who lets the miserable captive die.*
> *Should this man suffer punishment? Or would*
> *You say that what he did was just and good?"*

The king replied, "Destroy the wretch; by not acting he has another
man's blood on his hands."

Mazdak kissed the ground before the king and left his presence. At the
court gates he addressed the crowd, "Take the grain that has been hoarded
and hidden away; put it at men's disposal in the streets and throughout the
town; let each man take his share!" The hungry mob ran to loot the gran-
aries, and soon there wasn't a single grain left in either the city's or the
king's warehouses. When they saw this the overseers went to the king and
said, "The king's granaries have been plundered, and Mazdak is respon-
sible for this!"

Qobad summoned Mazdak and demanded that he account for the
looting of the warehouses. Mazdak replied, "I told the suffering citi-
zens what I'd heard from the king. I talked to the king of the world
about the poisonous snake, and about the man who had the antidote.
The king told me that the man who had the antidote had committed
a sin, and that if someone shed his blood there would be nothing
wrong in this. For a hungry man bread is the antidote to his sufferings,
one that he won't need when he's well fed again. If you are a just ruler,
your majesty, you won't hoard grain in your granaries. How many
hungry men have died with empty bellies because of those granaries!"

The king's heart was hurt by his words, and they stayed in his mind.
He questioned Mazdak and listened to the answers, and saw that
Mazdak's heart and soul were full of such ideas. Mazdak talked of what
the prophets and just religious leaders had said, but his arguments went
beyond all boundaries. Crowds collected about him and were led astray
by his talk. He said that those who had nothing were equal with the

powerful, and that one man should not own more than another, since the rich were the weft and the poor the warp. Men should be equal in the world, and why should one man seek to have more than another? Women, houses, and possessions were to be distributed, so that the poor would have as much as the rich. "By the power of the pure faith I proclaim equality," Mazdak said, "and what is noble will be distinguished from what is base; any man who follows any faith but this will be cursed by God."

Young and old, the poor flocked to him; he confiscated wealth from this man and gave it to that, and the wise were deeply troubled by his talk. But Qobad rejoiced in his words and followed his teachings. Mazdak sat at his right hand, and the court had no notion of where the chief priest was. The poor and anyone who lived by the sweat of his brow were with him; his faith spread throughout the world, and no one dared to stand against him. The nobility faced ruin and gave what they had to the poor.

Kesra Opposes Mazdak and Kills Him

One morning Mazdak came from his house to the king and said, "A great number of my disciples and the leaders of my faith have gathered at your door; will you see them, or should they be sent away?" Qobad told his chamberlain to grant them audience, but Mazdak said, "This hall is too small to accommodate such a large number, it would be better if the king went out onto the plain." The king gave orders that his throne be taken from the palace to the plain. A hundred thousand of Mazdak's followers were gathered there, and they came confidently before the king.

Mazdak said to the king, "Your majesty, you are above all wisdom, but you should know that your son Kesra is not of our faith, and who has the right to oppose us? He must promise in writing to abandon his evil ways. There are five things that lead us away from justice, and the wise cannot add another to them. These five are envy, the longing for vengeance, anger, desire, and the fifth, which becomes a man's master, greed. If you can conquer these five demons, the way to God lies open to you. It is these five that make women and wealth the ruin of the true faith throughout the world. If women and wealth are not to harm the true faith, they must be held in common. It is these two that generate envy, greed, and desire, and secretly they link up with anger and a longing for vengeance. Then demons corrupt the wise, and to prevent this these two must be held in common." As he finished speaking he seized Kesra's arm, and the king of Iran stared at him in astonishment. Angrily Kesra pulled his arm away and indignantly turned his eyes from Mazdak.

Qobad laughed and said, "Why are you so concerned about what Kesra believes?" Mazdak said, "He secretly denies the true faith; he's not of our religion." Qobad said to Kesra, "This is not the right way, to deny the true faith." Kesra replied, "If you give me time, I can show you how false and dangerous all this is, and then the truth will be plain to you." Mazdak said to him, "How many days are you asking the king, whose splendor fills the world, to grant you?" Kesra replied, "Give me five months, and in the sixth I will answer the king." This was agreed to, and the king returned to his palace.

Kesra sent messengers to find knowledgeable men to help him in his cause. One went to Khurreh-ye Ardeshir where the wise sage Hormozd lived, and another to Estakhr to summon Mehr-Azad, who came with thirty of his companions. These venerable seekers after wisdom sat together and discussed all manner of things, then they made their report to Kesra. When he had heard them out, Kesra went to Qobad and talked with him about Mazdak. "The time has come for me to learn which is the true religion," Kesra said. "If Mazdak is right, then Zoroaster's faith will disappear. I will accept his faith as true and choose in my soul as he has chosen. If the way of Feraydun, of Esdras and Jesus and the Zend-Avesta, is mistaken, then Mazdak's words are to be believed and no one in the world should be our guide but him. But if all he says is perverse, and he does not follow the way of God, hand him over to me, together with his followers, and I shall separate their skins and the marrow in their bones from their bodies." He swore this before Zarmehr, Khordad, Farayin, Banduy, and Behzad, and then returned to his palace determined to keep his oath.

When the sun displayed its crown on the following morning, and the ground became like a sea of ivory, the king's son and the priests and sages he had summoned arrived at the king's palace, talking matters over as they came. Mazdak delighted Qobad's heart with his words, and then a Zoroastrian priest addressed Mazdak in front of the assembly and said, "You are a seeker after knowledge, but the new religion you have made is a pernicious one. If women and wealth are to be held in common, how will a son know his father, or a father his son? If men are to be equal in the world, social distinctions will be unclear; who will want to be a commoner, and how will nobility be recognized? If a laboring slave and the king are the same, when a man dies, who is to inherit his goods? This talk of yours will ruin the world, and such an evil doctrine should not flourish in Iran. If everyone is a master, who is he to command? Everyone will have a treasure, and who is to be its treasurer? None of those who established religions have talked in this way. You have secretly put together a demonic faith; you are leading everyone to hell, and you don't see your evil acts for what they are."

When Qobad heard the priest's words, he sprang up and shouted his approval. Kesra added his support, and Mazdak's impious heart was filled with apprehension. The assembly rang with voices saying, "Mazdak should not sit next to the king, he is destroying our religion, he has no place in this court!" The king turned away from Mazdak's teachings in disgust, and his mind was filled with regret for what he had done. He handed Mazdak and his followers, who included a hundred thousand men of good standing, over to Kesra, and said, "Do with these men as you will, and never mention Mazdak to me again."

In Kesra's palace there was a garden with a high wall around it. It was dug up from end to end, and Mazdak's followers were planted there head down, with their feet in the air, like trees. Kesra said to Mazdak, "Go to my garden and see there trees of a kind no one has ever seen or heard tell of before." Mazdak went to the garden expecting to see fruit trees, but when he saw what was there, he gave a cry of despair and fainted. Kesra had a tall gallows built, and the impious Mazdak was strung up alive and head down. He was killed with a shower of arrows. If you have any sense, you will not follow Mazdak's way.

The nobility were once more assured of their wealth, their women folk, children, and splendid gardens. For a while Qobad was ashamed of what he had done and cursed Mazdak's memory. He distributed large amounts of wealth to the poor, and gave gifts to the country's fire-temples.

Kesra Is Made Qobad's Heir and Is Named Nushin-Ravan

The king was so pleased with Kesra for showing such wisdom that from then on he always consulted with him and listened to his advice. When he had ruled for forty years, the fear of death entered his heart, and he wrote a document on silk, acting as his own scribe. He began with praise of God from whom faith and ability come, whose commands are always fulfilled secretly or openly, whose sovereignty no one has fathomed, and whose followers are never cast down. He continued, "Whoever sees Qobad's handwriting here should listen only to Kesra's advice. I have bestowed the glorious throne on Kesra, and may he flourish after my death. May God be pleased with my son, and may the hearts of his enemies be confounded. Never swerve from his commands; rejoice and grow wealthy beneath his rule." He placed his golden seal on the letter, and entrusted it to Ram-Borzin.

Qobad was in his eightieth year, but he was not content to die. The splendor faded from his face and eyes; death came to him, and the world felt his absence. His body was wrapped in brocade and prepared with roses, musk, camphor, and wine. They built an imperial tomb for him and placed a royal couch and crown there. They laid the king on the golden couch and closed the tomb forever.

When the chief priest had ended the period of mourning, he made the king's letter public. It was read before the court, and the crown prince was seated on the throne amid the court's acclamations. Taking his place there, Kesra was hailed as the new king; jewels were poured over his head, and he was given the name Nushin-Ravan. So ends the reign of Qobad; now I shall set before you the reign of Kesra, who ruled with justice and glory, and who became renowned for his righteousness and generosity.

Kesra Nushin-Ravan promised a just administration and set about making the tax system more equitable. He toured his country's provinces, and secured the border areas against invasion. In particular, he built a wall between Iran and central Asia, to keep out attacks from that direction. Skirmishes across the western frontier with the Roman empire, in which Kesra was mostly the victor, led to a treaty, which included the provision that Kesra marry the Roman emperor's daughter.

THE REIGN OF
KESRA NUSHIN-RAVAN

The Story of Nushzad

You should understand that both king and subject need a partner, clothes, food, and somewhere to sleep. If this partner is a noble and sensible woman, she will be a treasure to her husband, especially if she is tall and has musky hair that reaches to her feet, and if she is wise and modest, with a soft and eloquent voice. Such was the king's wife: as tall as a cypress tree and as lovely as the moon. She was a Christian, and the whole town was filled with talk of her beauty.

She gave birth to a boy, with a face as radiant as the sun, more splendid than Venus shining in the night sky. Kesra called him Nushzad, and the child was protected from the strong winds of heaven. He grew to be like an elegant cypress, an accomplished young man, and an ornament to the kingdom. When he learned about hell and the way to heaven, Esdras, Jesus, and the path of Zoroaster, he rejected the Zend-Avesta and washed his face with the waters of Christianity. He chose his mother's beliefs over his father's faith, and the world was astonished at this. The king grieved that this rose had produced only thorns; the doors to the young man's palace were closed, and it became his prison. He was confined to Jondeshapur, far from both the Persian capital and the west, and his companions were criminals in chains.

It happened that when the king was returning from an expedition to the west he complained of fatigue and the pains of travel, and he became so weak that he halted at the River Jordan. Someone took the news to Nushzad that the imperial splendor was shrouded in darkness, that the great king Kesra was dead and had entrusted the world to another. Nushzad rejoiced to hear of his father's death, and may his name be cursed for this. As a wise man once said, "If you rejoice at someone's death, make sure that you never die!"

Kesra Nushin-Ravan's Illness and Nushzad's Rebellion

When Kesra's son heard that the throne was vacant, he threw open the
doors of his palace, and a crowd of senseless criminals who had been
imprisoned by Kesra flocked to him. Nushzad freed them all, and the
town was in an uproar. All the Christians there, priests and bishops
alike, joined him, and soon he had a force of thirty thousand men,
armed and ready for war. The Roman emperor wrote him a letter, as
murky as his behavior, recognizing him as the lord of Jondeshapur and
as the emperor's ally and co-religionist. Nushzad's fortunes had been at
a low ebb, but now they revived and he filled the town with evil men.

News of what Kesra's son was up to reached Ctesiphon. The com-
mander in charge of the city's defenses sent a horseman to Kesra, pass-
ing on all the secret reports he had heard. Kesra was saddened by the
news and his mind grew dark with apprehension. Talking privately with
his chief priest about the matter, he finally came to a decision. He sum-
moned a scribe, and with a frown on his face and cold sighs on his lips,
he dictated a letter filled with anger and sorrow to Ram-Borzin.

He began with praise of God who created the world and time, who
maintains the sun and Saturn and the moon in their places, who
bestows glory and sovereignty on men, whose rule is limitless and can-
not be diminished, beneath whose rule everything exists from the least
straw to elephants and lions, from the dust beneath an ant's feet to the
River Nile. He continued, "I knew of the emperor's letter, of the evils
my son has instigated, and of the criminals who have broken out from
the prisons and rallied to his cause. It would be better for a man to leave
the world than to see such a day. And we are all of us born for death,
including Kesra and Nushzad. No one, neither the ant and the mos-
quito nor the lion and the hippopotamus, escapes Death's beak and
talons. If the earth were to open and reveal what is hidden within her,
we'd see her lap filled with past kings and with the blood of warriors,
and the pockets of her skirts stuffed with wise men and beautiful
women. Whether you wear a crown or a helmet, the point of Death's
lance will pierce it. If those men who have gathered around Nushzad at
the rumor of my death can escape death themselves, then there is sense
in what they do, but it is only evil men who rejoice at a just king's
death.

"Nushzad has taken leave of his senses and is in league with some
devil: he flared up when he thought his desires had come to fruition,

but he cannot destroy my power on the strength of a rumor. If the throne were vacant, he would be its new occupant; his conduct is worthy of his faith and his malignant soul. But if my son's faith is impure, this is no cause for fear, and I care nothing for the wealth he has squandered, or for those who have rallied to his cause. They are an idle, lowborn, malignant rabble, unworthy to be my subjects. Talk of what they've done doesn't interest me, and you should not be concerned by it. I fear only God, who is beyond all knowledge, and to whom we must not be ungrateful: it is he who has given me victory and glory, power and the imperial crown, and if my praises had been equal to his gifts my power would have been even greater. Would that the seed of my body had found another womb in which to sleep; when it woke my enemy appeared, and I fear that I have brought these sorrows on myself. But if God is not angry with me, I am not concerned about the outcome of all this. As for the men who have flocked to his cause, I despise them. It is the emperor's letter that has muddied the waters in this way; they think that because he is a co-religionist and an ally, he will support them. A man loses his senses and pays no attention to the faith of his ancestors; but when this fool turns his head away from justice I shouldn't curse him since he is from my blood and body, and to curse him is to curse myself.

"You are to equip an army to fight them, but proceed cautiously and slowly, and if matters deteriorate and you have to fight, do so without rashness. It would be better to capture him than to kill him; it may be that he will repent of his sins. But if he is intractable and stoops to low tricks, don't hesitate to use your sword and mace against him. When someone we love is drawn to contemptible things, it is useless to try to separate him from his desires, and a noble man who rebels against the world's king deserves a wretched death. Don't be afraid to kill him; he has rebelled against our crown and embraced the Roman emperor's religion.

"As for the rebels who make up Nushzad's army, think of them as so much wind; they're malcontents, like gossiping women. The Christians among them will give up if you shout at them loudly enough, that's their way, and in the end they'll renounce that cross of theirs. The rest are slaves and malignant fools with not a noble thought in their heads, blown hither and thither by every wind. But if you capture Nushzad in battle, don't say these things to him. His womenfolk support him, so make his palace his prison and let him live with those who are happy to obey him. Give him free access to his wealth, women, food, and palace furnishings; he mustn't be in need of anything. But when you're victorious, don't hesitate to put to the sword any of the lords of the marches who have supported him: it's right that the king's enemies be fed to the crocodiles. And there are others, the seed of Ahriman, who oppose my rule in their hearts, who ignore the righteous things I have done, and whom Nushzad's rebellion has brought to light. But even if he has turned to evil ways, he is still my son, and my heart reminds me of this. Publicly brand the tongues of those who led Nushzad astray with their evil councils; my curses on their mouths and tongues! They are men who looked for me to weaken, who followed Ahriman and went by devious paths; they do not deserve to live in my kingdom, whose glory and crown belong to me."

Ram-Borzin Prepares for Battle Against Nushzad; Piruz's Words to Nushzad

The king's seal was set on the letter and a messenger quickly set off with it. He told Ram-Borzin all he had heard from King Kesra and handed over the letter with its orders to prepare for war. At cockcrow, the morning after the old man had read the letter and heard what the messenger had to say, the din of drums was heard before his palace and Ram-Borzin led the army out from Ctesiphon.

The news reached Nushzad, who mustered his troops and gave them pay and provisions. The Roman priests and patriarchs, with Shemas at their head, took their places in his army, whose hands were soaked in blood. A cry sounded from the gateway of Nushzad's palace, and his men surged forward, like a wave of the sea before the wind. They marched out of the city to the plain, their heads filled with warfare, their hearts with poisonous hatred. When they caught sight of the dust raised by Borzin's forces, they drew up their ranks in battle formation, and the brass trumpets were blown. The dust sent up by the cavalry obscured the sun, and the blows of heavy maces split the granite rocks. Nushzad, a Roman helmet on his head, was in the center of his forces, surrounded by so many Roman priests that their horses' hooves hid the ground. The earth seemed to seethe, and the air above their heads to groan in anguish.

A brave warrior, whose name was Piruz-Shir, came forward and cried out, "Nushzad, who turned your head away from justice? You have deserted the faith of Kayumars, Hushang, and Tahmures, and Christ the Deceiver himself was killed when he abandoned God's faith! Don't follow the faith of someone who didn't know what he was doing. If God's *farr* was with him, how were the Jews able to overcome him? Have you heard what your noble father did to the Romans and their emperor? And now you're fighting against him and lifting your head up to the skies! For all your handsome face and *farr* and strength, for all your massive shoulders and great mace, I see no wisdom in you: your soul is dark and bewildered. I pity that head and crown of yours, and your fame and lineage, which you are flinging to the winds. You are no mammoth or ravening lion, and you cannot withstand the might of Kesra's forces. O prince, I have never seen a picture in a king's palace that portrayed a horseman like you, with your reins and stirrups, your mighty arm and thigh, your ardor, and strength, and mace. No Chinese painter ever saw such a painting, and the earth has never seen a prince like you. Young man, don't burn Kesra's heart like this, don't muddy the splendor that illuminates the world. Dismount from your horse, ask for quarter, throw your mace and Roman helmet to the ground! If far away from here a cold wind blew black dust in your face, the king's heart would ache for you, the sun would weep for you. Don't sow the seeds of rebellion in this world, such quarrels don't become a king; but if you ignore my advice and choose the way of pride and confrontation, I hope my words come back to you often enough, and that your evil advisors' talk turns to wind."

Nushzad answered him, "Feeble old man, your head's filled with wind, you can expect no surrender from my army of heroes, nor from me, a king's son. I reject Kesra's faith and cleave to my mother's way. Her faith is that of Christ, and I shall not swerve aside from his glorious path. If Christ who brought our faith was killed, this does not mean that God's glory had abandoned him; his pure soul went to God because he saw no nobility in this dark world. If I am to be killed, I am not afraid, since death is a poison against which there is no antidote."

This was Nushzad's answer to the old warrior Piruz, and the air became thick with arrows. The drums and trumpets sounded and the two armies closed with one another. Nushzad urged his horse forward

like fire and pushed back the left flank of the king's army; he killed
many of their warriors and no one dared to oppose him. Ram-Borzin
was roused to action and gave orders for arrows to rain down like
springtime hail. Nushzad was wounded in the attack and recalled the
words of Piruz; he retreated to the center of his army, his body pierced
by arrows and his face sallow with pain. He said to his Roman war-
riors, "It is a sad and shameful thing to fight against one's father." He
groaned and wept, and asked for a bishop, to whom he told everything
that was in his heart.

> "It's I who brought this sorrow on my head:
> Send tidings to my mother when I'm dead,
> And say that Nushzad's earthly course is run,
> The good and evil of his life are done.
> Tell her she should not grieve for me, and say
> That in this world all things must pass away.
> This was my lot, and how could I have known
> Delight here, or the glory of a throne?
> All life is born to die, and when you see
> The truth of death you will not mourn for me.
> It's not my death I grieve for now, but rather
> That I've provoked the anger of my father.
> Build no great tomb for me, and do not bring
> The musk and camphor that preserve a king:
> Grant me a Christian grave." He spoke and sighed,
> And so the lionhearted Nushzad died.

The Story of Bozorjmehr

It's unwise to think of dreams as meaningless. You should consider
them as a kind of revelation of hidden things, and this is especially so
when the king of the world sees them. The stars, the moon, and the
heavens gather their scattered languages together into one path, so
that bright souls can see in dreams all that exists, like fire reflected in
water. One night, as King Nushin-Ravan slept, he saw a majestic tree
growing before the throne, and his heart was so delighted by it that
he called for wine and music. All was peace and pleasure, but then a
boar with sharp tusks sat down beside him and wanted to drink from
Nushin-Ravan's goblet.

When the sun rose in Taurus, and the lark's song was heard on every side, Kesra sat on his throne, and his heart was filled with melancholy because of his dream. A dream interpreter was summoned, and the high priests took their places in the court. The king explained to them what he had seen in his dream, but the dream interpreter gave no answer, because he had no knowledge of such a dream. A person who confesses his ignorance avoids having to make a judgment. When the king received no answer from this expert, his heavy heart looked for another solution. He sent distinguished men to every quarter, each with a chest of gold containing ten thousand coins to help them search throughout the world for a knowledgeable dream interpreter who could say what the king's dream meant, and he eagerly awaited their return.

One of these envoys was Azad-Sarv, and he traveled from Kesra's palace to Marv. He scoured the city and came across a priest with the Zend-Avesta before him; he was teaching little children the scriptures, and shouting at them in his anger and irritation. One older boy, whose name was Bozorjmehr, was studying the Zend-Avesta, poring over it with love. The envoy drew rein, and asked the teacher about the king's dream. The man replied, "This is not my business; the Zend-Avesta's the only branch of knowledge I care about." But when Bozorjmehr heard the envoy's question, he pricked up his ears and smiled. He said to his teacher, "This is sport for me: interpreting dreams is what I'm good at." The teacher yelled at him, "Have you done your exercise properly?" But the envoy said, "Perhaps he knows something; don't discourage him." The teacher was irritated with Bozorjmehr and said, "Say what you know then." But the boy answered, "I won't say anything except in front of the king, in his court."

The envoy gave him a horse and money and everything he needed for the journey. The two traveled together from Marv, as splendidly as pheasants strutting beneath the flowers. And so they went forward, chatting about the king, his commands, his *farr*, the crown and court, until they reached a place where there was water. They dismounted under the trees, and ate and rested. Bozorjmehr slept in the trees' shade, with a sheet pulled over his face. The envoy was still awake, and as he watched his companion, he saw a snake slither beneath the sheet and seem to sniff eagerly at the sleeping youth, from head to foot: then it gently glided away toward the trees. As the black snake eased its way to the top of a tree trunk, the boy lifted his head from sleep, and when the snake heard him moving it disappeared among the branches. The envoy was astonished and repeatedly murmured the name of God over the boy. To himself he said, "This clever child will reach an exalted position in the world." Then they galloped on, until they reached the king's court.

Bozorjmehr Interprets the King's Dream

The envoy preceded the youth to Kesra's throne and said, "I traveled from the king's court to Marv, searching like a pheasant through a rose garden, and I found a child at school, whom I have brought here as quickly as I could." Then he told the king what the youth had said, and he also described the strange incident involving the snake. Kesra called the boy forward and talked to him about his dream. The boy's head seemed so filled with words that they tumbled from his mouth: "In your palace, among the women of your harem, there is a young man who has dressed himself as a woman. Clear the court so that no one will realize what we're going to do. Then have your women walk before you, and as they set one foot before another we'll ask that foolhardy intruder how it is that he's found his way to the lion's couch."

The court was cleared of strangers, and the palace door locked. The king's women, in all their tints and scents, smelling of jasmine, filled with grace and modesty, walked slowly before Kesra. But no man was seen among them, and Kesra was as enraged as a lion. Bozorjmehr said, "This is not right; there is a young man somewhere among these women. Have them walk before you again, but with their faces unveiled." Once more the women paraded before the king, and this time a young man was discovered among them, tall as a cypress and with a face like a Kayanid. His body trembled like a willow, since his heart had despaired of life's sweetness.

There were seventy women in the harem, each as elegant as a cypress tree. One, who was cypress-tall and whose body was like ivory, was the daughter of the lord of Chaj. When she was living in her father's house, a young man, whose face was like jasmine and who was as enticing as musk, had fallen in love with her. He had paid court to her like a slave, following her wherever she went. The king asked her, "Who is this young man foolhardy enough to live in Nushin-Ravan's harem? And who has been looking after him?" She replied, "He is my younger brother, and we're both from the same mother. He dressed like this because he was ashamed before the king; he didn't dare look you in the face. If my brother veiled his face from you, it was out of respect for you, and you shouldn't think it was for any other reason." Nushin-Ravan was astonished at her explanation and at their behavior. He turned angrily to his executioner and said, "These two deserve to be in their graves." The man hurried them away and they were hanged in the king's harem, with their bodies upside down and covered in blood.

The dream interpreter was given a purse of coins, horses, and clothes; the king was amazed at his knowledge, turning his words over in his mind. They wrote his name down as one of the king's advisors, among the priests who give counsel; the heavens looked kindly on Bozorjmehr. Day by day his good fortune increased, and the king delighted in his presence.

Kesra's heart was just, and his heart and mind were ennobled by knowledge; he kept priests at his court, and experts in all branches of knowledge. There were always seventy savants who slept and ate in his palace, and whenever he rested from the labors of administering justice and from his banquets, he asked for some new discourse from one of them, and in this way his heart gained in knowledge. At this time Bozorjmehr was still a young man, eloquent, ingenious, and handsome. He learned from these priests, astrologers and wise men, and soon he surpassed them all.

Bozorjmehr became Kesra Nushin-Ravan's vizier, and much of Ferdowsi's account of Kesra's reign consists of Bozorjmehr's advice on how to rule. This advice, combined with Kesra's own naturally just and careful character, ensured Persian prosperity during his reign. The emperor of China went to war with Iran's neighbors in Soghdia, and he and Kesra, although mutually suspicious of one another, concluded a treaty of friendship. The emperor sent an envoy to Kesra, with a letter suggesting that the Persian king marry his daughter.

Nushin-Ravan Sends Mehran-Setad to See
the Emperor of China's Daughter

King Kesra Nushin-Ravan summoned a scribe, talked at length about
the emperor of China, and then dictated an answer to the emperor's
letter. He began with praise of God, who is victorious and who main-
tains the world, who is our guide to good and evil, who raises
whomever he wishes from misery to the high heavens, while another
man lives in wretchedness because God does not desire his prosperity.
The letter continued: "I am grateful to him for all benefits, and if I do
evil, it is his wrath that I fear: may my soul be divided from my body
if my hope and fear turn away from him. The envoy bearing the
emperor of China's kind message arrived here, and I heard all he had
to say concerning a marriage and the emperor's daughters who live
secluded in his palace. I will be happy to become allied to you, espe-
cially if it is by marrying your veiled daughter. To this end I am send-
ing you a wise ambassador, and when he arrives he can tell you of my
secret thoughts about this alliance. May your soul and body always be
filled with sobriety, may your heart be happy, and your friendship
toward us continue." When the scribe's pen ceased to move and the ink
was dried, he folded the letter and sealed it with musk. Kesra gave the
emperor's envoy a robe of honor, and his escort was astonished by its
quality.

Then he chose a wise high priest whose name was Mehran-Setad,
and as his companions a hundred eloquent and noble Persian horsemen.
To Mehran-Setad he said, "Travel with joy and victory, kindness and
justice; your thoughts and speech must be astute and eloquent, with
wisdom to guide you. First examine his harem, and see that you can
accurately distinguish the women there. Don't let a well made-up face
or splendid clothes, or fine jewelry deceive you; there are many young
women in his private apartments, all of them tall and splendid and
crowned. Someone born from a serving girl is no good to me, even if
her father is the king. Look to see which of them is modest and acts
appropriately, someone whose mother is from the emperor's family, who
is of true royal lineage. If she is as lovely in her body as in her descent,
she will make the world happy and be happy herself."

Mehran-Setad listened to the king and called down blessings on the
throne and crown. He set out on an auspicious day in the month of
Khordad, and when he arrived at the Chinese court he kissed the

ground and paid homage to the emperor, who welcomed him and assigned him splendid living quarters. But the emperor was troubled, and he went to the apartments of his wife, the empress. He told her of what Nushin-Ravan had said and talked to her at length about his wealth and army. He said, "This King Nushin-Ravan is young and intelligent, and fortune smiles on him. It would be a good idea to give him a daughter as a bride; it would increase my standing with him. You and I have a daughter in purdah here who is the crown of all princesses, but I love to see her face and could not bear to be parted from her. I've four other daughters born from servant girls. I'll give him one of them, and that'll save me both from war with him and from gossip." The empress said, "No one in the world's as cunning as you are!"

Having made this decision, the emperor slept until the sun rose above the mountains. Then Mehran-Setad appeared before his throne and handed over Kesra's letter. When the emperor read the letter he laughed with pleasure, both because of the alliance, and because a bride was to be chosen. He gave the Persian envoy the key to his harem and said, "Go and see who is hidden there." Four servants who were in the emperor's confidence accompanied him. The envoy took the key and entered the private apartments, while the servants told him tales of what to expect. They said, "Neither the sun nor the moon nor any wind have ever set eyes on those you will see." The apartments were arranged like a paradise, one that contained the sun and the moon and was filled with luxury. Five young women sat there with crowns on their heads and treasure at their feet,

> All but the great queen's child, whose elegance
> Did not require such gaudy ornaments:
> Her dress was old and plain, her head was bare,
> Crowned only with her coiled and musky hair,
> While her unpowdered and bewitching face
> Shone with a lovely God-created grace:
> She seemed a cypress with the moon above,
> Filling the women's rooms with light and love.

Mehran-Setad knew he had never seen anyone as lovely as she was, and his quick mind saw that the emperor and empress were being far from honest. The young woman covered her eyes with her hands and veil, and this increased Mehran-Setad's anger at their duplicity. He said to the servants, "The king has plenty of crowns, thrones, and bracelets; I choose this one, who has no crown or fine adornments, since she is worthy to be elevated in such a fashion. I undertook the pains of this journey to make a good choice; I didn't come here for Chinese brocade."

The empress said to him, "Old man, you have not said one pleasing word. There are women here who have splendor, beauty, and good sense, who delight the heart and are of marriageable age, tall like cypresses, with faces as lovely as springtime and who know how to serve a king, and you have chosen an immature child—this is not sensible of you!" Mehran-Setad replied, "If the emperor had deceived me, then my king would also say I wasn't sensible. I choose this young woman, who has no ivory throne, no crown or torque or jewelry. If your majesties do not approve, I shall return home as soon as I am permitted to do so."

The emperor considered his words, astonished by his understanding and by his decision. He saw that this old man's mind was clear, and that he was a great personage who was fit to carry out such delicate tasks. The wise ruler sat with his advisors and emptied the court of strangers. He ordered astrologers with Western charts in their hands, together with the great men of the country and all who felt benevolent toward the throne, to search for the will of the heavens. A priest studied the stars as they affected the emperor's alliance with the king and said at last, "Do not trouble your heart about this matter, it can only end auspiciously and will not deliver the world into your enemies' hands. This is the secret of the high heavens and of the favorable stars that turn there; a king who will be an ornament to the throne will be born from this daughter of the emperor and from the king's loins. Princes will pay homage to him, as will the noblemen of China."

The Emperor Sends His Daughter with Mehran-Setad to Nushin-Ravan

When they heard this, the emperor's heart rejoiced and the splendid empress smiled with pleasure. Once their hearts were set at rest, they sat the envoy down before them and told him whatever he needed to know about the empress's daughter. Mehran-Setad accepted her from her father, in the king's name. Servants came joyfully before the king bringing her splendid dowry, which included gold coins, jewels, torques, crowns, turquoise seals, an ivory throne, another throne of Indian aloes wood encrusted with gold and gems, a hundred finely saddled horses, a hundred camels laden with Chinese brocade, forty pieces of golden brocade woven with emeralds, a hundred camels laden with carpets, and three hundred serving girls. The emperor waited until the company had mounted in the Chinese fashion, with banners in their hands, and then he ordered that a throne covered in gold and silver cloth encrusted with gems be placed on an elephant's back. A hundred men lifted it into place, and beside it there was a banner of Chinese brocade so huge that it hid the ground. A golden litter was draped in brocade, and within it was the uncut jewel, the emperor's daughter, while the three hundred beautiful serving girls accompanied her with happiness in their hearts. Fifty servants and forty eunuchs formed an escort, and this was the manner in which the emperor sent his daughter to the Persian king.

When this had been accomplished, a scribe came forward bearing musk, rosewater, and silk, and the emperor dictated a letter of great splendor. He began with praise of the Creator, who maintains the world, who is vigilant and all-seeing, and whose creatures fulfill the destinies he appoints for them. He continued, "The Persian king is like a crown to me, and my alliance with him is not simply for my daughter's sake. I have always heard from those who are wise and noble, and from priests who have insight into such matters, about his glory and greatness, and this is why I have sought to be allied with him. No ruler in all the world is as just as he is; none has his magnanimity, or is as victorious and powerful as he is, none has his glory and might, and his faith in God nourishes his knowledge and understanding. I have sent my child to King Kesra, according to our custom, and have told her to act as his slave, as is fitting when she is in his women's quarters, to imbibe wisdom from his glory, and to learn his court's ceremonies and manners. May good fortune and wisdom guide you, and may greatness and knowledge be your support."

They set a seal of Chinese musk on the letter, which the emperor gave to the envoy and called down blessings on him. Then he gave Mehran-Setad a robe of honor more splendid than any given before by a king to a messenger. He also delighted Mehran-Setad's companions with presents of gold coins and musk. He traveled with his daughter and her wealth, the cavalry and richly caparisoned elephants, as far as the shore of the River

Oxus, and there heartfelt tears fell from his eyes. He waited until they had crossed over the river and gained the further shore. Then, with his heart filled with sorrow at being parted from his daughter, he turned back from the Oxus.

When the good news came from Mehran-Setad, people happily gathered at the court with presents, calling down blessings on the king of Persia and the emperor of China. They decorated the towns and roads of the route, and the road to Amui and Marv was as resplendent as a pheasant's feathers. By the time the travelers reached Gorgan and Bestam, the ground had become invisible beneath the finery and press of people; all the men, women and children of Persia crowded the road where the Chinese idol was to pass. They rained down jewels on her from the houses' upper storeys, and silver coins and saffron were scattered in her way. Bowls of sweet-smelling scents were set out, and the world re-echoed with the sound of drums and trumpets. The horses' manes were soaked in musk and wine, they trod on sugar and silver, and such was the din of flutes and harps and lutes that there was no place where a man could be quiet and sleep.

The princess was brought into the women's apartments, and Kesra looked into the litter. He saw a cypress tree with the full moon above it, crowned by her sweet-smelling hair that fell in cunningly woven braids; its musky ringlets framed the roses of her face, which shone as brightly as the planet Jupiter. King Kesra stared at her and repeatedly said the name of God in his wonder at her beauty. He selected apartments that were worthy of her, and a throne was prepared in her honor.

An Indian Rajah Sends the Game of Chess to Nushin-Ravan

One day, when the king's audience hall was hung with Byzantine brocade, the royal crown suspended above his throne, and the room was thronged with priests and lords of the marches from Balkh, Bamyan, and Karzeban crowned and seated on ivory thrones, the court learned that an envoy from an Indian king was approaching with a caravan of horsemen from Sind, elephants shaded by parasols, and a thousand laden camels. As soon as the king heard this, he sent an escort to welcome the caravan. The envoy entered the court and made his obeisance and called down God's blessings, as is the custom of noble men, and spread many jewels before the king as an offering, as well as ten elephants, earrings, and a parasol decorated in gold, with gems woven into its fabric. Then he unpacked the goods in his train and brought them all before the king. There were great quantities of gold and silver, musk, ambergris, fresh-cut aloes wood, rubies, diamonds, and glittering Indian swords; everything that Qanuj produced was there, and the servants hurried to lay his wealth before the throne. Kesra examined the presents that the Indian rajah had labored to collect, and had them taken to his treasury.

Then the envoy presented a letter written on silk to Nushin-Ravan, from the Indian king, together with a chessboard and its pieces, made with such skill that they were worth a treasury in themselves. The rajah had written: "May you reign for as long as the heavens turn. Set this chessboard and its pieces before your most learned men, to see if they can understand this subtle game, the names of its pieces, and where each one's home is on the board. See whether they can comprehend what the pawns and elephants do, and what the moves of the rook, the knight, the king, and his advisor are. If their intellects can fathom this subtle game, we shall gladly send the tribute and taxes that the king has demanded. But if the famous sages of Iran are all deficient in such knowledge, if their knowledge is not equal to ours, then Iran should no longer demand tribute from us. It is we who should accept tribute from you, since knowledge is the best of all things that confer glory."

Kesra listened carefully to what was said; then they set the board before him, and he looked at the pieces. On one side they were of painted ivory, and on the other of teak. The great king asked about the game, the pieces, and the board. The envoy answered, "Your majesty, the rules are those of war: see if you can work out the moves of the rook and the elephant, and how the pieces are drawn up for battle." The king said, "Give us a week, and on the eighth day we'll be happy to play this game with you." Fine apartments were set aside for the envoy, and all his needs were taken care of.

Priests and learned men came and they pored over the chessboard and its pieces. They tried various solutions and discussed the possibilities with one another, but none of them could work out the game's rules, and, frowning, they gave up the attempt. Bozorjmehr came to the king and saw that he was very disappointed by their remarks. But the vizier knew how to resolve the matter, and he said to Kesra, "Your majesty, I shall take wisdom as my guide and solve the riddle of this subtle game." The king said, "You are the man for this problem: may your soul see its way to a solution. Otherwise the rajah of Qanuj is going to say, 'The king has no one who can fathom such secrets,' and this will be a defeat for our priests, our wise men, and the court."

Bozorjmehr took the chessboard and pieces, and for a day and a night he studied them carefully, moving the pieces to left and right and taking note of their positions. Then he hurried from his apartments to the king and said, "Victorious king, I have studied this board and its pieces, and by the good fortune of your majesty, I now understand the game. Summon the rajah's messenger, and whoever else wishes to see this; but first you must witness it, because the game is exactly like a battle."

Overjoyed by his words, the king said that Bozorjmehr was a man able to solve all difficulties and favored by fortune. He summoned the rajah's envoy and seated him appropriately. Bozorjmehr addressed him, "You are the envoy of a rajah whose face is as splendid as the sun, and may wisdom be your soul's companion. What did your master say about these chess pieces to you?" The envoy replied, "When I left, the rajah said to me, 'Take these pieces of ivory and teak before the throne of the crowned king and tell him to have his priests and wise men examine them; if they can understand this subtle game, and play it correctly and elegantly, then, as far as we're able to, we shall send the purses of gold, the slaves, and the tribute they demand. But if the king and his advisors cannot understand the game, if their souls are not equal to it, then the king has no right to demand tribute from us. If he despairs of understanding the game, he will realize how fine our hearts and souls are, and he will send us his surplus wealth.'"

Bozorjmehr brought out the chessboard and said to the assembled priests and advisors, "You are wise, and your hearts are pure; take note of what he has said and of his master's views." Then the knowledgeable vizier set out a battlefield: the king's place was in the heart of his forces, his horsemen were to his right and left, and his infantry, armed with lances, stood before him. The clever vizier was next to the king, to show the way when battle was joined. As the horsemen attacked from both sides, the warlike elephants were there on the left; infantry went ahead of the horsemen, to watch for ways forward. When Bozorjmehr set out the army's ranks, the whole assembly was astonished. The Indian envoy was dumbfounded and dispirited. This man of magic was bewildered, and he brooded in his heart on what he had seen:

"This man has never been in India, nor
Has he so much as seen the game before—
How did he understand its rules? The earth
Can't show another man of equal worth."

Kesra was so pleased with Bozorjmehr that it was as if the heavens themselves were smiling on him. He praised his vizier at length and ordered that he be given a goblet filled with splendid jewels, a saddled horse, and a purse of gold coins.

Bozorjmehr Invents the Game of Nard, Which Nushin-Ravan Sends to India

Bozorjmehr went to his own home, where he shut himself away with a board and a pair of compasses. Carefully considering the game of chess, which the Indians had sent, he cudgeled his brains until he conceived of the game of nard. He had two dice made of ivory, with designs on them the color of teak. He made a board similar to a chessboard and set the combatants out on either side. The two armies were distributed in eight stations, where the pieces were drawn up ready to take the opposing city. The battlefield was divided into four sections, and there were two noble and magnanimous kings, equal in their forces and obliged not to harm one another. At their command the armies set off from each side, ready for war. If two pieces came on a solitary piece, that piece would be lost and its side would suffer a setback. The two kings were in the thick of the fighting, each overtaking the other in turn, and sometimes the battle was in the mountains, sometimes in the plains, and so the two kings and armies advanced until one was defeated. When he took his game to the king and explained it to him in detail, Kesra was astonished. He thought long and hard about the game and then said, "Your soul is clear and bright; may your good fortune remain young and vigorous!"

He ordered that two thousand camel drivers bring their animals to the court gates, and there they were loaded with goods from Byzantium, China, Central Asia, Makran, and Persia. When they were ready to set off, the king summoned the rajah's envoy, and talked with him at length about the nature of knowledge. He wrote a letter filled with wisdom and splendor, which began with praise of God, his refuge from evil. It went on, "To the king of India, from the Lake of Qanuj to Sind: your wise envoy, with his elephants and parasols, arrived at our court and delivered your message and the game of chess to us. We asked for time, and one of our learned men considered the matter deeply, until he discovered the game's rules. This wise man has now come to Qanuj, and to your majesty, bringing with him two thousand camels laden with royal gifts. We send the game of nard as an exchange for chess, and now we shall see which is the finer game. You have many pure-souled Brahmins with you; let us see if they can understand this game. Send the goods that my messenger has taken such pains to bring to you to your treasury. If the rajah of Qanuj and his advisors cannot fathom our game, he must send us an equivalent number of camel-loads of goods: this is the agreement between us."

The shining sun rose in the sky, and Bozorjmehr set off from the court. As he approached the rajah's kingdom with his gifts, the letter, and the game of nard, Brahmins gladly came to guide him. His head was filled with thoughts of the coming contest. When he was admitted into the rajah's presence, and saw his crown and the splendor of his court, he praised him at length in Pahlavi, then handed over the king's letter. He talked in detail about his journey, the game of chess, and the trouble he had taken to understand it; then he conveyed the greetings of the King of Kings, and the rajah's face opened like a blossoming flower. Next he produced the game of nard, pointing out the dice and its pieces, and put forward his king's proposal; lastly he said that when the king's letter had been read, he was sure that the rajah would not act unjustly. The rajah's face turned pale at this talk of chess and nard.

The Indian Sages Are Unable to Understand the Game of Nard

A nobleman conducted Bozorjmehr to suitable quarters, a hall was prepared for feasting, and wine and musicians were called for. The rajah asked for seven days' grace, and the country's sages gathered together to examine the game of nard. For a week the most intelligent of their men, young and old, competed against one another in trying to work out how the game of nard was played. On the eighth day their chief priest said to the rajah, "No one can make head or tail of this game; wisdom will have to help our souls if we're to construct a game from these pieces."

On the ninth day Bozorjmehr came forward with a frown on his face and hope in his heart. He said, "Kesra did not tell me to stay here for a long time; I must not disappoint my king." The Indian priests were discouraged by this; frowning in sorrow, they confessed their inability to fathom the game. Bozorjmehr sat himself down and the sages watched him intently as he set out the game and taught them how the pieces moved, which was the commander, how the war was fought, how the troops were drawn up, and how the king gave his orders. The rajah and his country's sages were astounded. All of them acclaimed Bozorjmehr, and called him a priest of the pure faith. The rajah questioned him about every branch of knowledge, and he answered each question appropriately. The raja's sages and advisors cried out, "This is truly an eloquent and wise man, quite apart from the business of chess and nard!"

They brought two thousand camels and loaded them with Qanuj's treasures; there were aloes wood and ambergris, camphor and gold, robes and cloth woven with jewels. All this was sent, together with a year's tribute, from the rajah's court to the Persian king's. Then the rajah asked for a crown to be brought from his treasury, together with a robe made of cloth of gold from head to foot, and these he presented to Bozorjmehr, praising him as he did so. He also gave many gifts to Bozorjmehr's companions. The two thousand camels laden with tribute and presents made a caravan the like of which no man had ever led before, and as Bozorjmehr traveled home from Qanuj he lifted his head up to the heavens with pride. He was happy to be carrying the rajah's letter, written on silk in Devanagari script, which said, "The rajah and his nobles bear witness—and not out of fear, but as their true opinion—that no one has ever seen a king like Nushin-Ravan, or heard from learned priests of one like him; and there is no one more knowledgeable than his vizier, whose wisdom is guarded by the heavens. We have sent a year's tribute in advance, and if more is required we shall send that too; we have sent all that was agreed according to our wager."

When the king learned that his wise advisor had been successful and was on his way home, he was overjoyed and gave orders that the noblemen in the city and army be informed, so that they could go together to welcome him. Bozorjmehr made a triumphal entry into the city, like a victorious prince, and when he approached the throne, the king heartily congratulated him, embracing him and questioning him about the rajah and the difficulties he'd encountered along the way. Bozorjmehr told the king about his journey and his good fortune, and then laid the rajah's letter before the throne. The scribe Yazdegerd was summoned, and when he read the rajah's letter the whole company was astonished at Bozorjmehr's knowledge and good fortune. Kesra said, "Thanks be to God for my wisdom, and for my knowledge of what is good; kings bow as slaves before my crown and throne, and their hearts and souls are filled with love for me."

Borzui Brings the Book of Kalileh and Demneh from India

The King of Kings, Nushin-Ravan—may his name live forever—always kept learned men and priests at his court, and they were an adornment to his reign. There were eloquent doctors, scholars, nobles, and men skilled in various professions. One such was the doctor Borzui, who was advanced in his skill and an eloquent speaker. He had some expertise in every branch of knowledge and was famous throughout the world for this. One day, during a royal audience, he came before the king and said, "Your majesty, you love knowledge, and your inquiring mind delights in learning things. Today my spirit was alert and at ease, and I read in an Indian book that a plant grows in the mountains there that looks like silk from Byzantium. If someone gathers this plant and prepares it in the correct way and then sprinkles it on the dead, they will begin to talk. Now with the king's permission, I shall make this difficult journey; I shall employ all my knowledge to see if I can find this wonder. If a corpse can live again, this is only to be expected now that Nushin-Ravan rules the world."

The king responded, "This is not possible, but we should inquire into it nevertheless. Take a letter from me to the ruler of India, and study the nature of these Indian idol-worshippers. Find a companion for this search, and ask good fortune to help you too; these mysterious words you've read perhaps point to some new wonder in the world. Take all your requests to the Indian king; you will certainly need him to provide you with a guide." Then Nushin-Ravan threw open the gates to his treasury and provided Borzui with three hundred camels laden with royal goods—gold coins, brocades, silks, seals, crowns, musk, and ambergris. Borzui set off and arrived at the Indian court, where he handed over his king's letter and spread the goods he had brought before the rajah. After reading the king's letter, the rajah said, "Kesra has no need to send me presents in this way; my people and my realm are themselves presents he has bestowed on me. Given his just rule and *farr,* his glory and good fortune, it would be no surprise if the world-ruler could resurrect the dead. The Brahmins who live in the mountains will help you carry out your plan. My vizier, my wealth, my treasurer, and all that's good and evil in India, are at your disposal; I measure my greatness by how I am able to aid you."

They provided him with suitable apartments close to the rajah, as well as with a cook, food, fine clothes, and carpets. He spent that night with the wise men of Qanuj, discussing his plans. When day broke over the mountains and the world-illuminating torch appeared, the rajah summoned his learned doctors, and those who could offer advice. Borzui set off for the mountains on foot, with a knowledgeable guide, and the doctors accompanied him. He gathered plants that were dry, fresh, withered, or flourishing, and he made various concoctions from them; but when he sprinkled these on the dead not a single corpse came to life, and it was clear that the mixtures were powerless. Though he walked over the whole mountain, his efforts were fruitless, and he knew that the dead could be revived only by that king who is eternal and rules all things. He was tormented by the pains of his journey, by the shame he would feel before his king and the courtiers, by thoughts of the wealth that had been given to the rajah, and by the foolish things he had said. He was sick at heart when he remembered the book he had read and said to himself, "Why did that foolish, senseless man write such ridiculous things, which could only lead to trouble and reproaches?"

He turned to the learned men who had accompanied him and said, "You are experienced, well-regarded men: do you know of anyone more knowledgeable than yourselves, who might outdo you in wisdom?" They all agreed on their answer: "There is an old sage, who surpasses us in both years and wisdom, and who is more knowledgeable than every master." Borzui replied, "You are noble and magnanimous men, and I ask you to take yet more trouble and to guide me to this sage. It may be that this eloquent and wise old man can help me in my search."

As they led him to this man Borzui's heart was preoccupied with worries, his mind with what he would say. When he met him, he eloquently described his troubles that had begun with the book he had read and with the words he had heard from various savants. The old man spoke to him about the different kinds of knowledge, and then said,

"When I was young I also read the book
You mention, and like you began to look
For this same plant; my time was vainly spent,
Until I saw that something else was meant.
Let me explain: the plant that you have tried
So hard to find is speech, the mountainside
Is knowledge, and the corpse is any man
Who's ignorant, since only knowledge can
Give life to us; if there's no knowledge there
You won't find life within us anywhere.
The plant you seek's a book called Kalileh,
Its language is the guide to wisdom's way—
You'll find this book, if you search carefully,
Locked away in the rajah's treasury."

Borzui was overjoyed when he heard these words, and it seemed to
him that all his troubles disappeared like the wind that blows and is
gone. He called down blessings on the sage and hurried to the court,
traveling as fast as fire. When he reached the rajah he bowed down
before him and said, "May you live for as long as the world remains.
Great king, there is a book called in the Indian tongue *Kalileh;* it's kept
under seal, in your treasury, in the archives there, and it is a guide to
wisdom. If it will cause you no distress, I ask that you order your treas-
urer to give this book to me."

The king's soul was upset at this request, and for a while he pon-
dered what to do. Then he said to Borzui, "No one has ever asked me
for this, but if King Nushin-Ravan wanted my body or my soul, or
one of my nobles or subjects, I could not withhold any of them from
him. But read the book here, from beginning to end, so that those who
hate me cannot say that I allowed it to be copied." Borzui replied, "I
want no more than you wish to grant me, your majesty." The king's
treasurer brought the book of *Kalileh and Demneh,* and guided Borzui
through it. Throughout the day he committed to memory whatever he
read, and went over it again at night until the dawn broke. He was
delighted by the book, and he washed his soul in its wisdom. He
secretly wrote the book out in Persian, and this is how it was sent to
Nushin-Ravan. As soon as Nushin-Ravan's reply came saying, "The

ocean of knowledge has reached us," Borzui went to the rajah and asked for permission to return home.

The rajah made much of him and gave him an Indian robe of honor, two costly bracelets and two sets of earrings, a torque set with royal gems, an Indian turban, and an Indian sword made of iron that glittered like silk. Borzui left Qanuj having learned a great deal and in high spirits; when he arrived home he made his obeisance before the king, told him what he had seen and heard at the rajah's court, and explained that the plant he had sought had been knowledge. The king said to him, "You have done well, and the book called *Kalileh* has given my soul new life. Take the keys from my treasurer, and choose whatever you wish." Wise Borzui went to the treasury, but he gave the treasurer little enough to do. There were gold and jewels to right and left, but he wanted no more than a suit of royal clothes. He clothed himself in fine fabrics and quickly made his way back to Kesra's court. As he bowed before the throne the king said to him, "You have been through so much, so why did you leave my treasury without taking either money or jewels? A man who has endured a great deal deserves a great deal." Borzui replied, "A man who wears his king's clothes has found the way to good fortune and the throne of greatness. And then unworthy men will see these clothes, and their evil hearts will be darkened, while our friends' faces will rejoice in our good fortune. I have one request of the king, and this is so that I shall be remembered in the world: when Bozorjmehr writes out this book, may he recall the trouble that Borzui took to obtain it. If the victorious king so commands, may he start the book with a mention of me, so that after I die learned men will not forget the difficulties I went through." The king said, "This is a noble desire, one that is fitting for a man with a free spirit. Your words exceed your station, but they are justified by the pains you have taken." Then he said to Bozorjmehr, "This request should not be denied," and when the scribe had cut his pen and was ready to write, he began his account with mention of Borzui.

This copy was a royal one, and the book existed only in Pahlavi script at that time. It was kept with care in the king's treasury, so that no one unworthy could look at it. It was read in Pahlavi until men spoke Arabic, then the caliph Mamun renewed the book, so that its sun could shine on other men. He had the heart of a learned priest and the

mind of the Kayanid kings, and he was skilled in all kinds of knowl-
edge. *Kalileh* was translated into Arabic, in the form in which you now
hear it recited. It remained in Arabic until the time of King Nasr; his
vizier and librarian was Abul Fazl, and he gave orders that the book be
translated into Persian and Dari, and so the matter was settled. Then
Nasr was guided by wisdom and desired that there might remain some
memorial to himself in the world. He had a man recite the whole
book to Rudaki, who strung its rich pearls, turning prose into verse.
For a man who is literate, this is an added adornment to the tales, and
for the ignorant it is a blessing: verse satisfies both the soul and the
mind.

Nushin-Ravan Is Angry with Bozorjmehr and Has Him Imprisoned

Now hear what happened to Bozorjmehr, who was raised from the
earth to the heavens, and brought down to base earth again by the
same man who had raised him up.

One day Kesra rode out from Ctesiphon to hunt horned sheep and
deer on the plain. The flock of sheep dispersed, leaving Kesra behind,
and he came on a grassy spot shaded by trees. Bozorjmehr was with him,
keeping him company out of affection and in order to serve him. The
king dismounted, intending to rest; none of his servants were nearby, but
the one kind face that was there was enough. He stretched out and
turned from side to side on the grass; then he laid his head down, with
Bozorjmehr watching from a little way off. The king always wore an
armband encrusted with jewels, and as he lay sleeping his arm was
uncovered. A black bird swooped down from the clouds, perched beside
the sleeping king, and saw the jewels on his naked arm. The bird saw no
one else there; the men in the king's entourage were off hunting by
themselves, and the sleeping king seemed to be alone with no one
nearby to advise him. Seeing the armband, the bird pecked open the
jewels' settings, and as the precious pearls and topazes fell out, he ate
them one by one. Then he flew up and disappeared from sight.

Bozorjmehr's heart was filled with foreboding at what the heavens
had brought. He knew that fate brings prosperity and hardship, and
that now a time of hardship had come. When the king woke and saw
Bozorjmehr biting his lip, he thought that this man whom he had
treated so well had acted disrespectfully toward him, and said, "You

dog, who told you a man's nature could be hidden? I'm not some celestial being like Hormozd or Bahman; my body is made of earth, air, and fire." But although the king tired out his tongue reproaching Bozorjmehr, he received no answer from him but sighs. Bozorjmehr seemed to shrivel away before his king and the turning heavens, because he had seen the signs of his downfall, and in his fear the wise counselor remained silent. The soldiers in the king's entourage were now all around the meadow where their master had rested. The king mounted his horse and looked at no one on the way back to his palace; he bit his lip as he rode, and when he dismounted he muttered to himself in anger. He ordered his men to harden their hearts against the vizier and to confine him to his palace.

Bozorjmehr sat in his palace, deprived of the king's favor. One of his relatives, a young, energetic man who waited on King Nushin-Ravan, lived there with him. This man followed Nushin-Ravan about his palace, and was quite forward in his conversations with the king. One day Bozorjmehr asked him how he served the king, and told him he should look for ways to improve his skills. The servant replied, "You are our chief priest, so let me tell you what happened today. After he finished eating I went forward and poured water on his hands, and he found the floor was wet from my ewer. He looked at me with such fury that I said to myself, 'I'll never eat or sleep again!' When the king of the world became angry with me like that, my hand holding the ewer went weak and I dropped it." Bozorjmehr said to him, "Go and get some water, and pour it as you did over the king's hands." The young man brought warm water and bit by bit poured it over the hands of the vizier, who said, "Next time, when you pour the water for him to wash his hands, try to do it smoothly, with no violent movements, and when the king raises his hands to touch his lips with perfume, stop pouring."

The next day, when King Nushin-Ravan was eating, the young man stood there filled with apprehension until he once again had to bring the ewer and basin for the king to wash his hands. He performed his task just as the knowledgeable vizier had told him, pouring the water not too slowly and not too quickly. The king said to him, "Your service has improved: who taught you how to do this?" He answered, "Bozorjmehr taught me how to do this properly, in the way the king has just seen." The king said, "Go to that clever man and ask him, 'What evil nature was it, what despicable ambition, made you choose

to sink down from the splendid and honorable rank you held?'"
Hearing the king's words, the young steward ran to his uncle with grief
in his heart. He told him what the king had said, and Bozorjmehr qui-
etly answered him: "In ways that can be seen, and in ways that cannot
be seen, my state is finer than the king's." The servant went back to the
king and told him what Bozorjmehr had said. Nushin-Ravan started up
in fury and ordered that Bozorjmehr be kept chained in a dark pit, and
then told the servant to ask this foolish man how his days passed when
he was imprisoned in this way. With his face covered in tears the young
man asked Bozorjmehr the king's question, and the good man's answer
was, "My days pass by more easily than the king's do." The messenger
ran to the king like the wind and told him what Bozorjmehr's answer
was. The king raged like a leopard. He drove all love for Bozorjmehr
from his heart and ordered that he be imprisoned in a metal chest with
spikes on the inside and with his head held by iron bands. He could not
rest by day or stretch out to sleep at night; his body was in constant pain
and his heart was in torment.

After four days the king of the world said to his servant, "Go to that
wise man once more; be quick taking my message and bringing his
answer. Ask him how he finds his body, now that its shirt is made of
sharp spikes." But when the servant gave him the obstinate king's mes-
sage, Bozorjmehr said to the young man, "My days are better than
Nushin-Ravan's days." Nushin-Ravans' face turned pale when he
heard this reply; he chose a man in the palace who was honest and
would understand what Bozorjmehr meant by his words. With him he
sent an executioner, and said, "Go, and say to this malignant man that
either he returns me a proper answer, not some foolishness about the
spike-lined chest where he's chained being better than the king's
throne, or this executioner will use his sword to show him how the
Day of Judgment will arrive."

The man came to Bozorjmehr, and his heart was moved to pity by
the sage's plight; he repeated the king's words for Bozorjmehr who
said,

> "Whether our lot is vile or glorious
> Fortune has never shown her face to us.
> But, king or commoner, we know that we
> Must leave this earth soon for eternity.

No man has an abiding foothold here
And, good or bad, our lives will disappear:
Then kings know fear, and cling to life, and grieve—
But wretchedness is never hard to leave."

The messenger and the executioner returned to their proud sovereign and told him what they had heard. The king's heart was troubled by this answer, and he gave orders that Bozorjmehr be taken from his prison to his palace again.

And so the heavens turned for a while; Bozorjmehr's face became wrinkled, his wealth could not assuage his grief, and he wasted away in sorrow.

The Emperor of Byzantium Sends a Sealed Casket, and When Bozorjmehr Guesses What Is Inside It He Is Released

At this time, the emperor of Byzantium sent an envoy to the king, with a letter and gifts and a locked strongbox. The envoy said, "The message from my master is as follows: 'The king has many wise priests at his court; if, without opening it, they can say what is inside this locked box, we shall send tribute and presents beside, according to our custom. But if your clever priests cannot penetrate this mystery, the king should not demand any more tribute from us, and neither should he send armies into our realm. Answer as seems fitting to you.'"

The world's king said to the envoy, "Even this is not hidden from God; with his grace I shall solve the problem, and I have clear-thinking advisors to help me. Spend a week as our guest, and give yourself freely to wine and pleasure." The king was bewildered as to what to do. He summoned his courtiers and wise men, and each of them looked at the keyless casket from every angle, but all of them had to confess their ignorance of what was inside it. The king became worried when none of the group had had any success. He thought, "This secret of the heavens is a problem for Bozorjmehr." But, embarrassed by the suffering his wise counselor had been through, he frowned and his face turned pale. His painful thoughts prompted him to have a suit of clothes brought from the treasury, and a fine horse with a royal saddle. He sent these to Bozorjmehr with a message: "I cannot deny the suffering you have endured; it was the high heavens that had me hurt you in this way. Your talk infuriated me, and you put your own body at risk. Now something has happened that is troubling my heart. The emperor of Byzantium has sent me one of their priests, a famous man in his own land, who has a golden casket with him that's completely closed, with a lock, and a seal of musk. The emperor says that our counselors should explain what is hidden inside the casket. I thought that this secret is something the soul of Bozorjmehr could understand."

When Bozorjmehr heard these words, his heart was filled with his old sufferings. He left the place where he had been confined, washed his head and body, and prayed before God who rules the world. He was an innocent man and his king was quick to anger, and Bozorjmehr was afraid that he would be harmed by the king again. It was still dark night when the king's message reached him and day had not yet dawned. As the sun showed his crown and night veiled her face, Bozorjmehr peered up toward the stars, and when the shining sun rose in the sky he washed the eyes of his heart with the water of wisdom. He sought out a wise man on whom he could rely and said to him, "My affairs are in a wretched state because the sufferings I have been through have darkened my eyes. Watch for who meets us on the road, and ask them about their lives, but don't inquire as to their names."

Bozorjmehr set out from his house, and there was a beautiful woman hurrying toward him. His companion described everything he couldn't see, and Bozorjmehr said, "Find out if this lovely woman has a husband." When she was asked, the woman answered, "I have a husband, and a child too, at home," and Bozorjmehr smiled at her words as he rode forward on his high-stepping horse. Then another woman appeared, and Bozorjmehr's guide asked her, "Do you have a husband and child, or do your arms embrace nothing but the wind?" She said, "I have a husband, but no child; and now that you have heard my answer, get out of my way." And at that moment a third woman appeared and she too was questioned: "You have a lovely face, and a proud, provocative walk; who keeps you company?" "I've never," she replied, "had a husband, and I don't want to show my face to anyone." Now when Bozorjmehr heard these answers, he turned them over in his mind.

His face was melancholy as he hurried forward. When he arrived, he was taken to the king, who commanded him to approach the throne. And then the king's heart was filled with sorrow, and he sighed deeply, because he realized that his wise advisor could no longer see.

The king apologized at length for his anger against this innocent man, and then talked about Byzantium and its emperor and the locked casket. Bozorjmehr said to the world's king, "May you shine for as long as the heavenly bodies shine. We should call an assembly of wise men and priests, as well as the envoy from Byzantium and have the casket placed before the king and his courtiers. Then by the power of God who gave us thought and has made my soul delight in truth, I shall say what is inside the casket, without touching either the box itself or its lock. Even if my eyes are now dark, my heart is bright, and my soul is armored with knowledge."

The king was happy to hear his words, and his heart revived like a flower in the springtime. He drew himself up as his worries fell away, and he had the envoy and his casket summoned, together with his priests, advisors, and sages, whom he seated before Bozorjmehr. The he addressed the envoy: "Give us your message, and make your demands." The envoy repeated what his emperor had said: "A victorious king should have wisdom, knowledge, and a good reputation. You have the *farr* and strength of a world-conqueror, greatness, knowledge, and might, priests who seek out the truth, and heroes who support you here at your court or take your part in the world at large. Let your clever courtiers see this locked and sealed casket, and let them in their wisdom say clearly what is hidden there. Then we shall send you tribute and taxes, since my country is wealthy enough to do this; but if they cannot do this, then they should no longer ask us for tribute."

Bozorjmehr then invoked God's blessing and said, "May the world's king always be happy, understanding, fortunate, and generous! I thank the Lord of the Sun and Moon, who shows our souls the way to wisdom, who alone knows what is open and what is secret. He has no need of knowledge, but knowledge is my desire. There are three shining pearls inside the casket, within a number of coverings; one is pierced, one is half pierced, and iron has never touched the third." When the envoy heard this he brought the key, while Nushin-Ravan watched. There was a box inside the casket, and inside this there were layers of silk, in which three pearls were hidden, just as the Persian sage had said. The first of them was pierced, the second half pierced, and the last untouched. All the priests who were present cried their congratulations, and showered Bozorjmehr with jewels. The king's face cleared, and as a reward he filled Bozorjmehr's mouth with splendid pearls. His heart was tormented by the thought of what he had done before; he writhed within and frowned to think how he had treated this man who had shown him such love and loyalty.

When Bozorjmehr saw that the king's soul was suffering, he spoke of those things from the past that he had kept hidden—the armband and the black bird, his anxiety for the jewels, and the king's sleep. Then he said to the king, "This was fated to happen, and there is no point in suffering regret because of it; the heavens bring us good and evil, whether to the king, or to his priests, or to Bozorjmehr. The signs of the seeds that God has sowed in the stars are written on our foreheads. May Nushin-Ravan's soul rejoice and always be free from pain and sorrow. However glorious a king might be, it is his vizier's job to be an ornament to his court. The king's business is hunting and warfare, wine and rejoicing, generosity, justice, and feasting; he knows how his predecessors reigned and follows their example. It is the vizier who must accumulate wealth, maintain the army, combat gossip, and hear suppliants for justice; it is his heart and soul that are troubled by worries about the administration and treasury."

As Kesra Nushin-Ravan's life drew to a close he nominated his son Hormozd as his successor and wrote a document to him setting out his advice and final wishes.

He began by invoking God and continued, "This is the advice of the son of Qobad. Understand, my son, that this world is faithless and filled with sorrow, hardship, pain, and adversity. And whenever you are happy here and your heart is free of sorrow, and you rejoice in your life, remember that you must leave this fleeting world. When thoughts of my departure came to me in the bright days and the long nights, I searched to see who would be worthy of the crown. I have six wise

sons, all of them are generous and just, and they delight my heart. I
chose you because you are the oldest, and you have wisdom and will be
an adornment to the crown. Qobad was eighty when he made me his
successor; I am now seventy-four, and I name you as the world's king.
In doing this I seek only rest and the public good, in the hope that my
soul will be blessed. I hope too that God grants you nothing but hap-
piness and prosperity. If you make men secure by your justice, you will
also ensure your own security, and heaven will be your reward: great is
the man who sows the seeds of righteousness.

"See that you are always patient, since it is not becoming for a king
to rush into decisions. A king who is alert and seeks for instruction
keeps his good reputation forever. Have no dealings with lies, because
if you do, your luck will wither away, and keep your heart and mind far
from haste because haste sends wisdom to sleep. Do good and strive for
the good, and in all things, good and evil, attend to the words of the
wise. Do not let evil come near you, for it will certainly have its effect
on you; dress appropriately, eat appropriately, and pay attention to your
father's advice. You come from God; see that you turn to him if you
would have him as your guide. If your justice makes the world prosper,
your throne will be secure and your subjects will be happy. If men do
well, reward them so that they forget the pains they took. Keep the wise
happy and close by, and make the world dark for those who are malev-
olent. Consult with the wise on every subject, and do not complain
about the difficulties that kingship imposes on you. If the wise can
always reach you, you will be able to keep your crown and throne.

"Do not let your subjects live in wretchedness, and see that the
country's nobles benefit from your justice. Do not look kindly on
those of low character, and entrust no task to an unjust man. Incline
your ears and heart to the poor, and take their sorrows on yourself; in
this way you will sow seeds of righteousness in your orchard, and your
enemies will become your friends. When a powerful man acts justly
and from the heart, the world is happy in his reign, and he too is made
happy. Do not withhold your wealth from the deserving, and be gen-
erous to the virtuous. If you follow my advice your crown will keep
its eminence. May he who bestows all benefits look kindly on you,
and may your good deeds be a refuge for you. Do not forget my
words, even though you can no longer see me. May your mind remain
fresh and strong, your heart happy, your body pure and safe from all

malevolence. May wisdom always guard you, and may your mind be filled with good thoughts.

"When I have left this great world, build me a tomb like a palace, in a place where few men go, and so high that the vultures cannot fly over it. Its entrance must be high in the vault, as high as ten lariats would reach, and over it must be written that this is my court, together with an account of my greatness, my wealth, and my armies. See that the chamber is spread with carpets and cushions, preserve my body with camphor, and sprinkle musk on my head for a crown. Bring five unused brocades of cloth of gold from my treasury, and wrap me in them according to the custom of the Kayanids and our ancestors. Construct an ivory couch and place it there, and over it suspend my crown. Then to its right and left set out all my gold dishes, goblets, and jewels: twenty goblets are to be filled with rosewater, wine and saffron, and two hundred with musk, camphor, and ambergris. Do not exceed or fall short of what I order you. The blood must be drawn off from the trunk of my body, so that it dries, and then it must be filled with camphor and musk. Then close the door to the chamber, since no one must see the king. If the tomb is built in this manner, no one will be able to find his way to me.

"Let my children and family, and all those who will grieve for my death, abstain from feasts and festivals for two months, since this is the custom when a king dies. And it would be right if all who are noble and benevolent would weep for the death of their king. See that you do not disobey the commands of Hormozd, or so much as draw breath without his knowledge."

Everyone wept when they heard of this document. Kesra Nushin-Ravan lived for one more year after he had written it, and when he died these words of his were his memorial; see that you preserve his memory. Now I shall tell of the crown of Hormozd, and place him on his throne.

THE REIGN OF HORMOZD

As Hormozd established his power and was finally able to reign as he wished, his evil nature became apparent and he strayed from the paths of righteousness. One by one, he destroyed his father's confidants and advisors, men who had lived peacefully and with no fear of danger. There were three in particular who had been scholars at Nushin-Ravan's court—one old man and two younger men. The first was Izad-Goshasp; the second, the wise Bozorjmehr, a man blessed with the divine *farr;* and the third Mahazar, also wise and of a serene and cheerful character. These three had served Nushin-Ravan's throne as courtiers and viziers, but Hormozd feared that one day they would feel no gratitude toward him, and he was determined to bring each of them down into the dust.

He had Izad-Goshasp thrown into prison for no reason. The chief priest at that time—a man called Zardhesht—was filled with anxiety for Izad-Goshasp's fate. It was as if an arrow had wounded his heart, and this good and noble priest became pale with worry. After a day in which Izad-Goshasp had had neither a servant, food, clothing, or any companion, he sent a message to the chief priest: "You have always been as dear to me as my own marrow and skin; I am now friendless in the king's prison, and no one visits me. I'm hungry and my aching stomach longs for nourishment. Send me some food, some antidote to the pains that gnaw at me." The priest's heart was moved to sympathy for his friend's situation, but he sent a cautious reply, "Despite your chains, be thankful you have not been physically harmed yet." He grieved inwardly and pondered what to do. He sent some food to the prison, but his heart trembled with apprehension at what he was doing, and he said to himself, "If that unchivalrous and luckless ruler finds out that his priest has sent something to the prison, my life won't be worth a copper coin.

The king will find some way to harm me, and his face will turn pale
with anger against me." But his heart was wrung for Izad-Goshasp's suf-
ferings, and his face was sallow with grief. He ordered his cook to take
food to the prison, and then he mounted his Arab horse and rode there
himself. The two men embraced, and their eyelashes were as wet as the

clouds in spring; they talked at length about the king's evil disposition.
A table was set before Izad-Goshasp, who took the sacred barsom in his
hand and murmured his prayers while Zardhesht listened. He talked of
his wealth and his palace, and then said,

> "Now go directly to Hormozd and say
> On my behalf, 'Don't turn your head away
> But think of all that I have undergone,
> Protecting you as if you were my son:

Is my reward to be imprisoned here,
To live in chains, consumed with grief and fear?
My heart is innocent and will display
The wrongs it has endured on Judgment Day.'"

As the priest was returning home, one of the king's spies ran and told Hormozd all he had heard, and the king decided on an evil course. He hardened his heart against Izad-Goshasp, and sent someone to the prison and had him killed. He continued to act toward Zardhesht as if nothing had happened, but he had the priest's words repeated to him at length and began to consider how to kill him.

He ordered his cook to prepare a dish that had been secretly poisoned. When the priest came to court for the royal audience, the king said to him, "Don't leave us today; I have found a new cook." The priest sat, and a table was set before him, and his face turned pale. He knew that the table signified his end, and he was not mistaken in this. The cooks brought in the dishes and the king ate some of everything. Then the poisoned dish was brought in, and the priest looked at it and knew in his heart that what was being offered to him as nourishment was poison. Hormozd watched and said nothing: he stretched out his hand to the poisoned dish, in the way kings do when they want to bestow a favor on one of their subjects. He took some brains from the dish and said to the priest, "What a fine brain you have. I've reserved this tender morsel just for you. Open your mouth and eat it; it will nourish you well." The priest replied, "By your soul and mind—and may you reign forever—do not order me to eat this morsel. I am full; don't urge me to eat more." Hormozd said, "By the sun and the moon, by your king's pure soul, take this food from my fingers; do not break my heart by denying me." The priest replied, "The king orders me and I have no choice."

He ate the morsel and, tormented by pain, rode quickly to his own house. He told no one of the poison he had eaten, but lay down on a mattress, groaning in agony. He ordered that antidotes for poison be brought, from his own treasury or from the town, but when he ate them they had no effect, and he complained bitterly to God about Hormozd. The king sent one of his confidants to watch the priest and see whether the poison had taken effect or his plan had failed. The priest saw the envoy, and tears coursed down his cheeks as he spoke: "Tell Hormozd that I say this to him: 'Your fortunes will decline, and you and I shall both go before our heavenly judge. From now on you will not be safe from harm, because God's justice will find you out. You are a malevolent man, and I bid you farewell; evil will come to you from the evil you have done.'" The envoy wept to hear these words and reported them to the king. Hormozd regretted what he had done, and he brooded on the truth of the priest's words. He sighed deeply, but could see no way to avoid the pains the priest had spoken of. Then the priest died, and the wise men of the country wept bitterly for him. This is the way of the world, which is full of pain and sorrow. Why strive for a crown, or glory in wealth? For the moments of pleasure pass, and time counts our every breath.

Hormozd Kills Sima-Borzin and Bahram Azar-Mahan

The sad incident of the chief priest put the whole country into a turmoil of distress. This bloodthirsty king, who was unworthy to sit on the throne, gave no thought to the evils that were to come. He prepared to shed more blood and decided to use Bahram Azar-Mahan for this purpose. At dead of night he summoned him, had him kneel before him, and said, "If you want to be safe and never suffer because of my anger or irritation, when the sun rises tomorrow and makes the mountaintops glisten like armor, come with the nobles of Iran and stand before my throne. I will question you about Sima-Borzin; make your heart pliant to my wishes when you answer. I will say, 'Who is this friend of yours? Is he evil, or is he a God-fearing man?' And you will say, 'He is evil, malevolent, the spawn of Ahriman.' After that you can ask me for whatever you desire—slaves, a throne, a seal of authority, a crown." Bahram replied, "I shall say that he is a hundred times worse than you have said." And in this way Hormozd sought for some excuse to ruin Sima-Borzin, even though he was a nobleman and had been a favorite of Hormozd's illustrious father.

When dawn's ivory veil appeared, and the sun rose in the sign of the Twins, the king sat on his ivory throne, above which was suspended his precious crown. The nobility of Iran presented themselves at court and when the chancellor drew back the curtain they went in together to the king, with Bahram Azar-Mahan and Sima-Borzin among them. One by one they sat according to their rank, and a number of them stood before the king. Hormozd said to Bahram Azar-Mahan, "This Sima-Borzin, who is here at this audience, is he worthy of his wealth or is he

an extortionate man? Someone with an evil character does not deserve
to be wealthy." Bahram Azar-Mahan knew what the king's question
meant, he knew it root and branch. He understood that Sima-Borzin
was already a man to be mourned, and that he would receive nothing
but a tomb, without so much as a shroud, from the king. He answered,
"Your majesty, think nothing of Sima-Borzin. He is the cause of Iran's
ruin, and would that his body had neither marrow nor skin to it. His
talk is all slander, which he uses to stir up quarrels."

When Sima-Borzin heard these words he said to him, "We are old
friends—don't vilify me in this way; don't make common cause with
demons like this. What have you seen in me, either in word or deed,
since we've been friends, which is the work of Ahriman?" Bahram
Azar-Mahan answered him, "You will be the first to harvest the seeds
you have sown in the world, and this fire you lit will give you back
nothing but black smoke. When Kesra summoned you and me to sit
before his throne with the priest Bozorjmehr and that noble courtier
Izad-Goshasp, he asked us who was worthy of the crown, who had the
divine *farr*, whether his older or younger son was more worthy of the
crown, and to which of them he should give it. We all stood and
answered him together, saying, 'This prince who was born of a Turk
is not worthy of the throne, and no one wants him as king. He is
descended from the emperor of China and has an evil nature, and in
his face and stature he looks like his mother.' But you said that
Hormozd was worthy to be king; well, this is the reward you've
received from that worthy man. This is why I have spoken against you
and cursed you."

Hormozd shrank back in shame when he heard this man's true
words. In the darkness of the night he had both men sent to his prisons
and muttered angrily against them. On the third night, when the moon
rose above the mountains, the king got rid of Sima-Borzin: he had him
killed in the thieves' prison, but all that he gained by this was sorrow
and curses. Learning of this honorable man's death Bahram Azar-
Mahan sent a message to the king: "Your crown is higher than the
moon's sphere. You know how hard I have tried to keep your secrets,
and that before that noble king, your father, I always spoke in your
favor. If you summon me to your throne I shall give you some advice
that will benefit Iran and keep those who are wise safe from harm."
Hormozd sent one of his confidants to fetch Bahram to the court in the

darkness of the night, and the king spoke kindly to him, then said, "Tell me what this advice is, which will improve my fortunes."

Bahram answered, "I have seen a simple black chest in the king's treasury: within it there is a casket, and within that there is a document written in Persian on white silk, and it is this on which the Persians' hopes depend. It is written in the hand of your father, the great king, and you should look at it." Hormozd sent someone to the treasurer saying, "Search among my father's treasures for a simple sealed chest: on the seal is the name Nushin-Ravan (may his soul live eternally). Find it quickly and bring it here to me now, in the darkness of the night." The treasurer hurried to find the chest, and ran with it to the king, with its seal still intact. The king broke the seal, repeatedly invoking the name of Nushin-Ravan as he did so. He looked in the chest and hurriedly pulled out a sheet of silk; then he stared at the words that Nushin-Ravan had written there:

> "For twelve long years, unequaled among men
> Hormozd will rule this land as king; but then
> Disturbances will fill the world, his name
> Will be obscured and lose its former fame.
> Foes will attack, and one will prove to be
> An evil and malignant enemy:
> The forces of Hormozd will flee and fail.
> His rival will dethrone him and prevail,
> His wife will put his eyes out, mourners' cries
> Will rise above his body to the skies."

When Hormozd saw this message in his father's handwriting, he was terrified and tore the silk in pieces. His face turned pale and his eyes filled with bitter tears. To Bahram he said, "You live by doing evil! What did you want to do with this document—tear the head from my body?"

Bahram said to him, "You are born of a Turkish woman, and you can never be sated with bloodshed. Your ancestry is from the emperors of China, not from Kay Qobad, even though Kesra bestowed the crown on you!" Hormozd knew that if this man stayed alive he would need no prompting to shed his king's blood; hearing these unwelcome words, he had Bahram taken back to the prison. On the next night, when the moon rose above the mountains, the executioner killed him in the prison. Now there were no wise advisors or priests left at his court.

Saveh Shah Attacks Hormozd

When Hormozd had reigned for ten years, voices rose against him in every country. Saveh Shah advanced from Herat, with elephants, war drums, wealth, and an army. To number his troops, count to a thousand four hundred times: he had one thousand two hundred war elephants, and you would say there was no way left unblocked on the earth. From the plain of Herat to Marvrud the land was filled with his warriors, as dense as warp woven with weft. He marched on Marv, and the land disappeared beneath the dust raised by his troops. He wrote a letter to Hormozd, saying, "Gather your armies and make a way for us; provide us with foraging, and remember our swords. I wish to travel through your kingdom; my troops cover the rivers, the mountains, and the plains." When the king read this letter, he grew pale at the thought of such an immense army.

And from the opposite direction the emperor of Byzantium led his army toward Persia, subduing the land as he did so. The Byzantine army was a hundred thousand strong, and included their renowned, warlike cavalry; they re-conquered the territory called Qeisar-Navan, which Nushin-Ravan had conquered. From every country armies led by famous noblemen were approaching. An army came from Khazar, and the land on their route was blackened by the mass of men. They were led by the experienced warrior Bedal, who marched with his own wealth and men and overran the countryside from Armenia to Ardebil. And an innumerable army came up from Arabia, led by young, proud riders like Abbas and Hamzeh. As they came they plundered the land that had provided Hormozd with regular tax revenues. They reached the Euphrates and left not a blade of grass still growing in the province.

Hormozd's days grew dark as messages came in from his forces, and this once-flourishing king seemed to wither away. He sent out messengers summoning the Persian nobility to his palace, laid the private information he had gathered before them, and said, "No one can remember a time when Iran has been attacked by so many different armies." The nobles were perplexed as to what to do and made various suggestions; then they said, "You are a clever and capable monarch, listen to our opinion in this matter. You are the wise king and we are only your subjects, we don't think of ourselves as learned people. You must consider what is to be done, and who can be our country's savior."

The priest who served Hormozd as vizier said, "Your majesty, you are knowledgeable and you accept knowledgeable advice. If the army from Khazar attacks, we will make short work of them. We can parley with the Byzantine Romans, and we'll utterly destroy the Arabs. My heart has no fear of Arabs. It hurts the eyes just to look at them, they eat snakes and lizards and they have no skill at fighting. It's Saveh Shah you should worry about, he's the real threat to us. Troubles come to us from the road to Khorasan, where our armies and wealth are being destroyed. When the Turks cross the Oxus and attack, we should respond without delay." Hormozd asked the priest how he thought they should deal with Saveh Shah. The priest replied, "Prepare your army, since it's an army that gives a king confidence. Summon the keeper of the muster rolls and have him tell you how many men under arms you have." The keeper brought in the rolls; the army came to a hundred thousand men, and this number included both infantry and cavalry. The priest said, "With an army like this we need not worry about Saveh Shah. If you act chivalrously and righteously, and avoid all evil, you will be able to save your subjects as a king should."

The king said, "The Byzantine emperor will not try to attack us. I'll return him the cities that Nushin-Ravan conquered, and he'll go back to where he came from." He found an envoy who was both a warrior and a scribe, a wise, eloquent, and clever man, and instructed him, "Tell the emperor I no longer require tribute from Byzantium, and that if he wishes to prosper, he should not set foot on Persian soil." As soon as the envoy passed on the king's message, the emperor returned to Byzantium and gave up all thoughts of war. Hormozd also sent an army commanded by the splendid and just warrior Khorad against the forces of Khazar. When they reached Armenia the enemy blocked their way and gave battle. The Persians killed a great number of them and brought back large amounts of plunder from the area. Once Hormozd knew that Khorad and his army were victorious, he concentrated all his thoughts on the one remaining problem—Saveh Shah.

Mehran-Setad Recommends Bahram Chubineh to Hormozd

The king had a wise, contented servant called Nastuh who said to the king, "May you live forever, and may evil always be far from you. You should ask Mehran-Setad what he remembers of former days. He sits in a corner, conning the Zend-Avesta; he's grown old and weak and has no hopes of the world now. I recently spent a day and a night with him and told him about Saveh Shah, his war elephants, and his huge army, but when he answered me he spoke only of former times. I asked him what he remembered, and he said that he would tell what he knew if the king of the world asked him."

The king immediately sent a courtier, who brought the old man in a litter to the king. When the old man entered, his heart filled with wisdom, his head with talk, Hormozd asked him what he remembered about the warlike Turks. "Your majesty, you are eloquent and eager to learn," Mehran-Setad said. "When the emperor of China sent your mother to Persia, I went with a hundred and sixty brave warriors to ask for her hand. Your father was a wise and just king, and he didn't want the daughter of some concubine. He said to me, 'Ask only for the daughter of the empress; a servant's child wouldn't be suitable for our court.' I went to the emperor and greeted him. He had five daughters, all as lovely as the spring, all tints and scents and beauty they were. He sent me to his harem; they had made the girls' faces up and put chaplets of roses in their hair, all except for your mother, who wore nothing on her head, and had none of the bracelets and necklaces and jewels the other girls were wearing. She was the only one who was the empress's daughter, and she was the one who had no make-up or finery on. Her mother really loved her and was tormenting herself with the thought of her daughter going off to some distant land; she didn't want to endure having to say goodbye to her when she left the emperor's palace. I chose her, out of all the emperor's daughters, and I didn't so much as glance at the others. The emperor told me to choose another one, saying all five were good, accomplished girls. But I said that she was the one I had to have, and that it would be my ruin if I chose a different one.

"Then he called for his learned counselors, and when they had knelt before his throne he asked them to cast his daughter's horoscope, to see what the stars held in store for her. One of his astrologers said, 'May you see nothing but good and hear nothing but righteousness. A child like a raging lion will be born from this girl and the Persian king; tall and strong-armed, in bravery like a lion, and in generosity like a rain cloud. He will be black-eyed, quick to anger, and impatient, and when his father dies he will be king. He will use up much of his father's wealth, but few enough of his days will be spent in evil. Then a fierce king will arise, and attack with an army of Turks, intending to overrun Persia and the Yemen. The Persian king will fear him and his victories; but the king will have a subject living far away, a proud, loyal horseman, tall and wiry, his head covered in black curls, talkative, with a large nose, dark-skinned, quick and fierce in his quarrels. This ambitious man will be named Chubineh, and he will be descended from champions. This subject of the king's will bring his army to the court slowly, then suddenly attack the Turks and break their army's power.'

"I've never seen a happier man than the emperor of China was when he had heard the astrologer out. He gave his daughter, who was the crown of all his daughters, to Nushin-Ravan, and, as the king's representative, I accepted her and started on my homeward journey. He gave us so many jewels that we had difficulty transporting them. He came with us as far as the Oxus, and there placed his beloved child in a boat; then he turned back from the shore, his heart filled with sorrow at parting from her. Now I have told the king all that I saw. Search your country for this man, and tell your envoy to hurry because the king's victories are in his hands. Don't entrust this matter to anyone else, friend or foe." When he had said this, his spirit left his body, and the whole company wept for him.

The king was astonished, and bitter tears rained down from his eyelashes. He said to the Persians there, "Mehran-Setad remembered these true accounts, and when he had told them to me he died, entrusting his soul to God. I am grateful to God that I have learned from this old man such pressing news. Search among our nobility, and the commoners too, until you find the man he spoke of; do your utmost to find him." Among his listeners was a well-known nobleman who was in charge of the king's stables; his name was Rad–Farrokh and he lived only to serve the king. He came to the king and said, "In my opinion the description this praiseworthy sage gave fits Bahram, the son of Bahram, who was Goshasp's son. He is a fine, proud horseman: I have not seen a more able lord of the marches riding in the plains. You gave him Barda' and Ardebil to rule, and he has become a great warrior there, with his war drums and cavalry."

Bahram Chubineh Arrives at Hormozd's Court

Hormozd sent for Bahram and had him told of Mehran-Setad's prediction. The ambitious chieftain hurried from Barda with his warriors, and as soon as he arrived, Hormozd had him admitted into his presence. Bahram looked at Hormozd's face and greeted him respectfully; the king gazed at him for a while, and formed a good opinion of what he saw. He saw the attributes Mehran-Setad had described; he smiled and his face relaxed again. Then he questioned him and made much of him, and had a fine building set aside for him to stay in.

The next morning, when night laid aside its musky cloak and the sun showed her face, the lord of the marches made his way to the court, and the nobles opened a way for him. The king called Bahram forward and sat him on a throne in front of the other courtiers. He questioned him about Saveh Shah and said, "Should I make peace with him, or send an army to confront him?" The warrior answered, "Making peace is not the way to deal with Saveh Shah. If he's determined on war, trying to make peace will only lead to your destruction: a malignant man will become more audacious when he sees you have no stomach to fight. If you stick to feasting when you should be fighting, one of your subjects will take over this realm." Hormozd asked, "Then what should we do? Wait, or march against him?" Bahram replied, "It's a good omen if this malcontent acts unjustly, because justice and injustice can't be together in one place. Attack this evil enemy, bring water to quench his fire; if you don't, the ancient heavens will choose a new ruler here. If we use the strength and skills we have, God will not reproach us and we shall not be ashamed when heroes ask us about our deeds. If there were only ten thousand Persians left alive and we fled from battle, those enemies who love to find fault with you would say that you ran away without fighting. If we can rain down arrows on the enemy and make our bows like the clouds in spring, if a hundred thousand maces and swords are shattered in the lines of battle, and still we are not victorious and must despair of our fortunes, then will be the time to obey the enemy, when we have neither minds nor souls nor bodies left to us."

When the king heard Bahram's words he laughed, and the throne seemed to shine with splendor. The courtiers left the king's presence, and their hearts were filled with anxiety. They said to Bahram, "When the king questions you don't be so foolhardy in your answers. Saveh Shah has such a huge army with him that not an ant or a mosquito can find its way through such a mass of men. After the things you've said in front of the king, who will dare to lead our armies?" But Bahram said to them, "My lords, if the king commands it, I am ready to lead our armies." The king's spies immediately went to Hormozd and told him what Bahram had said, adding ten new words for every one he'd spoken.

Hormozd Makes Bahram Chubineh the Commander of His Army

The Persian king was pleased to hear this, and he no longer feared Saveh Shah's forces. He made Bahram the commander of his army, lifting this warrior's head to the clouds, and all those who looked for renown in the wars hailed Bahram as their chief. Bahram came before his king, armed and ready for combat, and asked permission to review the army's troops, to see who was eager for war and who would hold back when there was glory to be won. The king replied, "You are their commander, responsible for whatever good or evil comes of this."

Bahram went to the plain where the king reviewed his warriors and ordered that the Persian army appear before him. He chose the best of them and registered the names of twelve thousand armed cavalry, whose horses were protected with barding. He enrolled men who were in their forties, and refused to consider those who were older or younger. Bahram had overall charge of the army, and he made his second in command a man called Yalan-Sineh, whose heart longed for war. He was to lead the troops into battle, curveting his horse, reminding the men of their lineage, and filling their hearts with courage. Another of his subordinates was Izad-Goshasp, who would not turn his horse back from a raging fire: his responsibility was to watch the baggage and to see that the two flanks of the army coordinated their attack. The rear of the army was commanded by Hamdan-Goshasp, a man who could seize lions by the tail when he rode. Then Bahram addressed his army:

> "Noble and valiant warriors, see that you
> Act righteously in everything you do—

If you would have God turn your present night
To dawn and victory with his glorious might,
See that in darkness when the trumpets sound
You leap into the saddle from the ground,
And ride as if the sun itself arose
At midnight to do battle with our foes.
Don't dream of rest until the battle's done,
Rest is for when our victory is won."

The king rejoiced to hear of Bahram's preparations and his speech, and threw open the doors of his treasury. He made weapons available to Bahram and had his warhorses brought into the town from their pastures, saying that the new commander could choose any of them for himself. Then he said, "You've heard what quantities of troops and arms and treasure Saveh Shah commands, and that the earth trembles when he takes the field, and yet you have chosen only twelve thousand armed men, together with their horses protected by barding, and I don't know if they will be sufficient on the day of battle. And instead of young swordsmen you've asked for men in their forties."

Bahram replied, "Your majesty, you speak truly and are favored by fortune. You have heard tales of the great men who ruled the world before us, and how, when fortune promised victory to them, a few troops were sufficient. If the king will permit me, I shall give you some examples. When Kay Kavus was imprisoned in Hamaveran with a huge army, Rostam chose twelve thousand of the finest cavalry he could find; he freed Kavus from confinement, and the force he had chosen was undefeated. In the same way Gudarz, the chieftain of the Keshvad clan, took twelve thousand armed cavalry with him in his war of vengeance for the death of Seyavash. And the great Esfandyar took twelve thousand warriors against Arjasp; he was able to raze the enemy's fortress and accomplish all his aims with them. If an army has more men in it than this it becomes uncontrollable and the commander is distracted on the battlefield. As for your saying that forty-year-olds can't fight better than younger men, a man of forty has experience, and his courage is the greater for it. He knows what loyalty is and remembers the bread and salt he's received; the heavens have turned many times above his head. He fears shame and the mockery of his detractors, and because of them he won't avoid fighting; a grown man's soul is steeled by thoughts of his wife and children and family. A young man is easily tricked, and when he must wait, he has no patience; he has no wife or children or fields to think of, and he confuses what's important with what doesn't matter. Because an inexperienced man has no wisdom, he can't see things as they really are. If he's victorious on the day of battle, he's happy and laughs and wastes his time, and if victory isn't his, the enemy will see nothing of him except his back."

At these words, the king felt as refreshed as a rose in the spring. "Go, put on your armor," he ordered Bahram, "and make your way to the reviewing ground." The commander left the king and asked for his belt, cuirass, and helmet. He strapped barding onto his horse and tied a lariat to the stirrups. The king came to the reviewing ground with his vizier, bringing arrows, polo mallets, and balls. His commander appeared and prostrated himself in the dust before his king, who gave him his blessing, and in response the commander kissed the ground. Then the king held up a banner, on which was depicted a purple dragon; this was the banner that had gone before Rostam in his wars, and the king lifted it lightly and kissed it, laughing as he did so, and handed it to Bahram. He called down many blessings on the banner and said to Bahram, "This banner belonged to the man my ancestors always called the first of champions, whose name was Rostam, who conquered the world, and was victorious and pure of soul. It is his banner you hold in your hand, and may you be victorious and loyal to your king! I believe you are another Rostam, in your courage, heroism, and loyalty." Bahram called down blessings on the king and said, "May you be victorious, and your soul remained untroubled!" Then he left the reviewing ground for his lodging, grasping Rostam's banner in his fist; the army's warriors dispersed, and their commander was content.

Bahram Chubineh Marches Against Saveh Shah

When the first light of dawn appeared above the mountains and the sun's glittering yellow shield shone there, the army's commander came before his king, his arms folded over his chest in submission, to say, "I have all I could wish, and by your *farr* I am the crown of the age, but I have one request to make of your majesty. It is that you send someone trustworthy with me, a scribe who can report back the name of anyone who distinguishes himself in battle and brings the enemies' heads

down into the dust, so that his fame may live in the world." Hormozd
replied, "The scribe Mehran is young, eloquent, and intelligent," and
he gave orders that Mehran accompany the army. Then the com-
mander, alert as a male lion, at the head of his experienced, courageous
troops, immediately set off from Ctesiphon.

Hormozd said to his vizier, "He is a brave man and will triumph on
the battlefield. But what do you think will happen then? We should dis-
cuss this at length." The vizier replied, "May you live forever, since this
is what you deserve. This champion, with his great strength and stature,
with his quick tongue and confident spirit, will surely be victorious and
overthrow the king's enemies. But I fear that in the end he will turn
against the king who has favored him. He's very forward in his speech,
and he acts like a lion when he talks with your majesty." Hormozd said,
"You're the most suspicious man alive! Don't confuse poison with its
antidote. If he defeats Saveh Shah, he deserves a crown and a throne.
This is my hope, that he reign as a prince, praised and successful." The
vizier was abashed, and held his tongue. But in his heart the king pon-
dered what he had said, and before long he chose a spy from among his
courtiers, someone who could follow up on this suspicion. He said to
him, "Hurry after the army commander, and report back to me on what
you see." The man sped after Bahram, and no one knew of his mission.
He was both a guide to what was happening and an interpreter of
omens, someone who told the king what the outcome of everything
would be.

As Bahram rode from Ctesiphon at the head of his army, with his
lance in his hand, he saw a seller of sheep's heads in the distance. The
man had a tray on which were a number of dressed heads. Bahram
urged his horse forward and spitted one of the heads on his lance, lift-
ing up the lance as he rode and then flinging the head down at will. He
took this as a sign and said, "This is how I shall deal with Saveh Shah's
head; I'll throw it down in the road before his troops, and then I'll
destroy his whole army." The man the king had sent saw this and inter-
preted it appropriately, thinking, "This man has fortune on his side, and
his efforts will gain him a throne: but then when he has what he wants
in his grasp he'll stubbornly defy his king." He returned, and reported
this to the king who grew anxious and worried. The man's words
seemed worse than death to him; he became dejected, like a green leaf
that shrivels and turns black.

He called for a young messenger to hurry after Bahram, instructing him, "Go and tell the army's commander to halt where he is tonight. At dawn he is to return here to me, where I'll clear the court and give him some advice. I've remembered a number of useful things I have to tell him." The young messenger caught up with Bahram and told him what he had heard from the king, but Bahram answered, "Tell him, 'You're a wise king, and people don't summon armies back when they are on the march. To return as you suggest would be a bad omen, and our enemies would be strengthened to hear of it. I'll come to your court once I'm victorious and I've made your army and country glow with splendor.'" The messenger returned and told the king what warlike Bahram had said. The king was pleased at this answer, and the messenger's efforts had no result.

At dawn Bahram called down blessings on the army and marched them as far as Khuzestan; no one along their route came to any harm. When they pitched camp a woman with a sack full of straw ran between the ranks; a horseman came and bought the sack from her, but he refused to pay and tugged at his reins and rode off. The woman went wailing to Bahram and said, "I had a little straw and I thought I could sell it, so I brought it to your army; but now a horseman has stolen it from me. He has an iron helmet on his head." They immediately searched for the man and dragged him before Bahram, who said to the thief, "You will lose your head for this sin you've committed." He was dragged stumbling in front of the tents, and his head, arms, and legs were smashed to pieces. Bahram split him in two with a sword, to terrify anyone else there who was inclined to act unjustly. A proclamation was made in front of Bahram's pavilion: "Whoever steals one stalk of straw will find no mercy; I shall split his body open with my sword. Buy whatever you need with silver coins."

Hormozd Sends Khorad-Borzin to Saveh Shah with a Deceitful Message

But Hormozd was constantly troubled by his thoughts, thinking now of Saveh Shah and his wealth and war elephants, then of the anxieties and fear he felt because of Bahram. His soul was full of sorrow, his fearful heart was split in two with worry. In night's darkness, after the moon set, the king said to Khorad-Borzin, "Contrive to reach our enemy: go as quickly as you can and don't rest on the way. Observe his army, who and

how many they are, and who their leaders and warriors are." Then he
had a letter written, filled with advice for his dangerous adversary, and it
was accompanied by innumerable royal presents. He said to his envoy,
"Travel toward Herat; on your way you will meet with Bahram's army.
Turn aside from your destination and tell Bahram that I'm sending flat-
tering messages to Saveh Shah in order to lure him into a trap, and that
Saveh Shah is not to learn of his identity or intentions."

Khorad-Borzin set out and talked with Bahram as his king had
ordered, and from there he traveled on to where Saveh Shah was camped
with his elephants and wealth and army. He praised and flattered him, and
passed on Hormozd's secret message, amplifying it in every way, so that
Saveh Shah would march on Herat. This he did, pitching camp by the
river there. A scout then saw Bahram's troops and ran to Saveh Shah say-
ing that a mighty army was approaching. Saveh Shah was alarmed by this
news; he summoned Hormozd's envoy from his tent and spoke to him
angrily, "You deceitful devil, haven't you seen how far you could fall, up
there on the heights? You've come from that wretched king of yours to
tempt me into an ambush. You're bringing up a Persian army to attack
me; they've pitched camp on the plains of Herat!" Khorad-Borzin
answered, "Don't misconstrue things when you see a few troops in front
of you. This is some lord of the marches who's going somewhere, or it's
someone who's fled from his own country and is seeking asylum with
you, or it's a merchant who's traveling with an escort to be safe on the
road. Who would be foolish enough to oppose you, unless the mountains
and oceans are going to fight?" Saveh Shah was satisfied by this answer
and replied, "Let us hope things are as you say."

Night came quickly from the mountains as Khorad-Borzin
returned to his tent. He made preparations for flight, to avoid the
destruction that was certain to descend on him otherwise. As the dark-
ness deepened, Saveh Shah sent his wise young son with an escort to
his enemy's leader. As he drew near the Persian force, the young prince
dispatched a horseman to inquire as to who these troops were, and why
they were advancing on this territory. A Turk rode forward like the
wind and called out, "Mighty warriors, who is your commander, who
leads this army, who is the finest fighter among you? Because our
crown prince, whom Saveh Shah loves more than his own eyes and
heart, wants to see him, without an escort." A warrior came to Bahram
and told him what he had heard, and the commander came out of his

tent and stood there beneath his glittering banner. When the prince saw him he urged his horse forward, so that it was covered in sweat. He asked, "Where have you ridden from, and why have you pitched camp here? I've heard that you've fled from Persia, that you're a fugitive who has blood on his hands." Bahram replied, "God forbid that I think of opposing Persia's king. I have come here with my army from Baghdad, at the king's orders, to fight. When news of Saveh Shah's army reached the royal court, he told me to march out and block their way with maces, lances, swords, and arrows."

The prince immediately returned to his father and told him what had happened. Saveh Shah grew suspicious at his words and sent for the Persian envoy. But he was told, "Khorad-Borzin has fled, weeping bitter tears of regret that he had come here." Saveh Shah asked his son, "How did that wretch find a route to go by? The night was dark, there is a huge army here; how could our sentinels be so negligent?"

Saveh Shah Sends a Message to Bahram Chubineh

Then Saveh Shah sent an old man, a fine orator, to Bahram, with orders to say, "Don't be such a fool as to lose your reputation here. You should at least realize one thing, that this king of yours is trying to get you killed. He's sent you to fight with someone who has no equal in all the world. He's said to you, 'Go and block his advance,' but haven't you heard the unsettling news that if a mountain is in my way, I can flatten it with my army and elephants?" When Bahram heard these words, he laughed at the man's blustering tactics. He answered,

> *"If secretly the world's king wants to kill*
> *His slave, I cannot contradict his will;*
> *If it would please him, then it's right that I*
> *Find my grave here: I am prepared to die."*

The messenger returned to Saveh Shah and gave him the warrior's answer. Saveh Shah said, "Go and question the Persian again. Say, 'Why do you need to talk so much? Why have you come here? Ask from me whatever you wish.'" The messenger went to Bahram and said, "Tell us whatever it is you're hiding. My king's star is in the ascendant, and he is looking for subjects like you."

Bahram replied, "Tell him this: 'If you want war, stop all this pretense. But if you want to make peace with the world's king, then I shall entertain you in the borderlands here, and I shall obey your commands. I shall give your troops gold and silver, and crowns and belts of office to those who are worthy of them. I shall send a horseman to the king and he will come halfway to meet you. He will provide you with foraging, as one ally to another. If you want friendship, the king will treat you well. But if you've come here to fight, then you should realize you've entered the sea and it's a sea monster you'll be fighting with; you'll retreat from the plains of Herat in such a wretched state that our nobility will weep for you. I wish you pits before you, winds at your back, rain to accompany you! It's your bad luck that has brought you here, intending to bring down evil on your head.'"

The messenger hurried back like the wind and recounted every detail of what Bahram had said. Saveh Shah was enraged to hear this reply; the cold words ate at his heart, and his face turned pale. He said to his envoy, "Go back again, and take that demon my answer. Say, 'There's no fame to be had from fighting with you, and it'll give me no satisfaction to kill you. I've courtiers crowded at my door like your king; the least of my servants are your superiors. But if you appeal to me for my protection, I'll lift your head above them all; you'll find immense wealth, and all your army will be well equipped. An ambitious man like you doesn't try to prove his courage by pointless, idle talk.'" Once more the messenger returned to Bahram and passed on his master's urgent, heartfelt message. And again Bahram replied, "I cannot hide my answer from your lord. Say this to him, 'If indeed I'm as lowly as you say, I feel no shame because of it. The King of Kings is ashamed to fight with someone as insignificant as you; it's my unimportance that has made me the leader of this army, which I've brought here in order to destroy Saveh Shah's forces. I'll cut your head off and take it to my king, and it's not even worth spitting on my lance to display as I ride there. It would shame you if I asked for your protection, and so in my insignificance I've come to attack you. You won't see me except on the battlefield, with my purple banner fluttering behind me; and when you see the dragon embroidered there, that will be the sign of your death; I shall sheathe my lance in your head and helmet.'"

After hearing such hostile talk, Saveh Shah's envoy turned his back on Bahram. He told Saveh Shah all he had heard and seen, and the Turkish king's head seethed with longing for vengeance. He ordered that his war drums be readied, and his towering elephants be led onto the plain; all the land became black with dust from his army's hooves, and the squeal of trumpets rang out. When Bahram heard that the enemy's troops were approaching, and that the plain had turned red, yellow, and black with their banners, he ordered his men to mount, and he came forward armed, with his mace in his hand. Behind him was the city of Herat, ahead an army with drawn swords. He coordinated the right and left flanks of his forces, all of whom were eager for battle. It seemed that all the world was made of iron, and that the stars were glittering lances.

Saveh Shah looked at the troops ranged against him: Herat was to the rear of Bahram's men, and Saveh Shah's own situation was hemmed in and unfavorable. He said to his horsemen, men of long experience who sympathized with his cause, "That Persian commander has tricked me: he delayed until his army had occupied the city and he's left the reed beds to us." He drew up his army's ranks in the narrow space left to them; the sky was darkened and the earth disappeared. He had forty thousand men on his right flank, but they were so hemmed in that they could hardly wield their swords, and there were another forty thousand in the rear. Because of the limited space many of his troops could do nothing. In the van of his army were his elephants, blocking the way like a wall. Saveh Shah was distraught that his army was unable to maneuver: it seemed that fortune had turned against him, and that his throne would soon be vacant.

Saveh Shah Sends Another Message to Bahram Chubineh

Once again Saveh Shah sent a messenger—a glib, deceitful warrior from the plains of Herat—to Bahram, saying, "The heavens have no love for you; be wise, open your heart's eyes, and listen to my advice. There are two peerless nobles in the world, shining like the sun in the heavens, armed all year round and ready to fight: I, the rightful ruler of the world, am one, and the other is my son. My troops outnumber the leaves on the trees, supposing they could be counted; if I could count my elephants and warriors, they would make the number of raindrops that fall in the spring seem laughable to you. I own more armor and tents and pavilions than you can imagine; the mass of my horses and warriors would terrify the very mountains and deserts. Kings are my servants, or worthy to be counted as such; if the seas could flow here and the mountains run, they would not be sufficient to move the treasures and troops I've accumulated. All the nobles of the world, except that Persian lord of yours, call me king.

"My soul can see clearly enough that your fate is in my hands. If I advance my armies, there will not be space for an ant or a mosquito to pass. I've a thousand armored elephants, and horses flee at the scent of them; who in all Iran can stand before me and block my way? My men occupy the land from here to Ctesiphon, and the number there will grow. Who has deceived you, what fool has tricked you? You've no mercy on yourself, or if you have, it's hidden away because it can't tell good from evil. When did a wise man ever talk so foolishly? Forget this war and come over to me. I won't keep you waiting long for my response: I'll make you a lord, I'll give you my daughter, you'll be an honored man here. You'll be a nobleman, free of all the miseries a subject must endure. When the Persian king is killed in battle, his crown and throne will be yours; I'll go on toward Byzantium, and leave all this land and its wealth and armies in your possession. I say this because I like you, your deeds show you possess the divine *farr,* and you know how to lead an army in war because your father and grandfather were both army commanders. This message is not a trick; I want to help you. Today you're opposing me with your contemptible little army, but even if you don't fall in with my wishes, this is the only message you'll ever hear from me."

Bahram Chubineh's Answer to Saveh Shah

The envoy spoke and Bahram listened, and when he answered his words were somber. He said, "Among those who have pride and nobility you're a byword for evil; an idle king who talks too much has no one's respect. Your previous messages, and this one, show me you're a great talker, certainly; someone whose luck is running out will try to save himself with speeches. In your pointless prattle I can hear that your heart is fearful, that you're terrified of being defeated. When you say you'll kill our king and give me his throne and army, you remind me of how, when a poor man is driven from a village, he will always claim that he was the village headman, that everyone else was his inferior and he was in charge. But the sun will not shine on our deeds for two more days before I send your bloody head spitted on a lance to my king.

"As for your talk about my being grateful to you and hailing you as an honorable king because you'll give me your child in marriage and the throne of Iran, where I'll be your ally, my answer is that my lance is now next to your ear and that I shall cut your head off with my sword. And when you're gone your head and crown and treasure, as well as your daughter and all you've taken such pains to accumulate, will be mine. And your boasts of having more crowns and thrones and elephants and cavalry than anyone can count remind me of the noble-man who, when he was in the thick of battle, said that a thirsty dog barks louder the further away from water he is. Devils must have cap-tured your heart to make you come to fight against my king, but you'll writhe in pain when God punishes you and you remember the evil deeds you've committed. And then you claim that crowned kings are your servants, that all the cities of the world are yours and bear witness to your greatness; well, the way's open to those cities, and servants and kings alike can take it. But if you knock at their gates the only sover-eignty they'll grant you is over waste reed beds. You talk about pardon-ing me, but you've forgotten my courage; you can pardon me when you see my lance, then you won't be calling me your subject. When my army's drawn up for battle I don't care a copper coin for your troops and ambition and elephants and throne. If you're a king, why do you lie so much? That's no way to win glory in the world. I've told my king that in three days' time, when the sun lights up the sky in splendor, he will see your head spitted on a lance before his throne."

The envoy's cheeks turned sallow, as if his once-flourishing fortune were now old and decrepit. He took the message to Saveh Shah, whose face darkened when he heard it; but his son said, "What do such boasts matter? We should weep with pity for their contemptible army." The son went to his pavilion and gave orders for cymbals and Indian bells, elephants and war drums, and directed that the heavens be filled with their din. While his son was preparing for battle in this way, Saveh Shah was filled with anxiety. He said to his son, "All our army loves you, but don't attack until dawn." The two armies retreated to their tents, and sentries were posted before the pavilions. On each side camp fires flick-ered, and the world was filled with the noise of the two armies.

Bahram's Dream: He Draws Up His Army for Battle

Bahram was alone in his tent when he summoned the Persian commanders, and they discussed the coming battle until nightfall. Then the Turks and Persians alike slept, and ambitious men who were eager to conquer the world forgot its claims. As Bahram slept within his tent, his heart was preoccupied all night with the coming battle.

> *And in the lion-warrior's mind it seemed*
> *As though the Turks had won; great Bahram dreamed*
> *His army was destroyed, and when he tried*
> *To flee, the paths were blocked on every side:*
> *On foot now and alone, he scoured the plain*
> *For warriors who could help him, but in vain.*

He was uneasy when he woke, and his mind, which was usually so resourceful, was filled with foreboding. The night was dark, and sorrow was his companion: he hid his dream and mentioned it to no one.

At that moment Khorad-Borzin arrived after fleeing from Saveh Shah. "Your one hope is to retreat and quickly," he said. "No one in all the world has ever seen an army as massive as Saveh Shah's. What makes you so confident? Look at the devil's trap you're falling into. Don't throw Persian souls to the winds, think of our brave warriors' lives. Find it in your heart to have pity on your own life, because you have never faced anything like this before!" Bahram replied, "All men from your town can do is sell fish, from summer to winter. Your calling is to handle nets by a lakeshore, you're not a man for maces and swords and arrows. But when the sun raises its head above the mountains, I'll show you how I fight with Saveh Shah."

When the sun rose in the sign of Leo and the world turned as white as a Roman's face, trumpets were sounded and the earth trembled with the pounding of horses' hooves. Bahram drew up his army and mounted his horse, flourishing his well-tried mace in his hand. There were three thousand armored and experienced cavalry on the right flank of his forces, and he sent as many warlike horsemen to the left flank. One side was commanded by Azar-Goshasp, and the other by Goshasp; in the rear was Yalan-Sineh, whose men were armed with maces and were to attack last. The van was commanded by Hamdan-

Goshasp, whose horse's hooves spread fire in the reed beds. Each of them commanded three thousand cavalry, eager for war.

A herald announced Bahram's message to his troops: "Great warriors with your golden helmets, if anyone flees from this battle, even if he's faced by a lion or a leopard, I swear by God I shall cut his head from his body and give his corpse to the flames." There were two paths from the camp, by which one could easily retreat, and Bahram had both blocked with a high wall of earth, while he himself took up his position in the center of the army. When the king's scribe saw this, he came to Bahram and said, "This is beyond all reason; your foolish boasting has gone on long enough! Look at the armies drawn up here—we're like a white hair lost on a black ox's hide. Things will go badly for Iran in this battle, our land will be destroyed, we'll be overrun by Turks, and not a field or a river or a mountain will remain to us!" Bahram yelled at him,

> *"Stick to your ink and paper, who told you*
> *To count our troops? Do what you're hired to do!"*

The scribe went to Khorad-Borzin and said, "Bahram's been bewitched by some devil!" The two scribes looked for a way to flee, fearing the catastrophe they felt sure would come. They went to a hill overlooking the battlefield and fixed their eyes on Bahram's helmet, to see how he fared when the fighting began in earnest.

When Bahram had drawn up his troops ready for battle, he turned aside, groaning in anguish, from the battlefield. He prostrated himself in the dust before God and cried out,

> *"O Lord of truth and justice, if you see*
> *My cause as wrong, protect my enemy,*
> *But if it is your cause for which I fight*
> *Make my heart calm, strengthen my army's might,*
> *Give us a joyful victory, and bless*
> *The world with riches, peace, and happiness."*

Still weeping, he mounted his horse, his ox-headed mace in his fist.

Bahram Chubineh Fights Against Saveh Shah

Now Saveh Shah addressed his troops: "Begin your magic, so that the hearts and eyes of the Persians will tremble, and no harm will come to you." All his magicians set about their business, and fire darted through the air: a wind rose up and a black cloud poured down arrows. Bahram cried out, "Noble lords and Persian warriors, take no notice of this magic; go forward to war with rage in your hearts. If the only hope they have is sorcery and magic, we should weep for the poor wretches!" A cry went up from the Persian side, and they readied themselves for combat. Saveh Shah saw that the magic had done him no good and he attacked on the left, like a wolf falling on a lamb. When he had broken their ranks he turned toward the center, where Bahram was. Bahram saw his men flee; he charged forward and with his lance unseated three horsemen. He shouted, "This is how to fight, this is our custom and how we carry it out. Have you no shame before God, or before our noble warriors?" Then like a hungry lion he made his way over to the left flank and shattered the enemy's ranks so thoroughly that their leader's banner disappeared. From there he turned back toward the center and said to his commander, "This is a desperate business; if the battle goes on for much longer, our army will be scattered; look for some way to retreat." They went and searched, but there was no way back; the road was blocked by a wall of earth. Bahram said to his commanders, "We have an iron wall ahead of us: any man who can get through it will reach safety and take his soul back to Iran and our king. Prepare your hearts to shed blood now: lift your shields above your heads and draw your swords. No one should despair of God's help, even if the bright day turns dark before us."

For his part Saveh Shah addressed his officers, "Bring the elephants forward, into the thick of the fighting, make the Persians' world dark and desperate." Seeing the elephants in the far distance, Bahram grew anxious and drew his sword. He said to his warriors, "Place your helmets on your heads and have your bows from Chach ready. By the head and soul of the world's king, beloved of our chieftains, crown of our nobility, I order whoever has a bow to make it ready immediately. Shoot three of your poplar arrows tipped with heads that draw blood into the elephants' trunks, then flourish your maces and go forward to kill the enemy." Bahram placed his steel helmet on his head and drew back his bow: a hail of arrows rained down and his army charged forward. The elephants' trunks were wounded by the arrows, and the plain grew sodden with their blood. Maddened by their wounds, the elephants turned back and trampled their own troops. Fortune had turned against them; Saveh Shah's army was in turmoil and many died. Bahram's troops pursued the elephants, and the earth was like a Nile of blood.

There was a pleasant hill near the battlefield, to the rear of the struggling army, and Saveh Shah had gone there to sit on a golden throne and observe the battle. He saw his army like a moving mountain of iron, the soldiers' heads covered in dust, their souls downcast, and behind them came the maddened elephants, trampling the troops as they stampeded. With tears in his eyes, Saveh Shah tried to comprehend how his army had been routed. He mounted a dun Arab horse and fled, fearing for his life. Bahram came after him like a raging elephant, his lariat on his shoulder, his bow in his hand. He called to his troops, "Fortune has turned against them; this is no time for reminiscing and talking. Pursue them with your swords, rain arrows down on them, show your mettle as cavalry." He made his way to the hill where Saveh Shah had sat crowned on his golden throne, and saw him fleeing in the distance. He sped after him, moving like a cloud across the sky, and selected an arrow with a glittering head, flighted with four eagle feathers. Placing the thumbstall against the deerskin string, he leveled the bow with his left hand and drew back the string with his right. The Chachi bow groaned as it bent, and as he pulled the deerskin string back to his ear, that too cried out. The arrow sped from his hand and pierced Saveh Shah's spine. Saveh Shah's head descended into the dust, and the earth beneath him ran with his blood. And so this famous king, with his armies and golden throne and golden crown, was vanquished. This is the way of the turning heavens, which show neither love nor kindness: don't pride yourself on your high throne, and take care to stay far from all harm.

When Bahram reached him, he dragged him facedown through the dust and cut off his head; none of Saveh Shah's men came near him as he did so. Later, seeing his headless body lying in the road, they lamented their loss; the land was filled with wailing, the sky with their distress. Saveh Shah's son said, "This was the work of God; Bahram's good fortune was with him. Our army had no room to maneuver, and that was what killed so many of us. The elephants trampled many of our war-

riors, and not one man in ten survived. Men either perished beneath the
elephants' feet, or had their heads cut off on the battlefield."

Bahram Chubineh Kills a Magician

When this evil day had passed, not one of the enemy could be seen
alive, except for those who had been taken prisoner; their bodies were
wounded by arrows, their souls by sorrow. The way was filled with
barding and helmets, heads that the helmets had betrayed to death,
Indian swords, arrows, and bows. The ground was like a sea of blood
from the dead, and everywhere saddled horses stood ownerless. Bahram
searched diligently for the Persian dead, asking Khorad-Borzin for help:
"Share my troubles for a day: look to see who among the Persians has
been killed, whom we have to mourn for." Khorad-Borzin went over
the whole site, peering in every tent and pavilion. For some time a fine
cavalry commander named Bahram was missing; he was a nobleman
and descended from Seyavash. Khorad-Borzin desperately searched
high and low but could find no trace of him; he turned over the
wounded and dead, but found nothing. Bahram Chubineh was very
distressed, but eventually the man appeared, like a key to open a locked
door, and leading a weeping red-haired Turk whose heart was eaten up

with sorrow. When Bahram saw Bahram, he said, "May you never lie beneath the dust!" Then he turned to the ugly Turk and said, "You, with the hellish face so far from heaven, what kind of a man are you? What's your name and tribe? Your mother should weep for you now."

The man replied, "I'm a magician: I'm the opposite of a straightforward, honorable man. When my lord goes to war against someone and gets into difficulties, I set to work. At night I show people things in their sleep, and this disturbs even those who are calm and careful by nature. It was I who sent you the nightmare that bothered you so much. But I should try for something stronger, because my spells didn't work. Our stars let us down, and all my efforts dispersed like so much wind. If you'll spare me, you've found a very skillful assistant." Bahram carefully considered the man's words, but his heart was troubled, and his face turned sallow. At first he thought, "This man would be useful on the day of battle, if I got into difficulties." But then he thought, "But what use was magic to Saveh Shah? All benefits come from God," and he ordered that the man's head be cut off. When the man had been killed, Bahram stood up and said, "O Lord of justice and righteousness: all greatness, victory, and the divine *farr*, might and imperial power, misery and joy, come from you. Blessings on the warrior who follows your way."

Then the chief scribe came forward and spoke: "O terrifying champion, neither Feraydun nor Kesra Nushin-Ravan ever saw a warrior like you. All the cities of Iran flourish because of you, all our champions are your slaves. Through you the throne has found good fortune, through you its subjects are exalted. You are a commander born of commanders: happy the mother who bore such a son! Your lineage is splendid and your mind is splendid; you are the pillar that supports all our country." Then all the nobles and the champions of the army left the battlefield.

Bahram Chubineh Sends Saveh Shah's Head to Hormozd
Darkness braided its hair, and the braids covered men's eyes in sleep; night's ebony curtain appeared, and the world rested from the din of drums. Swiftly the heavens turned, as if they thought the night tarried too long, until a golden ship arose from the water, bringing back sorrow and driving away sleep.

Bahram ordered his men to sever the heads of all the slain Turkish nobles and chieftains and to place a banner behind each head. The prisoners and heads were gathered together and taken from the battlefield. Then Bahram summoned his scribe and dictated a letter to the king describing the enemy's innumerable army; the changing fortunes of battle; the stratagems, fighting, and maneuvering against the enemy's forces; the Persians' struggles and prowess; and the cavalry who fought all day without respite. He selected an eloquent envoy from among his soldiers to take the letter and trophies. First he spitted Saveh Shah's head on a lance and put it with the banner Saveh had carried in battle; likewise, he spitted the heads of the Turanian nobles on lances and sent them with banners of the Chinese cavalry. He ordered that all these be taken directly to the Persian king. The prisoners and plunder he deposited untouched in Herat, awaiting the king's orders as to what was to be done with them. With the heads he also sent a number of horsemen to learn whether the king wished him to attack Parmoudeh, Saveh Shah's son.

For their part, the Turks and Chinese warriors made their way to Turan, naked and bereft of their weapons, horses, and baggage. When news of this reached Parmoudeh, he flung the crown from his head. The Turks bitterly lamented their dead nobles, smearing their heads with dust; they wept, and no one ate or rested or slept. Parmoudeh summoned the warriors and, weeping bitter tears, asked them how their innumerable army had been defeated in battle. Their spokesman replied, "We thought their army of no account, but no one has ever seen a horseman like Bahram when he fights. In battle he's greater than Rostam, and no warrior will stay to oppose him. Their army was not a hundredth of ours, but the best of our warriors was a child compared to them. God guided him, and if I say more you will not want to hear it." Parmoudeh brooded in his heart on Bahram's deed. Then, seething with rage, he decided to attack. He still had a hundred thousand warriors under arms, so he led his army out on to the plains and marched toward the Oxus.

The champion's letter reached Hormozd as he was sitting with his advisors and saying, "My wise counselors, it is now two weeks since we have heard anything from Bahram. What do you think of this? What should we do? We must discuss the matter." And at that moment the chamberlain entered and gave Hormozd the good news: "May the king reign prosperously forever. Bahram has defeated Saveh Shah and made the world splendid by his victory." Bahram's envoy was summoned, and seated in a higher place than the king's advisors. He said, "Great king, the battle turned out as you would wish. May you live peacefully and happily, because your enemies' fortune has grown old. The heads of Saveh Shah and his younger son, whom his father called his crown prince, are spitted on lances at your door, and all the city stares at them."

The king heard this and stood up, but immediately he bowed before God, and said, "O Judge and Guide, it is you who have destroyed our enemies. I was in such despair, and had no hope that my enemy would be overcome. It was not my commander who did this, or his army, it was God who accomplished this victory." Then he brought out a hundred and thirty thousand coins that he had inherited from his father and distributed a third of the sum to the poor, mostly to his own courtiers and servants. Another third he gave to the fire-temples, for the priests who conduct the rites to celebrate the festivals of No-Ruz and Sadeh, and the last third was given to individuals who would undertake to rebuild ruined caravanserais in the desert, so that men could travel there safely and without fear. Then he remitted four years of taxes on both the poor and the nobles who sat on ivory thrones.

Next, he sent a letter to the ruler of every province, saying that Bahram had been victorious and had cut off Saveh Shah's head. Hormozd worshiped God for seven days, and on the eighth he summoned Bahram's messenger and again sat him higher than the other courtiers. He planted a sapling in the garden of greatness by writing a fine answer to Bahram's letter. He sent him a silver throne and a pair of golden shoes, as well as other goods, and wrote a charter making him lord of Khatlan and Badakhshan, as far as the River Barak. He ordered him to give the plunder from the battlefield to his soldiers, except for Saveh Shah's personal treasure, which was to be sent to the royal court; and he directed Bahram to attack Parmoudeh immediately, before he became a formidable enemy.

Before he left the envoy was given a robe of honor. When he reached Bahram, the commander welcomed him warmly and did what the king had ordered, distributing the spoils of war to his soldiers, except for the evil Saveh Shah's treasure, which he sent to the king's court under the care of trustworthy men. Then the commander and his army marched out to war.

Bahram Chubineh's Battle with Parmoudeh, the Son of Saveh Shah; Parmoudeh Flees to His Castle

When Parmoudeh learned that Bahram was ambitious for the imperial throne, he deposited all his gold and silver coins and his jewels in a castle that he felt was safe and secure. Then he crossed the Oxus with his army and went forward confidently to battle. The two armies were soon face to face, and each of them pitched camp in the environs of Balkh. There were two parasangs distance between the two, a space appropriate for a battlefield.

The next day Bahram, who was eager for battle, hurried out to observe Parmoudeh's forces. Parmoudeh was also watching, and saw him as Bahram chose a high hill and ranged his army in front of it, covering the plain. Parmoudeh was taken aback at this show of force and the sight of Bahram before his troops, his warlike head lifted up to the sky. Filled with anxiety, he said to his men, "This leader is like a lion in his pride and ferocity, and the black earth where he stands will run with blood. His troops can't be numbered, and anyone would be reluctant to confront them. When night falls we'll attack, and thereby drive fear and anxiety from our hearts."

When Bahram marched from Persia against the Turks, an astrologer had said to him, "Start no enterprise on a Wednesday; if you ignore this advice, you will be harmed, and nothing you do will bring any profit to you." Between the two armies, to one side of the battle plain, there was a garden; on Wednesday Bahram went there, saying, "Today will be a day of pleasure." His men brought fine carpets, wine, musicians, and food. Bahram sat there drinking until one watch of the night had passed. A scout went to Parmoudeh and said, "Bahram is in that garden, drinking." Parmoudeh chose six thousand of his horsemen and sent them to encircle the garden without showing any light. But Bahram realized what was being planned and he said to Yalan-Sineh, "Make an opening in the garden wall." Then he and Izad-Goshasp and the other warriors who were with him mounted their horses and rode though the breech in the wall: who knows how they managed it? Trumpets sounded at the garden door, the commander urged his horse forward as a second breech was quickly made in the wall, and the enemy forces were thrown into a turmoil. Bahram fought with a javelin in his hand, like a man who was half-drunk; he was so eager for blood that no one he encountered escaped him. The commanders' cries and the sounds of iron against steel rang out, and from the garden to Parmoudeh's camp the way was littered with headless corpses.

When Bahram reached his encampment again, he too decided on a night attack, and with half the night gone he led his men out onto the plain. They reached the Turkish lines without being seen by the sentries and announced their approach with the squeal of trumpets and the din of drums. The Turkish warriors leaped up, and the tumultuous noise would have deafened a savage lion. Right and left in the darkness close combats began; in the night and with long lances everywhere men did not know friend from foe; sparks glittered from swords and seemed to burn the earth and air. Few Turks remained alive, and their blood made the stones there resemble nothing so much as coral. Their leader fled like wind-blown dust, his mouth dry and his lips turned blue, and kept going until dawn broke and night drew back her skirts. But Bahram pursued him, and when he reached him he roared like a lion:

> "Don't mix with warriors if all you can do
> Is run away when danger threatens you.
> You're just a little boy; you should have stayed
> Sucking your mother's milk if you're afraid."

And Parmoudeh replied, "How much blood must you shed before you'll be satisfied? When they fight, leopards on land and crocodiles in the rivers eventually become sated with blood: but you've never had enough, you're like an insatiable lion. You cut off the head of Saveh Shah, whom the turning heavens loved while he lived, and you destroyed his armies in such a way that the sun and moon felt pity for them. I am that warrior king's son, and you should know that you killed me too when you killed him. But we are all born from our mothers for death, whether we are Turks or Persians. You can pursue me as I flee, but you won't catch me until the end of time. If I return armed either of us might be killed in combat. Don't be so headstrong and fiery; this is not how an army commander should act. I shall return to my castle and try a new tack: I'll write to your king, in the hopes that he will grant me his protection. If he accepts my petition and helps me, I shall be the slave of his court and give up all hopes of sovereignty. I'll rid my mind of all thoughts of war and vengeance and make a pact of peace with him."

When Bahram heard him speak in this way, he turned back. After his army had rested from battle for a while he went to King Parmoudeh's abandoned camp and toured the area, cutting the heads from the bodies of the dead Turkish noblemen. These he heaped up together and the pile was like a mountain in height and breadth. Everyone still calls this place "Bahram's Hill." Then he dragged all the Turks' armor and equipment to this hill, and finally wrote a letter to Hormozd concerning Parmoudeh and his enormous army. He wrote about the Turks and their warlike king, who out of fear of Bahram's sword had resorted to a trick, and how the king had had to flee ignominiously from the battle. For his part, Parmoudeh closed the doors to his castle and sat conferring anxiously with a crowd of advisors. Many men gathered outside his castle gates, but no one knew what his plans for war were.

Parmoudeh Asks Bahram Chubineh for Asylum

Bahram said, "We should press ahead with this war." He told Yalan-Sineh to select three thousand horsemen, and directed Azar-Goshasp to take four thousand. The two of them were to attack whomever they could find, in the hope that when he saw the plains flowing with blood, Parmoudeh would be lured out of his castle. For three days they scoured the land in front of his castle in this way, and on the fourth, as the sun rose, Bahram sent a message to Parmoudeh, saying, "Lord and king of the Chinese Turks, why have you chosen this castle of all places in the world? Where now is Saveh Shah's ambition to rule the earth? Where are his treasures and power, his elephants with their barding, his clear-minded nobles? Where are his sorcerers' tricks and stratagems, that you've now hidden yourself away like this? The land of the Turks wasn't enough for you. The world had never seen anyone as fine as your father, but now you're holed up in this castle like a woman, beating your hands against your head in desperation, and with bitterness in your heart. Open your castle gates and ask for mercy, ask to be allied with my country's king, and send out whatever wealth you have. I will speak for you at the king's court, and if you have some secret that's lighting up your dark soul, reveal it to me; don't hold yourself aloof now that your situation's so desperate. If you want war, no army's going to help you when you've no money, but if you've allies enough and treasure and cash enough then beat your war drums and come out and fight!"

When the envoy had delivered this message, Parmoudeh replied,

"Say to him, 'Don't struggle to know the world's secrets. Because your first trial turned out well, you have become overconfident of the world's ways. Don't be so vain of victory; you may be young, but the world is old. No one knows the secrets of the turning heavens because they never show us their true face. Ridicule does not become a nobleman, and remember that I too once possessed an army, elephants, and war drums. The high heavens weave lies, and you should not give your heart over to presumptuous pride. My father was a brave, experienced warrior, and you saw him on the day of battle; the earth was the slave of his horse's hooves, and the heavens turned as he willed. But he sought what he should not have sought, and his evil designs brought him torment. Merit is obscured by ridicule, and our enemies laugh at us. You say that you have more cavalry and elephants than grain in the hopper of a mill, but this was true of him too; his good luck deserted him, and you will not always be prosperous and hailed as the light of the world. You should fear your fate, for it can turn an antidote into poison. Any man who makes bloodshed his profession will have enemies plot against him, and they will spill his blood as he has spilled the blood of other warriors. If you raise destruction's smoke over the land of the Turks, they will want vengeance sooner or later. I shall not present myself before you because I fear for my life. You are a slave and I am a king; how can I grovel before a slave? And I shall not fight you without an army, because my friends would say I was crazy to do so. If the straits I'm in force me to ask for quarter from your king, there is no shame in that; and then the doors to my treasury and my castle will be yours and you can do as you wish with this noble land.'" The envoy delivered his message, and Bahram was satisfied when he heard it.

Bahram Chubineh Writes to Hormozd, Asking That Parmoudeh Be Granted Safe Conduct

Bahram wrote a favorable letter to his victorious king, saying, "The Chinese emperor is besieged and asks for your favor: he requires a sealed letter of safe conduct, and when he receives it he will come to establish peace between you. He has fallen from greatness into misery and desires our protection."

When this letter arrived, the king's joy seemed limitless. He summoned his courtiers and sat the envoy on a royal throne; as the man read the letter out jewels were poured over him. Hormozd said to his courtiers, "Thanks be to God: I shall pray for three watches of the night, because the emperor of China will be my subject and the high heavens will be my crown. The leader of the Chinese Turks lifted his head up to the heavens and thought of himself as the king of the world, but now he pays homage to me. I give thanks to the Lord of the Sun and Moon, who has granted me this authority. I shall bestow hoarded wealth on the poor, so that goodness will come of this, and you too should praise God, and act with righteousness." He called over Bahram's envoy and spoke to him kindly and at length. He asked for a jewel-studded belt, clothes made of gold cloth, a horse with a bridle worked with gold and jewels; these he handed to the envoy, and added a purse of gold coins and many other presents. Then he declared that Bahram was the chief of all champions, and had a scribe write a proclamation on silk: "Parmoudeh the emperor is my ally; he is under the protection of Hormozd. May God, whose slaves we are, witness this seal and proclamation."

Then he wrote a letter as affectionate as heaven's grace to his ambitious commander: "Allow Parmoudeh and his army to come to my court, and send here whatever is valuable among the spoils you have taken from his army: may God be your guide in this matter. Search out where the enemy might still be hiding, and may your good fortune enable you to capture them and burn their houses. If you think more efforts are required and you need more troops, ask for them and I shall send you as many as necessary. Give me the names of those Persians who have acted well and valiantly in this war, so that they may be rewarded. I shall give your men the border areas, and you will receive a crown of authority over them."

Bahram Chubineh's Anger Against Parmoudeh

When this letter reached Bahram, his heart was rejuvenated. He was astonished, and summoned the Persian troops to see the gifts he had been sent; everyone who saw them congratulated him. Then he read them the letter, and such a cry of congratulation went up that the ground seemed to shake. He sent the warrant of safe conduct to Parmoudeh in his castle and brightened the darkness of his soul. That nobleman descended from his castle, blessing Hormozd's name as he did so. Everything of value in the castle was recorded. The proud commander of the castle immediately mounted his warhorse and marched with his men out of the castle, ignoring Bahram. When Bahram saw that, despite having captured this king, he was being treated with contempt, he sent men to bring Parmoudeh before the army on foot. Parmoudeh said to him, "I was the lord of any assembly and now I am a suppliant with no power; I have descended from my ivory throne to a wretched state. You are a malevolent man, and today you have not acted well toward me in having me brought before your troops like this. I have a warrant of safe conduct and I intend to travel to the king, in hopes that he will treat me as a brother and lighten the burden of my sorrows. What business have you with me, now that I have handed over to you my royal throne and wealth?"

Parmoudeh's words enraged Bahram and he lost all sense of proportion; he struck at Parmoudeh violently with his whip, as a man might strike an inferior; he had his legs bound in iron fetters and confined him in a tent. When Khorad-Borzin saw this, he said to himself, "Good sense is no friend to this commander." He went to the chief scribe and said, "This terrifying champion has less sense than the wing of a mosquito, and that's why he has no respect for anyone else. Someone should tell him that this is not the way to act, and that there's no greater danger to a man than his own anger." The two of them went to Bahram, their faces dark with foreboding, their lips filled with advice. They said, "You have thrown away the fruits of your labors; God forbid that a nobleman's head be filled with fire like this!" Bahram knew that he had acted in an ugly fashion, that he had done something as foolish as throwing sun-baked bricks into water. He regretted his actions, held his head in his hands in shame, and had Parmoudeh released from his fetters. He sent Parmoudeh a horse with a gold-worked bridle and an Indian sword in a golden scabbard, and went to him to alleviate his distress. He stayed with him while he prepared to leave, watched him mount his swift horse, and accompanied him along part of his route. But he saw that the king's face did not relax or grow cheerful. When the time came for them to separate, he said, "I think you're angry with me in your heart. If this is so, say nothing about it to Persia's king; it will not do your reputation with him any good."

The emperor replied, "My complaints are against fortune, and I have addressed them to God. Don't think of me as someone who will gossip about everyone, but if your king learns nothing of this, he does not deserve to be king. The turning heavens put me in fetters: I shall not say that some slave injured me." Bahram turned pale at these words; he writhed inwardly but managed to swallow his anger. He said,

"As far as you are able to, don't sow
Destruction's seeds—you'll reap them when they grow.
I tried to make your situation better;
I wrote on your behalf, and in my letter
I did not tell the king of all you'd done
In trying to renew the war he'd won."

The emperor replied, "That evil has gone by, and the past is as wind. When a man is defeated in war he has to be patient and make peace. But peace and anger seem to be the same to you, and it's clear you have little enough good sense. If a man follows his lord, he doesn't stumble at every turning. It's God's way we should follow, and cleanse our hearts of darkness. The evil you've done has gone, like the wind: it would be better if you said no more about it."

Bahram said, "I'd hoped this matter would remain secret. But if the sin I've committed is going to produce trouble, I won't try to hide it under a silk veil. When you get there say whatever you want to; my reputation won't be harmed by it." The emperor replied, "I consider any king a fool who takes no account of good and evil, and who is silent when his subjects act in ways that are wrong. Seeing such things from a distance, anyone—enemy, well-wisher, or ally—would say that you are an impulsive and contemptible lout, and that the Persian king is feeble-minded." Bahram was enraged, and his face turned pale. Khorad-Borzin saw this and was afraid that his bloodthirsty master would kill Parmoudeh in his fury. He said to Bahram, "My lord, swallow your anger, and turn back. What the emperor has said is true; you should listen to him and drive evil thoughts from your mind. If you had not spoken so coldly toward him, you heart would not now be so troubled." Bahram replied, "This vicious, talentless son can't wait to rejoin his father." The emperor spoke again: "Don't do this evil to yourself; greatness grows old with anger. People like you, with heads full of dust and hearts full of smoke, think ill of everyone and get on with no one, and their pride is perversity and foolishness. You try to frighten me with talk of the King of Kings, but it is right that my pain and peace should come from him. He is my equal, a nobleman as I am; he's not some malevolent slave. He is wise, dignified, of good lineage, and he remembers those who are wellborn. I command you, by the head and army of the Persian king, to turn back now, and to say nothing further to worsen your situation."

When he heard this, Bahram turned back to his army's encampment. Khorad-Borzin, the chief scribe, and other learned men wrote a letter to the king, recounting everything that had happened, publicly and privately. In the anger of the moment Bahram said to his chief priest, "Go immediately into the castle, hurry like the wind, and see what kind of treasure is there." The scribes went with trepidation in their hearts, and worked from sunrise until three watches of the night had passed: many pages were blackened with ink, but still the work was not finished. There was hardly room to move in the castle, so many undisturbed ancient treasures were there. From the times of Afrasyab and Arjasp there were gold coins, pearls from the sea, and gems from mines whose excavation was heaven's work. Famous treasures were there, like the belt of Seyavash, which had three bands of jewels on each boss, and also his earrings, the like of which no commoner or nobleman in all the world has ever owned. Kay Khosrow had given them to Lohrasp, who had in turn given them to Goshtasp, and Arjasp had placed them in the castle at a time that no one now remembers. No astrologer or learned man could compute the wealth gathered there: one by one each item was recorded, and Bahram sent an eloquent, honest, and alert scribe to gather everything of value that was in the castle and bring it to one place on the plain.

Among the valuable objects were a pair of earrings and a pair of boots with gold thread braided on them and jewels at the end of each braid. There were also two bolts of Yemeni cloth of gold weighing seven *man* each. In his perversity and arrogance Bahram ignored his duty and set these things aside. Then he ordered Payda-Goshasp to take the treasures to the king, with an escort of a thousand troops. He demanded ten caravans of camels from the emperor and counted off the goods as they were loaded. With the emperor at the head and the baggage train following on behind, the caravans made their way to court.

The Emperor Arrives at Hormozd's Court

While the king of the world sat in state, with a crown on his head and a mace in his fist, news came that the emperor and his train of ancient treasures were approaching. The king went on horseback to the courtyard of his palace to see the emperor's face, and also to see whether, when the emperor caught sight of him, he and his escort would dismount. He waited anxiously for the outcome, as the emperor and Payda-Goshasp came into view. The emperor dismounted and ran toward the king. There was a pause, and then Parmoudeh remounted his black Arab horse. The King of Kings urged his own horse forward and the two conferred together for a moment in the courtyard, but as Parmoudeh tried to follow the king into the palace the chamberlain caught at his horse's bridle. Parmoudeh quickly dismounted, and showed his duplicity by this act of homage. The king too dismounted, took him by the hand, and led him forward to the throne. He showed him great kindness and questioned him; the two talked for a long time together. Apartments worthy of his rank were set aside for him and decorated, and Parmoudeh was provided with everything he could need. His men were given quarters near him, and a scribe was placed at his disposal. The king sent servants to take care of the treasures that had accompanied Parmoudeh.

Hormozd Learns of Bahram's Behavior and Allies Himself with Parmoudeh

A mounted messenger arrived with a letter from the chief scribe, which read: "May the king reign in prosperity forever, and all his actions be generous and just. Know then that the army's champion has taken two bolts of Yemeni cloth, a pair of boots encrusted with uncut jewels, and the earrings of the noble Seyavash that have come down to us as a reminder of his greatness. Since the champion underwent great hardships, this should not be a cause for surprise." The king turned to Parmoudeh and asked him to recount what he had seen, and Parmoudeh confirmed what the scribe had written. Hormozd burst out in fury,

> *"This overbearing man has lost his way,*
> *Forgetting it's his business to obey.*

He dares to strike the Chinese emperor
As though he were some base inferior,
And then he takes these earrings—as if he
Were heir to some imperial family.
His good deeds have dispersed like wind-blown dust,
His justice is now shown to be unjust."

He summoned Parmoudeh to the place of honor at his side, and the two sat feasting until night came and spread its dusky curls over the assembly. Hormozd turned to Parmoudeh and said, "You have suffered a great deal from my country." Taking Parmoudeh's hand in his, he said, to the emperor's astonishment, "Renew our treaty, and let us set our agreement on a new basis." Then they swore a solemn oath, by God and their souls, that Hormozd would not turn his heart aside from the emperor, and that he would not change his mind in this for anything that Parmoudeh did. They swore by the throne and crown, by the sun and moon, by the sacred fires of Azar-Goshasp and Azar-Panah, by God who is above all and who maintains Venus and Jupiter in their courses, that when Parmoudeh returned to his people he would not turn aside from Hormozd or from his courtiers. When they had sworn this oath, they rose and retired to their sleeping quarters.

As the yellow sun rose above the mountains the two kings awoke. Hormozd had prepared a robe of honor, woven from gold and silver, together with a horse and crown. He sent these to the emperor and then accompanied him for two stages of his return journey. At the start of the long third stage he said his farewells to Parmoudeh and turned back.

When Bahram learned of the gifts Parmoudeh had received from the king, and that he was returning in triumph, he went out to meet him accompanied by his Persian noblemen. He had a stock of fodder made ready for Parmoudeh at every stage of the route he would take, in the towns and villages, as well as on the plains and mountains. Bahram came before him prepared to apologize humbly for his former behavior. He greeted him respectfully, but the emperor of China turned his head away and refused to accept any of Bahram's gifts, including the fodder he had provided for him and the slaves and purses of gold he had brought. Bahram rode with him, but the emperor would not cast a glance at him, and so they went forward for three days during which time Parmoudeh did not address a word to him. On the fourth day the emperor sent Bahram a message, "Go back, you have tired yourself out enough." Bahram angrily turned back toward Balkh, and there he stayed for a while, regretting his former actions, his heart filled with sorrow.

Hormozd Sends Bahram Chubineh a Spindle and Woman's Clothes

King Hormozd was dissatisfied with Bahram, and his impetuous behavior filled the king's soul with foreboding; first, because Bahram had intentionally mistreated the emperor, and second, because of his presumptuousness in taking spoils to which he was not entitled. He therefore wrote him a letter: "Base devil that you are, you no longer know yourself. You think you have no need of your superiors and do not understand that our abilities come from God. You see yourself seated on the sphere of heaven; you have disobeyed my orders and followed your own inclinations. You have forgotten the troubles I have endured, as well as the army and wealth I command. You do not act as a commander should, but raise your head up proudly to the skies. Now a royal gift has come that is worthy of you, something that is appropriate for the way you are acting." When Hormozd had sealed the letter he gave orders that a black spindle case containing a spindle, raw cotton, and various other unworthy objects be prepared. Then he asked that a purple blouse woven from hair be brought, together with a woman's red coif, and a pair of woman's yellow pants. He chose a messenger who was suitable to take such a present and said to him, "Take these to Bahram, and tell him, 'You are a worthless, useless wretch. You put the emperor of China in chains and you enjoy humiliating your superiors, but I shall bring you down from that throne you've placed yourself on, and I shall not consider you as a man from now on!'"

The messenger memorized the speech and traveled as fast as the wind. When Bahram saw the letter and gifts, he chose silence and patience. He said, "So this is my reward, and this is how my king treats me. But this cannot be the king's idea; it must be because of gossip by those who hate me. The king rules over his subjects, and if he despises me that is his right, but I did not think my enemies would gain access to him so quickly. Everyone has seen what I have done since I set off with all speed from the king's court, with only a small army at my command; everyone knows the difficulties and trials I have undergone.

If contempt is my reward for enduring such hardships, and if fortune can only treat me with scorn, I shall complain to God that the heavens have utterly withdrawn their favor from me."

Then he prayed to the Lord of Justice from whom all benefits come, and put on the red and yellow clothes. He set out the black spindle case and the other objects the king had sent, and ordered the king's nobles who were in his army to present themselves before him. His dark soul was filled with conflicting thoughts as they entered, young and old, and saw the manner in which he was dressed. They were all bewildered, and each man's heart was filled with anxiety. Bahram said to his men, "This is the gift the king has sent me. He is our ruler and we are his slaves, and our hearts and souls are filled with love for him. What do you think is the significance of this, and how should I answer our country's king?"

They all began to speak at once, saying, "You are a great champion, and if this is what the king thinks of you, then his courtiers are dogs. Remember what that wise old man said when he was grieved by Ardeshir's negligence: 'I despair of our king's throne and crown, since he pays no attention to whatever I do, for good or ill.'" Bahram replied, "Do not say such things. It is the king who confers honor on his army; we are his slaves, he is the provider, and we are his suppliants." But the Persians answered, "We shall serve no more. None of us will call him the king of Iran, or Bahram his army's commander." They went out on to the plain, and for some time Bahram spoke with them, and his lips were always filled with conciliatory words.

Bahram Sees His Fortune
After two weeks Bahram went out of his castle and onto the plain. He saw a thicket of trees ahead of him that seemed a fine place to pause and drink wine. A wild ass was there, and no one has ever seen a more splendid animal. Bahram rode after the wild ass, but without tiring his horse. After riding across open country for a while, they reached a narrow defile, and when Bahram followed the ass through it a wide desert appeared on the other side. The ass sped ahead and Bahram rode after him across the burning plain, until a magnificent castle appeared in the distance. Bahram rode toward it, with the ass still leading the way. Izad-Goshasp was riding after him, and when they reached the castle, Bahram gave him his horse's reins and said, "May wisdom always be

your companion." Then he entered the castle on foot, and went forward without a guide.

Izad-Goshasp waited for a while at the palace gateway, and then Yalan-Sineh, who had been following them on his swift-paced horse, arrived. Izad-Goshasp said to him, "Go into the castle and see where our commander has got to." Anxious to find his master, his heart filled with trepidation, Yalan-Sineh entered the castle. He saw an arch and a hall more splendid than any he had ever seen or heard of in Iran. In the hall there was a golden throne, its feet encrusted with jewels, and on it was laid a tapestry of Byzantine brocade embroidered with figures picked out in jewels on a golden ground. A woman with a crown on her head was sitting on the throne; in stature she was like a cypress tree, and her face was as lovely as the spring. The army's commander was seated on another golden throne, and around him were numerous serving girls as beautiful as idols, with fairy-like faces. As soon as the woman saw Yalan-Sineh she said to one of the serving girls, "Go quickly, dear friend, and tell that lionhearted warrior he is not permitted to be here. He should stay with his companions, and Bahram will come to him soon enough." And immediately she sent the serving girls to Bahram's escort, to take their horses to the stables, where they and their saddles would be taken care of.

At the command of this beautiful hostess, a gardener opened the door to the gardens, and a Zoroastrian priest came forward, praying quietly, the sacred barsom in his hand. Tables laid with many kinds of food were set about the garden. Once the men had eaten, their horses were brought at the gallop, and as he was leaving, Bahram addressed the woman who had entertained them, "May Jupiter protect your crown." She answered him, "Be victorious, always patient-hearted, careful in your councils."

As Bahram left the garden, his eyes rained down bitter tears. His nature had changed, his answers had changed, and his head seemed to lift itself up to the Pleiades. Again he followed the wild ass until it led them out of the thicket. When he reached the town again, he said nothing to his soldiers of what had happened. Khorad-Borzin watched him and said, "My lord, tell me truly, what was this marvel that you saw in the hunting grounds, this thing that no one has ever seen or heard of?" But Bahram gave him no answer: deep in thought, he made his way to his palace.

Bahram Adopts the Customs of a King

On the next day, when the foothills of the mountains turned to silver and the golden lamp of heaven appeared, a carpet of Chinese brocade was spread out, so that the ground looked like the heavens. Golden seats, with cushions made of gold-worked brocade, were set about the palace, and the commander of the army took his place there on a golden throne. He sat enthroned in state, like a King of Kings, with a royal crown on his head. The chief scribe saw all this and realized that it was an act of defiance. He went to Khorad-Borzin and told him what he knew, what he had seen, and what he had heard. Khorad-Borzin now knew that matters had reached a crisis and said to the scribe, "Don't take this lightly. We should say nothing, but in the darkness of the night we should go to the king." Once they had made their decision, they fled from Balkh under cover of darkness.

When Bahram heard of what they had done, he said to Yalan-Sineh, "Take a hundred horsemen and go after those two fools." Yalan-Sineh rode as quickly as wind-blown dust. He soon caught up with the chief scribe and closed in on him like a wolf. He stripped this innocent man of all he had and brought him back in heavy chains, so that Bahram could kill him. Bahram said to him, "Devil's spawn, why did you leave me without permission?" He answered, "My lord, Khorad-Borzin frightened me. He said that if I stayed, only my enemies would be happy; that he and I were in danger of being killed unless we fled." Because Bahram's honor seemed to be impugned before his men, he replied, "We must discuss the good and bad of this." He compensated the scribe for his injuries, returned his wealth to him, and said, "From now on consider more carefully what it is you're doing, and don't try to flee again."

Khorad-Borzin Informs Hormozd of Bahram's Actions

But Khorad-Borzin rode on undetected to the king's court, and there

> He told him all he'd witnessed, every word
> Of all the secret gossip that he'd heard—
> He told him of the thicket, the wild ass
> That guided Bahram, and the narrow pass,
> The jeweled castle and its lovely queen,
> The serving girls, the wonders that he'd seen.

He detailed all of this, and when he'd done,
Answered his monarch's questions one by one.

Hormozd was astonished by his words, and everything he heard went straight to his heart. Then he remembered the priest who had foretold that someone would arise who would disobey him, and a cold sigh came from his heart. Immediately he summoned the chief priest and sat him down with Khorad-Borzin, to whom he said, "Tell this man what you saw on that road." Khorad-Borzin did as his king commanded him and went over everything once again. The king said to the chief priest, "What can this mean? We must consider all the parts of it: there was an ass in a thicket and it went ahead as a guide; a castle in the middle of an arid desert, a crowned woman on a golden throne with serving girls standing before her as if she were a queen. All this is like a dream that someone tells in an ancient tale."

The priest answered the king of the world, "That wild ass was a demon in disguise, and when it summoned Bahram away from righteousness, falsehood appeared in his heart. Understand that the castle was made by magic, that the woman on the throne was an evil sorceress who showed Bahram the way of rebellion and promised him the crown and throne of sovereignty. When he returned from seeing her, he became drunk with ambition, and you should accept that he will never submit to you again. Your best course is to find some way to recall the army from Balkh to your court."

Now the king regretted the spindle case, the raw cotton, and the unworthy clothes. Not many days passed before a messenger arrived from Bahram, bringing a basket filled with daggers whose points were bent back. This he placed in front of the king, who stared at the iron weapons. He ordered that the daggers' blades be broken and flung in the basket; then he sent them back as a sign of conflict and warfare. When Bahram, whose judgment was clouded now, saw the daggers broken in half, he called the envoy and his Iranian advisors to him and had them gather round the basket. He said, "Look at this gift from the king, and don't think of it as something of no importance." His men brooded on what the king had done, and on their commander's words. They said, "The king's first present to us was a spindle and brightly colored clothes, and his next was broken daggers—this is worse than wounds and curses. Such a king should never rule, and may his memory be forgotten. If Bahram should once again ride his horse back to that court, curses on him and curses on the father who sired him."

Hearing their words Bahram realized that the soldiers' hearts were weary of the king, and he said to them, "Be careful and clear-headed, because Khorad-Borzin has told the king everything that had been kept hidden. Now each one of you must look to save his soul by swearing fealty to me. I must send lookouts onto the roads, or my luck will be at an end and one by one every man in this army will be killed." He said this, but his plans were quite otherwise: pay attention, and you will be astonished. He sent horsemen throughout the countryside to intercept any letters from the king that might encourage the Persians to fight against him. For some time no one received a letter from the king.

Bahram Takes Counsel with His Advisors; His Sister Gordyeh's Intervention

Then Bahram summoned the nobles of the army and put before them much that he had kept private. Hamdan-Goshasp, the chief scribe, war-like Yalan-Sineh, Bahram who was descended from Seyavash, and the wise counselor Payda-Goshasp were all present. He addressed this band who were eager for battle and had lost their way: "Anyone would be pleased to have you as advisors. Our superior is needlessly angry with us, and has deserted all precedent and good custom. We cannot simply weep over our troubles, like a man who hides his wounds from his doctors; what remedy do you suggest? If we hide our problems from the wise, simple matters become difficult; we are suffering, and it is time to put our troubles before knowledgeable men. We left Iran with a tiny army, eager for battle, and no one in the world will ever see a more numerous army than that of our enemies. Saveh Shah and Parmoudeh marched on Persia, but they considered us of no more importance than a wax bauble, as their real goal was Rome. But Parmoudeh and Saveh Shah were over-taken by events the like of which the world has never known. Even though we underwent all manner of hardships and left them neither their wealth nor their elephants, the king has restored their power and is now threatening war with us. What can we do now to escape his trap, to slip free of his chains? Think of your own lives, and of what balm you can bring to these wounds. I have unburdened my soul to you and told you the secrets of my heart."

In Bahram's private quarters his virtuous sister Gordyeh lived; this wise woman was her brother's confidante and comfort. Listening from behind the curtain separating her from the company, she heard her brother's words and sprang up, her heart quivering with anger. She stepped into the assembly, her head filled with all she wished to say, her tongue with ancient precepts. When he heard his sister's voice, Bahram fell silent, and out of fear the Persians gathered there also stopped speaking. Gordyeh addressed them: "You are noble and ambitious men, why do you remain silent at his words, although you bleed inwardly? You are Persia's leaders, her wise men, her magicians; what's your opinion of all this, what game do you intend to play on this blood-soaked plain?"

The horseman Izad-Goshasp spoke: "You remind us of the ancient heroes, and even if our tongues are sharpened in anger they are silent before the flood of your opinions. All your deeds are from God; they are brave, knowledgeable, and filled with wisdom. We don't have to be like leopards eager for war with anyone. Let no one ask for more from me, this is the extent of my answer. But if you make war, I will be with you, I'll ride at the head of your cavalry. If my commander approves of me, this will keep me young forever." Bahram saw that Izad-Goshasp was trying to position himself between the two factions. Then he turned to Yalan-Sineh and said, "What thoughts are you keeping hidden?" He replied, "Noble commander, whoever follows God's ways will not turn to evil when he gains victory and glory. If he does so, congratulations will turn to curses, and the turning heavens will hate him. God has given you glory and good fortune, an army, wealth, a diadem, and a throne, and, if you strive for more than this, ingratitude will fill your heart with sorrow."

Next he turned to Bahram, the son of Bahram, and said, "You are a wise man and reason is your friend, what do you think of this search for a throne and crown? Will it end well, or in pain and sorrow?"

> Then Bahram smiled at him, and threw his ring
> Into the air. "A slave can be a king,"
> He said, "for just as long as this will stay
> Up in the air. And there's no simple way
> To gain a royal crown: make no mistake,
> This is an arduous task to undertake."

Then Bahram Chubineh said to Payda-Goshasp, "You're a lion in battle, a man who rides his horse hard, what do you say to this business of mine? Am I worthy of the throne?" Payda-Goshasp replied, "You are like the heroes of ancient times. A priest once gave good advice for a situation like this: he said that if a man is knowledgeable and farsighted and becomes king, his soul will ascend to the heavens. It's better to risk all to be the possessor of the world's wealth than to live a long life as a slave."

Next he turned to the chief scribe and said, "You're an old, cunning wolf; open your lips and give me your opinion." But for a while the chief scribe was silent; he sat sunk in a multitude of thoughts. Finally he said to Bahram, "A man who seeks to satisfy his ambition will do so if he is worthy of what he aims at. Fate's reach is long and sure, and our efforts will bear fruit if God approves of them." Then Bahram said to Hamdan-Goshasp, "You have had experience of life's good and bad fortune. Whatever you say here in front of us will disappear like the wind and have no evil consequences for you. Give us your opinion of this business, say whether you think it will turn out badly or well." Hamdan-Goshasp replied,

> "You're valued by great men, and yet you fear
> Evils to come, troubles that are not here.
> What have imperial crowns to do with you?
> Thank God, and do what you were born to do.
> Don't reach up for the dates if you're afraid
> Their thorns will injure you. Stick to your trade!
> A country's king can never be at peace,
> The fears and trials he faces never cease."

Their remarks distressed Bahram's sister, and her soul was shrouded in darkness. She said nothing to her brother from the time the sun set until half the night had passed. Then Bahram said to her, "You are a chaste, good woman; what do you think of what has been said here?" But Gordyeh wept and gave him no answer; she was not happy with the words that his advisors had spoken. She turned to the chief scribe and said, "You have an evil nature, like a wolf's. Do you think none of the noble warriors of the world has ever longed for the crown and throne, for mighty armies, for victory and good fortune? Isn't being

king easier than being a slave? One should weep for this knowledge of
yours! But we should follow the customs of the ancient kings, we
should listen to their words." The scribe answered her, "If my opin-
ions are not acceptable then you should say and do whatever seems
right to you; let your heart guide you."

Gordyeh turned to Bahram and his conceited knights and said,
"There's no goodness in your knowledge or your opinions; your pride
is taking you down a mistaken path. How many times the throne has
been unoccupied, but no subject ever glanced at it. They maintained
the world in chivalry and had no eyes for the throne. Anyone with
intelligence knows that proud sovereignty is finer than being a humble
subject, but no one attempted to seize the Kayanid throne; men stood
before it ready to serve their kings. A stranger to the royal blood would
disgrace the crown, and it is lineage that makes a man worthy of great-
ness. Let us begin with Kavus, who tried to find out the ways of God,
to count the stars and hunt down the secrets of the turning heavens.
His perverse thoughts left him wretched and sorrowful in Sari, and
heroes like Gudarz and Rostam were troubled in their souls by this.
And then he went to Hamaveran and his legs were placed in heavy
gyves; but no one ever coveted his throne, they felt only sorrow and
sympathy for him. When the Persians said to Rostam, 'You are worthy
of the Kayanid throne,' he yelled at the man who had spoken, 'May I
see you in your narrow grave! How can a champion presume to sit
with the ceremonial that attends a king? Should I occupy a golden
throne while our king is imprisoned? My curses on such a suggestion!'
He chose twelve thousand warlike cavalry and rescued Kavus from his
chains, as well as Giv, Gudarz, and Tus.

"No subject ever sought the throne, no matter how fine his family
was. And when this Turk Saveh Shah came seeking the royal seal and
crown, the world's Creator prevented him from reaching Iran. You're a
slave, so what has put it into your head to desire the throne of the King
of Kings? This Yalan-Sineh curvets his horse and boasts that he will
make Bahram, the son of Goshasp, into a king, and so leave a name for
himself in the world. But the wise old king Nushin-Ravan was reju-
venated by the sight of Hormozd, and the great of the world are his
allies or his subjects. In Persia there are three hundred thousand horse-
men, all famous fighters and all the king's slaves sworn to carry out his

commands. The King of Kings chose you as his commander, as was right since your ancestors successfully fought against their enemies, and you return evil for this good fortune. Well, you should realize that it's yourself you're hurting. Don't make ambition king over good sense; no sensible person will call you wise if you do this. I may be a woman, and much younger than my brother, but I give a man's advice. Don't throw away the deeds of your ancestors, and God forbid that you remember my advice when it is too late."

The whole company was dumfounded by her words, and Bahram bit his lip. He knew that she spoke the truth, and that the way she sought was the right one. But Yalan-Sineh said, "My lady, don't talk in this company about kings and their customs. Hormozd will soon be gone, and our commander deserves the throne. Since Hormozd is as we know him to be, you should consider your brother to be the king of Iran. If Hormozd is so proud of the Kayanid crown and their customs, why did he send that spindle as a royal gift? We've had enough talk of Hormozd, anyway. He's of Turkish lineage, and I curse his people; may they disappear from the earth! You talk about Kay Qobad's line, whose crown and throne lasted for a hundred thousand years, but their rule is finished now, and there is no point in invoking their name. As for Hormozd's son, Khosrow Parviz, he is not worth mentioning. The best of his entourage are your brother's slaves and servants, and if Bahram tells them to, they will shackle their master's feet for him."

Gordyeh answered him,

> "You plot the devil's work in all you do
> And devils lie in wait to ambush you!
> Stop trying to destroy us; all I see
> From you is empty talk and vanity.
> My father was the governor of Rey
> But if my brother acts now as you say
> And carries out your treacherous design,
> He will annihilate his tribe and mine.
> All that we have achieved, at so much cost,
> Will be dispersed upon the winds and lost.
> You servile wretch—go! Be my brother's guide,
> Lay waste our lives, spread ruin far and wide!"

When she had said this, she began to weep and went to her own apartments; in her heart she was now a stranger to her brother. Everyone said, "This wise and eloquent woman speaks so well that her words seem to come from a book; her wisdom surpasses Jamasp's." But Bahram was displeased, and his sister's words angered him. His dark heart was filled with foolish thoughts, and he constantly dreamed of the royal throne. He thought, "Ambitious men can only win this fleeting world through hardship." Then he ordered a meal prepared and called for wine and musicians. "Sing a song of heroes," he said to the singer. "We'll have the song of the Seven Trials while we drink our wine, the one that describes Esfandyar's expedition to the Brazen Castle and the tricks he played in those bygone days." His companions drank Bahram's health a number of times, saying, "May the province of Rey flourish, since a commander like you hails from there, and may God create more as you are!" When the drinkers' heads were confused with wine and night came, the meeting broke up.

Bahram Has Coins Struck in the Name of Khosrow Parviz

The sun lifted its lance into the sky, and the dark night quailed before its brilliance. Bahram called for the chief scribe, and together they wrote a splendid letter to the emperor of China. Bahram wrote, "The need to apologize wracks me with pain; my heart is filled with regret and cold sighs. From now on I shall respect your country, and if I become lord of all the world, I shall treat you as my younger brother. Wash all thoughts of vengeance from your soul, and do not keep China and Iran separate from one another." Then he turned to other business.

He opened his treasury and distributed silver, horses, and slaves to his army; his secret aim in this was to further his ambitions. He chose a worthy warrior from among his troops and made him the governor of Khorasan. Sunk in thought, he himself set off from Balkh to Rey on the day of Khordad in the month of Dey. He turned many ideas over in his mind, and then gave orders that coins were to be minted in the name of Hormozd's son, Khosrow Parviz. He selected an eloquent, trustworthy merchant, one who was suitable to carry out a delicate task, and told him to take a purse of these coins to Ctesiphon. There he was to buy fine Byzantine brocades, worked in silk on a gold ground, so that the coins would be taken to the king and he would see them.

Bahram Writes to Hormozd, and Khosrow Parviz Flees from His Father's Court

He wrote a letter to Hormozd, filled with boasting and vanity. He mentioned many matters—Parmoudeh and Saveh Shah's army, the battles he had fought, and the king's present of a black spindle case and a woman's coif. Then he wrote, "In my dreams I never see the splendor of the king's face; when your noble son Khosrow Parviz sits on the throne, I shall level the mountains and make them plains if he orders me to, and turn the deserts to an Oxus of his enemies' blood." In this way he hoped to have the innocent prince killed. He said to the merchant, "When Hormozd sees the coins, he will be alarmed, and when he no longer has Khosrow Parviz to help him, he'll see the fate I have in store for him. Once I have established my authority over the country I shall tear the Sasanians up by the roots. God did not create the earth for them, and it's time they forfeited his favor."

A messenger took his letter to Baghdad, and when Hormozd read it, his face turned as pale as fenugreek. Then news came of the coins minted in his son's name, and sorrow was piled on sorrow. He writhed inwardly and became suspicious of his son. He confided his suspicions to Ayin-Goshasp, saying, "Khosrow has become rebellious and wants to separate himself from me. He's had coins minted in his own name, and what could be more contemptuous of my authority than this?" Ayin-Goshasp said, "May your horse and the battlefield never be without you!" Hormozd said, "I'm going to get rid of the wretch immediately." Secretly they summoned a man and sat him down with the king that night. Hormozd said to him, "Do as I say: banish Khosrow from the face of the earth." The man replied, "I shall do it; I'll use spells to drive all pity from my heart. Have poison brought from the king's treasury, and when he's drunk at night, I'll mix it with his wine. This will be better than shedding his blood." But the chamberlain learned of this, and could not sleep from anxiety. He hurried to Khosrow and told him the secret plan. When Khosrow Parviz heard that the king of the world was secretly plotting to kill him, he fled in the darkness of the night from Ctesiphon and seemed to disappear from the face of the earth. Not wanting to lose his precious head to no purpose, he made all haste to Azerbaijan.

When news reached the country's governors and lords of the marches that Khosrow had fled with a few horsemen from the king's court, they made inquiries as to where he might be. Men like Badan-Piruz and Shir-Zil, both just warriors with the strength of elephants, Shiran and pious Vastui, Khanjast from Oman, Bivard from Kerman, and Sam, who was descended from Esfandyar, from Shiraz—one by one they came with their warriors and sought out Khosrow Parviz.

Khosrow said to them, "I fear the king and his courtiers, but if you will go to the fire-temple and there solemnly swear to protect me, never to break this oath, I shall stay here with confidence and have no fear of Ahriman's designs against me." The warriors went to the fire temple and swore as he had requested, saying that they would hold him as dear as their own eyes. As soon as he felt safe, Khosrow sent out spies to find out what his father said about his flight, and whether he was plotting anything new. When Hormozd learned that Khosrow had fled, he immediately had Gostahm and Banduy, Khosrow's maternal uncles, thrown into prison, as well as all of Khosrow's other relatives, and there was much talk about this.

Hormozd Sends Ayin-Goshasp to Fight Against Bahram; He Is Killed

At this time the king said to Ayin-Goshasp, "We seem to have no recourse, and pain is our companion. Now that Khosrow has gone, what shall we do against that wretched slave Bahram?" Ayin-Goshasp said, "Your majesty, this business of Bahram has gone on for long enough. It's my blood he secretly wants to shed, because I was the first person to humiliate him. Send me to him with my legs in shackles; it may be that this will benefit you." The king replied, "I can't do that; it would be the work of Ahriman. No, I'll dispatch an army, with you at its head, and you can win glory in battle. But first send someone to him to sound out what he is thinking. If he is ambitious for sovereignty, for the crown and throne, good fortune will finally desert him. But if he is prepared to be my subject and prefers peace, I'll give him a portion of the world to rule, and place a hero's crown on his head. Let me know immediately what he is up to; don't delay, be as quick as you can."

Ayin-Goshasp set about putting the wise king's plan into action. There was a man from his town who was a prisoner in the king's jail, and when he heard that Ayin-Goshasp was going to war, he sent someone to him with a message saying, "I'm a fellow townsman of yours imprisoned here. If you beg me from the king, I'll accompany you on this expedition. I'll fight before you, as your protector in battle, if only I can get out of this narrow prison." Ayin-Goshasp sent someone to the king to say on his behalf, "One of my fellow townsmen is languishing in your jail; give him to me, your majesty, so that he can come with me on this expedition." The king said, "That evil good-for-nothing? When is he ever going to fight in front of you in a battle? He's a violent criminal, a lout, and a thief; you must be hoping for a bribe from him! Well, at the moment I don't want to deny you anything, even though there's no worse blackguard than he is." And he handed this bloodthirsty devil over to Ayin-Goshasp.

Ayin-Goshasp led his army out, and they marched as quickly as the wind as far as Hamedan, where they halted. Ayin-Goshasp made inquiries as to whether anyone there understood the stars and could foresee the future. Everyone said, "You'll be pleased with the astrologer who comes to you. There is a rich old woman who lives here who seems to know all the secrets of the stars. Whatever she says comes to pass, and she can tell you in the summer what will happen in the autumn." Ayin-Goshasp sent someone with a horse to fetch her, and when she arrived he questioned her about the king's business, and about his own military expedition. Then he said to her, "Whisper in my ear whether I will die in bed, or by my enemy's dagger." As he was talking privately with this old woman about his own affairs, the man whom he'd begged from the king passed in front of the woman, glanced at his commander, and went on. The old woman said, "Who was that man? We should weep for the harm he'll do to you. Your sweet life is in his hands; my curses on him, skin and bones!"

When Ayin-Goshasp heard this he remembered something he had heard long before, something an astrologer had told him that he had forgotten: "Your life is in the hands of a neighbor, who is a thief, a lout, and a worthless wretch. He will confront you during a long journey; you will cry out for help, and he will shed your blood." He wrote a letter to the king, saying, "That man I begged from you should not have been freed from prison; he is something worse than devil's spawn. You told me this, but I did not have your royal *farr* and so could not see the truth. As soon as he arrives, have his head cut off." He sealed the letter and when the seal was dry, he summoned his fellow townsman. He heaped praises on him, gave him some money, and called down God's blessings on him. Then he said, "Quickly and secretly take this letter to the king. If he gives you an answer, bring it straight to me; don't stay with the king."

The young man took the letter and set off, brooding as he went. He said to himself, "I was chained and imprisoned, I couldn't move, and I'd no food. God got me out of that terrible mess, and now my blood and brains are boiling at the thought of going back to Ctesiphon." He went gloomily along the road for a while, and then he opened the letter to the king. When he read his commander's letter he was bewildered at the ways of the world. He said, "This is my neighbor who begged me from the king, who said it was a noble deed to spare me, and now he wants to shed my blood. Did this idea come to him in a dream? Well, now he's going to find out what bloodshed means, and all his troubles will be over." His head whirling, he turned back and traveled as fast as the wind. As he approached the commander he saw that there was no one about: Ayin-Goshasp was resting in his tent, brooding on the king and what fate had in store, and there was no servant, or companion, or sword, or horse nearby. When his neighbor entered the tent Ayin-Goshasp knew that he had come to shed his blood. The man clapped his hand on his sword, and Ayin-Goshasp tried to soften him with words. He said, "Young man, you're mistaken, wasn't it I who begged you from the king when you'd despaired of life?" The man replied, "You did, but what did I do to make you want to destroy me?" As he said this he struck at Ayin-Goshasp's neck with his sword, and the commander's days of feasting and fighting were at an end.

He brought the severed head out of the tent, while the army was still unaware of what had happened. Knowing he would be condemned for shedding his commander's blood, he made his way as quickly as he could to Bahram Chubineh. He said to him, "Here is the head of your enemy, who was planning to kill you. He'd led an army here against you, not knowing what you intended." Bahram asked, "Whose head is this? Who should weep over it?" The man replied, "This is Ayin-Goshasp, who came from the king's court to fight against you." Bahram said to him, "This noble man had come from the king's court to make peace between me and the king, and you cut his head off while he was sleeping. You will receive such a punishment from me that all who see you will weep for you." He ordered that a gibbet be erected before his door, in view of the army and the countryside, and there the wretch was strung up alive, so that he understood in his heart what he had done.

When it was known that Ayin-Goshasp was dead, some of the horsemen he had brought with him went over to Bahram, and others to Khosrow Parviz, hoping to revive their fortunes in the world. The army was like a shepherdless flock that disperses on a day of wind and snow.

Gostahm and Banduy Blind Hormozd

When Hormozd learned of his commander's fate, he was so downcast that he gave no audiences and no one saw him with a wine glass in his hand. He found no peace, he could neither eat nor sleep, and his eyes were always filled with tears. Repeatedly he gave orders that no one was to be admitted to him. One of the courtiers said that Bahram was preparing for war and was intent on seizing the imperial throne. Another said that Khosrow Parviz was so angry with the king that he was leading an army against Iran. The chieftains were bewildered, and each one had a different opinion of what was happening. When these rumors spread throughout Ctesiphon, the king's rule lost all authority. His servants became anxious and quarrelsome, and those who had blessed him now cursed him. Few of his men remained at their posts at court, and to the king's heart the world had become a narrow place.

Banduy and Gostahm learned that the king's *farr* had darkened. The prisoners freed themselves from their chains and appointed one of their number to find out what was happening and who among the warlike chieftains was still at the court. When they learned how matters stood, they cast aside all pretense of loyalty and broke out of the prison. Such a tumult arose that the whole plain rang with it, and the troops who were in the city stood powerless against them. Now armed, and with followers and weapons, Gostahm and Banduy marched determinedly on the palace; they washed all trace of shame from their eyes. Then a detachment of troops appeared from the bazaar, heading toward the palace. Gostahm addressed them, "If you wish to join us, renounce your loyalty to the king, because Hormozd has turned aside from all good sense and from the true path; from now on you should not call him a king. Punish him, make Persia's glory as bitter as colocynth for him. We shall have you as our vanguard and place a new king on

Persia's throne, and if you do not falter in this enterprise we shall put Persia in your hands, while we ourselves will retire to some corner of the world with our companions."

At Gostahm's words, as one man the troops cursed the king and cried, "May there never again be a king who seeks to shed his son's blood!" Roused by his speech, they became shameless, setting fire to the palace gates and swarming into the audience hall where they snatched the crown from the king's head and dragged him down from the throne. Then they put hot irons into his eyes, and the bright lamps of his life turned dark. They left him, still alive, in this state and looted all the wealth that was there.

THE REIGN OF KHOSROW PARVIZ

By night, Banduy and Gostahm quickly sent a messenger with a
change of horses to Khosrow, who was then at the fire-temple called
Azar-Goshasp, to tell him what had happened. But when the envoy
described the tumult in Baghdad, the young man's face turned as pale
as fenugreek. He said, "Any man who ignorantly leaves the ways of
wisdom and has no fear of the turning heavens will lead a profitless life.
If this evil you describe were to please me, my sleep and food would
turn to fire. Even though my father tried to shed my blood and I fled
from Iran, I am still his slave and will listen to all he has to say."

Immediately he set off with a large number of troops from Barda',
Ardebil, and Armenia, traveling as quickly as fire. When news reached
Baghdad that a new claimant to the throne was on his way, the town grew
peaceful again, and Khosrow was encouraged by this calm. The city's
chieftains came out to welcome him; they seated him on an ivory throne
and placed a golden torque about his neck and a splendid crown on his
head. Khosrow entered the town in sorrow and went sighing to his father,
his face a witness to the grief he felt. When he saw him, he wept and paid
him homage; the two were closeted together for a long time. Khosrow
said, "You are a scion of Nushin-Ravan, but misfortune has dogged your
reign. You know that if I had been here to support you, not even a
needle would have been permitted to scratch the tip of your finger.
Think of what your orders are for me, now that sorrow has come to you
and my heart is filled with grief. If you command me, I shall be a slave
guarding you; I have no desire for the crown or the army and will cut my
head off before you if you order me to." Hormozd replied,

> "You are a wise man, and you know this day
> Of hardship and despair will pass away.

I've three requests to make of you, no more;
Grant me these three and I'll not ask for four.
First, that as day breaks, in the morning light,
You'll sing to me, and drive away the night;
Next that you'll send a warrior to me,
A veteran of our warlike cavalry
Who'll talk of wars and hunts; and see he brings
A book that tells the exploits of our kings,
So that in hearing them I'll find relief
From my incessant pain and constant grief.
Thirdly, see that your uncles understand
They're your inferiors here, and that this land
Is yours to rule, not theirs; blind them, and make
Their days a darkness for my sorrow's sake."

Khosrow replied, "May anyone who does not mourn for your blinded eyes perish, and may your enemies be swept from the earth! But consider, Bahram Chubineh has become a formidable warrior, and he has innumerable cavalry and swordsmen with him. If I dispose of Gostahm, I'll have no one to turn to for help against Bahram. As for horsemen who've known battles and banquets to recite the stories of ancient kings for you, I'll send new ones to you constantly. I wish your heart wisdom and relief from the pain you suffer." He left his father's presence in tears, and told no one of his secret thoughts. The son was a kinder man than the king, and as a sage once said,

"A sweetly spoken youth is finer than
A difficult and quarrelsome old man."

But in the end the virtuous and the vicious both lie beneath the dust.

Bahram Chubineh Learns That Hormozd Has Been Blinded and Leads His Army Against Khosrow Parviz

Bahram was astonished when he learned that the king's eyes had been put out with hot irons, that the light had died away from the garden's two narcissi, that Hormozd's good fortune was at an end and his son now sat on his throne. For a while he was taken aback and brooded on this turn of events, but then he ordered that the armies' drums be sounded and his great banner be brought out onto the plain. The baggage was loaded, the cavalry mounted, and Bahram prepared to do battle with Khosrow Parviz. Audaciously he led his army, which was like a moving mountain, as far as the bank of the River Nahravan.

Khosrow grew anxious when he learned of Bahram's aggressive advance, and sent out spies. He said to them, "First you must find out how his army feels about his intentions, whether they're with him in his desire for war, or whether they're moving against us reluctantly. Then notice whether Bahram stays mainly in the center of the army or moves about among his troops. Also, learn how he holds audience, and whether he ever thinks of going hunting while they're on the march." The spies set off on their mission without the army being aware of this, and when they returned they went secretly to Khosrow and said, "From the nobles down to the young recruits, his soldiers are with him in everything he does. When his men are on the march, he is always moving among them, sometimes with the right wing, sometimes the left, and then with the baggage train. He has everyone's confidence and has no need of outside help. He holds court like a king, and hunts in the same fashion. All his behavior is that of a king, and he constantly reads the book of *Kalileh and Demneh*."

Khosrow said to his vizier, "We have a long business ahead of us. Bahram terrifies the monsters in the oceans when he rides out against his enemies. He learned how to act like a king from my father, when he was king of the world; he's taken *Kalileh and Demneh* as his vizier, and no one has a human advisor who's better than this." To Gostahm and Banduy he said, "Sorrow and trouble are my partners now." Men like Gerdui, Shapur, Andian, the leader of the Armenians, as well as other nobles, sat with the king in secret council. After their deliberations Khosrow Parviz led his army out from Baghdad, and pitched his pavilion on the plains. The two armies were now close together: on the one side the commander, and on the other the king. When the world's light declined in the sky and night spread its dark curls, sentries were posted on each side. Then, as night grew dry-lipped and sick at heart and fled from day's dagger, the din of drums began from both camps, and the sun rose to guide them to battle. The king ordered Banduy and Gostahm to put on their iron helmets, and he went forward with his nobles to the riverbank.

When the sentry reported to Bahram that the enemy's forces were within two bowshots, he summoned his advisors. He mounted his white charger, a proud, fine horse with a black tail and brazen hooves. Grasping an Indian sword, whose blow was like lightning from a cloud, Bahram rode forward, glittering in glory; Izad-Goshasp was on his left, and Ayin-Goshasp and Yalan-Sineh, both longing for combat and filled with courage, accompanied him. There were also three Turkish warriors in his retinue, men who had sworn loyalty to Bahram, saying that if they saw the king become separated from his men, they would bring him dead or as a captive to Bahram.

On the one side Khosrow waited, on the other Bahram, and between them flowed the River Nahravan. The soldiers on both sides watched, to see how Bahram would approach the king.

Khosrow Parviz and Bahram Chubineh Address One Another

Bahram and Khosrow met, the face of the one was open and confident, the other's closed and apprehensive. The king, dressed in a Chinese cloak of gold-worked brocade, sat on his ivory-colored horse. Gerdui preceded him as a guide, and he was accompanied by Banduy, Gostahm, and Khorad-Borzin, who wore a golden helmet; they were all covered in iron, gold, and silver, and wore golden belts studded with rubies. When Bahram saw the king, his face turned pale with anger. He said to his warriors, "So this miserable son of a whore has risen up from wretchedness and stupidity to be a man; he's become powerful and is ready for battle. He's learned how to be an emperor, but I shall bring his days in the world to an end soon enough. Look at his army from one end to the other, and see if there's a single warrior there worthy of the name. I can see no horseman there who'd dare to confront me. Now he will see how men fight: headlong horses, swords and maces, weapons' blows and the hail of arrows, warriors' cries and the give and take of battle. No elephant can keep its ground when I lead my army in an attack; the mountains tremble at my war cry, and savage lions flee. We'll put a spell on the waters with our swords and fill the desert from end to end with blood." Then he urged on his piebald horse, and it leaped forward like a winged bird. To his army's astonishment he advanced to the river's edge and stood opposite the young king; a few Persians, all prepared to fight against Khosrow, accompanied him.

Khosrow turned to his companions and said, "Which of you can recognize Bahram Chubineh?" Gerdui said, "Your majesty, look at the man on the piebald horse, the one wearing a white cloak and a black sword belt, who's riding at the center of that group of warriors." Seeing Bahram, Khosrow knew immediately what kind of a person he was and said, "You mean the dark, tall man, on the piebald charger?" Gerdui said, "Yes, that's him, a man who's never had a benevolent thought in his life." Khosrow replied, "If you ask a hunchback a question, you'll get a rough answer. And can't you see that that man, with his boar's snout and half-closed eyes, is obviously evil and an enemy to God? I can see no humility in him, and no one is going to be able to treat him as a subject." But still hoping to turn the time from one of fighting to one of feasting, he addressed Bahram from a distance: "You're a proud warrior, but what are you doing here on the field of battle? You're an ornament to the court, the throne and crown depend on you, you're a pillar of the army in warfare, a shining torch at feasts, an ambitious God-fearing warrior; may God never abandon you! I have considered your position and weighed well the things you have done. I shall treat you and your army as my guests and refresh my soul with the sight of you; then I shall name you the commander of Iran's armies, as is just, and pray to God for your welfare."

Bahram heard him out. He let the reins in his hand drop and saluted Khosrow from his horse, then stood silently before him for a long while. Finally, still mounted on his piebald charger, he said, "I rejoice in the life I lead, and fortune favors me. I don't wish you greatness, because as a king you know neither justice nor injustice, and when the king of the Alans rules it's the most miserable wretches who support him. I've considered your position too, and I have a noose ready and waiting for you. Soon I'll construct a tall gibbet and tie your two hands together with my lariat; then I'll string you up as you deserve, and turn your days to bitterness."

When Khosrow heard Bahram's answer, his face turned as pale as fenugreek. He said, "Ungrateful wretch, no God-fearing man would speak as you do. A guest approaches, and you greet him with curses when you should be welcoming him. This was never the way of kings or noble warriors; neither Arabs nor Persians have ever acted like this, not if you go back for three thousand years. A wise man would be ashamed of such behavior. Think again, don't follow this ungrateful course. When a guest greets you kindly, you must be a devil to answer in such a fashion: I fear that I shall see you fall on evil days, ruined by your own obstinacy. Your well-being is in the hands of that king who lives eternally and rules all things; but you are an ungrateful sinner against God, and you'll bring contempt on your body, terror on your heart. When you say I'm king of the Alans, you only mention a third of my lineage; in what way am I unworthy to rule, how is this crown unsuitable for my head? Nushin-Ravan was my grandfather, Hormozd my father; who can you name who is more entitled to the crown than I am?"

But Bahram answered him, "You're evil, and you talk and act like a fool. You prattle about being a guest, but your nature is wicked and all you can do is repeat old stories. What do you know about what kings say? You're neither wise nor a good warrior. You were king of the Alans and now you're a contemptible wretch, lower than a slave of slaves. You're the most wicked man in the world; you're not a king and you have no right to lord it over other chieftains. The people have proclaimed me king, and I shall not leave you space on the earth to set your foot down. You say that bad fortune's in store for me, and that I'm unworthy of sovereignty, but I say that you're unfit to be a king, and may you never occupy the throne again! The Persians are your enemies, and they'll fight till they tear you up by the roots and flay the skin from your body and fling your bones to the dogs!"

Khosrow said to him, "You villain, what has made you so angry and insolent? Ugly talk is a fault in a man, and your nature has had this trait from the beginning. Fortunate the man who lives by wisdom, but wisdom has deserted your brain, and when a devil's hard-pressed he'll say anything. But I wouldn't want a fine warrior like you to be destroyed by anger: you should drive anger from your heart, control yourself, and put a spell on your rage. Remember the just God who rules all things, and in doing so make wisdom your guide. There's a mountain of troubles ahead of you, and, if you look, you'll see it's higher than Bisitun; the desert thorns will bear fruit before someone like you becomes king. Your heart's filled with thoughts of sovereignty, but we'll see what God wills. I don't know who has taught you this villainy and these councils of Ahriman, but whoever it was wanted to bring about your death with his words." Then Khosrow dismounted from his ivory-colored horse, removed the precious crown from his head, and turned lamenting toward the sun. His heart was filled with hopes of God's grace, and he said, "Bright Lord of Justice, it is you who makes the tree of hope bear fruit. You know this slave who stands before me, and that one should weep for the shame he has brought to the crown." And then he went aside to pray, and opened the secrets of his heart to God:

> "If I'm to give up my authority
> And see my lineage lose its sovereignty,
> I'll be your servant, and my one desire
> Will be to tend your temple's sacred fire.
> I'll take no food but milk, the clothes I wear
> Will be of wool and animals' coarse hair;
> I'll have no gold or silver, and I'll stay
> Within your temple's precincts night and day.
> But if my sovereignty's to stay with me,
> Guide my great army on to victory
> And do not hand my crown and throne to one
> Who's shown himself a slave in all he's done.
> If I achieve my heart's desire, I swear
> This horse and crown, the royal jewels I wear,
> My clothes of cloth of gold—all these will be
> Devoted to your temple's treasury;
> Over your temple's lapis dome I'll pour
> Ten purses of gold coins, and when I'm sure
> That I am once again Iran's sole king,
> I'll add ten thousand more gold coins, and bring
> The captives from this war, so that they'll be
> Your temple's slaves in perpetuity."

This sorely pressed man stood again after he had prayed, and quickly went back to the riverbank. He called out to Bahram Chubineh, "You have no wisdom, no manners, no royal *farr*; you're the hellish slave of some monstrous irascible demon who has blinded you. You've found rage and revenge instead of wisdom, and hell's demons applaud you for it; thorn brakes seem cities to you, hell seems an orchard; wisdom's torch has died before your eyes, and taken all the light from your heart and soul. Some wily magician has raised your ambitions and shown you the abyss, but the leaves of the tree for which you reach are poisonous, and its fruit is bitter. None of your family has ever shown such pride and ambition; God has not granted you the exalted position you crave, and you should not dream of things that can never be. A crab cannot sprout an eagle's wings, and an eagle cannot fly beyond the sun. I swear by God and by the throne and crown that if I find you without your army, I shall do you no harm. I have heard your savage language, but it is God who gives us victory and on him I rely. If I am not worthy to be a king I've no wish to live as anyone's subject."

Bahram replied, "You're foolish and in thrall to Ahriman. Your father was a God-fearing man, but you didn't respect him for what he was, and you pushed him ignominiously from the throne. You want to be a wise and capable king in his place, but you're perverse and an enemy to God, who will send you nothing but evil. It's true that Hormozd was unjust at times, and the land groaned beneath his oppression, but you're unworthy to be his son and to rule Iran and Turan. You don't deserve a throne, or even life; good fortune has so deserted you that a tomb is all you're good for. I shall avenge Hormozd, and I shall be king in Iran. And tell me again the story that everyone agrees on, about how you thrust hot irons into the king's eyes, or that you at least gave the orders for this to be done. From now on you'll see that sovereignty is mine, and I rule the heavens, from the sun to Pisces."

Khosrow said, "God forbid that a man should rejoice at his father's pain. It was written thus; what had to be came to pass, and there is no point in discussing it endlessly. You call yourself a king, but when death comes you won't even have a shroud to your name. You've your horse and barding, and because of these you hope for a sovereignty that will never exist. You've no home, no wealth, no country, no lineage; you're a king who's filled with wind. For all your army and wealth and false titles, you'll never know the splendor of a royal throne. Subjects have never sought to be king because they knew they were not worthy of the throne and crown. God created sovereignty out of justice, ability, and lineage; he bestows it on the most worthy person, the wisest, and the most compassionate. My father made me king of the Alans, and I was troubled enough by you then; now God has conferred imperial sovereignty, greatness, and the royal crown and throne on me. I shall do good in the world, so that my name shall not disappear after my death. When Hormozd ruled justly, the world rejoiced in his reign, and I as his son have inherited his throne, as is right, and with the crown and royal belt I have found good fortune. But you—you are filled with sin and deceit: first you attacked Hormozd, and all the evil in his reign was from you and your tricks and plots and lies. If God wills it, I shall avenge him and turn your sun to darkness. Who is worthy of the crown? If I am not worthy of it, who is?"

Bahram replied, "You're a warrior, and whoever snatches sovereignty from you is worthy of it. The Ashkanians ruled when Babak's daughter gave birth to Ardeshir. And isn't it true that Ardeshir became powerful and seized the throne through killing Ardavan? But five hundred years have passed since then, and the Sasanian crown has grown cold. Now it is time for me to possess the throne and crown, and my victorious fortune will ensure this. I look at your face and your fortune, your army, your crown, and your throne, and I stretch out my hand against the Sasanians as a savage lion leaps on its prey. I shall erase their names from the records and trample the Sasanian throne beneath my feet. If one listens to those who know the truth, it's the Ashkanians who deserve to rule. The truth is that you're a Sasanian and your lineage is a contemptible one, because Sasan was a shepherd, and the son of a shepherd. Didn't Babak employ him as a shepherd for his flocks?"

But Khosrow answered, "You ungrateful criminal, wasn't it the Sasanians who raised you up in the world? Your words are nothing but lies from one end to the other, and no honor will come from such talk." Bahram replied, "It's no secret that Sasan was a shepherd." Khosrow said, "When Dara died, he was unable to bequeath the crown to Sasan; but though fortune turned against him, the race survived, and no justice will come from your unjust chatter. And this is the intelligence and good sense and glory with which you hope to gain the imperial throne?" As he spoke, he laughed and turned away toward his own army. But one of the three savage Turks, who were as wild as wolves, and who had promised Bahram that on the day of battle they'd seek fame by bringing the king before him dead or alive, rode fearlessly forward and flung a lariat of sixty coils, which caught on Khosrow's crown. Gostahm severed the rope with his sword and the king's head was unharmed. Bahram turned on this wretched Turk and said, "You deserve to be in your grave for this! Who told you to attack the king; didn't you see me standing there parleying with him?" Then he returned to his camp, his soul filled with sorrow, his body with disquiet.

*V*ehemently, Gordyeh tried once again to dissuade her brother from his plans, but to no avail. Bahram attacked the king's army at night, and Khosrow Parviz was forced to flee back to Ctesiphon. There he consulted with his blind father Hormozd, who advised him to ask the emperor of Byzantium for help. As they were talking, news came that Bahram's army was approaching, and Khosrow fled westward into the desert. Khosrow's advisors, Gostahm and Banduy, remained behind and, unbeknownst to Khosrow, strangled Hormozd. Then they set out after Khosrow, who had taken refuge in a monastery. Bahram's army reached the monastery, but through a ruse of Banduy's Khosrow was once again able to flee westward. Banduy fell into Bahram's hands and was imprisoned, but he managed to escape. Bahram crowned himself king. Khosrow meanwhile had reached Byzantium and entered into lengthy negotiations with the emperor there, using Gostahm as his go-between. Eventually, the emperor agreed to help him against Bahram Chubineh.

The Emperor of Byzantium Sends Khosrow Parviz an Army and His Daughter

The emperor selected a hundred thousand of his troops, all fine men ready for battle, and these he assigned to Khosrow Parviz, together with armor, cash, and warhorses. In this way the king's long wait came to an end. The emperor had a daughter named Mariam, who was a wise, dignified, and intelligent young woman. He affianced her to Khosrow, with the rites of his religion, calling down God's blessing on her. Gostahm received her from the emperor, and with all due ceremony he handed her over to Khosrow. The emperor presented them with such a dowry that the splendid horses carrying it were exhausted by the weight. There were gold vessels and imperial jewels, rubies, and clothes embroidered with gold-worked designs, carpets, and Byzantine silk brocades bearing figures woven in gold. There were also bracelets, torques and earrings, and three splendid crowns encrusted with jewels.

Four golden litters were prepared, their facings studded with gems, as well as forty closed couches of ebony, glittering with gems like a rooster's eyes. Following them came serving girls as lovely as the moon, and five hundred young male servants mounted on horses with trappings of gold and silver. Then there were forty handsome, charming Byzantine eunuchs, together with four wise and famous philosophers; to these last the king told everything that was necessary. He also spoke with Mariam in secret, advising her on obedience and her duties, on when she should be generous, on her food, and on what behavior was appropriate. When the gifts were reckoned up their value was estimated at more than three hundred million dinars.

The emperor consulted with astrologers as to when would be the best time for the journey and set off on an auspicious day. After two stages of the journey he gave orders that Mariam come to him, and he spoke with her at length. He said, "Keep yourself secluded, and do not loosen your belt until you reach the Persian border; Khosrow must not see you naked before then, since this could lead to unforeseen consequences." He then bade her an affectionate farewell. To his brother Niatus, who was in charge of the Byzantine troops sent to Khosrow, he said, "Mariam is of your own blood, and so I have entrusted her to you. I am giving my daughter, my wealth, and a well-equipped army into your safekeeping." Niatus accepted the charge, and when he and the king had spoken together, he wept as they turned aside from one another.

Niatus, bearing his sword and mace, marched at the head of the army. Khosrow heard of their approach and set out from the town where he was waiting. As the dust sent up by the approaching troops became visible, followed by their banners and their splendid armored cavalry bearing down toward him like the wind, Khosrow laughed from his heart, as a flower blossoms in the spring. His spirits lifted and he dug his heels into his horse's flanks. He saw Niatus and embraced him, questioning him at length about the emperor who had gone to such trouble on his behalf and offered him so much wealth. Then he went over to the litter, where he saw Mariam and glimpsed her face beneath her veil; he questioned her too, and kissed her hand, rejoicing in his heart to see her beauty.

Khosrow brought the army to his royal pavilion, where he had a private chamber prepared for Mariam. He sat talking with her for three

days, and on the fourth, as the sun lit up the world, he had a splendid
tent prepared, and there he summoned Niatus and his subordinates
Sergius and Kut, as well as the other Byzantine commanders. He asked
them, "Who are your leaders, your finest warriors?" Niatus chose sev-
enty men to lead the attack on the day of battle, and each of them had
a thousand picked cavalry following his banner. When Khosrow saw
this fine force of cavalry all eager for war, he praised God who has cre-
ated time and the world, and called down his blessings on Niatus and
the army, as well as on the emperor and his country. To the command-
ers he said, "If God is with me in this battle, I shall show my mettle,
and make the earth as splendid as the Pleiades. May our thoughts now
be only of friendship; the heavens are with us, and the kindness of
noble men is as an orchard for us to rest in."

*K*hosrow Parviz traveled to Azerbaijan, where the people welcomed him.
Bahram Chubineh's attempts to rally support began to fail, and there
were a number of skirmishes between Bahram and Khosrow's allies.
For a while, Khosrow became separated from the main body of his army.

Khosrow Fights Against Bahram Chubineh

At that moment a cry went up from the sentries, and Bahram was told
that a group of men was approaching. Eager for conquest, with his wits
about him, Bahram mounted his horse, he grasped his sword, and fas-
tened his lariat to his saddle. From his horse's height he surveyed the
little group of men who were approaching, and then chose a few of his
own warriors. He said to Yalan-Sineh, "That wretch wants to prove his
worth in battle: I know it can't be anyone but him who would dare to
fight against me. He's come to attack me with his handful of men, and

he's walking into the mouth of a monster. There can't be more than twenty warriors with him, and I don't recognize any of them. If he confronts me and I don't overcome him, I'm a nobody." To Izad-Goshasp and Yalan-Sineh he said, "Men don't hide their bravery; we don't need more than four of us to defeat them." There was a man there called Janforouz, who preferred night to day; Bahram put him in command of his troops, while he and three companions went out to confront the enemy.

When Khosrow saw Bahram, he said to the Persians, "Their men are coming. Don't let your hearts fail now, because I'm finally face to face with my destiny. I'm here with my mace, and there is that malignant Bahram; fight against these rebels to my rule! There are fourteen of you, three of them; God forbid that they defeat you!" Niatus and his Byzantine companions had no choice but to prepare for combat. Other men made their way into the mountains where they could look down on the two groups, and everyone said, "Why is the king throwing his life away like this? Why should he leave behind all his fine cavalry and go into battle alone?" They raised their hands to the heavens in horror, believing that Khosrow was as good as killed already.

Bahram urged his horse forward and Yalan-Sineh and Izad-Goshasp accompanied him. When Khosrow's companions saw the enemy, most of them were like a flock of sheep scattering before a wolf. The king stood his ground as they fled, but he too had no choice but to wheel his horse about as Izad-Goshasp bore down on him. Gostahm, Banduy, and Gerdui were still with him: the royal hero called on God's help and said to Gostahm, "What is the point of my fighting if my men flee from me?" Gostahm replied, "Their cavalry are upon us, you can't fight them alone!" Khosrow looked back at their pursuers and saw that Bahram rode ahead of the rest. To save his skin, he cut away the straps of his horse's black barding, so that it could flee more quickly. His companions lagged behind, but his enemies began to close on him. As he rode, he came up against a mountain in which there was a narrow defile. He turned and his three enemies faced him; behind him was the defile, which narrowed to a cul-de-sac. The world's king was alone, cut off from his companions. He dismounted from his horse and began hurriedly to climb the mountain, but there was no way forward and the watching warriors despaired of his life. There was no place to make a stand, and no way to escape, and Bahram came rushing toward him. He called out to Khosrow, "Deceitful fool, now the abyss is opening beneath your glory! Why did you deliver yourself into my hands?"

When the king saw the desperate straits he was in, with his enemy's sword behind him and the rock ahead, he prayed aloud to God, "O world Creator, you are above the turnings of fate! Help me in my distress! It is you I turn to, not Saturn or Mercury."

> Before the echo of this prayer had died,
> Redoubled from the flinty mountainside,
> Sorush appeared; Khosrow stared in dismay—
> The angel's clothes were green, his horse was gray.
> He paused, then lifted Khosrow by the arm,
> And set him down where he was safe from harm
> (There's no surprise in this; the miracle
> Was God's, with him all things are possible).
> Now Khosrow wept and asked: "What is your name?"
> The angel said, "I am Sorush. I came
> In answer to your faith, and soon you'll be
> The world's king, glorious in your sovereignty:
> You'll reign for thirty-eight long years if you
> Act righteously in everything you do."
> He vanished, and the world has never known
> A vision like the one Khosrow was shown.

Bahram was astonished at all this and called repeatedly on God, saying, "When I fight with men I hope I'll never lack for bravery, but now I think I am fighting with the spirit world, and I must weep for my bad fortune."

On the other side of the mountain Niatus prayed to God for help, while Mariam scored her face with her nails in her anxiety for her husband. The hearts of the Byzantine troops on the plain and in the foothills were filled with foreboding, and when Niatus lost sight of Khosrow, he drew Mariam's golden litter aside and said to her, "Stay where you are. I fear that the Persian king has been killed." At that moment, Khosrow appeared in the distance on the mountainside; all of the army rejoiced, and Mariam's heart was freed from dread. Khosrow

came down from the mountain and told Mariam what he had seen: "My lovely Byzantine princess, it was God who saved me," he said. "I didn't flee out of cowardice or hang back from the fight. I was trapped in a rocky defile and called on the Creator for help, and he revealed to his slave secrets he had kept hidden. I saw things that the great Feraydun, Tur, Salm, and Afrasyab did not dream of, and they are portents of victory and royal power." The king told her what he had experienced, and then he ordered his army to prepare for battle and to remember Khosrow as they fought. For his part, Bahram was filled with consternation and regretted all he had done.

The Battle Between Khosrow Parviz and Bahram Chubineh

Khosrow's army came down from the foothills, and the world turned black with the dust sent up by its cavalry, while from the other direction Bahram led his army forward, so that there was no brightness left in the day. Bahram said, "Whoever leads an army needs to be wise, brave, and capable; the warriors who have seen my lance and my heroic spirit have chosen me over Khosrow, and I shall hurl the name of Nushin-Ravan into the dust." Making wildly for the king, he went ahead of the main body of his army, readied his bow, and notched an arrow to the string. Quickly he loosed the arrow toward the king's waist, but the arrow faltered in its flight, and when a slave saw it strike, he was able to pluck it out from the brocade in which the king was clothed. The king rushed forward against Bahram and lunged with his lance. Bahram's body was protected by a cuirass and the lance split with the impact; nevertheless, Bahram was terrified by the blow. The king sprang forward once again, bringing his sword down on Bahram's helmet; his sword, too, broke in pieces, and the blade stayed lodged in the helmet. Everyone who saw this or who heard the clash of metal on metal praised the king's courage. Their warriors followed the two, and battle was joined. Banduy hurried over to the king and cried, "Your crown is more exalted than the moon; this army is like a host of ants or locusts, covering all the desert and wastelands. It is not right that blood should be shed needlessly, or that a king attack his subjects. If anyone asks us for quarter, it would be better to grant it than to kill or wound him in battle." Khosrow replied, "I've no desire to avenge myself against those who repent of their sins; they are all under my protection, they are the jewels in my crown."

Night came down from the dark mountains, and the two armies separated and went back to their camps. The cries of the sentries and the jingling of bells meant that few of the soldiers fell asleep. Ambitious Banduy selected a brave herald with a strong loud voice and ordered him to mount his horse and get ready to wake anyone who slept. The two went out into no-man's land between the two armies and, when they were close to the enemy's camp, the herald cried out: "You slaves who have sinned and whose luck has run out, even if you have sinned more than any other man and distinguished yourself in battle against him, the king swears by God that he will forgive the crimes you have committed in public and in secret." When this cry was heard in the darkness everyone pricked up his ears, and Bahram's famous warriors prepared to steal away.

When the bright sun appeared above the mountaintops, and day made the land shine like silk, the plain was empty of people; they had crept away in the night, unbeknownst to Bahram. No one was to be seen in the tents, except a few of Bahram's closest friends and advisors. As Bahram walked among the empty tents and realized what had happened, he said to his companions, "Fly from this place, don't wait for disaster to strike." He asked the cameleers for three thousand camels, fine mounts that would foam at the mouth and bear heavy burdens. He loaded them with all the portable wealth he had—carpets and provisions, gold and silver, his ivory throne, bracelets, gold torques and crowns—then he mounted his horse and prepared to retreat.

Bahram Chubineh Flees to the Emperor of China

Bahram and his remaining soldiers trusted neither the road nor the loyalty of the countryside they were traveling through. With terror in his heart, Bahram took his gold and silver by trackless ways. Yalan-Sineh and Izad-Goshasp rode to one side of the army, telling stories of ancient kings as they went; Bahram rode ahead, his heart filled with regret and anguish. A humble village, too lowly to supply the wants of a nobleman, came into view in the distance. Because their throats were dry with thirst, Bahram stopped at an old woman's house. Politely they asked for bread and water. The crone heard them out and set an old basket containing barley bread in front of them, together with a tattered water skin. Yalan-Sineh handed the barsom to Bahram, but he was so sunk in sorrow he forgot to observe the ritual silence while eating. They ate the bread, asked for wine, and murmured their prayers. The old woman said, "You want wine, do you? I've wine and an old dried gourd: I split the gourd when it was fresh, and I dried it to use as a cup, and placed it over the wine." Bahram said, "As long as there's wine, we don't need any finer cup than that." The old woman went and brought her cup, which delighted Bahram. He filled it with wine, to please her, and said, "Now, mother, tell us what news you've heard about the world's business." The crone said,

"My brain's grown tired with all I've heard today:
So many folks from town have come this way
And all they'll talk about is Bahram's battle
Against the king, and such like tittle-tattle.
He had to run away, so people claim,
And hasn't got a soldier to his name."

Bahram said, "Tell me then, do you think Bahram was wise to do what he did? Or do you think he's an ambitious fool?" The woman said,

"Good sir, what devil's darkened your clear eyes?
Bahram rebelled, and everyone who's wise
Just laughed at him; nobody reckons he
Could win against a royal enemy."

Bahram said, "If he asks you, tell him to drink wine from a gourd, and keep a basket of barley bread for him till the next barley harvest comes round." This was Bahram's supper, and he stayed there that night, hoping to find some rest for his spirit, though he was unable to.

*H*ere, Ferdowsi unexpectedly breaks off his narrative for a moment to insert a lament for the death of his son.

Ferdowsi's Lament for the Death of His Son

Now that I'm more than sixty-five years old,
It would be wrong of me to hope for gold.
Better to heed my own advice, and grieve
That my dear son is dead. Why did he leave?
I should have gone; but no, the young man went
And left his lifeless father to lament.
I long to overtake him; when I do
I'll say, "I should have quit the world, not you,
And in your going, my belovèd boy,
You left your father destitute of joy.
You were my help in all adversity;
Why, now I'm old, have you abandoned me?
Did you perhaps find younger friends, who led
You from my side, to travel on ahead?"
At thirty-seven, his unhappy heart
Despaired and he was ready to depart;
When difficulties came he'd always shown
Me kindness, now he's left me here alone.
He went, while grief and bitter tears remain,
And inward suffering, and heartfelt pain.
He's gone into the light, and he'll prepare
A place to welcome his dear father there:
So many years have passed, and surely he
Is waiting there impatiently for me!
May God illuminate your soul, my son,
And wisdom keep you safe where you have gone.

N *ow that Bahram had fled, Khosrow Parviz had no more need for his Byzantine allies, who returned home. Bahram reached China, where he ingratiated himself with the emperor by killing a rebellious chieftain who was threatening the court, and then by slaying a lion that had killed one of the emperor's daughters. Bahram's reward was to be married to another of the imperial daughters. Khosrow Parviz sent a letter to the emperor demanding Bahram's extradition; the emperor's response was to put Bahram in charge of an army to invade Iran.*

Khosrow Sends Khorad-Borzin to the Emperor

When the king learned that this wolf Bahram had emerged from his thicket once more and was at the head of an army whose dust obscured the sky's brightness, he said to his counselor Khorad-Borzin, "Hurry to the emperor, and speak to him with all the persuasiveness you can muster. In Persia and beyond, you are the most knowledgeable of men, and you have the most eloquence." He opened the doors to his treasury and brought out such jewels, swords, and golden belts that Khorad-Borzin murmured the name of God in wonder. He took these objects as gifts and made his way to the Oxus; from there he continued by a secret route. When at last he reached the palace, he selected a messenger to announce his arrival to the emperor.

As soon as he heard the news, the emperor had the audience hall prepared and gave orders that the envoy be admitted. Khorad-Borzin entered humbly, made his obeisance before the emperor, and said briefly, "Your slave will speak when you order him to." The emperor replied, "Eloquent talk will make an old man's heart young again: tell us the profitable things you have to say. What's said is the marrow of a meeting, things left unsaid are only the skin." These words reminded Khorad-Borzin of the ancient enmity between their countries. He began his speech by invoking the world's Creator, who has made the heaven's sphere and the earth and time, and both the weak and the powerful; then he spoke of the certainty of death, and the history of the Persian kings. He continued: "Now the king of Persia is your relative, and his happiness and sorrow depend on your good and bad fortune. In the time of great kings, his mother's father was the emperor of China. Now in these days, when many things have changed, our alliance is renewed. May God who bestows victory keep you, and may the nobles of the earth be as your slaves." The emperor listened to him, then said, "You are a wise man; if there is another like you in Persia he must be eloquent enough to praise the heavens!" A place was set aside at court for the envoy, and the emperor kept him close by. At his command the gifts were counted out to the court treasurer, and the emperor said to him, "May you never want for wealth in the world. If there is something I can give you in exchange for all you have brought, tell me what it is. But you are more splendid than all gifts; you are the crown of the world's wise men."

Khorad's lodgings were beautifully decorated with all kinds of fabrics, and he was always welcome to join the emperor at table, out hunting, during the court festivities, or to drink wine with him. He waited for a chance to make his case; one day he saw an opportunity and bravely spoke up: "Bahram has an evil nature," he said. "He's more malevolent than Ahriman himself. He sells men of experience and understanding for profit, and for a paltry profit at that. It was Hormozd who promoted him, who lifted him up above the sun's sphere. Before that no one had heard of him, but then he was successful in everything he touched. He might act very well toward you now, but in the end he will betray you, as he betrayed the Persian king; he has no respect for either kings or God. If you send him to the Persian king, you'll lift the king's head above the moon with happiness. All Persia and China will then be yours, and you can have your palace anywhere you wish." The emperor was astonished at these words. His eyes darkened, and he said, "If you would keep my goodwill, don't say such things. I'm not a suspicious man and I don't break my word; a man who breaks his word has the dust as his shroud." When Khorad heard this, he knew that his mission had failed and that Bahram had encouraged the emperor with hopes of conquering Persia: to talk further with him would be a waste of breath.

Having lost hope of winning over the emperor, he decided to approach the empress, and he looked for someone with access to her. He met with a palace chamberlain and beguiled him with stories about Khosrow Parviz. Then he said to him, "I need to meet with the empress; help me be introduced to her as a scribe." The man replied, "There's no hope of that; Bahram Chubineh's her son-in-law, and all the power he has here is derived from her. You're a learned man—seek some other way, and tell no one of your secrets." Khorad-Borzin could see no solution to his difficulties.

There was an old Turk named Qalun, who was held in contempt by the other Turks; he wore sheepskins, and lived off whey and millet. Khorad-Borzin summoned this man to his fine quarters, where he gave him gold and silver coins, clothes, good meals, and entertained him with men of standing and importance. Khorad was cautious and patient, sly, and careful, and while he was cultivating Qalun he also continued to question the chamberlain of the empress's palace. This man, who visited the empress day and night, was tight-lipped and revealed nothing, but one day he said to Khorad, "You're a scholar, and a learned man, and if you had some knowledge of medicine too, and were famous for it, you would be as welcome as a new crown on the empress's head, because her daughter is ill." Khorad replied, "I have some medical knowledge. If you tell the empress, I will do my best in this business." The chamberlain hurried to the empress and said that a new doctor had arrived. She replied, "May you live in happiness for this news: bring him here, and don't stand scratching your head, get on with it!" He ran to Khorad-Borzin and said, "See that you do this secretly. Go to her and don't tell her your name; just be an amiable doctor."

Khorad went to the empress and saw that her daughter was suffering from a liver complaint. He asked for pomegranate juice and a particular kind of cress that grows on the banks of streams, and with these he tried to bring down the fever in her brain. By God's will, after seven days the girl was well again, and as resplendent as the new moon. The empress brought a purse of gold coins from her treasury and five lengths of gold cloth. She said, "Take these worthless gifts, and ask for anything else you desire." Khorad replied, "Keep these things for now; I shall ask for your help when I need it."

Khorad-Borzin Sends Qalun to Bahram Chubineh

For his part, Bahram had reached Marv, where he had drawn up an army as splendid as a pheasant's feathers. A messenger from the emperor reached him, saying, "Let no one go into Persia, because if Khosrow Parviz learns of our plans, he'll change his disposition toward us; have it announced that if anyone crosses into Iran without a sealed order from me, I'll have him hacked in two, and I swear by God that I won't let him ransom his life with silver."

For three months Khorad watched these secret preparations. Then, sick at heart, he summoned Qalun and made much of him. He said, "Every man in the world has some kind of secret in his heart. You used to beg door to door in China for coarse barley bread and millet, and sheepskins to wear; now your food is fine bread and lamb, and you dress in white silk. Look how you were and how you are, how men's curses have turned to congratulations! Now your life is drawing to an end; you've seen many days and nights, mountains and plains. There is something I want you to do. It's dangerous, and you may gain a throne from it, or you may end up in the black earth. I've obtained a copy of the emperor's seal, and I want you to travel quickly to Bahram and stay in Marv. There you're to put on your black sheepskin, and take a knife with you. Wait for the day of the month that is called Bahram, because he believes that's an inauspicious day for him. I've watched him for years, and on that day he never wants a crowd of people near him; he hides himself away wrapped in Chinese brocade. Say that you're bringing the great lord Bahram Chubineh a message from the emperor's daughter; see that you keep the knife in your sleeve until he calls for you. When you're admitted say, 'Her majesty ordered me to whisper her message in your ear, so that no one else may hear it.' And when he asks, 'What message?' run to him and plunge the knife into his gut, and then look for some way to escape. Whoever hears him cry out will flee from him—to the stables, or to look to the carpets or treasury; no one's going to harm you for this murder. And if you are killed for this, you've already experienced the good and bad that this world has to offer. But it's likely that no one will pay any attention to you, and if you can get away with this, you have bought the world and paid its price; King Khosrow Parviz will give you a city, a portion of the world for your own."

Qalun said, "I'll need a pass to get to him. I've reached the age of a hundred; how much longer am I going to live in want? My body and soul are ready to sacrifice themselves for you, since you've looked after me in the days of my wretchedness." When Khorad heard this he hurried to the empress and said to her, "The time has come, your majesty, for me to ask for your help. Two of my men have been thrown into chains, and I need your assistance to set them free. Get me a copy of the emperor's seal; you'll be giving me my life back if you do this." The empress said, "He's in a drunken sleep; I'll take an impression of his seal from his finger." She asked Khorad for clay, and then she went to her husband's bedside and impressed his seal ring on the clay; this she gave to Khorad, who thanked her and handed it over to the old man, Qalun.

Bahram Chubineh Is Killed by Qalun

Qalun took the impression of the seal and made his way quickly to Marv. There he waited until the day of Bahram, the one Bahram thought of as inauspicious. Bahram was alone in his house with a slave, eating a meal of pomegranates, apples, and quinces. Qalun went there and said to the doorman, "I'm not a warrior or a free man; I've been sent by the emperor's daughter. Her ladyship told me a secret to whisper in the king's ear: by his grace, she is pregnant, and unwell. If you could announce me, I'll give the message to his majesty." The doorman hurried to Bahram and said, "An ugly messenger dressed in a sheepskin is here; he says he has a message for your majesty from the emperor's daughter." Bahram said, "Tell him to show his face in here."

Qalun approached and put his head inside the door. Bahram saw a weak old man standing there and said, "If you've a letter, bring it here." Qalun replied, "It's something she said, that's all. I don't want to say it in front of anyone else." Bahram said, "Be quick, then, come and tell me in my ear; don't stand on ceremony." Qalun went forward with the knife in his sleeve, and then his treachery became apparent: he bent as if to whisper in Bahram's ear and plunged the knife into him, and the house was immediately in an uproar. As Bahram cried out, "Ah, I'm dead," people came running to him. He said, "Grab that man! Ask him who sent him here." Everyone who was in the house descended on the old man; they broke his legs, and the servants slapped and punched him, but no matter how hard they hit him he never opened his lips, though they tormented him from midday to midnight. By then his arms were also broken; they flung him into the courtyard, and with grief in their hearts they returned to Bahram.

Blood flowed from his wound; his cheeks were flushed and sighs escaped his lips. At that moment his sister Gordyeh came to him, tearing out her hair in her anguish. Distracted with grief, she laid her wounded brother's head against her breast and cried out,

> *"You were a knight whose presence spread such fear*
> *That lions would slink away when you came near;*
> *Who felled this pillar of the world? Who planned*
> *This crime and put the dagger in his hand?*
> *Alas for your ambition and your might,*
> *Your prowess that put savage lions to flight;*
> *You bowed to neither God nor king; whose blow*
> *So cruelly laid your mammoth body low?*
> *Who wrenched the roots up of this mountainside?*
> *Who felled this cypress in its noble pride?*
> *Who stretched his hand out to this princely crown*
> *And flung it so contemptuously down?*
> *Who filled this sea with earth? Who shattered this*
> *Great rocky peak and made it an abyss?*
> *We're strangers here, with no one to protect*
> *Our lives and wealth, or treat us with respect—*
> *My lord, I said to you repeatedly,*
> *'Do not uproot the tree of loyalty,*
> *Because if one Sasanian girl remains*
> *And crowns herself, it will be she who reigns,*
> *And all the provinces in Persia's land*
> *Will willingly submit to her command:*
> *Their hearts will not betray this family.'*
> *But you ignored my words, my lord, and me.*
> *Regret your actions, and the paths you trod,*
> *And take your guilty soul from here to God.*
> *Evil has come to our great house; I weep*
> *That all our foes are wolves, and we are sheep."*

When the wounded man heard her words, and understood the wisdom of her heart, and saw her face scored by her nails, her hair torn from her head, her heart filled with anguish, and her eyes with tears, he spoke sadly and falteringly: "Your advice lacked for nothing, but now my life draws to an end. Your advice had no effect on me; a demon misled me. There never was a king greater than Jamshid—the world lived in awe and hope of him—and yet he was misled by demons and made the earth a dark and fearsome place for himself. There was King Kavus, who ruled the world and was blessed by fortune, and he too was destroyed by a wretched demon; he ascended into the sky to see the turning spheres, the moon, and the sun, and you know the evil that came to him because of this. A demon misled me too, and I strayed from righteousness. I regret the evil I have done, but I trust that God will pardon me. Thus was it written on my forehead; why should I grieve for old sorrows again? The waters rise above my head, and all my joys and sorrows are as so much wind. Thus was it written, and what had to be came to pass, neither more nor less. I remember the words of advice you gave me. They are like jeweled earrings in my ears, but now that justice and injustice come to an end for me, do not repeat those words any more. Turn your face toward God, trust that fortune will smile again for you. The only friend you have against evil is God; speak with no one of either sorrow or joy. This is the portion I have had in the world, this and no more; now it has come to an end, and I must depart."

Then he said to Yalan-Sineh, "I hand the army over to you; pray for good fortune. Look after my virtuous sister; there is no finer advisor in the world than she is. Don't be separated from one another, stay always together. Don't remain in this enemy land; I have traveled here and am sickened by it. Go immediately to Khosrow Parviz; tell him your story and hear what he says. If he forgives you, have only him as the sun and moon of your lives. Build me a tomb in Persia, and destroy the palace I made for myself at Rey. I undertook so much for the emperor of China, and I had no thanks for it; this was not a just reward for my pains, that he should send some devil to kill me. Thus has it always been for the Persians; there has always been some evil demon guiding them."

Bahram had a scribe come and write a letter on silk. He said, "Tell the emperor: 'Bahram has gone; he has gone wretchedly and in sorrow, and with his ambitions thwarted.' Write, 'Look after those I leave behind and save them from their enemies, since I never did you any harm, and sought only righteousness and wisdom on your behalf.'" Then he spoke at length to his sister, first pressing her beloved head against his chest, then putting his mouth to her ear; in this fashion, his eyes filled with blood and he gave up his soul.

Everyone there wept bitterly for him, and their hearts were filled with anguish. His sister was loud in her laments, going over in her mind all he had said to her, and her heart was split in two with grief. They constructed a narrow coffin of silver and put a muslin undershirt on him, then wrapped his warlike body in brocade. Lastly they sprinkled camphor over the body until his head was hidden beneath it.

*K*horad escaped back to Iran, where he was warmly welcomed by Khosrow Parviz. The emperor of China wished to honor Bahram Chubineh's memory by proposing marriage to his sister Gordyeh, and he sent a letter to her to this effect.

Gordyeh Consults with Her Advisors and Flees from Marv

This young, wise woman sat and deliberated with her advisors. She said, "A new proposal has come to me, and it will always be remembered in my heart. The emperor of China has asked for my hand in the most ornate language. He has no faults; he is a great king, a brave man, and the lord of Turan. But whenever the Turks and Persians have tried to ally themselves in this way, the result has been sorrow and trouble. Look at Seyavash and Afrasyab; what did Seyavash gain except exposure to the burning sun? No mother ever bore such a fine young man, and yet he was destroyed. And what did Seyavash's son do but raise the dust of battle over Iran and Turan? We must arrange matters so that we flee in secret from these Turks to Persia. I have been worried about this for some time and have written a letter to Gerdui, asking him to intercede for us with Khosrow Parviz, and to tell him all that we've suffered."

Everyone there said, "You are our mistress, an iron mountain cannot make you quail, we will follow wherever you lead. You are more clever than a wise man, more intelligent than a knowledgeable vizier. We are all your servants and yours to command, and we will support you in your response to the emperor's request." She reviewed her troops, and had money made ready. She watched the army as it passed before her and chose one thousand one hundred and sixty men, champions who would not desert even if each faced ten enemies. She paid them and then returned to her house, where she said to the army commanders, "Once a man has decided on a journey his heart should be steadfast through good and bad fortune. He does not fear the might of the enemy, even if severed heads rain down on him from the clouds. We are strangers in Turan; we have no friends or allies here, we are weak and helpless among these Chinese noblemen. We must travel in darkness when our enemies are bewildered by sleep. Don't be anxious about the journey, even if a Chinese army attacks us, for surely their chieftains will come after us with their heavy maces. And if they come, stand together and give blows as good as those you receive. If any of you are not with me in this, you can stay here."

With one voice they replied, "We are your servants, and we will not turn aside from your commands." Then they prepared for battle against the Chinese forces; Yalan-Sineh, Mehr, and Izad-Goshasp mounted their horses and said, "It is better to die with honor than to live with the Chinese triumphing over us." Meanwhile Gordyeh visited the camel caravans and asked to see camels paraded before her; she chose three thousand of them and loaded them with their baggage. When night fell Gordyeh mounted her horse; she sat like a proud warrior, grasping a mace in her hand. Her horse was covered with splendid barding, and she wore armor and a helmet and a sword at her side. Her army rode forward like the wind, through the dark night and the bright day.

The Emperor Sends Tovorg After Gordyeh: She Kills Him

Many of the Persian soldiers threw themselves on the mercy of the Chinese emperor. His brother Tovorg came to the emperor and said, "You are a warlike lord; though many Persians have appealed to us for quarter, their army is making its way to Iran. If they escape, this will shame you forever, and your soldiers and people will laugh at you." The Chinese emperor's face clouded with fury and he said, "Hurry, and get an army together; see how far they've gone. When you catch up with them, don't use force at first, but try to see what persuasive talk will do. They don't know how we go about these things; it may be that you can break their determination by talk. Speak kindly to them, make much of them, treat them respectfully and chivalrously. But if one of them should attack you, then play the man and don't hesitate to fight: make Marv their graveyard and its earth as bright as a pheasant's feathers with their blood."

Tovorg set off with six thousand Turkish cavalry and on the fourth day caught up with the Persians. When their lionhearted leader saw them, she felt no anxiety. She hurried over to the leader of the caravan of camels and had the baggage placed behind the troops, and then inspected the plain where it was likely that a battle would be fought. She donned her brother's armor and mounted a high-stepping charger. The two armies drew up their forces, face to face, and every man there was ready to sacrifice his life. Tovorg, whom the emperor referred to as an old wolf, was at the head of his men, and he called out to the Persians: "Isn't that noble woman somewhere in your ranks?" Because Gordyeh was dressed in heavy armor, Tovorg did not recognize her, and once again he called out, "Where in this company shall I find the sister of the murdered king? I need to talk with her, both about the days that are gone by and about new matters." Gordyeh replied, "I am the person you're looking for, and I'm ready to ride my horse against a ravening lion."

When Tovorg heard her, and saw her seated on her warhorse, her mien as threatening as a lion's, he was astonished and said, "The emperor has chosen you from all his realm, so that you will be a reminder to him of that great knight Bahram. He said that if you listen to his words he will reward you handsomely. He said to me, 'Hurry to her, and tell her that if she is not pleased with my offer then I can change my mind. Talk to her and come to an agreement with her, and only if she won't accept your advice should you detain her.'"

Gordyeh said, "Let us move aside from the main body of the army. There I'll answer everything you've said." Tovorg came forward from his troops, to where the valiant warrior stood. When she saw that he was alone, this resourceful woman glared at him from beneath her dark helmet. "You saw Bahram; you admired him as a horseman and a warrior," she said. "He was a mother and a father to me, but his days have come to an end. Now I shall test your mettle and fight against you.

then, if you think I'm ready for a husband tell me, and we'll see if there is a husband who pleases me." She urged her horse forward, and Izad-Goshasp rode behind her. She lunged with her lance at Tovorg's waist, and split the fastenings of his armor, piercing his body. Yalan-Sineh led her troops in a general attack, and the Chinese army was thrown into confusion; many were killed, or hurled to the ground, or wounded. The Persians pursued them for two parasangs, and few of them remained mounted; the plain was like a river of blood, with headless bodies and others sprawling in the dust.

After her victory she crossed into Persia, and there wrote a letter to her brother Gerdui, explaining all that had happened to Bahram and herself.

Gostahm Revolts Against Khosrow Parviz and Proposes Marriage to Gordyeh

At this time Khosrow Parviz sent a messenger into Khorasan and said to him, "Speak with no one on your journey, but go straight to the lord of the marches, Gostahm, and say that he is to come to me as soon as he reads my letter." When the messenger reached Khorasan he went to Gostahm's court and repeated the king's message. But knowing that Khosrow Parviz was young and bloodthirsty, when Gostahm received this order he gathered his forces together and went to cities ruled by men of authority, visiting Sari, Amol and Gorgan. In a drunken rage the king killed Gostahm's brother, Banduy, and when Gostahm heard about this, he bit his hand, dismounted from his horse, tore at his clothes, and heaped dust on his head. He knew that the king wished to destroy him, in revenge for his part in the death of the king's father, Hormozd. He rode like the wind, lamenting and mourning, to the forest of Narvan, gathering men as he went. Near the mountains at Amol he hid his army in the woods and began a series of raids on the area. Wherever there were men without work, he gave them bread, and they joined with him. Whenever he heard that the king's troops were nearby, he attacked and destroyed them.

Meanwhile Gerdui went to Khosrow Parviz and told him of his sister Gordyeh's exploits, and of how she had defeated the emperor's forces at Marv. Gostahm too heard that Bahram's days had come to an end, and that Gordyeh had left China's savage ruler and defeated his forces in battle. Gostahm led his forces out to welcome her, and when she heard

of this, Gordyeh and her chief advisors set off from Amui. When he saw
her troops in the distance, Gostahm urged his horse ahead of the main
body of his men. He came before Gordyeh lamenting for Bahram, and
then told her of his grief for Banduy, wiping his tears away with the
sleeve of his robe. He saw Yalan-Sineh and Izad-Goshasp, and as he wept
he dismounted from his horse. He told them how the king had killed
Banduy, and how evil days had befallen him. He said, "It was as though
the king had forgotten that he is the son of Banduy's sister, and that
Banduy had shed his own blood for him. He cut off Banduy's hands and
feet, just as one would expect from a man of his nature. What hopes can
you have of such a man? He will do worse than this to you and your
friends, and meat will be cheap in the town when he butchers you. As
soon as he sees Yalan-Sineh in the distance he'll be eager for revenge,
because you were Bahram's commander, and it was through him you
became powerful in the world. Whoever knows Khosrow Parviz avoids
him; the best thing for him is a sharp knife at his throat! But join with
me, and we'll plan something." Hoping to save themselves from harm, all
those who heard him accepted his suggestion. Then he spoke earnestly to
Gordyeh about Bahram's exploits, and at his words she softened, and
many thoughts filled her mind. All of her men went over to Gostahm,
and hope brightened their dark forebodings.

One day Gostahm said to Yalan-Sineh, "What would this woman
say to being married?" Yalan-Sineh replied, "I'll prepare her mind for
the idea." Seeking out Gordyeh, he said, "I know the world, and I have
seen you are a wise woman. It was right that you put off the emperor
and chose to come back to Persia. What do you think of Gostahm as
a husband? He's the king's uncle, and a powerful commander."
Gordyeh answered, "If I take a Persian husband, my family won't die
out." Yalan-Sineh gave her to Gostahm, who was a fine warrior, and
of noble lineage. Gostahm thought her as sweet as a fresh apple, and in
his good fortune he had no suspicion of disaster. His days were
renewed in fighting against the armies the king sent, and as they were
defeated his confidence increased.

Gostahm Is Killed by Gordyeh

As time passed the king became more alarmed by Gostahm. One day
he burst out to Gerdui, "Gostahm has married Gordyeh; her warriors
went over to him, and I think they did it on her advice. One of my

informants has come from Amol and told me of everything they'd kept hidden." He talked in this way until night fell, and men's eyes grew weary, tired out by his words. As the servants brought candles and wine he cleared the hall of strangers and sat alone with his advisor, Gerdui. The two of them talked over the business of Gordyeh at length, and Khosrow said, "I've sent any number of armies against Amol, and the men have either been killed or returned wounded and complaining about their misfortunes. I can only see one solution to this, because so far my plans have weakened the crown and throne. When Bahram Chubineh forgot his duty, Gordyeh always supported us. I've an idea, but don't spread it abroad. I must write a letter to Gordyeh, one that's as beguiling as a stream of wine in the garden of paradise. I'll say to her, 'I shall be your friend everywhere and in every way. For a long time my tongue has not revealed the secrets of my heart, but now it's time to speak out, and Gerdui is my confidant in this. Find some means to get rid of that wretched miscreant Gostahm; if you can put him beneath a gravestone, my heart and household are yours. When you have done this I'll give provinces to your army and your companions, every-one you wish, and they will rule in those lands. You will have the golden chamber in my women's apartments, and all my desire for vengeance will be at an end. I swear I will do these things; I will add more oaths to this oath, and if I break my word, may all my alliances fail.'"

Gerdui responded, "Long may you flourish, as shining as Venus in the sign of Virgo! You know that, compared with your life, I set no value on my soul and children, or my land and friends, precious though they are to me. I'll send someone with this letter to Gordyeh and make her dark soul bright again. I shall send my own wife, and this will allay any suspicions; this is a woman's work, especially a clever woman's. The more I consider this, the more I see the message must be sent to my sister. This matter will soon be over with, and to your advantage; we must do neither less nor more than you have said."

Khosrow was overjoyed when he heard this, and all his worries disap-peared like the wind. He asked that paper and ink made from musk be brought from the treasury, and then he wrote a letter as lovely as a gar-den, as a rose whose petals are like the beloved's cheeks. It was filled with promises and oaths, adulation and advice, and when the ink on the greet-ing had dried, the letter was sealed with black musk imprinted with the name of King Khosrow Parviz. Gerdui also wrote a letter filled with advice and other matters; the king's letter was placed inside his, and the two were wrapped in silk. His resourceful wife heard all these words, took the package, and rode to the forest of Narvan as one woman bearing a message to another.

Gordyeh's face lit up like the springtime to see her. They talked about Bahram for a while and tears dropped from their eyes. Then the messenger handed over her husband's letter, with the king's hidden inside it. When this lionhearted woman saw the king's missive it was as if she saw the moon before her. She smiled and said, "If someone has five friends, this will be no trouble." She kept the letter secret from the court, but read it to five of her confidants, who took one another's hands and swore to aid her. She hid the five in her sleeping apartments, and when night came she extinguished the lights and placed her hand over her husband's mouth. The five accomplices rushed to the bedside and struggled with the man, who was drunk, until finally they suppressed his cries and smothered him. The town was soon in an uproar, and fires were lit in the streets. When she heard the noise, this intrepid woman put on her Byzantine armor; she called her Persians to her in the darkness and told them she had killed Gostahm. Then she showed them the king's message and encouraged them to be of good heart. Her men acclaimed her for what she had done and scattered jewels on the letter.

Gordyeh's Letter to Khosrow Parviz

This fearless woman asked for ink and a pen case, and sat with her advisors. She wrote a letter to the king concerning his enemies and allies. She began with praise of those who cleanse their hearts of vengeance and continued, "The deed that the king commanded has been accomplished, and all that his allies would wish has come to pass. Gostahm's forces are in disarray, by the grace of the world's king. What orders have you for me now; what will you demand of your slave?"

When the letter reached Khosrow, his approval of Gordyeh flourished again. He summoned an eloquent messenger, one who knew all the ancient stories, and wrote a letter as beautiful as a painting by the Chinese master Arzhang. In it he summoned her to his court and called her the moon's diadem. The messenger came to Gordyeh like the wind and told her what Khosrow had said, and when that lionhearted woman read the king's letter she was like a rose that blossoms in springtime. She mustered her troops and gave them their provisions, and at daybreak the baggage was loaded.

A great company of men came out to greet her, and when she reached the court she found the king's heart filled with anxiety to please her. She and her chieftains brought before him innumerable gold coins and jewels, brocades woven with gold, crowns and belts, golden thrones and golden crowns, and all these were counted out to the king's treasurer. The king looked at this elegant cypress, whose face was as lovely as the spring, and whose walk was like that of a pheasant, and had her conducted to the harem, where she was a given a rank higher than all his other women. Then he sent for her brother, his vizier, Gerdui, and asked for and obtained her hand in marriage, according to the rites of their religion. He rewarded her companions with robes of honor, as well as gold and silver, and every kind of wealth.

The Destruction of the City of Rey

Many long days passed, and Gordyeh wanted for nothing. One day, when Khosrow Parviz was drinking wine with the wise men of the court, and with his noblemen and warriors, a goblet was discovered with the name of Bahram written on it. The king ordered that it be thrown away, and everyone cursed Bahram, the goblet, and the man who had brought it there. He said, "Let Bahram's town, Rey, be trampled beneath war elephants' feet, its inhabitants driven out, and let it be turned to a wasteland." His vizier said to the king, "You are a living memorial of the Kayanid kings, but consider, Rey is a great town and it would be wrong for it to be trampled beneath elephants' feet. God would not approve of this, and neither would the wise men of the world." The king replied, "Then the place needs an ill-natured governor, an incompetent fool, someone who is ignorant and foul-mouthed." A courtier called Bahman said, "If the king wishes, we will look for such an incompetent, but we need some kind of guide." Khosrow said, "He should have red hair, a crooked nose, and an ugly face; he must be an infamous man, with a sallow complexion, someone who's malevolent, short in stature, his heart filled with anguish, base in his nature, vengeful and with a lying tongue; his eyes should be green and squinting, he should have big teeth, and he should lope along the road like a wolf."

The priests were astonished to hear Khosrow talk in this way, and wondered how they would find such a man. People searched the world, inquiring among both rich and poor, and then one day a man came to the king and said, "I saw someone of this description on the road. If the king commands me, I shall bring him here, and he can be sent to Rey." The king gave orders that the man be brought to the court, and when he entered everyone laughed at his appearance. Khosrow said to him, "Well, fool, tell us about how evil you are." The man replied, "I never stop doing evil things, and there's not an atom of wisdom in me. Tell me to do one thing and I'll do another, and I'll fill men's bodies and souls with anguish. I live off lies and I'm incapable of doing good." The king said to him, "And may your evil star keep you that way."

His name was written down in the court records as the governor of Rey, and this shameless man rose to greatness because he was so ugly. He was given a motley army and went off to his new post, taking his evil reputation with him. When he arrived in Rey he banished all shame from his heart. He gave orders that all the gutters on the roofs be torn down, and he took pleasure in watching this done. Then he had all the cats killed, which annoyed the city leaders. Everywhere he went he had a herald go in front of him shouting, "If I see a gutter in place, or a cat in a house, I'll burn the house down and stone its inhabitants." He searched everywhere and, if he found as much as one silver coin, he made its owner wretched. Mice took over the houses, and people despaired of the city. When it rained there were no gutters to carry away the downpour, and there was no one to care for the city. And that is how this ugly, shameless wretch sent from Khosrow's court caused a flourishing city to fall into ruin. The sun beat down on men's heads, and all the city was filled with pain and anguish, while the world ignored their sufferings.

This went on until spring and the month of Farvardin, when the land is adorned with flowers, the world becomes moist with dew, and the mountains and valleys are filled with tulips. The nobility went to their gardens to enjoy themselves, and the foothills of the mountains were dotted with deer and sheep. When Khosrow opened the gates to his gardens, he saw the fountains were filled with doves; he ordered that trumpets be blown, and bowls filled with sweet scents were set down there. He and his courtiers sat on the grass and called for wine, while they chatted amicably together. Gordyeh brought a little kitten, which she had dressed up just like a child. Sitting on a pony, on a gold saddle ornamented with jewels, the kitten had earrings hanging from its ears, and its nails had been painted as red as tulips. Its face was as sweet as springtime; its black eyes looked sleepy, because it had drunk some wine. A golden bridle hung from the pony, and Gordyeh led the kitten around the garden as if he were a child. The king of Persia burst into laughter at this sight, and all his courtiers copied him. He said to Gordyeh, "My beauty, what do you want from me? Tell me what it is you wish for."

This resourceful woman bowed before the king and said, "Great king, give me Rey: consider wisely, and free its sorrowful inhabitants' hearts from their grief. Recall that shameless wretch from Rey. Know him for what he is, a faithless, evil man. He has driven the cats from their houses and destroyed the town's gutters one by one." Khosrow laughed at his wife's words and said, "You are as lovely as the moon and strong enough to destroy an army. Recall that malevolent wretch, that Ahriman, from Rey." And so her good fortune grew in the shadow of the royal tree.

*K*hosrow Parviz's Byzantine wife, Mariam, bore him a son, Shirui. But the court astrologers predicted that the country would suffer as a result of this child, and that the army would never acclaim him as their leader.

THE STORY OF
KHOSROW AND SHIRIN

When Khosrow Parviz had been a fearless young man, in the period while his father was still alive, he had loved Shirin, and had cherished her more than his own sight. In all the world only Shirin pleased him, and he had eyes for no other beautiful women, or for the daughters of the nobility. But then his time was taken up with traveling about the world, and by his battles with Bahram; he seemed to have forsaken his love, and the beautiful Shirin wept day and night for him.

Khosrow Parviz Goes Hunting, Meets with Shirin, and Takes Her to His Harem

One day Parviz decided to go hunting, and the expedition was arranged as had been customary with former kings. Three hundred horses with golden bridles were led out; there were one thousand six hundred loyal footmen carrying javelins, and one thousand four hundred more who carried staves and swords and wore brocade beneath their armor. Following them came five hundred falconers, with sparrow hawks, merlins, and falcons, and then three hundred horsemen leading cheetahs. There were also leopards and lions, whose mouths had been muzzled with gold chains, and a hundred dogs with golden leashes, for running down deer. After them came two thousand musicians, all mounted on camels and wearing golden crowns; they had prepared songs to celebrate the hunt. There were thrones, tents, and pavilions, loaded on camels, as well as stalls for the animals. There were two hundred slaves with censers that burned aloes wood and ambergris, together with two hundred young servants carrying narcissi and crocuses, and they carried these so that the wind bore their scent to Parviz. In front of them went men who scattered water in which musk had been mixed, so that the wind would not suddenly stir up the dust and disturb the king.

When Shirin heard that this entourage was approaching, with the king at its head, she put on a golden dress scented with musk, and over it a surcoat of red Byzantine brocade with a gold ground worked with jewels. She made her cheeks the color of pomegranates, and on her head she placed a crown of imperial splendor. She went up from her royal chamber onto the roof of her palace, and the days of her youth brought her no pleasure. She waited there, with the tears trickling down her cheeks, until Khosrow Parviz approached. When she saw the king's face she stood so that he could see her, and she spoke gently to him about their former days; her eyes were like narcissi that droop with sorrow, and they bathed her cheeks' rosy color as she wept. Beautiful, and in tears, she reproachfully addressed the king:

> "My lord, my warrior, my king, who lives
> Favored by all that heaven's fortune gives,
> Where is your love now? Or your tears that I,
> And I alone, could comfort once and dry?
> Where are the endless nights we turned to day
> With tears, and smiles, and amorous sweet play?
> Where are our oaths and promises, and where
> Are all the vows we vowed we'd always share?"

And as she spoke her tears fell onto her imperial clothes. Tears welled too in Khosrow's eyes, and his face turned as yellow as the sun. He sent a horse with a golden bridle for her, and forty reliable Byzantine servants, to accompany her to the golden, bejeweled apartments of his harem.
From there he went to his hunting grounds, taking wine and musicians to entertain him, and when he had had his fill of hunting in the plains and hills, he set off in high spirits for the city. All the roads and buildings were decorated to welcome him, and a confused din of trumpets and songs of welcome resounded through the air. He made a royal, imposing figure as he strode into his high castle; Shirin came forward from the inner apartments and kissed his feet, the ground before him, and his chest. The king turned to his chief priest and said, "I want you to think only well of me: marry me to this beautiful woman, and give the good news to the

world." Then he married her according to the ancient rites that were customary in those days.

Khosrow Parviz's Nobles Give Him Counsel

When the nobility and army learned that Shirin had joined Khosrow Parviz's harem and that this old relationship had been renewed, the city was filled with discontent, foreboding, and curses. No one approached Khosrow for three days, and when the sun rose on the fourth day Khosrow summoned his nobles to an audience with him. He said, "I have not seen you for a few days, and this has worried me. I am troubled that something troubles you, and your sorrows fill me with anxiety." When he had finished speaking everyone present held his tongue; no one gave him an answer. Then, one by one, they looked at the chief priest, who, when he perceived this, stood and addressed Khosrow. "You are just and righteous, my lord," he said. "You became king when you were still a young man; you have seen a great deal of both good and evil fortune, and you have heard much good and evil in the world, concerning the great and their actions. But now the lineage of our nobility has been polluted; our greatness has been sullied by this alliance. If the father is pure and the mother is worthless, you should realize that purity cannot issue from them. No man seeks righteousness from a perverse source, which can only harm righteousness. Our hearts are saddened that this vicious demon has become the great king's consort. Is there no other woman in Persia, apart from this one, who pleases the king? If Shirin were not present in the king's harem, his face would shine with righteousness everywhere. Your ancestors, who were wise and just men, never heard of such a matter." The chief priest spoke at length, but the King of Kings gave him no answer.

At dawn the next day the court prepared to assemble. One said, "The chief priest didn't know what he was talking about." Another said, "What he said was full of wisdom." A third remarked, "Today the king will answer him; let's hope he has a good reply ready." All the counselors made their way into the king's presence, and the nobles took their places there. Then a man came in bearing a bowl that glittered like the sun, and he took it to each of the noblemen in turn. Warm blood had been poured into the bowl, and he offered it gently to each of them, but each man turned his face away. A murmuring spread through the assembly and everyone looked at the king, afraid of what he would do. Finally the king said to the Persians gathered there, "Whose blood is this, and why has it been placed in this bowl?" The chief priest said, "This blood is polluted, and everyone who sees it loathes it." He picked up the bowl and had it passed from hand to hand. Then it was cleansed and made shining again with water, and earth was used to scour it.

When the polluted bowl had been purified and shone again, it was filled with wine, with which musk and rose-water were mixed, and it glowed like the sun. Khosrow Parviz said to the chief priest, "Is the bowl what it was, or has it changed now?" The priest replied, "May your majesty flourish, good has been distinguished from evil. At your command what was hellish has become heavenly, and you have made what was ugly beautiful." Khosrow said, "In this land Shirin was considered to be like that bowl of polluted blood; but the bowl in my harem is now filled with wine; it is my scent that fills her now. Shirin's reputation suffered because of me, and it was because of me that she never sought for a partner among the nobility." All his nobles called down blessings on him, saying, "May the earth never be deprived of your reign. Greatness is increased by your greatness, and those you ennoble are the earth's nobility; you are our king, priest, and guide, and the very shadow of God on earth."

Shirin Kills Mariam; Khosrow Parviz Imprisons Shirui

Then the king's magnificence increased, and if before he had shone like the moon, he was now as splendid as the sun. He spent all his time with Mariam, the daughter of the emperor of Byzantium, and she was his favorite of all the women in his harem. Shirin was tormented by this, and her cheeks were always pale with jealousy. Finally, she poisoned Mariam, and the Byzantine princess died. Shirin did this alone, in secret, and no one was aware of what she had done; and a year after Mariam died, Shirin was given the golden apartments in the harem.

When Mariam's son, Shirui, was sixteen he had the stature of a thirty-year-old: his father brought him teachers, so that he could learn to be an accomplished nobleman, and a priest supervised him day and night, according to the king's orders. One day the priest came from the king to the prince and saw that he sat idly playing. In front of him lay his book, *Kalileh and Demneh*, but in his left hand the loutish youth held the dried paw of a wolf and in his right a buffalo's horn, and he sat there willfully banging the one against the other. The priest's heart was troubled by this pointless game; he took the wolf's claw, the buffalo's horn, and the youth's loutish behavior as a bad omen. He had seen the boy's horoscope, and had heard more details from the vizier and court treasurer, and he feared what fate held in store for the prince. He went to the chief priest and said, "All the prince cares about is trivial games." Immediately the chief priest passed this on to Khosrow, who was troubled by the report; his cheeks turned sallow at the thought of his son, and he brooded on what fate would unfold. He remembered the astrologer's words; his heart was troubled, and his vitals were twisted within him. He said, "We must wait to see what the heavens bring forth."

By the twenty-third year of the king's reign Shirui was strong and fully grown; he had become refractory and uncontrollable, and Khosrow grew anxious about him. The king's smiling soul was clouded with sorrow, and he had the prince confined to his palace, along with his companions and those who sought him out for advice; this group came to more than three thousand in all. The place was provided with clothes, food, and furnishings, the rooms were decorated appropriately, and slaves and servants were there in attendance. The king sent wine and limitless gold, and forty men were set to watch over the revelers, who passed their time in feasting and pleasure.

The Tale of the Musician, Barbad

As time passed the king's greatness increased, and no one received bad treatment at his court. In the twenty-eighth year of his reign news of this reached the musician Barbad, who was told, "The king favors musicians, and if you compete with his current musician, Sarkesh, he'll give you a higher rank than him." When he heard this, although he wanted for nothing, ambition flared up in him; he traveled from his own country to the king's court and presented himself to the musicians there. When Sarkesh heard him play, he was astonished at the newcomer's skill, and his heart grew dark. He went to the court chamberlain and gave him gold and silver and other gifts. He said, "There's a musician at the door who surpasses me in youth and skill: he mustn't enter Khosrow's presence, because if he does, he'll be looked on as a novelty and I'll be thought old-fashioned." The chamberlain agreed to refuse entry to their naïve visitor. And so when Barbad appeared, he was rudely received. The chamberlain would not admit him to the court, and no one came to help him. Despondently he left the court gates and, carrying his lute, made his way to the royal garden, where the king would go for two weeks of festivities at the New Year.

The gardener there was named Marduy, and Barbad liked him as soon as he saw him. That very day, the two became firm friends, and Barbad said to him, "It's as if you're the soul and I'm the body of one person. I have a favor to ask, something that will be easy for you to do. When the world's king comes to this garden, hide me somewhere so that I can see him; I want to watch his face for a moment, during the festivities." Marduy said, "I'll do it; set your mind at rest."

As Khosrow approached the garden, the gardener's heart glowed with excitement. He hurried to Barbad and said, "The king is coming here for the celebrations." Barbad dressed himself all in green and took his lute in his hand, ready to sing of glory and battles. He went to where the king was to sit, since a new site was selected each spring. There was a green cypress tree there, with abundant foliage and branches interlaced like warriors in a battle. Barbad climbed this tree and waited for the king to arrive. The king came from his palace to the spot that had been prepared for him. A young serving girl with a bewitching face gave him a goblet, and the red wine within rendered its crystal invisible. At the moment the yellow sun set and purple night came on, Barbad took his lute and sang the heroic song he had prepared. Hidden in the tree, he sang his beautiful lay, the one we now call "Dad-Afarid," and the king was astonished at the sweetness of his voice. The whole company was amazed, and everyone expressed a different opinion as to what was happening. The king ordered the company to search the area thoroughly, and they looked high and low but came back empty-handed. One experienced man came forward and said, "It should be no surprise that the king's good fortune has made even the green plants and flowers his musicians: may his head and crown flourish forever!"

The beautiful serving girl brought another goblet, and as the king took it from her, Barbad suddenly struck up another song, "The Heroes' Battle." The skillful musician sang and Khosrow listened, drinking his wine as the song progressed. Then he ordered that the singer be found, and that the garden be turned upside down if need be. They searched everywhere in the garden, taking flaming torches beneath the trees, but they saw nothing but willows and cypresses and pheasants strutting among the flowers. The king asked for another goblet of wine and leaned his head forward to listen. Again a song began, accompanied by the lute's sound; it was the one that is called "Green on Green" today, and is used for magical incantations. Khosrow Parviz stood to drink to the voice: he asked for a goblet that held a deep draught of wine, and he drained the bright liquor in one motion. He said, "If this were an angel compounded of musk and ambergris, or a demon, he wouldn't sing these songs, or know how to play the lute in this way. Search the garden again, left and right, till you find where he is. I'll fill his mouth and arms with jewels, and make him the chief of my musicians."

When Barbad heard the king's generous words, he came down from the branches of the cypress tree, and went forward confidently, in all his glory. He approached the king and bowed down, rubbing his face in the dust. Khosrow said to him, "What manner of man are you, tell me!" He replied, "Your majesty, I am your slave and live in the world only at your command." Then he told the king all that had happened, and of the man who had befriended him. The king's happiness at seeing Barbad was like that of a spring garden in the moonlight, but he said to Sarkesh, "You've no talent, you're as bitter as colocynth, and Barbad is like sugar. Why did you keep him away from me? Now he's come, you've no place in this assembly."

Then he drank wine to the sound of Barbad's voice, draining his goblet of its ruby contents, until his head became sleepy, and he filled Barbad's mouth with pearls of the first water. And so Barbad became the king's musician, and a respected man among the country's nobility.

> Now Barbad's tale is done: I wish for you
> Good fortune and good friends in all you do.

Khosrow Parviz Becomes Unjust

Despite his splendid throne, the great palace he built at Ctesiphon, and all his imperial glory, the world's king was dissatisfied, and he raised dust clouds of strife over Iran and Turan. This king who had been so just became unjust, and he rejoiced in the injustice of his inferiors.

There was a man called Farrokhzad, the son of Azarmegan, who became Khosrow's chamberlain. He was always frowning, and he acted malevolently toward those under his control, stealing people's wealth and pitting them against one another. He set himself ever new tasks, and all his efforts went to gathering ever more wealth. Men's former blessings turned to curses, and they said that the ruler who had been like a sheep had become a savage wolf. Since the populace had neither water nor bread nor any means of support, they fled from Persia to enemy lands, and the land was filled with curses against all those who had any part in this oppression.

And then there was Goraz, a man devoid of virtue, who fulfilled all Khosrow Parviz's dreams and desires, and guarded the frontier against Byzantium. His mind was a demon's, unjust and shameless, and when the once-just king became unjust, he was the first to betray Persia. The next was Farrokhzad, Khosrow Parviz's favorite and his chamberlain, who would let no one near the king. When the king's days were numbered, Farrokhzad's heart became corrupt: he allied himself with the wily Goraz, and their plot spread from province to province. Goraz wrote to the emperor of Byzantium and stirred up evil desires in him. He wrote: "Rise now, and take Persia; if you do, I will be the first to come to your aid." As soon as he read this, the emperor mustered an army and set off with it toward the Persian frontier.

The Army Deserts Khosrow Parviz and Frees Shirui

When the king heard of this serious development, he dismissed it as of no importance. He knew it was Goraz's doing, and that he had been in secret communication with the Byzantine emperor. Earlier he had summoned Goraz to the court but Goraz had made excuses and acted as if the king could not enforce his orders, even though he was afraid of him. The king sat in council with the Persian nobles, and they considered various ways to rid themselves of this problem. Then the king had a clever notion: he wrote a letter to Goraz saying, "I'm delighted with what you have done, and have praised you before our nobles. When you receive this letter may it brighten your dark spirits. Wait with your forces where you are until I advance, and with one army on this side and another on that, we shall trap the Byzantine emperor between us. We'll bring him back as a prisoner to Persia, and take all his army into captivity."

Then the king chose a cunning courtier, someone who could act as a spy, and said to him, "See that one of the Byzantine scouts catches sight of you and questions you. Then he'll take you to the emperor, or to their army's commander. When you're asked who you are, refuse to answer, then say, 'I'm just a poor man trying to make a living, and I've traveled a long way to deliver this letter to Goraz.' Tie the letter to your right arm, and if they take it from you, so much the better."

The man tied the letter as instructed and left the court. As he approached the Byzantine marches, a man caught sight of him and took him, with his face covered in dust, his cheeks sallow, and his lips purple, before the emperor. The emperor addressed him, "Where is Khosrow Parviz? You had better tell us the truth!" The poor man mumbled in a bewildered way and hung his head in fear. The emperor said, "Search this malevolent, ill-spoken wretch." They found the letter and opened it, and then looked for someone in the area who could read Pahlavi correctly. When a scribe was found who was able to read it, the emperor's face turned black as pitch. He said to himself, "This was a trap set by Goraz; I was marching straight into an ambush. This king with his army of three hundred thousand men and innumerable war elephants wanted to corner me: may his life end in darkness and sorrow!" And he withdrew his forces, forgetting all thoughts of conquest.

Goraz and Farrokhzad then made common cause and encouraged the army to revolt against Khosrow Parviz.

Farrokhzad knew that the king was aware of his treachery, and he did not dare approach the throne. He waited by the door and sounded people out, trying to win allies for when the army would declare itself against the king. He told his ideas to everyone and won many people over, saying that another man should occupy the throne, because Khosrow Parviz had forfeited *farr*, glory, and good fortune.

An experienced old man in Farrokhzad's employ said to his master, "The king blames you for the army's disaffection. You shouldn't pro-

ceed any further in this matter until another king is available, otherwise
the country will go to rack and ruin. We must consider his sons—
which of them has the dignity for this position and will cause the
fewest problems? Then we must place him on the throne in triumph
and pour gold dinars over his crown as is customary. Since Shirui is his
eldest son, he is the obvious choice, even though he's imprisoned at
the moment."

Everyone expressed the same opinion, and not many days passed
before the dust of Tokhvar's intrepid army rose up. Farrokhzad went
out along the road to greet him and his numerous troops, and the two
conversed for a long time. Farrokhzad went over the injustices that the
king had committed and then said, "The army must act with chivalry
and discretion and install a new king." The commander replied, "I'm
not a man for talk, but when I fight I make the world a hard place for
my enemies. When this king was young, he was loved by champions
and lords of the marches alike, but may no man make his days as dark
as this king has done. He lost everything when he became unjust and
rejoiced in the injustice of his inferiors."

At this Farrokhzad chose Tokhvar, from all the Persians, as his
accomplice and said to him, "Now we must go to where those poor
wretches are imprisoned and fearlessly free Prince Shirui, who is
young, brave, and ambitious. His jailer is an army commander, and he
and six thousand cavalry veterans keep him and his companions under
surveillance." Tokhvar replied, "I take no account of this commander.
If Khosrow Parviz's luck revives, every champion in Persia will find
himself on a gibbet or imprisoned in a pit; no one will escape injury."
Having said this he urged his horse forward, and it leaped to the fray
like lightning. The commander set to guard Shirui came out to oppose
him, but he was driven back and killed in the battle. Still in his armor,
Tokhvar went straight to the place where Shirui was confined and
called out to him. Shirui knew why this proud warrior had come, and
when he saw his face glowing after the battle, the young man's heart
beat faster with anxiety. Weeping, he said, "Where is Khosrow Parviz?
It's not your business to set me free." Tokhvar said to the prince, "If
you're a man don't stay here like a lion clawing at its cage. If you're not
with us, then declare yourself and withdraw. If we lose one out of six-
teen brothers, that's of no importance; there are still fifteen more of
you. All of the others are worthy to rule, and the throne will rejoice

in their reign." Shirui wept in bewilderment, uncertain whether to set foot outside of the building or not.

Khosrow Learns of the Army's Defection

Meanwhile Farrokhzad acted as court chamberlain and admitted no one to the king's presence, so that he would not hear of what was going on. When the tent of the sun was tattered, and noblemen went to their sleeping quarters, Farrokhzad summoned the city's sentries and all those who had authority over them. Confidently they came to the king's court, where Farrokhzad said to them, "The cry of the watchmen must be different tonight from last night. As each watch of the night goes by, all the watchmen must cry out in the name of Qobad." They agreed: "We will do this and drive the name of Parviz from our minds."

When night's black tent was pitched, the watchmen's cries went up from the city and bazaar, and all of them called in the name of Qobad. The king was sleeping in the darkness of the night, and Shirin was next to him in his bed. When she heard the cries, she was troubled and her heart beat faster. She said, "Your majesty, what can be happening? Listen! We must talk." The king woke at the sound of her voice and said in his irritation, "Your face is as lovely as the moon, but why are you talking when I'm asleep?" Shirin replied, "Open your ears, listen to what the watchmen are crying!" Khosrow heard their voices and his face grew pale as fenugreek. He said, "Three watches of the night have gone by, and now you will learn the truth of the astrologers' words. When this brat was born I secretly named him Qobad; publicly his name was Shirui, but in private, Qobad. Under cover of the night's darkness we must make for China, or Machin, or Makran; we must flee secretly, and ask for soldiers from the Chinese emperor." But his star was waning, and this talk of flight was empty chatter. Tricks did not help him in the night's darkness; he had underestimated the seriousness of what was afoot. He said to Shirin, "My time has come, and those who hate us have triumphed over our plans." She replied, "May you thrive forever, safe from your enemies' hands. Think of some ruse in your wisdom; God forbid that your enemies prevail. As soon as dawn breaks they are sure to come to the palace."

Then the king asked for armor, two Indian swords, a Byzantine helmet, a quiver full of arrows, and a golden shield from his treasury, as well as a slave who would fight in his defense. In the darkness he made his way to his garden, just at the time when the crow wakes up from sleep. Among the trees there was no space for a couch: he hung his golden shield from a branch, in an area where few men came. He sat among the narcissi and crocuses, with an Indian sword placed firmly beneath his knee. As the sun lifted its glittering lance, the king's malevolent enemies made their way to the palace. They went from room to room but found no sign of the king; they looted his treasuries and gave no thought to his suffering.

Khosrow Parviz Becomes His Son's Prisoner

Khosrow stayed in the garden, in the shade of a tall tree, and by midday he had grown hungry. There was an under gardener working there who had never seen the king's face. The sun-like sovereign said to him, "Cut a jeweled link from my belt: there are five gold bosses on each link. Take the link to the bazaar; buy me some meat and some bread with it, and see that you go by an unfrequented road." Now, for a man who knew about such things, the jewels on the link were worth thirty thousand gold coins.

The gardener hurried off to a baker's shop and tried to buy bread with the gold link. The baker said, "I don't know what this is worth, but I'm not letting you go!" The two went together to a jeweler and asked him to put a value on the link. When this knowledgeable man saw the piece, he said, "But who would dare to buy this? This is a piece from Khosrow's treasury; each year a hundred new ones of this kind are made. Who did you steal this from? Did you snatch it from a slave while he was asleep?" The three of them then took the gold and jewels to Farrokhzad, who immediately took this link severed from a golden belt to Prince Shirui and showed it to him. Shirui addressed the gardener: "If you don't tell me where the owner of this is, I'll cut your head off, and the heads of all your family too."

He replied, "Your majesty, he's in the garden, dressed in armor, with a bow in his hand. His stature is like a cypress tree's, and his face is like the spring; he seems a prince in every way. All the garden shines with his splendor, and in his armor he's like a shining sun. His golden shield hangs from a branch, and a slave stands in front of him, bow in hand. He cut this link and gave it to me, and said, 'Run and bring me bread and food from the bazaar.' I ran here from his side just a moment ago." Shirui knew that this was Khosrow, whose appearance was unique. Three thou-

sand horsemen went like the wind from the palace to the stream's bank.
When Khosrow saw them in the distance he quailed but drew his sword
for combat. The soldiers saw the king's face, and they turned back,
weeping. One by one they went before Farrokhzad, and each told the
same story saying, "We are slaves and he is Khosrow: misfortune is a new
thing in this king's life. No one would oppose him, not so much as by a
cold sigh, whether in a garden or on the field of battle." Farrokhzad took
a number of guards from the palace and went to the king. He went for-
ward alone and said to Khosrow: "If the king will grant me audience,
and forgive me for what has happened, I will come and explain the sit-
uation. If not, I shall go back to the palace." Khosrow said, "Say what
you have to say; you're neither my comforter nor my enemy."

Farrokhzad said, "Look more wisely on what's happening. You
could kill a thousand warriors but finally you'll tire of combat. All the
land of Persia is against you; all men are united in their enmity for you.
Come, and see what the heavens will show; it may be that their long-
ing for revenge will turn to clemency." Khosrow replied, "You are right,
this has always been my fear, that unworthy men should come and lord
it over me and make me the butt of their ridicule." Listening to
Farrokhzad's words, the king had grown sick at heart, and he remem-
bered that in earlier times an astrologer had said to him "Your death will
occur between two mountains, and at the hands of a slave, far from
other men. One mountain will be of silver, and another of gold, and
you will sit between the two with your heart trembling in fear. The
heavens will be gold above you, and the earth will be of iron, and for-
tune will be against you." "And now," Khosrow thought, "this iron
armor is like the earth for me, my shield is the golden heavens; and the
treasures that have been piled in these gardens, which so delighted my
heart, are the two mountains. My days have come to an end. Where
now is my star that lit the world with splendor, and my power and hap-
piness that made my name more exalted than crowns?"

They brought an elephant before him; his soul was darkened by
grief as he sat in the saddle and was escorted from the garden. He
called out in Pahlavi from the elephant's back, "My treasure, even if
you are Khosrow's enemy, do not make common cause with those who
are against me. Today I am in the clasp of Ahriman, and you were no
help to me in my distress; stay hidden, and show your face to no one."

Then Qobad ordered his men to treat him well, to have him taken to Ctesiphon, and installed in his vizier's palace, where Galinush would watch over him with a thousand cavalry. When the turning heavens brought his reign to an end, Khosrow Parviz had ruled for thirty-eight years: this happened in the month of Azar, on the day of Dey, at the time when fires are lit, fowls roasted, and wine drunk.

Then Qobad came forward and placed the crown on his head and sat in peace and prosperity on the throne. From all of Persia the army paid him homage, and he gave them a year's pay from the king's treasury. He reigned for no more than seven months; you can call him a king if you wish, or something worthless. But this is the treacherous world's way, and you should not look on it with trusting eyes.

Barbad's Lament for Khosrow Parviz

When Barbad heard that the king had been unjustly forced to quit the throne and that he was now powerless, he traveled from Jahrom to Ctesiphon, his eyelashes wet with tears, his heart swollen with grief. He came to the palace and saw the former king, whose once ruddy face was now as pale as fenugreek. He stayed with him for a while, and then went weeping to the audience chamber. He mourned in Pahlavi, his cheeks sallow with grief, and his heart filled with pain. When the king and those who were there in the palace, including the guards, heard his lament, they all wept, consumed with the fire of their pity. This is what Barbad sang:

> *O great Khosrow, great in your majesty,*
> *In warlike pride, in magnanimity—*
> *Where is that greatness now, your high renown,*
> *Your glory and your throne and royal crown?*
> *Where is your chivalry, your power, my king*
> *Who sheltered all the world beneath your wing?*
> *Where are your wives now, your musicians, all*
> *The nobles who once thronged your audience hall?*
> *Where now is Kaveh's banner, and the lords*
> *Who flourished in the air their glittering swords?*
> *Where are your valiant warriors and your priests,*
> *Where are your hunting parties and your feasts?*

Where is that warlike mien, and where are those
Great armies that destroyed our country's foes?
Where is your armor, wondrous to behold,
Studded with jewels, fashioned from shining gold?
Where is Shabdiz, your fiery stallion who
Galloped with such impatience under you?
Where are your glorious gold-shod cavalry,
Whose swords sought out one sheath—the enemy?
Where is that generous, never-failing store
Of your largess? Your eagerness in war?
Where are the camels, horses, elephants,
Their howdahs, trappings, and magnificence?
Where is that wise nobility of mind,
That eloquence, at once adroit and kind?
Why are you left deprived, in this sad state,
Who read you this page from the Book of Fate?
Once you desired a son—to be your friend,
A prop to your old age—and in the end
Grief came to you from him: a king's son gives
His father strength and shelter while he lives,
But to the King of Kings this son brought pain
And his success destroyed his father's reign.
Count Persia as a ruin, as the lair
Of lions and leopards. Look now and despair,
You were the best of Sasan's line, no one
Will ever reign again as you have done,
And as your seed degenerates, this land
Degenerates beneath an alien hand.
It is the shepherd's fault when wolves descend
And ravage all the sheep he should defend.
God keep your soul, and may each enemy
Of yours die gibbeted in agony!
I swear by God above, my noble king,
By Mehregan, by New Year and the spring,
That if my hand plays any song again
I should be stricken from the roll of men.
I'll burn my instruments and never face
The enemies who've dealt you this disgrace."

Then he cut off his four fingers and went back to his house with his hand mutilated; there he built a fire and burned all his musical instruments.

The Nobility Demand That Khosrow Parviz Be Killed; His Death at the Hands of Mehr Hormozd

All those who had allied themselves with the prince trembled day and night at what fate would bring, since Shirui was a coward and untried in the world's ways. The throne was like a snare to him, and his astrologers knew that his greatness would not last. Those who had been so eager to bring about this evil went to Qobad and talked of what had happened. They said, "We have said this once, and now we repeat it: your mind is set on other things than sovereignty. If two kings are enthroned in one land, one must take precedence and the other be his inferior, and their subjects will rue the day that father and son rule together. We are opposed to this arrangement; do not mention it to us again." Shirui was a slave in their hands, and he was afraid of what would come of this. He answered, "Only a contemptible fool would put his head deliberately into a trap. You must go to your homes and debate what is to be done. Search out someone in the world who can secretly deliver me from this difficulty." The king's enemies looked for someone who would secretly do away with him, but no one had the courage to attempt such a feat, or to bear the mountain of guilt that would come from killing such a monarch.

They searched everywhere until they found a man traveling by road who had blue eyes and sallow cheeks; his body was covered in hair and his face was flushed purple. This evil man's feet were dusty, his belly was wasted with hunger, and his body was naked. No one in the world, rich or poor, knew his name. This ugly wretch—and may he never see the joys of paradise—made his way to Farrokhzad and said, "I'm the man for this business; fill my belly and he's my prey!" Farrokhzad said, "Go, and do it if you can, and speak not a word of this to anyone. I'll have a purse of gold coins waiting for you, and treat you as one of my own." Then he gave him a sharp, glittering dagger, and the man immediately set off on his errand. He found the king, with his feet shackled, in the audience hall.

Khosrow trembled when he saw his assailant, and tears fell from his eyes. He said, "What ugly name is yours? Even your mother should weep to set eyes on you." The man replied, "They call me Mehr

Hormozd; I'm a stranger in this land and have no friends or compan-
ions here." Khosrow said, "And so my end has come at the hands of a
lowborn criminal. His face is inhuman, and no one in the world could
expect kindness from such a man." The king said to a servant boy stand-
ing near him, "Go lad, and fetch me a bowl of water mixed with musk
and aloes; and bring me a fine set of fresh clothes." The boy heard him
but didn't know what this signified; he quickly brought the king a
golden bowl, a ewer, and fresh clothes. Khosrow took the sacred bar-
som in his hands and prayed: this was no time for idle chat or frivolity.
He dressed himself in the clean clothes and asked pardon for his sins;
then he drew a previously unworn cloak over his head so that he would
not see his murderer. Dagger in hand, Mehr Hormozd locked the doors
to the king's apartments; quickly he went forward and slashed through
the king's clothes, plunging the blade into his vitals.

So turns the world, keeping its secrets hidden, and both the pru-
dent, harmless man and the idle boaster find nothing there but vanity.
Whether you own treasures or live in pain and sorrow, you cannot
remain in this fleeting world. Choose righteousness and benevolence if
you would be remembered with praise.

When news spread in the roads and bazaars that Khosrow had per-
ished in this way, evildoers made their way to where his fifteen sons
were kept chained in the palace and murdered these innocents on the
same day. Shirui did not dare say anything, but grieved over these
events in secret. This then was the end of Khosrow, who had been the
lord of such armies and ruled with such splendor. He had no rival as
the King of Kings, and no one had ever heard of such a monarch from
former times.

The Story of Shirui and Shirin,
the Wife of Khosrow Parviz

I have finished the tale of Khosrow Parviz, and now I will begin that
of Shirui and Shirin. Fifty-three days after the king was killed, Shirui
sent someone to Shirin with this message: "You are an abomination, a
magician who knows all spells; there is no one in Iran more culpable
than you. It was your sorcery, which could bring the moon down from
the heavens, that bewitched the king. Tremble now and come before
me. You'll strut so confidently about the palace no longer." Shirin was
enraged by his message, and its ugly, threatening language. She said,

"May no man flourish who spills his own father's blood! I shall not see that criminal even from a distance, neither on a day of sorrow nor on one of feasting." She summoned a scribe and had a document written in Pahlavi; she dictated her will to this man and listed her wealth there.

She had a little poison in a coffer, the like of which could not be found anywhere in the whole country. From then on she kept it on her person, and this cypress of the meadows proceeded to sew her own shroud. She sent a message back to Shirui: "You wear the crown, haughty in your majesty, but the words you've spoken are like leaves in the wind. May the heart of any malevolent wretch who talks about magic and rejoices in such things be brought low! If the king had cared for such sorceries, he'd have kept a witch in his harem so that he could see her face to face; but he kept me there, to delight his heart when he looked on me as evening fell. He would call me from my apartments, and his soul rejoiced to see me. Shame on you for this talk; such lies don't suit a sovereign. Remember God, who is benevolent, and don't say such things before men again."

They took her message to Shirui, who flared up in anger at this innocent woman, and said, "You've no choice but to come! No one in the world is as impudent in her speech as you are." When she heard this, Shirin was troubled and her cheeks turned sallow. She replied, "I will only come to you in the company of others; you must be surrounded by wise and respectable men." Shirui summoned fifty old men, wise in the world's ways, and then sent a messenger to Shirin who said, "Rise, come now, and leave off your excuses." Shirin heard, and dressed herself in blue and black and came before the king. She went straight to the garden called Shadegan, where there was a place set aside for free men to speak; she sat there veiled, as was customary for nobly born women. Shirui sent someone to her with this message: "It is now two months since Khosrow died; be my wife now, as is worthy of you, and in this way you will not be shamed before your inferiors. I shall treat you as my father did, and even more respectfully and kindly than he did."

Shirin replied, "First act justly toward me, and then my soul will be yours: then I will not bridle at your questions, or resist your orders or the wishes of your splendid heart." Shirui agreed to this, and told her to say what she had in mind. The noble woman spoke from behind her veil: "May you be prosperous and victorious, your majesty. You said that I am an evil woman and a sorceress, and that there is no purity or righteousness in me." Shirui replied, "This is true, but such an outburst is not to be taken seriously." Then Shirin said to the nobility gathered in the garden of Shadegan, "What evil have you seen from me, what darkness of soul, or deceit, or foolishness? For many years I was the queen of Persia, and in this time I always supported her brave warriors. I sought only righteousness, and all trickery and deceit were far from my mind. Through my intercession many men gained land and a fair portion of the world's goods. Let those who have lived protected by my shadow and that of my crown and glory say what they saw and heard, and their words will confirm all I did." The nobles who were there affirmed Shirin's goodness and said that there was no other woman like her in all the world, either in public life or hidden away.

Shirin said, "My noble lords, who have traveled the world and know its ways, there are three things that are honorable in a woman and that adorn the seat of greatness. First, that she possess both modesty and wealth, so that she may make her husband's house a place of beauty and contentment; another is that she bear him fine sons, and so augment his splendor; and the third is that she be beautiful of face and of good stature, and that her hair envelope her like a cloak. When I married Khosrow and felt my life to be renewed in the world, he had come from Rome disheartened and despoiled of his wealth, with hardly a home to call his own in this country. But then his reign became so splendid that no one in the world had ever seen or heard of its like. And I bore him four sons—Nastud, Shahryar, Forud and Mardanshah—who rejoiced his heart. Jamshid and Feraydun did not have such sons, and may my tongue turn mute if I am lying."

Having said this she drew back her veil from her face, which shone like the full moon, and the night behind it was her hair. "The third quality is a face such as you see before you, and if anyone believes that I am lying, let him raise his hand. One of my secret attributes was my hair, which no man in the world has ever seen. And here I display to you all my magic, which is not from sorcery or tricks or malevolence; no one has seen my hair before, and none of the nobles have even heard tell of it." The elders were dumbfounded at the sight of her, and they moistened their lips.

When Shirui saw Shirin's face, his soul seemed to take leave of his body. He said to her, "I must have no one but you; you are the only wife in all Iran whom I desire." The beautiful woman answered him, "There are matters I still require from Persia's king. May your reign be long, but I have some requests, if you will grant them." Shirui replied, "My soul is yours; I will grant whatever you wish." Shirin said, "Give me, piece by piece, before this company of nobles, all the wealth that I have owned in this land, and sign this document witnessing that you lay no claim to it." Immediately Shirui did as she requested, and when her requests were fulfilled Shirin went from the garden of Shadegan, walking before the nobles gathered there, to her own home, where she used her wealth to free her slaves and rejoice their hearts. The rest of her possessions she gave to the poor, bestowing most on people of her own household. She gave a portion to the fire-temples, for the celebration of the new year and summer festivals. There was a convent, which was in ruins and had become the lair of lions, and this she rebuilt, dedicating it to the memory of Khosrow, for the good of his soul.

Then she sat in its garden, unveiled, on the ground, divested of her finery. She called her servants to her and sat each one down with kindness. She said in a loud voice, "All of you who have generous hearts,

hear what I have to say, since no one will see my face again. Say only
the truth; wise people do not lie. From the time that I joined Khosrow
and was introduced into the golden apartments of his harem, from
when I became the first of queens and the glory of the king, what sins
did I commit? Don't speak merely for form's sake—what do such
things matter to a desperate woman?" Everyone stood and said:
"Queen among queens, you are eloquent, wise, and enlightened in
your soul; we swear by God that no one has ever seen a woman like
you before, or heard such a voice from behind the veil. From the time
of Hushang until now, no one like you has ever sat on the throne." All
her servants and slaves said together, "You are praised in China and the
west and in Taraz; who would dare to speak ill of you, and how could
you ever commit an evil act?"

Shirin responded to them, "This criminal, whom the turning heav-
ens mock, killed his own father for the sake of a crown and throne,
and for this may he never know happiness or good fortune again. Does
he think he can evade death, having killed his father in such a wretched
fashion? He has sent me a message that has darkened my anguished
soul. I have told him that while I remain alive I shall devote myself to
God; I have told him my intentions, but his evil desires have filled me
with sorrow, and I fear that after I die he will publicly slander me." The
company wept, both at her words and for Khosrow Parviz.

The king was told of what this innocent woman had said, and he
asked her again what she desired. Shirin sent a messenger to him saying
that she had only one more wish, that the entrance to Khosrow's tomb
be opened for her, and that she be allowed to look at him once more.
Shirui responded that it was fitting for her to look on the king again.
The guards opened the tomb and Shirin began a mourning lament. She
laid her face against Khosrow's face and spoke to him the words they
had spoken to one another in times past; then she drank the mortal poi-
son she carried, which began to cloud her soul. Her clothes scented
with camphor, she sat beside the king and leaned her back against the
tomb's walls. So she died, and her death was praised by the world.

When Shirui heard of this, he fell sick, and the sight of Shirin's
body filled him with grief. He ordered that another tomb be con-
structed, and there she was laid, her head crowned with musk and
camphor. Then Shirui sealed Khosrow's tomb, and not many days
passed before he too was given poison: the world had had its fill of

kings. He was born shamefully and died shamefully, leaving the throne to his son. So a man may reign for seven months, and in the eighth he finds that his crown is made of the camphor with which the dead are anointed.

*S*hirui was succeeded on the throne by his son Ardeshir, who ruled for six months and was then murdered. Goraz seized the throne, but he too was murdered after a reign of less than two months. Two royal princesses, Puran-Dokht and Azarm-Dokht, reigned briefly, the first for six months, the second for four months; they were succeeded by Farrokhzad, who was poisoned after a month. A grandson of Khosrow Parviz, Yazdegerd III, then became the last Sasanian king of Iran.

THE REIGN OF YAZDEGERD

After the death of Farrokhzad, Yazdegerd became king, in the month of Sepandormoz, on the day of Ard. He sat in splendor on the imperial throne and placed the crown on his head. He said, "By the revolutions of the turning sky, I am the descendant of Nushin-Ravan; from father to son the realm is mine, and the sun and the constellations Virgo and Pisces are favorable to my reign. I shall confer greatness on the lowly, and I shall not harm the mighty. I do not seek for glory and knowledge, or for warfare and valor, since time and good fortune, wealth, the royal crown, and the throne stay with no man. It is a good reputation we must strive for, not our own pleasure; pleasure is to be ignored, and reputation made our goal." And so he ruled for sixteen years, while the moon and sun passed over his head.

Sa'd, the Son of Vaqas, Invades Iran, and Yazdegerd Sends Rostam, the Son of Hormozd, to Fight Against Him

Omar, who was then the commander of the Arab armies, sent Sa'd, the son of Vaqas, with an army against the king. Hearing news of this Yazdegerd gathered troops from all quarters and ordered the son of Hormozd to lead them against the invader. This man's name was Rostam; he was an astute, intelligent man and a fine warrior. He was also a very knowledgeable astrologer, who paid attention to the advice of priests. He set out with the nobility under his command, and everyone who was capable of fighting well accompanied him.

For thirty months they skirmished, until the army made a stand at Qadesiya. Rostam was a just, kind man; in his capacity as an astrologer he said to himself, "This battle will turn out unfavorably; these times are unfavorable to kings, their current cannot flow in such channels."

He took his astrolabe and observed the stars, and when he saw the day of disaster that loomed he buried his head in his hands. He wrote a letter to his brother, beginning with praise of God, who brings both good and evil fates to pass. Then he continued:

> "*A wise man will be saddened when he learns*
> *Of how the moving sphere of heaven turns:*
> *Caught in the evil clutch of Ahriman,*
> *I am the time's most sad and sinful man;*
> *This house will lose all trace of sovereignty*
> *Of royal glory, and of victory.*
> *The sun looks down from its exalted sphere*
> *And sees the day of our defeat draw near:*
> *Both Mars and Venus now oppose our cause*
> *And no man can evade the heaven's laws.*
> *Saturn and Mercury divide the sky—*
> *Mercury rules the house of Gemini:*
> *Ahead of us lie war and endless strife,*
> *Such that my failing heart despairs of life.*
> *I see what has to be, and choose the way*
> *Of silence since there is no more to say:*
> *But for the Persians I will weep, and for*
> *The House of Sasan ruined by this war:*
> *Alas for their great crown and throne, for all*
> *The royal splendor destined now to fall,*
> *To be fragmented by the Arabs' might;*
> *The stars decree for us defeat and flight.*
> *Four hundred years will pass in which our name*
> *Will be forgotten and devoid of fame.*

> "*They've sent a messenger who says to me*
> *They'll leave our sovereign all his territory*
> *From Qadesiya to the river; but,*
> *For trade's sake, they require a highway cut*
> *Through our domains, no more than this. They'll pay*
> *Us taxes, offer hostages, obey*
> *Our king as theirs. But these are words, not acts,*
> *And have no correspondence with the facts:*

There will be war, and in this conflict I
Know many lion-warriors will die.
And all of my commanders, to a man—
Like Merui from wide Tabaristan,
Like Armani and Kalbui, all those
Who fight with heavy maces to oppose
Our enemies—reject their words and say,
'Who are these upstarts who have dared to stray
Across Mazanderan's and Persia's borders?
For good or bad then, issue us your orders
And let our swords and maces drive them back;
We'll press them hard enough when we attack!'
They cannot know the fate the stars foretell,
These stars which always treated us so well!
As soon as you have read this, don't delay
But make plans quickly and be on your way;
Gather together our nobility,
Their wealth and slaves, horses and property—
Azerbaijan must be your refuge now.
If Persian troops come from Zabol, allow
Them all you can in clothes and charity,
Treat them with friendly hospitality,
But watch the turning heavens—it's from there
That we are granted comfort and despair.
Say to our mother all I've said, but then
Tell her she'll never see my face again.
Give her my greetings, comfort her and see
She does not grieve too desperately for me.
If someone brings sad news of me, don't let
Your sorrow weaken you; we should not set
Our hearts on this world where our wealth is won
By pain and is another's when we're gone.
Devote your heart to God, and as you pray
Ignore this fleeting world which fades away.
The king will not see Rostam any more,
Since fate has driven me to fight this war.
Have all our people pray throughout the night,
Both young and old, until the morning light;

Be generous to the poor, and in your sorrow
Trust in God's help, give no thought to the morrow;
And as for me, my fate's to fight, to lead
Our armies in our country's hour of need:
May Persia flourish! But I know that I
Will not survive this battle, and must die.
When once the king is threatened, give no thought
To wealth or life, to all that you have sought,
Do not be weak or hesitant but strive
With all your strength to keep the king alive,
Since of this noble line the king alone
Still lives; the House of Sasan and its throne
Depend on him, and after him the race
Of Sasan will be gone, and leave no trace.
Alas now for their crown, their court, and for
Their throne that will be shattered in this war.
Farewell now: live for the king, be his shield,
Defend him, sword in hand, and never yield!

"But when the pulpit's equal to the throne
And Abu Bakr's and Omar's names are known,
Our long travails will be as naught, and all
The glory we have known will fade and fall.
The stars are with the Arabs, and you'll see
No crown or throne, no royal sovereignty:
Long days will pass, until a worthless fool
Will lead his followers and presume to rule:
They'll dress in black, their headdress will be made
Of twisted lengths of silk or black brocade.
There'll be no golden boots or banners then,
Our crowns and thrones will not be seen again.
Some will rejoice, while others live in fear,
Justice and charity will disappear,
At night, the time to hide away and sleep,
Men's eyes will glitter to make others weep;
Strangers will rule us then, and with their might
They'll plunder us and turn our days to night.

They will not care for just or righteous men,
Deceit and fraudulence will flourish then.
Warriors will go on foot, while puffed-up pride
And empty boasts will arm themselves and ride;
The peasantry will suffer from neglect,
Lineage and skill will garner no respect,
Men will be mutual thieves and have no shame,
Curses and blessings will be thought the same.
What's hidden will be worse than what is known,
And stony-hearted kings will seize the throne.
No man will trust his son, and equally
No son will trust his father's honesty—
A misbegotten slave will rule the earth,
Greatness and lineage will have no worth,
No one will keep his word, and men will find
The tongue as filled with evil as the mind.
Then Persians, Turks, and Arabs, side by side
Will live together, mingled far and wide—
The three will blur, as if they were the same;
Their languages will be a trivial game.
Men will conceal their wealth, but when they've died,
Their foes will pilfer everything they hide.
Men will pretend they're holy, or they're wise,
To make a livelihood by telling lies.
Sorrow and anguish, bitterness and pain
Will be as happiness was in the reign
Of Bahram Gur—mankind's accustomed fate:
There'll be no feasts, no festivals of state,
No pleasures, no musicians, none of these:
But there'll be lies, and traps, and treacheries.
Sour milk will be our food, coarse cloth our dress,
And greed for money will breed bitterness
Between the generations: men will cheat
Each other while they calmly counterfeit
Religious faith. The winter and the spring
Will pass mankind unmarked, no one will bring
The wine to celebrate such moments then;
Instead they'll spill the blood of fellow men.

These thoughts have dried my mouth, my cheeks turn pale,
I feel my sickened heart within me fail,
For since I was a soldier I've not known
Such dark days to beset the royal throne;
The heavens have betrayed us, and they spurn
Our supplications as they cruelly turn.
My tempered sword, that fought with elephants
And lions, will now I know be no defense
Against these naked Arabs, and all I see
Has only multiplied my misery.
Would that I had no knowledge, did not know
The good and evil that the heavens show.
The noble warriors who are with me here
Despise the Arabs, and they show no fear,
They think they'll turn the plain into a flood,
An Oxus flowing with these Arabs' blood;
None of them knows the heavens' will, or how
Immense a task awaits our armies now.
When fate withdraws its favor, why wage war?
What is the point of fighting any more?

"My brother, may God keep you safe; may you
Comfort the royal heart by all you do.
My grave is Qadesiya's battlefield,
My crown will be my blood, my shroud my shield.
The heavens will this; may my death not cause
Your heart to grieve too much at heaven's laws.
Watch the king always, and prepare to give
Your life in battle so that he may live—
The day comes soon when heaven's sphere will be,
Like Ahriman, our bitterest enemy."

He sealed the letter and summoned a messenger, saying to him, "Take this quickly to my brother, and tell him everything that is appropriate."

Rostam's Letter to Sa'd, the Son of Vaqas

He also sent a messenger, who rode like lightning, to Sa'd. The letter was written on white silk, and the scribe's script glittered like the sun. It was addressed "From the son of Hormozd the king, Rostam, the benevolent and foremost warrior of the world, to Sa'd the son of Vaqas, who seeks war and has made the world a dark and narrow place for himself."

The message began, "May the great God, whom we must fear, who has founded the turning heavens, and whose rule is one of justice and love, bless our prince, who is an adornment to the crown, the throne, and the royal seal, who is lord of the sword and crown, and whose glory binds Ahriman's evils. A contemptible business has been set afoot, involving pointless suffering and warfare. Tell me who your king is, and what kind of man you are, and what your customs and intentions are. You're a naked commander leading a naked army; on whose behalf are you fighting? Bread satisfies you, but you hunger for something more; you've no elephants, no thrones, no baggage train. Simple life in Iran would be enough for you; the crown and royal seal belong to another man, who has elephants, treasures, glory, power, and who is king by right of descent from father to son. When he appears, the moon is absent from the sky, and no king on earth has his stature. When he smiles at a banquet he gives away the ransom of the Arabs' leader, and his treasures remain undiminished by the gift. He has twelve thousand hunting dogs, cheetahs, and hawks, all with golden bells and ears decorated with jewels; in a year the plains where the Arabs live could not provide the food that his dogs and cheetahs run down in the hunt. His dogs and cheetahs eat more than you, and the cost is as nothing to the king.

"Is there no shame in your eyes, have you no wisdom or benevolence? And with your appearance, your lineage, your customs and character, you hope to gain the crown and throne? If you have ambitions in the world, and your words are not mere idle chatter, send me an experienced, eloquent warrior who can explain to me what your intentions are, and who has led you to the Persian throne; then we'll send a knight to the king to make your requests known.

"Don't make war against the king, because the end can only be a sorrowful one for you. He is descended from the world-ruler Nushin-Ravan, and his justice makes old men young again; his ancestors were kings and he is king, and time cannot show his equal. Do not make all the world curse you: a just, wise man who is not of royal lineage will not seek the throne. Look carefully at the advice I give you in this letter, and do not close your eyes and ears to wisdom." The letter was sealed and he handed it to the nobleman Piruz, the son of Shapur, who took it to Sa'd, the son of Vaqas. The Persian nobles waited, untroubled in their spirits, dressed in armor lavishly covered in gold and silver, with their golden shields and golden belts.

Sa'd's Answer to Rostam's Letter

Sa'd went out with his warriors to welcome the noble messenger. They brought him to their camp, and Sa'd questioned him about the king, his advisors, his army, and its commander. They spread a simple cloak for Piruz to sit on, and Sa'd said, "Our business is with swords and spears; men worth the name don't talk about brocade, or gold and silver, or sleeping and eating." The noble Piruz handed over the letter and repeated Rostam's words. Sa'd heard him out and read the letter, which astonished him.

He wrote an answer in Arabic, setting out things that were good and things that were ugly. He wrote about jinns and human beings, about the words of the Hashemite prophet, about the unity of God and the Qur'an, about what was promised and what was threatened, about God's support and the new ways; about the burning pitch and icy cold of hell; about the houris and streams, the camphor and water, the trees and wine and honey of paradise. Then he wrote, "If the king accepts this true faith, he will prosper in both this world and the next. He will keep his crown and royal earrings and live forever in splendor. Mohammad will intercede for his sins, and his body will be like distilled rosewater. Sow seeds that you will reap in paradise; it is wrong to plant hatred in the garden of disaster. I would not exchange the sight of one hair of one houri from heaven for the person of Yazdegerd himself, together with the wide earth and its orchards, castles, palaces, throne rooms, feasts and festivals. In this fleeting world your eyes have been dazzled by crowns and wealth; you trust in the ivory throne, in cheetahs and hawks and royal benevolence, but this world is not worth one gulp of sweet water, so why should it trouble your heart so much? Any man who opposes me in battle will see nothing but a narrow grave, and hell; if you join with me, your place will be in paradise. Consider carefully which you will choose." He set the Arab seal on the paper and invoked the name of Mohammad. He told Sho'beh Moghaireh to take the letter to the warrior Rostam.

The Persian commander was told, "A weak, old man is coming as a messenger; he has neither a horse nor armor, and he can hardly see.

He carries a thin sword on his shoulder, and his clothes are tattered."
Rostam had a brocade tent prepared and spread with Chinese carpets
woven with gold; his troops were drawn up as thickly as ants or locusts.
A golden chair was placed there, and Rostam seated himself on it;
around him were gathered sixty of his warlike cavalry officers, dressed
in purple clothes woven with gold and wearing golden shoes, torques,
and earrings. The tent itself was royally adorned.

When Sho'beh reached the tent, he did not set foot on the carpets. He stood humbly in the dust, leaning against his sword as if it were a staff. Then he sat on the earth and paid no attention to anyone; he did not even look at the Persian commander. Rostam greeted him, "May your soul rejoice, your spirit know wisdom, and your body flourish." Sho'beh replied: "Your name is well known; if you accept the true faith, I will be satisfied." Rostam bridled at these words; he frowned and his face turned sallow. He took the letter from him and handed it to a scribe, who read it to him. Rostam answered, "Tell your master, 'You are not a king, and you have no right to seek a crown. Speech is not a trivial matter for wise men, and you don't know what it is you're undertaking.' If Sa'd wore the Sasanian crown it would be an easy matter for me to fight on his behalf; but you should realize that your star is faithless. How can I explain to you that today will be a day of disaster? If Mohammad himself were your leader, I could speak according to the old faith about this new faith. But the hunchbacked sky will deal harshly with me. Return in peace, since there is no place for talk on the day of battle. Tell your master that it is better to die honorably in battle than to live while an enemy triumphs over you."

Rostam's Battle with Sa'd; the Death of Rostam

Rostam ordered that the trumpets be sounded and his army surged forward like the sea. A cloud of dust rose up, and there was such a din of war cries that the sharpest ears were deafened. Like fire glimpsed through a purple curtain, diamond lances glittered in the darkened air, spears struck against helmets, and men's heads were trampled by horses' hooves. The battle continued for three days; then thirst made men's blows grow weaker and their horses too faint to fight. Rostam's lips were dry as dust; his mouth was parched and his tongue swollen and split. Both men and horses were so tormented by thirst that they ate damp clay. A cry like thunder went up, from Rostam on the one side and from Sa'd on the other: the two of them rode out from the body of their men and faced each other alone beneath a tall cypress tree. Rostam gave another thunderous cry and struck a sword blow against Sa'd's horse: the horse collapsed beneath him, and as Sa'd disentangled himself, Rostam lunged at him with his sharp sword, to prevent him from rising. He intended to sever Sa'd's head from his body, but the dust of the battlefield hid Sa'd from his sight. He jumped down from his leopard-skin saddle and tied his horse's bridle to his belt, but while he was blinded by dust, Sa'd attacked and struck Rostam's helmet a mighty blow with his sword. Blood poured from Rostam's head, filling his eyes, and the ambitious Arab triumphed over him. Sa'd thrust his sword into Rostam's chest and neck and hurled his warlike body into the dust.

The two armies were unaware of what was happening to their leaders, and began to search for them. When they saw Rostam lying bloody in the dust and his pavilion slashed into pieces, the Persians fled, and many of their noblemen were slaughtered. Many died of thirst while still in the saddle, and in this way the lives of many local kings came to an end. The remnant of the army sought their king, riding hard by day and night. At this time Yazdegerd was in Baghdad, and his soldiers flocked to him there.

Yazdegerd Consults with the Persians and Goes to Khorasan

Hormozd's other son, Farrokhzad, rode furiously to the Tigris, his eyes awash with tears. He reached Kerkh and attacked the enemy with such force that not an Arab warrior remained alive there. At the same time, troops poured out of Baghdad onto the plain and joined battle, but when the dust of combat rose into the sky the Persians were driven back. Farrokhzad retreated and made his way to the king, his armor and weapons smeared with the grime of battle. He dismounted from his horse and made his obeisance before the king, his eyes filled with bitter tears, his heart with anguish. He said, "What are you waiting for? You are putting the Persian throne at risk: of all the royal lineage, no one remains alive but you, there's no one else who's worthy to assume the crown and throne. You are one man and your enemies are a hundred thousand: how in all the world can you go on with this war? Go to the forests of Narvan; there men will join you until you have an army, and then like young Feraydun you will be able to make new plans for the future." The king listened to Farrokhzad's words, and turned over the alternatives in his mind.

The next day the king sat on his throne and placed the Kayanid crown on his head. He summoned an assembly of the wise, the nobility, and learned priests. He said to them, "What do you think of this proposal? What would you say that ancient precedents advise? Farrokhzad tells me to flee with an escort to the forests of Narvan, saying I have followers and supporters in Amol and Sari. When our armies have grown in size, that will be the time to return and give battle. Do you agree with this suggestion?" With one voice they answered, "This is not advisable!"

The King of Kings replied, "I agree with you; my heart cannot go along with this idea. Am I to save my own head and abandon Persia's nobility and its mighty armies, the land itself, and its throne and crown? This is neither noble nor chivalrous nor sensible. It's better that I fight with the enemy than endure such shame; a leopard-like warrior of ancient times once said, 'Never turn your back carelessly on an enemy, because this can only lead to evil days.' In the same way that the king's subjects owe him allegiance in good times and in bad, so the world's king must not abandon them to their sufferings while he flees to safety and luxury." The nobles called down blessings upon him, and said, "This is the way of true kings! Now consider your orders, and tell us what you wish of us."

The king answered, "My heart is destroyed by anxieties. We will travel to Khorasan, and there restore our strength after our enemies' attacks. We have many men there, many champions ready to fight for us. There are noblemen and Turks in the Chinese emperor's service; they will side with our cause, and I will marry a daughter of the emperor to make our alliance stronger. With their help I will have a mighty army of both our nobility and warlike Turks. Mahuy is lord of the marches there, and he has many men, war elephants, and wealth. He was a lowly shepherd, a laborer in the fields, and I promoted him because he spoke well and had a warlike nature. He had no status and I made him a lord of the marches with war elephants and an army and his own territory. He's a nobody, but he owes his good fortune to my court, and learned men have said it's an ancient precept that one should be wary of those to whom one has done evil, and trust in those whom one's generosity has lifted up to the heavens from nothingness."

Farrokhzad clapped his hands together and said, "My God-fearing king, don't trust men who have a lowly nature. There's a new proverb that says however much you try to mold a man's character, you don't have the key to change what God has made, and you won't alter what he is. May you know nothing but sovereignty and greatness!" The king replied, "You're a lion in combat, but no harm can come from this attempt of mine."

Night passed, and at dawn the court set out from Baghdad toward Khorasan, their hearts prepared for hardship. The Persian nobles who accompanied the king were grief-stricken. They invoked blessings on him, praying that the land never lose him, and a cry of sorrow went up from the army when they saw the king was leaving. Persians and subjects of the Chinese emperor alike came forward weeping to the king, their eyes flowing with tears, and said, "How can our hearts rejoice in our land without sight of the king? We shall abandon our homes and sons and wealth and share your hardships with you. We have no desire to live without your throne, and may good fortune never turn against you." Eloquent representatives of the Chinese emperor's men bowed their faces to the black earth and said, "We left our land and sought refuge with you; now we shall go with burning hearts to the emperor, fleeing before the Arabs to the Persian marches." The king's eyes became wet with tears and he sorrowfully addressed his noblemen: "All of you, pray to God, praise him endlessly, that I may see you all once again, and that this Arab attack be short-lived. You are my strength, inherited from my father, and I would not have you harmed, or share with me in an evil fate. We shall see if the heavens can turn toward benevolence again, but make your peace with them since there is no escaping what they will." Then he spoke to the Chinese merchants and said, "Do not stay in Persia long, because the Arabs will bring harm to you and your affairs." Everyone turned away, filled with grief and anguish, weeping and lamenting.

Farrokhzad, Hormozd's son, took command of the army and summoned experienced Persian warriors to serve. The king traveled, weeping and in sorrow, preceded by his commander and the troops. They went stage by stage to Rey, and there rested for a while, consoling themselves with wine and music. From Rey, partly hopeful and partly despairing, they pushed on like the wind to Gorgan; from there they took the road to Bost, their faces filled with frowns, their hearts with anxieties.

Yazdegerd's Letter to Mahuy and the Lords of the Marches of Khorasan

The king summoned an experienced scribe and vented the emotions of his heart. As he traveled toward Marv, he wrote a letter to Mahuy, the son of Suri, who was the governor there. It was a message filled with pain and bitterness, with his heart's desires and his eyes' tears. He opened the letter in the name of the Creator, the lord of knowledge from whom all benefits derive, who makes Mars and the sun turn in the heavens, who rules over both elephants and ants, who raises the lowly as he wishes and needs no precedent for his actions. He continued: "What evil days have befallen us! Our kingdom has lost its glory: Rostam was killed on the day of battle, at the hands of Sa'd, the son of Vaqas, a man who has no country, no lineage, no knowledge, and no wealth, and grief hems us in. Now that their armies are gathered like magpies before Baghdad, summon your troops to service and prepare them for war. I shall follow this letter like the wind and come to you trusting in your probity and generosity." He chose an intelligent man, capable of giving good advice, as his messenger.

The king had the army's drums sounded, and they pushed on from Bost and Nayshapur to Tus. When Mahuy learned of their approach, he went forward to meet the king with a mighty army, all of whom were armored and bore lances. When he saw the splendor of the king's entourage, with the royal banner and so many soldiers clustered about him, Mahuy quickly dismounted, and acted more like a slave than a subject, going meekly forward over the hot earth, his eyes flowing with tears of humility. He kissed the earth and made his obeisance, then waited humbly before the king for a long time. Farrokhzad's heart was filled with happiness when he saw Mahuy's face and his army's ranks, and he spoke with him at length. "I hand this king, descended from the Kayanid royal line, over to your protection," he said. "See that not a breath of wind is allowed to harm him. I must go to Rey, and I don't know when I shall see the royal crown again, since many others like me have been killed on the battlefield by the Arabs. There was no knight in all the world like Rostam, no wise man had ever heard of his equal, and yet he was killed by one of these crows with their black turbans, and the day of his death was a disaster for me. May God give him a place among the blessed, and that black crow a place where he'll be tormented by the lances of hell." Mahuy replied, "You are a great warrior; the king is as my own eyes and soul to me, and I accept your request that I protect him."

At the king's command, Farrokhzad set off for Rey, and soon the

malevolent Mahuy forgot all thoughts of kindness. He spent his nights
dreaming of the throne, and his manner and bearing changed. He pre-
tended to be ill and neglected to serve the king as he should.

Mahuy Encourages Bizhan to Attack the King; the King Flees to a Mill

There was a successful warrior named Bizhan, whose family was from
Tarkhan. His seat was in Samarqand, and he had many allies in the area.
When the evil Mahuy was seized by ambition, he wrote a letter to
Bizhan: "You are descended from a warrior race, and here is an oppor-
tunity for you to profit from battle. The king of the world, with his
crown and throne and army, is here. If you attack, his head and crown
and throne will be yours, together with his treasures and the black
parasol held over the royal head." Bizhan considered the letter, and saw
that the world was ambitious Mahuy's to take. He said to his vizier, "As
the most honest of my men, what's your advice on this matter? If I
lead my army out to help Mahuy, my situation here will be ruined: the
Chinese king will have contempt for me and think of me as an oppor-
tunist and a time server. And if I don't do this, people will say I am a
coward and afraid to fight." His vizier answered, "You are a lionhearted
man, and it will be shameful for you to have offered friendship to
Mahuy and then to back out of it. Send your ally Barsam to fight this
battle; if you fight just because Mahuy encourages you to, serious men
will call you frivolous." Bizhan said, "You're right, it's best for me to
stay where I am. Send Barsam with ten thousand cavalry to Marv, and
we'll see whether he can seize Persia's treasures in his fist."

Glittering like a pheasant's feathers, the army set off from Bokhara
and arrived at the city of Marv in a week. Yazdegerd had no notion of
Mahuy's treachery: when it was still dark, at the time the roosters crow,
the sound of war drums rang out, and as day broke a horseman came
galloping to the king, saying, "Mahuy says an army of Turks is attack-
ing, led by the Chinese khan, and they are so numerous it seems the
earth could not bear their weight. What are the king's orders?" The king
leaped up and strapped on his armor, and the two armies came face to
face. When Yazdegerd saw the Turks' forces, he clapped his hands
together and drew his sword; he appeared before the army, massive as an
elephant, and the ground was awash with blood like the Nile. But when
the king attacked the Turks, none of his warriors followed him; they all

turned their backs on their monarch and abandoned him to the enemy cavalry. And as Mahuy too drew back from the fight, leaving him in the midst of the enemy forces, Yazdegerd realized his treachery. The king fought furiously, striking out with his sword, urging his horse on with his stirrups, and killing many of the enemy's renowned warriors; but when he became more hard-pressed, he turned his back on the battle and fled. With many Turks in pursuit, a Kaboli sword in his grasp, he rode like lightning flashing from a cloud.

There was a mill by the River Zarq, and there the world's king dismounted and concealed himself from his enemies. Their cavalry were searching everywhere, and all the area was filled with talk of him. The king had abandoned his horse with its golden saddle, his mace, and his sword in its golden sheath, and when the Turks came on these they cried out in their excitement, while the king hid himself away, sitting on dry straw, in the mill. This is the way of the deceitful world, raising a man up and casting him down. When fortune was with him, his throne was in the heavens, and now a mill was his lot; the world's favors are many, but they are exceeded by its poison. Why should you bind your heart to this world, where the drums that signal your departure are heard continuously, together with the caravan leader's cry of "Prepare to leave"? The only rest you will find is that of the grave. So the king sat, without food, his eyes filled with tears, until the sun rose.

The miller opened the mill door, carrying a load of straw on his back. He was a humble man, called Khosrow, who possessed neither a throne, nor wealth, nor a crown, nor any power. He made his living from the mill and had no other occupation. He saw a warrior like a tall cypress tree, seated on the stony ground as a man sits in despair; a royal crown was on his head, and his clothes were made of glittering Chinese brocade. Khosrow stared at him in astonishment and murmured the name of God. He said, "Your majesty, your face shines like the sun; tell me, how did you come to be in this mill? How can a mill full of wheat and dust and straw be a place for you to sit? What kind of a man are you, with this stature and face of yours, and radiating such glory, because the heavens have never seen your like?"

The king replied, "I'm one of the Persians who fled from the army of Turan." The miller said in his confusion, "I've never known anything but poverty, but if you could eat some barley bread, and some of the common herbs that grow on the riverbank, I'll bring them to you,

and anything else I can find. A poor man is always aware of how little
he has." In the three days that had passed since the battle the king had
had no food. He said, "Bring whatever you have, and a sacred barsom."
The man quickly brought a basket of barley bread and herbs and then
hurried off to find a barsom at the river toll house. There he met up
with the headman of Zarq and asked him for a barsom. Mahuy had
sent people everywhere searching for the king, and the headman said,
"Now, my man, who is it who wants a barsom?" Khosrow answered
him, "There's a warrior sitting on the straw in my mill; he's as tall as a
cypress tree, and his face is as glorious as the sun. His eyebrows are like
a bow, his sad eyes like narcissi; his mouth is filled with sighs, his fore-
head with frowns. It's he who wants the barsom, to pray; if you saw
him, you'd be astonished. I put an old basket with barley bread in it in
front of him."

The headman said, "Run from here and tell Mahuy what you've
said. But God forbid that evil-minded man should show his foul nature
once he's heard this." And he immediately handed him over to a man
who took him to Mahuy. Mahuy questioned him and said, "Who
wanted a barsom? Tell the truth now!" Fearfully, the miller said, "I was
carrying some materials I needed on my back, and I opened the mill
door in a hurry, and it was as if I saw the sun shining in front of me.
He had eyes like a deer's when it's afraid—they were as dark as the third
watch of the night. The mill seemed filled with sunlight because of
him; his crown was studded with uncut jewels, and he was dressed in
Chinese brocade. He's like the springtime itself, and no landowner has
ever planted a cypress as fine as he is."

Mahuy considered in his heart all he had heard and knew that this
was none other than Yazdegerd. He turned to the miller and said,
"Leave this assembly immediately and cut the man's head off; if you
refuse I'll cut your head off here and now and leave not one member
of your family alive." The noblemen gathered there heard his orders and
they all seethed with anger; their eyes were filled with tears and every-
one spoke vehemently against Mahuy's plan, including his own son.

Yazdegerd Is Killed by the Miller Khosrow
When Mahuy had heard his son out, he turned to the miller and said,
"Get on with it; go now, and spill our enemy's blood." The miller
heard him but could make no sense of what he was being told. It was

the night of the thirtieth day of the month of Khordad, when the miller returned to his mill and the king. Mahuy left the court, his eyes filled with tears, his heart with fury, and sent horsemen after the miller, saying to them, "The crown and earrings, his seal ring and the royal clothes must not be stained with blood; remove his clothes from his body."

The miller wept and his face had turned sallow as he made his way home. He prayed, "O bright Creator, thou who art above the heavens' turning, make this man's soul and body suffer for this evil command he has given me!" His heart was filled with shame and fear as he approached the king; his cheeks were stained with tears, and his mouth was as dry as dust. He came up to the king like someone about to impart a secret in a man's ear and plunged a dagger beneath his ribs. The king sighed at the wound, and his head and crown fell down to the dust, beside the barley bread that lay before him.

> A man who understands the world soon says
> There is no sense or wisdom in its ways:
> If this is how imperial blood is spilled
> And innocents like Yazdegerd are killed,
> The seven spheres grow weary of their roles—
> No longer do they cherish mortal souls.
> The heavens mingle their malevolence
> With kindnesses in ways which make no sense,
> And it is best if you can watch them move
> Untouched by indignation and by love.

The wretched Mahuy's knights saw that the royal tree was felled from the throne and battlefield, and each of them went forward to gaze at his face. They undid the clasp of his purple cloak and removed his crown and torque and golden boots. Then, as they stood again before the king, they spoke at last and said, "May Mahuy's body be like his, weltering in its blood on the ground."

Quickly they took the clothes and jewels to Mahuy and said, "The king knows neither peace nor war now." He ordered that the body be thrown into the river, at night, when men are sleeping. Two callous servants hurried to carry out his command; unaware of its rank, they dragged the bloody body outside and threw it in the mill pond. When day followed night two religious ascetics came into view, and one of them approached the bank. He saw the naked body floating there, and ran horrified back to the monastery door, where he told the other monks what he had seen. "The king is lying naked and drowned in the Zarq mill pond," he said, and monks and priests came running from the monastery doors, crying out in grief for the king. One of them said, "No one has ever seen such an event, or heard of it, not from before the time of Jesus, that a wretched slave, a man of no account, should give a king hospitality and then murder him. May Mahuy be cursed for this! Alas for your head and crown and noble stature, for your heart and knowledge and wisdom! Alas for this scion of Ardeshir, for this young warlike knight! You were alive, healthy, and wise, and now you have taken news to Nushin-Ravan that you who ruled the world and sought out its crowns have been killed with a dagger plunged into your liver, and have been thrown naked into a mill pond."

Four of the monks stripped off their habits and went into the water. They dragged the body of the young king, the descendant of Nushin-Ravan, to dry land, and everyone there, young and old, wept as they did so. In a garden the monks built him a tomb that towered up to the clouds. They dried the dagger wound and treated the body with unguents, pitch, camphor, and musk; then they dressed it in yellow brocade, laid it on muslin, and placed a blue pall over it. Finally, a priest anointed the king's resting place with wine, musk, camphor, and rosewater.

Mahuy Assumes the Throne

A man came to Mahuy and said, "The king of the world is now one with the earth. Byzantine priests and monks have filled the land with mourning for him. Young and old, they went weeping to take his body from the mill pond. They built a great tomb for him in a garden." Evil and shameless, Mahuy said, "Until now, Persia has never been kin to Byzantium." He gave orders that all who had built the tomb or who had mourned for the king be killed, and the area be plundered; this was Mahuy's notion of pleasure and appropriate behavior.

Then he looked about him and saw that in all the world there was no remaining descendant of the royal line. This shepherd's son possessed the king's crown and seal ring, and he longed to rule. He called his confidants to him and told them all that was in his heart. He said to his vizier,

"You are an experienced man, and you must know that a day of battle is looming. I have neither wealth, nor name, nor lineage to boast of, and I see that my life is at risk. The name on this seal ring is Yazdegerd's, and my sword is unable to pacify the people. All of the cities of Iran were his to command, but no wise man calls me king, and my seal's authority is not respected by the army. There were other alternatives to the things I did in secret; why did I shed the blood of the king of the world? I spend my nights tormented by anxiety, and God knows the state in which I live." His advisor said, "The deed is done, and the world is full of talk of it. Look to your own affairs, because you have cut the thread of the warp now. He lies in his tomb, beneath the dust, and has the cure for all the poisons that afflicted his soul. Call together men of experience and speak to them sweetly and plausibly. Say, 'The king gave me this crown and seal ring, as marks of authority. He did this because he knew an army of Turks was approaching. He summoned me in the darkness of the night and said, "When the dust of battle rises, who knows who will emerge victorious? Take this crown and seal ring, and it may be that some day they will be of use to you. This is all I have in the world, see that you hide them from the Arabs. Follow my precepts in all you do, and do not give my throne to the enemy." I have this crown as an inheritance from the king, and it is at his command that I sit on the throne.' In this way you will put a good face on your deception: who will know whether this is the truth or a lie?"

When Mahuy heard his words he said, "Wonderful! You are a true vizier, there is none better!" He summoned the commanders of his army and spoke to them as his vizier had suggested. They knew that what he said was untrue, and that he deserved to have his head cut off for his impudence. One of the champions there said, "This is your business, whether what you say is true or not." Mahuy sat on the royal throne and became ruler of Khorasan by this ruse. He gave grants of land to the nobility, and said, "By virtue of this seal ring I am the world's king." He distributed the world's lands while the stars looked on in astonishment: he gave his elder son Balkh and Herat, and sent armies out in every direction. He promoted evil men, as might be expected of a scoundrel of his character, making criminals governors everywhere, and wise men had to bow their heads and obey them. On all sides, truth was humiliated and lies flourished. When this wretch had gathered together a large enough army and collected sufficient wealth, his heart rejoiced; he gave cash to his troops and planned to fight against Bizhan. He sent soldiers, under the command of an experienced warrior named Garsetun, as an advance guard to Amui. His troops marched on Bokhara and he said, "I must take Samarqand and Chach by the authority of this seal ring and crown, and by the command of Yazdegerd, the world's king, the lord of the seven spheres. I shall be revenged upon Bizhan, since it is he who has brought misfortune on Iran."

Bizhan Fights Against Mahuy and Kills Him

News reached Bizhan that Mahuy had seized the imperial throne, sent orders far and wide sealed with the royal insignia, and subdued the countryside. Now he was heading toward the Oxus with an army eager for battle. Bizhan took his head in his hands at this turn of events, and then he summoned his troops to prepare for war. Information came that Mahuy's army had taken Samarqand; they were crossing the Oxus in boats, and the dust sent up by their troops hid the sun. Bizhan led his men out and prepared for battle; when Mahuy saw his opponent's ranks, their armor, helmets, and golden shields, their lances and maces and Chachi axes, his soul seemed to desert his body. Sick at heart, he drew up his troops; the air was obscured with dust, and the earth was invisible beneath the mass of combatants.

When battle was joined Bizhan planned to close in on Mahuy, but Mahuy realized this and, wailing in fear, he fled from the center of his army. Bizhan ordered his ally Barsam to lead men to the flank to cut him off. He said, "Mahuy is afraid of battle. Don't take your eyes off him, he mustn't be allowed to get back to the Oxus." Barsam watched Mahuy's banner; frowning and cursing, he led his men in pursuit of him as far as the sands of the River Farab. There he caught up with the fugitive and urged his horse forward. When they were face to face, instead of striking at him with his sword, Barsam reached out and caught Mahuy by the belt, and threw him easily to the ground. Then he dismounted, tied Mahuy's arms, and flung him on his own horse in front of the saddle. His companions arrived at this moment, and the whole plain was filled with talk of his exploit. They told him, "Don't bother taking him prisoner; you should cut his head off with an axe." Barsam answered, "This is not the way to act, because Bizhan doesn't know I've captured him."

Immediately Bizhan was informed that this vile slave, this ambitious traitor, the regicide Mahuy had been taken prisoner. Overjoyed to hear this, he exulted in his victory and banished care from his mind. A canopy was set up on the soft sand, and Mahuy was quickly brought there. When this sinner saw Bizhan, good sense deserted him; he became senseless with fear and began to scatter sand over his head. Bizhan addressed him, "You low-born wretch, may no subject ever again act as you have done! Why did you kill our just king, the lord of victory and the throne? From father to son he inherited kingship and was a king himself, the living emblem of Nushin-Ravan." Mahuy said, "From an evil person you should expect nothing but murder and sedition. Cut off my head for the wicked deed I've done, and fling it before this assembly." He was afraid that he would be flayed alive, and that his body would be dragged along, weltering in its blood.

Bizhan knew his secret terror, and he paused a while before answering. Then he said, "I want to cleanse my heart of hatred for you. With this chivalry of yours, this knowledge and understanding and character, you coveted the crown and throne." He cut off Mahuy's hands with his sword and said, "These hands have no equal in crime." Then he cut off his feet so that he couldn't move from the spot. Finally, he gave orders that Mahuy's ears and nose be cut off, and that he be sat on a horse, and left wandering the hot sands till he died of shame. He had a herald go about the camp and announce at each tent, "May those slaves who would kill their king think better of their foolishness; may those who wouldn't give their lives for the king be as Mahuy is, and may they never know glory!" Mahuy had three sons with his army, each with his own crown and throne. There and then a fire was lit, and the father and his three sons were burned in it. None of his family survived, or if they did, anyone who met them drove them away; may the nobility curse this family forever, and hate them for their murder of the king.

After this came the era of Omar, and when he brought the new faith, the pulpit replaced the throne.

After sixty-five years had passed over my head, I toiled ever more diligently and with greater difficulty at my task. I searched out the history of the kings, but my star was a laggard one. Nobles and great men wrote down what I had written without paying me: I watched them from a distance, as if I were a hired servant of theirs. I had nothing from them but their congratulations; my gall bladder was ready to burst with their congratulations! Their purses of hoarded coins remained closed, and my bright heart grew weary at their stinginess. But of the renowned men of my district, Ali Daylami helped me, and that honorable man Hosayn Qotayb never asked for my works for nothing. I received food and clothing, silver and gold from him, and it was he who gave me the will to continue. I never had to worry about paying taxes and was able to wrap myself in my quilt in comfort, and when I reached the age of seventy-one, the heavens humbled themselves before my verses. Now I have brought the story of Yazdegerd to an end, in the month of Sepandormoz, on the day of Ard, and four hundred years have passed since the Hejira of the Prophet.

> I've reached the end of this great history
> And all the land will fill with talk of me:
> I shall not die, these seeds I've sown will save
> My name and reputation from the grave,
> And men of sense and wisdom will proclaim,
> When I have gone, my praises and my fame.

GLOSSARY OF NAMES

The following is a list of the names in the stories in this book, together with a brief description of who or what they designate.

Persian names are pronounced with a more even stress than is common in English, and to an English speaker's ear this often sounds as if the last syllable is being stressed. A slight extra stress on the last syllable of names will bring the reader closer to a Persian pronunciation.

Persian has two distinct sounds indicated in English by the letter "a." One is a long sound (as in "father") and this has been indicated here by the accent "ā" (e.g., Zāl). The other is a short sound (as in "cat") and this has been indicated by the standard "a" (e.g., Zav). The vowel given as "i" is a long vowel, like the second vowel in "police." The vowel given as "u" is also a long vowel, like the first vowel in "super." "Q" and "gh" are pronounced approximately as a guttural hard "g," far back in the throat. "Zh" is pronounced like the sound represented by the "s" in "pleasure." "Kh" is pronounced like the Scottish "ch" in "loch."

ABBĀS . . . . an Arab warrior who attacks Iran during the reign of Hormozd.

ABUL FAZL . . . . the librarian of the Samanid king Nasr.

ABU BAKR . . . . the successor of the Prophet Mohammad as the leader of the Moslem community.

AFRĀSYĀB. . . . . a king of Turān, the brother of Aghriras and Garsivaz.

AGHRIRAS . . . . the brother of Afrāsyāb and Garsivaz.

AHRIMAN . . . . the evil god of the universe.

AHVĀZ. . . . . a city in southeastern Iran.

AJNĀS . . . . a warrior of Turān.

AKVĀN DIV. . . . . the name of a demon who tries to kill Rostam.

ALĀNĀN. . . . . a fortress of Turān.

ALĀNS . . . . a tribe living near the Caspian Sea.

ALBORZ . . . . the mountains to the south of the Caspian Sea. The word "borz" simply means "high (ground)," and in some of the *Shahnameh*'s early stories the mountains referred to seem to be the Himalayas rather than the mountains now called the Alborz.

ALI DAYLAMI. . . . . a man who supported Ferdowsi during his writing of the Shahnameh.

ALTOUYANEH . . . . the site of a major Sasanian victory over the Romans. It seems likely that the victory referred to is the one that took place near Edessa in 259 C.E., when the Roman emperor Valerian was captured by Shāpur I.

ALVĀD . . . . a warrior from Sistān.

ĀMOL . . . . a town near the Caspian.

AMOURIEH . . . . the area between the River Jordan and the Mediterranean.

AMUI. . . . . a plain to the north of the River Oxus.

ANDARIMĀN . . . . a warrior from Turān.

ANDIĀN. . . . . an Armenian chieftain.

ARASH . . . . an Ashkāniān (Parthian) king.

ARD. . . . . the twenty-fifth day of every month in the Zoroastrian calendar.

ARDAVĀN . . . . the last Ashkāniān king, defeated by Ardeshir.

ARDEBIL. . . . . a town in northwestern Iran.

ARDESHIR. . . . . another name for Esfandyār's son, Bahman. Also Ardeshir, the brother of King Shāpur Z'ul Aktāf, who acts as regent on the death of Shāpur.

ARDESHIR BĀBAKĀN. . . . . . . the founder of the Sāsāniān dynasty.

ARESTĀLIS. . . . . Aristotle.

ĀREZU . . . . the bride of Salm.

ARJĀSP. . . . . a king of Turān.

ARMANI . . . . a Persian warrior.

ARMENIA . . . . the country of the Armenians to the northwest of Iran.

ASHKĀSH . . . . a Persian warrior.

ARNAVĀZ . . . . the sister of Jamshid.

ARVAND . . . . the name of a river.

ARZHANG . . . . a demon of Māzanderān.

ASHK . . . . the name of the founder of the Ashkāniān dynasty.

ASHKĀNIĀN . . . . the Parthians; the dynasty that ruled Iran from 247 B.C.E. to 224 C.E., i.e. from the defeat of the Seleucid heirs of Alexander until the advent of the Sāsāniāns.

ASPORUZ . . . . a mountain in Māzanderān.

ĀTEBIN . . . . the father of Feraydun.

AVESTĀ . . . . see Zend-Avestā.

AYIN-GOSHASP . . . . a scribe at the court of Hormozd.

AZĀDEH . . . . a slave belonging to Bahrām Gur.

AZĀD-SARV . . . . Nushin-Ravān's envoy, who discovers Bozorjmehr.

AZAR . . . . the ninth solar month, and the ninth day of any month, in the Zoroastrian year.

AZAR-GOSHASP . . . . the name of a fire-temple in Balkh. Also of a companion of Bahrām Chubineh.

AZARM-DOKHT . . . . a Sāsāniān queen who reigned for four months. The sister of Purān-Dokht.

AZARMEGAN . . . . the father of Farrokhzad, the chamberlain of Khosrow Parviz.

AZAR-PANĀH . . . . apparently the name of a fire-temple, but unattested outside of the Shahnameh. According to some mss. the name of a scribe at the court of Nushin-Ravan.

BĀBAK . . . . a ruler of Estakhr; the maternal grandfather of Ardeshir.

BADAKHSHĀN . . . . an area in the northeast of Afghanistan, famous for its remoteness and its rubies.

BĀDĀN-PIRUZ . . . . a supporter of Khosrow Parviz when he is out of favor with his father Hormozd.

BĀDĀVAR . . . . a royal treasury. The name means literally "windfall."

BAHMAN . . . . Esfandyār's son, and Sāsān's and Homay's father. Also the name of an angel.

BAHMAN . . . . a son of Ardavān, the last Ashkāniān king.

BAHMAN . . . . a courtier of Khosrow Parviz.

BAHMAN . . . . a winter month, and the second day of every month, in the Zoroastrian calendar.

BAHRĀM . . . . a warrior of Irān.

BAHRĀM . . . . also called Ardavān: the last Ashkāniān king. A descendant of Seyāvash; a cavalry commander under Bahrām Chubineh. Also the name of the twentieth day of each of the Zoroastrian months.

BAHRĀM BAHRĀM . . . . a minor Sāsāniān king.

BAHRĀM BAHRĀMIĀN . . . . . . a minor Sāsāniān king.

BAHRĀM CHUBINEH . . . . a champion in the service of Hormozd and Khosrow Parviz. He rebels against his monarchs and attempts to seize the throne for himself.

BAHRĀM GUR . . . . a Sāsāniān king: the son of Yazdegerd the Unjust.

BAHRĀM HORMOZD . . . . a minor Sāsāniān king.

BAHRĀM PIRUZ . . . . a nobleman in the service of Bahrām Gur.

BAHRĀM SHĀPUR . . . . a minor Sāsāniān king.

BAHRĀM AZAR-MAHĀN . . . . . an advisor at the courts of Kesrā Nushin-Ravān and Hormozd.

BALĀSH . . . . a minor Sasanian king.

BALKH . . . . a town in northern Afghānistān.

BALUCHISTAN . . . . a province covering modern south eastern Irān and eastern Pakistan.

BĀMYĀN . . . . a valley in northern Afghanistan.

BANDUY . . . . a maternal uncle of King Khosrow Parviz. Also an advisor to Nushin-Ravān.

BARAK . . . . the name of a river and a town in northeastern Afghanistan.

BARĀNUSH . . . . A Roman commander captured by Shāpur I. Also a Roman emperor contemporary with Shāpur Z'ul Aktāf. The historical origin of both figures is probably the emperor Valerian captured by Shāpur I in 259 C.E.

BĀRBAD . . . . a musician who serves King Khosrow Parviz.

BARDA' . . . . a town in Azerbaijan.

BARKEH-YE ARDESHIR . . . . . a town founded by Ardeshir.

BĀRMĀN . . . . two warriors of Turan go by this name; one is a son of Viseh and is killed by Qāren, the other accompanies Sohrāb on his expedition against Irān.

BARMĀYEH . . . . the ox that nourishes the young Feraydun. Also a brother of Feraydun.

BARSĀM . . . . the son of Bizhan, the governor of Samarqand during the reign of Yazdegerd III.

BARSOM . . . . sacred rods used in Zoroastrian ceremonies.

BARZIN . . . . a warrior of Irān.

BEDĀL . . . . a warrior chieftain from Khazar.

BEH ĀFARID . . . . a daughter of Goshtasp, and sister to Esfandyar, Pashutan, and Homay.

BEHZĀD . . . . the name of Seyavash's horse.

BEHZĀD . . . . the father of Mehr-Piruz, a warrior of Bahrām Gur. Also an advisor to Kesrā Nushin-Ravān.

BESTĀM . . . . a town in northern Iran.

BISITUN . . . . a mountain in south east Irān, about thirty miles from the city of Kermanshah. In medieval Persian verse the name is sometimes used simply to mean any large mountain.

BID . . . . a demon of Māzanderān.

BITQUN . . . . a vizier of Sekandar. When Sekandar visits Queen Qaydā feh, he pretends to be Bitqun.

BIVARD . . . . a contender for the crown, after the death of Yazdegerd the Unjust.

BIZHAN . . . . a Persian hero, the son of Giv.

BOKHĀRĀ . . . . a city in Transoxiana.

BORZIN . . . . the name of a priest of Zoroaster who built the fire-temple named after him.

BORZUI . . . . a doctor who brings the book Kalileh and Demneh from India. Also the name assumed by Bahrām Gur when he visits India in disguise.

BOST . . . . an area to the east of Sistān; lying between Persia and India.

BOZORJMEHR . . . . meaning "Great Light." The vizier of Kesrā Nushin-Ravān. The modern form of the name is Bozarjomehr.

CHĀCH . . . . a city in Turkestan famous for the bows made there. Chachi is its adjectival form.

CHĀJ . . . . a town near Birjand in eastern Iran.

CHORASMIA . . . . the area to the south of the Aral Sea.

CTESIPHON . . . . the Sâsâniân capital, on the River Tigris.

DĀGHUI . . . . this area, which must lie somewhere between Persia and Turān, has not been further identified.

DAMĀVAND . . . . an extinct volcanic peak; the highest mountain in Irān.

DAMUR . . . . a warrior of Turān.

DĀRĀ . . . . the son of King Dārāb, defeated by Sekandar.

DĀRĀB . . . . the son of Bahman and Homāy. The father of Dārā and Sekandar.

DARI . . . . a name for the Persian language of eastern Iran and Afghanistan.

DASTĀN . . . . another name given to Zāl, the son of Sām and father of Rostam.

DAYLAM . . . . a city in Gilān, to the south of the Caspian Sea.

DEHESTĀN . . . . an area to the east of the Caspian.

DELAFRUZ . . . . the name of a thorn-cutter encountered by Bahrām Gur.

DELAFRUZ-E FARROKHPAY . . . a servant girl who helps Shāpur escape from captivity in Rome.

DELĀRĀY . . . . the wife of Dārā and mother of Roshanak.

DEZHKHIM . . . . a warrior of Māzanderān.

DILMĀN . . . . a province south of the Caspian.

EBLIS . . . . the devil.

ERMĀN . . . . Ermāni, an area to the north west of Irān, identified with present day Armenia.

ESDRAS . . . . identified with the Hebrew prophet Ezra.

ESFAHAN . . . . a city in central Iran.

ESFANDYĀR . . . . a Persian prince: the son of Goshtāsp, and father of Bahman.

ESMAIL . . . . a son of Abraham, whose descendants claimed the right to rule in the Yemen at the time of Sekandar.

ESRĀFIL . . . . the angel of death.

ESTAKHR . . . . a city in central Iran.

EUPHRATES . . . . one of the major rivers of Mesopotamia. For many years the de facto border between the Sāsāniān and the Roman empires.

FARĀB . . . . a town on the River Oxus.

FARĀMARZ . . . . Rostam's son.

FARĀNAK . . . . the mother of Feraydun.

FARĀYIN . . . . a supporter of Kesrā Nushin-Ravān against Mazdak.

FARHĀD . . . . a warrior of Irān.

FARIBORZ . . . . a Persian prince, the son of Kay Kāvus.

FARIGIS . . . . the daughter of Afrāsyāb and bride of Seyāvash.

FARROKHZĀD . . . . the brother of Rostam the son of Hormozd (who leads Yazdegerd III's armies against the Arab invaders).

FARROKHZĀD . . . . the chamberlain of Khosrow Parviz. This is apparently a different Farrokhzād from the man who reigned briefly after the death of Queen āzarm-Dokht.

FARSHIDVARD . . . . a warrior of Turān, and an associate of Piran.

FARSHIDVARD . . . . a miserly landowner, encountered by Bahrām Gur.

FARYĀN . . . . an Arab king who reigns on the borders of the lands ruled by Queen Qaydāfeh.

FARVARDIN . . . . the first month of the Persian year, which begins at the spring equinox in late March.

FERAYDUN . . . . a Persian king.

FILQUS . . . . Philip of Macedon, the father of Nāhid, and grandfather of Sekandar (Alexander the Great).

FOOR . . . . an Indian prince who fights against Sekandar.

FORUD . . . . Seyavash's son.

GALINUSH . . . . Khosrow Parviz's jailer, after he is imprisoned by his son.

GARSETUN . . . . an ally of Māhuy, the warlord who reigns briefly after the murder of Yazdegerd III.

GARSHĀSB . . . . a Persian king, Zav's son; the Persian army commander of the same name seems to be a different person and the father of Nariman is yet another bearer of the same name.

GARSIVAZ . . . . a warrior of Turān, the brother of Afrāsyāb and Aghriras.

GAZHDAHAM. . . . . a warrior of Irān, the father of Gordāfarid.

GERDUI . . . . a counselor to Khosrow Parviz. Brother of Gordyeh and Bahrām Chubineh.

GHASSĀNID. . . . . an Arab tribe.

GHUR . . . . the area north of Kandahār, in Afghanistan.

GILĀN . . . . a province to the south of the Caspian Sea.

GIV . . . . a warrior of Irān, the son of Gudarz.

GOLBĀD. . . . . a warrior of Turān.

GOLNĀR . . . . Ardavān's treasurer and Ardeshir's lover.

GOLSHAHR . . . . the wife of Piran, Afrāsyāb's counselor.

GONBADĀN. . . . . a castle in Khorasan.

GORAZEH . . . . a Persian nobleman.

GORĀZ. . . . . a warrior of Irān.

GORĀZM . . . . Goshtasp's son and Esfandyâr's brother, he slanders Esfandyār out of jealousy.

GORDĀFARID. . . . . a female warrior of Irān.

GORDYEH . . . . the sister of Bahrām Chubineh and of Gerdui. She is briefly the wife of Gostahm, whom she murders, and then of Khosrow Parviz.

GORGĀN. . . . . an area to the east of the Caspian.

GORGIN . . . . a warrior of Irān.

GORGSARĀN . . . . an unidentified area in Turān. There is a village of this name near Balkh, but this is too deep in Persian territory to be Bizhan's place of imprisonment. The word means "wolf-headed."

GORUI . . . . a warrior of Turān.

GOSHTĀSP . . . . a Persian king, the son of Lohrāsp.

GOSTAHAM . . . . a warrior of Irān.

GOSTAHM. . . . . a maternal uncle of Khosrow Parviz and a major participant in the struggles for the throne during Khosrow's and his father Hormozd's reigns. Also the name of a Persian warrior during the reigns of Yazdegerd the Unjust and Bahrām Gur.

GOSTAHOM. . . . . a Persian prince, the son of Nozar.

GUDARZ. . . . . a warrior of Irān, the father of Giv, the son of Keshvād.

GURĀBĀD . . . . an unidentified town or village near the border of Sistān and Irān. There are villages in modern Irān that have this name, but none of them are near Sistān.

HABASH . . . . the name given collectively to the tribes of Africa.

HAFTVĀD . . . . the father of the girl who finds the "Worm" of Kerman; he rebels against the Sāsāniān king Ardeshir.

HAMĀVAN. . . . . a mountain in Khorāsān.

HĀMĀVERĀN . . . . Sudābeh's country of origin, usually identified with the Yemen.

HAMDĀN-GOSHASP . . . . a Persian commander under Bahrām Chubineh.

HAMEDĀN . . . . a city in western Iran.

HAMZEH . . . . an Arab warrior who attacks Iran during the reign of Hormozd.

HARUM . . . . a town inhabited entirely by women, visited by Sekandar.

HEJĀZ . . . . Western Arabia.

HEJIR. . . . . a warrior of Irān.

HEJIRA. . . . . the flight of the prophet Mohammad from Mecca to Medina in 622 C.E., which marks the beginning of the Moslem calendar.

HEND . . . . India.

HERĀT . . . . a town in western Afghānistān.

HIRBAD . . . . the keeper of King Kavus's harem.

HIRMAND . . . . a river that marks one boundary of Zābolestān; its modern name is the River Helmand.

HOMĀ . . . . a mythical bird, said to bestow sovereignty on whomever its shadow touches.

HOMĀY . . . . daughter of Goshtāsp, sister to Esfandyār, Pashutan, and Beh Āfarid. Also, the name of Bahman's daughter.

HORMOZD . . . . the good god of the universe.

HORMOZD . . . . a Sāsāniān king; the son of Nushin-Ravān and the father of Khosrow Parviz. A name for Āhura Mazdā, the good principle of the universe. An advisor to Nushin-Ravān.

HOSAYN QOTAYB . . . . a man who supported Ferdowsi during his writing of the Shahnameh.

HOSHYĀR . . . . a Persian astrologer.

HUMĀN . . . . a warrior of Turān.

HUSHANG. . . . . a Persian king, the grandson of Kayumars.

IRAJ. . . . . the youngest son of Feraydun.

ESFAHÂN . . . . one of the chief cities in central Irān.

IZAD-GOSHASP . . . . a councilor of Nushin-Ravān, put to death by Hormozd. Also an army commander under Bahrām Chubineh.

JAHAN . . . . a son of Afrāsyāb.

JAHROM. . . . . a town in southern Iran.

JĀMĀSP . . . . vizier to the legendary kings Lohrāsp and Goshtasp.

JAMSHID . . . . a Persian king.

JANDAL . . . . King Feraydun's councillor.

JĀNFOROUZ . . . . a warrior in Bahrām Chubineh's army.

JĀNUSHYĀR . . . . an advisor to King Dārā, whom he kills.

JARAM . . . . an area near Badakhshān.

JARIREH . . . . Piran's daughter; Forud's mother.

JAVANUI. . . . . a priest sent as an envoy by the Persian nobility to Monzer, the guardian of the young Bahram Gur.

JAZA'. . . . . a tyrannical ruler of the Hejaz.

JEDDAH . . . . a coastal town in the Hejaz.

JEZ . . . . Mesopotamia.

JONDESHAPUR. . . . . a city in western Iran.

JORM. . . . . a magical site, from which a voice speaks to the mourners of Sekandar.

JUYA . . . . a warrior of Mazanderan.

KA'ABEH . . . . the central Moslem shrine, in Mecca.

KABOL, KABOLESTAN . . . . . . eastern Afghanistan and its chief city.

KAJARAN . . . . a town near the Persian Gulf, in southeastern Iran.

KAKUI . . . . a champion of Turan.

KALAT . . . . the town in Turan where Forud and his mother live.

KALBUI . . . . an ally of Rostam (the son of Hormozd) at the battle of Qadesiya.

KALILEH AND DEMNEH. . . . . the name of a book of advice cast in the form of animal fables.

KAMUS. . . . . a western ally of Afrasyab, killed by Rostam.

KANARANG . . . . a demon of Mazanderan.

KARIMAN . . . . an ancestor of Nariman, and therefore of the family of Zal and Rostam.

KARZEBAN . . . . a town in Khorasan.

KARUKHAN. . . . . a warrior of Turan.

KATAYUN . . . . a Byzantine princess who marries Goshtasp; the mother of Esfandyar.

KAVARESTAN . . . . the area of Transoxiana.

KAVEH. . . . . a blacksmith who leads the insurrection against the demon-king Zahhak.

KAVIANI . . . . an adjective from Kaveh, applied particularly to the banner made from Kaveh's leather apron.

KAY ARASH. . . . . a Persian prince, son of Kay Qobad.

KAY ARMIN . . . . '. . a Persian prince, son of Kay Qobad.

KAY KAVUS. . . . . a Persian king, son of Kay Qobad.

KAY PASHIN . . . . a Persian prince, son of Kay Qobad.

KAY QOBAD . . . . a Persian king.

KAYANID . . . . the name of the Persian royal house.

KAYD. . . . . an Indian king.

KAYUMARS . . . . the first Persian king.

KAZHDAHOM . . . . a Persian nobleman.

KEBRUI . . . . a village headman who becomes drunk at the court of Bahrām Gur.

KENĀM-E ASIRĀN . . . . a city built in the reign of Shāpur as a home for Roman prisoners.

KERKH. . . . . a town in Mesopotamia.

KESHMIHAN . . . . a city near Marv, in Transoxiana.

KESHVĀD . . . . Gudarz's father; the tribe to which Gudarz belonged.

KESRĀ . . . . see Nushin-Ravān.

KHANJAST . . . . a supporter of Khosrow Parviz when he is out of favor with his father Hormozd.

KESHVĀD . . . . a warrior of Irān, the father of Gudarz.

KHALLOKHI . . . . a town in Turkestan famous for its musk, and for the beauty of its inhabitants.

KHĀQĀN . . . . the title of the emperor of China.

KHARRĀD. . . . . a Persian chieftain at Kay Khosrow's court.

KHARRAD . . . . the warrior who captures Ardavān when he is defeated by Ardeshir.

KHATLĀN . . . . the area around Samarqand.

KHAZAR . . . . an area of Turkestān.

KHAZARVAN . . . . a warrior of Turān.

KHAZRAVĀN . . . . a chieftain who fights in the armies of Bahrām Gur.

KHERRĀD. . . . . a warrior of Irān.

KHEZR. . . . . a Qur'anic (and probably pre-Qur'anic) figure; in medieval legend the guardian of the waters of immortality.

KHORAD-BORZIN. . . . . a confidant of Hormozd. Also, the name of a fire temple.

KHORASAN . . . . A province including modern Khorasān, in north eastern Irān, but also the area to the north and south of the Oxus.

KHORDĀD . . . . a Zoroastrian angel.

KHORDĀD . . . . a supporter of Nushin-Ravān against Mazdak. The name of the third month and the sixth day of every month in the Zoroastrian calendar.

KHORRAMĀBĀĀD. . . . . a city built by Shāpur, in western Iran.

KHOSROW . . . . Seyāvash's and Farigis's son. A Persian king.

KHOSROW . . . . a claimant to the Persian throne after the death of Yazdegerd the Unjust. The name of the miller who kills Yazdegerd III. Also a legendary king.

KHOSROW PARVIZ . . . . a Persian king, the son of Hormozd, father of Shirui, husband of Mariam and Shirin.

KHOTAN. . . . . northeastern central Asia.

KHURREH-YE ARDESHIR . . . . a town in Pars, built by King Ardeshir.

KHUZESTĀN . . . . the southeastern province of Iran.

KIĀNUSH . . . . a brother of Feraydun.

KOHANDEZH . . . . a number of sites in Iran and Transoxiana bear this name, which means "ancient fortress." It is unclear which of them is meant in Ferdowsi's text.

KOLĀHVAR . . . . a warrior of Māzanderān.

KONDROW . . . . Zahhāk's treasurer.

KUFAH . . . . a city in southern Iraq.

KULĀD GHANDI . . . . a demon of Māzanderān.

KUT . . . . a Byzantine warrior.

KUCH . . . . the name of a tribe and of an area in south eastern Irān, near Kermān.

LAHĀK . . . . Pirān's brother.

LOHRĀSP . . . . a Persian warrior who is chosen by Khosrow to succeed him as king. The father of Goshtāsp.

MĀH . . . . the bride of Tur.

MĀH-ĀFARID . . . . the wife of Iraj.

MĀHAZĀR . . . . a counselor to Nushin-Ravān.

MĀHUY . . . . the governor of Khorāsān in the time of Yazdegerd III; after Yazdegerd's death he proclaims himself king.

MĀHYĀR . . . . a Zoroastrian priest who is one of the two murderers of King Dārā. Also a jeweler whose daughter ārezu marries Bahrām Gur.

MAJUJ . . . . see Yajuj and Majuj.

MAKRĀN . . . . southern Afghānistān and the south of what is now Pakistan.

MALEKEH . . . . the daughter of the Persian princess Nobahār and her Arab abductor Tāyer.

MĀMUN . . . . an Abbasid caliph (reigned 813 C.E. to 833 C.E.).

MANDAL . . . . an Indian king.

MĀNI . . . . a prophet and painter who appeared in the reign of Shāpur.

MANIZHEH . . . . a Princess of Turān. Afrasyāb's daughter.

MANUCHEHR . . . . a Persian king, the grandson of Iraj.

MARDĀNSHĀH . . . . one of Shirin's sons.

MARDUY . . . . a gardener who befriends the musician Bārbad.

MARGH . . . . a town in northwestern India.

MARIAM . . . . a daughter of the emperor of Byzantium; a wife of Khosrow Parviz; the mother of Shirui.

MARV . . . . a city in northern Khorāsān.

MARVRUD . . . . a town in Khorāsān, halfway between Balkh and Marv.

MAYAM . . . . an indefinite area to the east and north of Irān.

MĀZANDERĀN . . . . modern Māzanderān is the area to the south of the Caspian Sea. Various locations for Ferdowsi's Māzanderān have been suggested.

MAYSĀN . . . . a city in Mesopotamia founded by Ardeshir.

MAZDAK . . . . a prophet and social reformer who appeared in the reign of King Qobād, and was opposed by Qobād's son Kesrā Nushin-Ravān.

MEHRĀB. . . . . the king of Kābol, Rudābeh's father.

MEHRBANDĀD. . . . . a farmer encountered by Bahrām Gur while Bahrām is out hunting.

MEHR-AZĀD . . . . an advisor to Nushin-Ravan.

MEHRAK. . . . . a rebel who looted King Ardeshir's palace while the king was fighting against Haftvād of Kerman.

MEHRĀN-SETĀD. . . . . an envoy sent by Nushin-Ravān to China.

MEHR-BORZIN . . . . a warrior during the reign of Bahrām Gur.

MEHR-HORMOZD . . . . the murderer of Khosrow Parviz.

MEHREGĀN. . . . . a festival celebrating the autumnal equinox.

MEHRNUSH. . . . . one of Esfandyār's sons.

MERDĀS . . . . the father of Zahhāk.

MERUI . . . . an ally of Rostam (the son of Hormozd) at the battle of Qādesiya.

MILĀD . . . . a warrior of Irān.

MILĀD . . . . a city in western India.

MONZER . . . . an Arab prince who brings up Bahrām Gur.

MOSHK . . . . one of four sisters, all musicians, whom Bahrām Gur incorporates into his harem.

MORDĀD . . . . a Zoroastrian angel.

NĀHID. . . . . the daughter of Filqus, wife of Dārāb, and mother of Sekandar.

NAHRAVĀN . . . . a city in Mesopotamia; also a river of undetermined location (the word ravan means "flowing," nahr "channel").

NĀRVAN . . . . a forested area near the Caspian Sea.

NASIBIN . . . . a town in Mesopotamia, known for its monasteries and Christian population.

NASR . . . . an Arab chieftain of the Hejāz, befriended by Sekandar; also a Sāmānid king.

NARIMĀN . . . . the founder of the royal house of Sistān, to which belong Sām, Zāl, and Rostam.

NASTIHAN. . . . . a warrior of Turān.

NASTUD . . . . one of the sons of Shirin.

NASTUH . . . . a servant to King Hormozd.

NAYSHĀPUR . . . . a town in northeastern Iran.

NĀZ. . . . . one of four sisters, all musicians, whom Bahrām Gur incorporates into his harem.

NERSI . . . . a Sāsāniān king (Nersi   Bahman), the father of the princess Nobahār. Also, the brother of Bahrām Gur, who acts as regent in Bahrām's absence.

NIĀTUS . . . . the brother of the emperor of Byzantine; he is put in charge of the troops the emperor lends to Khosrow Parviz.

NIMRUZ . . . . the ancestral homeland of Sām, Zāl, and Rostam; also called Zābol, Zābolestān, Zāvol, Zāvolestān, and Sistān.

NISĀ . . . . a town founded by the Parthians, about halfway between the Caspian Sea and Marv.

NOBAHĀR . . . . the daughter of King Nersi; she is abducted by the Arab chieftain Tāyer and gives birth to a daughter, Malekeh.

NO'MAN . . . . the son of Monzer, Bahrām Gur's Arab guardian.

NOSHĀD . . . . a city built by Dārā.

NOZAR . . . . the son of Manuchehr, the king of Irān.

NUSHĀZAR . . . . one of Esfandyār's sons.

NUSHIN-RAVĀN . . . . also called Kesrā; a Sāsāniān king, the son of King Qobad and father of King Hormozd. The modern form of his name, which means "eternal soul," is Anushirvān.

NUSHZĀD . . . . Nushin-Ravān's son, by the daughter of the Roman emperor, who adopts his mother's faith (Christianity) and rebels against his father. Also, the father of Mehrak, a rebel against Ardeshir.

OMAR, IBN AL-KHATTĀB . . . . the second of the caliphs who succeeded the prophet Mohammad; in his reign Iran was invaded by the Arab armies bringing the new religion of Islam.

ORANDSHĀH . . . . an ancestor of Lohrāsp.

ORDIBEHESHT . . . . a Zoroastrian angel.

OXUS . . . . the river that traditionally marked the boundary between Iran and central Asia.

PAHLAVI . . . . the form of Persian spoken before the Arab conquest in the seventh century C.E.

PĀRS . . . . a province in central southern Irān, and the homeland of the country's two most important pre-Islamic dynasties, the Achaemenids and the Sasanians.

PARMOUDEH . . . . the son of Sāveh Shāh, leader of the central Asian Turks and the emperor of China.

PARTHIAN . . . . see Ashkāniān.

PASHIN . . . . the son of the legendary king Kay Qobad, and the ancestor of Khosrow, who is placed on the throne by the Persian nobility after the death of Yazdegerd the Unjust.

PAYDĀ-GOSHASP . . . . a warrior chieftain and companion of Bahrām Chubineh.

PIRUZ . . . . the envoy of Rostam (the son of Hormozd), to the Arab armies. Also, a Persian noble who opposes the accession of Bahrām Gur to the throne. Also, a minor Sāsāniān king.

PIRUZ-SHIR . . . . a warrior who reproaches Nushzād when he rebels against his father, King Nushin-Ravān.

PULĀD . . . . a warrior of Iran.

PURĀN-DOKHT . . . . a Sāsāniān queen.

QĀDESIYA . . . . the site of a decisive battle between the Sasanian and Arab armies, in 637 C.E.

QAHTĀB . . . . an Arab conqueror of the Hejāz.

QALUN . . . . a Turk who is suborned by Khorad Borzin to kill Bahrām Chubineh.

QANUJ . . . . a city in northern India.

QĀREN . . . . a number of warriors are called this; it was the name of one of the chief families of Sāsāniān Iran.

QAYDĀFEH . . . . the Queen of Andalusia during the time of Sekandar. Also the name of a Roman province.

QAYDRUS . . . . a son of Queen Qaydāfeh.

QAYSIĀN . . . . an Arab tribe.

QAYTUN . . . . the king of Egypt during the time of Sekandar.

QEISAR-NAVĀN . . . . a border area between Roman and Persian territory.

QOBĀD . . . . Another name for Shirui, the son of Khosrow Parviz. Also Kay Qobād, a legendary Persian king. Also a Sasanian king, the father of Nushin-Ravān.

QUR'ĀN . . . . the holy book of Islam.

QOTAYB . . . . an Arab tribe. Also the father of Nasr, a chieftain befriended by Sekandar.

RĀM-BORZIN . . . . a confidant of Kesra Nushin-Ravān and the commander of his armies during Nushzad's rebellion.

RESHNAVĀD . . . . a Persian general during the reign of Homāy.

REY . . . . a city in northern central Iran, to the south of modern Tehran.

ROSHANAK . . . . the daughter of Dārā and wife of Sekandar.

ROSTAM . . . . the preeminent hero of the epic; the son of Zāl and Rudābeh and father of Sohrāb.

ROSTAM, SON OF HORMOZD . the commander of the Persian armies under Yazdegerd III.

RUDĀBEH . . . . a princess of Kābol; Zāl's wife and Rostam's mother.

RUM . . . . the West.

RUMI . . . . of the West.

PASHANG . . . . two men bear this name; one is a king of Turān, and the father of Afrāsyāb, the other is a Persian, the nephew of Feraydun and the father of Manuchehr.

PASHUTAN . . . . Goshtasp's son, and Esfandyār's brother.

PILSOM . . . . Pirān's brother.

PIRĀN . . . . a nobleman of Turān; counselor to Afrāsyāb.

PULĀD . . . . a warrior of Irān.

QAJQAR . . . . a town in Turān.

QALUN . . . . a warrior of Turān.

QANNUJ . . . . a town in northern India.

QARĀ KHĀN . . . . an advisor to Afrāsyāb.

QĀREN . . . . a Persian army commander, also called Qāren-e Kāvus.

QOBĀD . . . . two men bear this name; one is a Persian warrior, the other a Persian king.

QOM . . . . a city in central Irān.

RAKHSH . . . . Rostam's horse.

RUDAKI . . . . the tenth-century Persian poet who versified Kalileh and Demneh.

RUZBEH . . . . a priest and counselor to Bahrām Gur.

SABĀK . . . . the ruler of Jahrom who joins Ardeshir, the founder of the Sāsāniān dynasty, against the remnants of Ashkāniān power.

SA'D, THE SON OF VAQĀS . . . the commander of the Arab armies that invaded Iran during the reign of Yazdegerd III.

SADEH . . . . a festival commemorating the discovery of fire.

SAHI . . . . the bride of Iraj.

SALM . . . . Feraydun's eldest son.

SĀM . . . . the father of Zāl.

SAMANGĀN . . . . a border town, between Irān and Turān.

SAMARQAND . . . . a city in Transoxiana.

SANGLAKH, PLAIN OF . . . . . . a mythical area, "sanglakh" means "stony."

SANJEH . . . . a demon of Māzanderān.

SĀRI . . . . a town to the southeast of the Caspian.

SARKESH . . . . a musician at the court of Khosrow Parviz.

SARUCH . . . . a plain near Kermān, in south eastern Irān.

SĀSĀN . . . . a Persian prince who flees to India and lives there as a shepherd; the ancestor of Ardeshir, the founder of the Sāsāniān dynasty. In the story of Bahman and Homāy, he is Bahman's son; in the story of Dārā, he is Dārā's son.

SĀSĀNIAN . . . . the dynasty that ruled Iran from 224 C.E. to 642 C.E.

SĀVEH SHĀH . . . . a central Asian Turkish leader, also referred to as the emperor of China, who attacks Iran during the reign of King Hormozd.

SAVORG . . . . Sekandar's regent in India.

SEKANDAR . . . . Alexander the Great. The Arabic version of his name was (Al-) Eskandar; Sekandar is Ferdowsi's usual adaptation of this.

SEND . . . . approximately modern Pakistan; the sea adjacent to it.

SEPANDORMOZ . . . . the twelfth month of the Zoroastrian calendar.

SEPAHRAM . . . . a warrior chieftain of Turān.

SEPANDARMEZ . . . . a Zoroastrian angel.

SEPANJĀB . . . . an area in Turkestan.

SEPED . . . . an unidentified mountain in Turān.

SEPINOUD . . . . an Indian princess who marries Bahrām Gur; the daughter of King Shangal.

SERGIUS . . . . a Byzantine warrior.

SEYĀVASH . . . . son of Kay Kāvus and father of Kay Khosrow and Forud.

SEYĀVASHGERD . . . . the city Seyavash founds in Turān.

SHABDIZ . . . . a horse belonging to Bahrām Gur. Also a horse belonging to Khosrow Parviz.

SHABRANG . . . . Bizhan's horse (the name means "Color of Night").

SHABRANG . . . . a horse belonging to Bahrām Gur.

SHĀDEGĀN . . . . the garden where Khosrow Parviz's wife, Shirin, answers Shirui's accusations against her.

SHAGHĀD . . . . Rostam's brother.

SHAHD . . . . an unidentified place, and body of water, in eastern Iran.

SHĀHEH . . . . a mythical city in Hāmāverān.

SHAHRIVAR . . . . a Zoroastrian angel.

SHAHRNAVĀZ . . . . a sister of Jamshid.

SHAHRGIR . . . . a warrior who captures Qaydrus, one of the sons of Qaydafeh, the queen of Andalusia. Also a commander in Ardeshir's army.

SHAHRYĀR . . . . one of the sons of Shirin.

SHĀHUY . . . . the son of Haftvād, a warlord who rebels against Ardeshir.

SHAMĀSĀS . . . . a warrior of Turān.

SUS . . . . Susa, in south western Irān.

SHANGAL . . . . the king of India during the reign of Bahrām Gur.

SHĀPUR . . . . a warrior of Irān.

SHĀPUR . . . . the name of a number of Sāsāniān kings, the most significant of whom are Shāpur I, the son of Ardeshir, and Shāpur Z'ul-Aktāf.

SHĀPURGERD . . . . a city built by King Shāpur I to accommodate Roman prisoners.

SHAVRAN . . . . a Persian warrior, the father of Zangeh.

SHAYBĀN . . . . an Arab tribe.

SHEGNĀN . . . . a contender for the Persian throne after the death of Yazdegerd the Unjust.

SHEMĀS . . . . a Christian general who helps Nushzād in his rebellion against his father, King Nushin-Ravān.

SHEMIRĀN . . . . a maternal ancestor of Bahrām Gur.

SHEMR . . . . a warrior whom Bahrām Gur places on the throne of Turān.

SHIDĀSB . . . . the chief minister of King Tahmures.

SHIDEH . . . . a son of Afrasyāb.

SHIDUSH . . . . a Persian warrior.

SHIRKHUN . . . . a warrior from Sistān.

SHIRĀN . . . . a supporter of Khosrow Parviz when he is out of favor
with his father, Hormozd.

SHIRĀZ . . . . a city in southern Iran.

SHIRIN . . . . a wife of Khosrow Parviz.

SHIRUI . . . . a warrior of Turān.

SHIRUI . . . . the son of Mariam and Khosrow Parviz; he reigns as king
for seven months.

SHIR-ZIL . . . . a supporter of Khosrow Parviz when he is out of favor
with his father, Hormozd.

SHO'AYB . . . . an Arab chieftain defeated by Dārāb.

SHO'BEH MOGHAIREH . . . . . the Arab envoy to Rostam, the son of Hormozd.

SHURESTĀN . . . . an area near the lands of the Arab king Monzer; the name
means "place of bitterness" and is used to refer to a salt
desert.

SHUSHTAR . . . . a city in southeastern Iran.

SIĀMAK . . . . the son of King Kayumars.

SIMĀ-BORZIN . . . . an advisor of Nushin-Ravān, killed by Nushin-Ravān's
son Hormozd.

SIMORGH . . . . the fabulous bird which rears Zāl.

SIND . . . . north western India.

SINDOKHT . . . . the wife of Mehrāb and the mother of Rudābeh.

SISANAK . . . . one of four sisters, all musicians, whom Bahrām Gur
incorporates into his harem.

SISTĀN . . . . a province of southeastern Iran and southern Afghanistan,
lying largely to the east of the modern Persian province of
the same name. Also the ancestral homeland of Sām, Zāl,
and Rostam; also called Zābol, Zābolestān, Zāvol,
Zāvolestān, and Nimruz.

SOGHDIA . . . . Transoxiana generally, and in particular the area around
Samarkand.

SOHRĀB . . . . the son of Rostam.

SORUSH . . . . a Zoroastrian angel. Also, an Indian astrologer. Also, the
seventeenth day of every Zoroastrian month.

SUDĀBEH . . . . the daughter of the king of Hāmāverān.

SU . . . . a legendary fountain where it is prophesied that
Yazdegerd the Unjust will die.

SURI . . . . the father of Māhuy (the governor of Khorāsān) during
the reign of Yazdegerd III.

SUSANAK . . . . one of four sisters, all musicians, whom Bahrām Gur incorporates into his harem.

TABARISTĀN . . . . the area to the south of the Caspian Sea.

TAHMINEH . . . . the daughter of the king of Samangān; Sohrāb's mother.

TAHMURES . . . . a Persian king, the son of Hushang known as the Binder of Demons.

TALIMĀN . . . . a warrior of Irān.

TĀLQĀN . . . . a town in Transoxiana.

TARĀZ . . . . a town in Transoxiana.

TARKHĀN . . . . an area in Transoxiana.

TĀYER . . . . an Arab chieftain who attacks Ctesiphon at the beginning of the reign of Shāpur Zu'l-Aktāf and abducts the princess Nobahār.

TAYNUSH . . . . a son of Qaydāfeh, queen of Andalusia. Also, a Roman envoy to the court of Yazdegerd the Unjust.

TERMEZ . . . . a town in Transoxiana.

TIGRIS . . . . the river forming the eastern boundary of Mesopotamia.

TOCHVAR . . . . a warrior of Turān; advisor to Forud.

TOKHVĀR . . . . a member of the conspiracy to place Shirui on the throne in place of his father Khosrow Parviz.

TOVORG . . . . a brother of the emperor of China, who tries to detain Gordyeh after her bother Bahrām Chubineh is murdered. Gordyeh kills him.

TUR . . . . Feraydun's second son.

TURĀN . . . . the country to the north of the Oxus.

TUS . . . . a Persian prince, the son of Nozar.

UKHAST . . . . a warrior of Turān.

ULĀD . . . . a landowner and warrior of Māzanderān.

VASTUI . . . . a supporter of Khosrow Parviz when he is out of favor with his father Hormozd.

VISEH . . . . a warrior of Turān.

YAJUJ AND MAJUJ . . . . monstrous beings defeated by Sekandar. Identified with Gog and Magog.

YALĀN-SINEH . . . . a warrior and companion of Bahrām Chubineh.

YĀNUS . . . . a younger brother of the Roman emperor captured by Shāpur; he leads an army against Shāpur and is defeated in battle by him.

YAZDEGERD . . . . the name of three Sāsānian kings; Yazdegerd the Unjust, the father of Bahrām Gur; Yazdegerd II, the son of Bahrām Gur; and Yazdegerd III, a descendant of Nushin-Ravān and the last Sāsānian king. Also a scribe at the court of Nushin-Ravān.

ZĀBOL/ZĀBOLESTĀN ...... another name for Sistān, the homeland of Sām, Zāl, and Rostam.

ZĀDSHAM .... an ancestor of Afrāsyāb.

ZAHHĀK .... a demon-king brought down by Kāveh and Feraydun.

ZĀL .... also called Zāl-e Zar and Zāl-Dastān, Sām's son, the father of Rostam.

ZANGEH .... a Persian warrior.

ZARASP .... a Persian warrior, the son of Tus.

ZARDHESHT .... the chief priest at the opening of the reign of Hormozd.

ZARMEHR .... an advisor to Nushin-Ravān.

ZARQ .... a village, and also the name of the river, where Yazdegerd was killed.

ZAREH .... a country and sea near North Africa.

ZARIR .... a Persian prince, son of King Goshtāsp.

ZAV .... a Persian king.

ZAVĀREH .... a warrior of Irān, the brother of Rostam.

ZĀVOL/ZĀVOLESTĀN ...... another name for Sistān, the homeland of Sām, Zāl, and Rostam.

ZEND-AVESTA .... The Zoroastrian sacred text. Ferdowsi often, anachronistically, refers to it before the advent of Zoroastrianism.

ZHENDEH-RAZM .... a warrior of Turān.

INDEX OF HEADINGS